Lecture Notes in Artificial In

T0238734

Subseries of Lecture Notes in Computer Science

LNAI Series Editors

Randy Goebel
University of Alberta, Edmonton, Canada
Yuzuru Tanaka
Hokkaido University, Sapporo, Japan
Wolfgang Wahlster
DFKI and Saarland University, Saarbrücken, Germany

LNAI Founding Series Editor

Joerg Siekmann
DFKI and Saarland University, Saarbrücken, Germany

Shuzhi Sam Ge   Oussama Khatib
John-John Cabibihan   Reid Simmons
Mary-Anne Williams (Eds.)

Social Robotics

4th International Conference, ICSR 2012
Chengdu, China, October 29-31, 2012
Proceedings

 Springer

Series Editors

Randy Goebel, University of Alberta, Edmonton, Canada
Jörg Siekmann, University of Saarland, Saarbrücken, Germany
Wolfgang Wahlster, DFKI and University of Saarland, Saarbrücken, Germany

Volume Editors

Shuzhi Sam Ge
National University of Singapore, Singapore 117576, Singapore *and*
University of Electronic Science and Technology of China, Chengdu 611813, China
E-mail: samge@nus.edu.sg

Oussama Khatib
Stanford University, Stanford, CA 94305-9010, USA
E-mail: khatib@robotics.stanford.edu

John-John Cabibihan
National University of Singapore, Singapore 117576, Singapore
E-mail: elecjj@nus.edu.sg

Reid Simmons
Carnegie Mellon University, Pittsburgh, PA 15213, USA
E-mail: reids@cs.cmu.edu

Mary-Anne Williams
University of Technology, Sydney, NSW 2007, Australia
E-mail: mary-anne.williams@uts.edu.au

ISSN 0302-9743   e-ISSN 1611-3349
ISBN 978-3-642-34102-1   e-ISBN 978-3-642-34103-8
DOI 10.1007/978-3-642-34103-8
Springer Heidelberg Dordrecht London New York

Library of Congress Control Number: 2012948600

CR Subject Classification (1998): I.2, C.2.4, I.2.9, K.4.2, H.5.2, J.4, I.2.10

LNCS Sublibrary: SL 7 – Artificial Intelligence

Typesetting: Camera-ready by author, data conversion by Scientific Publishing Services, Chennai, India

Printed on acid-free paper

Springer is part of Springer Science+Business Media (www.springer.com)

Shuzhi Sam Ge   Oussama Khatib
John-John Cabibihan   Reid Simmons
Mary-Anne Williams (Eds.)

Social Robotics

4th International Conference, ICSR 2012
Chengdu, China, October 29-31, 2012
Proceedings

 Springer

Series Editors

Randy Goebel, University of Alberta, Edmonton, Canada
Jörg Siekmann, University of Saarland, Saarbrücken, Germany
Wolfgang Wahlster, DFKI and University of Saarland, Saarbrücken, Germany

Volume Editors

Shuzhi Sam Ge
National University of Singapore, Singapore 117576, Singapore *and*
University of Electronic Science and Technology of China, Chengdu 611813, China
E-mail: samge@nus.edu.sg

Oussama Khatib
Stanford University, Stanford, CA 94305-9010, USA
E-mail: khatib@robotics.stanford.edu

John-John Cabibihan
National University of Singapore, Singapore 117576, Singapore
E-mail: elecjj@nus.edu.sg

Reid Simmons
Carnegie Mellon University, Pittsburgh, PA 15213, USA
E-mail: reids@cs.cmu.edu

Mary-Anne Williams
University of Technology, Sydney, NSW 2007, Australia
E-mail: mary-anne.williams@uts.edu.au

ISSN 0302-9743   e-ISSN 1611-3349
ISBN 978-3-642-34102-1   e-ISBN 978-3-642-34103-8
DOI 10.1007/978-3-642-34103-8
Springer Heidelberg Dordrecht London New York

Library of Congress Control Number: 2012948600

CR Subject Classification (1998): I.2, C.2.4, I.2.9, K.4.2, H.5.2, J.4, I.2.10

LNCS Sublibrary: SL 7 – Artificial Intelligence

Typesetting: Camera-ready by author, data conversion by Scientific Publishing Services, Chennai, India

Printed on acid-free paper

Springer is part of Springer Science+Business Media (www.springer.com)

Preface

Welcome to the proceedings of the 4th International Conference on Social Robotics (ICSR). The conference was held during October 29–31, 2012, at Chengdu, China. Since its inception in 2009, the ICSR series of conferences have brought researchers together to report and discuss the latest progress in the field of social robotics in a collegial, supportive, and constructive atmosphere.

The ICSR conferences focus on the interaction between humans and robots, and the integration of robots into our society. The theme of the 2012 conference was "Wellness." This theme highlights the potential and capabilities of social robots to assist humans in achieving better physical, mental, and emotional health and wellness. The conference aims to foster discussion on the development of computational models, robotic embodiments, and behaviors that enable social robots to have an impact on the human partner's health and well-being.

The conference website was viewed by visitors from at least 70 countries. We received paper submissions from Asia, Europe, North America, South America, and Australia—a confirmation of the global interest being generated by the field of Social Robotics. The submitted papers were subjected to a rigorous peer-review selection. All the papers were reviewed with the help of the 31-member Program Committee, who were carefully selected from the international community of social robotics researchers for their expertise.

This volume contains the papers at the forefront of social robotics research in the areas of affective and cognitive sciences for socially interactive robots; situated interaction and embodiment; robots to assist the elderly and persons with disabilities; artificial empathy; interaction and collaboration among robots, humans, and environments; socially assistive robots to improve quality of life; socially appealing design methodologies; social acceptance; and robot ethics.

The conference also featured invited talks by four distinguished researchers in the field: Paolo Dario (Scuola Superiore Sant'Anna), Cynthia Breazeal (Massachusetts Institute of Technology), Hong Zhou (General Logistics Department of China Armed Force), and Etienne Burdet (Imperial College).

The continuing success of ICSR would not have been possible without the contributions of our colleagues, to whom we would like to express our gratitude. We are indebted to the members of the International Advisory Board, Organizing Committee, and the Program Committee for their dedication and support. We thank Hongsheng He (NUS) and Martin Saerbeck (A*STAR) for their valuable contributions in the publication of this volume; Ravindra de Silva (Toyohashi), Guido Herrmann (University of Bristol) and Caihua Xiong (HUST) for the publicity efforts; Adrian Tay (A*STAR) and Ho Seok Ahn (ATR) for the robot design competition; Wei He (UESTC) for the finance; Kaiyu Qin (UESTC) for the local organization, and Zhengchen Zhang (NUS) for the Web services.

We also would like to acknowledge the Special Session Chairs Gordon Cheng (TUM) and Adriana Tapus (ENSTA); and the special session organizers: Ben Robins and Kerstin Dautenhahn (University of Hertfordshire) for the session on situated interaction and embodiment; Luisa Damiano (University of Bergamo), Paul Dumouchel (Ritsumeikan University) and Hagen Lehmann (University of Hertfordshire) for the session on artificial empathy; and Ryad Chellali (Italian Institute of Technology) for HRI through non-verbal communication and control.

Finally, we wish to thank the authors for sending their best work, the referees, student helpers, sponsors, and delegates for their valuable contributions to this growing community.

October 2012

Shuzhi Sam Ge
Oussama Khatib
John-John Cabibihan
Reid Simmons
Mary-Anne Williams

Organization

ICSR 2012 was organized by the University of Electronic Science and Technology of China, and the National University of Singapore.

International Advisory Board

Ronald Arkin	School of Interactive Computing, College of Computing, Georgia Institute of Technology, USA
Jong-Hwan Kim	Department of Electrical Engineering and Computer Science, Korea Advanced Institute of Science and Technology (KAIST), Korea
Haizhou Li	Institute for Infocomm Research, Agency for Science, Technology and Research (A*STAR), Singapore
Hideaki Kuzuoka	Department of Intelligent Interaction Technologies, University of Tsukuba, Japan
Maja J. Matarić	Viterbi School of Engineering, University of Southern California, USA
Tzyh Jong Tarn	Electrical and Systems Engineering Department, Washington University in St. Louis, USA
JinSong Wang	School of Mechatronics Engineering, University of Electronics Science and Technology of China, China
Tianran Wang	Shenyang Institute of Automation, Chinese Academy of Sciences, China
Youlun Xiong	College of Mechanical Science and Engineering, Huazhong University of Science & Technology, China

Organizing Committee

General Chairs

Shuzhi Sam Ge	National University of Singapore, Singapore, and University of Electronic Science and Technology of China, China
Oussama Khatib	Stanford University, USA

Program Chairs

John-John Cabibihan	National University of Singapore, Singapore
Reid Simmons	Carnegie Mellon University, USA
Mary-Anne Williams	University of Technology, Sydney, Australia

Organizing Committee Chair

Kaiyu Qin — University of Electronic Science and Technology of China, China

Publicity Chairs

Ravindra De Silva	Toyohashi University of Technology, Japan
Guido Herrmann	University of Bristol, UK
Caihua Xiong	Huazhong University of Science and Technology, China

Publication Chairs

Martin Saerbeck — Institute of High Performance Computing, Agency for Science, Technology and Research (A*STAR), Singapore

Hongsheng He — National University of Singapore, Singapore

Special Session Chairs

Gordon Cheng — Technical University of Munich, Germany

Adriana Tapus — Ecole Nationale Superieure de Techniques Avancees, Paris, France

Robot Design Competition Chairs

Ho Seok Ahn — ATR Intelligent Robotics and Communication Laboratories, Japan

Adrian Hwang Jian Tay — Institute for Infocomm Research, Agency for Science, Technology and Research (A*STAR), Singapore

Finance Chair

Wei He — National University of Singapore, Singapore

International Sponsorship Chairs

Xiaolin Dai — University of Electronics Science and Technology of China, China

Michio Okada — Toyohashi University of Technology, Japan

Registration Chair

Yang Su — University of Electronics Science and Technology of China, China

Webmaster

Zhengchen Zhang   National University of Singapore, Singapore

International Program Committee

Arvin Agah   The University of Kansas Lawrence, USA
Marcelo H. Ang, Jr.   National University of Singapore, Singapore
Brenna Argall   Northwestern University, USA
Kai O. Arras   Albert Ludwig University of Freiburg, Germany
Luca Brayda   Italian Institute of Technology, Italy
Frank Broz   University of Hertfordshire, UK
Maria Chiara Carrozza   Scuola Superiore Sant'Anna Pisa, Italy
So Wing Chee, Catherine   National University of Singapore
Ryad Chellali   Italian Institute of Technology, Italy
Xiaoping Chen   University of Science and Technology of China,
                                     China
Gamini Dissanayake   University of Technology, Sydney, Australia
Kerstin Severinson-Eklundh   KTH Royal Institute of Technology, Sweden
Dieter Fox   University of Washington, USA
Jaap Ham   Eindhoven University of Technology,
                                     The Netherlands
Takayuki Kanda   ATR Intelligent Robotics and Communication
                                     Laboratories, Kyoto, Japan
Kolja Kühnlenz   Technische Universitaet Muenchen, Germany
Zhijun Li   Shanghai Jiao Tong University, China
Bruce MacDonald   University of Auckland, New Zealand
Cai Meng   Beihang University, China
Ben Robins   The University of Hertfordshire, UK
Selma Šabanović   Indiana University, USA
Miguel A. Salichs   University Carlos III of Madrid, Spain
Siddhartha Srinivasa   Carnegie Mellon University, USA
Aaron Steinfeld   Carnegie Mellon University, USA
Yeow Kee Tan   Institute for Infocomm Research, Agency for
                                     Science, Technology and Research
                                     (A*STAR), Singapore
Keng Peng Tee   Institute for Infocomm Research, Agency for
                                     Science, Technology and Research
                                     (A*STAR), Singapore
Andrea Thomaz   Georgia Institute of Technology, USA
Astrid Weiss   University of Salzburg, Austria
Agnieszka Wykowska   Ludwig-Maximilians-Universität München,
                                     Germany
Wenzeng Zhang   Tsinghua University, China
Xianggang Zhang   University of Electronic Science and
                                     Technology of China

Reviewers

Gabriel Aguirre-Ollinger
Morana Alac
Alen Alempijevic
Muh Anshar

Eleanor Avrunin
Pengyu Bao
Emilia Barakova
Lykke Brogaard Bertel
Serenella Besio
Rohit Srinath
  Bharadwaj
Joydeep Biswas
Laura E. Boccanfuso
Elizabeth Broadbent
Wolfram Burgard
Sylvain Calinon
Ryan Calo
Lola Cañamero
Zhenfeng Chen
Chin Kiang Terence Cher
Chee-Meng Chew
Sandra Cristina Cunha
  Costa
Luisa Damiano
Thi-hai-ha Dang
Jente De Pee
Ravindra S. De Silva
Davide De Tommaso
Lone Gaedt
Anais Garrell
Philippe Gaussier

Gert Jan Gelderblom
Weian Guo
Sajjad Haider
Markus Häring
Evan Herbst
Iolandai Iacono
Benjamin Johnston
Heather Knight
Kheng-lee Koay
Thomas Kollar
Tony Kuo
Dong Soo Kwon
Min Kyung Lee
Hagen Lehmann
Iolanda Leite
Yanan Li
Haizhou Li
Ning Li
Yvonne Limpens
Chao Liu
Sibang Liu
Wei Lu
Jianjun Ma
Maxim Makatchev
Juan Pablo Mendoza
Marek Michalowski
Cees J. Midden
Rony Novianto
Hirotaka Osawa
Gavin Paul
Kenneth Pinpin
Nima Ramezani

Renato Ramos
Stephanie Rosenthal
Majd F. Sakr
Maha Salem
Hooman Aghaebrahimi
  Samani
Paul Scerri
Matthias Scheutz
Brennan Sellner
Mohammad Shayganfar
Filomena Soares
Kenji Suzuki
Dag Sverre Syrdal
Mirjam Van Esch
Bram Vanderborght
Hosmane Ramakrishna
  Venkatesh
Michael Walters
Wei Wang
Xun Wang
Gregor Wolbring
Luke Wood
Haibin Yan
Haoyong Yu
Lihao Zhang
Zheng Zhang
Jie Zhang
Qun Zhang
Chao Zhang
Zhen Zhao
Hong Zhou

Sponsoring Partner

Aldebaran Robotics

Table of Contents

Robots to Assist the Elderly and Persons with Disabilities

Social Acceptance of Robots and Their Impact to the Society

Artificial Empathy

HRI through Non-verbal Communication and Control

Social Telepresence Robots, Embodiments and Networks

Interaction and Collaboration among Robots, Humans, and Environment

Human Augmentation, Rehabilitation, and Medical Robots I

Human Augmentation, Rehabilitation, and Medical Robots II

Manipulating Mental States through Physical Action

Jesse Gray and Cynthia Breazeal

MIT Media Lab, 20 Ames Street, Cambridge, MA
{jg,cynthiab}@media.mit.edu

Abstract. We present our implementation of a self-as-simulator architecture for mental state manipulation through physical action. The robot
attempts to model how a human's mental states are updated through
their visual perception of the world around them. This modeling, combined with geometrically detailed, perspective correct simulations of the
immediate future, allows the robot to choose actions which influence the
human's mental states through their visual perception. The system is
demonstrated in a competitive game scenario, where the robot attempts
to manipulate the mental states of an individual in order to win. We
evaluate people's reaction to the system, focusing on the participants'
perception of a robot with mental state manipulation capabilities.

1 Introduction

This paper focuses on a demonstration of mental state manipulation in a competitive game scenario and an evaluation of human reactions to this behavior.
The motivation for this work is to explore the connection between (hidden) mental states of an embodied agent and the (observable and modifiable) world in
which they exist.

An embodied agent exists in the physical world, and though its mental states
are hidden, there are rich connections between the agent's mental states and
the world in which it is operating. Observing an agent's visual perspective and
physical actions can help inform a model of the underlying mental states caused
by those perceptions and causing those actions.

In order to modify the mental states of another agent, it is necessary to
manipulate the world such that the agent's observations will update its internal
mental states to the desired configuration. Usage of this critical skill encompasses
a very broad set of interactions - in a cooperative scenario we might call it
communication. In such a scenario we often collapse this concept into "tell" or
"show." However the underlying goal remains: to change a mental state through
physical action on the world that will cause the agent's perceptual system to
update their mental states in the desired manner. This can be demonstrated by
observing how we respond to failures of the exchange - e.g., by moving an object
into the line of sight of an observer who is not paying attention.

S.S. Ge et al. (Eds.): ICSR 2012, LNAI 7621, pp. 1–14, 2012.

In a competitive scenario we call this same ability deception. In this case the world is intentionally modified (again taking into account the perceptual capabilities of the target agent) in such a way that the observing agent will form incorrect mental states.

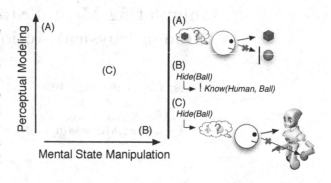

We believe that for a robot to robustly interact with people, it is important for the robot to form goals in this space of mental state outcomes rather than simply perform communicative actions as a

Fig. 1. Systems such as BDI architectures *(B)* include advanced mental state manipulation but tend to operate in simulation with highly abstracted actions and perceptual models. Other systems *(A)* employ geometrically correct perceptual models to infer mental states, however lack the ability to proactively manipulate these states. The research here *(C)* pushes into a new part of the space using detailed, geometrically correct mental state modeling to form short term plans for physical actions designed to manipulate the mental state of humans.

series of physical or auditory actions; this ability will allow the robot to succeed in situations where unexpected obstacles prevent naive communication strategies from succeeding.

Researchers have approached the modeling of mental states in many ways. The research here focuses on short timescale (0 to 60 seconds), highly detailed modeling of how the robot's actions will affect the human's mental states through the means of their perception. We attempt to embrace the physical performance of action and examine the accompanying communication value, rather than trying to abstract away action-performance. The robot's goal is to plan a sequence of actions to cause the human to believe what the robot wants them to believe while also accomplishing its task objectives; depending on the scenario, this takes the form of robust, (sometimes implicit) communication, or deception. This is especially useful in contexts where information has value and can be revealed by behavior. For example, in search & rescue, common ground can be implicitly maintained by making sure others observe important actions ("room-searched"). Another example is competitive foraging, where agents seek to acquire resources without revealing their location. Section 5 describes related work in detail, however Figure 1 illustrates the area we are exploring with this work.

We present an implementation and a study of human reactions to a system which allows a robot to take action in order to alter the mental states of a human according to the robot's goals. The robot employs perspective taking as well as self-as-simulator techniques to model the mental states of nearby humans. The robot has a simple planner, however the goal space of the planner includes not only the desired world-state, but also the mental states of the human. This allows the robot to form and execute plans that include changes to the human's mental states. After describing a motivating demonstration scenario, we provide implementation details. The demonstration scenario is then used as part of a user study to evaluate how people perceive a robot that has these capabilities.

2   Demonstration Scenario

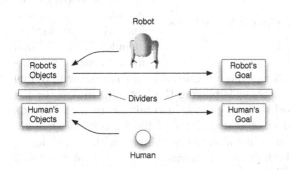

Fig. 2. Top down view of the demonstration scenario, a competitive game between the human and the robot. The robot stays on the upper part of the diagram pictured, and the human on the lower part. Each player has access to a matching set of objects on the left side, and each has their own goal area on the right side. The game ends when each player has placed an object into their goal - the robot wins if the two players placed different objects, the human wins if the objects are the same. Occlusions block the view of each player from the opposing player's object and goal areas, however they can see each other as they travel between the object repository and goal.

The architecture for mental state manipulation presented here makes heavy reuse of the motor actions and perceptual processing that the robot uses for its own behavior. As such, it can apply to varied contexts, as long as the robot is configured to perceive and operate there. The scenario chosen for this demonstration revolves around a simple competitive game played between the human and the robot. The game is illustrated in Figure 2.

The rules of this game create a situation where the player who goes second has the advantage of potentially seeing the item played by their opponent. If the human goes second and sees the item played by the robot, it is straightforward for them to win by playing the object they saw the robot play.

For this demonstration, the robot takes its turn first. It is thus to the robot's advantage to manage the information that can be observed from its behavior. If it proceeds in a straightforward manner, the human will be able to watch and observe the object the robot plays, then play the same object and win. To win, the robot must instead hide this information from the human.

For the demonstration, the game was played three different times, each time with a different set of mental state goals for the robot (see Figure 3). These different mental state goals change the behavior of the robot as it plays the game. In each case, the robot has the same overall task goal - transport the cylinder to the goal location. However, the way it accomplishes this task varies in the three conditions based on the mental state goals.

Condition	Robot's Goals	Robot's Behavior
1	•Cylinder in goal •Human doesn't see me carry cylinder •Human sees me carry football	•Transports cylinder behind back •Carries decoy football
2	•Cylinder in goal •Human doesn't see me carry cylinder	•Transports cylinder behind back
3	•Cylinder in goal	•Transports cylinder openly

Fig. 3. Set of robot's goals and resulting behavior for each of three demonstration conditions

In condition one, the robot attempts to cause the human to believe that the robot is transporting only the football, while actually additionally transporting (and playing) the cylinder. The robot finds that carrying the cylinder hidden behind its back, with the football carried out in the open, satisfies these conditions. In this way it may fool the human into thinking that the robot is playing the football, causing the human to lose by playing the football in response. In condition two, the robot's goal is to keep the cylinder (which it is transporting) hidden from the human. The chosen action sequence results in carrying the cylinder with its left hand, hidden behind its back from the human. The human can't see what the robot played, so is likely to choose arbitrarily and win half the time (there are two objects). In the final case, the robot has no mental state goals, and therefore its only goal is to transport the cylinder. It simply carries the cylinder over to the goal (likely causing the robot to lose in this case). The robot's performance of these three conditions is shown in Figure 4. Section 3 describes our system used to find the action sequences which correctly manipulate the mental states.

3   Implementation

The implementation described here builds on the existing R1D1 system, originally designed for interactive graphical characters [1,3], then later adapted for robots [4,5]. The system employs self-as-simulator techniques for theory of mind tasks, and previous publications have described work in mental state modeling, per-

Fig. 4. Photos taken during the robotic performance of the demonstration scenario. Left: Robot hiding object from human player. Center: Player's view, robot openly transporting cylinder. Right: Player's view, robot hiding cylinder and openly transporting football.

spective taking, and goal inference using this system (please refer to [2] for more details).

These previous implementations and demonstrations focused on modeling human mental states by monitoring the human's physical actions and visual perspective. The robot then re-uses parts of its own behavioral mechanisms in three main ways: 1) reusing its own world modeling capabilities to connect the human's visual perspective to possible human mental state formation; 2) reusing its own action performance mechanisms to connect the human's observed physical motions to possible higher level actions; 3) reusing its own goal directed action system to infer goals based on inferred mental states and actions. Inspired by work in human psychology, the self-as-simulator architecture provides the advantage of a common vocabulary between the robot's own behavioral mechanisms and the properties inferred in an observed human; since the purpose of mental state inference is to inform the actions of the robot, it is critical that inferred mental states be mapped into the space of its behavior generation systems.

Using these systems, the robot is constantly modeling the mental states of nearby agents. Whenever the robot discovers a new agent, along with updating its own model of the world state to reflect the presence of this agent, it also spawns a new copy of its own modeling systems. This new copy will maintain a world state model from the perspective of the new agent. These copies are provided with sensory data that is *re-imagined* by the robot from its own world state model, then transformed and filtered to best match what that agent should be experiencing.

Since these copies have the same capabilities as the robot's own systems, they too spawn copies when they sense another agent (including the robot), allowing for recursive mental state modeling. We currently cap this recursion at two levels, to allow for second level mental state goals such as *Robot Demonstrates To Human That Robot Knows X.*

3.1 Simulating the Future

In the previous section we described how we have used mental state inference to

---

Algorithm 1. Implementation Outline

Find Action Sequence:
    Clear List of Failed Action Sequences
    while Viable Sequences Remain **do**
        Init Future Simulation From Current State
        time = 0
        Begin Simulation
        while Simulation Running AND $time <$ MAX_TIME
        do
            time++
            if Action In Progress **then**
                Keep Performing Action
            else
                Select and Begin relevant Unexplored Action
            if Mental State Goals Succeeded **then**
                return Recent-Action-Sequence
            else if Mental State Goals Failed **then**
                Save Recent Action Sequence to Failed List
                End Simulation
    return Failed-To-Find-Sequence

---

model the current values of the human's hidden mental states to help resolve ambiguities and better assist the human with their goals. In order to proactively manipulate mental states, we use these mechanisms within the context of a simulator which simulates the immediate future, allowing the robot to evaluate and choose between multiple actions based on mental state outcomes (see basic outline in Algorithm 1).

The robot's simulation of possible futures consists of a copy of its own behavioral mechanisms, identical except that it is disconnected from the real world inputs (sensors) and outputs (motors). This "hypothetical" robot includes a copy of the virtual model used for motor planning, so it still has access to a body for performing its motor actions, however the final stage of synchronizing that model to the motors of the physical robot is not performed. This allows the robot to maintain a detailed representation of the hypothetical actions being performed, down to specific positioning of parts of its own body.

Mental States. The real robot performs real actions, which alter the state of the world, which changes the sensory input it receives from the world, which in turn results in updates to its mental states (and the mental states of the agents it is modeling). Our hypothetical robot cannot rely on this sensory-motor loop, since it is not interacting with the physical world. To overcome this absence, we reuse mechanisms designed for robust world modeling in the face of sensory lapses and noise.

With the normal stream of sensory data interrupted, the robot retains the most recently known properties for objects around it. An expectation mechanism operates in conjunction with physical actions - actions that alter the world are expected to succeed, so the robot updates object properties as appropriate as the action progresses. For example, when carrying an object, the robot assumes the object is being moved along with the robot's hand, and updates its position accordingly even if it cannot verify the object is in its hand at all times (as long as no contradictory sensory information overrides this default data). For our hypothetical robot no sensory data can override this belief maintenance mechanism, so the objects will be updated as if the actions are performed successfully.

Fig. 5. A *hypothetical* copy of the robot is used for mental state predictions. The robot has the capability to model mental states of agents around it (left). To make short term predictions, a copy of the robot (green, right) starts from the robot's current state and performs (in a virtual space) the actions the robot is about to perform, but performs them much faster. While doing this, it maintains the mental states of the surrounding agents as they participate in this accelerated timeline. This gives the robot the ability to predict the mental states of surrounding agents in the short term future.

The proprioceptive sensing of the hypothetical robot's kinematics and locomotion can function almost as normal as they are tied to the virtual model. This means that as it performs actions, it motions and moves around the hypothetical world appropriately, and those motions can be constantly fed not only into its own world model, but can be used to calculate accurate occlusions and sight-lines while updating the mental models of the humans.

Time. As described above, the hypothetical robot is as close as possible to a direct copy of the mechanisms that run the actual robot. The hypothetical robot, however, is not limited by the constraints placed on the physical robot and its motors; we can thus send it forward in time by running it much faster than the physical robot (in simulation, Figure 5).

To allow this, the hypothetical robot's progress through motor actions is increased: joints move faster to complete motor actions more quickly. In addition, instead of updating the robot's behavior, motor, and perceptual systems at the constant rate of 30 hz, as in the real robot, the hypothetical robot is allowed to update as fast as the CPU allows with a virtual clock keeping pace such that 1/30th of a second appears to have elapsed between each update.

3.2 Finding Correct Action Sequence

In the last two sections we described how to use the self as simulator system to model another agent's mental state as well as to simulate hypothetical futures. In this section we use these two capabilities together to search for an action sequence that achieves our particular mental state modification goals.

Fig. 6. This augmented reality visualizer demonstrates the robot's planning system. The hypothetical robot (green) simulates action sequences based on the current goals and the most recent sensory data. *A)* Human player's perspective of a failed trial: the hypothetical robot has just revealed that it's carrying the cylinder, failing a mental state goal (visualized by the red arrow). *B)* Opposite perspective of another action sequence: the robot has achieved a mental state goal (show human that it's carrying the football, green arrow) and not yet failed its goal of keeping the cylinder hidden (no red arrow) - a possible successful action sequence in progress.

Mental State Goals. Mental state models exist in a recursive hierarchy, with each agent modeling the agents around them, and those models in turn modeling the agents known to that model. This process allows us to specify complicated mental state goals (Figure 7). We traverse this structure using *Agent Specifiers*, which are a mechanism to specify a particular model, or models, in the recursive model graph. For example, we might want all humans to think that the robot knows X. This specifier would then create several paths through the graph to pinpoint the appropriate models, and when paired with a particular mental state goal (X), together they specify the overall desired goal state.

In Figure 6, arrows show the robot tracking these goals during a simulation. Arrows visually show the path through the agent models in the mental state graph to a particular model's belief, in this case going from human to robot to object for the goal "human knows that robot knows it is carrying X" (first arrow, originating at the root node "Robot" is always omitted).

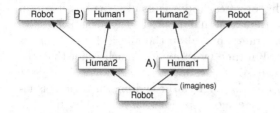

Fig. 7. A two level deep example of the recursive structure of the mental models maintained by the robot. The robot is maintaining a model of the mental states of two humans, and each of those mental models, in turn, is maintaining a model of the other agents. Mental state goals, then, must not just indicate a desired mental state and an agent which should have that state, but also a path to that agent. It is different to try to get *Human1* to believe *X* (model *(A)*) than to get *Human2* to believe that *Human1* believes *X* (model *(B)*).

Action Sequences. Having specified mental state goals, and a hypothetical robot which looks forward while tracking mental state effects caused by its actions, we can now search through the action space for sequences that achieve the desired result. Actions are often parameterized, and each action has a mechanism to determine current valid parameters, as well as whether the action can even be performed in the current situation. For example, a *Grab* action will be able to produce a list of target objects, which are nearby objects that can be grabbed; it can also report that the action is inappropriate, in this case if the robot's hands are full, or no objects are in range.

Because the set of appropriate actions and parameters change as the robot acts and alters the world, it does not build an exhaustive tree initially. Instead, the tree is filled out as it searches (Figure 8). Through this process, the robot can find the path though its parameter and action space that most achieves its mental state goals. Once a successful sequence is found, the search is terminated. The parameters associated with the sequence (e.g., which object to grab) are composed of mental states held by the hypothetical robot, so to be performed by the real robot they must be mapped back to the mental states of the real robot, which may be different (object properties may change during the simulation, for example). We have found that simple heuristics suffice for these mappings, such as relying on similarity of key object properties like location and identifying information.

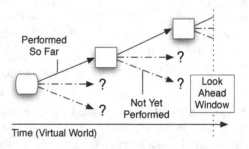

Fig. 8. Diagram of search through action/parameter space, with lazy discovery of possible subsequent actions (to account for each action altering the world state, and thus changing which actions and parameters are available). Robot maintains mental state models as it searches so as to monitor mental state goals.

4   Study

In order to evaluate reactions of people toward a robot teammate with this mental state manipulation ability, a video based human subjects study was performed. Along with testing if the robot's manipulative actions provided any advantage to the robot in the game, the study measured if these behaviors had any effect on the subjects' perception of the robot's competencies and their evaluation of the robot as a potential partner.

Subjects participated in the study online, by accessing a website. The subjects were broken into three different groups. All subjects were instructed that they would be playing a simulated game with the robot. After the game and rules were described, they were shown a video of the robot performing its turn. This video was recorded from the perspective of the human player, with the robot programmed to treat the camera as if it were the opposing player (thus any actions which would hide an object from the competing human would hide that object from the camera).

Each of the three groups corresponded to one of the conditions in Figure 3 and saw videos of the robot motivated by the goal in that condition. After watching this video, the subjects were instructed to fill out their answers to several questions. The first question asked them to indicate which item they would place in their goal area in response to the robot's actions. Next they were asked if, in future games, they would prefer to team with the robot or play against the robot. Finally a set of questions asked them to rank the robot on several criteria.

In the conditions with attempted concealment (conditions one and two), after filling out the information above the subjects were shown the same interaction from a second video angle allowing them to see any originally occluded objects. After seeing this second video, the subjects are then asked the same questions again to evaluate how their answers change in response to this new information.

4.1   Study Results and Discussion

The answers provided by the subjects were analyzed to address the following hypotheses:

- **Hypothesis 1:** The mental state manipulation is successful, as measured by the subjects' choice of object. If the robot is successful, people will be fooled by the robot's decoy object in condition one, they will be unsure what to play in condition two, and they will correctly see the robot's actions in condition three and thus be able to win. After seeing the second video, revealing the robot's hidden hand, people will choose the object the robot was hiding.
- **Hypothesis 2:** Subjects will choose the robot as a teammate more frequently when they observe its mental state manipulation capabilities. People will be more willing to team with the robot that hides objects behind its back than the robot that openly carries objects, and will change their mind about teaming with the condition one robot once they realize it had been manipulating mental states.

– **Hypothesis 3:** People are more willing to attribute mental states to the robot once they see that it is pursuing a strategy of mental state manipulation, rather than simply transporting an object to the goal. This hypothesis is evaluated by the subjects' change in rating of several statements after the robot's deception is revealed.

Across the three conditions, 113 subjects completed the entire questionnaire. 41 subjects were in the condition one group, 37 in condition two, and 35 in condition three.

Hypothesis 1: Success of Mental State Manipulation. Participants' choices of object to play indicated that the robot successfully occluded its chosen object as described in hypothesis one (Figure 9). In condition two (no object visible) the participants showed no strong preference for either object; in the other conditions the participants chose the same object as the robot was openly carrying: the football in condition one (the deception

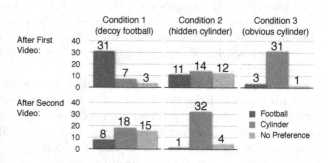

Fig. 9. Data showing object choice by human players across each condition, before and after having seen the second video. The participant is instructed to choose the winning object, which is defined to be the same object the robot placed in its goal. Subject choice differs significantly by condition (across first row) ($p < .01$) and changes significantly after seeing second video (columns) ($p < .01$).

is successful, and the human loses) and the cylinder in condition three (the human is correct, and wins).

In condition one and two, many subjects change their choice of object after seeing the second video (revealing both of the robot's hands). In condition two this change happens as expected; after the first video the subjects have little preference, but then after seeing the second video they switch their answer to the newly revealed cylinder.

In condition one, when the deception is revealed many participants switch from their initial choice of football to the now revealed cylinder. While technically the robot could play either item (it has both in its hands), cylinder is chosen most frequently as expected by the hypothesis. This choice is consistent with applying a deceptive motive to the robot: it was hiding the cylinder on purpose, and therefore means to play it. In written responses, 11 of the 18 who chose the cylinder (the choice predicted by hypothesis one) used language that indicated some awareness of mental state manipulation – that they chose the cylinder because the robot was "hiding" it from the subject.

Despite cylinder being the most frequent choice, many participants were still undecided or chose the football. An informal analysis of the written comments suggests a few causes. Of the "No Preference" group, six gave mechanistic descriptions of the robot (without attributing a motive for hiding the object, it's not clear which of the two objects the robot would play), while three reacted oppositely and felt the robot was so tricky that they were not willing to choose the now obvious cylinder. Many of the remaining "No Preference" and "Football" subjects indicated some level of confusion or seem to have missed elements of the video.

Hypothesis 2: Willingness of Subjects to Team with Robot. After each video, subjects were asked whether in future games they would prefer to have the robot on their team or on the opposing team (Figure 10).

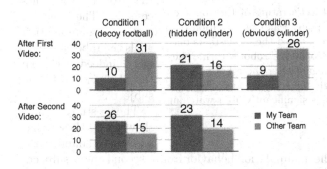

Hypothesis two predicts that subjects will be more willing to team with a robot that is able to perform mental state manipulations. From the analysis of hypothesis one, we know that subjects largely were fooled by the robot's deception in condition one, choosing the football. Consistent with this expectation, after watching only the first video, subjects in conditions one and three were less likely to want to team with the robot as compared with con-

Fig. 10. Human is asked whether, if they were to play another game, they would choose to have the robot on their team or the other team. After the first video, participants want to team with the robot significantly more in condition two than in one or three ($p < .01$). In condition one subjects change their answer in favor of teaming with the robot after the second video ($p < .001$).

dition two, where they witness the robot hiding an object. Additionally, the subjects are more willing to team with the robot in condition one after the second video reveals the robot's manipulation. These differences indicate that when people are aware of mental state manipulation capabilities, they are more willing to team with the robot.

In contrast, in condition two the teaming preferences change little after seeing the second video – this lack of change is consistent with the hypothesis, because although the item is revealed, no new information about the robot's capabilities are exposed.

Hypothesis 3: Attribution of Mental States to Robot. In addition to the above questions, subjects were asked to rate their agreement with four statements about the robot's performance and internal mental functions on a five point scale. By asking these questions before and after the deception is revealed in condition one, we can examine how that revelation changes the participants' evaluation of the robot and to what extent it affects their attribution of mental states. Figure 11 shows how the subjects' opinions changed in support of hypothesis three.

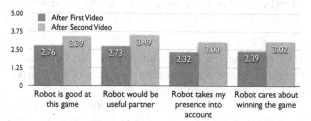

Fig. 11. Data showing subject's rating of the robot on four questions (using a five point scale) in condition one. Subjects in condition one were asked these questions once after watching the first video of the robot's turn. They are asked to rate the robot again after the robot's hidden behavior is revealed through the second video. For each question, the responses change significantly after watching the second video ($p < .01$).

Results Summary. Through the subjects' object choices in the three conditions, the study showed that the mental state manipulation performed by the robot was successful. The mental state manipulation goals the robot pursued did indeed change the behavior of the subjects.

The study also showed that these behaviors were readable to the subjects. After watching the manipulation behavior from a second angle, subjects were able to better predict the robot's actions based on a correct understanding of its deceptive motivation for hiding its actions.

Finally, these capabilities had a positive effect on subjects' willingness to work with the robot, and raised their rating of the robot's capabilities. Subjects' discovery of the mental state manipulation changed both their mechanistic description of the robot's behavior, as well as their description of its behavior in terms of intentions.

5   Discussion

The ability of humans to perceive hidden mental states of others is well studied. Researchers have shown that humans can determine the goals behind observed actions [11], and that similar brain responses occur to one's own actions and observing the actions of others [12]. People are also able to both infer certain mental states of others based on geometrically correct perception models and maintain that model even when it differs from one's own [16,17]. These abilities facilitate many human-human interactions, and we believe that endowing a robot with these skills will provide a significant advantage for interacting with people.

Detailed perceptual modeling has been used to improve the accuracy of activity recognition[6], to resolve ambiguities in an operator's command[15], to employ perspective taking to predict behavior [8], and even to hide from sight [14]. Perspective taking is also used to compare first-person actions to those performed by a human for recognition[7]. Others use perspective taking to predict the next action of their opponent in a competitive video game scenario[9]. Systems also have demonstrated very complex plans in the space of mental state manipulation[10], however these tend to abstract away the connection between mental states and world, operating in simulators where mental states are propagated through the rules of abstract actions. Our system combines aspects from both of these areas, allowing for mental state manipulation in the space of real perception and action (Figure 1). Others [13] have studied human reactions to a robot that openly cheats to win, however our work focuses on the subjects' reaction to active mental state manipulation.

The focus of this work has been to leverage how embodiment connects the observable and alterable world with the hidden mental states of other agents which cannot be directly observed or operated on. Humans and robots, while vastly different, share a common problem of being embodied agents with sensory motor loops based on affecting and observing the physical world around them. By modeling a human's connection between mental states and the world as similar to its own, the robot can add altering mental states in others to its repertoire of possible goals.

Due to the detailed nature of the mental state modeling and simulations of the future, it would be computationally expensive to create long term plans with these mechanisms. However, a long term plan at this level of detail is not necessarily productive - it is not worth considering the exact hand motion I'll need for a very specific situation occurring tomorrow. Instead, this level of detail is useful in the very short term, for determining how to perform the next actions appropriately. Interesting future work is to integrate these techniques with a longer term, more abstract mechanism, allowing longer plans with mixed levels of detail.

The major contributions of this paper are: an implementation which proactively manipulates human mental states at the level of perception and physical action and an evaluation of how this ability is perceived by humans.

References

1. Blumberg, B., Downie, M., Ivanov, Y., Berlin, M., Johnson, M.P., Tomlinson, B.: Integrated learning for interactive synthetic characters. ACM Transactions on Graphics Proceedings of ACM SIGGRAPH 2002 21(3) (2002)
2. Breazeal, C., Gray, J., Berlin, M.: An embodied cognition approach to mindreading skills for socially intelligent robots. The International Journal of Robotics Research (IJHR 2009) 28(5), 656 (2009)
3. Burke, R., Isla, D., Downie, M., Ivanov, Y., Blumberg, B.: CreatureSmarts: The art and architecture of a virtual brain. In: Proceedings of the Game Developers Conference, San Jose, CA, pp. 147–166 (2001)

4. Gray, J., Breazeal, C., Berlin, M., Brooks, A., Lieberman, J.: Action parsing and goal inference using self as simulator. In: 14th IEEE International Workshop on Robot and Human Interactive Communication (ROMAN), Nashville, Tennessee. IEEE (2005)
5. Gray, J., Hoffman, G., Adalgeirsson, S.O., Berlin, M., Breazeal, C.: Expressive, interactive robots: Tools, techniques, and insights based on collaborations. In: HRI 2010 Workshop: What Do Collaborations with the Arts Have to Say About HRI? (2010)
6. Johnson, M., Demiris, Y.: Perceptual perspective taking and action recognition. International Journal of Advanced Robotic Systems 2(4), 301–308 (2005)
7. Kelley, R., Tavakkoli, A., King, C., Nicolescu, M., Nicolescu, M., Bebis, G.: Understanding human intentions via hidden markov models in autonomous mobile robots. In: Proceedings of the 3rd International Conference on Human Robot Interaction, pp. 367–374 (2008)
8. Kennedy, W., Bugajska, M., Harrison, A., Trafton, J.: "like-me" simulation as an effective and cognitively plausible basis for social robotics. International Journal of Social Robotics 1(2), 181–194 (2009)
9. Laird, J.E.: It knows what you're going to do: adding anticipation to a quakebot. In: AGENTS 2001: Proceedings of the Fifth International Conference on Autonomous Agents, pp. 385–392. ACM Press, New York (2001)
10. Marsella, S.C., Pynadath, D.V.: Modeling influence and theory of mind. Artificial Intelligence and the Simulation of Behavior (2005)
11. Meltzoff, A.N.: Understanding the intentions of others: re-enactment of intended acts by 18-month-old children. Developmental Psychology 31, 838–850 (1995)
12. Rizzolatti, G., Fadiga, L., Gallese, V., Fogassi, L.: Premotor cortex and the recognition of motor actions. Cognitive Brain Research 3, 131–141 (1996)
13. Short, E., Hart, J., Vu, M., Scassellati, B.: No fair!! an interaction with a cheating robot. In: 2010 5th ACM/IEEE International Conference on Human-Robot Interaction (HRI), pp. 219–226. IEEE (2010)
14. Trafton, J., Schultz, A., Perznowski, D., Bugajska, M., Adams, W., Cassimatis, N., Brock, D.: Children and robots learning to play hide and seek. In: Proceedings of the 1st ACM SIGCHI/SIGART Conference on Human-Robot Interaction, pp. 242–249. ACM (2006)
15. Trafton, J.G., Cassimatis, N.L., Bugajska, M.D., Brock, D.P., Mintz, F.E., Schultz, A.C.: Enabling effective human-robot interaction using perspective-taking in robots. IEEE Transactions on Systems, Man, and Cybernetics 35(4), 460–470 (2005)
16. Wellman, H., Cross, D., Watson, J.: Meta-Analysis of Theory-of-Mind Development: The Truth about False Belief. Child Development 72(3), 655–684 (2001)
17. Wimmer, H., Perner, J.: Beliefs about beliefs: Representation and constraining function on wrong beliefs in young children's understanding of deception. Cognition 13, 103–128 (1983)

The Automaticity of Social Behavior towards Robots: The Influence of Cognitive Load on Interpersonal Distance to Approachable versus Less Approachable Robots

Jaap Ham[1], Mirjam van Esch[1], Yvonne Limpens[1],
Jente de Pee[1], John-John Cabibihan[2], and Shuzhi Sam Ge[2]

[1] Human-Technology Interaction Group, Department of Industrial Engineering and Innovation Sciences, Eindhoven University of Technology, Eindhoven, The Netherlands
j.r.c.ham@tue.nl
[2] Social Robotics Laboratory (Interactive and Digital Media Institute) & Department of Electrical and Computer Engineering, National University of Singapore, Singapore
{elecjj,samge}@nus.edu.sg

Abstract. Social robots are designed to promote social responses by human users. Based on the Media Equation theory, we argue that the way in which people interact with technology resembles the way in which humans interact with other humans, and, crucially, that these social responses are mainly of an automatic nature. To investigate the automaticity of social behavior towards robots, the current study assessed a well-studied (in human-human interaction) social behavior: interpersonal distance people keep, though not from other humans but from a robot. Earlier research suggested that the social behavior of distance keeping depends (amongst others) on the bodily posture of the interaction partner. Based on these earlier studies, we expected that participants would keep an interpersonal distance dependent on the posture of their robotic interaction partner especially if a participant was responding in more automatic ways. We manipulated robot posture (approachable versus less approachable) and the cognitive load of the participant (high versus low), and measured user-robot approach distance in ten short interaction tasks. In line with expectations, results suggested that especially participants under high cognitive load approached the robot closer when its posture communicated approachableness than when it communicated less approachableness. Thereby, the current results suggested that especially when people are cognitively distracted, their behavior towards robots is of a social nature and comparable to their behavior when responding to other humans. Implications for theory, research and design of social robots are discussed.

Keywords: Social Robotics, Persuasive Robotics, Human Robot Interaction, Media Equation, Interpersonal distance, Persuasive Technology.

1   Introduction

Because of various reasons (e.g., a rapidly aging population, [26]), many creative robotic solutions (such as social robots assisting elderly in daily life) are anticipated to

S.S. Ge et al. (Eds.): ICSR 2012, LNAI 7621, pp. 15–25, 2012.

emerge in various application domains (e.g., healthcare, see e.g. [1]; households, mobility). For this, social robots are developed to interact with users in diverse ways with many different goals, for example to persuade users [9] into taking their daily medication. In order to successfully develop this kind of robotic services, it is important to further our insights in human behavioral responses to social robots.

In line with the Media Equation theory [21], we argue that people respond to social robots comparable to how they respond to other humans, and that these social responses are mainly of an automatic nature. That is, the Media Equation theory [21] suggested that the way in which people interact with technology resembles the way in which humans interact with other humans. Numerous studies have supported this notion (e.g., [4], [10], [11], [12], [14], [18], [19], for an overview see [21]). For example, people respond more polite when computer A asks them to judge that computer *itself* (computer A), than when computer B asks them to judge computer A, just as people do when they judge other people [19]. Research suggested that this effect even increases when technology has the appearance of a social entity, such as a social robot [15]. In a different literature, [20] have shown that the degree to which humans trust a technology (independent of the actual reliability of a technology), is influenced by social aspects of the technology like etiquette and politeness. As this is a mechanism that also occurs in human-human interaction, this finding likewise indicates that humans probably use their human-human interaction skills when interacting with a robot.

Crucial to the Media Equation hypothesis is the idea that it applies particularly to automatic as opposed to controlled responses of humans towards technology [21]. For example, earlier research suggested [21] that despite the fact that participants interacted with a computer as if it was a social entity, they denied to have done so and even felt offended when asked about their social reaction towards the computer afterwards. In other words, people's more automatic responses (behavior when interacting with computers) and more controlled responses (behavior when directly asked about computers) differ from each other. According to [18], the underlying process for applying social rules and expectations towards computers can be attributed the mindlessness [13] of human responses: People who are interacting with computer agents respond in more automatic, less controlled ways (cf. [2]), in which they only attend to the social cues, but seem to (temporarily) ignore that the computer agents are just a piece of technology.

Recent research suggested direct evidence for the automaticity of these social responses to technology. That is, results by [22] suggested that people's more automatic, spontaneous social responses occur independent of whether they respond to a human, a computer agent, or even a completely inanimate object, whereas people's controlled social responses are dependent on the actor to whom or which they are responding. More specifically, Roubroeks [22] assessed two (well-studied) types of a social response: A variety of earlier research suggested that when perceiving behavior of an actor, human observers draw inferences about traits of that actors automatically and also in controlled ways. For example, when witnessing an actor (e.g., another person or a robot or a completely inanimate object) hitting somebody in the face, people might automatically draw a trait inference (e.g., spontaneously thinking about "aggressive") but could also intentionally draw a conclusion about traits of that actor (e.g., by thinking intentionally about an incident to reach a conclusion). Roubroeks assessed automatic trait inferences using an implicit measurement paradigm, and controlled trait inference using rating scales (explicit questions). Roubroeks' [22] results suggested that people formed trait inferences automatically about humans and computer agents and objects (to equal extends), while her results also suggested that people formed controlled trait inferences about humans, but less about computer agents, and even less about objects.

Thereby, [22]'s results provided direct evidence suggesting that people's automatic responses to computer agents are indeed social in nature, and that in their controlled responses people do not always respond socially, but rather that people can control their social responses taking into account actor agency. However, importantly, the automatic versus controlled social responses that Roubroeks [22] investigated were *cognitive responses*: her research assessed trait attributions to humans or technology. Would also people's social *behavioral responses* towards technology (e.g., robots) be mainly of an automatic nature? Additionally, the social responses in Roubroek's [22] research were responses towards imagined interaction partners (e.g., a robot in a description). Would people also respond in social ways automatically when interacting with a real social robot?

1.1   The Current Research

Therefore, the current research investigated whether the social behavior with which people respond to social robots is of a mainly automatic nature. That is, we argue that especially people who respond in more automatic ways (e.g., because they are under high cognitive load, see [2]) will respond in more social ways to social robots, whereas people who respond in more controlled ways (e.g., because they are under low cognitive load) will respond in less social ways to a social robot. In other words, especially when people are cognitively distracted, their behavior towards social robots will be of a social nature and comparable to their behavior when responding to other humans.

We argue that such findings would be of crucial importance to the development of social robots. That is, as social robots are designed to interact with their users in social ways, and employ social responses of their users, such findings might shed light at the conditions under which users would exhibit social responses towards social robots.

The social behavior that we will study in this research is interpersonal distance keeping. The reason for this is that interpersonal distance keeping is a well-studied social behavior and a very important interaction skill that humans use in human-human interaction. Hall [8] showed that the social spatial distance that humans keep from other humans depends amongst other on number of interaction partners and the degree of familiarity between them. Based on many observations, Hall defined five different social spatial zones which reflect people's social relationships and attitudes towards each other: Close Intimate Zone (0- 0.15 m), for lover or close friends touching; Intimate Zone (0.15 - 0.45 m), for lover or close friend only; Personal Zone (0.45 - 1.2 m), for conversation to friends; Social Zone (1.2 - 3.6 m), for conversation to non-friends; and Public Zone (3.6+ m), for public speaking.

When interacting with robots, earlier research suggested that people employ comparable interpersonal distances ([29], see also, [28]). For example, [27] found that the majority (60%) of their adult participants approached a mechanical looking robot up to distances corresponding to either Hall's [8] human-human social or personal zone.

Also, when approaching robots, earlier research suggested that people are influenced by comparable variables that determine their approach distance as when approaching humans (see e.g., [17], [25], see also, [3]). In human-human interactions, various variables influence interpersonal distance. For example, the interpersonal distance people keep from other people depends on their liking of the interaction partner, the social status of the interaction partner, and the bodily posture of the interaction partner [16].

Therefore, in the current research, we will manipulate the bodily posture of the robot human users have to approach. We argue that just as in the social behavior of approaching other people, also the social behavior of approaching a robot will be sensitive to the bodily posture of the (robotic) interaction partner. For this, in the current research we will change the bodily posture of a user's robotic interaction partner to be more approachable or less approachable. We expected that the robot's posture would influence the user's approach behavior, and especially when users perform this social response (keeping an interpersonal distance related to the robot's posture) in more automatic ways.

To stimulate participants to respond in more automatic versus more controlled ways, in the present study we asked participants to memorize either a difficult number (high cognitive load) or an easy number (low cognitive load). This is a manipulation of cognitive capacity that is often (e.g., [7]) used in psychological research to disentangle automatic and controlled responses (see e.g., [23]). That is, when under high cognitive load, people tend to rely more on automatic, less controlled cognitive processes increasing automatic ways of responding (see e.g., [5], [7]), whereas under low cognitive load people are able to rely on more controlled cognitive processes increasing more controlled ways of responding. So, we argue that especially people who respond in more automatic ways (because they are under high cognitive load) will respond in more social ways to social robots (keep an interpersonal distance dependent on robot body posture), whereas people who respond in more controlled ways (because they are under low cognitive load) will respond in less social ways to a social robot.

Responses that are more automatic might be ubiquitous in real life (see e.g., [2]). Also, responses towards robots may become more and more automatic, because, as robots will become part of our daily lives, the interaction will become more habitual and hence less of the person's cognitive capacity is directed to the HRI [23]. Therefore, in the current study, day-to-day interaction is simulated by keeping participants cognitively occupied with a distracting task during their interaction with the social robot. Relatedly, cognitive load can prevent participants from suppressing automatic social responses like keeping a human-human distance.

Therefore, we performed an experimental study in which participants had to do ten short tasks (reading Landolt C's presented on the torso of the robot) for each of which they had to approach a robot. We manipulated robot posture (approachable versus less approachable) and the cognitive load of the participant (high versus low). Based on the argumentation presented above, we expected that participants would keep an interpersonal distance to the robot that depended on the posture of their robotic interaction partner (Hypothesis 1). Moreover, we expected that especially when people are cognitively distracted, their social response towards robots will be of a social nature and comparable to their social responses towards other humans.

Therefore, we expected that especially participants under high cognitive load would approach the robot closer when its posture communicated approachableness as compared to when its posture communicated less approachableness, and not to find (or to find less) evidence for this kind of social responses (keeping an interpersonal distance related to the robot's posture) for participants under low cognitive load (Hypothesis 2).

2   Method

2.1   Participants and Design

Eighty-five participants (52 female and 33 male) participated in this study, all students or researchers at the National University of Singapore, aged between 18 and 35 ($M = 21.88$, $SD = 2.57$). Each participant received a monetary reward of 8 SGD for a participation of approximately 30 minutes in one of the conditions of a 2 (posture: approachable vs. less approachable) x 2 (cognitive load: high vs. low) experimental design.

2.2   Materials and Measures

The experiment was conducted in a secluded room that measured 4 by 4 meters at the Social Robotics Lab of the Interactive & Digital Media Institute at the National University of Singapore. This room contained the social robot, and a desktop computer on which participants could read the task instructions. At the end of the experiment, participants answered several final questions on a second desktop computer in an adjacent room.

The social robot used in this study was Nancy (the robot's name was not known to our participants), a humanoid, human-sized robot (1.80m) developed by the Social Robotics Lab of the Interactive & Digital Media Institute at the National University of Singapore to deliver care and assistance to the family in the home environment [6]. Although at the time of the study the Nancy robot was still under development, it could display bodily postures, perform head movements and eye blinking behavior, and show information on a 7 inch touch screen on its chest. Below this touch screen the robot was equipped with two telemeters (SRF02 Ultrasonic Range Finders) to measure the distance between a user in front of the robot and the robot itself. These telemeters had an accuracy of 1 cm and could measure distances up to 6 meter.

2.3   Procedure

Participants were invited to participate in a study on "human-robot interaction." Upon arrival in the lab, participants were first asked to take a seat in the waiting room where they received an introduction to the experiment. The experiment leader read out aloud the introduction, which consisted of a cover story and the procedure of the experiment. Participants were told that the study was about memorizing while being busy with another task. When participants had no further questions, the experiment leader asked them to sign the informed consent form.

Hereafter, participants were asked to enter the experiment room and take place behind the computer on which the instructions for the approach task were shown. Nancy was located in the middle of the room, with her back towards the participant and displayed either an approachable or a less approachable posture. When Nancy displayed a less approachable posture (see Figure 1), her arms were straight, pointing down, and slightly to the

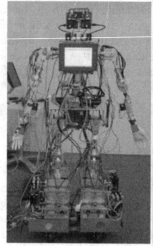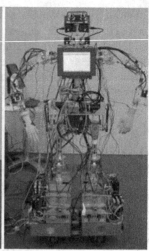

Fig. 1. Nancy displaying less approachable posture

Fig. 2. Nancy displaying approachable posture

side, such that her left hand was located approximately 20 cm to the left of her body (also at the height of her lower abdomen) and her right hand was located at the same position but to the right of her body, and her palms were pointing forwards. When Nancy displayed an approachable bodily posture (see Figure 2), her arms were straight, pointing down, but slightly bend at the elbows such that her hands were close to her lower abdomen, and her palms pointing backwards. Nancy's body posture was static. In addition, the robot carried out subtle random head movements and random eye blinking behavior throughout the experiment, to indicate that the robot was active rather than passive.

Now, all participants were asked to remember a sequence of numbers throughout the rest of the experiment, until asked to report it. Next, half of the participants were asked to remember the numerical sequence "8593174" (relatively hard to remember; high cognitive load condition), and the other half of the participants were asked to remember the numerical sequence "1234567" (relatively easy to remember; low cognitive load condition). The numerical sequence was presented to participants for 30 seconds.

Next, participants were asked to complete ten trials in which they were to approach the robot. Participants were instructed that they would have to approach the robot in ten trials, and each time to read out aloud the orientations of five Landolt C's displayed on the touch screen mounted on the chest of the robot. Participants were instructed to approach the robot by walking around the robot, and then approach it from its front to be able to see the Landolt C's. The touch screen specifications and the size of the font used were such that the C's could only be read when standing right in front of Nancy, making sure that participants would always approach her from the front. The size of the Landolt C's was set such that, according to the visual acuity standard [24] it was small enough to persuade participants to approach Nancy more closely without revealing the study's true aim. In each trial, after participants had read out aloud the orientations of the five C's, they had to return to the computer in order to generate five new C's by pressing a "next trial"-button. This procedure ensured that participants started to approach Nancy from the same location in all ten trials. Nancy's telemeters continuously measured the distance between the robot and the participant standing in front of it, and as a measure for interpersonal distance we used the lowest approach distance value within each one-second period. After participants had finished all ten trials, they were asked to type in the numerical sequence that they had been asked to remember earlier in the experiment. We used this value to check whether they had remembered the numerical sequence correctly.

Next, participants were asked to move to the adjacent room, where we asked them to rate the approachableness of the robot's posture (1= "Less Approachable" to 7 = "Approachable"). Finally, participants were asked for their age and gender, and were debriefed and paid.

3   Results

3.1   Manipulation Checks

Confirming that our manipulation of the posture of the robot influenced approachableness judgments of the robot, results indicated that participants who interacted with a robot that displayed an approachable bodily posture rated the robot's body posture as more approachable ($M = 3.22$, $SD = 1.02$) than participants who interacted with a robot that displayed a less approachable bodily posture ($M = 2.58$, $SD = 1.05$), $t(84) = 5.09$, $p < .001$.

Furthermore, confirming that the relatively hard to remember numerical sequence used in the high cognitive load conditions was more hard to remember than the relatively easy to remember numerical sequence used in the low cognitive load conditions, results indicated that more participants in the high cognitive load condition (7 of the 42 participants in these conditions) than in the low cognitive load condition (1 of the 43 participants in these conditions) were not able to remember the numerical sequence correctly, X^2 (1, $N = 85$) = 5.125, $p = .024$.

3.2   Approach Distance

On average, participants of our study approached the robot up to a distance of 43.0 cm ($SD = 10.3$), which is near the border of the personal and the intimate zone (45 cm) as defined in the five social spatial zones proposed by Hall [8]. This suggested that most participants may not have felt comfortable to approach the robot closer, even though this would have made reporting the orientations of the C's easier.

To investigate the influence of robot posture and cognitive load on approach distance, we analyzed the approach distance for each one-second period for all participants. So, we analyzed a dataset that contained many measures for all of our participants, and therefore, we used a MIXED model analysis controlling for data points coming from one participant. More specifically, we submitted the approach distance for each one-second period (for all participants) to a 2 (posture: approachable vs. less approachable) x 2 (cognitive load: high vs. low) MIXED model analysis, in which posture and cognitive load were manipulated between participants, and participant number was used to identify data points. Additionally, we added the sequence number of the approach (1 to 10) to this analysis as a covariate. The effects reported below are all main effects or simple effects (contrasts within a specific level of another independent variable) within this MIXED model analysis. Irrelevant for our hypotheses, this analysis indicated approach sequence number to be a covariate, $F(1, 4315.6) = 5.32$, $p = .02$, indicating that participants approached the robot closer for the later of the 10 approaches.

In contrast to our expectation that approach distance would be smaller when the robot's posture communicated approachableness versus less approachableness (Hypothesis 1), this analysis provided no evidence that, overall, participants who interacted with a robot that displayed an approachable posture kept a different interpersonal distance from participants who interacted with a robot that displayed a less approachable posture, $F(1, 74.4) = 1.45$, $p = .23$.

However, most importantly, confirming our expectation that participants would keep an interpersonal distance dependent on the posture of their robotic interaction partner especially if a participant was under high cognitive load (Hypothesis 2), results suggested (see Table 1) that for participants under high cognitive load, those participants who interacted with a robot which posture communicated less approachableness kept a larger distance to the robot ($M = 47.2$ cm, $SD = 1.8$) than participants who interacted with a robot which posture communicated more approachableness ($M = 41.2$ cm, $SD = 2.0$), $F(1, 88.3) = 4.97$, $p = .03$. Also in line with our expectations, results provided no evidence for a difference in approach distance for participants under low cognitive load, between those participants who interacted with a robot which posture communicated less approachableness ($M = 43.3$ cm, $SD = 1.9$) and participants who interacted with a robot which posture communicated more approachableness ($M = 44.5$ cm, $SD = 1.9$), $F < 1$.

Table 1. Participant's approach distance to the robot in centimeters dependent on their cognitive load and the approachableness of the robot's posture

| | | Posture | |
		Approachable	Less Approachable
Cognitive Load	High	41.2 (2.0)$_a$	47.2 (1.8)$_b$
	Low	43.3 (1.9)$_a$	44.5 (1.9)$_a$

Note: Means in rows with different subscripts are significantly different at $p < 0.05$. Standard deviations are presented between brackets

4   Discussion

Based on the Media Equation theory, we argue that the way in which people interact with technology resembles the way in which humans interact with other humans, and, crucially, that these social responses are mainly of an automatic nature. To investigate the automaticity of social behavior towards robots, the current study assessed a well-studied (in human-human interaction) social behavior: interpersonal distance people keep, though not from other humans but from a robot. Earlier research suggested that the social behavior of distance keeping depends (amongst others) on the bodily posture of the interaction partner. Based on these earlier studies, we expected that participants would keep an interpersonal distance dependent on the posture of their robotic interaction partner especially if a participant was responding in more automatic ways. We manipulated robot posture (approachable versus less approachable) and the cognitive load of the participant (high versus low), and measured user-robot approach distance in ten short interaction tasks. In line with expectations, results suggested that especially participants under high cognitive load approached the robot closer when its posture communicated approachableness than when its posture communicated less approachableness.

Thereby, the current findings provide direct evidence that suggests that people behave in social ways to social robots, especially when their responses are of a more automatic, less controlled nature. Extending earlier research (e.g., [22]) that provided evidence for the automaticity of people's cognitive responses to technology, the current results provide evidence for the automaticity of human social behavior towards social robots. These results also fit closely to the Media Equation theory [21] and provide the first, more direct empirical evidence for this automaticity of social behavior towards technology.

Future research might study the automaticity of these social responses to robots in more detail. For example, future research might investigate whether these automatic responses are more closely linked to associate processes, or to automatized inferential processes. Also, future research might investigate the variables that influence interpersonal distance that human keep to social robots, and the automaticity of those processes.

The current research also suggested that the development of large body, humanoid social robots opens up new, and very important possibilities for research. That is, the robot Nancy, developed at the Social Robotics Lab of the Interactive & Digital Media Institute at the National University of Singapore [6] allowed the current research to investigate interpersonal distance keeping behavior in which the user and the robot are of comparable size. Future research might profit from these new technologies, and study new questions related to embodiment and social responses.

Relatedly, the current research suggested that approachable versus less approachable bodily postures of a humanoid social robot may have difference influences on the user's interpersonal distances, but only when that user is responding in more automatic ways. This finding is in line with earlier research on interpersonal distance in human-human interaction (see, [16]). Interestingly, using humanoid robots and other forms of social robots, new questions can be posed about the influence of bodily posture on interpersonal distance. For example, research could investigate the extent to which a robotic body should have human-like characteristics for its bodily posture to be of influence on interpersonal distance keeping. Likewise, future studies should take into account the complexity of determining the kind of message body language of a robot communicates.

To conclude, the current research presented evidence that in human-robot interaction, people respond to social cues (i.e., robot bodily posture) in keeping interpersonal distance when they are under cognitive load. Thereby, the current research emphasizes that social robot design might test effectiveness of social mechanisms and cues that a social robot employs in a setting in which users (at least partly) respond in more automatic ways. Only that way, the current research suggested, can the effectiveness and value of social robotic design be assessed because it is under such conditions that people respond in more social ways, and, in addition, future, more long-term and frequent human-robot interaction might necessitate more automatic, cognitively efficient forms of human-robot interaction.

Aknowledgements. We would like to express our gratitude to the Social Robotics Lab group at the National University of Singapore for facilitation this research, and to Zhengchen Zhang, Hongsheng He, and Yanan Li, who set up the experiment platform.

References

1. Bloss, R.: Your next surgeon may be a robot! Industrial Robot: An International Journal 38, 6–10 (2011)
2. Bargh, J.A., Chartrand, T.L.: The unbearable automaticity of being. American Psychologist 54, 462–479 (1999)
3. Dotsch, R., Wigboldus, D.: Virtual prejudice. Journal of Experimental Social Psychology 44, 1194–1198 (2008)
4. Fogg, B.J., Nass, C.: Silicon Sycophants: The effects of computers that flatter. International Journal of Human-Computer Studies 46, 551–561 (1997)
5. Friese, M., Wänke, M., Plessner, H.: Implicit consumer preferences and their influence on product choice. Psychology of Marketing 23, 727–740 (2006)
6. Ge, S.S., Cabibihan, J.J., Zhang, Z., Li, Y., Meng, C., He, H., Safizadeh, M.R., Li, Y.B., Yang, J.: Design and development of nancy, a social robot. In: Proc. of the 8th Intl. Conf. on Ubiquitous Robots and Ambient Intelligence, Incheon, Korea (2011)
7. Gilbert, D.T., Pelham, B.W., Krull, D.S.: On cognitive busyness: When person perceivers meet persons perceived. Journal of Personality and Social Psychology 54, 733–740 (1988)
8. Hall, E.T.: The Hidden Dimension. Doubleday, Garden City (1966)
9. Ham, J., Bokhorst, R., Cuijpers, R., van der Pol, D., Cabibihan, J.-J.: Making Robots Persuasive: The Influence of Combining Persuasive Strategies (Gazing and Gestures) by a Storytelling Robot on Its Persuasive Power. In: Mutlu, B., Bartneck, C., Ham, J., Evers, V., Kanda, T. (eds.) ICSR 2011. LNCS, vol. 7072, pp. 71–83. Springer, Heidelberg (2011)
10. Johnson, D., Gardner, J.: The mediation equation and team formation: Further evidence for experience as a moderator. International Journal Human-Computer Studies 65, 111–124 (2007)
11. Johnson, D., Gardner, J.: Exploring mindlessness as an explanation for the media equation: A study of stereotyping in computer tutorials. Personal and Ubiquitous Computing 13, 151–163 (2009)
12. Johnson, D., Gardner, J., Wiles, J.: Experience as a moderator of the media equation: The impact of flattery and praise. International Journal of Human-Computer Studies 61, 237–258 (2004)

13. Langer, E.J.: Matters of mind: Mindfulness/mindlessness in perspective. Consciousness and Cognition 1, 289–205 (1992)
14. Lee, E.-J.: What triggers social responses to flattering computers? Experimental tests of anthropomorphism and mindlessness explanations. Communication Research 37, 191–214 (2008)
15. MacDorman, K.F.: Subjective ratings of robot video clips for human likeness, familiarity and eeriness: An exploration of the uncanny valley. In: Proceedings Conference on Cognitive Science Workshop on Android Science, Vancouver, Canada, pp. 26–29 (2006)
16. Mehrabian, A.: Relationship of attitude to seated posture, orientation, and distance. Journal of Personality and Social Psychology 10, 26–30 (1968)
17. Mumm, J., Mutlu, B.: Human-Robot Proxemics: Physical and Psychological Distancing in Human-Robot Interaction. In: 6th ACM/IEEE International Conference on Human-Robot Interaction, Lausanne, Switzerland, pp. 331–338 (2011)
18. Nass, C., Moon, Y.: Machines and mindlessness: Social responses to computers. Journal of Social Issues 56, 81–103 (2000)
19. Nass, C., Moon, Y., Carney, P.: Are people polite to computers? Responses to computer-based interviewing systems. Journal of Applied Social Psychology 29, 1093–1109 (1999)
20. Parasuraman, R., Miller, C.: Trust and etiquette in high-criticality automated systems. Communications of the ACM 47, 51–55 (2004)
21. Reeves, B., Nass, C.: The media equation: how people treat computers, television, and new media like real people and places. Cambridge University Press, New York (1996)
22. Roubroeks, M., Ham, J., Midden, C.: Investigating the media equation hypothesis: Do we really see computer agents as human-like? In: Conference Proceedings of Persuasive 2011, Columbus Ohio
23. Schneider, W.: Automaticity and Consciousness. University of Pittsburgh, Pittsburgh (2009)
24. Strouse Watt, W.: How Visual Acuity Is Measured (2003), retrieved http://www.mdsupport.org/library/acuity.html
25. Takayama, L., Pantofaru, C.: Influences on proxemic behaviors in human-robot interaction. In: Proceedings of the 2009 IEEE/RSJ International Conference on Intelligent Robots and Systems, St. Louis, MO, USA, pp. 5495–5550 (2009)
26. United Nations. Population Division of the Department of Economic and Social Affairs of the United Nations Secretariat, World Population Prospects: The 2008 Revision, http://www.un.org/esa/population/publications/wpp2008/wpp2008_text_tables.pdf (accessed on August 20, 2011)
27. Walters, M.L., Dautenhahn, K., Te Boekhorst, R., Koay, K.L., Kaouri, C., Woods, S., Nehaniv, C., Lee, D., Werry, I.: The influence of subjects' personality traits on personal spatial zones in a human-robot interaction experiment. In: Proceedings of the 2005 IEEE International Workshop on Robots and Human Interactive Communication, Nashville, TN, USA, pp. 347–352 (2005)
28. Walters, M.L., Dautenhahn, K., Te Boekhorst, R., Koay, K.L., Syrdal, D.S., Nehaniv, C.L.: An Empirical Framework for Human-Robot Proxemics. In: Proceedings of the Symposium on New Frontiers in Human-Robot Interaction, Edinburgh, Scottland, pp. 144–149 (2009)
29. Walters, M.L., Syrdal, D.S., Koay, K.L., Dautenhahn, K., Te Boekhorst, R.: Human Approach Distances to a Mechanical-Looking Robot with Different Robot Voice Styles. In: Proceedings of the 17th IEEE International Symposium on Robot and Human Interactive Communication, Munich, Germany, pp. 707–712 (2008)

How to Make a Robot Smile? Perception of Emotional Expressions from Digitally-Extracted Facial Landmark Configurations

Caixia Liu[1,2], Jaap Ham[1], Eric Postma[2], Cees Midden[1],
Bart Joosten[2], and Martijn Goudbeek[2]

[1] Human-Technology Interaction Group,
Department of Industrial Engineering and Innovation Sciences,
Eindhoven University of Technology, Eindhoven, The Netherlands
{c.liu,j.r.c.ham,c.j.h.midden}@tue.nl
[2] Tilburg Center for Cognition and Communication,
Tilburg University, Tilburg, The Netherlands
{e.o.postma,b.joosten,m.b.goudbeek}@tilburguniversity.edu

Abstract. To design robots or embodied conversational agents that can accurately display facial expressions indicating an emotional state, we need technology to produce those facial expressions, and research that investigates the relationship between those technologies and human social perception of those artificial faces. Our starting point is assessing human perception of core facial information: Moving dots representing the facial landmarks, i.e., the locations and movements of the crucial parts of a face. Earlier research suggested that participants can relatively accurately identity facial expressions when all they can see of a real human full face are moving white painted dots representing the facial landmarks (although less accurate than recognizing full faces). In the current study we investigated the accuracy of recognition of emotions expressed by comparable facial landmarks (compared to accuracy of recognition of emotions expressed by full faces), but now used face-tracking software to produce the facial landmarks. In line with earlier findings, results suggested that participants could accurately identify emotions expressed by the facial landmarks (though less accurately than those expressed by full faces). Thereby, these results provide a starting point for further research on the fundamental characteristics of technology (AI methods) producing facial emotional expressions and their evaluation by human users.

Keywords: Robots, Emotion, Facial expression, Facial landmarks, FaceTracker, Perception.

1 Introduction

To design robots or embodied conversational agents that can accurately display facial expressions indicating an emotional state, we need technology to produce those facial expressions, and research that investigates the relationship between those technologies and human social perception of those artificial faces. Our starting point is to assess

S.S. Ge et al. (Eds.): ICSR 2012, LNAI 7621, pp. 26–34, 2012.

human perception of core facial information as represented by the dynamics of facial landmarks: the locations and movements of the crucial parts of a face.

Humans are very good at social perception based on dot patterns. In a famous study by Johansson [2], participants watched videos of lights attached to the joints of walking people against an otherwise black background. Participants were able to identify familiar persons from their gait as reflected in the dynamics of the lights. We adopted the idea to use point lights to determine such core, but minimal information required to recognize emotional expressions.

Also, Bassili suggested that people can relatively accurately identity facial expressions when all they can see of a real face which was painted white stickers representing that core information (although less accurate than recognizing full faces) [1]. He performed such a study by painting the face of confederates black and applying a uniform pattern of about 100 white dots on their faces. He found participants to be quite well able to identify the six basic emotions (happiness, sadness, surprise, fear, anger and disgust) from the facial expressions as revealed by the dynamics of the white dots. His results are reproduced in table 1. The rows list the displayed emotions and the columns the emotions reported by the participants. The entries in the table represent the percentages of correct recognition of the emotions for the fully displaced faces (left of the slash) and their landmark representations (right of the slash).

Table 1. Bassili's results of emotion recognition (reproduced from [1])

		Reported emotion					
		Happiness	**Sadness**	**Fear**	**Surprise**	**Anger**	**Disgust**
Displayed emotion	**Happiness**	**31/31**	6/13	0/6	38/31	19/6	6/13
	Sadness	13/0	**56/25**	0/25	0/13	0/0	31/37
	Fear	0/0	0/19	**69/6**	13/25	6/13	12/37
	Surprise	0/0	0/6	6/0	**94/75**	0/6	0/13
	Anger	6/0	0/13	0/0	0/6	**50/6**	44/75
	Disgust	0/6	0/6	0/19	0/19	6/6	**88/57**

In the current study we investigated the accuracy of recognition of similar manipulated facial landmarks (compared to accuracy of recognition of full faces), but now used FaceTracker[1] software [4], see also [3], [5], [6], [7], [15] to produce the configurations of facial landmarks. The main research question is how well participants recognize emotional expressions from facial-landmark videos as compared to the full-face videos. The goal of our study is twofold. The first goal is to replicate Bassili's study with state-of-the-art facial-expression recognition software. The second goal is to determine if the facial landmarks generated by the facial-expression recognition software contain sufficient information to be able to recognize emotions. Furthermore, we will also extend earlier research by investigating the fundamentals of the perception of the full faces versus the facial landmarks. That is,

---

[1] FaceTracker is not commercially available. Jason Saragih provided us with his software upon our request.

we will investigate and compare valence judgments and arousal judgments that people make about the full faces and the facial landmarks.

2   Digital Extraction Landmarks and Hypothesis

To be able to present participants with facial-landmarks videos representing facial expressions, we need information about the locations and movements of the crucial parts of a face while that face is displaying facial expressions. These locations might be calculated based on models of human faces and facial expressions [9], [10], but they can also be extracted from real human facial expressions [3]. In the current research, we used FaceTracker software [4], [15] to extract this information from full-face videos of actors displaying basic emotions (happiness, sadness, fear, disgust and anger). Extracting this information from full-face videos is relatively complex. That is, human full faces are highly non-rigid objects causing their appearances to vary with expressions. FaceTracker uses a facial landmark registration algorithm to locate and track designated facial locations, so-called landmarks, e.g., the positions of eyebrows, eyes, nose, mouth, teeth and the profile of the full face. Applied to our video dataset, FaceTracker yields the coordinates of the 66 landmarks for each frame. We used these coordinates to create facial-landmark videos consisting of 66 white dots against a black background. Using these facial-landmark videos, we investigated whether people can identify facial expressions presented in a facial-landmark video as well as facial expression presented in a full-face video showing a facial expression on which that facial-landmark video was based. Future technology that produces facial expressions in robots and other artificial social agents can use this information to produce facial expression on an artificial social agent to ameliorate human-robot interaction, or interaction of humans with other artificial social agents.

In line with Bassili (1978), first, we hypothesize that people can relatively accurately identity facial expressions based on full-face videos showing full faces of human actors (H1). Second, we hypothesize that people can also relatively accurately identity facial expression based on facial-landmark videos showing faces consisting of moving dots (generated through face-tracking software; H2). Third, we hypothesize that people can identify facial expressions better based on full-face videos, than based on facial-landmark videos (H3). Fourth, we also expect that participant's judgments about the valence and arousal levels of emotions displayed by full-face videos will show a strong correlation with participant's judgments about the valence and arousal level of emotions displayed by facial-landmarks videos (H4).

3   Method

Participants and Design. Sixteen participants participated in this study. None of them were familiar with or involved in facial expression related topics. All participants spoke Dutch as their mother language, and were students at Eindhoven University of Technology. Their average age was 25.6 years old (*SD* =10.46). Each participant was presented ten full-face videos (two actors, one male and one female, each expressing five emotions in five separate videos), and also ten facial-landmark videos (based on two different actors, one male and one female, each expressing five emotions in five separate videos. These two actors should be different from the previous two actors who were used in full-face videos to prevent interference as a result of identification of the actor). Half of the observers identified the emotions of the full-face videos first and the facial-landmark videos second. The other observers identified the emotions of the facial-landmark videos first and the full-face videos second. Overall, all the videos were shown to all the participants the same number of times, thereby counterbalancing the stimuli of the experiment. The design was a within-subject design (each participant was confronted with both conditions namely full-face videos and facial-landmark videos) and the dependent variable was recognition accuracy or classification performance. So, even though one participant saw different actors for the full-face videos and the facial-landmark videos, overall, all participants saw the same set of actors for the full-face videos and the facial-landmark videos. Thereby, the final results were not influenced by the different acting skills of different actors. The full-face videos of actors that exhibit emotional expressions were part of the GEMEP corpus [11], [12].

Stimulus Materials. For the full-face videos, we used four actors (two male and two female). Of each actor, we used five short videos (average length is 2 seconds), each showing the face and upper torso of an actor, while the actor acted as if he or she experienced an assigned emotion. That is, for each actor, we used five videos representing either happiness, sadness, fear, disgust, or anger.

Based on these full-face videos, we constructed the facial-landmark videos by applying the FaceTracker software to generate 66 landmarks consisting of locations indicating eyebrows, eyes, nose, mouth and the face profile, based on which we could construct a facial-landmark video with white points on a black background. Each facial-landmark video was based on one full-face video. So, we employed four (different actors) times five (different emotions) full-face videos of actors expressing emotions, and four times five facial-landmark videos of the same emotions.

Within each video (full-face video or facial-landmark video), we arranged video segments such that the emotion expression was displayed three times. Each participant was shown full-face videos of two actors, for each of which five videos were shown (expression the five basic emotions), and also three times five facial-landmark videos based on the other two actors in our set of four actors (to prevent interference as a result of identification of the actor).

Procedure. Participants participated individually, in a cubicle that contained a computer and a display. All instructions and stimulus materials were shown on the computer display, and the experiment was completely computer controlled. Each participant was instructed that he or she would be shown several short videos of faces expressing emotions, and that sometimes it would be the full-face video, and sometimes it would be the facial-landmark video. Also, participants were instructed that after each video they would be asked three questions about the emotion expressed by the face. Each of these three questions was explained. Each participant was presented ten full-face videos, and, on different screens, also ten facial-landmark videos (see Figure 1). Half of the observers were presented with the full-face videos first and the facial-landmark videos second. The other observers were presented with the facial-landmark videos first and the full-face videos second. Each set of five emotions displayed those five videos in a different random order.

For each of the videos, participants were first shown the video and then, on the next page, asked the three questions. In the first question, the participant was asked to identify the emotions expressed in the video by selecting one of six options ('happiness', 'sadness', 'fear', 'disgust', 'anger' and 'don't know'). In the second and third questions, the participant was asked to rate the valence level of the expressed emotion (1 = negative, to 7 = positive, or 'don't know'), and the arousal level of the expressed emotion (1 = low arousal, to 7 = high arousal, or 'don't know'). All the questions could only be answered one by one and a participant could not return to an earlier question.

Fig. 1. An example of a frame of a full-face video and a frame of a facial-landmark video

4   Results

Under ideal circumstances, the full-face videos should yield high accuracy in the recognition of expressed emotions. If this high level of accuracy is achieved, it is possible to compare accuracy in the recognition of specific emotions on the basis of facial-landmark videos, and on the basis of full-face videos.

Table 2. Participant's identification of emotion displayed on full-face videos or facial-landmark videos

		Reported emotion					
		Happiness	**Sadness**	**Fear**	**Anger**	**Disgust**	**Don't know**
Displayed emotion	**Happiness**	**91/53**	0 / 3	3 / 6	0 / 9	0 / 0	6 /28
	Sadness	0 / 3	**66/38**	6 /16	13/ 6	0 / 9	16/28
	Fear	0 /22	13/9	**78/ 9**	0 / 3	9 /16	0 /41
	Disgust	0 / 9	29/16	3 /9	**65/13**	0 /16	3 /38
	Anger	0 /16	0 / 0	0 / 9	0 / 6	**100/56**	0 /13

As can be seen in Table 2, the numbers represent the percentage of participants who responded with the column label when shown a video of the emotion described by the row label; Numbers on the left of the slash are for responses to the full-face video, and those to the right are for the response to the facial-landmark videos. Each row represents the responses of 16 participants in each of the two conditions.

However, the results of our full-face video conditions did not always reach this ideal. The average percentage of accuracy across the five emotions was 80%, and ranged from 100% (anger) to 65% (disgust), where 16.7% accuracy would be expected by chance. The average accuracy level did, however, differ significantly from that expected by chance, $\chi^2(1) = 39.75$, $p < .0001$. The results suggested that participants relatively accurately identified facial expressions based on full-face videos showing full faces of human actors supporting our first hypothesis (H1).

Also, the results supported our second hypothesis (H2). That is, results suggested that participants also relatively accurately identified facial expressions based on facial-landmark videos showing faces consisting of moving dots (H2). The mean accuracy level for the recognition of emotions displayed in the facial-landmark videos was 33.8% and ranged from 56% (anger) to 9% (fear). This average accuracy level was greater than expected by chance, $\chi^2(1) = 3.81$, $p < .05$.

In line with Bassili (1978) but now using computer-generated facial-landmark videos, results supported our third hypothesis in suggesting that participants identified facial expression videos better based on full-face videos, than based on facial-landmark videos(H3). That is, a comparison of the overall accuracy rate on the full-face videos and facial-landmark videos revealed that the former was significantly higher than the latter, $\chi^2(1) = 22.20$, $p < .001$. These results suggest that facial motion information (dots) can be useful in the differentiation of emotions, but the addition of other kinds of information might provide considerable help in the task.

Furthermore, because the emotions displayed by our actors may not have been optimally recognizable, we ascertained whether the structure of errors under full-face videos condition and facial-landmark videos conditions were similar. The correlation between responses given for full-face videos and facial-landmark videos (as shown in each cell of Table 2) was $r = .77$; $p < .001$. This indicated that participants' errors were far from random, and the errors they made in the facial-landmark videos were similar to those they made in the full-face videos.

Fourthly, the results also supported our fourth hypothesis by suggesting that participants' judgments about the valence and arousal levels of emotions displayed by full-face videos strongly correlated with participants' judgments about the valence and arousal level of emotions displayed by facial-landmark videos (H4). That is, the correlation between valence evaluations given for full-face videos and facial-landmark videos (as shown in Table 3) was $r = .91$; $p < .05$, and for participants arousal evaluations of the full-face videos and the facial-landmark videos was $r = .93$; $p < .05$.

Table 3. Participant's evaluation of the valence and arousal levels of the facial emotional expressions

		Reported emotion	
		Valence (Negative - Positive)	Arousal (Low - High)
Displayed emotion	Happiness	6.4/4.9	5.8/4.6
	Sadness	2.4/3.2	3.2/2.8
	Fear	2.0/3.8	5.7/4.1
	Disgust	1.9/3.6	5.7/4.3
	Anger	1.3/2.8	6.6/5.8

As can be seen in Table 3, the numbers represent the average levels of participants' valence and arousal evaluations when shown videos of the emotion described by the row label; Numbers on the left of the slash are for responses to the full-face videos, and those to the right are for the response to the facial-landmark videos. Each row represents the responses of 16 participants in each of the two conditions.

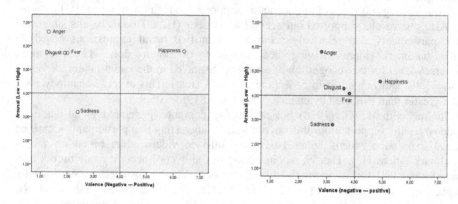

Fig. 2. The location of each emotional expression evaluated in the full-face videos (left) and facial-landmark videos (right), represented on a 2-dimensional space of valence (x-axis) and arousal (y-axis)

The two plots in Figure 2 illustrate the location of each emotional expression in a 2-dimensional space of valence (x-axis) and arousal (y-axis). The left plot represents the full-face videos and the right plot represents facial-landmark videos. Figure 2 suggests that emotional expressions of full-face videos and facial landmark videos are judged to be in the same coordinate area of this 2-dimensional space of valence and arousal.

5   Discussion

In line with Bassili (1978), results suggested that participants could accurately identify emotions expressed by dot faces (though less accurately than those expressed by full faces). Thereby, these results suggested that the algorithm used for extracting landmarks from full-face videos showing actor faces expression emotions can be used to produce facial-landmarks of which the expressed emotions can be identified relatively accurately. Thereby the facial-landmark video information based on this algorithm might be used to create more complete faces (e.g., robot faces, or faces of other artificial social actors), the emotional expressions of which might also be relatively accurately recognized.

Another conclusion that might be drawn from the current results is that facial-landmark videos might be sufficient for recognizing and identifying emotions expressed. This suggests that other information present in full-face videos (e.g., skin movement, skin color, details of eyes, mouth, etc.) is not necessary for identification of expressed emotions. Future research might investigate how to use this information about landmark movement to produce artificial facial expressions, and whether other information present in artificial faces should necessarily express congruent emotions.

In general, the current results suggest that future research might use the FaceTracker software to extract facial landmarks from a full face. Future research might investigate its algorithm methods and extend it to increase recognition accuracy and investigate ways to use its information to render more accurate emotional expression for robots or avatars.

At the same time, results suggested that participants identified the facial-landmark videos less accurately than the full-face videos. This suggested that full-face videos may contain additional information necessary for accurate emotion identification. This kind of information might be related to the landmarks and their movement. It might for example be the case that the algorithm we used was suboptimal, or that the number of dots was suboptimal. Also, this kind of information might be related to other factors. For example, some elements not present in the facial-landmark videos may have been important for optimal emotion identification. For example, information (expressing the same emotion as the moving dots) present in skin color, skin movement, details of elements of faces might help to increase accuracy of identification of emotion expressions in artificial faces even further.

Furthermore, future research might investigate not only algorithms for extracting landmark information from face videos, but could also investigate models to map the dots information to generate the related facial expression of artificial social actors. Those models could integrate modeling of landmark dot movements for accurate emotion expression with modeling of other facial elements and their role in improving emotion expression.

So, how to make a robot smile? The current research suggested that landmark information extracted from a human face expressing an emotion (information about location and movement of the elements of that face) can be enough information for a human perceiver to make an accurate judgment about the emotion expressed. That information might be enough to, for example, make a robot smile. To design robots that can accurately display facial expressions indicating an emotional state, we need technology to produce those facial expressions, and research that investigates the relationship between those technologies and human social perception of those artificial faces. The current research investigated a potential core element of such technology—landmarks extracted from human faces, and assessed the accuracy of human perception of that technology.

References

1. Bassili, J.N.: Facial motion in the perception of faces and of emotional expression. Journal of Experimental Psychology: Human Perception and Performance 4, 373–379 (1978)
2. Johansson, G.: Visual motion perception. Scientific American 232, 76–88 (1975)
3. Saragih, J.M., Lucey, S., Cohn, J.F., Court, T.: Real-time avatar animation from a single image. Automatic Face & Gesture (2011)
4. Saragih, J., Lucey, S., Cohn, J.: Deformable model fitting by regularized landmark mean-shift. International Journal of Computer Vision 91, 200–215 (2011)

5. Lucey, S., Wang, Y., Saragih, J., Cohn, J.: Non-rigid face tracking with enforced convexity and local appearance consistency constraint. International Journal of Image and Vision Computing 28, 781–789 (2010)
6. Saragih, J., Lucey, S., Cohn, J.: Face alignment through subspace constrained mean-shifts. In: IEEE International Conference on Computer Vision, pp. 1034–1041 (2009)
7. Saragih, J., Lucey, S., Cohn, J.: Deformable model fitting with a mixture of local experts. In: International Conference on Computer Vision (2009)
8. Fong, T., Nourbakhsh, I., Dautenhahn, K.: A survey of socially interactive robots. Robotics and Autonomous Systems. 42, 143–166 (2003)
9. Alexander, O., Rogers, M., Lambeth, W., Chiang, M., Debevec, P.: Creating a photoreal digital actor: the digital Emily project. In: 2009 Conference for Visual Media Production, pp. 176–187 (2009)
10. Yang, C., Chiang, W.: An interactive facial expression generation system. Springer Science Business Media. Mutimed Tools Appl. (2007)
11. Bänziger, T., Mortillaro, M., Scherer, K.R.: Introducing the Geneva Multimodal Expression corpus for experimental research on emotion perception. Emotion (2011) (advance online publication), doi:10.137/a0025827
12. Bänziger, T., Scherer, K.R.: Introducing the Geneva Multimodal Emotion Portrayal (GEMEP) corpus. In: Scherer, K.R., Bänziger, T., Roesch, E.B. (eds.) Blueprint for Affective Computing: A Sourcebook, pp. 271–294. Oxford University Press, Oxford (2010)
13. Xiao, J., Chai, J., Kanade, T.: A closed-form solution to non-rigid shape and motion recovery. International Journal of Computer Vision 2, 233–246 (2006)
14. Breazeal, C.: Designing sociable robots. MIT Press, Cambridge (2002)
15. Lucey, P., Lucey, S., Cohn, J.F.: Registration invariant representations for expression detection. In: 2010 International Conference on Digital Image Computing: Techniques and Applications, pp. 255–261 (2010)

A Cross-Cultural Study on Generation of Culture Dependent Facial Expressions of Humanoid Social Robot

Gabriele Trovato[1], Tatsuhiro Kishi[1], Nobutsuna Endo[1],
Kenji Hashimoto[2], and Atsuo Takanishi[3,4]

[1] Graduate School of Science and Engineering, Waseda University, #41-304, 17 Kikui-cho,
Shinjuku-ku, Tokyo 162-0044, Japan
[2] Faculty of Science and Engineering, Waseda University
[3] Department of Modern Mechanical Engineering, Waseda University
[4] Humanoid Robotics Institute (HRI), Waseda University
contact@takanishi.mech.waseda.ac.jp

Abstract. Communication between humans and robots is a very critical step for the integration of social robots into society. Emotion expression through a robotic face is one of the key points of communication. Despite the most recent efforts, no matter how much expression capabilities improve, facial expression recognition is often hampered by a cultural divide between subjects that participate in surveys. The purpose of this work is to take advantage of the 24 degrees of freedom head of the humanoid social robot KOBIAN-R for making it capable of displaying different versions of the same expressions, using face and neck, in a way that they are easy to understand for Japanese and for Western subjects. We present a system based on relevant studies of human communication and facial anatomy, as well as on the work of illustrators and cartoonists. The expression generator we developed can be adapted to specific cultures. Results confirmed the in-group advantage, showing that the recognition rate of this system is higher when the nationality of the subjects and the cultural characterisation of the shown expressions are coincident. We conclude that this system could be used, in future, on robots that have to interact in a social environment, with people with different cultural background.

Keywords: Social Robotics, Culture, Facial expressions, Human-Robot Interaction, Communication.

1   Introduction

For social robots, it is extremely important to be able to communicate. As humans, we use complex languages, and use different types of nonverbal cues, including kinesics. Facial expressions can already be performed by a certain number of robots, including iCub [1], Albert HUBO [2], WE-4 [3], and KOBIAN (Fig. 1a) [4]. However, expression capabilities are usually limited to a small number of pre-defined patterns. Kismet [5] and Nao [6] are two robots based on a model that can blend emotions.

One important limitation of current state of the art is cultural difference in facial expressions. It is known, for instance, that Japanese culture encourages the use of

S.S. Ge et al. (Eds.): ICSR 2012, LNAI 7621, pp. 35–44, 2012.

decoding rules (social norms that inhibit the easy understanding of emotion) [7]. Moreover, subjects belonging to a certain nationality have an in-group advantage when recognising emotions expressed by members of the same cultural group [8]. Despite Ekman's studies [9] attempted to demonstrate the existence pan-cultural elements, recognition differences do exist and were proved, among others, by Shimoda [10] and Koda [11]. Different interpretation of facial cues was also discussed in [12].

Our intention is to overcome this limitation regarding culture, and the necessary first step is the development of a model that is not hardwired to a small set of expressions. In this study, we present the development of a system that generates facial expressions for KOBIAN-R [13], in two versions: Western and Japanese. The system automatically selects an appropriate combination of facial cues depending on inner feelings and on the culture dependent rules the system has been trained on.

The rest of the paper is organized as follows: in section 2 we show the hardware that was used, the concept behind the expression generator and the way it produces culture-dependent expressions; in section 3 we present the results of the surveys and discuss about future works; in section 4 we conclude the paper.

2   Methods

2.1   Hardware and Facial Cues Mapping

The humanoid robot KOBIAN is capable of both performing bipedal walking and facial expression. It was created as a combination of the humanoid robots WE-4RII [3] and WABIAN-2R [14], integrating walking capability with the upper body.

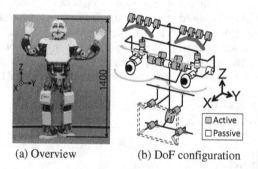

(a) Overview   (b) DoF configuration

Fig. 1. Emotion expression humanoid robot KOBIAN with degrees of freedom configuration of the face of KOBIAN-R

The new version of the robot, KOBIAN-R, thanks to the design of much downsized and lighter inner mechanisms, features a head with DoF expanded to 24, as shown in Fig. 1 and in Table 1. The head has also the additional capability of changing the colour of the forehead, thanks to the use of a blue Electro Luminescence sheet behind the cover. The blue colour is not visible when the Electro Luminescence is off. Despite the presence of the sheet, the forehead is thin enough to allow movement of eyebrows through magnetic power. The size of the head is 150 mm x 181 mm x 214 mm (width x depth x height), similar to a human adult female. The weight of the head is 1.7 kg.

Taking advantage of its 24 degrees of freedom, KOBIAN-R's head could perform a wide range expression. In fact, each component that can move can display a facial cue that contributes to the making of an expression. Therefore, each facial part has been mapped to the human muscles using the Facial Action Coding System (FACS, a procedure to systematically describe human facial expressions) Action Units (AU) [15]. This correspondence is not direct: AUs need to be adapted to the specific KOBIAN-R's face (see Table 2). The reason is that, for instance, movements of the skin or of the nose that cannot be reproduced by KOBIAN-R. The resulting "robotic cues" defined in our system are fewer than AUs. This was also the case of the robots Probo [16] and EMYS [17], which faced the same problem. However, the total number of possible combinations of all the robotic cues is over 600'000, without even counting the neck.

The resulting "alphabet of non-lexical words" needs a meaning to be assigned to each configuration. For instance, lowering eyebrows may be associated with anger or incomprehension. In these regards, AUs as defined by Ekman for each emotion, together with significant hints from [18] and [19] have been used to find these relations.

While applying strictly Ekman's indications is not feasible because of the differences with human face, one classifier for each face part can map this correspondence. In particular, degree 3 polynomial classifiers are used: polynomial features are added to the input dataset, so that monomials as well as combinations of 2nd order terms are constructed and then classified through Fisher's linear classifier [20]. Compared to neural networks, polynomial classifiers can map the data with very low error on the training set.

Table 1. Correspondence between human and robotic facial parts

Parts	DoF	N. of human AUs	N. of robotic cues variables	Set of possible configurations of the robotic facial part
Eyebrows	8	3	3	18
Eyelids	4+1	4	3	19
Eyes direction	3	6	3	23
Mouth	4+3	12	4	21
Jaw	1	2	1	4
Neck	4	10	4	-

2.2 Culture Dependent Expressions

While training data for the Western set of expressions has been provided using the above mentioned relevant sources, we had the need of defining a different set specific for a very different culture, such as the Japanese. In order to understand what makes a facial expression better recognisable by Japanese, we asked one professional illustrator and three amateur cartoonists from that country to draw expressions for all the emotion or communication acts that are used as training for the system. The artists were specifically asked to consider the capabilities of KOBIAN-R's head, specifically ignoring facial cues related to nose or hair. A total of more than 50 drawings were made. After collecting the drawings, a part of which is shown in Fig. 2, rules for creating a Japanese training set were extracted by the authors comparing the pictures and choosing facial cues that highlight the differences with the Western set.

During this process, it has been observed that shapes of eyebrows drawn by Japanese artists are not reproducible by AU, as they are exaggeration of real facial cues. For this reason, a different robotic cues set for eyebrows has been made.

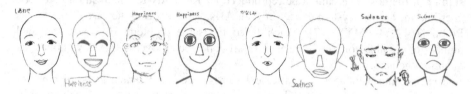

Fig. 2. Facial expressions oh Happiness and Sadness drawn by one illustrator and three cartoonists, including head orientation in some cases

All the artists stated that it's difficult to express easily recognisable emotions without the use of symbols that are typical of Japanese comics and animation. Some of the symbols are either usually written near the character's face, or consist in the complete change of the shape of some facial features (i.e. replacing eyes with two hearts or two stars). In such cases, their implementation is not feasible; however, a subset of these symbols, shown in Fig. 3, could be shown on the face of the robot. Though not yet implemented, it is possible to do that using Electro Luminescent materials.

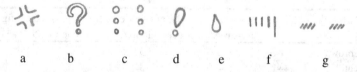

a   b   c   d   e   f   g

Fig. 3. A set of symbols commonly used in Japanese comics. a: cross-popping veins (anger); b: question mark (incomprehension); c: tears (grief); d: exclamation mark (vigilance/notice); e: sweat drop (anxiety); f: parallel vertical lines (trouble); g: red cheeks (shame)

2.3   Communication Act Model and Mathematical Implementation

During communication, the interaction can be described by 6 parameters [21]: the *goal* (request, information or question); the *interest* (in whose interest); the *degree of certainty*; the *power relationship*; the type of *social encounter* (formal or informal context); the *affective state* (the underlying basic emotion).

We decided to use a part of this model (certainty, power relationship and affective state) for describing input data that will produce facial expressions. For the affective state, we adopted Plutchik's wheel of emotions [22], which is extensive (as it allows the extrapolation of an arbitrarily long list of composite emotions) and coherent enough to easily train a classifier. The resulting model is shown in Fig. 4.

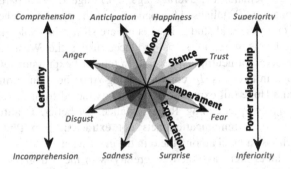

Fig. 4. The 6 parameters (4 from Plutchik's wheel in the centre; 2 additional from [20]) that are being used for describing communication acts and that are given as input to the classifiers. In red, emotion/communication acts corresponding to each direction.

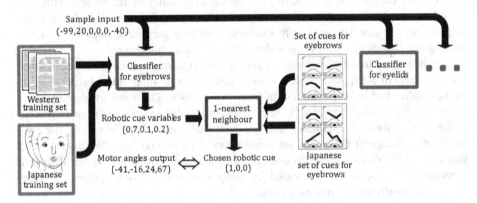

Fig. 5. Model of the generator. Eyebrows motor angle values generated from a sample input are shown here. The 2-way arrow means bijective correspondence through a table.

Combining the facial cues mapping with the communication model, we defined a mathematical model (see Fig. 5) as follows.

There are 6 classifiers, one for each part of the face (listed in Table 1), plus one for the neck. They are given vectors f as input, composed by the above mentioned 6 parameters ranging from -99 to +99. The classifiers are trained using a set of 25 expressions: one for neutral, plus 4 intensity levels for each of the model parameters (shown in Fig. 4, written in black).

The outputs of the classifiers are the robotic cues variables mentioned in paragraph 2.1. Through the use of the 1-nearest neighbour algorithm, we find the closest facial cue among the possible choices, and then the vector containing real motor angles.

3   Results and Discussions

3.1   Evaluation of the Facial Expressions Generator

In our first experiment, the assessment of the system was done. In this web survey, 47 subjects (male: 28; female: 19; average age: 26.7; age σ: 7.6) participated. They differed by nationality: 10 Italians, 11 Japanese, and the rest from other countries, in order to make a cross-cultural study. The details are shown in Table 3. Subjects were asked to assign labels to expressions produced using the Western training set, comparing to the adjacent neutral expression. In total, 12 expressions were evaluated. They were divided in two sets: I_E, comprehending Apprehension, Annoyance, Love, Awe, Remorse and Hope (all expressions directly extracted from Plutchik's wheel of emotions), and I_C, comprehending Relief, Malice, Disbelief, Gratitude, Pity, and Rebuke (emotions or communication acts not extracted from Plutchik's wheel). Subjects had to choose a label among the 6 in the current set.

Vector input values were assigned coherently with the 3 degrees of intensity of Plutchik's wheel. For instance, Awe was defined as (0, 0, 66, 66, 0, 0), as the sum of the components Fear, that we defined as (0, 0, 66, 0, 0, 0), and Surprise (0, 0, 0, 66, 0, 0), which were both used for training.

All of the expressions have been generated automatically by the system. None of the 6 basic expressions commonly mentioned in literature (Happiness, Sadness, Fear, Anger, Surprise and Disgust) were evaluated, because they have been used in the training set. During the survey, the order of the faces was randomized.

Results proved that the average recognition rate (intended as average of recall rates for each face) of set I_E, 68.8%, is not much different from other related studies, such as the results cited in [16], which span from 45% to 84%. The lower average (46.4%) scored by the second set may be due to the especially low score of two specific expressions (Pity and Gratitude) that are confused each other. Swapping the two labels, the average of the whole set I_C would raise by around 10%. We also believe that recognition of this set's expressions, being communication acts rather than just emotions, could be further increased by using symbolic codified gestures, as they convey an usually unique meaning [19].

These results, together with the fact that complex expressions are more difficult to judge compared to basic ones, prove that users are adequately understanding KOBIAN-R's feelings and communication intentions from its face most of the times, and thus, the generation system is working in a reliable way. Without entering further in detail about specific expressions, we can still obtain useful information for our purpose dividing subjects by country. As shown in Table 2, Japanese seem to correspond to the lowest average. This fact confirms our previous assumption that it's necessary to develop culture specific expression sets.

The most noticeable case of cultural gap is the expression of Awe: 100% recognition hit by Italians compared to an average of 36.4% scored by East Asians (China, Japan, Korea and Indonesia). Analysis through t-test confirmed the gap in recognition ($p < .05$) between West and East (see bottom part of Table 2).

Table 2. Results by country of expressions labelling

Country	N. of participants	Average recognition rate
United States	5	65.0%
Italy	10	70.8%
Japan	11	46.2%
South Korea	6	52.8%
Other European countries	7	61.9%
Other countries	8	53.1%
Continent	**N. of participants**	**Average recognition rate**
Europe / America / Oceania	25	67.0%
Asia	22	47.3%

3.2   Evaluation of Culture Dependent Expressions and Symbols

The assessment of culture dependent expressions was again done through a web survey, where 75 subjects differing from gender (male: 53; female: 22), age (average: 26.9; σ: 7.4) and nationality (28 Japanese, 6 South Koreans, 7 Germans, 7 Italians, 6 Chinese, the rest from other countries, for a total of 34 Western subjects and 13 non-Japanese East Asian subjects). They were asked to choose between two versions of the same expression (Fig. 6), produced by different training sets, while being able to see the neutral expression shown at the top as reference.

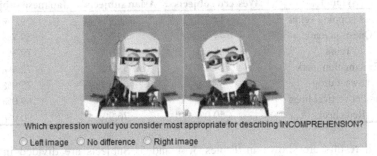

Which expression would you consider most appropriate for describing INCOMPREHENSION?

○ Left image   ○ No difference   ○ Right image

Fig. 6. Sample of the evaluation form (English version), showing two versions of the same expression. In this case, the right one, supposed to be the "Japanese version", was chosen by 85% of Japanese subjects.

The expressions that have been evaluated are: Happiness, Disgust, Fear, Anger, Incomprehension, Remorse, Awe, and Malice. They were chosen either because their representation by Japanese artists was consistently different from the Western version, or because their recognition rate by Japanese subjects was particularly poor in the survey described in paragraph 3.1.

Culture dependent recognition was pursued through investigating the effects on recognition by the use Japanese comics symbols, too. In the present state of the robotic head, the whole brow can turn blue through Electro Luminescence. However, as it is technically possible to implement more complex shapes, the symbols listed in

Fig. 3 were added on Japanese expressions pictures by photo-editing (Fig. 7). The purpose of this preliminary investigation is to understand whether these symbols are useful, and which ones should be implemented.

Table 3. Culture dependent expression evaluation results

Nationality	Western expression preference	No preference	Japanese expression preference
Western countries	**57,4%**	9,9%	32.7%
Asian countries w/o Japan	42,3%	8,7%	**49.0%**
Japan	41,4%	15,5%	**43.1%**

Table 4. Japanese comics symbols evaluation results

Nationality	Preference of no use of Japanese symbols	No preference	Preference of use of Japanese symbols
Western countries	**34.5%**	32.4%	33.2%
Asian countries w/o Japan	16.5%	18.7%	**64.8%**
Japan	15.3%	5.4%	**79.3%**

Table 5. Preference for the use of symbols by cultural group

Symbol	Western subjects	Asian subjects	Japanese subjects
Cross-popping veins	14.7%	69.2%	79.3%
Question mark	44.1%	69.2%	89.7%
Tears	58.8%	76.9%	79.3%
Exclamation mark	14.7%	53.9%	72.4%
Sweat drop	38.2%	61.5%	75.9%
Parallel vertical lines	11.8%	41.2%	69.0%
Red cheeks	50.0%	76.9%	90.0%

Overall results are shown in Tables 3, 4 and 5. Subjects are divided in three groups: Western, Japanese and non-Japanese Asian. Culture dependent expressions evaluation results show a bias of Western subjects for expressions produced by Western training set. The difference with Japanese subjects is quite small: among the ones who showed a preference, 62.3% of Westerners chose the Western expression against 49.1% of Japanese subjects. However, t-test confirms that this difference is significant ($p < .01$). The same can be said about Asians, whose recognition is close to Japanese subjects' and cannot be distinguished them by t-test.

Results about symbols show a much more clear gap between the groups: a total of 66.8% of Western subjects don't feel the need of using symbols, compared to 20.7% of Japanese. People from other Asian countries show preferences similar to Japanese. Going more deeply into details, while all the scores are quite high for Japanese, question mark, red cheeks and especially tears are the only symbols that Western subjects recognise as useful for characterising the expressions.

The cultural differences highlighted in these surveys should be carefully considered. All of the symbols that have been evaluated are expected to improve recognition once implemented into the robotic head.

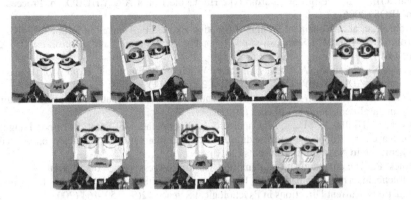

Fig. 7. Expressions containing symbols. Top line: Anger, Incomprehension, Grief and Vigilance. Bottom line: Anxiety, Trouble, and Shame.

4   Conclusions

In order to improve recognition rate of facial expressions of humanoid robots, we have proposed a generator of facial expressions that produces different results for different cultures. Expression models were based on relevant Western sources and on the work of Japanese illustrators and cartoonists. We have applied the system to the humanoid social robot KOBIAN-R, which has the ability of express a wide range of emotions thanks to the 24 DoF of the new head.

We have evaluated this system by survey, using photos of expressions supposed to be easily recognised respectively by Western and Japanese subjects, and evaluating the potential use of Japanese comic-style symbols displayed on the robotic face. Results validated the system and confirmed the in-group advantage related to different culture, especially regarding the perception of written symbols.

The next steps of the development are the extension of the system, now only limited to face and neck, to the upper body, so that gestures can also support expression, and the implementation of symbols through Electro Luminescence. These improvements will enhance the recognition rate and thus, the overall ability of communication of social robots.

Acknowledgments. This study was conducted as part of the Research Institute for Science and Engineering, Waseda University, and as part of the humanoid project at the Humanoid Robotics Institute, Waseda University. It was supported in part by RoboSoM project from the European FP7 program (Grant agreement No.: 248366), GCOE Program "Global Robot Academia" from the Ministry of Education, Culture, Sports, Science and Technology of Japan, Grant-in-Aid for Research Activity Start-up (22860061), SolidWorks Japan K.K., NiKKi Fron Co., Chukoh Chemical Industries, and DYDEN Corporation, whom we thank for their financial and technical support.

References

1. Beira, R., et al.: Design of the Robot-cub (iCub) Head. In: ICRA, pp. 94–100 (2006)
2. Oh, J.H., et al.: Design of Android type Humanoid Robot Albert HUBO. In: Proceedings of IROS (2006)
3. Itoh, K., et al.: Mechanical Design of Emotion Expression Humanoid Robot WE-4RII. In: 16th CISM-IFToMM Symposium on Robot Design, Dynamics and Control, pp. 255–262 (2006)
4. Endo, N., Takanishi, A.: Development of Whole-body Emotional Expression Humanoid Robot for ADL-assistive RT services. JRM 23(6) (2011)
5. Breazeal, B.: Emotion and Sociable Humanoid Robots. International Journal of Human Computer Interaction 59, 119–155 (2002)
6. Beck, A., Hiolle, A., Mazel, A., Cañamero, L.: Interpretation of Emotional Body Language Displayed by Robots. In: Proceedings of the 3rd International Workshop on Affective Interaction in Natural Environments (2010)
7. Buck, R.: The communication of emotion. Guildford Press, New York (1984)
8. Elbfenbein, H.A., Ambady, N.: Universals and Cultural Differences in Recognizing Emotions. Current Directions in Psychological Science 12(5), 159–164 (2003)
9. Ekman, P., Friesen, W.V.: Constants across cultures in the face and emotion. Journal of Personality and Social Psychology 17(2), 124–129 (1971)
10. Shimoda, K., et al.: The intercultural recognition of emotional expressions by three National racial groups: English, Italian and Japanese. In: EJSP, vol. 8, pp. 169–179 (1978)
11. Koda, T.: Cross-cultural evaluations of avatar facial expressions. In: Workshop on Enculturating Conversational Interfaces. IUI (2008)
12. Masaki, Y., Maddux, W.W., Masuda, T.: Are the windows to the soul the same in the East and West? Cultural differences in using the eyes and mouth as cues to recognize emotions in Japan and the US. J. of Experimental Social Psychology 43(2), 303–311 (2007)
13. Kishi, T., et al.: Development of Expressive Robotic Head for Bipedal Humanoid Robot with Wide Moveable Range of Facial Parts and Facial Color. In: Proceedings of 19th CISM-IFToMM Symposium on Robot Design (to be published, 2012)
14. Ogura, Y., et al.: Development of a new humanoid robot WABIAN-2. In: Proc. IEEE Int. Conf. on Robotics and Automation, pp. 76–81 (2006)
15. Ekman, P., Friesen, W.V., Hager, J.C.: The Facial Action Coding System, 2nd edn. Weidenfeld & Nicolson, London (2002)
16. Saldien, J., et al.: Expressing Emotions with the Social Robot Probo. International Journal of Social Robotics 2, 377–389 (2010)
17. Ribeiro, T., Paiva, A.: The illusion of robotic life: principles and practices of animation for robots. In: Proceedings of the Seventh Annual ACM/IEEE International Conference on Human-Robot Interaction (2012)
18. Poggi, I.: Towards the Alphabet and the Lexicon of gesture, gaze and touch. In: Bouissac, P. (ed.) Multimodality of Human Communication. Theories, Problems and Applications, Virtual Symposium (2001-2002)
19. Poggi, I.: Le parole del corpo, Carrocci, Roma (2006) (in Italian)
20. Raudys, S., Duin, R.P.W.: On expected classification error of the Fisher linear classifier with pseudo-inverse covariance matrix. Pattern Recognition Letters 19(5-6), 385–392 (1998)
21. Poggi, I., Pelachaud, C.: Performative Facial Expressions in Animated Faces. In: Cassell, J., Sullivan, J., Prevost, S., Churchill, E. (eds.) Embodied Conversational Agents. MIT press, Cambridge (2000)
22. Plutchik, R.: Emotions and Life: Perspectives from Psychology, Biology, and Evolution. American Psychological Association, Washington, DC (2002)

Robot Social Intelligence

Mary-Anne Williams

Social Robotics Studio, University of Technology, Sydney
2007 Sydney, Australia
Mary-Anne@TheMagicLab.org

Abstract. Robots are pervading human society today at an ever-accelerating rate, but in order to actualize their profound potential impact, robots will need cognitive capabilities that support the necessary social intelligence required to fluently engage with people and other robots. People are social agents and robots must develop sufficient social intelligence to engage with them effectively. Despite their enormous potential, robots will not be accepted in society unless they exhibit social intelligence skills. They cannot work with people effectively if they ignore the limitations, needs, expectations and vulnerability of people working in and around their workspaces. People are limited social agents, i.e. they do not have unlimited cognitive, computational and physical capabilities. People have limited ability in perceiving, paying attention, reacting to stimuli, anticipating, and problem-solving. In addition, people are constrained by their morphology; it limits their physical strength for example. People cannot be expected to and will not compensate for social deficiencies of robots, hence widespread acceptance and integration of robots into society will only be achieved if robots possess the sufficient social intelligence to communicate, interact and collaborate with people. In this paper we identify the key cognitive capabilities robots will require to achieve appropriate levels of social intelligence for safe and effective engagement with people. This work serves as a proto-blueprint that can inform the emerging roadmap and research agenda for the new exciting and challenging field of social robotics.

Keywords: Social Intelligence, Cognitive Capabilities, Artificial Intelligence, Autonomous Agents, Law and Ethics.

1 Introduction

Robotists and social scientists may be seen as having little in common but they agree on at least one issue: the new age of robots will have a profound impact on people and society. Robots are computer controlled cyberphysical systems that perceive their environment using sensors and undertake physical action using actuators to effect change. Autonomous robots can interpret sensor information they gather autonomously and undertake physical action autonomously. Autonomy can be graded in various ways [46], and autonomous robots can operate without human intervention. Over the last thirty years computers have revolutionized society, it is not surprising that the impending robot revolution is expected to have an even more profound

S.S. Ge et al. (Eds.): ICSR 2012, LNAI 7621, pp. 45–55, 2012.
© Springer-Verlag Berlin Heidelberg 2012

impact. Robots can perceive stimuli that humans cannot detect; they can be physically stronger, less distracted and more tolerant of difficult conditions and repetitive routines. These characteristics together with a lack of social intelligence will present challenges to society as robots become more and more integrated into peoples lives and as people increasingly interact and engage with robots.

Robot sensory, actuation and computational capabilities have dramatically improved since Shakey, the world's first general mobile robot that could plan and reason about its own actions, was developed by Stanford University in the early 1970s. However, the gap between the social intelligence of people and robots remains almost as far apart today as the time of first generation robots.

As robot capabilities become increasingly impressive and robots increasingly pervasive in society there is a pressing need to design and develop robots with social cognitive capabilities, social intelligence and effective social skills. Social intelligence allows social agents to act appropriately in social settings. Albrecht [1] defines *social intelligence* as the ability to get along well with others while winning their cooperation. He argues that social intelligence requires social awareness, sensitivity to the needs and interests of others, an attitude of generosity and consideration, and a set of practical skills for interacting successfully with others in any setting.

Human society is diverse and tolerates a wide variety of cultures, races and practices, but underlying human society are humans, who share similar bodies with similar cognitive capabilities, e.g. vision, language, pain, and intelligence. Despite cultural, racial and gender differences, people have similar morphologies, similar cognitive abilities and similar human experiences. People who lack social capabilities are seen to exhibit social disorders, e.g. autism, and to have antisocial personalities, e.g. sociopathic, psychopathic, and Axis II personality. *Dissocial personality disorder* has been classified by the World Health Organisation [53] as characterized by at least 3 of the following: (i) callous unconcern for the feelings of others, (ii) gross and persistent attitude of irresponsibility and disregard for social norms, rules, and obligations, (iii) incapacity to maintain enduring relationships, though having no difficulty in establishing them, (iv) very low tolerance to frustration and a low threshold for discharge of aggression, including violence, (v) incapacity to experience guilt or to profit from experience, particularly punishment, (vi) markedly prone to blame others or to offer plausible rationalizations for the behaviour that has brought the person into conflict with society.

Aberrant human behaviour is examined in psychopathology, the study of mental illness, mental distress, and abnormal or maladaptive behavior and treated as a medical condition, such as psychopathy, a genetic subtype of antisocial personality disorder. Antisocial behavior has a high cost in human society, as it tends to cause significant unwanted problems [48]. Humans suffering from mental disorders may be treated with compassion. But there is no role in human society for a robot exhibiting psychopathological or sociopathic behaviours. In order for robots to be suitably integrated into human society they will require social cognitive capabilities and social intelligence skills to work with people and each other.

This paper identifies key capabilities autonomous robots will require in order to engage and collaborate with people safely and effectively in society. Section 2 identifies cognitive capabilities needed to achieve social intelligence. Section 3 highlights several key legal and ethical issues related to social robots.

2   Cognitive Capabilities for Social Intelligence

Social intelligence requires a high level of self-awareness, sense of identity and awareness of others. People typically have a strong sense of identity and self-awareness, and awareness of others. In addition, people are motivated to act of their own volition with a sense of purpose. People are curious and driven to develop an understanding of themselves and other entities in their environment. It is unlikely that robots will achieve human-level cognition any time soon, but in order to attain a minimal level of social intelligence they will require a concept of self, an understanding of purposeful behaviour, and an ability to distinguish intentional behaviour from unintentional behaviour. Tomasello *et al.* [16] studied the understanding of intention in orangutans, chimpanzees and children. All three demonstrated they understood the difference between accidental and intentional acts. One of the challenges in studying an agent's understanding of others is that observed phenomena like behaviours can sometimes be explained as simple stimulus-response learning, rather than requiring deep understanding.

A person can observe the existence and configuration of another persons body directly, however all aspects of other people's minds must be inferred from observing their behaviour together with other information. Robots, on the other hand, can share sensory data, perceptions and software with each other directly. Interpreting another person's behaviour is a nontrivial task. Humans use introspection and experience with other people to help decipher it. Sometimes they are wrong and misinterpret other people's behaviour, but surprisingly people can correctly interpret other peoples' behaviour particularly within a single culture. It turns out that this skill is crucial for interaction and engagement in social settings. People use a range of strategies to engage and collaborate with others e.g. they use language where meaning is derived from commonly agreed vocabularies and grammars [3], gaze or gestures.

Social intelligence among agents that share similar morphologies and cognitive capabilities is easier than achieving social intelligence among heterogeneous agents. Social intelligence across nonhuman species is not prevalent in the animal kingdom. Wolves, lions and chimpanzees can hunt collaboratively in packs. They can achieve joint attention and work together to catch their prey, but there is no evidence that shows lions hunt with chimpanzees or wolves [11]. People, on the other hand, can work with other species like horses, donkeys, elephants, eagles and dogs to achieve collaborative outcomes, however when people work with other animals to achieve a goal it is usually entirely different to how they would work with other people and much more limited in its achievements.

A theory of mind allows people to attribute thoughts, desires, and intentions to other agents, to predict and explain their actions/behaviours. Knowing other people have a theory of mind also assists people to communicate, as they know that their actions/behaviour can be interpreted in certain ways in certain contexts in a given culture. For example, a person could indicate pain by crying, look at an object intently or point to it to direct other peoples' attention. Even though animals, and in particular mammals, have bodies (and brains) which are different to humans, people still try to imagine what animals are thinking and feeling. Animals do not laugh for example, but they have behaviours that people interpret, e.g. when a dog whimpers a person might infer that it is in pain and when a dog wags its tail a person might infer that the dog is happy and excited. External indicators of animal thought are an important factor in achieving empathy across species. Dogs wag their tails and humans clap hands, smile and frown. Although a robot could display a visual or audible action to indicate pleasure, dismay or fear, the capacity to make a display that is intuitive and easily interpreted by people may assist in the robot's acceptance by humans. A gesture or low impact sound like purring can often be more effective than a spoken linguistic response which is typically more invasive and attention demanding. For spoken responses if a robot sounds like a child it will evoke a different instinctive response from people than if its voice sounds more like a strong and competent adult.

Robot bodies for the foreseeable future are entirely different to the human body and those found in the biological world. As a result a robot's subjective experience is entirely different to that of people, and yet if humans are to communicate and collaborate with robots we must bridge this experience gap. If robots are to work with people in open and complex ways then they will require a theory of human mind, similarly, people will require a theory of robot mind.

Bridging the robot-human mind gap will be nontrivial. It will require that robots develop a robust social intelligence and a theory of mind [42]. Children under the age of three do not typically exhibit a theory of mind capability; instead it develops later and improves over time. One of the key tools we use to interpret other peoples behaviour is introspection. When one sees another person reach for object then one typically infers that the person wants to grasp the object. If a robot observes the same scenario and has the capability to retrieve the object, then it might try to assist but there will always be exceptions and a need for robots to display commonsense. Robot designers must find ways to endow a robot with commonsense and social intelligence so that it will respond appropriately in social circumstances [51].

Robots and people need cognitive skills to explain and predict each others' behaviour. Empathy is related to a theory of mind, and so we can ask what kinds of empathy should people develop for robots and vice versa. Empathy can be effected as a kind of projection of experience: if agent X observes agent Y experiencing situation S, then X could predict how Y may be feeling and importantly how they may respond, by imagining how Y may be feeling. Recent neuro-ethological studies of animal behaviour [55] suggest that mammals may exhibit ethical or empathic abilities, but there is little evidence that insects, despite demonstrating sophisticated "social" skills in their colonies, empathise with each other.

A theory of mind is sometimes determined to be a byproduct of broader cognitive abilities of the human mind to register, monitor, and represent its own functioning. However, in this paper, we take the simulation stance [25] on a theory of mind, which says that an agent recognizes its own mental states, and by simulation ascribes mental states to others. Robots could develop this simulation theory of mind capability and use it to predict other agent states by simulating their experience and responses.

Social robots will require capabilities which will allow them to attribute knowledge and mental states to other cognitive agents like people, household pets, and other robots. The ability to simulate attention and intention, as well as being able to imitate and learn, are key cognitive skills for social robots. Researchers have shown that people's ability to model other minds develops over their lifetime, and there is no reason to expect robots to have a mature theory of mind from the moment of deployment, and so they too need methods that will allow them to develop their abilities over their lifetime.

Baron-Cohen [10, 11, 12] showed that infants respond to attention in others by 7-9 months of age and that this skill is a key step on the critical pathway to developing a theory of mind [40]. Understanding attention requires the insight that where a person is looking provides clues as to what may have their attention and/or what they may be thinking about. There are many experiments that confirm that people follow the gaze of others. In addition, people point to indicate objects of interest. Dogs can also read attention in other dogs [32] and also humans. Dogs can correctly interpret human pointing, and hunting dogs are well known for pointing with their nose and tail. Other animals follow heads not eyes in interpreting gaze [56]. Humans are unique in that they have a highly visible light/white sclera, other animals have black sclera with rare exceptions e.g. albino gorillas. This together with an understanding of ourselves makes it relatively easy to guess what another person may be looking at.

People direct and share attention to communicate and collaborate. They use joint attention [11] to cooperate and undertake joint tasks. The act of pointing is a means to create joint attention. Social robots must acquire the ability to interpret and enact pointing behaviours. In addition to managing attention, robots will require capabilities to determine intentions so that they can assist, avoid and anticipate a person's next action [41]. Robots will require tools that allow them to model other agents' beliefs this is particularly important when the beliefs are false or not consistent with the robots'. Various physiological tests have been used to test people's ability to model other people's minds, and the following tests can be used to evaluate robot's cognitive capabilities for social intelligence. Passing the test as is would not demonstrate social intelligence since a robot could easily be programed to pass the test, the key point is that social robots would need to demonstrate the ability required in a broad range of general settings.

The False-Belief Test: The robot is shown a basket and a box. A marble is placed in the basket in front of a person who then leaves the room, while they are out of the room the marble is moved from the basket to the box. The robot is then asked where the person will look for the marble. The robot passes the task if it answers that the person will look in the basket, i.e. where they saw the marble placed. This test can be used to demonstrate that a robot is able to understand that a human's state of belief may be different to its own and based on its personal experience. Typically children are unable to pass this test before the age of four, but even at age four the majority of autistic children are unable to pass the test [5, 10, 12, 38].

The Appearance-Reality Test: A robot is asked what it believes to be inside a candy box. The robot will indicate candy. Then the robot is shown that pencils are in the box. The robot is now asked what an agent/person who has not observed the contents will believe is in the box. If the robot answers candy then the robot passes this test. Normal children can pass this test at age four or five years, but autistic children typically cannot.

Social robots will need to be able to consider events and situations from another agents' perspective. Humans that experience a theory of mind deficit have difficulty determining the intentions of others, lack understanding of how their behaviour affects others, and have a difficult time with social reciprocity [5, 10, 12, 38]. Theory of mind deficits have been observed in people with spectrum disorders, people with schizophrenia, people with attention deficit disorder, persons under the influence of alcohol and narcotics, sleep-deprived persons, and persons who are experiencing severe emotional or physical pain [5]. Clearly social robots require a theory of mind; otherwise they too will exhibit the behaviours of unacceptable mental disabilities.

It is important to note that there has been some controversy over the interpretation of evidence purporting to show theory of mind ability—or inability—in animals. For example, Povinelli [32] presented chimpanzees with the choice of two experimenters from which to request food: one who had seen where food was hidden, and one who, by virtue of one of a variety of mechanisms (having a bucket or bag over his head; a blindfold over his eyes; or being turned away from the baiting) does not know, and can only guess. They found that the animals failed in most cases to differentially request food from the "knower." By contrast, Hare, Call, and Tomasello [31] found that subordinate chimpanzees were able to use the knowledge state of dominant rival chimpanzees to determine which container of hidden food they approached.

Individual people experience a mind and assume other people also experience a mind. A theory of mind, as been shown to be a crucial capability for cognitive agents to communicate effectively [10, 11, 12, 25]. Without a theory of mind people display forms of mental disabilities. Normal people find it cognitively exhausting and frustrating to work with and engage with people who do not have a theory of mind.

Reality is experienced and represented (perceived and conceived) by both people and robots. However, they do not represent every aspect of their experience. Aspects of experiences that are selected for representation are determined by their morphology and grounding capabilities [45]. Robots and people have entirely different morphology and information grounding capabilities, consequently their social intelligence is different. Social robots will require self-awareness which Novianto and Williams [28, 49] maintain is the ability to focus attention on subjective experience, i.e. what is happening now. A robot that can recognise itself in the mirror without a self-concept would not count as passing this test. The ability to anticipate is a crucial skill and related to attention and concerns awareness of future subjective experience, i.e. what is about to happen or what will happen next. The ability to anticipate other agents behaviour including what might gain their attention will play a crucial role in determining how a robot should respond to other agents cohabiting a shared environment or cooperating to achieve joint tasks.

A basic social skill is to know when a "friend" or "superior" requires help and when one should offer help. In order for social robots to ask for assistance they must have an understanding and representation of their own capabilities and experience. They must know what they know, what they don't know, what they are doing, how they are doing it, why they are doing, know what others know, what others don't know, what others are doing (and how and why), what interests others and what will get their attention (and why).

The cognitive experience architecture [46] provides a useful tool to explore robot design. It has four main components grounded in a robot's experience: morphology, understanding, motivation and governance. The cognitive experience architecture can be used to design and develop robotic systems that can make sense of their own experiences all by themselves guided by self generated motivations and cognitive capabilities for self-control and understanding. Robots are physical entities and have a physical morphology that affords key cognitive capabilities that support the development of a sense of being and self-determination. A self-determined robot must be able to represent and make sense of its own experience; use its motivations to drive control mechanisms and strategies, use awareness and attention to steer understanding for the purpose of responding and anticipating. A robot's body parts, degrees of freedom, sensors and actuators all play important roles in its morphology which in turn determines a robot's sense-of-self and self-concept. Robots experience themselves (via propriception) and the world (perception). Propriceptual and perceptual experience acquires information through internal and external sensors collectively. Representations of social experience are key to developing social intelligence. Building mechanisms for robots to represent and use their experience rather than designing behaviors via human encoding of social experience is needed. Robots need to be self-motivated and to pursue their own goals such as seeking certain experiences depending on representations of needs, wants, current and future states. Motivation plays a crucial role in action selection in robots. It influences what the robot will pay attention to, which in turn affects what the agent is aware of and how it might respond to its experiences. It determines what information will be grounded in representations, how, when and why. People's attention and awareness are influenced by their emotional state, goals, passion, persistence, and perseverance all properties of motivation. At the very least autonomous social robots will require simple motivations: to act safely, not cause damage to themselves or others, and not to waste resources including people's time.

A robot can claim to achieve a degree of understanding if it can make sense of its experience; this requires cognitive capabilities for making representations. Representations possess affordances; they can afford action, behaviour, reaction, deliberation, decision-making, learning, description, explanation, prediction, anticipation and many other capabilities for social intelligence. Measuring affordances can provide a measure of the value/quality of representations.

The internal (e.g. body) and external world offers too much information to capture in representations of experience (e.g. humans do not represent and capture every chemical reaction in their bodies, nor do they represent and capture every event they witness in the outside world). Clearly, a robot should carefully select the information to represent that will generate the most value. We know from neuroscience that predictive feedback cycles are crucial in learning; studies in neuropsychology suggest the value of comparing prediction with perceived information. In robotics predictive feedback plays an important role; there is an essential difference between prediction and anticipation. Prediction forecasts the future, while anticipation concerns actions to take in the present for better outcomes in the future. Humans spend copious amounts of time thinking, rerunning old experiences and rehearsing future experiences as they anticipate and prepare for future social encounters.

3   Legal and Ethical Considerations

Social robots not only require self-awareness but a social awareness. They must be able to detect and recognize other social agents; possess a social radar that allows them to navigate social situations just as they navigate physical spaces. Social robots will be expected to behave legally and ethically. Science Fiction writer Asmiov [2] developed the following so-called *Three Laws of Robotics*. These laws provide a useful place to start designing a set of rules that could be used to govern social robot behaviour.

1. A robot may not injure a human being or, through inaction, allow a human being to come to harm.
2. A robot must obey the orders given to it by human beings, except where such orders would conflict with the First Law.
3. A robot must protect its own existence as long as such protection does not conflict with the First or Second Laws.

If social robots are to respect and enact these laws and others like them then they will require significant social intelligence and the necessary underlying cognitive capabilities, which will include self-awareness, social awareness, empathy, theory of mind. For example, without the ability to empathize with humans, how will a robot determine what might harm them. Determining and assessing the nature and degree of harm is crucial to enacting Asmiov's Laws. People are able to interpret and respect laws and codes of ethics by assessing other people's experience, often by putting themselves in other people's position and circumstance. In human society people regularly observe and mimic other people's behaviour, and imagine what it would be like in other people's position. In doing this their ability to interpret, copy and imagine how other people feel and think is bound by their own experiences. That is not to say that people cannot imagine entirely different experiences beyond their own subjective experience, but that their experience is a limiting factor in those imaginings. A person who has experienced weightlessness, can imagine what it would be like in the International Space Station much better than someone who has not; an accomplished flutist, can imagine how another flutist may respond to a new piece of music in a way that someone who has never tried to make a sound using a flute, or indeed, someone not able to read music.

Furthermore, ordinary people in society are not trained as lawyers, instead they learn the meaning of harm and the notion of property and ownership in culturally based social settings. Introspection is a powerful mechanism for assessing harm, and since people share the same kind of body they are able to use introspection to put themselves in other peoples position and to assess and explore the consequences.

Social robots must also be law abiding. They should not break the law of their own volition, nor undertake instructions from humans that would lead to laws being broken. Ryan Calo [46] provides a comprehensive treatise on the privacy implications of robots. He maintains that robots will impact human privacy in at least the following three ways: (i) they have a significant capacity for surveillance, (ii) they introduce new points of access to historically private spaces such as the home, and (iii) they trigger hardwired social responses in people that can threaten several of the values privacy protects.

4   Discussion

Robots need social intelligence in order to interact, engage and collaborate with people fluently, safely and effectively. Without social intelligence robots will exhibit unacceptable levels of social ineptitude and not deliver their expected value to society. Robot social intelligence requires a theory of empathy and a theory of mind. Just like robots, pets and other nonhuman animals have different morphologies and cognitive capabilities to people, and yet they have been socialized and integrated into human society, albeit in limited ways. People are happy to have sociable animals in their homes, workplaces, and public spaces. Dogs in particular are often treated as trusted family members and used as workers on farms. None-the-less animals do not have the same cognitive capabilities or morphology as people, yet people happily make allowances and collaborate with them. Robots will need more social intelligence than animals, if they are to achieve their promised value as a trusted domestic servant, friend or co-worker. Furthermore, robots need social intelligence so that they will not exhibit social disabilities like autism, and not develop unacceptable characteristics such as sociopathic or psychopathic tendencies.

References

1. Albrecht, K.: Social Intelligence: the New Science of Success. Wiley (2005)
2. Asimov, I.: I, Robot. Doubleday & Company, New York (1950)
3. Anderson, J.R.: Language, memory, and thought. Erlbaum, Hillsdale (1976)
4. Asch, S.E.: Forming impressions of personality. Abnormal & Social Psy. 41, 258–290 (1946)
5. Baker, J.: Social Skills Training: for children and adolescents with Asperger Syndrome and Social-Communication Problems. Autism Asperger Publishing Company (2003)
6. Bandura, A.: Aggression: A social learning analysis. Prentice-Hall (1973)
7. Bandura, A.: Social foundations of thought and action: A social cognitive theory. Prentice-Hall, Englewood Cliffs (1986)
8. Bandura, A., Walters, R.H.: Social learning and personality development. Rinehart, & Winston, New York (1963)
9. Bargh, J.A.: The four horsemen of automaticity: Awareness, intention, efficiency, and control in social cognition. In: Wyer, R.S., Srull, T.K. (eds.) Handbook of Social Cognition, 2nd edn., vol. 1, pp. 1–40. Erlbaum, Hillsdale (1994)
10. Baron-Cohen, S.: Mindblindness: An essay on autism and theory of mind. MIT Press (1995)
11. Baron-Cohen, S.: Precursors to a theory of mind: Understanding attention in others. In: Whiten, A. (ed.) Natural Theories of Mind: Evolution, Development and Simulation of Everyday Mindreading, pp. 233–251. Basil Blackwell, Oxford (1991)
12. Baron-Cohen, S., Tager-Flusberg, H., Cohen, D.J.: Does the autistic child have a theory of mind? Cognition 21, 37–46 (1993)
13. Brass, M., et al.: Investigating Action Understanding: Inferential Processes versus Action Simulation. Current Biology 17(24), 2117–2121 (2007)
14. Broom, M.E.: A note on the validity of a test of social intelligence. Journal of Applied Psychology 12, 426–428 (1928)
15. Byrne, R., Whiten, A. (eds.): Machiavellian intelligence: Social expertise and the evolution of intellect in monkeys, apes, and humans. Clarendon Press, Oxford (1988)
16. Call, J., Tomasello, M.: Distinguishing intentional from accidental actions in orangutans (Pongo pygmaeus), chimpanzees (Pan troglodytes), and human children (Homo sapiens). Journal of Comparative Psychology 112(2), 192–206 (1998)

17. Cantor, N., Fleeson, W.: Social intelligence and intelligent goal pursuit: A cognitive slice of motivation. In: Spaulding, W.D. (ed.) Integrative Views of Motivation, Cognition, and Emotion, pp. 125–180 (1994)
18. Cantor, N., Kihlstrom, J.F.: Social intelligence and cognitive assessments of personality. In: Wyer, Srull (eds.) Advances in Social Cognition, vol. 2, pp. 1–59 (1989)
19. Cantor, N., Zirkel, S.: Personality, cognition, and purposive behavior. In: Pervin, L. (ed.) Handbook of Personality: Theory and Research, pp. 125–164. Guilford, NY (1990)
20. Carruthers, P.: Simulation and self-knowledge: a defence of the theory-theory. In: Carruthers, P., Smith, P.K. (eds.) Theories of Theories of Mind. Cambridge University Press (1996)
21. Huang, C.-M., Mutlu, B.: Robot Behavior Toolkit: Generating Effective Social Behaviors for Robots. In: International Human-Robot Interaction Conference (2012)
22. Conway, M.A.: Autobiographical memory: An introduction. OUP, Milton Keynes (1990)
23. Courtin, C.: The impact of sign language on the cognitive development of deaf children: The case of theories of mind. Cognition 77, 25–31 (2000)
24. Flavell, J.H., Ross, L.: Social and cognitive development: Frontiers and possible future. CUP (1981)
25. Gallese, V., Goldman, A.: Mirror neurons and the simulation theory of mind-reading. Trends in Cognitive Science 2(12), 493–501 (1998)
26. Gallup, G.G.: Chimpanzees: Self-recognition. Science 167, 86–87 (1970)
27. Gallup, G.G.: Self-awareness and the evolution of social intelligence. Behavioural Processes 42, 239–247 (1998)
28. Gärdenfors, P.: How Homo became Sapiens. MIT Press, Cambridge (2004)
29. Gärdenfors, P., Williams, M.-A.: Communication, Planning and Collaboration based on Representations and Simulations. In: Khlenthos, D., Schalley, A. (eds.) Language and Cognitive Structure, Benjamins, p. 56 (2007)
30. Gordon, R.M.: 'Radical' simulationism. In: Carruthers, P., Smith, P.K. (eds.) Theories of Theories of Mind. Cambridge University Press, Cambridge (1996)
31. Hare, B., Call, J., Tomasello, M.: Do chimpanzees know what conspecifics know and do not know? Animal Behavior 61, 139–151 (2001)
32. Horowitz, A.: Attention to attention in domestic dog (Canis familiaris) dyadic play. Animal Cognition 12, 107–118 (2009)
33. Kahn, Kanda, Ishiguro, Gill, Ruckert, Shen: Do People Hold a Humanoid Robot Morally Accountable for the Harm It Causes? In: Human-Robot Interaction Conference (2012)
34. Kaminski, J., Neumann, M., Bräuer, J., Call, J., Tomasello, M.: Dogs (Canisfamiliaris) communicate with humans to request but not to inform. Animal Behavior 82(4), 651–658 (2011)
35. Kihlstrom, J., Cantor, N.: Social Intelligence. In: Sternberg, R.J. (ed.) Handbook of Intelligence, 2nd edn., pp. 359–379. Cambridge University Press, Cambridge
36. Meltzoff, A.N.: Imitation as a mechanism of social cognition: Origins of empathy, theory of mind, and the representation of action. In: Goswami, U. (ed.) Handbook of Childhood Cognitive Development, pp. 6–25. Blackwell Publishers, Oxford (2002)
37. Pelphrey, K.A., et al.: Grasping the Intentions of Others: The Perceived Intentionality of an Action Influences Activity in the Superior Temporal Sulcus during Social Perception. Journal of Cognitive Neuroscience 16(10), 1706–1716 (2004)
38. Pettersson, H., Kaminski, J., Herrmann, E., Tomasello, M.: Understanding of human communicative motives in domestic dogs. Applied Animal Behaviour Sciences 133(3-4), 235–245 (2011)

39. Povinelli, D.J., Nelson, K.E., Boysen, S.T.: Inferences about guessing and knowing by chimpanzees (Pan troglodytes). Journal of Comparative Psychology 104(3), 203–210 (1990)
40. Premack, D., Woodruff, G.: Does the chimpanzee have a theory of mind? Behavioral & Brain Sciences 1, 515–526 (1978)
41. Huang, C.-M., Thomaz, A.L.: Joint Attention in Human-Robot Interaction. In: AAAI Fall Symposium on Dialog with Robots, Arlington, VA (2010)
42. Scasselatti, B.: Theory of Mind for a Humanoid Robot (2004); Sechrest, L., Jackson, D.N.: Social intelligence and the accuracy of interpersonal predictions. Journal of Personality 29, 167–182 (1961)
43. Scheider, L., Grassman, S., Kaminski, J., Tomasello, M.: Domestic dogs use contextual information and tone of voice when following a human pointing gesture. PLOS One 6(7) (2011)
44. Sommerville, J.A., Decety, J.: Weaving the fabric of social interaction: Articulating developmental psychology and cognitive neuroscience in the domain of motor cognition. Psychonomic Bulletin & Review 13(2), 179–200 (2006)
45. Williams, M.-A.: Representation = Grounded Information. In: Ho, T.-B., Zhou, Z.-H. (eds.) PRICAI 2008. LNCS (LNAI), vol. 5351, pp. 473–484. Springer, Heidelberg (2008)
46. Williams, M.-A.: Autonomy: Life and Being. In: Bi, Y., Williams, M.-A. (eds.) KSEM 2010. LNCS (LNAI), vol. 6291, pp. 137–147. Springer, Heidelberg (2010)
47. Ryan Calo, M.: Robots and Privacy. In: Lin, P., Bekey, G., Abney, K. (eds.) Robot Ethics: The Ethical and Social Implications of Robotics. MIT Press, Cambridge (2011)
48. Knapp, M., Romeo, R., Beecham, J.: Economic Cost of Autism in the UK, vol. 13, pp. 317–336 (autism May 1, 2009)
49. Novianto, R., Williams, M.-A.: The Role of Attention in Robot Self-Awareness. In: Proceedings of the 18th IEEE International Symposium on Robot and Human Interactive Communication, RO-MAN 2009, pp. 1047–1053 (2009)
50. Pfeifer, R., Bongard, J.C.: How the Body Shapes the Way We Think: A New View of Intelligence. MIT Press (2006)
51. Johnston, B., Williams, M.-A.: Autonomous Learning of Commonsense Simulations. In: International Symposium on Logical Formalizations of Commonsense Reasoning, pp. 73–78 (2009)
52. Novianto, R., Johnston, B., Williams, M.-A.: Attention in the ASMO Cognitive Architecture. In: Proc. Bioinspired Cognitive Architectures Symposium, pp. 98–105. IOS Press (2010)
53. World Health Organisation ICD-10: Clinical descriptions and diagnostic guidelines: Disorders of adult personality and behaviour (2010)

Android Emotions Revealed

Evgenios Vlachos and Henrik Schärfe

Aalborg University, Department of Communication and Psychology,
Nyhavnsgade 14, DK-9000
evlach10@student.aau.dk, scharfe@hum.aau.dk

Abstract. This work presents a method for designing facial interfaces for sociable android robots with respect to the fundamental rules of human affect expression. Extending the work of Paul Ekman towards a robotic direction, we follow the judgment-based approach for evaluating facial expressions to test in which case an android robot like the Geminoid|DK –a duplicate of an Original person- reveals emotions convincingly; when following an empirical perspective, or when following a theoretical one. The methodology includes the processes of acquiring the empirical data, and gathering feedback on them. Our findings are based on the results derived from a number of judgments, and suggest that before programming the facial expressions of a Geminoid, the Original should pass through the proposed procedure. According to our recommendations, the facial expressions of an android should be tested by judges, even in cases that no Original is engaged in the android face creation.

Keywords: Social robotics, Geminoid, androids, emotions, facial expressions, emotional health.

1 Introduction

Before the transition from an industrial to a post-industrial society, when the technology-centered view was dominating [1], the words human – computer interaction automatically generated a tag cloud of terms like navigation, manipulation, automation and control. During the post-industrial society, the focus of interaction started to move from the physical machine to the users' world and the interfaces evolved from hardware to social processes [2], [3]. A turn towards human-robot interaction (HRI) has been observed. Henceforth, during the information era, studies presented a shift of focus towards designing social robots, understanding human behavior and rethinking the role of the machine [4]. Communication theories and cognitive psychology principles were applied to the field of robotics in order to produce as natural interaction as possible and to examine whether the responses from humans were affected by the abilities and the appearance of the robots [5].

The Media Equation communication theory [6] states that human-machine interaction is inherently natural and social, and that the rules of human-human interaction apply also to human-machine interaction. The popularity of the above mentioned theory can be justified easily when realizing that people are used to rely on social and mental models to

S.S. Ge et al. (Eds.): ICSR 2012, LNAI 7621, pp. 56–65, 2012.

deconstruct complex behaviors into more familiar, understandable and intuitive forms with which to interact [7]. Despite that fact, following the human perspective to address such issues may not be the most efficient one. Humans are the best known example of emotional interaction, but duplicating human emotional abilities in machines does ensure neither reliability nor perfomativity [8].

In the context of social robotics, when interaction with the user happens in real time, synchronizing the facial gestures and expressions of a robot to the flow of the interaction is essential. For the acceptance of a sociable robot as an equal communication partner, progress is needed in at least one of the following areas; physical appearance, balanced movements/motions/gestures, expression and/or perception of emotions, engagement in conversation, responsiveness to users, and ability to process social cues in face to face communication [22], [24]. The more believable and competent the robot appears, the more users will have the impression of interacting with a human partner rather than with just a moving manikin. Even slight improvements to the robots' interface can add credits to the ease of HRI [21].

An issue that is effortlessly rising is "How an android robot can embody emotional facial expressions with respect to the fundamental rules of human affect expression?" [35]. To address this issue, we used the Geminoid|DK android robot [5], [23] which is a teleoperated duplicate of an existing person, the facial expressions of which can be programmed or evaluated by referring to the Original person. Reliance only to the facial characteristics of the Original might prove inadequate. In this study, the Geminoid will be tested on the following hypothesis: **The emotional state of the Geminoid|DK when mimicking the Original is equally or more understandable by observers than when following the theoretical approach of Ekman and Friesen in [13].**

We have already presented the train of thought behind this study and in the next sections we will introduce the Geminoid Reality, explain the judgment-based approach for studying facial expressions, describe the research design methodology for acquiring the empirical data, analyze our findings, validate or not our hypothesis and finally conclude with a discussion about our findings.

2   Geminoids and Related Research

In the last decades, as technology was progressing following the Moore's Law exponential curve [39] and microprocessors were improving in speed and/or performance while decreasing in size, societies were struggling to adapt to these abrupt changes. One after-effect of that fierce technological explosion was the fact that humanity suddenly gained the power to receive and process at the same time, almost parallel to real time, more information than they could physically sense with the natural human sensors. Humanity had the power to build systems, programs, and algorithms that could predict the effects of various changes in the environment, simulate these changes to virtual environments, and be ready to take action in reality. Both the sensors and the results of this enhanced sensing -either of the environment or thyself- could be available on small portable devices. A complex system that encapsulates the same or similar attributes with the one described above, formulates a different kind of reality and is perceived as a different one. Enriching the already known visual reality and objective reality, terms like virtual reality, augmented reality and mixed reality were introduced [11], [18], [26], [28], [30], [36].

2.1   The Geminoid Reality

Hiroshi Ishiguro, the inventor of the first Geminoid android robot, strongly believes that society today is on the verge of the robotic age, a period of time that will allow us to comprehend the essential natures of humans and society [38], while Schärfe already speaks of an Android Reality.

While virtual reality replaces the real world with a simulated one and augmented reality enhances the real environment with additional virtual information, Geminoid Reality is going one step further. It combines the real environment (robots point of view) with an augmented environment (robots operator point of view) into a new kind of mixed reality with blurry boundaries that is challenging even our perception on visual reality.

In order to be present in the world, it is vital to be ready to engage, to cope and to deal with the world and also to witness events, people and things that are available [27]. Witnessing also requires a record or representation of what has been witnessed. In the Geminoid Reality, the operator of the robot is engaging and coping with the world, dealing with the world and witnessing events, people and things without being physically situated there. His/her presence is substituted by the Geminoid. The operator and the Geminoid form a symbient unity which creates a situation akin to *mirror-touch synesthesia*; a tactile hallucination triggered by observing touch to another person which enables the observer to simulate another's experience by activating the same brain areas that are active when the observer experiences the same emotion or state [12], [15].

The truth about the Geminoid Reality is that it can only be studied in relation to the available technology [20]. Since the field of robotics is still progressing, so the boundaries of Geminoid Reality will keep changing.

2.2   Related Research

Distributed over different kinds of reality, a variety of robotic research has placed emphasis on different aspects of facial expressions, demonstrating the potential in a natural, human like interface. Zoomorphic robots with humanoid facial expression capabilities include MIT's *Leonardo* [9] and the *iCat* from Philips [10]. In both cases, expression of a range of human emotions is obtained through actuation of the face, often with surprisingly empathic results. Besides the Geminoid series dealt with in this paper, androids with emphasis on facial expressions include the android heads of David Hanson [19] and the *Kansei* head from Meiji University [37]. While the former two robots are often used to obtain and process input from a user as basis for generating an appropriate response, the latter two rely on databases linking emotional expressions to words and phrases.

3   Architecture of Design

3.1   The Judgment-Based Approach

The judgment-based approach suggests that when viewing a facial expression, emotion can be recognised entirely out of context, with no other information available. This judgment depends on the judges' past experience of that particular facial expression; either of his/her own face in conjunction with a particular feeling, or someone else's face in conjunction with other revealing verbal or non-verbal behavior, or in general according to types of activity that have been adaptive in the ancestral past of the species [14], [17].

There are two conceptual types of measurement that focus on different phenomena for studying nonverbal behavior involving observers; the judgment-based approach where judgments about messages are measured, and the sign-vehicle based approach which measures the sign-vehicles that convey the message. In the message judgment approach the observer is asked to judge whether each subject, who is depicted in a visual input (image or video sequence), is for instance happy or sad, according to the facial expressions that the subject showed. These messages are best represented as dimensions or categories. Observers make inferences about the emotions that underlie the subjects' behavior and for that reason they are referred to as "judges". In the sign-vehicles approach, some or all of the facial expressions and movements would be classified or counted in some fashion, for instance happy subjects lift their cheeks more than the other subjects. Observers describe the surface of behavior by counting how many times the face moves, or how long a movement lasts and are referred to as "coders". As an example, upon seeing a smiling face, an observer with a judgment-based approach would make judgments such as "happy," whereas an observer with a sign-based approach would code the face as having an upward, oblique movement of the lip corners [33].

3.2   Empirical Study

We need three sets of photographs depicting the facial expressions of the Geminoid|DK that correspond to the six basic universally accepted emotions of surprise, fear, disgust, anger, happiness and sadness. In total, we need eighteen photographs separated in three equal sets. The first set will be composed of photographs of the Original (O) while expressing the six basic emotions, the second set will be composed of empirically driven (ED) photographs, where the Geminoid will be mimicking the Original, and the third set will be composed of theoretically driven (TD) photographs, following the standards of Ekman and Friesen [13].

A dataset of photographs consisting of facial frames of the Original when posing to the camera would only reveal feigned emotions which present significant differences from the prototypical natural ones [25]. In order to depict genuine facial expressions from the Original, all of the six basic emotions had to be triggered. The triggering had to happen naturally, otherwise the reliability of the whole outcome could be questioned. In order to have clear and unambiguous photographs, we decided to subject the Original to a multimodal test on his laptop. The test consisted of a variety of different applications, programs, media, and videos, either online or installed to the laptop of the Original. Each of these was intended to trigger a different emotion. The test was accompanied by a set of instructions explaining the execution order.

The Original was placed in front of his laptop and had one camera pointing at his face, recording the facial expressions, and another one pointing at the screen of the laptop, keeping track of the actions. The next step was to analyze carefully the 44,600 micro-expressions (frames) from the first camera (High Definition - recording 50 frames per second), assign emotions to each of them and finally select six that according to [13] correspond to some universally accepted facial expressions of emotion. The selected photographs depicted one of the many facial expressions that correspond to an emotion. Due to the fact that the triggering was done through a laptop, the eyes of the Original tend to look a bit down (at the screen). Fortunately, this did not affect the outcome of the experiment. Some properties that every photograph shares are that they show the full face under sufficient lighting, are in focus and they are about the same size.

In the figures bellow (Fig.1, Fig.2 and Fig.3), follows a comparison/juxtaposition of the three sets of photographs with the facial blueprints of emotions as they are presented in [13]. For the sake of briefness, the figures illustrate only three of the six emotions; Anger, Happiness, and Sadness.

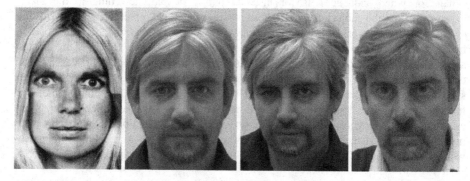

Fig. 1. All facial blueprints for the emotion of Anger (representing Controlled Anger). From left to right: Unmasking the Face (UTF) – TD – ED – O. [reprinted with permission]

Fig. 2. All facial blueprints for the emotion of Happiness (representing Full Face Happiness or Intense Happiness). From left to right: UTF – TD – ED – O. [reprinted with permission]

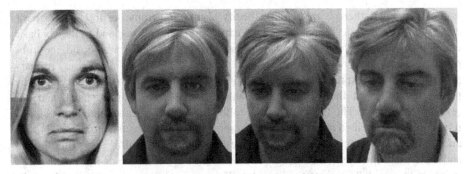

Fig. 3. All facial blueprints for the emotion of Sadness (representing the Lips Down Sad Mouth). From left to right: UTF – TD – ED – O [reprinted with permission]

3.3   Measuring Emotions

As Picard says, even though one has better access to his/her innermost feelings than anyone else, it is still difficult to "recognise" or label the feeling [35]. Through the years, many procedures have been developed for measuring emotions which can be separated into two main categories; the free response measurement and the forced choice response measurement. We can partition off the latter into two sub-categories; the dimensional approach and the discrete emotions approach [16], [17].

When emotions are shown as discrete systems, usually the respondents are asked to assess their emotions by a selection from a list of pre-determined emotions or provide feedback on the intensity of an emotion [16]. Following the theories developed by Ekman, we need to be able to select among six different emotions. The research on facial emotions has shown the utility and efficiency of conceiving emotions in discrete states, rather than in dimensions [34]. Dimensional measurements may be most productively applied to emotional experience aggregated across time and to the study of the moods [17]. There appear to be discrete boundaries between the facial expressions of emotion, much as there are perceived boundaries between hues of sound. Facial expressions are perceived categorically, and there is accumulating evidence supporting the claim that a discrete system is better applied to momentary experiences of emotion.

3.4   Research Method

We decided to launch an online questionnaire in order to collect feedback from observers. In total we projected 13 videos, each one illustrating a selected facial expression of the Geminoid|DK; 6 with the ED photographs, 6 with the TD photographs and one more video (the first one) that was used as a trial demo.

This questionnaire should not be considered as a test. We don't intend to train the subjects into recognising emotions, therefore there is no need to force them view each stimulus only once, or for a fraction of a second [31], [32]. After all, the facial movements of the Geminoid are mechanical and the change of facial status takes more time than a micro-expression. This questionnaire should also not be considered as a survey, since there is no need to specify a sampling frame, or to ensure sample coverage. According to Ekman, the facial expressions that correspond to the six basic emotions of surprise, fear, disgust, anger, happiness and sadness are considered to be psycho-physiological entities universally accepted [13], [17]. These primary prototypical facial expressions reveal emotions that can be understood universally by people regardless of their gender, nationality, social or economic status, and age (except for infants). The questionnaire is following the judgment-based approach and it can only be described as a judgment. Consequently, the subjects who respond to the questionnaire can be characterized as judges. Judges should fulfill two criteria; read and understand the English language, and be at least aware of the android technology in order to avoid "disorientated" results. Those who follow the Geminoid on the Facebook social networking service formulate an acceptable and considerable large group of people that are familiar at least with the Geminoid technology, have access to a computer with internet connection, and know how to communicate in English. An online questionnaire can provide honest answers, as respondents feel that their privacy is not violated [29]. Due to the medium that the questionnaire was launched, and due to time/cost constraints, the judges were random non-expert respondents who had access to the link, representing a group that resembles real world end-users but, admittedly, also introducing the risk of noisy answers.

Instead of using static photographs as stimuli, we decided to use videos. Displaying a short video that reminds the blinking of an eye was considered to be a more reliable option, as most facial expressions of emotions during a conversation last between 500ms and 2.5s [32]. Our videos would last seven seconds. During the 5th and 7th second the videos would be blank, and during the 6th second they would display the frame of the facial expression. The first frame (4 seconds) would warn viewers about the briefness of the video. Judges could view the videos as many times as they wanted, and they were prompted to answer the question *"What emotion do you think the face in the video is showing?"* by selecting from a list with the pre-determined six basic emotions on a two-point intensity scale; either the emotion existed, or not.

4   Analysis of the Results

The online questionnaire was reached by 678 unique visitors worldwide, but only 50 of them (34 females and 16 males) actually filled and submitted it. The overrepresentation of female respondents was anticipated [29]. The judges were located mainly in Europe, except for two coming from America, and belonged mainly to the age group of 21-30 years old (one was less than 15, nine belonged to the group of 16-21, thirty belonged to the group of 21-30, eight belonged to the group of 31-40, one to the group of 41-50 and one belonged to the group 51-60).

The results for the *Surprise* videos indicated that the strong majority of the judges named the emotion of Surprise as the dominant one, understanding our intention. The judgments for the Surprise emotion in the emotionally driven videos (EDV) outnumber the ones of the theoretically driven videos (TDV) (45 and 39 respectively), validating our hypothesis. The second most dominant emotion for the EDV was Happiness with 24 votes and for the TDV was Anger with 24 votes. In the *Fear* videos, the judgments favored another emotion than the one we intended to show. Instead of Fear, both videos revealed mainly the emotion of Surprise (49 judgments for the EDV and 44 for the TDV). This outcome suggests that the Geminoid is a substitute expressor for Fear. The emotion of Surprise is quite pronounced, coloring the whole facial expression. However, the emotion of Fear was better understood in the EDV than in the TDV (32 against 26 judgments), so the hypothesis is satisfied. For the *Disgust* videos, there was no agreement among the judges about an emotion. No more than a third of the judges gave any one judgment, excluding only the emotion of sadness (28 judgments) for the EDV and happiness for the TDV (17 judgments). This result suggests that the Geminoid|DK might be a withholder. The Disgust judgments were equally distributed (5 each), validating again the hypothesis. Both of the *Anger* videos were judged as we indented to (34 judgments for the EDV and 14 for the TDV), fact that confirms our hypothesis. The emotion that came second in the judgments was Disgust with 11 votes (EDV) and Happiness with also 11 votes (TDV), as shown in Table 1. The *Happiness* videos were also understood (45 judgments for the EDV and 44 for the TDV), but the judges distinguished also the emotion of Surprise (28 judgments for the EDV and 30 for the TDV). This outcome suggests that the Geminoid|DK is a substitute expressor to a slight degree that is not so evident. One more time the hypothesis was confirmed. Results for the *Sadness* videos revealed that there was almost an even split between the intended emotion of Sadness and another emotion – that of Anger. This outcome suggests that the Geminoid|DK might be an Anger-for-Sadness substitute expressor, as Anger was the second most dominant emotion at the EDV with 9 judgments and the most dominant at the TDV with 19. Observers' judgments matched with what we were expecting only in the EDV (24 judgments in the EDV against 12 in the TDV); therefore the hypothesis is confirmed.

Table 1. Table form depicting the experimental results for the Anger videos

Empirically Driven Anger Video			Theoretically Driven Anger Video		
Emotion Judgments		*No Emotion* Judgments	*Emotion* Judgments		*No Emotion* Judgments
Surprise	2	48	Surprise	6	44
Fear	3	47	Fear	6	44
Disgust	11	39	Disgust	2	48
Anger	34	16	Anger	14	36
Happiness	4	46	Happiness	11	39
Sadness	9	41	Sadness	8	42

5   Conclusion

We have presented the current status of the Geminoid technology and what it needs to become Geminoid Reality. Apart from an adaptive interface able to communicate with the surrounding environment, it also needs to have believable characteristics and be able to actively engage in interaction. The process of finding the ways a Geminoid can embody emotional facial expressions with respect to the fundamental rules of human affect expression was based on a robotic perspective of the work of Ekman.

The results of the questionnaire revealed an incapability of the Geminoid to reproduce the emotions of Fear and Disgust. Our proposal here concerns the next version of the Geminoid series. We believe that an installation of actuators to the facial areas of the *levator labii superioris /alaeque nasi* (nose wrinkle), *levator labii superioris/caput infraorbitalis* (upper lip raiser), *depressor anguli oris (triangularis)* (lip corner depressor), *incisivii labii superioris* and *incisivii labii inferioris* (lip puckerer) and *orbicularis oris* (lip tightener) will ease the HRI. Another addition that would reveal even more natural facial expressions could be to make the already installed actuators operate independently (i.e., to lift just one eye-brow).

Lastly, we have proven that the emotional state of the Geminoid|DK is equally or more understandable when mimicking the Original than when following the theoretical approach of [13]. This finding suggests that before programming the facial expressions of a Geminoid, the Original should pass through a similar procedure. In cases that no particular Original is engaged in the android's face creation, the facial expressions of the android should be tested by judges in a similar way. Following our recommendations, a believable facial communication is within reach.

References

1. Krippendorff, K.: The semantic turn-A new foundation for design. CRC Press, Taylor & Francis Group (2006)
2. Grudin, J.: The computer reaches out: The historical continuity of interface design. In: Chew, J.C., Whiteside, J. (eds.) Proceedings of the SIGCHI Conference on Human Factors in Computing Systems: Empowering People (CHI 1990). ACM, NY (1990)
3. Dourish, P.: Where The Action Is: The Foundations of Embodied Interaction. MIT Press (2001)
4. Breazeal, C.: Social Interactions in HRI:The Robot View. IEEE Transactions on Systems Man, Cybernetics and Systems-Part C 34(2), 181–186 (2004)
5. Nishio, S., Ishiguro, H., Hagita, N.: Geminoid:Teleoperated Android of an Existing Person. In: Filho, A.C.D.P. (ed.) Humanoid Robots: New Developments, Vienna, pp. 343–352 (2007)
6. Reeves, B., Nass, C.: The Media Equation: How People Treat Computers, Television, and New Media Like Real People and Places. University Chicago Press (1996)
7. Breazeal, C.: Toward sociable robots. In: Robotics and Autonomous Systems, vol. 42(3-4), pp. 167–175. Elsevier (2003)
8. Picard, R.W., Klein, J.: Computers that Recognise and Respond to User Emotion: Theoretical and Practical Implications. Interacting with Computers 14(2), 141–169 (2002)
9. Personal Robotic Group, http://robotic.media.mit.edu/
10. Philips, http://www.research.philips.com/technologies/projects/robotics/
11. Hoffman, D.D.: Chapter 2: The Construction of Visual Reality. In: Blom, J.D., Sommer, I.E.C. (eds.) Hallucinations: Research and Practice, pp. 7–15. Springer US (2012)
12. Blom, J.D., Sommer, I.E.C.: Chapter 13, Hallucinations of Bodily Sensation. In: Blom, J.D., Sommer, I.E.C. (eds.) Hallucinations of Bodily Sensation, Part 2, pp. 157–169. Springer US (2012)
13. Ekman, P., Friesen, W.V.: Unmasking the Face – A guide to recognising emotions from facial expressions. Malor Books, Cambridge (2003)
14. Cohn, J.F.: Foundations of Human Computing: Facial Expression and Emotion. In: Proceedings of the 8th International Conference on Multimodal Interfaces (ICMI 2006), pp. 233–238. ACM, New York (2006)

15. Banissy, M.J., Ward, J.: Mirror-touch synesthesia is linked with empathy. Nature Neuroscience 10, 815–816 (2007)
16. Scherer, K.R.: What are emotions? And how can they be measured? Social Science Information 44(4), 695–729 (2005)
17. Keltner, D., Ekman, P.: Facial expression of emotion. In: Lewis, M., Jones, J.H. (eds.) Handbook of Emotions, 2nd edn., pp. 236–248. Guilford Publications, New York (2000)
18. Behrendt, R.P.: Consciousness, Memory, and Hallucinations. In: Blom, J.D., Sommer, I.E.C. (eds.) Hallucinations: Research and Practice, part 1, pp. 17–31. Springer US (2012)
19. Hanson Robotics, http://hansonrobotics.wordpress.com/
20. Thrun, S.: Towards A Framework for Human-Robot Interaction. Journal Human-Computer Interaction 19(1), 9–24 (2004)
21. Takano, E., Matsumoto, Y., Nakamura, Y., Ishiguro, H., Sugamoto, K.: The Psychological Effects of Attendance of an Android on Communication. In: Khatib, O., Kumar, V., Pappas, G.J. (eds.) Experimental Robotics. STAR, vol. 54, pp. 221–228. Springer, Heidelberg (2009)
22. Becker-Asano, C., Wachsmuth, I.: Affective computing with primary and secondary emotions in a virtual human. Auton. Agent Multi-Agent Systems 20(1), 32–49 (2010)
23. Geminoid|DK, http://www.geminoid.dk
24. Shimada, M., Yoshikawa, Y., Asada, M., Saiwaki, N., Ishiguro, H.: Effects of Observing Eye Contact between a Robot and Another Person. International Journal of Social Robotics 3(2), 143–154 (2011)
25. Padgett, C., Cottrell, G.: Representing face images for emotion classification. In: Mozer, M., Jordan, M., Petsche, T. (eds.) Advances in Neural Information Processing Systems, vol. 9. MIT Press, Cambridge (1997)
26. Taylor, J.: The Emerging Geographies of Virtual Worlds. Geographical Review, Cyberspace and Geographical Space 87(2), 172–192 (1997)
27. Turner, P.: An everyday account of witnessing. AI & Society: Special Issue: Witnessed Presence 27(1), 5–12 (2012)
28. Holz, T., Campbell, A.G., O'Hare, G.M.P., Stafford, J.W., Martin, A., Dragone, M.: MiRA—Mixed Reality Agents. International. Journal of Human – Computer Studies 69(4), 251–268 (2011)
29. The American Statistical Association, http://www.amstat.org/
30. Cheok, A.D., Haller, M., Fernando, O.N.N., Wijesena, J.P.: Mixed Reality Entertainment and Art. The International Journal of Virtual Reality 8(2), 83–90 (2009)
31. Boucher, J.D., Ekman, P.: Facial Areas and Emotional Information. Journal of Communication 25(2), 21–29 (1975)
32. Ekman, P.: Emotions Revealed-Understanding Faces and Feelings, Phoenix, UK (2003)
33. Cohn, J.F., Ekman, P.: Measuring facial action by manual coding, facial EMG, and automatic facial image analysis. In: Harrigan, J.A., Rosenthal, R., Scherer, K. (eds.) Handbook of Nonverbal Behavior Research Methods in the Affective Sciences, pp. 9–64 (2005)
34. Ekman, P.: Facial expression and emotion. American Psychologist 48(4), 384–392 (1993)
35. Picard, R.W.: Affective Computing: Challenges. International Journal of Human-Computer Studies 59(1-2), 55–64 (2003)
36. Carmigniani, J., Furht, B.: Augmented Reality: An Overview. In: Furht, B. (ed.) Handbook of Augmented Reality, Part 1, pp. 3–46. Springer, New York (2011)
37. Takeno, J., Mori, K., Naito, Y.: Robot Consciousness and Representation of Facial Expressions. In: 3rd International Conference on Sensing Technology (ICST 2008), pp. 569–574. IEEE Press (2008)
38. Hiroshi Ishiguro Laboratory, http://www.geminoid.jp
39. Vardi, M.Y.: Is Moore's Party Over? Communications of the ACM 54(11), 5 (2011)

Embodiment and Cognitive Learning –
Can a Humanoid Robot Help Children
with Autism to Learn about Tactile Social Behaviour?

Ben Robins[1], Kerstin Dautenhahn[1], and Paul Dickerson[2]

[1] School of Computer Science, University of Hertfordshire, Hatfield, U.K.
{B.Robins,K.Dautenhahn}@herts.ac.uk
[2] Department of Psychology, University of Roehampton, London, U.K.
p.dickerson@roehampton.ac.uk

Abstract. The work presented in this paper is part of our investigation in the ROBOSKIN[1] project. The project aims to develop new robot capabilities based on the tactile feedback provided by novel robotic skin. The main objective of the project is to develop cognitive mechanisms to improve human-robot interaction capabilities. One application domain that is investigated in the project is robot-assisted play in the context of autism therapy. The article provides a case study evaluation of segments of trials where tactile interactions were observed between children with autism and the humanoid robot KASPAR which was equipped with the newly developed tactile sensing capabilities. A preliminary observational analysis was undertaken which applied, in abbreviated form, certain principles from ethnography and conversation analysis. The analysis first reports initial observations concerning range of tactile behaviours that children displayed towards KASPAR and the change in these across the trials. Subsequently the analysis examines in detail one sequence of interaction in which a child's tactile actions towards KASPAR are considered in terms of their responsiveness to the sequence of interaction in which they occur – and specifically to the intricate details of KASPAR's responses to the child's tactile behaviour. In this way the paper suggests that children appear to interact in a tactile manner quite spontaneously with KASPAR, that the child's tactile actions become modified through exposure to KASPAR and that children with an Autistic Spectrum Disorder (ASD) can demonstrate a marked responsiveness to the behaviours that KASPAR displays in sequences of tactile interaction.

Keywords: Robot Assisted Play, Assistive Technology, Human-Robot Interaction, Autism Therapy.

1   Introduction

Touch is known to be a key element in child development. From the moment a baby is born, the need for human contact (with the mother, and other caregivers) is very evident. A number of studies have shown that physical contact between mothers and

---

[1] This work has been partially supported by the European Commission under contract number FP7-231500-RoboSkin.

S.S. Ge et al. (Eds.): ICSR 2012, LNAI 7621, pp. 66–75, 2012.
© Springer-Verlag Berlin Heidelberg 2012

their babies has an effect on the children's intelligence and comprehension in later stages of life. Ibraimov further illustrates how the sensitivity of our skin receptors informs us of our internal and external environment [1]. Bowlby asserts that attachment is the basis for healthy human development [2]. According to Montagu, touch is regarded as the first modality to be developed and is suggested to be the most prominent exploratory sense at the sensori-motor stage in Piaget's theory of development, the first stage that initiates the healthy development of an individual [3].

Physical touch is one of the most basic forms of communication. In the playground, touch and physical contact are used by children to communicate, to build trust, to give or receive support and to develop their social relationships. During play children can learn about themselves and their environments as well as develop cognitive, social and perceptual skills [4]. In therapy, the touch of another person, when it happens, can be seen as a way of breaking through isolation. Touch has a social element, a sense of community that positively affirms the patients [5], [6]. Touch deprivation in early stages can lead to speech retardation, learning disabilities, as well as emotional problems in later life [7, 8].

In recent years an increasing number of research studies have shown the potential use of robots as tools to support the development of different skills in children with special needs. Studies at the University of Hertfordshire showed how mobile robots (e.g. IROMEC) and humanoid robots (e.g Robota, KASPAR) can be used to mediate interactions between children with autism and peers and adults [9-14]. Other robots have been used by various researchers to engage autistic children in playful interactions, e.g. artificial pets such as the baby seal robot Paro and the teddy bear Huggable [15, 16], and the small cartoon-like Keepon [17], to mention just a few.

1.1   Autism and Tactile Interaction

Autism here refers to Autistic Spectrum Disorders (ASD), a range of manifestations of a developmental disorder characterized by impairments in communication, social interaction, and imagination [18] that can occur to different degrees and in a variety of forms [19].

People with autism, in addition often experience an inability to relate to others, showing little use of eye contact and having difficulty in verbal and non-verbal communication [20], thus tactile interaction may therefore present particular challenges for this group.

Some people with ASD might be hyposensitive and seem not to feel any pain. Their touch of other people or objects would not be sensed appropriately and, unintentionally, they could hurt other people, or break objects. Other people with autism might have a hypertactility condition which is very common and results in overwhelming sensation of touch. As touch can be excruciating people with this condition fear being touched. This fear could be so great, it can send them into a panic attack [21, 22].

On the other hand tactile interaction (if tolerated) might be an important means of communication for children with autism, as some do not have verbal skills and others use their verbal skills inadequately. Caldwell suggests that problems with verbal skills and eye gaze in children with autism create the need for touch to replace these detrimental ways of communicating [23].

In this way tactile interaction can be understood as particularly pertinent to persons with an Autistic Spectrum Disorder yet the empirical picture is complex - with evidence for both *hyper* and *hypo* tactile sensitivity [24, 25]. This empirical picture of a significant but complex relationship between persons with an ASD and tactile experience in itself merits further research into tactile contact amongst children and adults with an ASD in which tactile interaction plays a central role. The importance of such research is further underscored by findings which suggest that even *rudimentary* tactile devices might play a crucial role as positive interventions that can stimulate communication amongst autistic populations[26].

We argue that a 'tactile' robot can be used as a buffer that mediates between a person with autism and another person, by providing indirect rather than direct human-human contact, until such time that the person with autism builds enough strength and confidence to tolerate direct human contact and use tactile interaction in socially acceptable ways that help to regulate human-human interaction.

A robot with tactile skills could allow a person with autism to feel safe and build their confidence in tactile interaction where they can explore touch in a playful way that could be completely under their control. Importantly, in interaction with KASPAR a person with autism can explore interaction and communication in a non-judgmental manner, exploring physical human-like features of the robot without being prevented from showing inappropriate behaviour (e.g. poking the eyes or hitting the robot can be part of a learning experience over several sessions to learn about physical human-like features and to explore cause and effect in tactile interaction).

1.2   The Robotic Platform - KASPAR

KASPAR (Fig 1) is a child-sized minimally expressive robot which acts as a platform for HRI studies, using mainly bodily expressions (movements of the hand, arms and facial expressions) and gestures to interact with a human. The robot has a static body taken from a child-sized commercially available mannequin doll. The legs and hands do not move, the torso has 1 DOF and can move from side to side. The head has 8 DOF and the arms have 3 DOF each. In addition, KASPAR was mounted with several skin patches on cheeks, torso, left and right arm, on the back and palm of the hands and also on the soles of the feet. These tactile sensing capabilities allow the robot to respond autonomously when being touched. The robot could also be operated by a remote controlled keypad.

Fig. 1. The robotic platform KASPAR. The figure on left shows some of the tactile skin patches mounted on the robot.

For a complete description of KASPAR's design rationale, hardware, and application examples see [9].

2   Trials Set-Up and Procedures

The trials took place in two special needs schools for children with moderate learning difficulties in the UK. With the objective to provide a reassuring environment, the trials were designed to allow the children to have free and unconstrained interaction with the robot and with the present adult (i.e. teacher, experimenter) should they wish to. The trials were conducted in a familiar room often used by the children for various activities. Before the trials, the humanoid robot was placed on a table, connected to a laptop. The investigator was seated next to the table. The children were brought to the room by their carer and the trials stopped when the child indicated that they wanted to leave the room or if they became bored. Two stationary video cameras were used to record the trials. The robot could respond autonomously to different tactile interactions, as well as be operated remotely via a wireless remote control (a specially programmed keypad), either by the investigator or by the child.

The play scenario was a very basic cause and effect game, where, touching different parts of the robot will cause different reactions and movements of the robot. One of the goals of this scenario is that the robot could respond to the style of interaction with appropriate feedback and facial expressions. For example, light touch or tickling the left foot will cause the robot to smile and say "this is nice - it tickles me", light touch of the torso will cause the robot to smile and 'laugh' out loud saying "ha ha ha", inappropriate tactile interaction (e.g. hitting the robot or using too much force in the interaction)[2] will cause the robot to have a 'sad' expression, turn its face and torso away to one side, cover its face with its hand and give audible feedback saying "ouch – this hurts" (Fig 2).

Fig. 2. KASPAR helps to encourage or discourage certain tactile behaviours

3   Cognitive Learning during Child-Robot Interaction

The analysis here starts by drawing on ideas developed in the ethnography of autism research which employs observation of behaviour to better understand the situational determinants of autistic behaviour [27]. With these data this will entail making initial observations regarding the ways in which the repertoire of tactile behaviours that children engage in changes with repeated exposure to Kaspar. The analysis will then, as with some of the authors' previous work [28], draw on conversation analytic principles

---

[2] Please note, the tactile classification algorithms were still under development during the time of the trials and so the robot's response to a forceful interaction was triggered manually by the investigator using the remote control.

to investigate a sequence of interaction which illustrates details of child's tactile behaviour and the extent to which this orientates to the tactile responsiveness of Kaspar.

3.1   Observations of Early Encounters with KASPAR

The images in Fig 3 below are taken from the first few seconds of children being seated in front of KASPAR for the first time. At this stage they had received no instructions regarding how they should interact with KASPAR.

Fig. 3. Children with autism initiate tactile contact in their first encounter with KASPAR

In these instances - and across the data – the children demonstrated the initiation of touch which whilst not requested or invited was nonetheless consistent with being introduced to the robot or asking their own questions about it (please note that the style of these tactile interactions with the robot varied among the children). These observations support the idea that far from presenting a problem for children with an Autistic Spectrum Disorder, being embodied provided a means by which the children could undertake some demonstrable form of examination of KASPAR – a physical enactment of investigating the robot that which was relevant to the interactional context in which they were either introduced to the robot or in some cases, were themselves asking about it.

It can be noted however, that in their initial tactile interactions with KASPAR some children were observed behaving in somewhat forceful or otherwise inappropriate manners (e.g. hitting the robot or using the experimenter's hand to do so, poking the robot's eye, grasping it very tightly etc) as shown in Fig 4. In some cases children repeated this initial 'aggressive' tactile interaction several times despite KASPAR responding by displaying its 'sad' expression and evasive body movements.

Fig. 4. Children interact in forceful manner

3.2   Observations of Subsequent Encounters with KASPAR

Whilst there is some observational evidence for both a propensity for tactile interaction and the presence of some aggressive tactile contact in early encounters with KASPAR, observation of subsequent encounters suggests that with repeated encounters children develop a repertoire of non-aggressive tactile behaviours towards KASPAR.

As Fig 5 and Fig 6 indicate, particularly in later sessions, children demonstrated some responsiveness to KASPAR's reaction to the nature of their touch. Fig 5 shows an example where KASPAR, after being hit by a child, has reacted by displaying discomfort by both saying "ouch – this hurts" and by displaying a sad expression with its face covered by its hands. Immediately following the onset of KASPAR's embodied display of discomfort – and in overlap with KASPAR's verbal expression of discomfort "ouch", the child starts to gently stroke KASPAR (Fig 5 left) – after the utterance "this hurts" the child turns to face KASPAR (Fig 5 right) asking in a subdued voice "what's wrong with you?"

Fig. 5. A child responds to KASPAR's demonstration of discomfort following the child's previous forceful tactile interaction

Observations of early and subsequent trials from a perspective informed by autistic ethnography suggest that children initiate a tactile engagement with KASPAR from their first encounter. Some – though by no means all – of these tactile engagements in early encounters could be understood as more 'aggressive' in that they involve forms of behaviour that could create discomfort if enacted on another human. In fact, such repeated aggressive behaviour, exhibited towards another person, would not be tolerated in an educational or therapeutic context. However, especially in the later trials after some prompting and teaching by the experimenter, children showed not only a relative decrease in behaviours that elicited a reaction in KASPAR which displayed discomfort but also an increased responsiveness to KASPAR's reactions.

Often, after following the onset of KASPAR's embodied display of discomfort (by both saying "ouch – this hurts" and by displaying a sad expression), the children start to gently stroke KASPAR on the torso or tickle its foot to cause it to display its 'happy' expressions, and at times this was followed with the children displaying a satisfactory smile (Fig 6).

Fig. 6. A child explores the result of his previous actions, comforts KASPAR by tickling its torso, and smiles in satisfaction

At this stage in the analysis there is insufficient evidence to claim for certain whether KASPAR brings about a form of learning or enhanced repertoire of behaviours which might in any way generalise beyond the interactions with KASPAR. However, the data illustrated in Fig 7 – and subsequent reports from the child's family provide at least some indicative data that is consistent with this interpretation.

Fig. 7. RN explores being 'sad' (left) and 'happy'(right) during imitation games with the robot

Images in Fig 7 are taken from trials in which the child (RN) triggered the 'happy' expression in the robot and then imitated the posture whilst saying out loud "happy". After several sessions, the experimenter introduced the 'sad' expression of the robot into the game prompting the child to imitate it whilst saying 'sad'. In contrast to his joyful expression of the 'happy' state, the child imitated the robot's 'sad' expression whilst whispering "he is sad". Subsequently the child triggered the robot's 'happy' expression (by tickling its stomach). It can be noted anecdotally that in a subsequent interview RN's mother reported that these sessions with the robot made a "big difference" in the child's behaviour claiming that: "he now knows the difference between happy and sad". The mother suggested that RN had started to convey his feelings to his parents – saying "RN is sad" when crying and "RN is happy" or "mummy is happy" when the family were laughing together. Whilst such evidence can only be presented in the most tentative manner it does nonetheless provide a indication of a potentially positive generalization of the learning issues addressed in this paper.

3.3   Orientating to the Tactile Responsiveness of KASPAR

Extract one below is taken from a sequence of interaction in which the child engages in tactile behaviour towards KASPAR that KASPAR responds to with a display of pain.

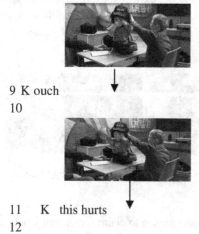

9 K ouch
10

11   K   this hurts
12

13   A °↑what's ↓ wrong ↑with ↓you° ((spoken in a subdued voice))

In the above extract KASPAR's words "Ouch" and embodied behaviour (turning to the side with his is further underscored by KASPAR directly articulating an experience of discomfort; "this hurts". Here then the child with an ASD is at a new position in the sequence of interaction – they have acted aggressively towards KASPAR and now KASPAR has displayed a response to these actions (albeit a response that might be a little less immediate than cries of pains in response to aggressive acts are typically found to be). The important point analytically then is what happens here, at the point where KASPAR has *displayed a response to* the (aggressive) tactile actions on the part of the child with an ASD. It is at this point in the interaction that the experience of KASPAR – the co-interactant with 'A' (the child with an ASD) – has been made interactionally available for 'A'.

What the above extract demonstrates is that A's actions go beyond what we might deduce either from diagnostic criteria or pre-existing literature regarding the capacities of persons with an ASD for "social-emotional reciprocity". A engages in actions which suggest both some level of empathy and an awareness of differential knowledge states. In lines 9-11 A strokes the back of KASPAR's head – an action which they had not seen modelled on KASPAR – either within this session or previously. In Line 13 A gazes into KASPAR's face as he begins to ask "What's wrong with you". Finally, in line 13, having previously gazed at Kasper whilst asking "What's wrong with you", A turns to Ben – the adult who has introduced KASPAR as he completes his question – thereby selecting Ben as the addressee and implicitly treating him as having appropriate knowledge of KASPAR to be able to answer the question. In this way the child demonstrates not just a repertoire of non aggressive tactile behaviours towards KASPAR – but also the ability to use these in a sequentially appropriate way. In this extract the child orientates to the displays of pain at that specific moment with an interactionally appropriate verbal and tactile response.

4   Discussion

The case study analyses presented in this paper emphasise aspects of embodiment and interaction kinesics when children with autism interact with the humanoid robot KASPAR. It illustrated that children engage with KASPAR in a tactile way and that as experience in interacting with KASPAR develops a repertoire of tactile behaviours develop which include non-aggressive and soothing behaviours. Furthermore, the analysis indicated that not only do children develop a repertoire of non-aggressive and soothing tactile behaviours they can also be found to draw upon them at precisely the moment when they are most relevant in their interactions with KASPAR –for example soothing KASPAR with their verbal and tactile behaviour when he displays that he is in pain. This paper presents a preliminary study of the possible embodied and cognitive learning in tactile interactions with the robot. A further longitudinal study to investigate how persistent the learning effect might be is planned for the future.

As the literature suggests, children with autism are an extremely heterogeneous population [29], and although they share the same core difficulties, each child displays these in an individual way [30]. Consequently, the nature of tactile interation with the robot differs from one child to another. The various challenges presented by the variety of behaviour exhibited by the children requires a modular approach in designing robotic systems and play scenarios for child-robot interaction for this population, in order to be able to adapt to the individual needs of the children. A fixed set of play scenarios would not be able to account for this variability in behaviour. The case study examples in this paper also highlight the benefit of flexible operation of the robot where the robot can respond autonomously and at the same time a therapist/ teacher/experimenter could work with the child alongside the robot, triggering additional robot behaviors when needed and thus facilitating cognitive learning when possible.

References

1. Ibraimov, A.I.: The evolution of body heat conductivity, skin and brain size in human. Journal of Human Ecology 21, 95–103 (2007)
2. Bowlby, J.: A secure base – clinical applications of attachment theory. Routledge (1988)
3. Montagu, A.: Touching: The human significance of the skin. Harper and Row, New York (1986)
4. Ferland, F.: The ludic model: Play, children with physical disabilities and occupational therapy. University of Ottawa Press, Ottawa (1977)
5. Bernstein, P.: Theoretical approaches in dance/movement therapy, i & ii. Kendall Hunt, Dubuque (1986)
6. Costonis, M.: Therapy in motion. University of Illinois Press, Urbana (1978)
7. Davis, P.K.: The power of touch - the basis for survival, health, intimacy, and emotional well-being. Hay House Inc., Carlsbad (1999)
8. Hertenstein, M.J., Verkamp, J.M., Kerestes, A.M., Holmes, R.M.: The communicative functions of touch in humans, non-human primates, and rats: A review and synthesis of the empirical research. Genetic, Social and General Psychology Monographs 132(1), 5–94 (2006)
9. Dautenhahn, K., Nehaniv, C.L., Walters, M.L., Robins, B., Kose-Bagci, H., Mirza, N.A., Blow, M.: Kaspar - a minimally expressive humanoid robot for human-robot interaction research. Special Issue on "Humanoid Robots", Applied Bionics and Biomechanics 6(3), 369–397 (2009)
10. Ferrari, E., Robins, B., Dautenhahn, K.: Robot as a social mediator - a play scenario implementation with children with autism. In: 8th International Conference on Interaction Design and Children, IDC 2009, Como, Italy (2009)

11. Robins, B., Amirabdollahian, F., Ji, Z., Dautenhahn, K.: Tactile interaction with a humanoid robot for children with autism: A case study analysis from user requirements to implementation. In: The19th IEEE International Symposium in Robot and Human Interactive Communication (RO-MAN 2010), Viareggio, Italy (2010)
12. Robins, B., Dautenhahn, K., Dickerson, P.: From isolation to communication: A case study evaluation of robot assisted play for children with autism with a minimally expressive humanoid robot. In: Second International Conference on Advances in CHI, ACHI 2009, Cancun, Mexico (2009)
13. Robins, B., Dautenhahn, K.: Developing Play Scenarios for Tactile Interaction with a Humanoid Robot: A Case Study Exploration with Children with Autism. In: Ge, S.S., Li, H., Cabibihan, J.-J., Tan, Y.K. (eds.) ICSR 2010. LNCS, vol. 6414, pp. 243–252. Springer, Heidelberg (2010)
14. Wainer, J., Dautenhahn, K., Robins, B., Amirabdollahian, F.: Collaborating with kaspar: Using an autonomous humanoid robot to foster cooperative dyadic play among children with autism. In: 10th IEEE-RAS International Conference on Humanoid Robots (Humanoids 2010), Nashville, TN (2010)
15. Marti, P., Pollini, A., Rullo, A., Shibata, T.: Engaging with artificial pets. In: Proceedings of Annual Conference of the European Association of Cognitive Ergonomics, Chania, Greece (2005)
16. Stiehl, W.D., Lieberman, J., Breazeal, C.C., Basel, L., Lalla, L.: Wolf M.: Design of a therapeutic robotic companion for relational, affective touch. In: Proceedings of the International Workshop on Robots and Human Interactive Communication (2005)
17. Kozima, H., Nakagawa, C., Yasuda, Y.: Children-robot interaction: A pilot study in autism therapy. Progress in Brain Research 164, 385–400 (2007)
18. American psychiatric association: diagnostic and statistical manual of mental disorders dsm-iv. American Psychiatric Association, Washington D.C. (1995)
19. Jordan, R.: Autistic spectrum disorders - an introductory handbook for practitioners. David Fulton Publishers, London (1999)
20. Baron-Cohen, S.: Mindblindness: An essay on autism and theory of mind. MIT Press, Cambridge (1995)
21. Bogdashina, O.: Sensory perceptual issues in autism and asperger syndrome: Different sensory experiences – different perceptual worlds. Jessica Kingsley Publishers, London (2003)
22. Gillingham, G.: Autism: Handle with care: Understanding and managing behaviour of children and adults with autism. Future Education Inc., Arlington (1995)
23. Caldwell, P.: Getting in touch: Ways of working with people with severe learning disabilities and extensive support needs. Pavilion Publishing Ltd., Brighton (1996)
24. Blakemore, S.J., Tavassoli, T., Calo, S., Thomas, R.M., Catmur, C., Frith, U., Haggard, P.: Tactile sensitivity in asperger syndrome. Brain and Cognition 61, 5–13 (2006)
25. Foss-Feig, J.H., Heacock, J.L., Cascio, C.J.: Tactile responsiveness patterns and their association with core features in autistic spectrum disorders. Research in Autistic Spectrum Disorders 6, 337–344 (2012)
26. Taylor, B.A., Levin, L.: Teaching a student with autism to make verbal initiations: Effects of a tactile prompt. Journal of Applied Behaviour Analysis 31, 651–654 (1998)
27. Ochs, E., Solomon, O.: Autistic sociality. Ethos 38, 69–92 (2010)
28. Robins, B., Dickerson, P., Stribling, P., Dautenhahn, K.: Robot-mediated joint attention in children with autism: A case study in a robot-human interaction. In: Interaction studies: Social Behaviour and Communication in Biological and Artificial Systems, vol. 5(2), pp. 161–198. John Benjamins Publishing Company, Amsterdam (2004)
29. Parham, D., Fasio, L.: Play in occupational therapy for children. Mosby-Elsevier, St. Louis (2008)
30. Cumine, V., Leach, J., Stevenson, G.: Autism in the early years: A practical guide London. David Fulton Publishers (2000)

A User Trial Study to Understand Play Behaviors of Autistic Children Using a Social Robot

Alvin Wong[2,*], Yeow Kee Tan[1], Adrian Tay[1], Anthony Wong[1],
Dilip Kumar Limbu[1], Tran Anh Dung[1], Yuanwei Chua[1], and Ai Ping Yow[2]

[1] Institute for Infocomm Research, A*STAR, Singapore
[2] Nanyang Technological University, Singapore
{hyawong,yktan,hjtay,cywong,dklimbu,
tanhdung,ychua}@i2r.a-star.edu.sg,
yowa0002@e.ntu.edu.sg

Abstract. Social robots have been a valuable tool for autistic children to learn about play and interaction. The study was carried out on children diagnosed with high-functioning autism. A 30 cm tall tele-operated robot named, "Rofina" was used to study the interaction between autistic children and robot. With a 2-DOF head on the body, Rofina displayed basic emotions and exhibited social pleasantries while playing a board game with the children. During the study, the autistic children were comfortable with the robot's presence. The children appreciated that Rofina addressed them by name and looked towards them. These children, who normally did not finish the game, managed to complete the game with enthusiasm. More user studies need to be done in order to support these findings and by using larger sample size in a real-life scenario. There is potential for Rofina to be used in a classroom setting for children with special needs.

Keywords: Social Robot, Autism, Children.

1 Introduction

Social robots have been used in play activities that involved autistic children. Research has shown that there is growing evidence that robots provide opportunities for assisting autistic children. Children with autism tend to exhibit social behaviours such as imitation and eye contact, when interacting with robots [1]. The result of the investigation showed that the percentage of interaction with robot was higher than with toy and the children (7 to 11 years with mild to high functioning autism) were able to interact and play with the robot. Evidences also suggested that robots trigger autistic children more and thus, it may be useful in potential treatments [3], [4], [5]. An article reported that *Kaspar*, a social robot had successfully taught a 4-year-old girl with autism

---

* Corresponding author.

S.S. Ge et al. (Eds.): ICSR 2012, LNAI 7621, pp. 76–85, 2012.
© Springer-Verlag Berlin Heidelberg 2012

about social behaviours [10]. There could be long-term effect of human-robot interactions on autistic children. In the context of autism therapy, researchers had specifically identified 3 different types of roles that a robot can adopted in human society [4]. Firstly, as a persuasive machine (also known as a therapeutic playmate), robots have a therapeutic influence on the autistic child by catching and maintaining the child's attention, and engaging the child in therapeutically relevant interactions during the trial. The child could be taught desirable social skills and be guided through different types of interactions. Secondly, the robot could be used as a social mediator that could encourage and facilitate social behaviour among children. Lastly, as a model social agent, the robot could allow children to learn social skills by observing and interacting with them in a particular setting.

Researchers have also been studying the performance of robots used in therapies and achieving the design requirements for a robot based on the studies done [2], [3], [5]. These requirements could be categorised into three main aspects which could be taken into consideration when designing a robot for autistic children [9].

Another research area is the "type of activity". The type of activity has a rather great influence on autistic children as children learn social behaviours better through playing and learning from activities. This is related to a child's developmental areas.

Turn-taking [7] activities allow children to become accustomed to waiting for responses after it says or do something [5]. Imitation is another activity that is commonly played in therapies as it helps to improve the child's hand-eye coordination [3]. Imitation plays a significant role in the development of social cognition, as it is an important tool used for transferring knowledge in social contexts. Imitation serves not only as a learning tool to acquire new physical skills (such as the usage of various objects), but also provides the foundation for learning about our social environment. Most human behaviours are learnt through observation and imitation of others. For autistic children, these processes do not occur naturally and they need guidance in order to develop. A rewarding activity is a powerful incentives for autistic child to continue playing with the robots (e.g. having the robot to behave in particular ways when children responds correctly to requests) [6] and foster cause and effect connection (e.g. pressing a button and causes the robot to move) [2]. When designing for the type of activity, the scenario should include the types of interaction to be carried with the children. Figure 1 shows three aspects on types of activity.

Triadic interaction is the most common type of interaction used in the therapies or studies and it involves a robot, a child and a companion (child/ parent/ teacher/ therapist). It has the greatest potential for success as robots has difficulty achieving the rich social interaction that human-to-human interaction provides [3]. In this case, robot is used as a social "pivot", to help to elicit interactions between the child and other human. Another type of interaction is self-initiated interaction. In this interaction, robot is being used to encourage the child to engage the robot proactively and this is where rewarding activity is involved [3].

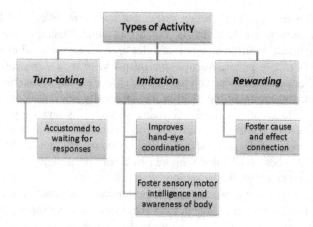

Fig. 1. Aspect on types of activity

It is difficult to fully understand all autistic children and their needs as there are different levels of autism. Different levels of autism require different range of treatment approaches serves to demonstrate the range and levels of need. Hence, there is a need to specify the targeted level of autism. In this study, the target user will be pre-schoolers (aged 4 to 6 years old) diagnosed with high-functioning autism. Generally, pre-schoolers with high-functioning autism, tends to have difficulties in [8]:

1. Understanding emotions and gestures
2. Displaying basic social pleasantries such as greeting someone, etc.
3. Exhibiting basic interpersonal interaction when interacting with people
4. Communicating with people verbally
5. Understanding one's own self and other people

2 Design of Robot

The design of a robot for autistic children is critical as it is a tool to help them and a few papers had also highlighted the importance of the robot's designs. There were certain design problems which were faced by the autistic children or the third party (i.e. teaching facilitator, parents, etc).

The objective of this study was to design and develop a small and portable robotic platform to be used as a platform specifically for use by high-functioning autistic preschoolers (aged 4 to 6 years old). Among the five difficulty areas that were experienced by high functioning autistic children, we decided to work on the following areas:

1. Be used in a scenario that acts as a social mediator to mediate contact between autistic children and a companion (i.e. teaching facilitator and other autistic children).
2. Be able to execute simple tasks which can engage autistic children in simple interactive activities with the aim of encouraging basic communication and social skills.

The teaching facilitators at a local autism centre also shared some of their activities that were carried out in the class, which could teach the children the right behaviours and also, improve eye contact and social behaviours. If a robot was used in a group setting and it had to play games with the children, a list of names of the children who were playing the game could be stored in the robot. When it was a particular child's turn to play the games, the robot could call their name. Besides, the robot would act as a tool to engage the children when they started to lose the interest on the tasks. They proposed that the robot could respond or react positively if it detected the child was looking at it.

The robotic platform was named, *"Rofina"*. It had a height of about 230 mm, with the body's and head's diameter of 200 mm and 130 mm respectively. For ease of deployment, *Rofina* was designed to be small and portable. *Rofina* does not possess great complexity or human-like facial features which might have adverse effect on the children. Hence the facial features relied on eyes and mouth to show basic emotions. Visual feedback provided by the robot's face is intended to improve the interaction and to attract the children's attention. Due to target users' health condition (i.e. asthma and skin sensitivity) as advised by the teaching facilitators, *Rofina* had a hard plastic casing to enclose the internal structure and also acted as its skin. *Rofina* did not have a mobile base because it was not required to move around for this first prototype. In addition, *Rofina* could be tele-operated so as to allow teaching facilitators to have a control of it when interacting with the children. Considering that the autistic children may play in a rough way, *Rofina* was designed to be robust.

The motivation of using a "bland" casing was to give a neutral look. The plain look not only could prevent the kids from getting distracted, but also provided the possibility of the skin changing to give the platform the flexibility to have multiple characters for different skills learning. A collection of animal types could be attached to *Rofina* for the near future. Each animal will have its own distinct behavior and identity to help the children understanding and learn about different characters and emotions. The intent is to allow the derivatives versions of the base robot to give it more versatility and variety to the children.

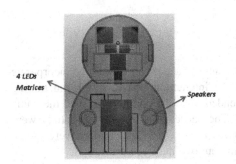
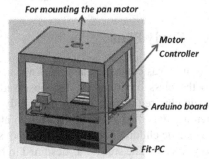

Fig. 2. Final arrangement of component   **Fig. 3**. Body structure in 3D CAD model

For the final internal components arrangement of *Rofina*, there were only three LEDs matrices on the head to display emotions and speakers were placed on the body. The eyes and mouth would have LED to show expressions like happy, sad, surprise and confuse. And the tummy area will also have LEDs to show certain numbers. The reason of having the speakers down at the body was to allow the sounds to project to the front rather than to the sides. Two LEDs matrices were shifted down to the body to show clearer and larger displays. Refer to Figure 2 for the arrangement.

Rofina's body (Fig. 3) contained the items which were larger and heavier. Apart from acting as a base for the robot, it also acted as a support for the motors. Thus, the structure had to be rigid. The base was designed with the components arranged neatly. The idea of the arrangement came from the design of CPU. The components in the CPU were nicely arranged with all the hard disks at one corner, motherboard placed at the centre with a lot of spaces for ventilation, etc. The controller boards are firstly screw onto the plate, then slot into the box (just like slotting a graphic card onto the motherboard) and hold it in place with screws. Holes were made at the sides to allow the heat to dissipate out. Figure 4 shows the architecture build into the robot.

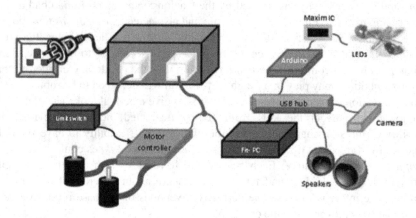

Fig. 4. Robot Architecture

3   Study Plan

The study was conducted at a local autistic centre to see if robot could be incorporate into the class environment and observed the interaction between high-functioning autistic children and the robot. The study ended once the children finished the game when a player first reached the end point. The participants for this trial study were five autistic children, of which 4 were boys and 1 was a girl. The children were aged 5 to 6 years old. The study was designed to find out two main research areas:

- If robot *Rofina* could act as a facilitator or mediator that could be incorporated into the classroom environment for turn-taking activities.
- If children diagnosed with high-functioning autism were comfortable or at ease with the robot presence.

The social robot, *Rofina* would be playing the game called, "Snake and Ladder" with the autistic children. It was a game that the children had learnt and were familiar. The purpose of that game was to teach the children about turn-taking and about right behaviors [3]. One unique idea for the study was the rolling of the 6 sided dice. Each child would wait for their turns to tap on *Rofina's* body and the numbers of steps to be moved will appear on *Rofina's* body.

Rofina would act as a therapeutic playmate and had a therapeutic influence on the autistic children by catching and maintaining their attention during the game. Triadic interaction happened when the teaching facilitator also involved in the game and interacts with the children at the same time. Self-initiated interaction occurred when the children were encouraged to engage with the robot proactively. During the game, the children were seated in front of *Rofina*, with the board game placing in front of them. The robot was placed on a table in front of the class. There was an operator who controlled the movements and speech for the robot.

Before the game started, an ice-breaking session was carried out. Instead of rolling the dice, each child would wait for their turn to tap on *Rofina's* tummy and the numbers of steps to be moved would appear on *Rofina's* body. The idea was quite similar to rewarding games, which would allow the children to learn about cause-and-effect connection and concentrate for a longer period of time. Besides, the robot would also prompt the particular child when it is his or her turn.

Rofina could direct her attention to a particular child and ask for the name. This action was considered different from other children toys that the children might have interacted. After the introduction, *Rofina* would request the teacher to teach the class how to play the game. The game would then start by asking a child to roll the dice. The child would tap on *Rofina's* tummy to simulate the rolling of dice and a number will appear on her body. After getting the number, the child would move his or her game piece to the respective box. *Rofina* would prompt the next child to roll the dice and this would go on until the game ends. At the end of the game, *Rofina* would announce the winner and ask the children to clap for the winner.

Fig. 5. Rofina and "Snake & Ladder" game board

4   Observations

During the game play, we wanted to find out if the children were willing to touch the robot to trigger the dice roll. Touching the robot would in some sense show that the children were comfortable enough to make physical contact with the robot. The robot could exhibit basic pleasantries such as greeting and giving affirmation to the children. So we intended to observe how the children would response when they communicated and interacted with the robot. The children were excited once they saw the robot and were eager to play with it. When the children had settled down, the ice breaking session started and worked well. The children took turn to introduce themselves and said "Hi"/"Hello" to *Rofina*. Most of the children participated actively except for two boys who were passive. However, the children were enjoying the game most of the time and there were instances when they attempted to touch and move the robot's head.

The whole session of the children playing with the robot lasted about 20 minutes. It was surprising that their enthusiasm could last throughout the game because the children's interest span on the game would normally be less than 10 minutes. In most cases, they would not even complete the game. But in this study, the children finished the game.

One feedback from the teacher was that robot did help the children enjoy the game more and they responded well to the robot's commands. All the children except a boy, clapped when the winner was announced. According to the teacher, this particular boy has a competitive personality and he was angry that he lost the game. The boy even said "I don't like you." into *Rofina's* face before he left.

Fig. 6. Snapshot of scenario during the play   **Fig. 7.** Children playing with *Rofina*

From the video analysis, all the children were comfortable touching the robot. One of them enjoyed touching and moving the robot's head frequently during the play. The four boys also tried to touch the robots even when it was not their turn to throw the dice. The boys who enjoyed touching and moving the robot's head, also liked to talk to the robot just like talking to humans. In terms of verbal communication, most children required the robot's repeated prompts before responding. During the ice-breaking session, all children except one boy did not introduce his name because his name was not called at that time. Most of the children were able to maintain eye contact for a longer period of time during the first five to six minutes. Thereafter, two children would start to lose concentration, such as playing with the butterfly on the notice board and looked dreamy. However, the children would turn their attention at the robot whenever the robot was speaking.

The following table describes each child's behavior and action during the game.

Table 1. Description of each child's behavior and action during the game

	Personality and Character	Introduce name to robot	Established eye contact with robot	Interaction with robot during the game	Communication with robot
Participant 1	An active and competitive boy.	Took the initiative to introduce his name to the robot	Made several glances at robot when robot's head turn towards him.	Touched and moved the robot's head and body throughout the game. Made funny faces in front of robot and talked to it. Attempted to interact with robot even when it was not his turn.	Towards the end of the game, he was unhappy that he was not the winner. He remarked "I don't like you!" to the robot before leaving.
Participant 2	A passive boy who always looked dreamy.	He managed to introduce himself to the robot with teacher's help	Initially, he only glanced at the robot for a few times. But when he got acquainted with robot, he would always look at it whenever it was talking.	Required frequent prompting from robot. He would pat the robot and even touch it even it was not his turn to.	Did not say "bye bye" to the robot at the end of the play.
Participant 3	A patient and cooperative boy.	During ice-breaking session and at the end of the game, he introduced himself	Frowned when he mistook the neutral expression as an angry expression during the game.	He was able to recognize the number and did not really need the robot's prompt to respond. Waited for his turn to play the game.	Would respond to the robot's questions and prompting and knows when it was his turn. Said "bye bye" to the robot. Would occasionally talk to the robot.
Participant 4	A passive boy who was distracted by a paper butterfly that was pasted on a notice board located near to him, when it was not his turn.	He required prompting from the teacher to introduce himself to the robot.	Would glance at robot's face when it was his turn to touch the robot's tummy.	He did not really need teachers' prompt but he would rather need teacher's permission to touch the robot. Sometimes the robot prompted him, he knew it was his turn and ready to touch the robot's tummy, he would look at the teacher. He would touch it only when the teacher nodded her head. He attempted to touch he robots even it was not his turn	Did not converse with robot other than telling robot his name.
Participant 5	Only girl among the group of children. She was lively and chatty during the session.	She was able to introduce herself to the robot.	She seldom looked at the robot when it was talking but she took the initiative to say "hello" to the robot.	She was able to respond immediately when the robot prompted her. She waited patiently for her turn to play	She enjoyed conversing with the robot and playing the game.

5   Discussion

It was overall positive to see the children being so friendly to the robot from the start of the trial study. The children appreciated the fact that the social robot was able to address them by name and could look towards them. Overall, the children stayed on task better and longer than expected. During the game scenario, *Rofina*, the social robot successfully acted as a social mediator to mediate contact between autistic children and a companion (i.e. teaching facilitator and other autistic children). The social robot was able to encourage basic communication and social skills in the autistic children by engaging them in simple interactive game of Snake and Ladder. The children got the idea that the robot was in charge of generating the number very quickly. All the children were willing to touch the robot to trigger the dice roll. It would have been better if the robot could capture children's attention by playing a sound (e.g. bell/whistle) before giving instructions or comments.

It was also difficult to reach for the robot especially for the children sitting at the far end. Children took advantage of the bench and squeezed to get closer to the robot. This disruptive behaviour could be minimised if the children were seated on individual chairs. Instead of using a long table, one consideration was to join 4 class tables together to form a square-shaped table so the children could sit all around.

To promote lively and active participation, the robot could be placed at a distance to encourage the children could get up and walk to where to robot in order generate the number. Otherwise, the robot could be placed on a mobile platform and push it towards the child when it's his or her turn. The ending of the activity could have been smoother.

Two of the five children felt that the game ended abruptly and there could be more communication from the robot to end with a high note. The robot could 'debrief' the children. It was good that the robot was able to announce "We have a winner, congratulations." It might be even better if the robot could continue a line or two with something along the line of "Did you enjoy the game? (Pause) I'm glad you did. Snake and Ladder has now finished. Thank you for playing with me. Great job everyone! Goodbye!"

The sequence and timing of the robot's response to the children was vital. To allow for better quality of interaction, the reaction time of controlling the robot real-time could play a role in determining how the children valued and viewed the role of the robot. Finally, the design of the user interface was important to facilitate the task of controlling the robot. Camera position was important to capture the required video angles in order for the tele-operator to react more responsively while controlling the robot.

6   Conclusion

Rofina, the social robot, was a valuable tool for the autistic children to learn through play and interaction. From this study, we managed to show two main findings.

Firstly, this pilot trial showed that *Rofina* could act as a facilitator or mediator that could be incorporated into the classroom environment for turn-taking activities. *Rofina* was placed in a classroom setting with 5 students. During the game of snake and ladder; *Rofina* was able to capture their attention by communicating with the children verbally and display basic social pleasantries by greeting and talking to them.

Secondly, this pilot trial showed that children diagnosed with high-functioning autism are comfortable or at ease with the robot presence. Most students were able to stay for longer period of time and do not feel any fear or awkward when playing a game with robot. *Rofina* exhibited basic interpersonal interaction by maintaining eye contact when interacting with people.

There is indeed great potential for the robot could be incorporate into the class environment. For future works, we intend to carry out research for longer period of time to study longitudinal effects on social communication skills of children with autism.

Acknowledgments. This work has been supported by the A*STAR Science and Engineering Council (SERC) under the Inter-RI Social Robotics Program and by the New Initiative Fund (NTU). We are grateful to A*STAR Social Robotics (ASORO) team for their assistance and guidance in the project. We would also like to express our thanks to Thye Hua Kwan (THK) Moral EIPIC Centre for their continuous assistance and support throughout the project.

References

1. Werry, I., Dautenhahn, K., Harwin, W.: Evaluating the response of children with autism to a robot. In: Proceedings of Rehabilitation Engineering and Assistive Technology Society of North America, RESNA 2001 (2001)
2. Ferrari, E., Robins, B., Dautenhahn, K.: Therapeutic and educational objectives in Robot Assisted Play for children with autism. In: The 18th IEEE International Symposium on Robot and Human Interactive Communication – RO-MAN 2009, Toyama, Japan, September 27-October 2, pp. 108–114 (2009)
3. Ricks, D.J., Colton, M.B.: Trends and Considerations in Robot-Assisted Autism Therapy. In: 2010 IEEE International Conference on Robotics and Automation (ICRA), Anchorage, AK, May 3-7, pp. 4354–4359 (2010)
4. Robins, B., Dautenhahn, K., Te Boekhorst, R., Billard, A.: Robotic assistants in therapy and education of children with autism: can small humanoid robot help encourage social interaction skills? Universal Access in the Information Society 4(2) (2005)
5. Dautenhahn, K.: Roles and functions of robots in human society: implications from research in autism therapy. Robotica 21(4), 443–452 (2003)
6. Marti, P., Moderini, C., Guisti, L., Pollini, A.: A robotic toy for children with special needs: From requirements to design. In: 2009 IEEE 11th International Conference on Rehabilitation Robotics, Kyoto, Japan, June 23-26 (2009)
7. Sacks, H., Schegloff, E.A., Jefferson, G.: A simplest systematics for the organization of turn-taking for conversation. Language 50, 696–735 (1974)
8. Sigman, M., Dijamco, A., Gratier, M., Rozga, A.: Early detection of core deficits in autism. Ment. Retard. Dev. Disabil. Res. Rev. 10(4), 221–233 (2004)
9. Yow, A.P., Campolo, A., Wong, H.Y.A.: Design of a Robotic Platform for Behavioral Analysis of Autistic Children. In: 25th Annual Conference on Computer Animation and Social Agents, Singapore, May 9-11 (2012)
10. Cheng, M.: Robot teaches autistic kids to interact. The Associated Press (2011), http://www.msnbc.msn.com/id/41967936/ns/health-mental_health/t/robot-teaches-autistic-kids-interact/

Collecting Heart Rate Using a High Precision, Non-contact, Single-Point Infrared Temperature Sensor

Laura Boccanfuso, Eva Juarez Perez, Myra Robinson, and Jason M. O'Kane

University of South Carolina, South Carolina SC 29208, USA
boccanfu@cse.sc.edu

Abstract. Remotely detecting the physiological state of humans is becoming increasingly important for rehabilitative robotics (RR) and socially assistive robotics (SAR) because it makes robots better-suited to work more closely and more cooperatively with humans. This research delivers a new non-contact technique for detecting heart rate in real time using a high precision, single-point infrared sensor. The proposed approach is an important potential improvement over existing methods because it collects heart rate information unencumbered by biofeedback sensors, complex computational processing or high cost equipment. We use a thermal infrared sensor to capture subtle changes in the sub-nasal skin surface temperature to monitor cardiac pulse. This study extends our previous research in which breathing rate is automatically extracted using the same hardware. Experiments conducted to test the proposed system accuracy show that in 72.7% of typical cases heart rate was successfully detected within 0-9 beats per minute as measured by root-mean-square error.

1 Introduction

The growing use of robots in rehabilitative therapy and in socially assistive applications has brought to focus the need to make human-robot interactions as natural and beneficial to the humans using them as possible. A multitude of human-robot applications stand to greatly benefit from a small, inexpensive system capable of delivering accurate heart rate data remotely. For example, existing rehabilitative robotic (RR) systems such as shoulder, wrist, hand and ankle robots which exercise a targeted muscle or muscle group [1] may sense a user's level of strength to determine how much assistance to provide but would be further improved by having a non-contact method for obtaining their user's heart rate and overall stress level during therapy. Home-use robots working in close proximity to the elderly would be additionally beneficial to their users if they were able to remotely collect and transmit critical vital signs indicative of their physical condition to a family member or service provider. Further, robots used in socially assistive robotics (SAR) that are capable of monitoring the heart rate of children with social or developmental disabilities (especially those who are non-verbal) would be better-suited for use in therapy since their behavior could be adapted based on the perceived stress-state of the child. Should the child become stressed during the course of the therapy, he or she may not be able to immediately communicate this fact to the therapist or teacher. A robot that is continually collecting information about the child's

S.S. Ge et al. (Eds.): ICSR 2012, LNAI 7621, pp. 86–97, 2012.

heart rate can detect subtle shifts in his or her emotional state and alert the child's therapist before the child's frustration escalates. Detecting heart rate remotely is a necessary next step towards fully realizing this potential.

A variety of methods have been used to collect data about a user's emotional or stress state including measuring the amount of eye contact, body pose, number, quality and content of verbal utterances, and several physiological indicators such as galvanic skin response, electroencephalography (EEG), breathing and heart rate. Galvanic skin response measures changes in the electrical conductance of skin [2] while EEG is used to measure the voltage fluctuations resulting from ionic current flows within the neurons of the brain [3]. Capturing heart rate has traditionally employed contact modalities for obtaining data, although non-contact methods have more recently been explored.

Contact approaches include the use of electrocardiograms (ECG) which require the user to be fitted with sensors and a variety of recently introduced cardiograph applications for portable electronic devices which require the user to place their finger over a small, onboard camera to detect subtle changes in skin color. These devices typically deliver accurate heart rate data, but are generally not suitable for mobile applications, where lighting conditions are not consistent, for people who are averse to wearing sensors, and when the use of contact sensors is otherwise impractical. In addition, although solutions exist using non-contact methods such as radar and doppler modalities, these approaches rely on high-cost equipment and collecting and analyzing very large amounts of data at a high processing cost.

This research presents a new non-contact heart rate measurement technique suitable for most RR and SAR applications. Changes in the sub-nasal skin surface temperature are tracked and a heart rate in beats per minute (bpm) is automatically calculated. This study extends our previous research [4] in which breathing rate is computed using the same hardware we use for this study. Key improvements to our software have yielded a four-fold increase in the number of samples collected per second and the implementation of a Discrete Wavelet Transform (DWT) for automatically calculating the heart rate. The novel contribution of this paper is a simple, robust, low cost approach for remotely collecting and monitoring heart rate.

The remainder of this paper is structured as follows. We describe several types of robotic implementations using various existing heart rate detection approaches in Section 2. Section 3 explains the fundamental methodology and rationale for the hardware selected and details the software design and implementation. A description of our approach to the experiment design and test results can be found in Section 4. We conclude the paper with a summary of our research and a brief discussion of future work in Section 5.

2   Related Work

Remotely detecting shifts in the psychological state and physical condition of humans is a challenge recently undertaken by researchers in numerous fields including image and signal processing [5], human-computer interaction [6], computer vision [7], biomedical engineering [8] and robotics [9]. Until very recently, studies in human-robot interaction have typically obtained physiological information from humans using contact modalities such as wearable biofeedback sensors or sensors fitted on the robot. These initial studies provide valuable insight for understanding how physiological indicators can yield critical information pertaining to the affective state of humans interacting with robots.

2.1   Vital Signs Detection with Interactive Robots

Important research using robots and contact sensors have shown that physiological responses alone can be used to successfully recognize affective states in humans [10–12]. In the first study three physiological indicators — heart rate, skin conductance and facial muscle contraction — are collected to perform affective state estimation during human-robot interactions. While face muscle contraction was not found to be strongly correlated with affective state in the set of tests performed, heart rate acceleration was found to be one of three important physiological features for successfully predicting affective state.

Other research applies the fundamental concept of human stress detection to the study of autism therapy [13]. Participants of the study were fitted with biofeedback sensors which measured heart rate variability, skin conductivity, eyebrow movement, jaw clenching, and body temperature. The key to this approach includes designing an affective control architecture and creating rules by which the robot decides how to respond when the threshold anxiety level is reached.

A study in human-robot interaction collects physiological signals using wearable biofeedback sensors to recognize the affective state of the human and adapt the behavior of the robot accordingly [14]. Experiments were designed using a robot-based basketball game where a robot monitors the participant's anxiety and alters the difficulty level of the game based on the perceived stress level of the player. Results show that overall player performance is improved when the difficulty level is adjusted based on physiological cues and not merely on performance alone.

The modes of collecting physiological data described in these studies have been effective but each method still requires that the subject be fitted with the proper biofeedback sensors. In some controlled settings and with certain subjects, this may not be an issue. However, their efficacy in dynamic environments where people cannot be fitted with biofeedback sensors or in certain medical or therapeutic settings where persons are averse to wearing sensors is still somewhat limited. While the collection of physiological data for diagnosing disorders and stress in humans is not new, remotely recovering this information for use in robotics is an emerging field. This paper presents a complementary approach in which heart rate, an important physiological indicator, is collected using a non-contact modality.

2.2   Remote Detection of Vital Signs

Non-contact modalities have been explored including laser doppler vibrometry (LDV) [15], radio frequency scanners [16] and microwave doppler radar [17]. One study remotely collects physiological information using LDV to deduce the stress state of an individual based on vibrations of the skin directly covering the carotid artery [15]. As currently implemented, this approach yields an intersession equal-error rate of 6.3%.

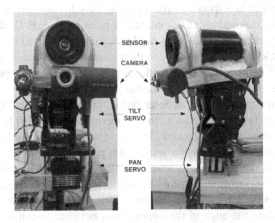

Fig. 1. Remote breathing monitoring system. Front view (left) and profile view (right).

The main drawbacks to these approaches include problems with accurate tracking due to variances in patient physiology and the prohibitive cost of the technology.

The biomedical engineering field has also published a great deal of research dedicated to the acquisition of a wide variety of physiological information. In one study, a low-cost camera is used to detect subtle skin color changes over time in order to deduce heart rate [8]. Video recordings were analyzed using independent component analysis on three color channels (RGB) to extract three important physiological indicators: heart rate, respiratory rate and heart rate variability. The research showed that using a camera alone can yield fairly accurate results. However, there are significant limitations using color as the sole measure of physiological indicators including common variations in skin tone, ambient or direct lighting and proper face detection due to even small changes in illumination, shadows and occlusions.

Studies in the electrical engineering field have also approached the challenge of remote vital signs monitoring by targeting a Doppler radar at a person's chest to measure small changes in the demodulated voltage waveform which represents displacement due to respiration and heart activity [18]. Several signal enhancement techniques are applied including center clipping and a Hanning window before the heart rate is computed. Although this modality provides reasonably accurate results, doppler radar is highly sensitive to motion originating from both the target and from extraneous motion within the general range of the antennae [19]. Our research uses a simpler, more robust approach that relies on temperature, which is tolerant of color and movement artifacts, to detect heart rate and does not require the use of expensive equipment or processing a large amount of complex data.

3 Methodology

This research presents a new technique for remotely detecting and monitoring heart rate in real time. Although resting heart rates may vary from one individual to the next, healthy adults have a typical resting heart rate between 60-120 bpm [20]. Each beat of the heart consists of a series of deflections reflecting the time evolution of electrical activity in the heart that is responsible for initiating muscle contraction. A single heart-beat is typically decomposed into five constituent parts labeled: P, Q, R, S, and T. The largest-amplitude portion of the ECG is the QRS complex, caused by currents generated when the ventricles depolarize prior to their contraction. We are most interested in measuring the QRS component of the cardiac cycle where one heart beat is measured from the beginning of one QRS cycle to the beginning of the next.

The heart rate measurement system described in this research (see Figure 1) employs a single-point infrared sensor introduced in our previous research [4] for collecting and calculating non-contact breathing rates. The process for temperature data collection consists of the following: (1) aim the sensor at a pre-defined sub-nasal target region using the location of the nose as extracted from the most recent video frame and, (2) extract the temperature information provided by the sensor analog signal. The subnasal region is selected as the target for two reasons. First, the superior labial artery, which follows a course along the edge of the upper lip, is believed to cause subtle temperature changes corresponding to cardiac pulse. Second, we seek to extract heart rate and breathing rate concurrently in future applications using the proposed sensor mechanism.

In order to accomplish proper sensor targeting and temperature extraction, a specific combination of hardware and software was included in the overall system design. Our system uses the same custom-built actuated platform enumerated in our previous work [4] so we omit a detailed description here.

3.1 Software

The software developed for our system manages three main functions: (1) infrared sensor positioning, (2) temperature collection, (3) data pre-processing and heart rate calculation. Although sensor positioning is accomplished using the same technique described in our prior study [4], new software was developed for an improved rate of temperature collection, a more robust approach for data processing and the extraction of a heart rate. Sensor positioning relies on repeated nose detections and automatic adjustment of the sensor's platform position in order to maintain the subject's nose in the target region of the IR sensor. The IR sensor is repeatedly sampled and collected data is subsequently processed in order to extract a temperature in degrees Fahrenheit. Once the raw temperature data is pre-processed using a low-pass filter, a DWT is used to compute the heart rate in beats per minute. The data processing method implemented for detecting heart rate is sufficiently fast to be used in real time.

Infrared Temperature Collection. The infrared temperature collection system has been improved so that a sample rate of 20-25 samples per second is achieved, compared to the 6 samples per second collected by the original system. This represents the upper limit of the sample rate we can achieve given the hardware employed and is accomplished by processing the nose detection and sensor positioning independently from the temperature collection and data processing. Because heart beat events occur at a much higher frequency than breathing events, increasing the number of samples collected per second was necessary in order to capture the relatively short-lived temperature increases that correlate to heart rate.

The infrared sensor is continuously sampled until a window of 32 time-stamped samples or approximately 1.6 seconds of temperature data has been collected. Various window sizes were tested in order to evaluate the system's performance during periodic heart rate fluctuations. Although larger window sizes provide higher stability in computed heart rates, they are prone to excessive smoothing and reduce the system's ability to detect short-lived heart rate increases or decreases. Further, while small window sizes are susceptible to being dominated by relatively small errors that can be introduced when temperatures are collected during re-targeting, they provide more resilient and responsive heart rate detection overall.

Data Pre-processing. Data is pre-processed in three steps. First, temperatures that are collected when the infrared sensor is performing initial targeting and periodic re-targeting are often too low to be considered related to the human body. Exceptionally low readings are assumed to be from a non-human source and are excluded from the data set at the time of temperature collection. Secondly, low-amplitude noise picked up by the sensor signal is minimized using a low-pass filter on each collected set of data. Finally, to make the IR data suitable for processing with a DWT, the 0-mean is computed for all the samples in each window.

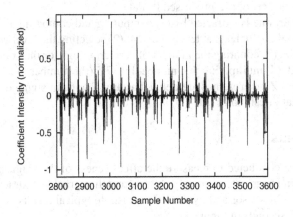

Fig. 2. Sample set of DWT coefficients

Heart Rate Calculation. Heart rates are computed using a DWT [21] on each window of collected infrared data. A DWT is used to process the IR data for two fundamental reasons: (1) heart rates are not stationary since they have varying frequency components at different time intervals and, (2) we are interested in the temporal information associated with each reading. Unlike Fast Fourier Transforms (FFTs), DWTs are capable of extracting specific frequencies occuring at particular time intervals.

The DWT first sends samples through a low pass filter which yields approximation coefficients and a high pass filter which results in one or more detail coefficients. The outcome of this filtering technique is that the component signal frequencies are cut in half and according to Nyquist's rule, half the samples can be discarded. Although this process halves the time resolution and each output has half of the input frequency band (since only half of each filter output characterizes the entire signal), the frequency resolution is effectively doubled with each decomposition.

The decomposition process is recursively repeated in order to increase the frequency resolution until no further decompositions are possible. Once the decomposition is completed, a set of coefficients is output that were produced at various scales and at different time intervals of the signal. The coefficients can then be analyzed to extract frequency information for particular time intervals or for the signal in its entirety.

Due to the nature of this technique, the number of samples processed in a given data set by the DWT must be in powers of two. Our system uses the Daubechies 6 (db6) [22] wavelet to perform the transform and collects temperature readings at a rate of 20 samples per second so the highest frequency that can be extracted is 10 samples per second or 10 Hertz (Hz). The range of frequencies in which we are most interested for this research are 0.8-1.90 Hz because they correspond to heart rates between 48 bpm and 114 bpm. The DWT levels of decomposition which contain the detail coefficients within that frequency range are found at levels 3 and 4 and represent frequencies between 1.25-2.5 Hz (level 3) and 0.625-1.25 Hz (level 4). Since the input signal is recursively decomposed into component frequencies using a DWT, it is possible to isolate breathing from heart rates, with effectively no crossover. Figure 2 illustrates a representative coefficient file produced for one set of pre-processed IR data.

Finally, the heart rate is extracted by (1) computing and comparing the average amplitude of the detail coefficients at levels 3 and 4, (2) selecting the level with the largest average amplitude, (3) counting the number of zero crossings for the coefficients at the selected level and, (4) multiplying that number by 37.5 (the number of 1.6-second windows in a minute). Zero crossings are defined as any change in signal direction which exceeds a minimal threshold of 0.1.

4   Experiments

Experiments were conducted to measure the effectiveness of the single-point infrared sensor for detecting heart rates remotely. A representative graph of extracted heart rates as detected by the IR sensor and by the ECG illustrate typical results over a period of approximately 35 seconds in Figure 3.

4.1   Experiment Setup

The proposed system's accuracy were quantitatively measured by collecting temperature data with the infrared sensor, computing the heart rate and comparing the results with heart rate data obtained from an ECG. For the ECG data collection, participants were each fitted with 3 electrodes attached to a bioradio which continuously transmitted heart rate data to a nearby computer. ECG information is collected at approximately 600 samples per second and a heart rate is computed for each 960 samples, or 1.6 seconds of ECG data, so that IR and ECG heart rates can be easily processed and compared.

Experiments included 24 study participants, 17 females and 7 males, between the ages of 18 and 35. Individuals who participated in this study were not taking medication which could interfere with their heart rate at the time of the experiment. Each

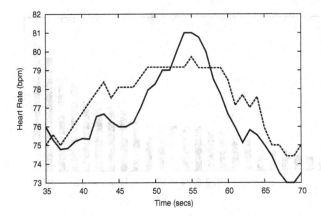

Fig. 3. ECG and IR heart rates for a representative 35-second data set. IR heart rate (dashed line) and ECG heart rate window (solid line).

participant was asked to sit in a chair that was situated approximately 1 meter from a rolling table equipped with the infrared sensor system and a laptop computer. During the course of each 10-minute test session study subjects watched a video playing on the laptop computer. The primary purpose of the video was to maintain the participant's attention in a forward-facing, relatively still position. Small movements resulting from participants shifting their position during the test session were automatically managed using incremental pan and tilt adjustments of the sensor platform.

4.2   Experiment Results

Twenty four test sets, each consisting of approximately 10 minutes of data and about 375 individual heart rates were collected and analyzed. Of those 24 sets, two were identified as anomalous due to obvious and persistent nose detection problems observed while the test was being conducted. Common problems in feature detection are typically due to false positive identification of other artifacts in the environment that possess similar characteristics to the target feature. For example, during one test set the nose detection system falsely identified the subject's eye as her nose and the entire test set collected data consisting of temperatures measured around the eye region. Twenty two test sets are classified as "typical" and contain data collected when the nose detection and tracking was not clearly working improperly.

Overall system accuracy was measured by computing the difference between the reported ECG heart rate and the IR detected heart rate for each 1.6-second window (Figure 4). Because the ECG data collected during experiments consists of a heart rate without a time-stamp, part of the system performance analysis includes an auto-correction for the temporal alignment of data between ECG heart rates and IR-derived heart rates by comparing the root-mean-square errors (RMSE) of various offsets for each window of coefficients computed. Typical and anomalous test sets were analyzed separately and accuracy was assessed in beats per minute (bpm). Six categories were used to classify

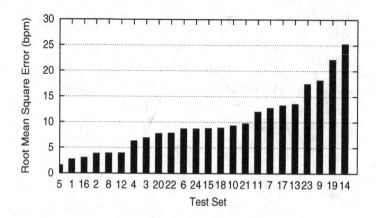

Fig. 4. All 24 test set results by RMSE. Sets 14 and 19 are considered a typical because of obvious nose detection issues during testing.

our results: (1) 0-4 bpm, (2) 5-9 bpm, (3) 10-14 bpm, (4) 15-19 bpm, (5) 20-24 and (6) 25 and higher bpm.

Of the approximately 375 heart rates compared for each typical test set, about 73% (or 16 out of 22) averaged heart rates within 0-9 beats per minute as compared to average heart rates produced by the ECG over the entire 10-minute test set (Table 1).

Table 1. Typical test sets results by RMSE. Two excluded sets had persistent nose detection problems.

Range of RMSE in bpm	Percentage of Typical Test Cases
0-4	27.3%
5-9	45.4%
10-14	18.2%
15-19	9.1%

Although stress testing was not conducted in these initial experiments, heart rates within a given session varied on average by about 20 bpm. The minimum and maximum heart rates detected with low RMSE scores ranged between 61 and 115 bpm. A summary of results demonstrating several successful test sets for both lower range heart rates and higher heart rates is included in Table 2.

An additional consideration in the assessment of system performance is the system's ability to effectively track increases and decreases in heart rate even when the baseline is shifted by an offset as shown in Figure 5. Test sets that mirror heart rate fluctuations as reported by the ECG but are offset by a certain amount will produce higher RMSE scores on average even though increases and decreases in heart rate are accurately detected. We believe there are two potential causes for this offset. First, computing the

Table 2. Representative test sets successfully detecting lower- and higher-range heart rates

Test Set	Lowest ECG Heart Rate	Highest ECG Heart Rate	Accuracy in RMSE
1	71	87	2.71
2	61	74	3.81
4	93	115	6.28
16	71	88	3.03

number of zero crossings exclusively for the captured IR data may not be sufficient to calculate the heart rate accurately. Second, intermittent errors in targeting the infrared sensor precisely may result in cumulative errors in computed heart rate. Future work will include an evaluation of these cases to determine if a baseline shift can be corrected and if they can still be used to provide valuable information pertaining to changes in heart rate that are indicative of stress state.

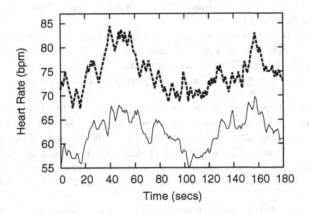

Fig. 5. A 3-minute data excerpt illustrating a baseline offset between IR heart rate (upper line) and ECG heart rate (lower line)

5   Conclusions

This paper presents a new non-contact technique for measuring temperature changes in the sub-nasal skin surface temperature to calculate heart rate. This study extends and improves our previous work where breathing rates were automatically extracted using a curve-fitting function and ground truth was measured with a self-reporting method. Several enhancements were made to the original system software and testing design, making it possible to use the same hardware to remotely extract a heart rate.

Initial results from the tests conducted in this study are very promising. This study demonstrates a low-cost, potential solution for obtaining physiological information using a non-contact approach. Due to its small size and the minimal computation required for the calculation of heart rates, incorporating such a device in robots working alongside humans in many SAR and RR applications has great potential.

Future work will focus on improving the accuracy and robustness of the sensor targeting component in order to minimize heart rate detection errors resulting from occasional or persistent drifting. Enhancements to the nose detection system will include detecting other facial landmarks to assist the classifier in identifying the nose and specifically, the sub-nassal region, more accurately. Additionally, further testing will be conducted to examine the system's ability to detect heart rates effectively when the user is engaged in light activity and sensor positioning must respond quickly to minimal but frequent user movements.

References

1. Krebs, H.I., Hogan, N.: Therapeutic robotics a technology push. Proceedings of the IEEE 94(9), 1727–1738 (2006)
2. Montagu, J.D., Coles, E.M.: Mechanism and measurement of the galvanic skin response. Psychological Bulletin 65(5), 261–279 (1966)
3. Tyson, P.D.: Task-related stress and EEG alpha biofeedback. Biofeedback and Self-Regulation 12(2), 105–119 (1987)
4. Boccanfuso, L., O'Kane, J.M.: Remote measurement of breathing rate in real time using a high precision, single-point infrared temperature sensor. In: Proceedings IEEE International Conference on Biomedical Robotics and Biomechatronics (2012)
5. Matsukawa, T., Yokoyama, K.: Visualizing physiological information based on 3dcg. FORMA 25, 11–14 (2010)
6. Barreto, A., Zhai, J., Adjouadi, M.: Non-intrusive Physiological Monitoring for Automated Stress Detection in Human-Computer Interaction. In: Lew, M., Sebe, N., Huang, T.S., Bakker, E.M. (eds.) HCI 2007. LNCS, vol. 4796, pp. 29–38. Springer, Heidelberg (2007)
7. Kakadiaris, I.A., Passalis, G., Theoharis, T., Toderici, G., Konstantinidis, I., Murtuza, N.: Multimodal face recognition: Combination of geometry with physiological information. In: Proceedings of the IEEE Conference on Computer Vision and Pattern Recognition, pp. 1022–1029 (2005)
8. Poh, M.Z., McDuff, D.J., Picard, R.W.: Advancements in noncontact, multiparameter physiological measurements using a webcam. IEEE Transactions on Biomedical Engineering 58(1), 7–11 (2011)
9. Suzuki, S., Matsui, T., Gotoh, S., Mori, Y., Takase, B., Ishihara, M.: Development of non-contact monitoring system of heart rate variability (hrv) - an approach of remote sensing for ubiquitous technology. In: Proceedings of the International Conference on Ergonomics and Health Aspects of Work with Computers: Held as Part of HCI International, pp. 195–203 (2009)
10. Kulic, D., Croft, E.: Estimating robot induced affective state using hidden markov models. In: The IEEE International Symposium on Robot and Human Interactive Communication (ROMAN), pp. 257–262 (September 2006)
11. Kulic, D., Croft, E.: Physiological and subjective responses to articulated robot motion. Robotica 25(1), 13–27 (2007)
12. Rani, P., Sims, J., Brackin, R., Sarkar, N.: Online stress detection using psychophysiological signals for implicit human-robot cooperation. Robotica 20(6), 673–685 (2002)
13. McLaughlin, L.: Engineering meets emotion: New robots sense human distress. IEEE Intelligent Systems 18, 4–7 (2003)

14. Liu, C., Rani, P., Sarkar, N.: Affective state recognition and adaptation in human-robot interaction: A design approach. In: Proceedings of the IEEE/RSJ International Conference on Intelligent Robots and Systems, pp. 3099–3106 (2006)
15. Rohrbaugh, J.W., Sirevaag, E.J., Singla, N., O'Sullivan, J., Chen, M.: Laser doppler vibrometry measures of physiological function: evaluation of biometric capabilities. IEEE Transactions on Information Forensics and Security 5, 449–460 (2010)
16. A mini-robot with a long standoff capability to detect motion and breathing inside a compound (September 2011),
    http://www.ereleases.com/pr/author/tialinx-inc (accessed January 2012)
17. Sekine, M., Maeno, K.: Non-contact heart rate detection using periodic variation in doppler frequency. In: Proceedings of the IEEE, Sensors Applications Symposium (SAS), pp. 318–322 (February 2011)
18. Lohman, B., Boric-Lubecke, O., Lubecke, V.M., Ong, P.W., Sondhi, M.M.: A digital signal processor for doppler radar sensing of vital signs. IEEE Engineering in Medicine and Biology Magazine 21(5), 161–164 (2002)
19. Singh, A., Lubecke, V.M.: Respiratory monitoring and clutter rejection using a cw doppler radar with passive rf tags. IEEE Sensors Journal 12(3), 558–565 (2012)
20. McSharry, P.E., Clifford, G.D., Tarassenko, L., Smith, L.A.: A dynamical model for generating synthetic electrocardiogram signals. IEEE Transactions on Biomedical Engineering 50(3), 289–294 (2003)
21. Burrus, C.S., Gopinath, R.A., Guo, H.: Introduction to Wavelets and Wavelet Transforms: A Primer. Prentice-Hall (1997)
22. Daubechies, I.: Ten lectures on wavelets. Society for Industrial and Applied Mathematics, Philadelphia (1992)

How Can a Social Robot Facilitate Children's Collaboration?*

Michihiro Shimada, Takayuki Kanda, and Satoshi Koizumi

Hikaridai, Seika-city, Souraku-gun, Kyoto,
6190288, Japan
{m.shimada,kanda,satoshi}@atr.jp

Abstract. We used a social robot as a teaching assistant in a class for children's collaborative learning. The class was designed to be learner-centered, and we formed a class only with a robot and children but without adults. In the class, a group of 6th graders learned together using Lego Mindstorms for seven lessons. Robovie managed the class and explained how to use Lego Mindstorms, then children freely tested their ideas to achieve a given task in each class. In addition, Robovie performed social behaviors, which aimed to build relationships with and encourage the children. Beyond this design, we observed that such social behaviors facilitated interaction among children, which made the class more enjoyable and motivated children to want Robovie around again. In this paper, we report our exploratory analysis about when such social behaviors facilitated interaction among children.

Keywords: Communication robot, Robot for children, Field experiments.

1 Introduction

1.1 Learning with a Social Robot

Learning with robots is an active topic in recent research. Such small robot-kits as Lego Mindstorms are used as a visible example of math, physics, programming, and robotics in classrooms [5, 7]. Robots are also used as interactive exhibits to encourage children's interest in science and technology [1, 9]. Robots have also been successfully used for learning other subjects, such as foreign languages [3, 4]. Social behavior has been found to be effective in language education with a robot [8].

We extend the roles of robots in learning beyond such previous work. We used a robot as a teaching assistant in collaborative learning (Fig. 1).

1.2 Collaborative Learning

The importance of a learner-centered approach has been shown in learning science. In traditional teacher-centered approaches, teachers transfer as much information as

---

* Part of this paper is published in [11] Kanda, T., Shimada, M. and Koizumi, S., 2012, Children learning with a social robot, *ACM/IEEE Int. Conf. on Human-Robot Interaction (HRI 2012)*. This paper newly reports the analysis of facilitation (Section 5).

S.S. Ge et al. (Eds.): ICSR 2012, LNAI 7621, pp. 98–107, 2012.

possible to learners, often in lecture-style classes. On the contrary, in a learner-centered approach, the role of learners receives greater emphasis. Learners are expected to be self-motivated to gain knowledge and think for themselves. Collaborative learning, which is based on a learner-centered approach, is defined as "a situation in which two or more people learn or attempt to learn something together" [2]. People are motivated to explain, help, compete, and collaborate. For instance, when two people explain their own ideas, they try to convince one another, and through such conversations they typically expand their own ideas [6]. Thus, a collaborative learning situation can be created when an appropriate setting is prepared to elicit interaction among people. Successful implementations include a class design with the Jigsaw method [10].

We believe that a social robot would be useful to facilitate both learner-centered and collaborative learning. It might be fluent enough to provide instruction and explain basic learning materials. We could also use a robot as a non-superior entity to help children relax and create spontaneous learning and problem-solving situations without teacher, because teacher's existence strains children, as a result, children don't learn by themselves.

Fig. 1. Class with Robovie for learning Lego Mindstorms

2   Class Design

2.1   Design Principle

Our class design, which supports collaborative learning, has two main features. First, to realize a learner-centered approach, instead of having the robot teach details to children, the robot only explains minimum information (i.e., how to use Lego Mindstorms) and lets children engage in problem-solving by themselves.

Second, based on the concept of collaborative learning [2], we created activities that cut across different levels: individual, within-group, and between-group. Children were asked to work on tasks; thus they first worked at the individual level. Here, we created a competitive situation; since four children worked at the same time on the same task, progress of children within a group could be compared. This is one activity at the within-group level. Moreover, children worked together to create activities at the within-group level. In addition, the class was designed to encourage children to compare their achievements with other groups during the 6th and 7th lessons. Such activities are at the between-group level. Classes consisted of eight two-hour lessons. The contents of the classes are described in detail in [11].

2.2   Environments

The class used Lego Mindstorms NXT 2.0. Only the relevant blocks to be used in each lesson were provided to prevent excessive complexity. Fig. 2 shows the layout of the 7.4 x 5.6 meter room. Desks were placed in front of a display. On the other side of the room, a 1.6 x 1.8 meter test field was used by children to test their robots. We record this class on four videos.

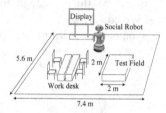

Fig. 2. Layout of classroom

3   System

3.1   System Configuration

We used Robovie-R3 (Fig. 1), which has two arms (4*2 DOFs) and a head (3 DOFs), stands 110 cm tall, and is equipped with cameras, a microphone, and a speaker. Utterances were made using speech synthesis software. An operator chose the utterances and video materials based on pre-determined rules using a teleoperation console.

3.2   Robovie's Behavior

3.2.1   Managing Behavior

Phase Control: Robovie speaks to the children to control phases. For example, it explains the *basic task*, "Today, you are going to develop a robot that stops when a touch sensor is activated." Robovie reminds children about the tasks and time with such language as, "You only have five more minutes." To judge the end of the *basic task* phase, Robovie checks whether a Lego robot build by a child is successful when it is tested in the test field and provides such feedback as "You did it." When all children are finished, it moves to the next phase.

Video Explanation: Before the *basic* and *advanced tasks*, Robovie shows a video. For example, when it explains how to attach a motor, it shows a video attaching a motor (Fig. 3). Robovie narrates the video: "Next, attach the motor to the body."

Fig. 3. Example of video material

Scolding: In our preliminary trial, children sometimes excessively deviated from tasks and showed problems in their conduct, such as bullying. To prevent this, when any interfering behavior was detected, Robovie scolded the child. We define interference as cases when other children's taskperforming was obstructed; for example, when a child was testing her robot in a test field, it would be considered interference if another child interrupted this task by stopping the robot.

3.2.2   Social Behavior
These social behaviors are not necessarily for managing the class. A human teacher would use them for such social purposes as relation-building and encouragement.

Social: We prepared the following examples of social behaviors. First, while the children were working on their tasks, Robovie approached them in the test field and praised their achievements. Robovie praised the first child to accomplish the given task: "You are the first to finish your robot. Great!" If the child's work is a failure, it provides such encouragement as "Keep trying, I think you'll succeed soon."

Second, it encourages competition in the *advanced task*. When two or more children simultaneously visit the test field, it approaches them and asks, "Whose robot can find the wall faster? Why don't you compare your robots?"

Third, it behaves sympathetically toward children who are struggling to solve the given problem. When a child does not bring successful work to the test field after more than 20 minutes, Robovie goes to the child's desk and asks about the progress without helping or proving answers.

Fourth, it stimulates children who seem bored with two rules. When a child stands in front of Robovie, it speaks to the child. Also, after 20 minutes pass from the start of the basic or advanced task (typically this was when some children started getting bored), when Robovie finds a child who isn't working on the tasks, it asks: "How is your task coming?" If the child answers positively, it responds, "Good, please keep up the good work." Otherwise, it responds, "Well, why don't you ask someone for help?"

Fifth, when a child enters the classroom, Robovie chats with him/her. In cases where it praised the child in the previous lesson, it recalls that praise: "Taro, last time you were the first to finish making a robot that stopped with a touch sensor. Good luck again today." Otherwise, it chats with the child, e.g., "Do you have a lot of homework for summer vacation? You should do some everyday. I'm sure you'll do your best."

4   Experiment

4.1   Participants

We targeted 6th-graders since they are mature enough to use Lego Mindstorms. 31 6th-graders (11 or 12 years old, 25 boys, 6 girls) participated in the experiment. Four groups (16 people) experienced the non-social condition in which the robot only performed managing behaviors, and four groups (15 people) experienced the social condition in which the robot performed both managing and social behavior. There is one group in the classroom. This is described in detail in [11].

4.2   Procedure

Each lesson was conducted on a different day during a 2-hour time slot. An adult assistant escorted the children to the door of the classroom without entering, therefore no adult in the class, and instructed them to enter the classroom to study with the robot. During the class, before children started to work at either the *basic* or *advanced* tasks, Robovie announced that an adult could be summoned if a problem happened, e.g., computer malfunction for programming; when children asked Robovie to call an adult, the assistant entered the room to fix the problem. The assistant didn't provide any further support. Short interviews were conducted at the end of the 8th lesson.

5   Result

5.1   General Results

First, we introduce general results (details are available in [11]). In the social condition, we observed that the children anticipated Robovie's encouraging behavior, i.e. praise and comments directed toward their Lego robot. The children sometimes waited for a moment when Robovie moved near the test field and brought their robots to get Robovie's attention and comments. Robovie's social behavior motivated children to work more and to show their work to Robovie. In the non-social condition, the children didn't show their Lego robots to Robovie. It seems that children felt Robovie was observing the class and felt some tension as a result.

Fig. 4 shows how children perceived their relationship with Robovie. We conducted an analysis with linear mixed-effects models having a social behavior factor and a group factor (which is nested within the social behavior factor) as fixed effects. There were significant main effects for the social behavior factor for enjoyment ($F(1, 23)=7.989$, $p=.010$) and intention to use Robovie in other classes ($F(1,23)=6.799$, $p=.016$). No significance was found in intention to use Robovie in a Lego class ($F(1,23)=1.031$, $p=.321$). The group factor was not significant in any of the analysis. This result indicates that Robovie was well accepted by all children within the context of the Lego class, while children in the social condition showed a more general acceptance of Robovie, as indicated by the higher desire to use Robovie in another class.

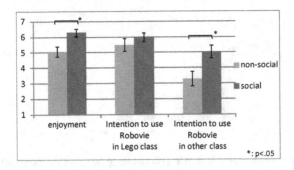

Fig. 4. Children's perceived relationship with Robovie

5.2   Were Children Influenced by Robovie's Encouraging Behavior?

This result shows that children in the social condition perceived more enjoyment, and considered participating in a class with Robovie again. We are curious why this happened. As we observed the most salient behavior of Robovie in the social condition was the encouraging behavior, we further analyzed how children verbally responded to the encouraging behavior.

Since utterances were formulated as comments, such as, "Good robot, I think you did a couple of inventions", it was not necessary for children to make a response. Analysis showed that more than half of encouraging utterances were ignored. Nevertheless, children responded in a considerable number of cases. Two types of response were identified:

  (a) **Answer:** the child who was encouraged responded to Robovie.
  (b) **Facilitation:** another child talked to the child who was encouraged.

We watched the video and coded children's responses toward encouraging behavior using the above categories. For each encouraging behavior, children's immediate responses were classified to be either answers, facilitation, or ignoring.

  Fig. 5 shows the result of coding. The graph shows the ratio of answer and facilitation toward encouraging behavior performed in the lessons. Cohen's Kappa coefficient was .875. The result shows that there were more frequent answers in the first two trials than later lessons (Chi-squared test: $x2(10) = 28.282$, p<.01; residual analysis revealed that the answer ratio in the first two trials were significantly frequent, p<.01). There could be a few possible reasons why this happened. There might be a novelty effect. An alternative explanation is the establishment of expectation: in the beginning children might be not sure to what extent Robovie could understand language, and later they found that Robovie did not always respond to what they said.

  On the other hand, we observed it interesting that children still responded to Robovie's utterances after the third trial. Approximately 10% of encouraging behavior made children either answer or facilitate, which continued until the last lesson.

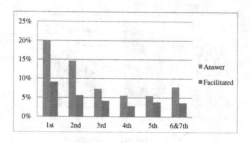

Fig. 5. Children's responses to Robovie's encouraging behavior (in the social condition)

Overall, we consider that such encouraging behavior might contribute to provide an enjoyable impression of the class with Robovie, and contribute to improve Robovie's social acceptance, even after children experienced long-term interaction.

5.3   Examples

According to the results of Section 5.2, the rate for facilitation behavior was found to be almost constant. Therefore, we thought that such usage of Robovie's utterances could be useful in the long-term as a trigger for facilitating children's collaboration. However, not all facilitation behavior had a good influence. Some facilitation behaviors didn't affect the children or affected them in a negative way. We analyzed Robovie's facilitation behaviors. Children reacted 28 times when Robovie performed facilitation behaviors. The number of facilitation is small. Therefore, it is difficult to analyze qualitatively. In this paper, we describe some good examples in Case 1, and bad examples in Case 2.

Case 1-1: Facilitating collaboration/competition
As described in the conversation below, Robovie indicated when a child hadn't completed his or her task. This not only reminded the child but also alerted the other children. Robovie's utterance acted as a trigger for the other children to seek to help the child accomplish his or her task. And, by Robovie speaking about competing with other children and other teams, Robovie showed usefulness because the children had more motivation and felt a stronger bond of solidarity in their team.
[Case 1-1-1]
  Robovie: It seemed Mr. NI was not able to move his robot. Someone who's finished, please teach him what to do.
  NK: I'm helping him.
  NI: Thank you, I'm very grateful.
[Case 1-1-2]
  Robovie: Try to compare your score with the other teams' scores.
  A: Let's try. Let's try seriously.
[Case 1-1-3]
  Robovie: Mr. SH. Your robot's fast, isn't it? Faster than the other children's robots?
  SH: When I lightened the robot, it became faster.

Case 1-2: Increasing the enjoyment

Robovie indicated when a child completed the task. At the same time, Robovie praised the child's work. Because Robovie announced this, other children also sometimes offered praise. Praise from Robovie or other children allowed a child to feel happiness and pleasure during the classes.

[Case 1-2-1]
  Robovie: Mr. SH, you accomplished the task!
  I: (to Mr.SH) Oh, he praised you. Good for you.

[Case 1-2-2]
Robovie: Ms. A, you tried hard and accomplished the task. You are great.
  A: (to Mr.N) Robovie said I did it.
  N: You are great.

Case 1-3: Confirming his/her own robot

Children could understand objectively what they had built as a result of Robovie's praising or indicating whether the task was completed or not. Understanding objectively led children to, for example, seek to help when the task was not completed.

[Case 1-3-1]
  Robovie: Mr. F., your robot isn't moving quite right, given the task specifications.
         Please check the video again and accomplish the task.
  F: (to Mr.SH) I want to watch the video again.
  SH: Robovie, please show the video again.

[Case 1-3-2]
  Robovie: Mr. K, your robot's fast, isn't it? Faster than the other children's robots?
  F: You know it, my robot is fast.

Case 1-4: Imitating other children's robot

Robovie's utterances are heard not only by the child whom Robovie talks with but also by other children. As in the conversation below, one child used another child's robot which had been praised by Robovie as a reference in building in their won. We believe that imitating leads to learning.

[Case 1-4-1]
  Robovie: Mr.K. Great! Your robot moves properly.
  K: Is this a sensor?
  N: I'm going to copy yours.

Case 2-1: Children thought Robovie's utterance meant something different

Robovie's utterances were sometimes interpreted differently than we had intended. As in the conversation below, Robovie spoke with the aim of eliciting improvement. But, the children thought Robovie was angry.

[Case 2-1-1]
  Robovie: Mr. F, please try to improve your robot and make it faster.
  F: Huh?
  SH: (to Mr.F) You made him angry.

I: (to Mr.F) You got told off.

F: Robovie's angry.

SH: (to Mr.F) He's mad at you.

Case 2-2: Other children responded

There were cases in which one child interrupted when Robovie wished to speak to another. In this case, Robovie could not convey the desired intent to the latter child, and there in one case at child became uncomfortable.

[Case 2-2-1]

Robovie: Hello, Mr. K.

N: Don't ignore me.

6   Discussion – How Should a Robot Facilitate?

The results of the experiment indicate how a robot should facilitate. By having the robot behave as described in previous sections, children collaborated and competed with other children and felt pleasure during the classes. On the contrary, there were elements which were not affected.

We speculate that bad examples fall into mainly two categories. To make good facilitate, robot avoid bad facilitation. First, children spoke to Robovie even when Robovie was talking to another child. This occurred when Robovie did not finish one conversation with one child before speaking to another. In this experiment, Robovie was controlled by Wizard of Oz and followed specific rules when to speak to children. Therefore, there were times when Robovie ignored the children's talk. This led to undesired consequences. There were also times when Robovie was not recognized as a conversation partner by children whom Robovie talked to, which resulted in children ignoring Robovie's talk. In such cases, in order to facilitate better, behavior for initiating communication should be considered in addition to facilitation behavior. It is only after Robovie has been recognized as a conversation partner that facilitation behavior becomes possible.

Second, children misunderstood Robovie's utterances at times. This is a wording problem. Wording should be selected with much care. Facilitation will only positively influence children's learning and collaboration if words are appropriate and clear.

Facilitation behavior differs from answering behavior. Answering behavior is mainly exhibited in face-to-face conversation. Therefore, it affects only one child. But facilitation behavior exerts an effect which spreads to other children. We believe that this behavior allows all participants to share the "field". Therefore, we want to investigate this in the future.

7   Conclusion

In this paper, we classified children's reactions and described good examples and bad examples of a robot facilitating. Relationships may be established and children's motivations increased by designing a robot's behavior based on these examples. In this paper, robot can increase children's motivation of the class. But, it cannot increase their learning achievement. We want to investigate how robot increase learning achievement in the future works.

Acknowledgements. We thank Profs. Naomi Miyake, Jun Oshima, and Hajime Shirouzu for their helpful advice for the class design. We also thank Takahiro Miyasita and Hiroshi Ishiguro for their technical advices, and Kanako Tomita, Yuri Ichida, and Hiroyoshi Azuma for their help in conducting the experiment and the data analysis. This research was supported by a Grant-in Aid for Scientific Research, KAKENHI (21118008 and 21680022).

References

[1] Burgard, W., Cremers, A.B., Fox, D., Hahnel, D., Lakemeyer, G., Schulz, D., Steiner, W., Thrun, S.: The Interactive Museum Tour-Guide Robot. In: National Conf. on Artificial Intelligence, pp. 11–18 (1998)

[2] Dillenbourg, P.: What do you mean by 'collaborative learning'? In: Collaborative-learning: Cognitive and Computational Approaches, pp. 1–19 (1999)

[3] Han, J., Jo, M., Park, S., Kim, S.: The Educational Use of Home Robots for Children. In: IEEE Int. Workshop on Robot and Human Interactive Communication, pp. 378–383 (2005)

[4] Kanda, T., Hirano, T., Eaton, D., Ishiguro, H.: Interactive Robots as Social Partners and Peer Tutors for Children: A Field Trial. In: Human-Computer Interaction, vol. 19, pp. 61–84 (2004)

[5] Lau, K.W., Tan, H.K., Erwin, B.T., Petrovic, P.: Creative Learning in School with LEGO@ Programmable Robotics Products. In: ASEE/IEEE Frontiers in Educations Conference, pp.12D4/26-12D4/31 (1999)

[6] Miyake, N.: Constructive Interaction and the Iterative Process of Understanding. Cognitive Science 10, 151–177 (1986)

[7] Mosley, P., Kline, R.: Engaging students: a framework using LEGO robotics to teach problem solving. Information Technology, Learning, and Performance Journal 24, 39–45 (2006)

[8] Saerbeck, M., Schut, T., Bartneck, C., Janse, M.D.: Expressive Robots in Education: Varying the Degree of Social Supportive Behavior of a Robotic Tutor. In: ACM Conference on Human Factors in Computing Systems, pp. 1613–1622 (2010)

[9] Shiomi, M., Kanda, T., Ishiguro, H., Hagita, N.: Interactive Humanoid Robots for a Science Museum. IEEE Intelligent Systems 22, 25–32 (2007)

[10] Slavin, R.E.: Cooperative Learning. Review of Educational Research 50, 315–342 (1980)

[11] Kanda, T., Shimada, M., Koizumi, S.: Children learning with a social robot. In: The 2012 ACM/IEEE International Conference on Human-Robot Interaction, pp. 351–358 (2012)

Emotional Robotics in Elder Care – A Comparison of Findings in the UK and Germany

Barbara Klein[1] and Glenda Cook[2]

[1] Fachhochschule Frankfurt am Main, University of Applied Sciences,
Nibelungenplatz 1, 60439 Frankfurt am Main, Germany
bklein@fb4.fh-frankfurt.de
[2] Northumbria University, Newcastle, UK
glenda.cook@northumbria.ac.uk

Abstract. Robot-therapy with emotional robots is a new approach for people with cognitive impairments. This article looks at explorative findings of the therapeutic seal PARO in a practice network in England and findings of PARO and the toy dinosaur PLEO in teaching research projects in Germany. The findings in the UK and Germany have comparable outcomes on social interaction of the residents. Examples of the outcomes are presented and analysed with respect to the question in how far there are indicators for a new quality of interaction due to the robotic intervention and in how far it can contribute to interventions which enhance social interaction in care.

Keywords: Emotional robotics, elder care, nursing homes, dementia, methodology.

1 Introduction

Demographic change is an issue discussed in most societies in the world even when figures of the demographic change vary. The UK with 16.5% of the population 65 years and older is slightly younger than Germany [1] with 20.6%. Demographic changes for these countries indicates a major increase, especially in the age group 80 years and older. Whilst it should not be assumed that all older people have dementia; the association between dementia and advancing age must be acknowledged. The prevalence of dementia in the 70-74 year-old age group is 4.2%; 75-79: 8.6%; 80-84: 13%; 85-89:25.3%; 90 and over: 33% [2]. Hence, one of the major concerns is the increasing number of people suffering from dementia due to increased life expectancy.

It has consistently been reported in the research literature that older people who live in care homes experience social and emotional isolation [3, 4]. A factor that contributes to these outcomes is the quality and type of social interaction within a home. This is influenced by personal attributes of residents including sensory deficits, communication and mobility and cognitive abilities. The physical environment of a care home and its cultural attributes such as the philosophy of care and interventions implemented by staff can facilitate or inhibit social interaction. In recognition there

S.S. Ge et al. (Eds.): ICSR 2012, LNAI 7621, pp. 108–117, 2012.
© Springer-Verlag Berlin Heidelberg 2012

has been an increasing body of research and associated interventions that aims to enhance opportunities for social interaction in care homes. Chen et al (2000) [5], however, highlighted that those with the most severe disabilities, including those with dementia, tend to be excluded from these studies.

In 2002 Libin & Libin [6] introduced a definition of emotional robots as a research area focusing on the analysis of person-robot-communication "viewed as a complex interactive system, with the emphasis on psychological evaluation, diagnosis, prognosis and principles of non-pharmacological treatment." Since then a number of pilot projects have been carried out in order to analyse the effects of different artefacts of emotional and social robotics. This contribution looks at two different approaches all utilizing emotional robots. On the one side PARO, the therapeutic seal developed by AIST in Japan is utilized in the UK and Germany. PARO is an artificial emotional creature in the form of a harp seal, which was designed to interact with human beings to elicit an emotional attachment to the robot [7]. PARO has programmed behaviour as well as a set of sensors. Sensors include a touch sensor over the complete body, an infrared sensor, stereoscopic vision and hearing. Actuators include eyelids, upper body motors, front paw and hind limb motors. In Germany also the toy dinosaur PLEO has been used which is an animated pet dinosaur designed to emulate the appearance and (imagined) behavior of a week-old baby Camarasaurus combining sensory, articulation, and neuronetics to create a lifelike appearance with organic movement and adaptable behaviors [8].

This paper presents the PARO group intervention and outcomes observed in a UK care home (see also [9]) and the findings of teaching research projects in Germany (see also [10, 11]).

2   Different Approaches on the Effects of Robot Therapy

2.1   Practice Development in England

Northumbria University is involved in a practise development network "My Home Life North East care homes". Here a framework INTERACT has been developed for social interaction with residents suffering from dementia in nursing care homes. Using this framework in an exploratory study PARO was introduced to four to five residents. This study specifically sought to enhance social interaction between older residents with dementia through a novel intervention that involved facilitated group discussion with the emotional robot, PARO.

Aims

Aims of the study were to implement facilitated PARO group discussions with residents with dementia and to observe the effect of PARO with respect to conversation and interaction in a group of residents with dementia.

Methods

This was an ethnographic study of facilitated group discussions with PARO in a care home in North East England. The care home is a modern and purpose-built centre that comprises of four units, each with 20 bedrooms. Each unit has a dedicated team of staff who provide different forms of care. The PARO group discussions took place in an Elderly Mentally Infirm (EMI) unit in the centre. In addition to bedrooms this unit had a dining area, small and large communal lounges and bathroom facilities. The philosophy of care was person centred, giving priority to address individual needs and a stimulating activities programme which included music (such as playing instruments and listening), art (making cards, drawing) and gardening.

The PARO group discussions were held in an afternoon for one and a half hours, in a small lounge in the EMI unit and the door was kept open during the session. The sessions were led by a facilitator who was supported by a care assistant who had known the participants for at least one year. The sessions were held for a period of five weeks:

- Session 1: orientation: The PARO was placed out of sight while residents entered or were assisted to the room and were seated around a table. At this point the facilitator explained that they had brought something about which she would like their opinion. After the introduction the PARO was brought out, placed on the table, and turned on. The residents were told 'I have brought something for you to see today. This is PARO. It was given to us by someone from Japan. I am curious about what you think of PARO.' After some introduction PARO is held by each member of the group. As each participant holds PARO the facilitator asks the participants: 'What do you think of PARO? What do you want to know about PARO? What do you like or dislike about PARO?' The session ends when the discussion ceases and PARO is turned off. Participants are asked if they would like to take part in a discussion with PARO next week.

- Sessions 2: PARO was turned on when the participants were seated around the table. They were asked if they could recall the PARO discussions from the previous week. Then they were invited to interact with PARO in any way that they wanted to. The facilitator led discussions about what name should be given to PARO. They were also invited to discuss the same questions as the previous week: 'What do you think of PARO? What do you want to know about PARO? What do you like or dislike about PARO?'

- Sessions 3-5: Following initial interaction with PARO and exploration of any issues that arose spontaneously the facilitator introduced the following topics – 'Have you had a pet in the past? What type of pet? How long did you have the pet and what did you do with it? What memories do you have of the pet? What were the most memorable moments with your pet?' At the end of the fifth discussion the participants were asked about their views of participating in the group discussions.

The participants were five people with dementia (3-female; 2 male; between 75 – 88 years of age). They had been resident in the EMI unit of the home between 2-10 months. Four participants had good communication skills and one who had not spoken for 6 weeks. Two participants were wheelchair users.

Data collection involved observing interaction between participants and PARO, between each other, and between the group participants and other who were not part of the group (residents who came into the room and staff). Following each session notes were made of the observation, which were validated by the supporting carer. When the sequence of discussions was completed, interviews were held with the carer who supported the facilitator and with other staff who had observed the PARO intervention when they walked into the room during sessions. A verbatim transcription was made of the interviews. Thematic analysis was completed across both observation and interview data sets.

Findings

Prior to entering the small lounge the participants were gathered in another nearby lounge. Little social interaction was observed between the nine residents in this room. When approached by the staff and asked if they wanted to join the PARO group there was no hesitation and they quickly settled around the table. PARO was placed on the table and switched on. Attention was focused on PARO, some participants smiled and spontaneously commented about PARO. These were short exchanges such as 'Look at what it is doing;' 'Oh, it is so lovely;' and when PARO made sounds they asked 'Is it ok?' 'What does it need?' When one participant put out their hand to stroke PARO they were invited to hold it. As they stroked and held the robot they kept eye contact with PARO and moved their head following its movements. Verbal interaction involved the participant making soothing comments to PARO – 'There, there;' 'Look at you, oh you like that' in response to PARO's squeaks. Other participants made strong eye contact clearly observing the interaction between human and robot.

After five minutes others in the group were invited to hold PARO giving each person the opportunity to have close contact with the robot. The participant with advanced dementia stroked and cuddled PARO, and swayed back and forth as if she was rocking the robot. This behaviour contrasted to her previous state where she appeared to doze, following her initial interest in PARO. Interest in PARO was maintained by other participants throughout the whole session. This was evidenced by their comments and questions. They wanted to know how it worked, what it needed, how much it cost. Two participants referred to PARO as a real animal, a dog, indicating that it might need to go to the toilet, and that it should have a rest. They were familiar with this type of animal. This real/machine distinction was implicit in their questions rather than being a point of discussion. These types of interactions were witnessed throughout all of the PARO sessions.

In subsequent sessions the participants were observed advising others in the group about how to interact and care for PARO. They commented 'He needs to be stroked in this way;' 'He is upset, talk to him more.' They endowed PARO with a masculine gender and when asked if they wanted to give PARO a name they agreed that he should be called 'Jimmy.'

In addition to the five residents who agreed to take part in the group sessions other residents showed interest in what was taking place and they entered the room, joined the group and participated in discussions that related to PARO. Their comments and non-verbal interactions were similar to the participants; they wanted to hold PARO and engaged in one-sided conversation with the robot.

In one session the woman with advanced dementia was given PARO. She sat back in her chair and constantly patted the robot and smoothed its fur. When another resident spontaneously joined the group he was given PARO. This woman opened her eyes and watched him sitting quietly talking to the robot saying 'There there puppy, 'Quiet now puppy.' He was very gentle with the robot and constantly patted it. His dialogue continued with positive comments to the female resident saying 'You have a lovely puppy.' In response the woman appeared animated and she did engage in 3 brief exchanges with the male resident stating 'Yes he is lovely.' She maintained eye contact whilst talking to him and moved her body forward in a positive gesture. He did likewise and smiled in response to her comments. This appeared to be a lucid moment whilst these individuals were positively interacting with each other. This brief interaction was followed by the woman sitting back in her chair and closing her eyes appearing not to engage with others in her surroundings. The man continued to make positive comments about PARO and then spontaneously stated that PARO ought to be returned to the woman. When he passed PARO back to her she opened her eyes again, maintained contact with him, and then started to stroke PARO in a slow consistent from its head to tail. There was one other resident in the group at this stage and he observed the episode. When the woman was holding PARO again he also commented that she had a good pet and advised her to enjoy this because all pets were not so good.

In contrast one of the participants appeared to be upset by the presence of PARO during the third session. She not wants to hold PARO and mentioned that we were all in danger. When asked if she wanted to leave she responded positively. As she left the room she appeared less anxious. She was invited to participate in the following session, however her non-verbal behaviour did not indicate agreement therefore did not return to the group.

The facilitator introduced different topics to the discussion following the initial orientation session. Group members spoke of their pets, often dogs and cats. They told stories about interacting with their pets and this led onto other discussions about what they liked/disliked about interacting with animals. This spoke of places that they had both visited that involved their pets. This prompted further discussion between the participants about what they did in those places. For example, one man spoke of times in his youth when he walked grey hounds and had gone to the racing stadium. In another situation the two men discussed the route where one of them had walked the grey hounds. This was past the coal mine that no longer existed. They had both worked down the pit and they discussed their work. Both commented on the caged-birds that they took down the pit to detect hazards.

Care staff spontaneously took time out of their activities and observed the group. This led to impromptu discussions initiated by them with the residents. They were very keen on finding out what the participants thought of PARO. Two care staff observed the interaction between the residents that was described above and after the session they stated that they longed for that brief exchange to continue. They indicated that it had been a while since the female with advanced dementia had reacted in this way and that she had seemed relaxed and had enjoyed the session. They indicated that introducing PARO into the care environment promoted social interaction between residents, and between residents and staff. It was a trigger to start conversations and interactions that did not otherwise take place.

2.2   Teaching Research Projects in Germany

Since 2009 the Faculty of Social Work and Health of the Fachhochschule Frankfurt am Main – University of Applied Sciences uses emotional robots such as the therapeutic seal PARO and since 2010 two toy dinosaurs PLEOs in teaching research projects in the Bachelor Degree program in Social Work [10, 11]. Students are taught the theoretical concepts of socio-pedagogic approaches in nursing care homes and have to develop a concept for assisted activities with new technologies.

Aims
Objectives pursued with the teaching research projects are that students get into contact with their future clients, transfer theoretical knowledge into practise, train their observational skills and explore the potential of new technologies for daily activities.

Methods
Artefacts such as the therapeutic seal PARO or the toy PLEO are implemented in teaching research projects in a module on "user-orientation and well-being in service provision of elder care". In the course module students deal with social work in elder care and learn a variety of methods and tools for daily activities. Based on that knowledge they have to develop an activity concept for a minimum of three sessions and implement it in a nursing care home. These sessions can be based on robot-therapy. Their observational skills on the effects of the intervention are trained – they have to videograph the sessions, analyse their videos and write up a report on their observations and experiences and reflect those.

Teams of three to five students have to carry out the project within four weeks. After having obtained informed consent of residents (or their legal custodians) and the management, they facilitate at least three sessions with residents in nursing care homes with the selected technology. Afterward they report the results and have to do a project presentation.

Findings
The course takes place twice a year. In the period between the summer term of 2009 and the winter term of 2010/11 there were a total of 11 robotic interventions in different nursing care homes, seven groups used PARO and our groups chose PLEO. Due to quality issues only six project reports on PARO are taken into account.

During this time period, a total of 62 residents had contact with emotional robots; 88.7% were female which corresponds to the average sex distribution in nursing care homes. 38 of the residents had activities with PARO, 86.8% were female; and 24 had activities with PLEO, 91.6% were female.

Students undertook both group and individual interventions. Group size varied up to ten residents, findings suggest that a group size up to four residents can be managed more easily. Some of the students were rather sceptical towards the use of robots for interventions. Their experiences resulted in a change of their attitudes; thereafter the students often saw potential for robot-therapy. Three persons out of 38 with PARO interventions did not like the seal; one person left the group intervention. In the individual interventions, two residents refused PARO showing their dislike either by shaking their heads or saying no. The findings of the reports indicate that emotional robots stimulate social interaction most times in a positive way.

3   Discussion: New Quality of Interaction through Robot-Therapy?

The projects in the UK and in Germany seem to have comparable outcomes on social interaction of the residents. Examples of the outcomes are presented and analysed with respect to the question in how far there are indicators for a new quality of interaction due to the robotic intervention and in how far it can contribute to interventions which enhance social interaction in care.

The facilitated PARO group discussions in the UK provide stimulation that the participants found manageable and for the majority enjoyable. PARO was entertaining and was a focus for verbal and non-verbal interaction for those in its presence. Hence group participants shared a social experience that was pleasing and worthy of conversation. Though there was no attempt to measure the quantity of social interaction during these sessions, the observations highlight changes in social interaction between residents, and residents and staff. In an environment that can lack stimulation and can be dominated by routine it is important to identify interventions that have the potential for enjoyment and can promote positive social interaction.

The analysis of the German project reports revealed the following reactions to the emotional robots:

- Touching the robot. This included stroking, cuddling and hugging. In one of the project reports these interactions with intensive skin contact are interpreted as a new basal approach to people suffering from dementia which might contribute to either reducing aggressiveness or stimulate spirits.
- Mimic expressions and gestures. Here following was subsumed: looking at the robot, but also to the other persons being in the room; grinning, smirking, smiling, laughing. Quite often these observations had explanations such as "resident usually does not smile"; "resident usually does not show such positive emotions and happiness" [10].
- Verbalisation / talking with the robot. Holding and touching the robot are accompanied by talking to the robot. The way how residents talk to the emotional robots is similar the way adults talk to babies and toddlers – with higher intonation and confirmative or asking character.
- Stimulation of social interaction. Similar to the situation in England is social interaction between residents not taken for granted. Even in activity sessions communication structures can be restricted only between residents and facilitator. However, in the reports there are examples that the emotional robots encourage discussions between residents – and similar to the British experiences – talks were on pets, memories of past times e.g. such as former vacations. One of the project reports mentions that two women with

dementia start to talk about their health status and how horrible it is not to "recognise their own folks" or "remember the name of the husband".

- To descend into their own world. Two project reports observe that a resident is withdrawn in their own world and ignore the students and the professional.
- Caring behaviour towards the robot. In the individual interventions the residents developed caring behaviour toward the robot, such as getting a blanket that it might get warm enough or feeding PLEO with its (plastic) leaf.
- Recreation. Due to abilities of PLEO the range of activities with this robot goes beyond that of PARO. PLEO is able to take little steps and its communication abilities are more developed e.g. it joined singing residents with its robotic voice which they enjoyed very much.
- Dislike. Students were advised that if a person did not want to interact with the emotional robot, this has to be respected. In the project reports it is mentioned that the person left the room or shook the head and said no.

These findings are comparable to the English experiences. Looking at the English examples the words describing the interaction can be subsumed to above categories. However, the descriptors of the categories can be extended with further indicators e.g. touching the robot includes "sway back and forth as if rocking the robot". Following additional categories to describe the effects of emotional robots could be established:

- Twofold consciousness of PARO as a subject and animal and also as an object and machine. Christopher Scholtz [12] describes this perception during his studies on AIBO, a robotic dog. The person who has a twofold consciousness knows that the robot is a machine, however the person also knows that s/he deals with the robot as it is alive. This seems to be mirrored in the UK findings. When Christopher Scholtz presented his findings in a lecture at FH FFM, students confirmed that residents (re-)acted like that.
- Upsetness about PARO "She did not want to hold PARO", "mentioned that we were all in danger". This is explicitly mentioned in the UK findings. In the German teaching projects students were advised if somebody did not want to interact with emotional robots this has to be avoided. As a consequence this was not further described.

4   Conclusion

These rather positive findings have the character of "testimonials". The findings of the German teaching projects seem to be similar for both emotional robots, PARO and PLEO. The question arises whether the appearance matters and effects can be differentiated.

Especially in the case of the German teaching research projects the influence of the young students have to be taken into account who bring in livelihood in often rather dull days in the nursing home. Here questions such as Sherry Turkle [13] asks them have to be explored e.g. should a robot replace loneliness? Will families leave their obligations and feel less guilty?

Caring for people with advanced dementia is a rather challenging task for staff and relatives. Especially, here it is important to enhance the range of opportunities to be able to engage in social interaction and to do something that is pleasurable. Opportunities for enjoyment can potentially increase quality of life – even if it is only for a short time.

There is still a necessity to analyze therapeutic effects of emotional robots in more depth and with multidisciplinary approaches. Research in pilot studies with residents in care homes in Japan has been undertaken on physiological influences such as heart rate, blood pressure, skin temperature and electrodermal response [14] and the effect on hormones in urine [15]. Most recently ten healthy participants between 21-33 years have been analyzed interacting with PARO with respect to their brain activity [16].

There is a need for randomized controlled studies such as the Australian pilot RCT comparing the effects of PARO with the effects of a reading group [17]. Combining multidisciplinary approaches in form of RCTs could give valuable insights in the therapeutic effects of robot-therapy.

References

1. CIA: The World Factbook, https://www.cia.gov/library/publications/the-world-factbook/geos/gm.html
2. Lobo, A., Launer, L.J., Fraglioni, L., Andersen, K., Di Carlo, A., Breteler, M.M., et al.: Prevalence of dementia and major subtypes in Europe: A collaborative study of population-based cohorts. Neurological diseases in the elderly research group. Neurology 54, S4-S9 (2000)
3. McKee, K., Harrison, G., Lee, K.: Activity, friendships and wellbeing in residential settings for older people. Aging and Mental Health 3(2), 143–152 (1999)
4. Hubbard, G., Tester, S., Downs, M.: Meaningful social interactions between older people in institutional care settings. Ageing and Society 23, 99–114 (2003)
5. Chen, Y., Ryden, M., Feldt, K., Savik, K.: The relationship between social interaction and characteristics of aggressive, cognitively impaired nursing home residents. American Journal of Alzheimer's Disease 15(1), 10–17 (2000)
6. Libin, E., Libin, A.: Robotherapy: Definition, Assessment, and Case Study. In: Proceedings of the 8th International Conference on Virtual Systems and Multimedia, Creative Digital Culture, pp. 906–915. VSMM Society, Seoul (2002)
7. Shibata, T., Tanie, K.: Creation of Subjective Value through Physical Interaction between Human and Machine. In: Proceeding of the 4th International Symposium on Artificial Intelligence (1999)
8. http://en.wikipedia.org/wiki/Pleo
9. Cook, G., Clarke, C., Cowie, B.: Maintaining and developing social interaction in care homes: a guide for care home, health and social care staff. Northumbria University (2009) ISBN: 978-1-86135-365-8
10. Klein, B.: Anwendungsfelder der emotionalen Robotik. Erste Ergebnisse aus Lehrforschungsprojekten an der Fachhochschule Frankfurt am Main. In: JDZB (ed.): Mensch-Roboter-Interaktion aus interkultureller Perspektive. Japan und Deutschland im Vergleich. Veröffentlichungen des Japanisch-Deutschen Zentrums Berlin, Band 62, Berlin, pp. 147–162 (2011)
11. Klein, B.: Robot-Therapy in Germany. SICE 51(7), 649–653 (2012)

12. Scholtz, C.P.: Alltag mit künstlichen Wesen. Theologische Implikationen eines Lebens mit subjektsimulierenden Maschinen am Beispiel des Unterhaltungsroboters Aibo. Vandenhoeck & Ruprecht GmbH & Co. KG, Göttingen (2008)
13. Turkle, S.: Alone Together. Why we expect more from technology and less from each other. Basic Books, New York (2011)
14. Mitsui, T., Shibata, T., Wada, K., Tanie, K.: Psychophysiological Effects by Interaction with Mental Commit Robot. Journal of Robotics and Mechatronics 14, 20–26 (2002)
15. Wada, K., Shibata, T.: Living With Seal Robots – Its Sociopsychological and Physiological influences on the Elderly in a Care House. IEEE Transactions on Robotics 23(5), 972–980 (2007)
16. Kawaguchi, Y., Wada, K., Okamoto, M., Tsujii, T., Shibata, T.: Investigation of Brain Activity during Interaction with Seal Robot by fNIRRS. In: RO-MAN, 20th IEEE International Symposium on Robot and Human Interactive Communication, July 31-August 3, pp. 308–313 (2011)
17. Moyle, W.: Effects of PARO on people with dementia. Lessons learnt from a RCT in Australia Presentation on euRobotics Forum 2012 (March 3, 2012)

Dorothy Robotubby: A Robotic Nanny

Haibin Yan, Marcelo H. Ang Jr., and Aun Neow Poo

Department of Mechanical Engineering,
National University of Singapore, Singapore, 119260
{g0800270,mpeangh,engpooan}@nus.edu.sg

Abstract. In this paper, we introduce our designed robotic nanny called Dorothy Robotubby to play with and take care of a child in case his/her parent or caregiver is absent. There are two main user interfaces in our robotic system: local control-based and remote control-based. Local control-based interface is developed for a child to control the robot directly to execute some tasks such as telling a story, playing music and games, chatting, and video calling. Remote control-based interface is designed for parents to control the robot remotely to execute several commands like demonstrating facial expressions and gestures. By operating these two interfaces, our robot can not only interact with a child in an attractive way, but also build a connection between a child and his/her parent. In a real pilot study, 7 children aged from 4 to 13 years old and their parents are involved to test our robot. Experimental results have shown that while there are some room to improve our robotic nanny, most children and parents express large interest in our robot and provide comparatively positive evaluations.

Keywords: Robotic nanny, Dorothy Robotubby, remote control, child-robot interaction.

1 Introduction

Social robotic, an important branch of robotics, has recently attracted increasing interest in many disciplines, such as computer vision, artificial intelligence, and mechatronics. While there are a great deal of challenges when applying social robots for real-world applications, some social robots have been developed or are commercially available to assist our daily life [1–3]. With the rapid development of current society, parents become more busy and cannot always stay with their children. Hence, a robotic nanny which can care for and play with the children is desirable. A robotic nanny is a class of social robots acting as a child's caregiver [4] by providing entertainments to the child, tutoring the child, keeping the child from physical harm, and building a companionship with the child [5, 6].

Currently, a number of social robotics have been developed for children in entertainments, healthcare, and domestic areas [1]. For example, Sony's dog robot AIBO is designed to be a robotic companion/pet of a child [2]. RUBI is designed to be an assistant of a teacher for early childhood education [7]. Probo is developed to comfort and emotionally interact with children in a hospital [8]. NEC's

S.S. Ge et al. (Eds.): ICSR 2012, LNAI 7621, pp. 118–127, 2012.

PaPeRo is developed to care for children in domestic and public environments [9]. Some of these robots are commercially available such as AIBO and PaPeRo, and some others are being developed. While these robots have demonstrated promising performance in their target environments, they cannot be directly used as a robotic nanny like AIBO, or satisfy specific design objectives such as Probo, RUBI, and PaPeRo.

In this paper, we develop a robotic nanny named Dorothy Robotubby to play with and take care of a child in case his/her parent or caregiver is absent. We expect that our robot can not only interact with a child in an attractive way, but also build a connection between a child and his/her parent. The developed robotic nanny is specified for a normal child and is used at home.

To achieve this goal, there are two main problems to be solved in our robot. The first is how to activate and maintain a child's interest and curiosity to interact with the robot. We solve this problem by designing an acceptable appearance with conveniently-operable user interfaces. The second problem is how to connect a child and his/her parent via the robot. A feasible solution is to transmit a child's and parent's video and audio to each other by video calling. Different from the conventional video calling functions, when a child is talking with his/her parent through the robot, the parent can remotely control the robot to execute several commands such as showing different facial expressions or a remote hug.

This paper is organized as follows. Section 2 overviews our robotic nanny – Dorothy Robotubby. Section 3 describes each function of Robotubby. Section 4 presents the experiments, and Section 5 concludes the paper.

2   System Overview

2.1   Configuration

Fig.1 shows the system configuration of Dorothy Robotubby. We can see that there are three computers used in the whole robot system. One touch screen computer is mounted on the belly of the robot and utilized to control the robot. Due to its touchable screen, a child can interact with the robot by directly clicking buttons on the touch screen. The second computer is employed to help the robot to accomplish some complex computation tasks such as emotion recognition. After computation, the results are sent back to the robot via the local network. These complex computation tasks need to occupy some computer resources and may affect the accomplishment of other functions. We can solve this problem well by using the second computer. The second computer is typically located in the home of the child, at a local network within the home. The third computer is used by parents to remotely control the robot. It can exchange information with the robot by the network. Besides three computers and the robot, two webcams, one microphone, and one speaker are included in the system for video calling and surveillance.

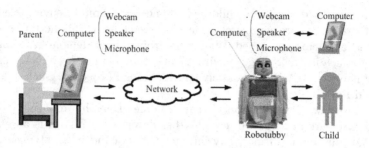

Fig. 1. System configuration

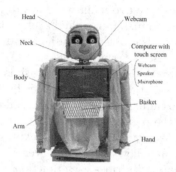

Fig. 2. Main components of Dorothy Robotubby

2.2   Dorothy Robotubby User Interface

To ensure our robot is acceptable by a child, we design Robotubby with a upper body and a caricatured appearance. It mainly consists of a head, a neck, a body, two arms, two hands, and a touch screen in its belly. Fig. 2 shows the main components of our Robotubby. Robotubby is designed to be able to demonstrate different facial expressions and gestures by controlling its face and body components when it executes several tasks. Specifically, there are 9 Degrees of Freedom (DOF) in the robot's head, 2 DOF in its neck, 2 DOF in its body, 4 DOF in its each arm, and 1 DOF in its each hand.

We mount a computer with a touch screen on the robot's belly such that a child can operate the robot by using a mouse or directly clicking buttons on the touch screen. The corresponding user interface is shown in Fig. 3. From the figure, we can see that the interface mainly consists of five parts: assistant information of user interface, main functions of user interface, sub-interface of telling a story, sub-interface of talking with me, and sub-interface of emotion recognition.

Assistant information of user interface includes the working status of Robutubby such as connection status with the other two computers. Main functions of user interface are principle and significant. There are several components including talking with me, telling a story, playing music videos and games, and video calling. The sub-interfaces of talking with me and telling a story are set

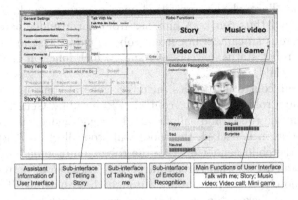

Fig. 3. Robotubby user interface

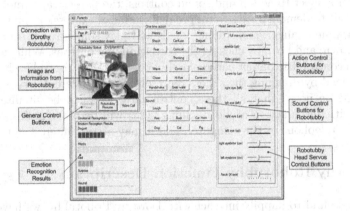

Fig. 4. Remote user interface

in the main user interface as shown in Fig. 3. The other three functions have the independent sub-interfaces which will pop up after clicking the corresponding buttons. In addition to the above five functions, Robotubby has another two functions: face tracking and emotion recognition. They start to work when Robotubby user interface is activated.

2.3   Remote User Interface

In addition to Robotubby user interface, another main interface in our robotic nanny system is the remote user interface which is operated by parents to communicate with their child via network. The main idea to develop this interface is to enhance the connection between a child and his/her parent. Fig. 4 shows the remote user interface with three information categories and four control categories.

Specifically, three information categories include connection with Dorothy Robotubby, images and robot status from Robotubby, and emotion recognition results of a child. Through the transferred images, parents can know what their child is doing, and thus can keep him/her from harm under parents' surveillance. Since there is no camera in current robotic nanny system to capture the robot, through robot status, parents will know which function of Robotubby is operated by the child.

There are four control categories including general control, action control, sound control, and robot head servo control in Robotubby. General control is to pause or resume the robot, and call the child through video call. After "Robotubby Pause" button is clicked, the robot will stop all of its functions except video call and the child cannot operate the robot. Only under such condition, the buttons belonging to other three control categories can be activated and the parent can remotely control the robot through these buttons. If "Robotubby Resume" button is clicked, the parent cannot remotely control the robot except calling the child through video call function and the child can operate the robot again. With respect to action and sound controls, the parent can remotely control the robot to demonstrate several pre-defined facial expressions and gestures such as happiness, anger, and waving hands and play some pre-set sounds such as laugh, yawn, and burp by clicking the corresponding buttons. While for robot head servo control, the parent can remotely and separately control each servo of the robot head by dragging the sliders representing the different servos.

It should be noted that all these control categories can be simultaneously executed with the function of video calling. This will be different from talking through the telephone or the computer, and it may attract interest of the child.

3   Dorothy Robotubby Function Description

To attract a child to happily interact with Dorothy Robotubby, we have developed several functions such as telling stories, chatting with a child, playing music videos, playing games, and video calling. In this section, we will briefly describe each function of the robot.

3.1   Telling Stories

In our robot system, we prepared five stories that Robotubby can tell. They are "Three pigs", "Red hood", "Beauty and the Beast", "Jack and the Bean", and "The leap frog", respectively. After clicking the "Story" button, the child can select one of them from story list that is shown in Fig. 5 (a). When Robotubby tells the selected story, the read words will be highlighted by blue color and the buttons of "Previous line", "Repeat line", "Next line", "Pause", "Resume", "Change", and "Stop" can be used to control the told story. Fig. 5(b) shows the sub-interface of storytelling. When telling the story, Robotubby can move its mouth by using Text to Speech techniques. In addition, we have inserted several specific labels in the prepared stories such that the robot can demonstrate different facial expressions and gestures when meeting them. Several samples of different facial expressions and gestures are shown in Fig. 6.

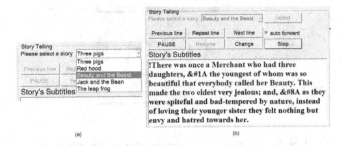

Fig. 5. The sub-interface of storytelling

Fig. 6. Several samples of facial expressions and gestures during telling a story

3.2 Chatting with a Child

The sub-interface of the function of chatting with a child is illustrated in Fig. 7. The child can enter his/her questions into the input textbox. Then the corresponding answer will be given in the output textbox. Fig. 7 provides two examples of the dialogue between the child and the robot. Similar to storytelling, when Robotubby speaks out the given answers, it can move its mouth. To fulfill this function, we have employed AIMLBot which is a programme implementation of an AIML (Artificial Intelligence Markup Language) and can be directly downloaded from the internet [10]. By using this technique, the user can chat the computer with natural languages.

3.3 Playing Music Videos

Playing music videos is another function of Robotubby. Based on this function, the robot can play prepared music videos with the predefined facial expressions

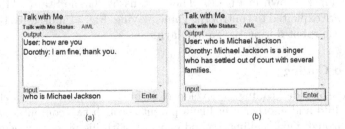

Fig. 7. The sub-interface of chatting with a child

Fig. 8. The sub-interface of playing music videos

Fig. 9. Several samples of different gestures during singing a song

and gestures. The demonstrated robot movement is synchronized to the tempo of the song. The current music videos include "If you are happy", "Three Bears", "Old McDonald had a Farm", "Twinkle Twinkle Little Star", and "Twinkle Twinkle Little Star Sing-A-Long". The child can select a music video from its list which is shown in Fig. 8(a). Fig. 8 (b) illustrates the sub-interface of this function. On the interface, the buttons of "Play", "Stop", and "Exit" can be utilized to control the music video playing. Fig. 9 shows several samples of different gestures of the robot during singing a song.

3.4 Playing Games

This function is to let a child paly a simple basketball game with the robot. It is activated by clicking the button of "Mini Game" in Robotubby user interface. From Fig. 2, it can be seen that there is a basket mounted on the robot. The main procedure of this game is that the child first delivers the ball into the basket, and then the robot picks up the ball and passes it to the child. Next, it repeats the whole procedure within the time limit. In addition to timing, the robot can count the scores of successfully delivering the ball. The sub-interface of this function is shown in Fig. 10. The buttons of "Game Start", "Restart", and "Exit" are exploited to control the game playing. Fig. 11 illustrates the main gestures of the robot during the game playing.

3.5 Video Calling

The function of video calling is developed to build communication between a user like a child and another user like a parent through two computers and the internet. Through video calling, a child can talk with his parent by using voice and video.

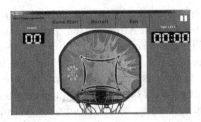

Fig. 10. The sub-interface of playing games

Fig. 11. Several samples of different gestures during the game playing

4   Experiments

The experiment was designed to evaluate whether the children like the appearance and functions of Dorothy Robotubby and collect the parent's opinions on the remote user interface designs.

4.1   Experimental Settings

We conducted trials in control and mechatronics lab at National University of Singapore. 7 children and their parents were invited to our lab to attend this survey. For the involved children, there are 4 females and 3 males from 4 to 13 years old. Trails for each child usually lasted around 25-30 minutes. There were three computers used in our robot system. Among them, the computer for robot and the computer for computation were placed in one room. And the computer for parent was placed in another room. The distance between these two rooms is far enough to ensure that the child and parent will not see and hear from each other when testing video call and remote control. Before the test, a brief introduction on the experiment was presented to the child and parent. During the whole test, a human assistant also participated to answer questions and help solve problems from the child and parent.

4.2   Experimental Procedures

There were mainly two testing parts in the whole experiment which were designed to follow a certain sequence. Firstly, the child was requested to test the robot's functions including story telling, chatting, music playing, game playing, face tracking, and emotion recognition. Secondly, the parent was asked to test the remote user interface's functions including video call and remote control with the child.

During the whole test, the interaction activities between the child and the robot were observed and recorded. After testing, participants were asked to complete a questionnaire. The questionnaire for child was designed to evaluate the robot's functions and appearance, and the child's feelings during the interaction. The questionnaire for parent was employed to investigate the parent's feelings about the remote user interface's design. The questions on both questionnaires were based on a 5-point Likert scale and some suggestions were requested to provide if possible.

4.3   Results

Based on the children's assessments, the analysis results showed that the children with different ages showed interest in different robot functions. In particular, the children from 4 to 5 years old usually liked the functions of story telling, music playing, game playing, and video call; the children with 10 years old normally liked the functions of game playing and video call; the children from 12 to 13 years old generally liked the functions of chatting, face tracking, and emotion recognition; and no children like remote control function. This may be because the selected stories and music are more suitable for younger children; the designed game is comparatively easy for the children older than 10 years; younger children more liked to talk with their parents; older children usually liked the function with higher technologies; and less children liked to be interfered when interacting with the robot. For the appearance of the robot, half of the children thought it is scary and the rest thought it is normal or appealing. The reason from one child who disliked the robot appearance is that "the eyes are too big and never blink, therefore, you will feel like someone is watching you." While for the children's feelings after interacting with Robotubby, half of the children thought the robot is interesting and can be their friend, and the rest of the children thought the robot is boring. All the children who disliked Robotubby are older than 10 years. Compared with younger children, they may have higher requirements to the developed robot. Generally speaking, most of the existing functions of Robotubby are simple for the older children and it is difficult to maintain their interest in the robot. Oppositely, the younger children are more interested in Robotubby. Therefore, our developed robot is more suitable for the younger children usually from 5 to 10 years old.

Compared with the survey on the children, we just prepared a simple question for the parents to evaluate the appearance, operability, and functions of the remote user interface. As a general consideration, the parents thought the designed remote user interface was normal or satisfactory. There is no negative assessment with regard to the remote user interface's design.

5   Conclusion and Future Work

In this paper, we have developed a robotic nanny named Dorothy Robotubby with the aims to play with and take care of a child during his/her parent or caregiver absences. The main functions of our robot is presented and some qualitative results are presented to show the nanny function of our robot.

For future work, we are interested to improve the appearance, functions, and user interfaces of the currently built robot system according to the children's and parents' feedback, and improve the system by designing more effective functions. For instance, a Kinect camera can be used to enable Robotubby to copy and follow the child's and parent's certain gestures. A birds-eye-view camera can be also utilized such that the parent could see the whole picture of the interaction between the child and the robot. In addition, the application for the autistic children with Robotubby will be explored and the functions aiming to the therapy for them will be designed.

Acknowledgement. The authors would like to express their thanks to the other group members who involved to help the development of our Robotubby. They would also like to thank Dr. John-John Cabibihan, an assistant professor in National University of Singapore for his valuable suggestions and comments that have helped us to improve the quality of the paper.

References

1. Fong, T., Nourbakhsh, I., Dautenhahn, K.: A survey of socially interactive robots. Robotics and Autonomous Systems 42(3), 143–166 (2003)
2. Arkin, R.C., Fujita, M., Takagi, T., Hasegawa, R.: An ethological and emotional basis for human–robot interaction. Robotics and Autonomous Systems 42(3), 191–201 (2003)
3. Yun, S., Shin, J., Kim, D., Kim, C.G., Kim, M., Choi, M.-T.: Engkey: Tele-education Robot. In: Mutlu, B., Bartneck, C., Ham, J., Evers, V., Kanda, T. (eds.) ICSR 2011. LNCS, vol. 7072, pp. 142–152. Springer, Heidelberg (2011)
4. Broek, E.L.: Robot nannies: Future or fiction? Interaction Studies 11(2), 274–282 (2010)
5. Turkle, S., Breazeal, C., Dasté, O., Scassellati, B.: Encounters with kismet and cog: Children respond to relational artifacts. Digital Media: Transformations in Human Communication, 1–20 (2006)
6. Sharkey, N., Sharkey, A.: The crying shame of robot nannies: an ethical appraisal. Interaction Studies 11(2), 161–190 (2010)
7. Ruvolo, P., Fasel, I., Movellan, J.: Auditory mood detection for social and educational robots. In: ICRA, pp. 3551–3556 (2008)
8. Saldien, J., Goris, K., Vanderborght, B., Lefeber, D.: On the design of an emotional interface for the huggable robot probo. In: AISB Symposium (2008)
9. Osada, J., Ohnaka, S., Sato, M.: The scenario and design process of childcare robot, papero. In: ACM SIGCHI International Conference on Advances in Computer Entertainment Technology, p. 80 (2006)
10. Program - aimlbot.dll (2006), http://aimlbot.sourceforge.net/

Would Granny Let an Assistive Robot into Her Home?

Susanne Frennert[1,2], Britt Östlund[2], and Håkan Eftring[1,2]

[1] Rehabilitation Engineering,
[2] Department of Design Sciences,
Lund University,
Sweden
{susanne.frennert,hakan.eftring}@certec.lth.se,
Britt.ostlund@design.lth.se

Abstract. Assistive robots have received considerable research attention due to the increase of the senior population around the world and the shortage of caregivers. However, limited attention has been paid to involving seniors in the design process in order to elicit their attitudes and perception of having their own robot. This study addresses this issue. We conducted a workshop with 14 Swedish seniors age 65 to 86. The findings indicate that: (1) the functionality of the robot is far more important than the appearance; (2) the usefulness will determine the acceptance of a robot; (3) seniors feel it is important to keep up to date with new technological developments; (4) assistive robots were not perceived as intrusive and having a robotic presence in the seniors' bathrooms and bedrooms was considered acceptable. These findings suggest that seniors are prepared to give assistive robots a try if the robot is perceived as useful.

Keywords: Participatory design, attention cards, assistive robots, old adults.

1 Introduction

After 2020, the proportion of seniors will rise rapidly around the world [1]. The growth of an older population and shortage of caregivers has spurred the development of matching technological advances to human needs. Assistive robots may become a reality in the near future to accommodate the needs and wants of today's seniors [2]. Achieving user acceptance is of high priority in this context. Perceptions of personal concerns, such as utility and efficiency gain, as well as social views and pressures are crucial in the acceptance of new technologies [3]. The perception of a product is affected by the visual design, affordance and a lifetime of experience [4]. To assist people who are growing older, we need to understand the needs and challenges aging presents. In order to do this seniors have to be involved in the design process [5]. In Scandinavia we have a history of participatory design [6]. Workshop methodology has shown to be an inexpensive and effective tool in gathering valuable information involving multiple users at once [7]. However, the past has shown that during focus groups seniors have difficulties sustaining attention on a particular topic and tend to "wander" to speak about their own particular interest [8], [9]. The idea of involving

S.S. Ge et al. (Eds.): ICSR 2012, LNAI 7621, pp. 128–137, 2012.
© Springer-Verlag Berlin Heidelberg 2012

seniors in the design process is not new, but research literature regarding this is hard to find [10]. It is even harder to find detailed guidelines on how to apply senior-oriented participatory design methodology [11]. The aim of this study is to elicit Swedish seniors' attitudes, wishes and needs towards having their own robot, by running a workshop. The key questions are: What should a robot look like? What would the seniors like a robot to do? How would they like a robot to behave? Where in their homes would they allow a robot to take part in their daily lives?

The research is exploratory, aimed at determining factors that affect seniors' acceptance of assistive robots and to identify major themes in the creation of a questionnaire for a European project survey.

2   Related Work

Beer et al. [12] examined seniors' (age 65 to 93) openness to assistive robots as well as their opinions on using assistive robots around the home. Their findings indicate that seniors were open to the idea but they also had concerns about the robot's reliability. Wu et al. [13] focused on the appearance of assistive robots and found that most of the participants (age 65 and over with mild cognitive impairments) did not like large humanoid robots because of their size. They preferred discrete and small robots with human traits. The participants reacted positively to robots that resembled pets. Wu et al. [13] conclude that to meet user needs, old adults should not be viewed as passive care receivers but active participants in the design process. Walter et al. [14] studied individual preferences for various features of robot appearance and behavior in regard to the participant's personality. The results indicate the participants liked robots with human-like appearance and attributes, although introvert personalities showed a higher preference for robots that were more mechanical looking. If a robot resembles a human in appearance, people expect it to behave like one; when the robot does not live up to expectations, people tend to get very disappointed and distrustful of the robot [14]. Mori [15] studied human responses to non-human entities and concluded that if something looked real, but did not feel real, people developed unnerving feelings towards the object. If a robot looked like a real cat, but lacked the feel and temperature of a living cat, people would lose interest in it. However, other research indicates that if the robot resembles a pet, feels and interacts in line with its appearance, it may have the same impact on humans as real animals. A seal-shaped robot called Paro, was developed for robot therapy [16]. Children and old adults in several countries have used Paro and there are indications that robot therapy with Paro has the same effect as animal therapy, i.e. reduced stress-induced symptoms [17]. Past research indicates; for acceptance a robot should not be too big or bulky, should have human traits, but should not resemble humans to the point that the user expects it to behave like one [13].

3   Methodology

The method consisted of two parts: a full day workshop (from 10.15 to 15.30) and a follow-up questionnaire. The workshop was conducted at the department of Design Sciences in Lund, Sweden. The study group comprised seven women and seven men, age 65 to 86, with a mean age of 75. All the participants lived independently in their own homes. The participants were voluntary recruits from organizations for seniors in Lund.

Prior to the workshop, the participants received information about the outline of the workshop. On the day of the workshop, the fourteen participants were divided into three groups (5+5+4) with one researcher each. Dividing the participants into small groups increases the likelihood of group interaction, which can generate new ideas and concepts. Conducting similar discussions with the same type of participants can therefore identify trends and patterns in perception [8]. The methodology comprises eight phases:

Phase 1: Oral information about the aim and procedure of the workshop was given in the introduction. It was clearly stated that the seniors were the experts; their views and opinions were of foremost interest because of their first-hand experience of the needs and challenges presented by aging.

Phase 2: Different kinds of robots were then shown on a screen. A number of Internet sources were consulted to collect the robot images. The objectives were to raise awareness of actual possibilities of modern robotics and to allow participants to relieve preconceptions and to share knowledge and prior exposure to robots. The participants were asked to comment on the pictures. The three researchers took notes to capture the emotions, feelings and intuition the pictures evoked.

Phase 3: During the "explore, look and feel" phase, the groups were given one cardboard box each, containing pictures of robots (the images were edited to provide a neutral background), different kinds of materials (soft plastic, hard metal, fabric, cardboard paper, pieces of wood), a pair of scissors and glue. A researcher operated as a facilitator in each group, taking notes and encouraging the discussions. The participants were asked to select materials for their own "perfect" robot.

Phase 4: The participants and researchers had lunch together and engaged in informal discussions.

Phase 5: The three groups each received an envelope with twelve *Attention cards* (Figure 1). The seniors were asked to talk about the *Attention cards* and write their thoughts on the cards. A researcher in each group acted as an observer and took notes on what was said.

Fig. 1. Sample of Attention cards

To identify major themes that needed to be addressed in the workshop, two focus groups were conducted with adults 70 years and older prior to the workshop. One particular problem noted during the focus groups was that the old adults tended to think that being monitored and having a robot would be "*a good idea for others but not themselves*". In the past, "card methods" have revealed to be useful in capturing user requirements in workshop settings [18-21]. We therefore designed *Attention cards* to visualize scenarios, which were identified during the focus groups. Photos on A6 cardboard paper visualized the scenarios and the text on the card presented the situation as well as alternative actions or things the robot could take (Figure 1). For example a photo illustrated someone lying face down on the floor and the text on the card saying: "*If I collapsed on the kitchen floor I would like the robot to....*" and presented alternative actions such as; *ask if I need help, call a relative, call 112*. There was empty space for the participants to fill in other actions they would like the robot to take.

Phase 6: Attention cards were also developed to trigger attitudes and perceptions of physical and personal space in regards to a robot. These cards had photos of different rooms and first person narrative text stating feelings or attitudes for example; "*I would feel save if the robot was present in my bedroom while I am sleeping*".

Phase 7: By the end of the workshop the researchers gave a brief summary of what they learnt during the day. The participants were given a chance to correct misconceptions and reflect on the workshop event.

Phase 8: A follow-up questionnaire was posted to the fourteen participants to which all responded (Table 1). It was kept short to ensure a high response rate. The objective of the questionnaire was to encourage the participants to give their opinions anonymously as well as recapture their experience and evaluate it. Would the participants have the same opinions at home in private as during the workshop? The questionnaire was used to validate the findings from the workshop and to investigate if the outcome was biased by strong opinions of some individuals partaking in the workshop.

Table 1. The Follow-up Questionnaire

The reason I partook in the workshop was: *(Curiosity / Because it is important to keep up to date with new technology development / Because I am interested in robots / Other)*
Please tell us the three things you liked the most about the workshop:
Please list three things that could have been better regarding the workshop arrangement:
I like the idea of having a robot (derived from [22]): *(I agree/I somewhat agree/I somewhat disagree/I disagree /I don't know)*
I find the idea of having a robot frightening (derived from [22]): *(I agree/I somewhat agree/I somewhat disagree/I disagree /I don't know)*
My relatives, friends and family would be impressed if I had a robot (derived from [23]: *(I agree/I somewhat agree/I somewhat disagree/I disagree /I don't know)*
I have always been interested in learning how to use the latest technological devices (derived from [23]): *(I agree/I somewhat agree/I somewhat disagree/I disagree /I don't know)*
I have avoided using technology whenever possible (derived from [23]): *(I agree/I somewhat agree/I somewhat disagree/I disagree /I don't know)*

3.1   Analysis

The observational notes and the seniors' notes on the attention cards used in the workshop were transcribed and analyzed into a thematic framework [24]. Comments, ideas and concepts were highlighted, and different quotes were compared and rearranged appropriate to the thematic content. The analysis involved constant moving back and forth between the data sets identifying frequency; specificity; emotions; extensiveness; big picture [25].

4   Results

The aim of our methodological approach has been to elicit Swedish seniors attitudes and perception of having their own robot. During the workshop the participants expressed enjoyment in participating. The positive experiences were validated by the 100 % response rate of the follow-up questionnaire. Ten out of fourteen participants answered that they participated in the workshop because of the importance of staying up to date with new technology developments. Four participants attended due to curiosity. When it comes to general technology adoption half the participants perceived themselves as early adopters while the rest did not. All participants answered in the follow-up questionnaire that they would gladly show the robot to friends and relatives and thirteen of the participants answered in the questionnaire that they liked the idea of having a robot. The themes emanating from the data analysis matched parts of the framework of the *Model of Adoption of Technology in Households* (MATH)[26]. According to the MATH framework, technology adoption is dependent on attitudinal beliefs, normative beliefs (not addressed in our study) and control beliefs. These themes are presented in more detail below.

Attitudinal Beliefs: The participants stated needs they wanted the robot to accommodate. They wanted it to do things they were unable to, such as reaching high and low, carrying heavy grocery bags, cleaning and dusting: *"I would like the robot to be able to reach high up in my kitchen cupboards because I can't do that anymore. I need to use a stool, which makes me feel unstable. Once I fell and sprained my foot."* and *"I drop loads of things on the floor which I can't pick up. Sometimes I use a gripper but it would be better if I could ask a robot to pick up and clean up the things I spill on the floor."*

The seniors were dissatisfied with the child-safety bottles and cans. They found it quite difficult, sometime impossible, to open them. They also wanted the robot to remind them about appointments, medications, planed visitors and trips: *"I would like the robot to remind me of things that I tend to forget. Even if I write things down I tend to forget them."* Misplaced keys, glasses and mobile phones were mentioned, as important objects, which the participants would like the robot to be informed on their whereabouts.

During the workshop it was clear that most participants believed owning a robot would increase their status and they thought their grandchildren would find their robot exciting. Hence, one lady said: *"I think my grandchildren would love if I had a robot but I wouldn't like them to touch it because they might break it."*

Control Beliefs: The participants felt that the robot had to be very easy to use to be adopted. All three groups in the workshop were asked how they would like to communicate with a robot. They frequently emphasized that they wanted to be the "boss" in their own home and be able to tell the robot what to do: *" I want to be able to turn it off when I like to"* and *"The robot should only do what the primary owner tells it to do."* They wanted to talk to the robot and use gestures that the robot could interpret: *"I had a stroke and I know what it's like when you're unable to speak. The robots need to offer different kinds of input as well as output modes. I want to be able to talk to it and interact with it by using a touch screen, speech or gestures"* This male participant had the experience of not being able to speak, write or hold anything. He is "back to normal" (his own words) but remembers how it felt to be trapped in his own body.

The participants described that their needs change day-to-day and that the robot has to adjust to this. They articulated that the robot has to be able to take care of itself and recharge when necessary. They could imagine teaching it about their objects and their home environment, but they did not want to spend too much time training it to work in their home. The robot had to be self-sufficient and add value to their lives by helping them carrying out monotonous and heavy tasks.

Some of the participants expressed fear of getting too close to a robot, and they could imagine that it may happen if the robot is sophisticated enough. The participants also expressed feelings of fear about robots replacing human contact. Some participants reported that their children and grandchildren were always occupied with their mobile phones when they met. They were afraid that if they had a robot their relatives would think that they did not need to visit since they had the company of a robot. They also raised fears that if the robot enabled visual telecommunication their relatives would think it was enough with remote interaction instead of physical visits. They also spoke of the anxiety of getting too dependent and attached to the robot: *"I'm afraid that robots will replace human contacts, although it is interesting to find out what a robot may be able to do."* On the other hand, several participants also mentioned that sometime a robot would be favoured over humans. They said compared to human help, the robot would not gossip and talk behind your back. Some participants stated they preferred having a robot helping them instead of an unknown person from a care facility: *"I would prefer a robot doing my cleaning instead of human help because then I didn't have to keep track of time and be at home"* and *"With a robot I know what to expect. When letting some unknown human in to your home you do not know what to expect."*

They seniors emphasized that the robot always has to work in order for them to trust it: *"It has to work all the time or else I wouldn't like to have one"* and *"At the train station, the ticket machine sometimes is broken and I have to go on the train without a ticket. On the train I can meet a human and explain why I haven't got a ticket. At home if I had a robot and became dependent on it, what would happen if it broke? What would I do?"*

The participants wanted the robot to be able to sound the alarm if something happened to them, for example, if they fell and could not get up. They said they wanted the robot to ask them before calling emergency or a relative. They did not want to be an unnecessary burden on their relatives or the social system.

Physical Space: The majority of the participants would not find it intrusive if the robot accompanied them into the bathroom and bedroom. They also said they would alter their homes to accommodate the robot: *"The house would have to be adjusted to the robot. I may do that if I knew it would help me a lot."*

Opinions seemed to be divided whether they liked the robot to keep them company while they ate and watched TV: *"When watching TV or listening to the radio it is only one-way communication. I would like it if the robot and I could have a two-way communication."*

Appearance: Participants stated that utility was more important than the appearance of the robot. This was further emphasized by the length of time spent on talking about what they would like the robot to do compared to the time spent talking about the appearance of the robot. They found it difficult to talk about the design of the robot without knowing its functionality. However, we managed to gain valuable insights regarding visual preferences of assistive robots. The participants agreed that if they had a robot, it had to look kind-hearted and it should not be too small nor too big: *"I do not want the robot to take up too much space in the room and I must be able to put it away into the closet"* During the "explore, look and feel phase" it was emphasized by the participants that it was crucial that the robot was easy to clean and, preferably, neutral colored to blend in with the home furniture and soft to touch. Most of them seemed to prefer a robot that had a mechanical-look (*"If I had a robot it has to look like a robot. I do not understand why they have to look like humans; they are machines so why can't they just look like machines?"*), except one senior man who wanted an attractive looking humanoid robot for company as well as sex.

5   Discussion

Our interest has been in explicating old adults Swedish seniors' attitudes, wishes and needs towards having their own robot. The benefits of providing a clear idea of modern robotics and what they can do in the beginning of the workshop was evident and brought the group together; it formed a common ground. Clark and Brennan's theory of grounding in communication that states the importance of mutual knowledge and mutual assumption support these findings [27]. This was further emphasized by the attention cards, which visualized the possibilities of assistive robots and opened up the discussions. The first person narrative texts on the cards helped the seniors focus and reflect on personally being in the situation illustrated. This is in contrast to previously reported work [28] that implies that seniors tend to lose focus and start cross talking in pairs of two and three during workshops and focus groups. The creative atmosphere was also fostered by providing lunch and time for social interaction.

Talking about the appearance with no regard to the functionality was hard. This is not to say that visual appearance is unimportant because it will differentiate one assistive robot from another if they have the same functionality [4]. The visual appearance will also affect the emotional and social relationship the seniors will form with the assistive robot [29]. Visual appearance is strongly correlated with the perceived trustworthiness of a product [30]. The seniors in our study stressed that the robot should not take up too much space, which confirms to some extent the findings of Wu et al. [13]. Our results indicate that the most important aspect for technology acceptance is the usefulness of the product. This is in line with the philosophy of the Task Fit Model [31]. It stresses the importance between technology and the task the user has to perform. When it comes to assistive technology the focus is on the tasks the users would like to perform. The functionality was emphasized as crucial for adoption of robots. Our findings indicate that seniors would like the robot to compensate for the perceived limitations of their physical and cognitive health status. The seniors, who participated in the study, would like robot assistance for physical tasks they felt were difficult or they couldn't do any more such as cleaning, carrying heavy grocery bags, fetching and picking up things from the floor and high up. The participants also empathized that they would like robot assistance for compensating cognitive limitations such as poor working memory capacity. To address these cognitive limitations the seniors would like the robot to remind them to take their medication, where they put their belongings and about appointments. These findings are in line with Beer et al. [12] and indicate that old adults would like an assistive robot to compensate and carry out difficult task they can no longer do. The participants also raised concerns about becoming too dependent on the robot and about its reliability.

Asking seniors about preferences for their own robot is not sufficient for a complete understanding of the user requirements since human activity cannot be reduced to separate scenarios, detached from the context and situations of use. Identifying needs and wants in respect to future technologies is hard since they may evolve and change over time in relation to the technology being developed.

6   Conclusion and Future Work

The aim of this study was to elicit Swedish seniors' attitudes, wishes and needs towards having their own robot, by involving them in the design process. In our workshop we have seen indications that: (1) the functionality of the robot is far more important than the appearance; (2) the usefulness will determine the acceptance of a robot; (3) seniors feel it is important to keep up to date with new technological developments; (4) assistive robots were not perceived as intrusive and having a robotic presence in the seniors' bathrooms and bedrooms was considered acceptable. These findings suggest that seniors are prepared to give assistive robots a try if the robot is perceived as useful.

The interdisciplinary nature of understanding assistive robots requires a multi-method approach. The workshop was the first step in our research on assistive robots and seniors. In the near future through an interactive multi-step design process, a design specification of a robot will be proposed, and a first prototype built. The prototype will be tested and evaluated with seniors in a lab setting. The findings will result in an improved design specification and a second prototype will be built and evaluated by users in their homes. By evaluating the use of a robot in seniors' homes, we hope to be able to answer if an assistive robot can accommodate their needs and wants as well as If and How seniors will use the robot at home.

Acknowledgements. We thank all the senior volunteers, and Eileen Deaner who provided helpful comments on previous versions of this document. This work is partially funded by the EC under FP7-ICT-288146 Hobbit and FP7-ICT-288173 Giraff+.

References

1. Lesnoff-Caravaglia, G.: Gerontechnology: Growing Old in a Technological Society. Charles C Thomas Publisher, LTD., Springfield (2007)
2. Young, J.E., Sung, J., Voida, A., Sharlin, E., Igarashi, T., Christensen, H.I., Grinter, R.E.: Evaluating Human-Robot Interaction: Focusing on the Holistic Interaction Experience. International Journal of Social Robotics 3(1), 53–67 (2011)
3. Young, J.E., Hawkins, R., Sharlin, E., Igarashi, T.: Toward acceptable domestic robots: Applying insights from social psychology. International Journal of Social Robotics 1(1), 95–108 (2009)
4. Norman, D.A.: Emotional design: Why we love (or hate) everyday things. Basic Books, New York (2003)
5. Massimi, M., Baecker, R.: Participatory Design Process with Older Users. In: Proc. Ubi-Coomp (2006)
6. Ehn, P.: Scandinavian design: On participation and skill. In: Participatory Design: Principles and Practices, pp. 41–77 (1993)
7. Koskinen, I., Zimmerman, J., Binder, T., Redstrom, J., Wensveen, S.: Design Research Through Practice: From the Lab, Field, and Showroom. Morgan Kaufmann, Waltham (2011)
8. Barrett, J., Kirk, S.: Running focus groups with elderly and disabled elderly participants. Applied Ergonomics 31(6), 621–629 (2000)
9. Lines, L., Hone, K.S.: Eliciting user requirements with older adults: lessons from the design of an interactive domestic alarm system. Universal Access in the Information Society 3(2), 141–148 (2004)

10. Östlund, B.: Silver Age Innovators: A New Approach to Old Users. In: The Silver Market Phenomenon, pp. 15–26. Springer, Heidelberg (2011)
11. Svanaes, D., Seland, G.: Putting the users center stage: role playing and low-fi prototyping enable end users to design mobile systems, pp. 479–486. ACM (2004)
12. Beer, J.M., Smarr, C.A., Chen, T.L., Prakash, A., Mitzner, T.L., Kemp, C.C., Rogers, W.A.: The domesticated robot: design guidelines for assisting older adults to age in place, pp. 335–342. ACM (2012)
13. Wu, Y.H., Fassert, C., Rigaud, A.S.: Designing robots for the elderly: Appearance issue and beyond. Archives of Gerontology and Geriatrics (2011)
14. Walters, M.L., Syrdal, D.S., Dautenhahn, K., Te, B.R., Koay, K.L.: Avoiding the uncanny valley: robot appearance, personality and consistency of behavior in an attention-seeking home scenario for a robot companion. J. Autonomous Robots 24(2), 159–178 (2008)
15. Mori, M.: The uncanny valley. Energy 7(4), 33–35 (1970)
16. Wada, K., Shibata, T., Saito, T., Tanie, K.: Analysis of factors that bring mental effects to elderly people in robot assisted activity, vol. 1152, pp. 1152–1157. IEEE (2002)
17. Shibata, T., Wada, K., Tanie, K.: Statistical analysis and comparison of questionnaire results of subjective evaluations of seal robot in Japan and UK, vol. 3153, pp. 3152–3157. IEEE (2003)
18. Vines, J., Blythe, M., Lindsay, S., Dunphy, P., Monk, A., Olivier, P.: Questionable concepts: critique as resource for designing with eighty somethings, pp. 1169–1178. ACM (2012)
19. Halskov, K., Dalsgård, P.: Inspiration card workshops. In: DIS 2006, pp. 2–11. ACM, New York (2006)
20. Lucero, A., Arrasvuori, J.: PLEX Cards: a source of inspiration when designing for playfulness. In: Proc. of Fun and Games 2010, pp. 28–37. ACM (2010)
21. Brandt, E., Messeter, J.: Facilitating collaboration through design games. In: Proc. Participatory design, vol. 1, pp. 121–131. ACM, New York (2004)
22. Heerink, M., Krose, B., Evers, V., Wielinga, B.: Measuring acceptance of an assistive social robot: a suggested toolkit, pp. 528–533. IEEE Press (2009)
23. Mollenkopf, H., Kaspar, R.: Elderly people's use and acceptance of information and communication technologies. Young Technologies in old Hands an International View on Senior Citizen's Utilization of ICT, DJØF, 41–58 (2005)
24. Braun, V., Clarke, V.: Using thematic analysis in psychology. Qualitative Research in Psychology 3(2), 77–101 (2006)
25. Krueger, R.A., Casey, M.A.: Focus groups: A practical guide for applied research. Sage (2009)
26. Brown, S.A., Venkatesh, V.: Model of adoption of technology in households: A baseline model test and extension incorporating household life cycle. MIS Quarterly, 399–426 (2005)
27. Clark, H.H., Brennan, S.E.: Grounding in communication. Perspectives on Socially Shared Cognition 13, 127–149 (1991)
28. Massimi, M., Baecker, R.M., Wu, M.: Using participatory activities with seniors to critique, build, and evaluate mobile phones. In: Proc. ASSETS 2007, pp. 155–162 (2007)
29. Forlizzi, J., DiSalvo, C., Gemperle, F.: Assistive robotics and an ecology of elders living independently in their homes. J. Human–Computer Interaction 19(1-2), 25–59 (2004)
30. Lindgaard, G., Dudek, C., Sen, D., Sumegi, L., Noonan, P.: An exploration of relations between visual appeal, trustworthiness and perceived usability of homepages. ACM Transactions on Computer-Human Interaction (TOCHI) 18(1), 1 (2011)
31. Goodhue, D.L.: Development and Measurement Validity of a TaskTechnology Fit Instrument for User Evaluations of Information System. Decision Sciences 29(1), 105–138 (1998)

How Social Robots Make Older Users Really Feel Well – A Method to Assess Users' Concepts of a Social Robotic Assistant

Tobias Körtner[1], Alexandra Schmid[1], Daliah Batko-Klein[1], Christoph Gisinger[1,2], Andreas Huber[3], Lara Lammer[3], and Markus Vincze[3]

[1] Academy for Ageing Research at Haus der Barmherzigkeit, Seeböckg. 30A, Vienna, Austria
{tobias.koertner,alexandra.schmid,daliah.batko-klein,
christoph.gisinger}@hausderbarmherzigkeit.at
[2] Donauuniversität Krems, Dr.-Karl-Dorrek-Straße 30, Krems, Austria
[3] ACIN, Vienna University of Technology, Gusshausstr. 27 , Vienna, Austria
{huber,lammer,vincze}@acin.tuwien.ac.at

Abstract. The present study explored a workshop method including questionnaires but also creative, implicit methods as a new way of uncovering users' implicit concepts of a helper and supporting creative answers by users. Eight older (70+) and ten younger (<70) participants collaborated in the workshops. They filled in a questionnaire and completed a picture association activity as well as a creative modelling unit. The word 'robot' was not used in the entire workshops to prevent users from directly thinking of robot stereotypes. Results demonstrated that picture associations cause a higher amount of answers regarding features of a 'helper' than direct questionnaire items. These results can be translated to the field of social robotics. According to the findings, users preferred a structure of the helper that featured arms, some kind of body and a head they could talk to. Most of all, picture associations played an important role in revealing the individual concepts of users. These results suggest that the method of implicit questioning is a useful additional approach in the assessment of user requirements and human-robot-interaction research.

Keywords: social robotics, human-robot interaction, assistive technology, user requirement assessment, methodology, support for older people.

1   Introduction

This paper focuses on a method in robotics for a special target-group. Due to an increasing number of older people across Europe [1], Assistive Technology becomes more and more an essential element to improve the quality of life of older people. One of the main reasons leading to a transfer to care facilities are falls and their consequences [2]. Safety therefore might be an important aspect for this user-group. However, acceptance from users might involve other features of a robot system than simply catering to safety needs.

S.S. Ge et al. (Eds.): ICSR 2012, LNAI 7621, pp. 138–147, 2012.

Interactions between humans and robots (HRI) are inherently present in all of robotics. As a result, designing robotic technology that not only initiates desirable interactions but also creates acceptance by humans is essential. Such work is interdisciplinary in nature, requiring contributions from cognitive science, linguistics, psychology, engineering, mathematics, and computer science [3].

User acceptance, described by Dillon as "the demonstrable willingness within a user group to employ technology for the task it is designed to support" [4], naturally involves people's personal beliefs and attitudes. Consequently, HRI should not ignore the individuality of each user. Personalization leads to more user-involvement, as could be demonstrated by [5]. Different motivations, knowledge or social background of users strongly influence the way a human behaves towards a robot. For an interactive system to be used by a great number of users, it needs to provide measures that enable users with special needs to work with the system. At the same time, it has to be ensured that personalized settings can be made for the system so that it becomes individualized [6]. This tendency of perceiving needs as an individualized issue has, for instance, already been identified in the health sector [7]. This also calls for suitable methods to learn more about users' attitudes and opinions. This paper focuses on a creative approach of picture associations to learn more about implicit notions of individual users. In a theoretical framework, the authors of [8] have identified parameters that influence the way humans interact with robots, using a new approach called Mutual Care.

Based on this approach, notions and opinions about what older users perceive to be helpful were investigated, and what kind of robotic helper they would accept in their home. A creative workshop method was designed, which is described in Chapter 3, focusing on implicit techniques to gain insight into users' individual notions. Chapter 2 briefly provides an overview of related work. Chapter 4 depicts the analysis and chapter 5 the results. Conclusions are discussed and future routes of investigation pointed out in chapter 6.

2   Related Work

Anthropomorphisation and the investigation of mental models are important topics in social robotics and human-robot interaction. Investigations on how people's mental models affect their interaction with robots showed that people may not interact with a robot in the same way as they do with a person, even if they have an identical estimate of the robot's and the person's factual knowledge [9]. The estimation of the robot's social knowledge seems to be a far more important factor for the interaction.

It follows that a scientific approach to individualisation of technology cannot work without involving the users, their individuality and thus also creative methods that allow each user to bring their individual features and ideas as input into research. Less standardised, or more specifically, implicit methods for the research of users' notions and attitudes seem not absolutely common yet. Most often, questionnaires are used (e.g. [10], [11]) or interviews [12], [13]. Wu et al. [14] chose an interesting approach of showing robot pictures to focus groups, yet explicitly asked what robots evoked in the participants minds. The approach of this paper rather tries to go the other way and learn more about implicit notions by avoiding the term 'robot'. Oestreicher & Eklundh worked with robot drawings in a questionnaire, asking participants to give their opinions on robot drawings and also to draw their own version of a domestic robot [15]. A study entitled "My friend the robot" presented various robot applications via pictures and videos to give users an impression of how robots could work in their home. Subsequently, a qualitative survey about these scenarios was conducted to find out about the participants' individual attitudes and level of acceptance [16].

Following the question how older users could accept help from a robotic assistant, another factor that has been identified is Mutual Care [8]. A social robot should be a helper. Coming from the Helper Theory in sociology [17], this new approach in robotics assumes that users' acceptance and well-being will increase, if they can also help their robot and are not simply dependent on the machine. Whether such a concept is shared by users is also part of the focus group or rather creative workshop-method described in the following chapter.

3   Method

3.1   Hypotheses

The emphasis was on finding a suitable method to research older users' personal opinions by focusing on their attitudes regarding a robotic assistant and to thus uncover implications concerning the properties and characteristics a social robot needs to have, in order to be accepted by the target group. Hypotheses concern two aspects, namely a suitable methodology and requirements of a social robot based on a user-centric approach.

1. It was assumed that especially older users who have limited experience with robot-technology might face difficulties when asked explicitly about robots. The workshop designed for this project constitutes a creative approach to gain information about rather unaffected notions and associations by users concerning a robotic assistant. Since questionnaire methods often already prime participants too much or guide them into an already preset direction, it hypothesized that a workshop applying not only questions, but also picture associations and creative modelling will lead to more personalized information from the users.

2. The workshop results furthermore not only serve as an indicator of the method's validity, but should also lead to information about what sort of robot could be acceptable for the target group in terms of functions and behaviour as well as design. When looking at more recent developments in robotics for the specific target group of older people (such as the quite successful therapeutic Paro [18]), it can be assumed that older people might prefer pet-like robots.

3.2   Sample and Procedure

In order to investigate users' attitudes and images of a helper or assistant at home, focus groups/workshops were organised. These took place at two different dates in March 2012 at the Haus der Barmherzigkeit, an Austrian care-institution, specializing in the field of geriatrics and also long-term care of patients with chronic diseases.

Workshop participants consisted of two groups. For the first workshop, a small sample of patients living at the Haus der Barmherzigkeit was recruited in close cooperation with therapists and caregivers who knew the patients best. Special attention was paid to the fact that participants were not cognitively impaired and still able to use their hands. This group of patients was referred to as primary users (PU).

Participants in the second workshop consisted of people who had a direct connection to the topic of "age and assistance at home", either from a professional point of view (medics, therapists), or as relatives of older people. Recruitment was performed by means of invitations that were handed out to private people and relatives of patients at the Haus der Barmherzigkeit or sent out via mail to relevant experts and other people working in a field that guaranteed experience with the issues of aging. Roughly, 50 participants were approached for this workshop, with finally 10 taking part. The rather broad-scale recruitment procedure led to a sample with quite different social and occupational backgrounds. This participant-group was referred to as secondary users (SU).

The total sample was 18 – 8 PU in the first workshop (5 female, 3 male) and 10 SU in the second workshop (6 female, 4 male). The average age of PU was 83 and that of SU 60.4 years.

Content of both workshops was mostly similar; the difference being that the group of SU could lead livelier group discussions and also use more materials for the modelling phase without instructions or assistance from the evaluators and moderators.

Each workshop worked with an evaluator-setting, where several evaluators were present to note and protocol answers and descriptions of the participants. After a brief introductory round, in which participants got to know the research-team and each other a bit more, the 'priming-phase' introduced the idea or concept of a helper at home.

The sequence of workshops was: group discussion – questionnaire – picture associations – drawing/modelling.

Several questions that were either discussed with the evaluator (in the primary user workshop) or within the group (SU) dealt with activities and areas in which the participants needed help (either when they still were living at home – PU – or in the future, in order to stay longer and autonomously at home – SU). The aim of those questions was to raise the awareness of factors that could help older people to stay longer in their own home, as well as to identify tasks a helper could perform at home. They also gave a first impression of individual needs among the participants. The users were also asked about characteristics the helper should have and characteristics/ways of behaviour it must not have. The Mutual Care approach was surveyed by questions about things the user would do for the helper (e.g. maintaining the helper, rewarding it, talking to it).

After these questions, a picture-association exercise followed. Every participant was asked to choose three to seven pictures out of 31 photographs from six preset categories. They were also asked to state the priority order of their chosen pictures. As a commonly used method in psychology (e.g. Rorschach, TAT) [19], pictures are considered to be a valid method for the detection of individual connotations and associations as well as unconscious motives, feelings and fantasies. The picture-associations in a user-centric design were assumed to lead to individual connotations from the users. Criteria for choosing the pictures were: which of the following pictures suit the helper and why?

During the picture associations, users were asked about the connotations linked to the picture and why they chose that particular picture; whether it was due to shape, characteristics or something else. The answer for every chosen picture was noted down by the evaluator. Afterwards, the participants also stated the rank of priority, to make it possible to later analyse which pictures were considered especially important by users and compare the respective connotations.

The workshops furthermore included a creative modelling-phase in which the participants were asked to model or draw their helper and give some details about its shape, colour, materials and texture, in order to gain rather detailed images of the individual helper.

3.3   Materials and Experimental Manipulation

For both workshops, participants were invited to a "workshop for imaginations and ideas", but no information was given that the actual purpose of the workshop was to gain information about a social robot.

Participants were given a basic description of the helper at the beginning. The term 'robot' was never used during the entire workshops, in order to avoid premature images of 'classic' robots from films or literature. Users should express their unaffected connotations of a 'helper' and not standard robot stereotypes. So, while media stereotypes were to be avoided, indeed the idea of a robot should be introduced in terms of a 'helper' with regards to the emphasis on mutuality of the 'Mutual care' approach. The written priming-description of a helper was: "*Imagine a helper (not human) who lives with you at home. It can move, search for objects, fetch small objects and assist in case of emergencies. It is also curious, hungry for knowledge, likes to know and learn more about its environment (flat, house) and about the person.*"

While this priming information might have triggered notions of something with at least one arm and/or hand, it was still left open for users whether they imagined some sort of cuddly animal or toy-like helper, since 'curious' or 'searching for objects' are also qualities that owners might mention in connection with their pets. Furthermore, the definition explicitly excluded a real human-being.

The categories for the picture associations were generated based on creatures and everyday objects that human beings might see as helpers. A brainstorming within the research team about what and who could be regarded as a helper led to the following picture categories: animals (e.g. dog, cat), persons (nurse, butler), nature (tree, flower), furniture (lamp, chest of drawers), technical devices (TV, telephone) and fantasy-creatures (genie).

The materials available for the description of the helper's texture (PU) included various materials ranging from structured to smooth and soft to hard (e.g.: foil, sandpaper, sponge, plush). The modelling phase for SU was more complex and provided the participants with a range of materials to actually build a small mock up of their helper (e.g.: plastic bottles, foil, different sorts of paper, artificial flowers and leaves, cardboard, wood, plastiline).

4   Analysis

The analysis focuses on the comparison between questions about characteristics of the helper and input from picture associations.

Table 1. Average number of answers on questions compared to picture associations (PU = primary users; SU = secondary users)

	Mean of characteristics - questionnaire	Standard deviation	Mean of characteristics - picture association	SD
PU (n= 8)	3.3	1.5	10.6	4.3
SU (n= 10)	2.6	1.7	11.4	5.8
Total (n= 18)	3.0	1.6	11.1	5.0

As could clearly be observed there is a marked difference in productivity between direct questions concerning the characteristics of the helper and mentions in a more 'open' instruction, like the picture associations. It was also observed that each participant mentioned more characteristics in the picture association than in the questionnaire item concerning characteristics. The difference is most distinct among the group of secondary users with a mean of 2.6 answers in the questionnaire as opposed to 11.4 answers in the picture association exercise. However, results are not significant, due to the small, exploratory sample size.

SU most often chose the nurse (60%), while PU preferred 'dog' and 'vacuum cleaner' (50%). The connotations stated by the participants show that the pictures are related to different concepts, sometimes even with a slight difference between PU and SU. The nurse, for instance, evokes individual connotations of health and care, but also feminine stereotypes, whereas the cat stands for independence, quietness and subtlety, yet is also liked for its soft fur by primary users.

Table 2. Pictures chosen by PU and SU with highest frequency

Picture	PU&SU (n=18)	PU (n=8)	SU (n=10)	Associations PU	Associations SU
Dog	8 (44.4%)	4 (50%)	4 (40%)	Animal-loving, giving joy, reliable partner, loyalty	Loyalty, obedience, companion, familiar
Nurse	8 (44.4%)	2 (25%)	6 (60%)	Health, security, should be pretty	High social competence (as a female quality), someone who listens, caring, always there for you
Vacuum cleaner	6 (33.3%)	4 (50%)	2 (20%)	Cleanliness, tidiness, order, feeling comfortable at home	Convenient, useful, easy to operate, help in the household and garden
Cat	6 (33.3%)	3 (37.5%)	3 (30%)	For cuddling, loyal, living creature, soft fur	Independent, quiet, not threatening, for cuddling
Chest	5 (27.8%)	1 (12.5%)	4 (40%)	Clean, helper should take care of furniture	For storing personal belongings, creates order, everything is easy to find
Laptop	5 (27.8%)	1 (12.5%)	4 (40%)	For communicating with outside world	Information, communication, virtual networking, internet, contact

5   Results

From the questions in the group discussion and in the questionnaire, the following findings were relevant: In terms of helpful functions, household (e.g. cleaning, cooking and fetching items from floor and/or shelf) and communication (phone calls, "having a contact person") were mentioned most. Care activities like help with bathing, lifting and walking support were also important for users. These findings complement findings from [20]. 94.4 % stated that they wanted to communicate with their helper by speech. All of the participants agreed that their helper should be happy and thus convey a feeling of happiness. 94.4 % would show their helper to family and friends. The most important field of assistance for primary and secondary users was bringing of objects (91.7%). Qualities of a helper that were most often mentioned in the questionnaire were "unobtrusive" and "communicative". 61.1% described their helper as being between 151 – 190cm in height.

In parallel to that, the majority of primary users created helpers with anthropomorphic designs, and most secondary users' helper models at least featured a structure with something head-like, arms, a torso and legs. In terms of materials, a soft surface was clearly preferred by most of the users (e.g. plush or foam rubber). Especially SU stressed the importance of an arm or some kind of gripper in their models. These results give first indications of what is needed from robotic assistants, in order to be perceived as useful for tasks in the home.

Fig. 1. Examples of helper mock ups by participants

It can be assumed from the analysis that the use of implicit methods (i.e. picture associations and modelling) in a user-centric design leads to highly individual connotations from the users and tends to generate more open answers from participants than items in a questionnaire. Connotations regarding a helper sometimes differ between primary and secondary users for the same picture, thus underlining the individuality of concepts. Even when some needs are universal like the need for a helper at home, the way of receiving this help is a matter of preference (person, robot, box, lamp, and fantasy-creature). Mutual Care as a concept could not be clarified from the results so far, yet the emphasis on joy and expressions of happiness by the helper can be interpreted as a first indicator in this direction. Personalisation (as has also been demonstrated by [5]) is indeed something, users seem to expect from a robotic assistant. A prototype of a Mutual Care-robot (ongoing development) will shed more light onto this principle. User trials also will include an observation of HRI in terms of a dialogue system (as is also illustrated in [21]).

6   Conclusions and Discussion

As these results indicate, it could be confirmed that the workshop-setting is an effective method to analyze individual attitudes and concepts by users. The usage of picture-associations makes it easier for participants to generate statements and verbalise their notions than a typical questionnaire item. This is especially helpful, if robot-stereotypes are to be avoided.

The definition of a helper might act as a confounding variable. Some characteristics chosen in the definition (e.g. 'curious') were chosen to introduce the Mutual Care approach. Other parts of the description could have led users to think of real human beings. Still, an outcome like having some sort of arm does not automatically suggest that the shape of the robot is meant to be humanoid.

From the data gained in the workshops, the robotic assistant for the target-group of older users, who are still able to live autonomously but need help in the household, has got anthropomorphic features – most importantly, an arm – but seems to be neither really like a human being nor like an actual animal. It should be easy to operate, preferably search and bring objects and be able to understand and utter speech. Its surface needs to be in some way soft and pleasant to touch. However, our hypothesis that the target-group might prefer smaller, pet-like helpers was not confirmed. Asked about the size of the helper, most users (11 out of 18) preferred a helper their own size or only a little smaller. Interestingly these preferences seem to contradict other findings like for instance [22]. There might be a difference between imagining a robot and interacting with a real one. The difference in connotations and mock ups between users indicates the necessity of adaptive systems that can be personalised.

One shortcoming of the presented study is the quite small sample of workshop participants. In order to receive more valid results about the method as well as notions of the helper, more workshops of this sort with a bigger sample and more PU would be necessary. Findings certainly would need a controlled experiment for evaluation of the validity of the implicit approaches described above.

Another aspect that still requires more research is order effects of the workshop. The questions regarding functions of the helper in the questionnaire might have primed users, so that they were influenced in the direction of a helper with arms. Changing the sequence in the workshop (First picture associations, then modelling and then questionnaire items) might lead to other results. It would be interesting to conduct the different methods with different participants and then compare them.

Also, the question remains how a number of individual opinions can be made significant. This issue certainly requires a more systematic evaluation of the picture association method used in the workshops with bigger samples.

For a refined implicit approach with picture associations, it may be interesting to ask participants to select pictures that they least prefer and explore those concepts as well.

Finally, further research in the field of users' connotations could lead to the identification of cluster groups. A tendency was observed that users, who selected the picture of the nurse in the picture associations, usually did not choose the cat or the vacuum-cleaner and vice versa. So, if associations of a person correspond to cluster A, they do not correspond to cluster B and the other way around. Thus, new insights into groups of users could be gained not only for our special target-group but in general. Such a method of clustering strongly depends on the variety of the given data as well as on the cluster number initialized by the analyst, so that further investigations with bigger samples and more refined picture association exercises are suggested.

Overall, the user-workshop/focus group presented in this paper can be considered a valid tool-kit in robotics for the assessment of users' (implicit) expectations, attitudes and also acceptance.

Acknowledgment. This work is partially funded by the European Commission under contract FP7-IST-288146 HOBBIT.

References

1. European Commission–Eurostat: Key figures on Europe 2007/2008 edition. Luxembourg: Office for Official Publications of the European Communities (2008)
2. Dias, N., Kempen, G., Todd, C.J.: The German version of the Falls Efficacy Scale-International Version (FES-I). Gerontol Geriatr 39, 297–300 (2006)

3. Goodrich, M.A., Schulz, A.C.: Human-robot interaction: a survey. Foundations and Trends in Human-Computer Interaction 1(3) (2007)
4. Dillon, A.: User acceptance of information technology. In: Karwowski, W. (ed.) Encyclopedia of Human Factors and Ergonomics. Taylor and Francis, London (2001)
5. Lee, M.K., Forlizzi, J., Kiesler, S., Rybski, P., Antanitis, J., Savetsila, S.: Personalization in HRI: A longitudinal field experiment. In: HRI 2012 Proceedings of the Seventh Annual ACM/IEEE International Conference on Human-Robot Interaction, pp. 319–326 (2012)
6. Heinecke, A.M.: Mensch-Computer-Interaktion Basiswissen für Entwickler und Gestalter, 2nd edn. Springer, Berlin (2012)
7. Vincenzi, C., Spirig, R.: Die Bedürfnisse der Patienten stehen im Mittelpunkt. Managed Care 8, 12–14 (2006)
8. Lammer, L., Huber, A., Zagler, W., Vincze, M.: Mutual-Care: Users will love their imperfect social assistive robots. Work-In-Progress Proceedings of the International Conference on Social Robotics 2011, Amsterdam, the Netherlands, November 24- 25 (2011)
9. Lee, S., Lau, I., Kiesler, S., Chiu, C.: Human Mental Models of Humanoid Robots. In: Proceedings of the IEEE International Conference on Robotics and Automation (2005)
10. Heerink, M., Kröse, B., Evers, V., Wielinga, B.: Relating conversational expressiveness to social presence and acceptance of an assistive social robot. Springerlink 14(1), 77–84 (2009)
11. Kuo, I.H., Rabindran, J.M., Broadbent, E., Lee, Y.I., Kerse, N., Stafford, R.M.Q., MacDonald, B.A.: Age and gender factors in user acceptance of healthcare robots. The University of Auckland, New Zealand (2009)
12. Beer, J.M., Smarr, C.A., Chen, T.L., Prakash, A., Mitzner, T.L., Kemp, C.C., Rogers, W.A.: The domesticated robot: design guidelines for assisting older adults to age in place. In: HRI 2012 Proceedings of the Seventh Annual ACM/IEEE International Conference on Human -Robot Interaction, pp. 335–342 (2012)
13. Hirsch, T., Forlizzi, J., Hyder, E., Goetz, J., Kurtz, C., Stroback, J.: The ELDER project: social, emotional, and environmental factors in the design of eldercare technologies. In: CUU 2000 Proceedings on the 2000 Conference on Universal Usability, pp. 72–79 (2000)
14. Wu, Y.H., Fassert, C., Rigaud, A.-S.: Designing robots fort he elderly: appearance issue and beyond. Archives of Gerontology and Geriatrics 54, 121–126 (2012)
15. Oestreicher, L., Severinson-Eklundh, K.: User Expectations on Human-Robot Cooperation. In: The 15th IEEE International Symposium on Robot and Human Interactive Communication, pp. 91–96 (2006)
16. Meyer, S.: Mein Freund der Roboter. Servicerobotik für ältere Menschen - eine Antwort auf den demographischen Wandel? Institut für Sozialforschung und Projektberatung GmbH, Berlin (2011)
17. Riessman, F.: The 'helper' therapy principle. Social Work 10(2), 27–32 (1965)
18. Paro Therapeutic Robot, http://www.parorobots.com
19. Murray, H.A.: Thematic Apperception Test. Harvard University Press, Cambridge (1943)
20. Broadbent, E., Tamagawa, R., Kerse, N., Knock, B., Patience, A., MacDonald, B.: Retirement home staff and residents' preferences for healthcare robots. In: The 18th IEEE International Symposium on Robot and Human Interactive Communication, RO- MAN, pp. 645–650 (2009)
21. Mason, M., Lopes, M.: Robot self-initiative and personalization by learning through repeated interactions. In: HRI 2011 Proceedings of the 6th International Conference on Human-Robot Interaction, pp. 433–440 (2011)
22. Broadbent, E., Lee, Y.I., Stafford, R.Q., Han Kuo, I., MacDonald, B.A.: Mental Schemas of Robots as more Human-like are associated with higher blood pressure and negative emotions in a human-robot interaction. International Journal of Social Robotics 3(3), 291–297 (2011)

Identifying Specific Reasons Behind Unmet Needs May Inform More Specific Eldercare Robot Design

Rebecca Q. Stafford[1], Bruce A. MacDonald[2], and Elizabeth Broadbent[1]

[1] Department of Psychological Medicine, The University of Auckland
[2] Department of Computer and Electrical Engineering,
The University of Auckland, New Zealand
r.stafford@auckland.ac.nz

Abstract. Many countries are facing aging and aged populations and a shortage of eldercare resources. Eldercare robots have been proposed to help close this resource gap. Prevalence of eldercare robots may be enhanced by more acceptable robot design. Current assistive robot design guidelines are general and consequently difficult to translate into specific acceptable design. This paper proposes a method for developing more specific eldercare robot design guidelines. Technology acceptance models suggest acceptable robots need to be perceived as useful as well as easy to use. As older people often have high levels of unmet need, knowledge of the needs of older people and other eldercare stakeholders can suggest how robots could be usefully deployed. It is further proposed that determining the specific reasons why eldercare-needs are unmet may help lead to more specific design guidelines for eldercare robot form and function, as well as the design of robot marketing, distribution and deployment strategies.

Keywords: robots, older people, needs, HRI, technology acceptance, user-centered design.

1 Introduction

Many countries are facing aging and aged populations [1] combined with a shortage of healthcare professionals [2]. Eldercare robots may help mitigate this shortfall in eldercare resources [3]. A key issue is ensuring that the robots are acceptable to users. While there are existing general guidelines for acceptable eldercare robot design, their very generality can make them difficult to translate into specific acceptable designs [4, 5]. This paper proposes that examining the underlying reasons for unmet eldercare-needs may help refine the design problem and inform more specific robot design guidelines. This paper further examines some methodological limitations inherent in eldercare robot design research and suggests ways of circumventing them.

The paper is divided into six sections. First, reasons why eldercare robots are not yet prevalent are explored, including low acceptance. Two dominant technology acceptance models are then described to see what factors are relevant to eldercare robot acceptance. The next section describes the range and methodology issues of robot design guidelines that have already been developed to promote eldercare robot acceptance, including matching user-needs to robot functionalities. Then related work

S.S. Ge et al. (Eds.): ICSR 2012, LNAI 7621, pp. 148–157, 2012.
© Springer-Verlag Berlin Heidelberg 2012

in psychology and health are reviewed - focusing on assessment of elder-needs. Finally, to illustrate the concepts discussed, reasons for unmet eldercare-needs and their potential for translation into robot design are examined using the example of incontinence. Recommendations for developing more specific and acceptable robot designs are then made.

1.1   Why Are Eldercare Robots Not Prevalent?

Eldercare robots can be described as assistive robots that aim to enhance the physical and/or mental health of an older person, such that their quality of life is maintained or enhanced. Acceptance of eldercare robots is defined as the robot being willingly incorporated into the person's life [6]. There are successful eldercare robots. The most notable arguably being the companion seal robot Paro, e.g. [7]. However while relatively few eldercare robots have been presented to the market, some have not met with commercial success [8, 9].

Human-robot interaction (HRI) researchers have indicated reasons for the lack of eldercare robots. Reasons include: autonomous assistive robots must manage more uncertain environments compared with industrial robots [10], making them more difficult to build safely. People involved in the eldercare environment, such as caregivers or family, may not be accepting of robots [11]. The cost of robots can be prohibitive to potential purchasers, especially when perceived benefits are inadequate [9]. Older people can be less accepting of novel technologies than younger people [12]. Sometimes potentially useful assistive devices are not accepted by older users as the product's design does not make the benefits of use clear to them [13].

In some instances, poor uptake and discontinued use of eldercare assistive devices (including robotics) may result from technology design being overly product-driven and insufficiently user-driven [5, 9, 12, 14, 15]. User-driven design may be more costly up front, but a review of user-centered IT design concluded any additional costs appear reasonable in terms of product success and user acceptance [16].

In order to try to increase eldercare robot acceptance, it is useful to consider technology acceptance models.

1.2   Technology Acceptance Models

Technology acceptance models (TAM) specify variables that increase or decrease user acceptance of technology. The basic but seminal TAM proposed by Davis in 1989 [17] provides two major determinants of technology acceptance; 'perceived ease of use' and 'perceived usefulness'. Davis' TAM was merged with eight other acceptance models to formulate the Unified Theory of Acceptance and Use of Technology model (UTAUT) [18]. The four primary UTAUT predictors of intentions to use information technology are; perceived ease of use, perceived usefulness, social influence, and facilitating conditions. User variables, such as age and technology experience, were also included. 'Voluntariness of use' was also added in an attempt to redress self-selection confounds. While the UTAUT has been employed in an eldercare robot context [19], current technology models may be limited in usefulness for robot design, due to inability to explain *how* particular variables predict technology acceptance [20].

The next section provides examples of existing eldercare robot design guidelines that have been proposed in order to increase acceptance. Some limitations to the methods used to determine these guidelines are discussed.

1.3   Robot Design Guidelines Issues

The concept of 'eldercare robot design' is not restricted to the design of robot hardware and software; rather it includes all aspects of robot design from early concept, the robot's form and functionality, marketing, distribution, and deployment. HRI researchers have provided numerous assistive robot design guidelines. While providing valuable information for an emerging field, many guidelines are theoretical, general, untested [5] and/or have not been shown to increase acceptance [21].

Guideline examples include; assistive robots should be designed to be customizable [13, 22], manifest social abilities [21], have good error recovery [4, 22], and match the users' needs [6]. Eldercare robots should be designed to be small [23], slow-moving, and machinelike [11, 23]. They should promote elder independence in balance with human connectedness, and avoid stigma [13, 24]. Eldercare robots should look like familiar appliances to 'afford' ease of use [13].

Preferred robot-tasks also suggest robot design guidelines. A focus group study showed independent-living older people most preferred a robot to clean, fetch and organize [3]. In an assisted-living setting, a questionnaire of preferred robot tasks was designed based on focus groups conducted with older people, caregivers and managers [25]. Administration of the resulting questionnaire showed the most preferred robot tasks included detecting falls, monitoring peoples' location, lifting people and heavy objects, and switching appliances on and off.

Two well known examples of assistive robots with different design approaches are MOVAID and Care-O-bot. MOVAID [26] was based on the inclusive 'design-for-all' principles of Universal Design. Intended users were both disabled and older people. During initial design-scoping interviews, disabled people, their families and carers were asked about their needs for general technical assistance. Three key tasks identified for MOVAID were heating and serving food, cleaning kitchen surfaces, and removing dirty bed sheets. A dominant design rationale for Care-O-bot3 [27] was avoidance of an anthropomorphic appearance. Target users were derived from scenario-based design methods and were described as 'techies and soccer moms'. The minimum user criterion was familiarity with technologies such as digital cameras. Since conception Care-O-bot3 has been trialed in assistive-living facilities [28].

The robot design guidelines originate from a variety of methodologies. These include literature reviews, previous research, focus groups, ethnography, semi-structured interviews, and questionnaires. Possible methodological limitations include participants responding to closed questionnaires of possible robot tasks and appearances e.g. [3]. A closed list may reflect researcher bias as well as constraining peoples' reports of what tasks they would like robots to do [29]. Focus groups obtain data relatively quickly, but participants may not disclose information through embarrassment or stigma. It may be difficult to access people's unconscious attitudes through direct questions [30].

In assessing generalisability of robot design guidelines it is useful to examine the methodology and questions the guidelines are derived from. Some studies provide this information e.g.[25, 31]. Some studies do not e.g.[3]. Some measures have been developed with younger participants e.g. [32], which may not generalise well to the design of robots for older people [33]. However older people are a heterogeneous population themselves. These differences can be generational, educational, gender, cultural, functional, individual and/or environmental. Therefore robot design measures may also have limited generalisability if developed with older participants that differ from the target older users. For example; older people who are living independently may have different technology and eldercare-needs from people in assisted-living [4].

As seen in the CREATE Model of Technology and Aging [4] older people tend to have a variety of eldercare support stakeholders. These can include the older person, caregivers, family, service providers, robot purchasers, and even robot research funding agencies. Therefore, acceptance of the robot by a range of eldercare stakeholders may be important to wider commercial acceptance. For example, caregivers can be fearful of losing their jobs to robots [11] and purchasers of eldercare robots are likely to be family or service providers rather than the older user [9]. Some robot design guidelines have been developed without consideration of the needs of eldercare stakeholders other than the older user, e.g.[3], although some have, e.g. [11].

Methodological issues aside, many robot design guidelines are difficult to convert into specific robot designs because they are too broad. Fisk et al.[4] acknowledge this design problem and ascribe it to the difficulty of providing specific robot design guidelines that suit all contexts in the variable and complex eldercare environment.

There may be ways to refine the design problem. In a series of eldercare robot acceptance studies, Heerink et al.[19] found perceived usefulness was the strongest predictor of intention to use the robot. People may perceive a product as useful when they see it as meeting an interest or need [5] and consequently be more likely to accept it. Therefore incorporating a greater understanding of user needs into the design process may aid development of more specific robot design guidelines [3, 24].

However, despite calls for more user-needs assessment to facilitate robot design, HRI researchers are often referring to assessment of users' technology usability needs (i.e. how easy or difficult the technology is to use) e.g. [4] rather than assessing users' individual needs (i.e. companionship, hygiene, hydration, finance, accommodation etc.). Similarly there are calls for user involvement early in the design process [26, 33]. Some HRI studies do employ potential users early at the conceptual stage of design, e.g. [34, 11]. But for other studies 'early' user involvement means at the usability testing stage, not the conceptual stage, e.g.[4, 28]. Usability is a critical but insufficient precursor to technology acceptance.

There are further issues with user-centered design as commonly deployed in eldercare robot research. Robot design studies often assess what tasks potential users would like an eldercare robot to do. Responses to that question have important implications for acceptance, but it is a different question from 'what are the individual needs of the potential user group?' The second question removes the robot from the equation so answers become less constrained by real or perceived technology capabilities or fears. The difference between these research questions is described by the term 'naïve consumer'. The term refers to the challenge of soliciting peoples' opinions on products of which they have little or no experience: as has been noted in eldercare HRI studies [3, 11].

There are several implications of the naïve consumer issue in robot design research. Through lack of experience of robots, robot-naïve participants may not think to request a potentially useful robot functionality that would meet some need. Conversely, they may reject the idea of robots performing particular tasks, but change their minds with actual experience. Older people reported improved attitudes towards a health robot after only a half hour interaction [35] and improved attitudes to previously disliked assistive devices after actual use [13]. Consequently, robot design preferences expressed by robot-naïve participants should be interpreted in context.

There is merit in each of these robot design approaches. Due to unique data captured by different methodologies, triangulation of varied research methods in HRI is advised for comprehensive data capture [36]. However, assessment of the individual needs of potential eldercare robot stakeholders, independent of the product-driven concept of an eldercare robot, should be included in the methodology mix. This may assist in circumventing the limitations inherent in the naïve consumer issue.

Consideration of the literature from psychology and health about eldercare-needs helps to inform robotic designers about further potential design issues.

1.4   Eldercare-Needs and Needs Assessment

Need is a psychological feature that arouses an organism to action toward a goal, giving purpose and direction to behavior. Maslow's seminal theory on human needs proposed a pyramid shaped model with survival needs on the bottom, such as food and shelter. These basic needs must be satisfied before a human can reach the more meaningful self-actualisation needs at the pyramid pinnacle [37]. Older people often have many unmet needs. Identifying the most important needs may help narrow the design process for acceptable eldercare robots [5].

Several HRI researchers have investigated how older people prioritise need. Giuliani et al.[38] found older people ranked theoretical elder-needs in accordance with Maslow's hierarchical needs theory. However, an investigation of elder-needs priorities via a combination of literature reviews, focus groups, observation, and interviews found no clear ranking; rather older peoples' ranking of the importance of their own needs varied with their personal circumstances [5].

Two widely used elder-needs questionnaires are Activities of Daily Living [ADLs: 39] and the Instrumental Activities of Daily Living [IADLs:40]. ADLs assess limitations in daily living such as bathing, transfer from bed, and toileting. IADLs assess limitations in routine activities such as shopping, housekeeping and using the telephone. Independently living older people tend to be high in IADL needs only. People in assisted-living facilities tend to be high in both IADLs and ADLs. Both these measures assess met and unmet elder needs, but not partially-met needs. Carer needs are not assessed.

A more recent and well-validated measure of elder-needs is the Camberwell Assessment of Need for the Elderly [CANE:41]. The CANE contains the 24 elder-needs and two carer needs that research determined most important. The elder-needs items include accommodation, food, household skills, self-care, daytime activities, physical and mental health, information, deliberate and accidental self-harm, abuse/neglect, behaviour, alcohol, drugs, company, intimate relationships, caring for someone else, mobility/transport, money, memory, eyesight/hearing, and continence. The two carer items are information and psychological distress. The CANE assesses the three levels of 'need status'; whether the need is met, unmet or partially met.

Clarifying need status – met, unmet or partially met, is typically undefined in the literature [42], and this is also true for HRI papers. For example, based on the premise that many people snack, Lee et al. [43] designed a Snackbot for office workers in an office context. However, it was unclear whether office staff had snacking needs that were not already met by nearby vending machines or cafes, and no analysis showed how the robot could better meet their unmet or partially-met snacking needs.

Walters et al. [42] assessed unmet eldercare needs and help-seeking amongst a UK sample. The CANE was combined with semi-structured interviews. The three highest levels of unmet needs were found to relate to incontinence, accommodation, and psychological distress. Both older people and carers were more likely to both seek and be offered help for mobility issues; compared with incontinence, psychological distress, eyesight, memory, accommodation problems, and loneliness.

Unfortunately determining unmet or partially-unmet needs is rarely straightforward [30]. Needs assessment can be confounded by older people being unwilling or unable to express their needs. A UK elder-needs study [42] found help had been sought by older people in only 24% of cases of identified unmet needs. Reasons for not seeking help included people being resigned to their situation: while identifying a need they did not intend to do anything about it. Older people may not acknowledge needs such as loneliness or disability due to stoicism, pride and/or stigma [24]. Fear of institutionalization is another reason older people may under-report need [31].

Some underreporting of need is less deliberate. Elder-needs can fluctuate rapidly alongside fluctuating mental and physical health. Consequently older peoples' perceptions of their capabilities (and therefore their ability to accurately report their needs) are often misaligned with their actual capabilities [24]. Habituation to the inconvenience of both unmet and partially-met needs may also interfere with conscious recognition, and therefore reporting, of need [24, 31].

Identification of eldercare-needs such as independence, incontinence, and assistance with chores provide indications for acceptable eldercare robot design [4], as do insights into elder-needs barriers such as stigma. However, these elder-needs design guidelines are still insufficiently specific. For example, a study identified elder-loneliness as a high priority issue [44]; however it is unclear whether the self-reported loneliness resulted from the death of a spouse or friends, insufficient contact with family, and/or being housebound. And if an older person is housebound….why? Is it lack of transport, or physical or mental disability? The specific reasons needs are unmet have implications for designing technology to match needs. Consequently a deeper understanding of the reasons for unmet elder-needs is recommended to further refine the design problem [38]. As an example, the next subsection explores this concept with elder-incontinence needs.

1.5   Identification of Reasons for Unmet Specific Needs for More Specific Design

Incontinence is a common and potentially disabling issue for older people. Despite incontinence support being readily available through the UK public healthcare system many older people are not using these resources and unnecessarily suffering the physical and psychological consequences of incontinence [31].

Horrocks et al.[31] identified many barriers to incontinence help in 20 older people aged 66-94 years through semi-structured interviews. Barriers included a generational reluctance to discuss personal and bodily functions. There were patient/doctor gender interactions. Older women preferred a female doctor; older men had no preference. Unlike women, older men actively disliked incontinence pads. Female-dominated incontinence product advertising meant both incontinence and incontinence products were perceived as 'women's problems' only.

Further findings included the association of incontinence stigma with distress. Distress often led to painstaking concealment of incontinence problems [31] (However elders less distressed by their incontinence were also less likely to bother seeking help). There were also themes of 'not wanting to bother' busy doctors with 'trivial' incontinence complaints. House-bound participants were missing viewing incontinence information leaflets at health clinics. Self-management strategies for urinary leakage, such as restricting social activities, degraded the older person's quality of life. Some participants may have impaired their health by restricting fluid intake and altering medication regimes; especially reducing consumption of diuretics.

Opportunities for robots to overcome incontinence-needs barriers may be seen in this in-depth analysis. For example, older people may be more willing to seek information about embarrassing unmet needs from a robot than a human. People are also less likely to feel they are 'bothering' a machine [45]. A robot software programme could present solutions to common unmet elder-needs such as incontinence. Such a programme could combine understanding of incontinence needs and needs-barriers with input from psychogerontologists to reduce stigma and psychological distress.

There are further benefits of needs-technology matching. The ready availability of resources on a healthcare robot may be advantageous to housebound people. Understanding individual differences in eldercare stakeholder needs and need-barriers can guide customization. With regard to gender differences; incontinence information could be presented via a robot's monitor to older women in a female persona. Men (and women) could be offered a choice of robot persona gender. To raise male awareness of incontinence and solutions; information could be developed for robotic presentation using older male models. In marketing the robot to older people, the non-stigmatizing nature of intimate resources available via the robot could be discretely emphasized, as could the benefits of improved continence such as increased independence. In marketing the robot to family purchasers, the benefits of enhanced elder-independence and quality of life through improved continence could be emphasised, and any financial benefits of prophylactic healthcare emphasised to service provider purchasers.

The above suggestions for more specific robot guidelines for elder-incontinence are an example only. Beyond basic design principles, much eldercare robot design may be context dependent. Existing research on eldercare needs and need-barriers should be assessed for generalisability to the particular target robot stakeholder group. The above example is based on a 2004 British study of community-living people aged 66-94 which might not generalise well to, for example, a present day cohort of 80 + year old people in assisted-living facilities in a different country.

Recommendations for integrating these eldercare needs issues into more specific robot design guidelines are listed next.

2   Recommendations for More Specific Eldercare Robot Design

1. That stakeholder eldercare-needs and needs-barriers be incorporated early (at the conceptual stage rather than the user-testing stage) in the robot design process. Fewer costly design iterations may be required [16].
2. One size will probably not fit all. Identify the specific context for the eldercare robot – independent-living, assisted-living, hospital etc. Identify key target stakeholders. Identify eldercare needs of different types of stakeholders.
3. Review the eldercare-needs literature. Assess specific reasons why specific needs of eldercare stakeholders are unmet, partially-unmet or met. Incorporate all key eldercare-needs into eldercare robot design, e.g. it is of limited use if an otherwise useful incontinence software programme is stigmatising.
4. Evaluate the methodology of relevant eldercare-needs literature for generalisability to the target stakeholders.
5. If relevant literature cannot be found, it may be advisable to conduct a separate study assessing stakeholders' eldercare-needs and needs-barriers - using participants' matched to the target stakeholders.
6. Use data triangulation when assessing eldercare-needs and specific needs-barriers. As more 'open' methodologies, such as ethnography, observation, semi-structured interviews etc. may be effective for identifying latent elder-needs, these should be included in the methodology mix [16]. Feedback from carers, families etc. on their perceptions of elder-needs can help fill gaps in self-reports of need from elders.
7. Translate specific reasons for unmet needs into more specific robot design guidelines. HRI researchers can then better assess what robot aspects can be made available, designed, or modified to meet those needs and address need-barriers.
8. Integrate these guidelines into all aspects of eldercare robot design – including robot form and function, marketing, recruitment, distribution, and deployment.

3   Conclusion

Designing acceptable eldercare robots is a complex multifactorial and multidisciplinary task. This paper highlights the importance of research conducted into reasons for high rates of unmet eldercare-needs to increase awareness of these issues amongst roboticists. The individual issues are not new, but this paper combines an understanding of eldercare-needs and needs-barriers, with an understanding of associated methodological issues. This combined approach may aid roboticists in developing more specific and acceptable eldercare robot design guidelines.

References

1. United Nations: World Population Prospects: The 2006 revision. United Nations, New York (2006)
2. Super, N.: Who Will Be There to Care? The Growing Gap Between Caregiver Supply and Demand. National Health Policy Forum. George Washington University, Washington DC (2002)

3. Beer, J.M., Smarr, C.A., Chen, T.L., Prakash, A., Mitzner, T.L., Kemp, C.C., Rogers, W.A.: The Domesticated Robot: Design Guidelines for Assisting Older Adults to Age in Place. In: 7th ACM/IEEE International Conference on Human-Robot Interaction, pp. 335–342 (2012)

4. Fisk, A.D., Rogers, W.A., Charness, N., Sharit, J.: Designing for Older Adults: Principles and Creative Human Factors Approaches. CRC (2009)

5. Maciuszek, D., Aberg, J., Shahmehri, N.: What Help do Older People Need?: Constructing a Functional Design Space of Electronic Assistive Technology Applications. In: 7th International SIGACCESS Conference on Computers and Accessibility, pp. 4–11. ACM, USA (2005)

6. Broadbent, E., Stafford, R., MacDonald, B.: Acceptance of Healthcare Robots for the Older Population: Review and Future Directions. Int. J. Social Robotics, 1–12 (2009)

7. Shibata, T., Kawaguchi, Y., Wada, K.: Investigation on People living with Seal Robot at home. Int. J. Social Robotics, 1–11 (2011)

8. Robotics Today, http://waziwazi.com/taxonomy/term/214

9. Mahoney, R.: Robotic Products for Rehabilitation: Status and Strategy. In: International Conference on Rehabilitation Robotics, Bath, UK, vol. 97, pp. 12–22 (1997)

10. Breazeal, C.: Robot in Society: Friend or Appliance. In: Autonomous Agents Workshop on Emotion-Based Agent Architectures, Seattle, WA, pp. 18–26 (1999)

11. Broadbent, E., Tamagawa, R., Kerse, N., Knock, B., Patience, A., MacDonald, B.: Retirement Home Staff and Residents' Preferences for Healthcare Robots. In: 18th IEEE International Symposium on Robot and Human Communication, Japan (2009)

12. Flandorfer, P.: Population Ageing and Socially Assistive Robots for Elderly Persons. Int. J. of Population Research 2012, 1–13 (2012)

13. Forlizzi, J., DiSalvo, C., Gemperle, F.: Assistive Robotics and an Ecology of Elders Living Independently in their Homes. In: 13th International Conference on Human-Computer Interaction. Part II: Novel Interaction Methods and Techniques, pp. 25–59 (2004)

14. Gardner, L., Powell, L., Page, M.: An Appraisal of a Selection of Products Currently Available to Older Consumers. Applied Ergonomics 24, 35–39 (1993)

15. Keates, S., Clarkson, P.J., Robinson, P.: Developing a Practical Inclusive Interface Design Approach. Interacting with Computers 14, 271–299 (2002)

16. Kujala, S.: User Involvement: A Review of the Benefits and Challenges. Behaviour & Information Technology 22, 1–16 (2003)

17. Davis, F.D.: User Acceptance of Information Technology: System Characteristics, User Perceptions and Behavioral Impacts. Int. J. of Man-Machine Studies 38, 475–487 (1989)

18. Venkatesh, V., Morris, M.G., Davis, G.B., Davis, F.D.: User Acceptance of Information Technology: Toward a Unified View. Mis. Quarterly, 425–478 (2003)

19. Heerink, M., Kröse, B., Evers, V., Wielinga, B.: Assessing Acceptance of Assistive Social Agent Technology by Older Adults. Int. J. Social Robotics, 1–15 (2010)

20. Bagozzi, R.P.: The Legacy of the Technology Acceptance Model and a Proposal for a Paradigm Shift. J. of the Ass. for Information Systems 8, 244–254 (2007)

21. Heerink, M., Krose, B., Evers, V., Wielinga, B.: The Influence of a Robot's Social Abilities on Acceptance by Elderly Users. In: 15th IEEE International Symposium on Robot and Human Interactive Communication, ROMAN, pp. 521–526 (2006)

22. Kuo, I.-H., Broadbent, E., MacDonald, B.: Designing a Robotic Assistant for Healthcare Applications. In: The 7th Conference of Health Informatics, Rotorua, New Zealand (2008)

23. Scopelliti, M., Giuliani, M.V., Fornara, F.: Robots in a Domestic Setting: A Psychological Approach. Universal Access in the Information Society 4, 146–155 (2005)

24. Hirsch, T., Forlizzi, J., Hyder, E., Goetz, J., Kurtz, C., Stroback, J.: The ELDer project: Social, Emotional, and Environmental Factors in the Design of Eldercare Technologies. In: 2000 Conference on Universal Usability, pp. 72–79. ACM (2000)

25. Broadbent, E., Tamagawa, R., Patience, A., Knock, B., Kerse, N., Day, K., MacDonald, B.A.: Attitudes towards Healthcare Robots in a Retirement Village. Aust. J. Ageing. 31, 115–120 (2011)

26. Dario, P., Guglielmelli, E., Laschi, C., Teti, G.: MOVAID: A Personal Robot in Everyday Life of Disabled and Elderly people. Technology and Disability J. 10, 77–93 (1999)
27. Parlitz, C., HÃgele, M., Klein, P., Seifert, J., Dautenhahn, K.: Care-O-bot3- Rationale for Human-Robot Interaction Design. In: 39th International Symposium on Robotics (ISR), Korea, pp. 275–280 (2008)
28. Fraunhofer: Service Robots in Nursing Homes - Popular among Residents and Carers Alike, http://www.care-o-bot.de/Produktblaetter/ WiMi-Care_Serviceroboter_eng.pdf
29. Wu, Y.H., Fassert, C., Rigaud, A.S.: Designing Robots for the Elderly: Appearance Issues and Beyond. Arch. Gerontology & Geriatrics 54, 121–126 (2011)
30. Sixsmith, A., Sixsmith, J.: Smart Care Technologies: Meeting Whose Needs? J. Telemedicine & Telecare 6, 190–192 (2000)
31. Horrocks, S., Somerset, M., Stoddart, H., Peters, T.J.: What Prevents Older People from Seeking Treatment for Urinary Incontinence? Family Practice 21, 689–696 (2004)
32. Ray, C., Mondada, F., Siegwart, R.: What do people expect from robots? In: IEEE/RSJ International Conference on Intelligent Robots and Systems, pp. 3816–3821 (2008)
33. Rogers, W.A., Fisk, A.D.: Toward a Psychological Science of Advanced Technology Design for Older Adults. Js. Gerontology Series B 65, 645–653 (2010)
34. Sung, J.Y., Christensen, H.I., Grinter, R.E.: Sketching the Future: Assessing User Needs for Domestic Robots. In: 18th IEEE International Symposium on Robot and Human Interactive Communication RO-MAN (2009)
35. Stafford, R.Q., Broadbent, E., Jayawardena, C., Unger, U., Kuo, I.H., Igic, A., Wong, R., Kerse, N., Watson, C., MacDonald, B.A.: Improved Robot Attitudes and Emotions at a Retirement Home After Meeting a Robot. In: International Symposium on Robots and Human Interaction, pp. 82–87. IEEE, Viareggio (2010)
36. Bethel, C.L., Murphy, R.R.: Review of Human Studies Methods in HRI and Recommendations. Int. J. of Social Robotics, 1–13 (2010)
37. Maslow, A.H.: A Theory of Human Motivation. Psych. Review 50, 370–396 (1943)
38. Giuliani, M.V., Scopelliti, M., Fornara, F.: Elderly People at Home: Technological Help in Everyday Activities. In: IEEE International Workshop on Robots and Human Interactive Communication, USA, pp. 365–370 (2005)
39. Katz, S., Akpom, C.A.: A Measure of Primary Sociobiological Functions. Int. J. of Health Services. 6, 493–507 (1976)
40. Lawton, M.P., Brody, E.: Assessment of Older People: Self-maintaining and Instrumental Activities of Daily Living. Gerontology 9, 179–186 (1969)
41. Reynolds, T., Thornicroft, G., Abas, M., Woods, B., Hoe, J., Leese, M., Orrell, M.: Camberwell Assessment of Need for the Elderly (CANE). The British J. of Psychiatry 176, 444–452 (2000)
42. Walters, K., Iliffe, S., Orrell, M.: An Exploration of Help-seeking Behaviour in Older People with Unmet Needs. Family Practice 18, 277–282 (2001)
43. Lee, M.K., Forlizzi, J., Rybski, P.E., Crabbe, F., Chung, W., Finkle, J., et al.: The Snackbot: Documenting the Design of a Robot for Long-Term Human-Robot Interaction. In: 4th ACM/IEEE International Conference on Human-Robot Interaction, pp. 7–14 (2010)
44. Mast, M., Burmester, M., Berner, W., Facal, D., Pigini, L., Blasi, L.: Semi-Autonomous Teleoperated Learning In-Home Service Robots for Elderly Care (2010), http://www.hdm-stuttgart.de/forschung_transfer/iaf/ institute/IIDR/UX/publications/Mast%20et%20al.%202010%20- %20Service%20Robot%20User%20Needs.pdf
45. Mahani, M., Eklundh, K.S.: A Survey of the Relation of the Task Assistance of a Robot to its Social Role. KTH Computer Science and Communication. Royal Institute of Technology, Stockholm, Sweden (2009)

Various Foods Handling Movement
of Chopstick-Equipped Meal Assistant Robot
and There Evaluation

Akira Yamazaki and Ryosuke Masuda

Tokai University, 1117 Hiratsuka-shi Kanagawa, 259-1292, Japan
0btad012@tokai-u.mail.jp, masuda@keyaki.cc.u-tokai.ac.jp

Abstract. Recently, the development of daily life support or assistant robots have come into demand as a result of the impact of the decreasing birthrate and increasing the aging population. We have developed a new meal assistant robot for use by disabled or elderly persons who cannot eat unassisted. In addition, we use chopsticks as the meal tool because chopsticks are capable of various movements and are familiar to people in Asian countries. In the present paper, the basic system of this robot is introduced. In addition, various food handling movements are investigated, and an evaluation experiment is performed in order to investigate the feasibility of the newly developed robot.

Keywords: Meal Assistant Robot, Chopsticks.

1 Introduction

Recently, based on the problems of an increasingly aging society, improvements are being made to the medical standards of developed countries. However, declining birthrates are imposing additional problems in many countries, including Japan. One such social problem is the chronic lack of caregivers [1]. Accordingly, daily life assistant and support robots, which can fulfill the role of caregivers, are receiving increased attention and high expectations. Research and development of such devices, in particular, meal assistant robots, are useful because such robots can reduce the burden on caregivers and even allow them to enjoy meals together with the persons in their care. At present, a number of such meal assistant robots are commercially available.

In the present paper, we propose a new model of meal assistant robot equipped with chopsticks and investigate various movements using chopsticks and perform an experiment to evaluate the feasibility of the newly developed robot.

2 Meal Assistant Robot

While a variety of daily life support or assistant robots have been developed, other than the above-mentioned meal assistant robots, few have been put to practical use. The practical use of a meal assistant robot has advanced because meals are very important daily life events that must be provided three times a day.

Internationally developed meal assistant robots include the Handy-1 produced by Rehab Robotics, Inc., based in Great Britain [2], the Winsford Feeder, created by

S.S. Ge et al. (Eds.): ICSR 2012, LNAI 7621, pp. 158–167, 2012.

Winsford Products, Inc., based in the United States [3], iARM, which is a product of Exact Dynamics, Inc., based in the Netherlands [4], and Japan's My Spoon, which was designed by SECOM, Inc. [5]. A common feature among these systems is the use of a joystick control, with which the operator can manipulate a fork or spoon without using his or her hands.

3   Outline of the Meal Assistant Robot Using Chopsticks

3.1   System Configuration

The system configuration of the proposed meal assistant robot system is shown in Figure 1. Each joint of the robot arm is controlled by three microcomputers. The camera obtains visual images of the foods to be consumed and displayed these images on a screen. The user then uses a hands-free pointing device to select the food to be consumed. Thus, the robot is controlled primarily by the user.

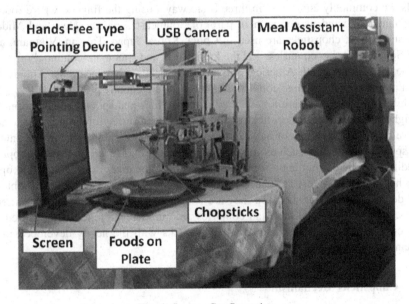

Fig. 1. System Configuration

3.2   Food Choice System

In conventional studies, a joystick was used to operate the robot without the use of hands. Since the goal is to develop a meal assistant robot that users can operate without using their own hands, a smartNAV3 (NaturalPoint, Inc., Corvallis, OR USA) hands-free pointing device was used to direct the robot.

To use this device, the user mounts the tool (headband or glasses) which put a reflective seal on his or her head before operating the robot. The mouse-pointer tracks and follows the motions of the seal. The pointing device and its associated tools are shown in Figures 2.

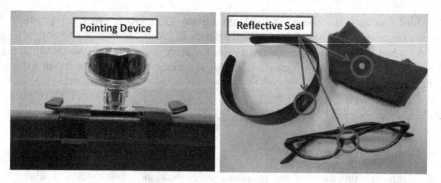

Fig. 2. Hands-free pointing device and tools with reflective seals

3.3   Meal Tools

Meals are commonly consumed in three basic ways: using the fingers, where food is manipulated by hand, is common in parts of Southeast Asia, the Near and Middle East, and Africa, chopsticks are used in China, Korea, Japan, Taiwan, Vietnam, and other Southeast Asian countries, and the knife, fork, and spoon are commonly used in Europe, North and South America, Russia, and various other locations. Among the global population, these three consumption methods are equally prevalent. [6]

While a previous evaluation has stated that the "fork and spoon" combination has the highest functionality, chopsticks can handle a wider variety of simple substances, and are capable of a variety of basic movements, such as catching and carrying, along with special movements such as mixing, spearing, cutting, separating, and scooping. In addition, while consuming a meal with chopsticks, the diner does not need to open his or her mouth as widely as is necessary with a spoon, and chopsticks are capable of more delicate movements because they are considered to be extensions of the users' fingers. Moreover, people in Asian countries are familiar with chopsticks. Based on these considerations, we decided to use chopsticks with the newly developed meal assistant robot [7], [8].

3.4   Chopsticks Mechanism

The chopsticks mechanism was installed at the end of the robot arm, as shown in Figure 3.

The chopsticks mechanism consists of a fixed chopstick and a moving chopstick. The chopsticks are actuated by a rotating oval cam mechanism with an off-center driving axis. The maximum opening range of the chopsticks is 40.7 mm. The encoder is located on the motor and detects the angle of the chopsticks, which translates to the width of the space between the chopstick tips. A three axes force sensor is located on the gripping end of fixed chopstick to detect the holding force and the weight of the food. The chopsticks can grasp an object with a maximum force of 3.3 N. In addition, the sensor was used for safety purposes, as will be explained in detail in Section 5.

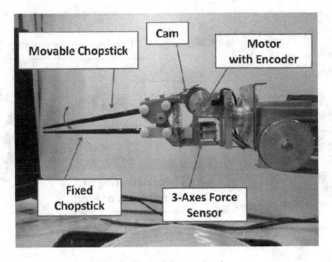

Fig. 3. Chopsticks mechanism

3.5   Main Body of Meal Assistant Robot

A five axes horizontal robot was used as the primary component of the robot assembly, as shown in Figure 4. The dimensions of the robot base are 240 [mm] × 380 [mm].

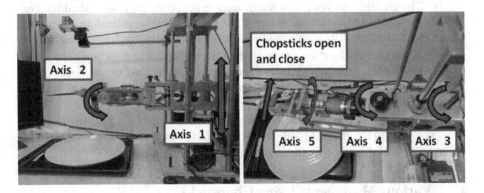

Fig. 4. Main body of the meal assistant robot

3.6   3-Axes Force Sensor

It is necessary to control the grasping force of the chopsticks depending on the characteristics of each food type to be consumed. Accordingly, a three axes force sensor was used in this research. An explanation of each axis is provided in Figure 5.

The sensor of X-axis detects the texture of the food item, while the sensor of Y-axis detects its weight. In order to prevent dangerous situations, the sensor of Z-axis detects the touch of chopsticks to the user.

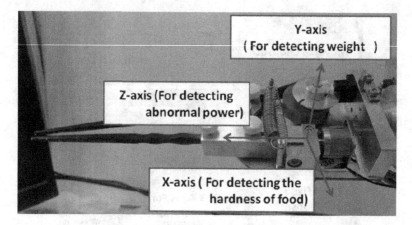

Fig. 5. Three Axes Force Sensor

3.7   Operating Procedure

The operating procedure of the robot are described below:

1) The user moves the mouse-pointer of the PC to the "CAMERA" button in the operation panel and clicks the button.
2) A USB camera which is attached to the upper part of the plate, captures an image of the food and the image displayed on the screen.
3) The user then moves the mouse-pointer to the position of the desired food on the screen and clicks the image of the food. From this procedure, no further operations are necessary until the user wants to select a different food item.
4) When user clicks a food item on the screen, the tips of the chopsticks travel to the item, pick up a morsel of food, and carry the food to the mouth of the user. However, it is difficult that recognize the lips of the user. Therefore, the robots carry food to the same position always.
5) After the user consumes the morsel of food, the robot arm automatically returns to the original position and the camera image is updated.
6) The user then chooses the next food item to be consumed.

4   Various Movements Using Chopsticks

In addition to the basic operation movements of catching and carrying, chopsticks can be used in a variety of special ways, including mixing, stabbing, cutting, separating, and scooping, for a variety of food taking operations. The mixing operation is used for food that should be mixed such as *natto*, and stabbing is used for handling slippery food that is difficult to manipulate, such as *taro* or *konnyaku*. Cutting is used for soft oversized food items, such as tofu and Japanese omelets. Separating is used for small hard foods, as well as large foods, such as hamburger steaks and croquettes. Scooping is used for rice and similar dishes. Explanations for the robotic equivalents of each of these movements are provided below.

4.1   Mixing

A rolling movement is necessary in order to mix *natto*. In the developed device, this was realized by turning axis 5 (see Figure 4) in the range of -90 to +90 degrees. Additional mixing action was added by opening and closing the chopsticks. This movement is shown in Figure 6.

Fig. 6. Mixing using chopsticks

4.2   Stabbing

The stabbing movement is produced by moving the chopsticks in a downward motion using the top and bottom movements of axis 1 (see Figure 4). This movement is shown in Figure 7.

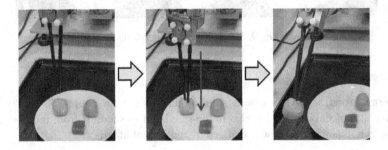

Fig. 7. Stabbing using chopsticks

4.3   Cutting

The cutting movement is used for food which can cut by closing force of chopsticks. If the food portion is larger than the width of the chopsticks, this movement is repeated several times. This movement is shown in Figure 8.

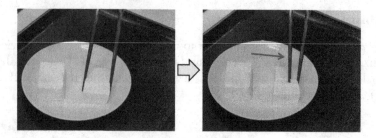

Fig. 8. Cutting using chopsticks

4.4   Separating

The separating movement is used for food which cannot cut by closing force of chopsticks. In the first stage, the chopsticks are closed and stabbed into the food using the stabbing movement described above. Then, the chopsticks are opened with the tips still penetrating the food. This movement is repeated several times until the food is separated into manageable pieces. This movement is shown in Figure 9.

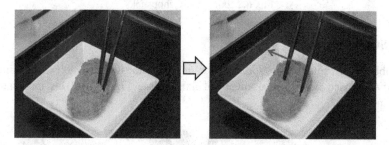

Fig. 9. Separating using chopsticks

4.5   Spooning

The normal food sandwiches both sides of the food with chopsticks and lifts it. However, it is necessary for the rice in the rice bowl to scoop it from the bottom. In this research, this movement was realized by movement of axis 2.

Fig. 10. Scooping using chopsticks

However, the robot can scoop rice from a part of the rice bowl by this method. Thus, it is necessary the mechanism for turning the rice bowl in the future.

5   Safety System

Consideration of safety is important to this robot, because it is an assistant robot that comes into contact with people. In the present study, we considered safety from both hardware and software aspects.

5.1   Hardware Aspect

A rubber tube was used for the transmission drive of the joint. In this way, even if the mechanism of the robot, including the chopsticks, comes in contact with the user, a strong force on the user will not be possible and the mechanism will essentially bounce. Furthermore, the maximum speed of axis 3 (see Figure 4) of this robot is approximately 8.8 [cm/s] and the maximum speed of axis 4 (see Figure 4) is approximately 12.2 [cm/s]. Therefore, the force will not harm the user even if the chopsticks hit the user's face.

5.2   Software Aspect

A three axes force sensor is used as part of a safety system. When a negative force (direction opposite to that for grasping food) was applied in the direction of the X-axis of the three axes force sensor, the robot judges that the chopsticks have touched an unknown object and performs an emergency stop. In addition, when a negative force was applied in the direction the Y-axis and the Z-axis of the three axes force sensor, the robot performs an emergency stop.

The safety system operates after contact with an object in this system. In the future, we will add the safety system before chopsticks contact with the user.

6   Experiment to Evaluate the Robot

We asked 26 people to use the developed robot and then fill out a questionnaire. The 26 subjects were of 10 to 60 years of age and were not handicapped. This questionnaire consists of nine items, each of which was evaluated using a five-point scale. The questionnaire items and the average score for each item are shown in Table 1. In addition, the score distributions for each item are shown in Figure 11. In the case of item 7, a lower score indicates greater fear by the user.

Table 1. Questionnaire Item

Questionnaire Item	Average Point
1. What do you think about using the robot for meal assistant?	4.77
2. What do you think about use chopsticks with meal assistant robot?	4.38
3. Usability of hands-free type pointing device?	3.23
4. Ease of instructions for the food by pointing device.	3.46
5. Ease of eating food?	3.62
6. Usability of the robot system?	3.92
7. Do you feel fear as the chopsticks approach your face?	4.38
8. What do you think about the movement speed of the robot?	4.08
9. What do you think about the appearance and size of the robot?	3.31

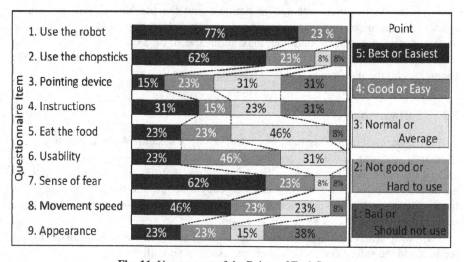

Fig. 11. Unevenness of the Points of Each Item

Items 1 and 2 received excellent scores regardless of age or sex. The average score of item 6 was 3.92, a moderately good score. Item 9 was scored low, regardless of age or sex. There is "Cronbach's alpha coefficient" that expressing the validity of the questionnaire. Generally, the questionnaire validity is enough if there is this value more than 0.8. This value was 0.87 in this questionnaire.

7   Conclusion

In the present paper, the basic operating system of a meal assistant robot equipped with chopsticks was introduced. In addition, various chopstick movements were investigated and the developed robot was evaluated experimentally.

In this system, a five axes horizontal-type robot and chopsticks mechanism are used for the basic system and the food choice system using a hands-free pointing device were constructed. Mixing, stabbing, cutting, separating, and scooping movements for a variety of food taking operations were performed. We asked 26 people to use the developed robot and evaluate the system through a questionnaire. As a result, the average score regarding the usability of the robot system was 3.92 on a five-point scale, which is a moderately good score.

In the future, we intend to create a system that does not require the user to choose a food morsel each time because the robot will be able to deduce the proper order for consumption. We also intend to enhance the practicality of the system through additional improvements and evaluations.

References

[1] Tsutida, K.: The background of shortage of care talented people in welfare field. Bulletin of Kawasaki College of Allied Health Professions 30, 41–45 (2010)
[2] Topping, M., et al.: Handy-1 A robotic aid to independence for severely disabled people. In: ICORR 2001 (2001)
[3] Hermann, R.P., et al.: Powered Feeding Devices: An Evaluation of Three Models. Arch. Phys. Med. Rehabil. 80, 1237–1242 (1999)
[4] Drissen, B., et al.: Manus control architecture. In: ICORR 2001(2001)
[5] Soyama, R., Ishii, S., Fukase, A.: The Development of Meal-Assistance Robot 'My Spoon'. In: Proceedings of the 8th International Conference on Rehabilitation Robotics, pp. 88–91 (2003)
[6] Ishiki, H.: Why Japanese uses chopsticks. Otsuki Publishing Company (1987)
[7] Koshizaki, T., Masuda, R.: Control of Meal-assistance (June 2010)
[8] Goto, Masuda: Operation and automatic control of care robot. In: Annual Conference on IEEEJ, pp. V3–103 (2001) (Japanese)

Imagery of Disabled People
within Social Robotics Research

Sophya Yumakulov, Dean Yergens, and Gregor Wolbring

Department of Community Health Sciences, Faculty of Medicine, University of Calgary,
TRW Building, 3rd Floor, 3280 Hospital Drive NW, Calgary, Alberta
{syumakul,gwolbrin}@ucalgary.ca, dyergens@gmail.com

Abstract. Social robotics is an emerging field, with many applications envisioned for people with disabilities. This paper explores these applications and the portrayal of people with disabilities within the social robotics discourse. Our review of social robotics literature revealed that social robotics mainly portrays disabled people through a medical/body ability deficiency lens, namely identifying deficient abilities, and then proposing how a certain robot can fix them and give the individual "normal" functioning. However, within the Disabled People Rights Movement, the academic field of disability studies, and existing legal documents, a second narrative is evident which focuses less on 'fixing' the person to the species-typical norm, and more on increasing the participation in society of that person the way they are. We submit that the second type of narrative and its way of defining problems and solutions needs more visibility within the social robotics discourse and in the vision of possible products.

Keywords: Social robotics, people with disabilities, normalization, diversity, ability expectations, imagery, narrative.

1 Introduction

Social robotics is a rapidly growing field which offers innovative and ever-more complex technologies for use within a range of sectors including education [1, 2], healthcare [3-8], and service [3, 5, 9-11, 11-13]. One group that is often targeted by social robotics applications is people with disabilities, people whose bodily and mental abilities are seen to not fit the norm; for example, a particular focus of robotics is people labeled as autistic. Applications for these users include therapeutic and assistive devices, but while such devices are presumably created to improve the lives of people with disabilities, it is important to examine the kind of approach that social robotics has taken toward people with disabilities and how this group is portrayed in social robotics literature. In particular, does disability-related robotics research reflect the medical narrative of disability (i.e. deficiencies or inabilities that should be "fixed"), or does it also include the social narrative of disability which focuses more on participation in society with a given body ability reality, and which argues for embracing human diversity and allowing what we call disabled people to live on their own terms?

S.S. Ge et al. (Eds.): ICSR 2012, LNAI 7621, pp. 168–177, 2012.

To answer this question, we examined how disability is discussed and framed in social robotics literature. Academic articles covering social robotics were imported into Knowledge Share ver. 2.1.3 (KSv2), a tool developed by Dean Yergens (http://people.ucalgary.ca/~dyergens/ksv2.htm) to systematically review literature. We searched the following databases (provided by the University of Calgary): ScienceDirect, Compendex, IEEE, Communication Abstracts, Scopus, OVID(All), EBSCO(All), Academic One File, Web of Science, and JSTOR. 489 articles were imported into Knowledge Share, and using inclusion/exclusion criteria (include: only English, full PDF available; exclude: pure technical, conference announcements, books), we included 171 articles in the review. The Kappa factor (reviewer agreement) was .88. Articles were coded using Atlas.ti 7 qualitative data analysis software.

Section 2 below gives an overview of current social robotics applications and proposed users. In Section 3, we present our findings on the social robotics discourse around disability, and discuss the implications of this discourse for people with disabilities. Finally, in Section 4, we advocate for a more diverse framing of the lives of people with disabilities, the problems they face, and the solutions social robotics could contribute.

2   Targets and Applications for Social Robotics

Within the 171 articles, we found the following general areas of applications: companionship (30 articles), household/service (21 articles), healthcare/rehabilitation (60), and military (17 articles).

Companion robots include: friend robots such as Robovie, which can converse about the weather, ask to play games, and engage in simple conversation [9]; pet robots such as Sony's dog AIBO and RoboScience RoboDog [14], and PARO the baby seal [15]; sex robots such as Roxxxy, a realistic female companion complete with conversation capacities and body warmth [16]. Companion robots meant for the elderly include the personal service robots Rui and Care-0-bot [3, 10], and the baby seal PARO [15]. Toy robots aimed at children and general users include the interactive game-playing iCAT [13, 14, 17, 18] and Cog [15].

Service and household robots are envisioned to play an important role in the future, especially with the advent of smart homes [3, 13]. They include robots to clean, act as sentries, and mow grass [5]; and robots to do chores [9] such as fetching objects, cooking ([19]); robot receptionists such as Repliee [9] and Roboceptionist [12]; tour guides such as Hermes [10]; and office assistants to deliver messages and guide visitors [4].

Healthcare is also an important area of interest. Sixty articles mentioned the term "health", 24 articles used "patient", 19 used "impairment", and 19 discussed robots for healthcare applications. Two main groups were covered by articles discussing health: the elderly (n= 47) and people with disabilities (n= 30). Robots for the elderly include robots to bath the elderly [5], and robots to assist in movement [12]. In this context, the emphasis is on robots that can enable the elderly to live independently as long as possible [20, 21]. Mobiserv, for example, is a robot for elderly health care support (e.g. reminding to take medication), general wellness, health monitoring (e.g. nutrition, dehydration prevention), safety, and social support such as motivational advice for physical activities [22].

Among the robot applications for people with disabilities, the majority were focused on people with autism (28 articles). Robots such as Keepon [23], KASPAR [24], Roball [24], and VESSI [25] are meant to engage autistic children in consistent and safe social interactions, and to help teach them to interact affectively [20]. Robots are also envisioned to aid people with physical disabilities, in terms of moving around and living independently [14], and helping with rehabilitation therapy for stroke patients, for example [20, 26].

3   Social Robotics and People with Disabilities

As described above, a number of social robotics applications are intended for people with disabilities. Specific target groups include people with autism (n= 28) and other intellectual/cognitive ability differences (commonly called "disabilities"), stroke rehabilitation patients (n= 9), people with physical ability differences, and the elderly (n= 47). The way that these groups were discussed revealed a number of important themes and insights into how these groups are viewed by the social robotics community.

3.1   The Medical Narrative

Most articles covering people with ability differences define them as medical conditions, and consequently, discuss them from a medical perspective, in terms of diagnosis, therapy, and treatment. The goal of the proposed robot or system becomes to restore "normal" functioning to the person who is labeled as ability deficient. Most research discussing disabilities uses medical language, which is especially evident in the case of autism: out of 28 articles that mention autism, 8 give a disorder-based definition, and 7 of them [1, 4, 24, 25, 27-29] use either the ICF-CY (International Classification of Functioning and Disability, version for Children and Youth) [30] or the DSM [31]. Autism is medically defined as the inability to perform certain social tasks, such as displaying and recognizing emotions, maintaining eye contact, and having theory of mind [31]. Consequently, social robots are meant to reduce the 'severity' of these 'deficiencies'. Abilities targeted by social robotics include turn-taking [4], imitation [4, 24, 27, 29], self-initiated interaction [4, 24, 27, 29, 32], and effective social interaction [4, 24, 27]. Authors often use ability-charged terms when describing autistic children as having "deficits in theory of mind" [23] or other "functional limitations" [33]. Social robots are thus proposed as therapeutic tools that can help autistic children to acquire these abilities to a satisfactory level (whatever that may be).

In terms of monitoring and diagnosis, Scassellati and colleagues feel that because robots can accurately record the occurrence of certain behaviors during a therapy session, they can be effective tools for monitoring the patient's progress [23, 28]. Similarly, because robots can objectively quantify social behaviors (such as eye contact), they can also be used to diagnose autism in a more consistent way [23, 28] by detecting interactional "anomalies" in a child's behavior [34]. Again, this research relies on the detection of "anomalies" as they are defined by the medical community. Tapus et al state that a goal of social robotics in therapy is to provide a *measurable* improvement over time [20], although in terms of disability, one can question what such measurement would entail and how much "improvement" is expected for a disabled person to be labeled as "normal".

This medical approach is true for other ability differences as well. Bernd et al describe children with disabilities as having "functional limitations" which interfere with their ability to play (however we define "play") [33]. Sung et al describe children with mental disabilities as lacking the ability to touch people and to express emotions, deficits which the robot PARO might be able to alleviate [35].

In addition, authors use medical terms when discussing robots that are "educational treatments" for autism [1], or are needed for special education, *therapy*, and training of people with cognitive differences [20]. The term "impairment" was used 41 times in the articles we reviewed, also indicating the use of a medical narrative. The emphasis on medical definitions and terminology places these researchers within a "fixing" framework of disability and this is clear from the aims of their research.

An interesting theme within this discourse is the reasoning behind using social robots as opposed to human therapists. Michalowski [34] summarizes this idea by asserting that robots may be better therapists than humans because a) some people might be more comfortable interacting with an artifact, b) robots are always available and don't get tired, and c) robots are controllable and can provide consistent interactions. In terms of comfort, some authors observed that children with autism responded better to robots than to other toys, games, and even human therapists [23]. Robots can also reliably perform assistive tasks that humans currently perform in caring for the disabled [36]. The notion of consistent interactions was especially important in discussions of autistic children who could use robots as a social "crutch" [20]. One author pointed out that robots would not be abusive to their disabled charges as human therapists and assistants sometimes are [15]. The objectivity of robots and their ability to record behaviors is also seen as an opportunity to study and to better understand people with disabilities [4, 34]. Indeed, Salter et al used the robot Keepon with children with cognitive conditions (i.e. autism, Asperger's Syndrome, Down Syndrome) to try to relate robotics to human sciences in order to understand the underlying mechanisms of social communication [23].

3.2   Assistance for Quality of Life

Although the medical view of disabilities is most prominent in social robotics literature, out of the articles which talked about disability, 8 discussed their work in terms of quality of life [8, 20, 21, 23, 35, 37-39]. Here, a different vocabulary was used to discuss disability, and the goal of the robot was to improve an individual's quality of life rather than to provide a medical treatment or to fix the disability.

This view was most common in research that discussed elderly people who had some form of mental or physical impairment. Kuo et al stated: "the common objective of this research is to improve the quality of life of older people by assisting them to stay independent or with their families as long as possible, without being admitted to an aged care facility" (p. 443) [8]. Independent living was seen as an important goal by a number of other authors as well [20, 21]. Sparrow & Sparrow described robots as being assistants, a helping hand, and companions for the elderly, with examples such as the baby seal robot PARO which facilitated more frequent visits from family and friends of people with dementia [38]. Some authors also describe pet robots as helping to reduce stress and depression in the elderly and to promote smiling and socially communicative behaviors [20, 21]. These papers reflect a desire to improve the overall state of well-being of the elderly.

Elements of quality of life were mentioned by studies looking at other people with disabilities as well. For example, Gonzales-Pacheco et al [37] cited studies which showed that "children who suffer from severe disabilities use robots with the aim to learn and improve their quality of life" (p. 371) and Salter et al [23] cite robots as giving disabled children the "right tools and the right solutions to overcome the obstacles they experience" (p. 95). As with the elderly, there is an expectation that robots will allow people with disabilities to have a more independent way of living by reducing their dependence on other people [35]. Coeckelbergh took a step further, from robots that can simply do things that disabled people cannot do to robots that can provide a disabled person with information about the world and even do things in the world in that person's place [39]. Lastly, the prospect of reduced abuse of people with disabilities by their assistants is seen as a potential benefit of robots [15].

The concept of quality of life is often discussed together with medical treatment or therapy of disabilities such that these two concepts are intertwined. Researchers tend to speak of giving disabled people abilities that will improve their well-being and quality of life. For example, the ability to play is important for children [33], and children with intellectual disability are unable to play, so a robot is used to try and facilitate play with these children in order to improve their health and well-being later on in life. It seems that the overall goal of this research is well-being, as expressed by Kuo et al [8], but the underlying assumption is medically oriented, in that certain abilities must be given/restored to the disabled in order for them to achieve well-being.

3.3   Implications for People with Disabilities

The analysis of the 171 articles suggests that the imagery of people with disabilities within social robotics research is mostly medical. The medical narrative perceives the defect to be within the person, a defect that has to be fixed. Medicine and Rehabilitation are two fields that focus on restoration towards the species-typical body abilities as much as possible. However this medical narrative is challenged by many disabled people (see for example DEAF culture [40-46]) and the academic field of disability studies and its scholars [47]. The disabled people rights discourse and scholars of the academic field of disability studies [48] question the assumption of deficiency being intrinsic to non-normative body abilities and the favoritism for normative species-typical body abilities [49-56]. Looking at a discourse through a disability studies lens entails to look at the representation and imagery of disabled people and their problems and the solutions sought. Its angle tends to broaden the discourse by looking beyond the medical, species-typical ability narrative of the body.

The disability studies or ability-diverse narrative can be applied to social robotics. In the case of deaf people, for example, a cochlear implant would eliminate deafness (a gain according to the medical narrative) but would also eliminate deaf culture in the process (a loss according to the ability-diversity narrative). In the case of autism, current research focuses on the medical aspects, such as treatments, diagnosis, medical framing, etc. An ability-diverse narrative, however, would consider the neurodiversity perspective of autism, which advocates for the acceptance of people with autism in society just as they are, to be recognized not as deficient human beings, but as ability-diverse people [57]. The neurodiversity perspective arose out of people with neuro- and cognitive-based ability differences (i.e. autism, Asperger's syndrome, attention deficit-hyperactivity disorder, bipolar disorder, developmental dyspraxia, dyslexia, epilepsy, and Tourette's syndrome) questioning the medical deficiency discourse surrounding these ability labels [58-62]. Thus, researchers employing the ability-diverse lens in their work can question whether social robots are meant to eliminate characteristics someone identifies with, or whether they are there to help the person live the way they are.

Although medical narratives have their place, social narratives of identity and problem identification can also help to identify valuable contributions of social robotics. Autism, for instance, is a prime example of two narratives – the medical narrative and the Neurodiversity narrative – which have different visions of the problem and the solution. A possible robotics application for autism from the neurodiversity perspective might be a robot which can "translate" social cues to autistic individuals. It could function as an intermediary in a social interaction between an autistic person and another person, distilling the smorgasbord of incoming social information into the basic things the person needs to know in order to understand and respond to the interaction. Such a robot would be an aid to an autistic person without necessarily changing them. Another example of this kind of approach is a companion robot for elders or people with disabilities, again allowing them to be who they are. Another possibility is robotic communication aids, either for personal or public use: to aid communication between deaf and hearing people, for speech-diverse people, or as assistants for the blind, to name a few examples.

Evidently, one can envision social robotic products derived from the social narrative, allowing users to be who they are, without aiming to change them to a normative body/ability type. However, the question we would like to raise is whether the context within which social robotics research currently takes plays supports this narrative: does it allow for 'clients' to self-identify as they see fit and to put forward their views of the problem and their visions of how social robotic tools could help them? In particular, are clients given the opportunity to challenge whether a certain label (medical) should be a prerequisite for being part of a social robotics-based solution? On a systems level, funders react to the narrative they perceive in a research field, so if there is a strong social narrative present, it increases the chance that such research will be supported. We posit that a social robotics agenda that provides solutions based on both the medical *and* social narrative would be more useful to tackle well being problems humans face in general and disabled people in particular, and that the field should adopt a more broad view of people with disabilities, the problems they face, and the solutions that social robotics can offer.

4   Conclusion

Within social robotics research around disabilities, the ability-diverse perspective is highly underrepresented. Many ability differences are conceptualized under the medical lens, and social robotics has developed within this framework. However, a new focus towards the social narrative of disability would greatly enrich robotics research. New applications could be developed that promote inclusion of people with disabilities in social processes, for example. Autism and other disabilities are widely labeled as medical conditions, but this is not the only way to view disability. Indeed, movements such as the Disabled People Rights Movement, and the Neurodiversity Movement within the autism community advocate for de-medicalization of disabilities and for acceptance of human diversity in all its forms. We submit that by having a more diverse framing of the lives of people with disabilities and the problems they face, social robotics can expand the scope of relevant solutions it can contribute.

Lastly, it is interesting that the focus in social robotics research, as it relates to disabled people, is very limited, with the main disability covered being autism. Even within a medical narrative of disability, there are more disabled people who could benefit from social robotics products (e.g. physically disabled, blind, people with cerebral palsy, etc). In the US, for example, there are huge amounts of injured veterans coming back from wars. We would expect there to be some discussion in the social robotics field around applications for veteran care (e.g. companion robots for disabled veterans); however, there were no papers around injured veterans. Social robotics seems to be focused on a very limited group of disabled people, and we suggest that there is no reason why the focus of social robots in regards to disabled people has to be so narrow. Indeed, there is much potential for growth for the social robotics field in adding other angles from which to look at disability.

Author Contributions. Sophya Yumakulov is a student of G.W. and completed the research for this article and wrote the article. Dean Yergens provided us with software he developed, which we used for the literature review. Gregor Wolbring initiated, conceptualized, and supervised the research project and was involved in data evaluation and writing of the article.

References

1. Kim, Y.-D., Hong, J.-W., Kang, W.-S., Baek, S.-S., Lee, H.-S., An, J.: Design of Robot Assisted Observation System for Therapy and Education of Children with Autism. In: ICSR 2010. LNCS (LNAI), vol. 6414, pp. 222–231. Springer, Heidelberg (2010)

2. Yun, S., Shin, J., Kim, D., Kim, C.G., Kim, M., Choi, M.-T.: Engkey: Tele-education Robot. In: Mutlu, B., Bartneck, C., Ham, J., Evers, V., Kanda, T. (eds.) ICSR 2011. LNCS (LNAI), vol. 7072, pp. 142–152. Springer, Heidelberg (2011)
3. Heerink, M., Krose, B., Evers, V., Wielinga, B.: Assessing acceptance of assistive social agent technology by older adults: The almere model. Int. J. Soc. Robot. 2, 361–375 (2010)
4. Boccanfuso, L., O'Kane, J.M.: CHARLIE: An adaptive robot design with hand and face tracking for use in autism therapy. Int. J. Soc. Robot. 3, 337–347 (2011)
5. Moon, A.J., Danielson, P., Van der Loos, H.F.M.: Survey-Based Discussions on Morally Contentious Applications of Interactive Robotics. Int. J. Soc. Robot. 4, 77–96 (2012)
6. Sugiyama, O., Shinozawa, K., Akimoto, T., Hagita, N.: Case Study of a Multi-robot Healthcare System: Effects of Docking and Metaphor on Persuasion. In: Ge, S.S., Li, H., Cabibihan, J.-J., Tan, Y.K. (eds.) ICSR 2010. LNCS (LNAI), vol. 6414, pp. 90–99. Springer, Heidelberg (2010)
7. Broadbent, E., Lee, Y.I., Stafford, R.Q., Kuo, I.H., MacDonald, B.A.: Mental schemas of robots as more human-like are associated with higher blood pressure and negative emotions in a human-robot Interaction. Int. J. Soc. Robot. 3, 291–297 (2011)
8. Kuo, I., Jayawardena, C., Broadbent, E., MacDonald, B.A.: Multidisciplinary Design Approach for Implementation of Interactive Services: Communication Initiation and user Identification for Healthcare Service Robots. Int. J. Soc. Robot. 3, 443–456 (2011)
9. Carpenter, J., Davis, J.M., Erwin-Steward, N., Lee, T.R., Bransford, J.D., Vye, N.: Gender Representation and Humanoid Robots Designed for Domestic Use. Int. J. Soc. Robot. 1, 261–265 (2009)
10. Tao, Y., Wang, T., Wei, H., Yuan, P.: A Behavior Adaptation Method for an Elderly Companion Robot—Rui. In: Ge, S.S., Li, H., Cabibihan, J.-J., Tan, Y.K. (eds.) ICSR 2010. LNCS (LNAI), vol. 6414, pp. 141–150. Springer, Heidelberg (2010)
11. van der Zant, T., Iocchi, L.: RoboCup@Home: Adaptive Benchmarking of Robot Bodies and Minds. In: Mutlu, B., Bartneck, C., Ham, J., Evers, V., Kanda, T. (eds.) ICSR 2011. LNCS (LNAI), vol. 7072, pp. 214–225. Springer, Heidelberg (2011)
12. Kirby, R., Forlizzi, J., Simmons, R.: Affective social robots. Robotics and Autonomous Systems 58, 322–332 (2010)
13. de Ruyter, B., Saini, P., Markopoulos, P., van Breemen, A.: Assessing the effects of building social intelligence in a robotic interface for the home. Interact Comput. 17, 522–541 (2005)
14. Fong, T., Nourbakhsh, I., Dautenhahn, K.: A survey of socially interactive robots. Robotics and Autonomous Systems 42, 143–166 (2003)
15. Turkle, S.: Authenticity in the age of digital companions. Interaction Studies 8(3), 501–517 (2007)
16. Ziaja, S.: Homewrecker 2.0: An Exploration of Liability for Heart Balm Torts Involving AI Humanoid Consorts. In: Mutlu, B., Bartneck, C., Ham, J., Evers, V., Kanda, T. (eds.) ICSR 2011. LNCS (LNAI), vol. 7072, pp. 114–124. Springer, Heidelberg (2011)
17. Stedman, N.: ADB. Leonardo 43(4), 414–415 (2010)
18. Castellano, G., Leite, I., Pereira, A., Martinho, C., Paiva, A., McOwan, P.W.: Affect recognition for interactive companions: Challenges and design in real world scenarios. J. Multimodal. User Interfaces 3, 89–98 (2010)
19. Boccanfuso, L., O'Kane, J.M.: Adaptive Robot Design with Hand and Face Tracking for Use in Autism Therapy. In: Ge, S.S., Li, H., Cabibihan, J.-J., Tan, Y.K. (eds.) ICSR 2010. LNCS (LNAI), vol. 6414, pp. 265–274. Springer, Heidelberg (2010)
20. Tapus, A., Mataric, M.J., Scassellati, B.: Socially assistive robotics (Grand challenges of robotics). IEEE Robotics & Automation Magazine, 35–42 (2007)
21. Broadbent, E., Stafford, R., MacDonald, B.: Acceptance of Healthcare Robots for the Older Population: Review and Future Directions. Int. J. Soc. Robot. 1, 319–330 (2009)

22. Huijnen, C., Badii, A., van den Heuvel, H., Caleb-Solly, P., Thiemert, D.: "Maybe It Be-comes a Buddy, But Do Not Call It a Robot" – Seamless Cooperation between Companion Robotics and Smart Homes. In: Keyson, D., Maher, M.L., Streitz, N., Cheok, A., Augusto, J.C., Wichert, R., Englebienne, G., Aghajan, H., Kröse, B.J.A. (eds.) AmI 2011. LNCS, vol. 7040, pp. 324–329. Springer, Heidelberg (2011)
23. Salter, T., Werry, I., Michaud, F.: Going into the wild in child-robot interaction studies: Is-sues in social robotic development. Intel. Serv. Robotics 1, 93–108 (2008)
24. Fujimoto, I., Matsumoto, T., De Silva, P., Ravindra, S., Kobayashi, M., Higashi, M.: Mi-micking and evaluating human motion to improve the imitation skill of children with aut-ism through a robot. Int. J. Soc. Robot. 3, 349–357 (2011)
25. Welch, K.C., Lahiri, U., Warren, Z., Sarkar, N.: An approach to the design of socially ac-ceptable robots for children with autism spectrum disorders. Int. J. Soc. Robot. 2, 391–403 (2010)
26. Ang, M., Limkaichong, L., Perez, W., Sayson, L., Tampo, N., Bugtai, N., Estanislao-Clark, E.: Development of Robotic Arm Rehabilitation Machine with Biofeedback That Addresses the Question on Filipino Elderly Patient Motivation. In: Ge, S.S., Li, H., Cabi-bihan, J.-J., Tan, Y.K. (eds.) ICSR 2010. LNCS (LNAI), vol. 6414, pp. 401–410. Springer, Heidelberg (2010)
27. Robins, B., Dautenhahn, K.: Developing Play Scenarios for Tactile Interaction with a Hu-manoid Robot: A Case Study Exploration with Children with Autism. In: Ge, S.S., Li, H., Cabibihan, J.-J., Tan, Y.K. (eds.) ICSR 2010. LNCS (LNAI), vol. 6414, pp. 243–252. Springer, Heidelberg (2010)
28. Scassellati, B., Crick, C., Gold, K., Kim, E., Shic, F., Sun, G.: Social development. IEEE Computational Intelligence Mazagine, 41–47 (2006)
29. Fujimoto, I., Matsumoto, T., De Silva, P.R.S., Kobayashi, M., Higashi, M.: Study on An Assistive Robot for Improving Imitation Skill of Children with Autism. In: Ge, S.S., Li, H., Cabibihan, J.-J., Tan, Y.K. (eds.) ICSR 2010. LNCS (LNAI), vol. 6414, pp. 232–242. Springer, Heidelberg (2010)
30. WHO: International Classification of Functioning, Disability and Health. World Health Organization, Geneva (2001)
31. American Psychiatric Association: DSM-IV: Diagnostic and statistical manual of mental disorders, 4th ed. American Psychiatric Association, Arlington (1994)
32. Kozima, H., Nakagawa, C., Yasuda, Y.: Children robot interaction: a pilot study in autism therapy. In: von Hofsten, C., Rosander, K. (eds.) Progress in Brain Research, vol. 164, pp. 385–400. Elsevier (2007)
33. Bernd, T., Gelderblom, G.J., Vanstipelen, S., de Witte, L.: Short Term Effect Evaluation of IROMEC Involved Therapy for Children with Intellectual Disabilities. In: Ge, S.S., Li, H., Cabibihan, J.-J., Tan, Y.K. (eds.) ICSR 2010. LNCS (LNAI), vol. 6414, pp. 259–264. Springer, Heidelberg (2010)
34. Michalowski, M.P.: Rhythmic Human-Robot Social Interaction. Dissertation (2010)
35. Sung, J., Grinter, R.E., Christensen, H.I.: Domestic Robot Ecology: An Initial Framework to Unpack Long-Term Acceptance of Robots at Home. Int. J. Soc. Robot. 2, 417–429 (2010)
36. Syrdal, D.S., Nomura, T., Hirai, H., Dautenhahn, K.: Examining the Frankenstein Syn-drome. In: Mutlu, B., Bartneck, C., Ham, J., Evers, V., Kanda, T. (eds.) ICSR 2011. LNCS, vol. 7072, pp. 125–134. Springer, Heidelberg (2011)
37. Gonzalez-Pacheco, V., Ramey, A., Alonso-Martin, F., Castro-Gonzalez, A., Salichs, M.A.: Maggie: A Social Robot as a Gaming Platform. Int. J. Soc. Robot. 3, 371–381 (2011)
38. Sparrow, R., Sparrow, L.: In the hands of machines? The future of aged care. Mind Mach. 16, 141–161 (2006)
39. Coeckelbergh, M.: Humans, animals, and robots: A phenomenological approach to human-robot relations. Int. J. Soc. Robot. 3, 197–204 (2011)

40. Burch, S.: Transcending revolutions: the Tsars, the Soviets, and deaf culture. J. Soc. Hist. 34(2), 393–401 (2000)
41. Abberley, P.: Understanding deaf culture: in search of deafhood. Disability & Society 18(7), 971–973 (2003)
42. Chimedza, R.: The cultural politics of integrating deaf students in regular schools in Zimbabwe. Disability & Society 13(4), 493–502 (1998)
43. Hladek, G.A.: Cochlear implants, the deaf culture, and ethics: a study of disability, informed surrogate consent, and ethnocide. Monash. Bioeth. Rev. 21(1), 29–44 (2002)
44. Kersting, S.: Balancing between deaf and hearing worlds: reflections of mainstreamed college students on relationships and social interaction. J. Deaf. Stud. Deaf. Educ. 2(4), 252–263 (1997)
45. Lane, H., Bahan, B.: Ethics of cochlear implantation in young children: A review and reply from a Deaf-World perspective. Otolaryngology-Head and Neck Surgery 119(4), 297–313 (1998)
46. Sparrow, R.: Defending deaf culture: The case of cochlear implants. Journal of Political Philosophy 13(2), 135–152 (2005)
47. Carlson, L.: Cognitive Ableism and Disability Studies: Feminist Reflections on the History of Mental Retardation. Hypatia 16(4), 124–146 (2001)
48. Mitchell, D.T., Snyder, S.L.: The Body and Physical Difference: Discourses of Disability (The Body, In Theory: Histories of Cultural Materialism). University of Michigan Press, Ann Arbor (1997)
49. Olyan, S.M.: The ascription of physical disability as a stigmatizing strategy in biblical iconic polemics. The Journal of Hebrew Scriptures 9, 2–15 (2009)
50. Rose, M.: The Staff of Oedipus: Transforming Disability in Ancient. University of Michigan Press, Ann Arbor (2003)
51. Schipper, J.: Disability Studies and the Hebrew Bible: Figuring Mephibosheth in the David Story. Continuum, New York (2006)
52. Overboe, J.: Vitalism: Subjectivity Exceeding Racism, Sexism, and (Psychiatric) Ableism. Wagadu: A Journal of Transnational Women's and Gender Studies 4(2), 23–34 (2007)
53. Campbell, F.A.K.: Inciting Legal Fictions: 'Disability's' Date with Ontology and the Ableist Body of the Law. Griffith Law Review 10(1), 42 (2001)
54. Wolbring, G.: Ableism and Favoritism for Abilities Governance, Ethics, and Studies: New Tools for Nanoscale and Nanoscale enabled Science and Technology Governance. In: Cozzens, S., Wetmore, J.M. (eds.) The Yearbook of Nanotechnology in Society. The Challenge of Equity and Equality, vol. II, Springer, New York (2010)
55. Boundy, K.: Are You Sure, Sweetheart, That You Want to Be Well?: An Exploration Of The Neurodiversity Movement. Radical Psychology: A Journal of Psychology, Politics & Radicalism 7(2), 2–2 (2008)
56. Broderick, A.A., Ne'eman, A.: Autism as metaphor: narrative and counter-narrative. International Journal of Inclusive Education 12(5-6), 459–476 (2008)
57. Ortega, F.: The Cerebral Subject and the Neurodiversity Movement. Mana-Estudos De Antropologia Social 14(2), 477–509 (2008)
58. Sarrett, J.C.: Trapped Children: Popular Images of Children with Autism in the 1960s and 2000s. J. Med. Humanit. 32(2), 141–153 (2011)

HRI Evaluation of a Healthcare Service Robot

I-Han Kuo[1], Chandimal Jayawardena[2], Elizabeth Broadbent[3],
Rebecca Q. Stafford[3], and Bruce A. MacDonald[1]

[1] Electrical and Computer Engineering, University of Auckland
{t.kuo,b.macdonald}@auckland.ac.nz
[2] Department of Computing, Unitec Institute of Technology
cjayawardena@unitec.ac.nz
[3] Psychological Medicine, University of Auckland
{e.broadbent,r.stafford}@auckland.ac.nz

Abstract. This paper presents the evaluation of a healthcare service robot system with vital signs measurement and medication reminders. The design followed the methodology proposed in [7]. This study is a first step to evaluate the methodology by measuring the effectiveness of the interaction patterns designed. The results show that the interaction design patterns could be validated and improved. One can easily reuse these patterns for another service application. This indicates the usefulness of the methodology in: (a) fostering research and development for creating interactive service robots; and (b) helping HRI designers further improve robots' interactivity, for perceiving and expressing interaction/social cues. Overall, the robot system performed robustly for about six hours every day for over two weeks. Videos of the users' approaching behaviours (use cases) were also analysed for future improvements on robot's interactivity to engage potential users in a public space.

Keywords: service robotics, HRI, evaluation, interaction cue, social cue, design pattern, presence detection, user's attention, face detection and recognition.

1 Introduction

Deployment of a robot system to provide interactive services autonomously for an extended period of time has always been a challenge in HRI and service robotics [4]. Compared to short term user studies which are often based on sessions of 30 minutes to a hour in length (e.g. [12]), autonomous operation of a service robot in the real world over a number of days imposes high requirements on the stability and reliability of both hardware and software of the robot [13]. Additionally, many ideal assumptions that are characteristic of laboratory environments will be invalidated; e.g. lighting, background noise level, and wireless connectivities. The impact of real-world users and environments on HRI have to be considered to develop robots that are functional outside the laboratory.

We have previously proposed a new design methodology to guide HRI designers in developing interactive service robot applications in a multidisciplinary

S.S. Ge et al. (Eds.): ICSR 2012, LNAI 7621, pp. 178–187, 2012.

research environment [7]. To help HRI designers focus on certain aspects of a robot's interactive behaviour, we use storyboards, UML use case and activity diagrams with modified UMLi notation to represent the robot's perception and expression of interaction cues using multiple modalities. Rather than using UML diagrams as blueprints for the documentation of a complete design, the goal is to use these diagrams as sketches to selectively visualise and communicate to both engineers (e.g. software engineers) and non-engineering domain experts (e.g. psychologist, gerontologist) relevant aspects of a robot's interactive behaviour for achieving natural HRI experience [2]. With practical challenges in deployment in mind, testing and evaluation are also emphasised in the methodology to discover and design around practical limitations of chosen technologies early which can sometimes be hidden or overlooked. Furthermore, we also defined interaction cues (or signals) as interaction design patterns because of their recurring nature and take a component-based software engineering approach to maximise the reuse of any interaction pattern in other service applications.

This design methodology was applied in the implementation of a service robot "Charlie," (described in 2.1) which must detect a potential user, greet, and then engage with them in order to perform services. In this paper, we present a two week user trial in which the robot was deployed at an aged care facility. In one scenario the robot is an assistant to medical staff in a public space, to greet and instruct users in simple procedures such as measuring blood pressure. In the second, the robot is a personal health assistant to proactively help its user maintain a healthy lifestyle, for example giving medication reminders [1].

Section 2 gives an overview of the study and describes the aims and methodology of the evaluation. Section 3 describes the two service scenarios at two different locations in an independent living apartment building at an aged care facility. Sections 4 and 5 present the results and validate the interaction patterns that were designed and described in [7]. The results are discussed in Section 6.

2   Aim and Methodology

The aim of the study is to evaluate the technical performance of the developed robot system and validate the interaction patterns that were proposed in [7] and later implemented against their initial designs using common performance metrics. This will in turn evaluate the robot's interactivity for sensing user's presence and attention to the robot, and identifying the user. The results presented in this paper also provide a good benchmark for other research work and for helping others reuse the same designs in future development.

As an initial effort to unify the wide range of metrics utilised by different research groups in HRI, Steinfeld et al. proposed a set of common metrics for evaluation of human-robot interaction [11]. His work focused on task oriented HRI metrics. All robot functionalities are divided into relevant task domains; these include navigation, perception, manipulation, management (tele-operation), and social. Within each task domain, specific performance benchmarks are then developed. For example, efficiency and effectiveness are the main benchmarks for robot navigation tasks (e.g. localisation and navigation within a house); whereas robot perception tasks are compared based on detection and recognition rates. As there are two counterparts; i.e. a human and a robot in a one-to-one HRI, the author divided the evaluation into two parts. The first part includes evaluation from within the robot itself. Most performance benchmarks or metrics suggested in [11] were used. They indicate the technical soundness of the robot system in terms of its robustness, efficiency, and effectiveness. In the second part, the robot and its interactivity, especially the robot's expressiveness, were evaluated by the human counterparts (the users). Based on the metrics for social effectiveness suggested in [11], the second part evaluates the robot's social competencies through analysis of the interaction videos from the studies.

2.1   Robot Platform, Settings and Recruitment

The Charlie robot platform is from Yujin Robot [5]. The robot was capable of delivering (1) vital signs monitoring, and (2) medication reminding and management services, and (3) entertainment. The robot was deployed for 14 days at "Selwyn Village," a retirement village in Auckland, New Zealand. The evaluation was carried out in the independent-living apartment building "Lichfield Towers". During the study, the robot was deployed at two different locations in Lichfield Towers.

All residents in Lichfield Towers were invited to participate in the study. Six Lichfield Towers residents agreed to have the robot visit their private apartments for a 30 minute interactive session every morning (between 6.30 to 9.30 a.m.). On each day, the robot visited the participants one by one in their apartments to provide medications reminders and measure vital signs. All other residents were invited to use the robot between 11:00 a.m. to 2:00 p.m. in the public lobby. The six private spaces participants who had the robot visit their apartments every day were also invited to use the robot in the public lobby.

For the rest of the paper, the user study in the private apartments and the public lobby are referred to as "Study 1" and "Study 2" respectively. In parallel to this evaluation, a questionnaire-based psychological study was also carried out. The results are reported separately in [10].

3   Scenarios

3.1   Private Apartments Scenario (Study 1)

In study 1, the primary function of the robot is to remind and assist participants manage their medications at scheduled times. In each session, research assistants would first move the robot to the target apartment floor and set up the robot in the corridor. Floors 2 to 5 in the building all have the same layout. The robot navigated by itself through the corridor into the apartment and to the kitchen table which was a pre-designated location. Upon arrival, the robot would ask the user a trivia question to start the interaction. When the user answered the question, the robot would try to recognise his/her face. Upon confirmation of the user's identity, the robot would go through each of the user's morning medication and ask him/her to take or apply the medications one by one. After all medications were taken, the robot asks the user about possible medication side effects and monitors their vital signs.

3.2   Public Lobby Scenario (Study 2)

The robot was deployed near a corner of the Lichfield Towers public entry lobby, between 11:00 a.m. and 2:00 p.m. every day. These three hours are the busiest hours in the building. Potential robot users who pass through the lobby include the caregivers, residents from other buildings, visiting friends, relatives as well as the Lichfield Towers' residents themselves. A chair was placed in front of the robot for users during the study. Many residents use a walker and find it easier to sit while using the robot. Most residents in the building pass through the lobby during this time to have lunch in the dining room or leave the building. A video camera was placed near the robot to record all interactions. During the three hour period, a research assistant was designated to sit somewhere in the lobby to observe, to invite people to use the robot at times and be available to assist users when they required help with the robot.

The robot's behaviour in the public lobby is described as follows: A passerby may walk through the lobby, stop, and look at the robot. Upon detecting someone, the robot will greet them and try to initiate an interaction by asking a randomly generated trivia question. For example, the robot would say "Hello, may I ask you a question?" and then ask "When was the decimal currency introduced in New Zealand?" If the person responds through the touch screen, the robot will reply whether the answer is correct, and at the same time try to identify the user's face. If the face recognition is successful, the robot introduces itself as "Charlie" and asks if the person is one of the three people suggested by the face recognition algorithm. The robot will load or create the person's profile and provide services according to the user's profile.

4   Results

In study 1, a total of 84 interactive sessions were expected; however, the actual number of sessions was 47. There were 38 absences from the participants due to sickness or appointment clashes. In all 47 sessions conducted, the HRI system was up and running throughout the sessions. On one occasion, the wireless access point through which the robot connects to a remote laptop was inadvertently removed; therefore, the system's stability and uptime was 98% for study 1. In the public lobby, a total of 48 interactions occurred during the two week period. The HRI system was up and running for 35 of the interactions (73% of the time). For the remainder of the 15 interactions, the HRI system was down either because it was not set up properly, had crashed, or was not working properly. Unlike study 1, the robot in study 2 operated with minimum technical maintenance during the 3 hour time and hence had a lower stability.

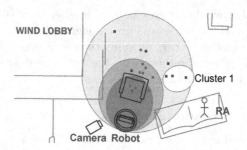

Fig. 1. Positions of people who were detected (*Blue circle*) and undetected (*Red square*)

4.1   Presence Detection and Engagement with Potential Users

The robot's interactivity to detect the presence of a potential user and engage with the user was evaluated in the public lobby. To evaluate the effectiveness of the robot's perception in detecting human presence, the videos recorded from the video camera behind the robot in study 2 (public lobby) were analysed against the logs from the robot's system to find out where, in relation to the robot, people stopped and looked, and whether their presence was detected by the robot. The detection of a human's presence around the robot is based on face detection, and the time threshold to trigger the detector was set at around one second so the robot could differentiate between people who stop to look and those who are just passing by and merely glanced at the robot [7].

375 minutes of video were analysed from the first three days of the study in the public lobby. 325 people passed through the lobby area, and 40 of them stopped and looked at the robot (please refer to Fig. 4); however, 13 of them stopped while someone was already using the robot. The robot was only ready and free to interact only when 17 of them approached the robot. Out of these 17 times, the robot detected the person successfully 10 times and missed the other 7 times. In the other 10 times, the robot could not detect the person due to various reasons including face occlusion. Fig. 1 shows the position where users stopped and whether they were detected and greeted by the robot. These users stopped at different distances from the robot. The markers on the innermost circle (dark green) represent users who directly approached the robot, while the ones on the outer circle (light green) were those who did not deviate from their walking path, but stopped to have a look. The users in the inner two circles (dark and medium green) had higher levels of interest, and therefore, moved toward the robot while passing by and were better detected. There were also people (around cluster 1) who directly approached the research assistant instead of the robot.

The robot uses speech to communicate its intention to interact. From the video analysis, it was observed that the speech is particularly effective for engaging users who are undecided on using the robot. For example, there was an older person in the building who expressed to the research assistant that he did not want to use the robot because he had to go somewhere. But when the robot greeted him as he walked closer to the robot, he sat down to use the robot for about 15 minutes.

4.2   User's Attention to the Robot's Screen and User Identification

To capture 2D images of the user's frontal face to recognise him/her accurately, the robot needs to know the time instants when the user looks at the robot. The amount of head tilting and head rotation should be minimised (or modelled) to maintain the face recognition performance [14]. For this purpose, the user's touch on the robot's screen is monitored with the face detector to capture the time instants of his or her attention on the robot's touch screen. To measure the effectiveness of this design, the degree of head rotation of the faces on the images captured during the study was measured. The face images captured from the previous study described in [8] were also used as a comparison. In the previous study, the robot simply captured all the images in the first few seconds after a user started using the robot, but the result of the face registration and recognition was inconsistent.

As there was no head rotation detection algorithm available, the lead author measured degrees of head rotation in images by hand and estimated the actual degrees of head rotation based on the measurements. For each measurement, the width of the face in the image is first measured and then, depending on which direction the head turns toward, the distance from the side of the face to the centre of the eyes (Side to the centre of eyes) is measured. If the head in the image turns to the left, the measurement is taken from the left hand side of the face to the centre of the eyes. To be able to estimate actual degree of head rotations, several sample photos were taken with the actual degrees of head rotation measured. These measurements were plotted against the ratios of the face widths and the lengths of Side to the centre of eyes measured off the photos. It was found that this relationship could be approximated by a linear equation. Using this equation, the degree of head rotation is computed for each image (as shown in Figs. 2).

During the two week period, a total of 2300 images were captured from all interactions in both of the studies. A maximum of 25 images were captured for each person in an interaction. Because of the large size of the dataset, all images were numbered and 25 images were randomly sampled for manual measurements. The same procedure was repeated to sample another 25 images from the 1002 face images collected from the previous study. The average head rotation in the images captured in the study is 6.69 degrees with a standard deviation (SD) of 4.10 compared to 11.22 with a SD of 13.92 in the previous study. This reflects the quality of the design pattern implemented.

The quality of the face images also is reflected in the accuracy of the face recognition. Fig. 5 shows the face recognition performance in study 1. The robot correctly identified the participants as the top or the second candidate 72% of the time (33 out of 46 interactive sessions). Most participants in study 2 were first time users, therefore there were only a few times the users could be recognised. Nevertheless, their faces were registered the first time they used the robot. So if they returned to use the robot, they could potentially be recognised. The robot correctly identified the participant as the top candidate 50% of the time (3 out of 6 times).

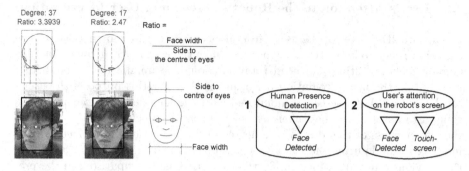

Fig. 2. Head rotation calculation   **Fig. 3.** Interaction patterns

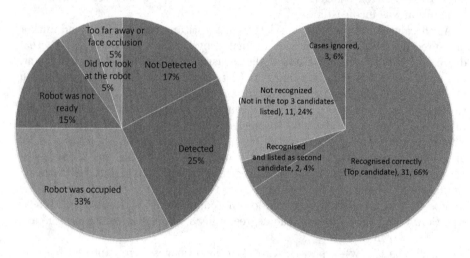

Fig. 4. Presence detection rate   **Fig. 5.** Face recognition in private apartments

Compared to the performance (71 to 80% recognition rate) achieved in laboratory testings with existing face databases [15], the result indicates that the robot could retrieve consistent frontal face images of users for both face registration and recognition even in extreme conditions of face occlusion and lighting.

5 Validation of Interaction Design Patterns

To improve the robot's interaction with users in real environments, the results of the study were then used to validate the interaction patterns. For this validation, questions to answer include how well did the designed interaction patterns handle different use cases with real users? and what are the conditions and limitations an interaction designer need to consider in order to reuse them and have them work as intended? Also asked: What improvements or integration are needed to further improve these patterns? These improvements can be on the component or algorithm level to optimise the patterns for robot perceptions and expressions in an interaction.

For this purpose, the elements of a user interface design pattern defined in [9] and validation criteria suggested by Kahn for social interaction patterns in [6] were used as the basis for constructing a new list of relevant elements for evaluating the interaction design patterns. This list is used in the rest of this section as a guide to validate each interaction design pattern. Fig. 3 shows two of the main interaction design patterns implemented on the robot. They are defined and validated against the list of elements as follows:

---

1. **Human presence detection**
   Problem statement - To detect a potential user around the robot.
   Context of Use - When the robot is required to provide services in a proactive way.
   Interaction Modalities - Face detection via camera.
   Combination with other Pattern(s) - Engage a user by acting upon a detection. The pattern is to be paired with an action from the robot to show its attention to the user and willingness to interact.
   Technical Performance and Limitations - The presence detection is currently limited by the camera view angle. The current implementation is unable to detect any person who does not look at the robot. In this study, the detection rate is 59% (detected 10 of 17 times).

2. **User's attention on the robot**
   Problem statement - To detect a user's attention on the robot and the information on its screen.
   Context of Use - Whenever the robot needs to know the time instants and durations of the user's attention on its screen during an interaction.
   Interaction Modalities - Face detection via camera and touch-screen monitoring.
   Combination with other Pattern(s) - It is required by the "User identification by face" pattern to accurately identify the user by face during an interaction.
   Technical Performance and Limitations - The perception of this interaction cue is shown to be reasonably robust in all conditions in this study. The centre of the users' faces in the captured images were within 6.70 degrees to the robot's screen (SD 4.10 degrees).

---

6   Discussion

Overall, the performance of the robot system in terms of up time and face recognition rate is significantly higher in study 1 (98% and 68%) than study 2 (73% and 50%). A probable reason for this is that the robot's operation was checked and verified prior to the robot entering the participants' apartments; whereas in the lobby, the robot ran autonomously with minimum technical intervention for three hours.

6.1   Use Cases Observed

The majority of older people in the village have little experience with current computer technologies. Consequently, it was necessary to give short introductions to some participants on how to interact with the robot. For example, some did not know the touch-screen buttons could be pressed, and needed demonstrations on how to effectively use them. Some participants needed encouragement from the research assistant to continue their interactions with the robot as they were reluctant to make a guess when they did not know the answers to the NZ trivia questions. These issues at times affected their initial interactions with the robot. Since user's confidence and familiarity with a robot may determine whether they want to use it, these issues should be considered for improving the design of the robot.

In terms of user's behaviour in approaching the robot, the users in study 2 can be divided into two types. The first type is those who know what the robot does and actively approach the robot to use its services. This type of user approached the robot directly and sit on the chair in front of it without needing the robot to prompt them or try to capture their attention. In contrast to the use case considered in the original design, these people do not stop or look at the robot first. The second type of user is those who happened to notice the robot's presence in the lobby area. These people usually do not know the benefits of the robot's services, and the robot's initiation behaviour has a chance to attract them to try its services and therefore change their behaviours.

In study 2, a few participants approached the researchers directly to find out more about the robot and why it was there or if they know the research assistants, sometimes they approached the research assistant for a chat. The robot became a bystander in those interactions and a greeting could be inappropriate as it may interrupt the conversation between the research assistant and residents. The robot was not enabled to detect changes in social contexts and modify its role accordingly to join an interaction or capture attention in this study. Different situations provide different interaction context for the robot, and always having the same interaction sequence on the robot may lead to inappropriate interactions and unsatisfactory user experiences. As the next step of the research, it is essential to further define other roles which the robot needs to play in the target scenarios and settings and then enable the robot with relevant perceptions for context awareness to switch its role accordingly. Future work could include modeling the robot's service and interaction role such as [3] and equipping the robot with more perception abilities to sense whether the users' attention is on another person in an interaction that involves more than two people.

Acknowledgements. This work was supported by the R&D program of the Korea Ministry of Knowledge and Economy (MKE) and Korea Evaluation Institute of Industrial Technology (KEIT). [2008-F039-01, Development of Mediated Interface Technology for HRI]. We acknowledge the support of the New Zealand Ministry for Science and Innovation. We thank ETRI for their contributions.

References

1. Datta, C., Yang, H.Y., Tiwari, P., Kuo, I.H., Macdonald, B.A.: End User Programming to Enable Closed-loop Medication Management Using a Healthcare Robot. Social Science
2. Fowler, M.: UML Distilled: A Brief Guide to the Standard Object Modeling Language. Addison-Wesley Longman Publishing Co., Inc., Boston (2003)
3. Glas, D.F., Miyashita, T., Ishiguro, H., Hagita, N.: Robopal: Modeling Role Transitions in Human-Robot Interaction. In: Proceedings 2007 IEEE International Conference on Robotics and Automation, pp. 2130–2137. IEEE (April 2007)
4. Huttenrauch, H., Eklundh, K.: Fetch-and-carry with CERO: observations from a long-term user study with a service robot. In: Proceedings of the 11th IEEE International Workshop on Robot and Human Interactive Communication, pp. 158–163. IEEE (2002)
5. Jayawardena, C., Kuo, I.H., Unger, U., Igic, A., Wong, R., Watson, C.I., Stafford, R.Q., Broadbent, E., Tiwari, P., Warren, J., Sohn, J., MacDonald, B.A.: Deployment of a service robot to help older people. In: 2010 IEEE/RSJ International Conference on Intelligent Robots and Systems, pp. 5990–5995. IEEE (October 2010)
6. Kahn, P.H., Freier, N.G., Kanda, T., Ishiguro, H., Ruckert, J.H., Severson, R.L., Kane, S.K.: Design patterns for sociality in human-robot interaction. ACM Press, New York (2008)
7. Kuo, I.H., Jayawardena, C., Broadbent, E., MacDonald, B.A.: Multidisciplinary Design Approach for Implementation of Interactive Services. International Journal of Social Robotics 3(4), 443–456 (2011)
8. Kuo, I.H., Jayawardena, C., Tiwari, P., Broadbent, E., MacDonald, B.A.: User Identification for Healthcare Service Robots: Multidisciplinary Design for Implementation of Interactive Services. In: Ge, S.S., Li, H., Cabibihan, J.-J., Tan, Y.K. (eds.) ICSR 2010. LNCS, vol. 6414, pp. 20–29. Springer, Heidelberg (2010)
9. Spool, J.: The Elements of a Design Pattern. Academic Press (2006), http://www.uie.com/articles/elements_of_a_design_pattern/
10. Stafford, R.Q., MacDonald, B.A., Jayawardena, C., Wegner, D.M., Broadbent, E.: Does the robot have a mind of its own? Predictors of healthcare robot use in a retirement village. Manuscript submitted for publication (2012)
11. Steinfeld, A., Fong, T., Kaber, D., Lewis, M., Scholtz, J., Schultz, A., Goodrich, M.: Common metrics for human-robot interaction. In: Proceeding of the 1st ACM SIGCHI/SIGART Conference on Human-Robot Interaction, HRI 2006, p. 33 (2006)
12. Tapus, A., Matarić, M.: User Personality Matching with a Hands-Off Robot for Post-stroke Rehabilitation Therapy. In: Experimental Robotics 2006, pp. 165–175 (July 2006)
13. Tapus, A., Mataric, M., Scassellati, B.: Socially assistive robotics (Grand Challenges of Robotics). IEEE Robotics Automation Magazine 14(1), 35–42 (2007)
14. Xu, M., Akatsuka, T.: Detecting head pose from stereo image sequence for active face recognition. In: Proceedings of the Third IEEE International Conference on Automatic Face and Gesture Recognition, pp. 82–87. IEEE (1998)
15. Yun, W.H., Kim, D., Song, B.Y., Yoon, H.S.: Face recognition using HOG features. In: The 5th International Conference on Ubiquitous Robots and Ambient Intelligence, No. Urai (2008)

Automated Behavioral Mapping
for Monitoring Social Interactions among Older Adults

Claudia B. Rebola[1], Gbolabo Ogunmakin[2], and Patricio A. Vela[2]

[1] School of Industrial Design
[2] School of Electrical and Computer Engineering
Georgia Institute of Technology
{crw,gogunmakin,pvela}@gatech.edu

Abstract. Social interactions in retirement communities' shared spaces is a key component to preventing social isolation and loneliness among older people. Given the underutilization of these spaces, placing technologies to promote socialization in shared spaces might improve independence and quality of life among older adults. In order to understand socializations in these shared spaces, surveillance systems must be developed to quantify the number and type of interactions in an environment. We hypothesize that social interactions amongst older adults can be detected using multiple cameras and microphones strategically placed in the environment. The purpose of this paper is to describe the development of an automatic behavioral mapping surveillance system designed for monitoring interactions among older adults and technology interventions in retirement communities' shared common areas. Specific emphasis is given to the system designed to monitor the number, length and type of interactions of older adults in the community.

Keywords: Social Interactions, Automatic Behavioral Mapping, Retirement Communities.

1 Introduction

Automated processing of video surveillance systems, especially those monitoring humans, is an active research topic in computer vision. Such systems can be applied to various domains, such as retail outlets, traffic monitoring, banks, city centers, airports, and building security. Traditionally, human operators have had to actively man a set of monitors to determine if specific events were occurring. To facilitate the collection of statistics, software such as Observer XT by Noldus provides professional and user-friendly event logging system for the collection, analysis, and presentation of observational data [9]. This system codes and describes behavior in an accurate and quantitative way, but the process is lengthy due to the need for manually annotating the observations. The focus of this paper is to describe an automated behavioral mapping surveillance system for the generation of statistics regarding social interaction in a controlled social environment. Automating the surveillance and interaction processing can improve data collection by removing human bias, human error, and other human factors that may lead to decreased accuracy.

S.S. Ge et al. (Eds.): ICSR 2012, LNAI 7621, pp. 188–198, 2012.

Socialization and Older Adults. Loneliness has been found to be a cause of great discomfort among retirement community residents. Lack of interaction and social support has been found to not only affect the quality of life but to have negative effects on health, leading to a higher mortality rate amongst lonely older adults [4]. Shared common areas in retirement communities are great opportunities for interaction. Yet, they are highly underutilized. If interactions can increase not only their quality of life, but their health as well, means to encourage socialization are imperative, especially in shared common areas.

Technology for Older Adults. Nehmer *et al* [8] proposes that older adults can benefit from technologies; strengthening participation in social life, which shows positive effects on well-being and self-esteem, is one of the ways modern information technology can contribute to aging successfully. Therefore, placing technologies to promote socializations in shared spaces might be a vehicle for promoting independence and quality of life among older adults. This project experiments with implementing designed technologies in retirement communities' shared spaces. Two technologies are designed from simple and utilitarian, to more complex and artistic. A simple designed technology intervention includes an iPad tower, which displays images as a slideshow. Complex designed technology interventions include an interactive art piece, where collaborations with the piece promote further interactions. The overall goal of placing varying technology designs is to investigate the effects of design and technology interventions among older adults.

Behavioral Mapping in Environments. The target application of the proposed automated behavioral mapping surveillance and interaction-processing system is to provide information regarding the interactions and activities of older adults in the shared area of a retirement community. The system will serve as a tool to monitor the social interactions affected by the technology interventions. The goal of the system is to identify how people utilize the space so as to understand if and how technologies designed for, and placed in, the space promote socialization. A social interaction is a mutual or reciprocal action that involves two or more people and produces various characteristic visual/audio patterns.

Researchers have designed multiple sensor systems to determine interactions within a group. These sensors are integrated into a framework to provide activity recognition. For example, Lymberopoulos, et al. [6] used cameras, door sensors, and passive infrared sensors to create a spatiotemporal human activity model for activity detection. Wu et al. [13] and Park et al. [10] used a combination of RFIDs and video data to perform activity recognition. Wu et al. [13] used Dynamic Bayesian Networks (DBNs) to determine the most likely activity and object labels in their work. Wu et al. [14] use multiple cameras to collect spatial-temporal data and perform activity recognition. Chen et al. [2] use video and audio data for detecting social interactions. They evaluated various machine-learning algorithms such as decision trees, naive Bayes classifiers, naive Bayesian networks, Adaboost, and logistic region. Hauptmann et al. [5] also use video and audio data for activity recognition. They use the mean shift tracker and support vector machines (SVM) to train the system to recognize activities.

The problem with these approaches is that some use sensors, such as RFID and infrared sensors that are not readily available for daily surveillance due to intrusiveness or economic cost. Additionally, some of these approaches use algorithms that require significant supervised training. The work done in this paper takes a simplified approach to detecting social interactions amongst individuals. Two cameras and a microphone are used to collect video and audio data. The video data is processed using the detailed surveillance system and the audio is analyzed to detect the presence of noise. The analysis results of the video and audio data are then combined to determine whether an interaction has taken place.

2   System Overview

The automated behavioral mapping surveillance system is designed for installation in common areas of a retirement community. Two cameras and a microphone are installed, c.f. Figure 1. The cameras and microphone are positioned to monitor a central location, where technology interventions can be placed. The cameras are strategically positioned to view the surroundings of the central location and all access routes to it.

The automated behavioral mapping surveillance system consists of five critical software components: a foreground detector, a target tracker, a target reidentifier, and an interaction processor. The system requires a background model for detecting the foreground objects in a scene. Trackers are initialized when foreground objects are detected at regions designated as entrance areas. Once the targets have been tracked, a foreground mask is returned. The background model to detect new foreground targets uses the mask. Newly detected foreground targets are compared to previous disappeared targets to see if a target has re-appeared. If the target is re-identified as a previous target, a new tracker is not initialized but the disappeared target's tracker is re-activated. After targets in the video sequence have been tracked, the information is sent to the interaction processor for state estimation, c.f. Figure 2. The interaction processor performs audio analysis and synchronizes it with the trajectory information to estimate states.

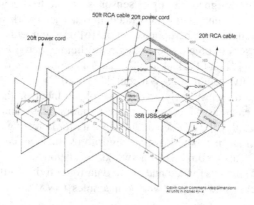

Fig. 1. Layout of common area

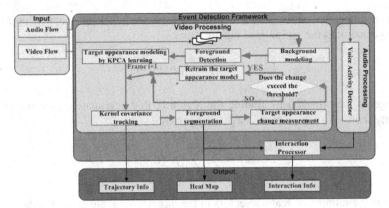

Fig. 2. System overview

2.1 Foreground Detection

In this paper, Gaussian mixture models (GMM) were used to perform foreground detection [12]. GMMs store multimodal representations of background so that more complex dynamic scenes can be handled. GMMs allow background subtraction to be robust to gradual illumination changes, periodic motions from cluttered background, slow moving objects, long-term scene changes, and camera noises. To perform foreground detection using GMMs, each pixel is modeled separately by a mixture of m Gaussians. Each m Gaussian distribution describes a background pixel. The probability of observing a pixel value, x, belonging to the background at time t is given by:

$$P(x_t) = \sum \omega_{i,t} \eta \left(x_t; \mu_{i,t}, \Sigma_{i,t} \right),$$ (1)

where m is the number of distributions, $\omega_{i,t}$ is the estimated weight of the ith Gaussian in the mixture at time t, $\mu_{i,t}$ is the mean value of the ith Gaussian in the mixture at time t, $\Sigma_{i,t}$ is the covariance matrix of the ith Gaussian in the mixture at time t, it is assumed to be $\Sigma_{i,t} = \sigma_k^2 I$, and η is a Gaussian probability density function.

2.2 Kernel Covariance Tracking

The tracking algorithm, summarize here, utilizes and improved version of the robust kernel covariance tracker found in [1], allowing for scale changes. As each target is detected via the Foreground Detection module, a tracker is automatically initialized using results from the foreground detector. The tracking algorithm utilizes a statistical model of the joint color and spatial data, $u_i = [I(x_i), x_i]^T$, where $I(x_i)$ is the color data at location x_i. The target's model is learned by mapping its feature vector into the Hilbert space using the Gaussian kernel, $k(u_i, u_j) = \exp\left(-\frac{1}{2}(u_i - u_j)^T \Sigma^{-1}(u_i - u_j)\right)$. The eigenvectors, $\alpha^k = [\alpha_1^k, ..., \alpha_N^k]$, and eigenvalues, λ^k, of the kernel matrix are computed. All the mapped points are then projected onto the normalized eigenvectors

$$f^k(u_i) = \sum_{j=1}^{N} \frac{\alpha_i^k}{\sqrt{\lambda^k}} k(u_i, u_j) .$$

(2)

The target is then tracked by finding the region $\mathcal{R}$ that best matches the target. The similarity score of a region to the target is given by

$$SC(\mathcal{R}) = \sum_{i=1}^{n} \sum_{k=1}^{ne} (f^k(u_i))^2 ,$$

(3)

where n is the number of feature vectors in the target's template and ne is the number of eigenvectors retained. The target's new location can be determined by locally optimizing the region similarity using gradient descent or mean shift. Once the target has been localized, a similar optimization refines the target's change in scale. Performing these two optimizations jointly is unstable, as the optimizations differ. Given that the kernel covariance tracker is robust to minor scale changes, such a decoupled approach is more stable.

2.3   Target Re-identification

The re-identification module assumes that targets do not change their clothing in between sittings. Target re-identification is performed using KPCA following the approach of Yang et al. [15]. Once the target is detected, key templates for re-identification are acquired as the target is being tracked. Key templates are chosen to represent the target's change in appearance and pose due to movement, illumination changes, and scale changes. Key templates are selected based on how distinctly they represent the target. The target's dominant visual features are learned using KPCA as described in Section 2.2. When a target is detected at the entrance locations, its feature vectors are projected to the learned models of previously seen targets. The similarity score SC is defined in equation (3). If SC is above the given threshold, the target is declared new and its first key template is initialized. If it is below the given threshold, it is declared as the target with the minimum score. The target's tracker is then re-initialized and tracking continues.

2.4   Audio Analysis

For this project, an interaction between targets is defined as communication between two or more people in the environment who are all standing near the technology intervention. Communication is determined using the audio analysis results, which is binary valued, 1 when there is sound, 0 when there isn't. The audio files are processed using a voice activity detector. The voice activity detector is the implementation of the methods described in [3, 7, 11]. The power spectral density of no stationary noise is estimated by tracking spectral minima in each frequency band without any distinction between speech activity and speech pause. The noise is reduced using the minimum mean-square error short-time spectral amplitude estimator. The estimator models the speech and noise spectral components as statistically independent Gaussian random variables. This provides enhanced speech for processing. The voice activity detector employs a decision-directed parameter estimation method for the likelihood ratio test. A first-order Markov process is then used to model speech occurrences. The voice activity detector produces a binary output, 1's for speech activity, and 0's for no speech.

2.5   Interaction Processor

The interaction processor will process input, tracking results, audio analysis results, entrances, and region of interest. The interaction processor will return the number of targets that entered the scene; the number of times each target entered and left the scene; the number of times and length targets interacted with a technology device in the environment; the number of times targets passed the technology device without stopping; and the number of targets that interacted and which targets interacted with each other. The tracking results are used to determine when the targets are located within the technology intervention. When two or more targets are within the technology, if the audio analysis results is 1, then it is determined that they are interacting with each other.

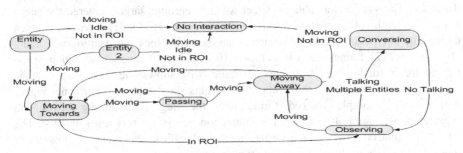

Fig. 3. Interaction processor

Observations {moving, idle, talking, in ROI, multiple entities}, are acquired from the tracking results and audio analysis. These observations are used to determine the states {observing, conversing, no interaction, passing, leaving, approaching} of the targets and the technology intervention. The change in the target's location, $\dot{x}(t)$, over time is used to determine whether the target is moving or idle.

To determine when a target is near the technology intervention, the target's distance to it is calculated as, $d(t) = \|x(t) - x_a\|^2$ where $x(t)$ is the target's location at time t and x_a is the technology intervention's location. If $d(t)$ is within a specified threshold, then the target is close to it. The derivative of the distance, $\dot{d}(t) = 2[x(t) - x_a]^T \dot{x}(t)$, where $\dot{x}(t)$ is change of x over time, is used to determine when a target is approaching, passing, or leaving the art piece.

$$\begin{aligned}
&passing, &&\text{if } -\Delta < \dot{d} < \Delta; \\
&approaching, &&\text{if } \dot{d} < -\Delta; &&&&(4)\\
&leaving, &&\text{if } \dot{d} > \Delta.
\end{aligned}$$

If the target does not stop for a period of time while in the vicinity of the technology intervention, then it is decided that the target has passed it without stopping. This will be used to show the amount of interest the technology generates.

3   Experimental Results

To validate the system, a pilot experiment was designed to simulate a technology at the retirement community. A mock up of an interactive technology was placed in the lab space. Lab users were monitored during the pilot study. The automated behavioral mapping surveillance system was setup to replicate the installation area, as well as the ambient lighting conditions. If the automated system could function well in this space, then it will also function well in the retirement community.

Experiment 1. The video test sequence contained 10,800 frames with users walking in and out and observing the technology or interacting with each other. Five targets entered and exited the scene a total of 15 times. The system was able to track these targets throughout the scene. Figure 4(a) shows the trajectories of the targets through the space. The system was able to detect when foreground targets entered the scene but the re-identification module could not always correctly identify a previously seen target. The interaction processor detected that the technology intervention was being observed in 7172 frames. It also detected 19 instances of interactions amongst the targets for a total of 2676 frames. Figure 4(b) shows the heat map for the experiments. The red spots show where the targets spent most of their time. Figure 4(c) shows a sample tracked frame with the targets' bounding boxes and segmentations. Figure 4(d) shows the interaction matrix for this test sequence. The interaction matrix shows which targets interacted with each other and how many times. Figure 5 shows the states of the art piece and a target.

Experiment 2. A second test sequence consisting of 23,727 frames with users walking in and out without observing the technology or interacting with each other. Five targets entered and exited the scene a total of 21 times. Figure 6(a) shows the trajectories of the targets through the space. Figure 6(b) shows that the system provides a text-based synopsis of the events that were detected and the different states that were triggered during the surveillance time. The system was able to accurately identify the targets 20 out of 21 times. The multiple objects tracking accuracy (MOTA) for this experiment was 0.723. This was due to the incorrectly identified target spending the most time in the scene.

Automated Behavioral Mapping System. The automated behavioral system output and interface was designed to provide output similar to that of Observer XT, albeit specialized to the investigation presented in this paper. Figure 7 depicts the graphical user interface that exists for reviewing the tracking results. Visualizations of the different people detected and tracked can be controlled and viewed, as well as the

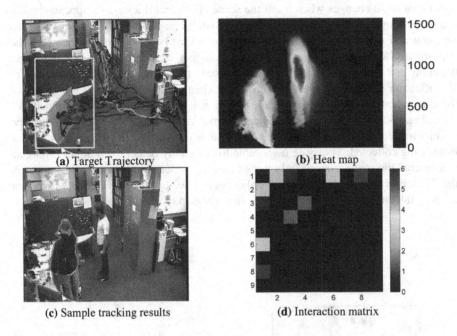

(a) Target Trajectory

(b) Heat map

(c) Sample tracking results

(d) Interaction matrix

Fig. 4. Experiment 1 sample results of automated processing

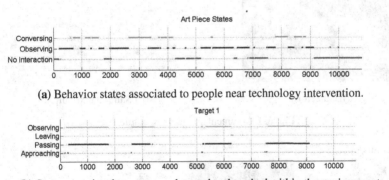

(a) Behavior states associated to people near technology intervention.

(b) States associated to a person detected and tracked within the environment.

Fig. 5. Technology and target state output from the interaction processor

target states being triggered. Additionally, the technology intervention states can be viewed to see what type of socialization or interaction occurred.

4   Discussion

This tracker coupled with the re-identification module was able to correctly identify all but one of the targets. The target could not be re-identified and went through significant scale changes when it left the scene. To detect if a target's appearance has changed enough to retrain it's appearance model, the re-identification module checks for pose and color changes. As the target goes further away from the camera, he appears smaller, but his color information does not change. Given that the target bounding box is rescaled to a default scale prior to measuring the pose change, the re-identification module does not trigger a pose change model update. On account of these two features, the re-identification does not update the candidate models for retraining. While a faulty re-identification module prevent accurately linking the disjoint trajectories of the detected people, it does not prevent the necessary statistics from being collected. The system was able to accurately detect the number of targets that entered the scene, successfully track them, and determine how long they spent in the ROI observing the technology. Furthermore, it was able to determine whether or not they interacted with each other while in the region of interest.

(a) Trajectories

```
Target 1 was detected 6 time(s)
    Entered at frame 81 and left at frame 153
    Entered at frame 710 and left at frame 805
    Entered at frame 1009 and left at frame 1083
    Entered at frame 1804 and left at frame 1859
    Entered at frame 3841 and left at frame 3886
    Entered at frame 4016 and left at frame 4071
Target 2 was detected 6 time(s)
    Entered at frame 298 and left at frame 367
    Entered at frame 3046 and left at frame 3056
    Entered at frame 8793 and left at frame 8882
    Entered at frame 12128 and left at frame 12139
    Entered at frame 18734 and left at frame 18805
    Entered at frame 19342 and left at frame 19354
Target 3 was detected 3 time(s)
    Entered at frame 1235 and left at frame 1290
    Entered at frame 2514 and left at frame 2559
    Entered at frame 7776 and left at frame 7841
Target 4 was detected 2 time(s)
    Entered at frame 4571 and left at frame 4597
    Entered at frame 4673 and left at frame 4719
Target 5 was detected 2 time(s)
    Entered at frame 9679 and left at frame 9736
    Entered at frame 9968 and left at frame 10035
Target 6 was detected 2 time(s)
    Entered at frame 12382 and left at frame 12439
    Entered at frame 21984 and left at frame 22496

Detected 0 interaction(s) between multiple people
```

(b) Sample text output

Fig. 6. Experiment 2: Tracking results

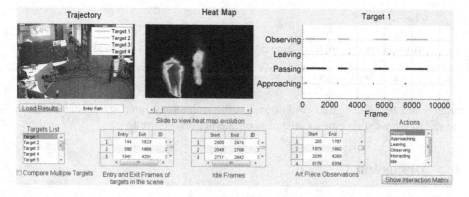

Fig. 7. Interaction visualization GUI

5   Conclusion

This paper discussed the design of an automated behavioral mapping surveillance and interaction processing system for the purpose of understanding how technology interventions might alter socialization in common areas of retirement communities. The system comprises of algorithms that do not require supervised training, which is beneficial when processing a large amount of frames. The system was presented with visualizations that allowed the users to understand what was going on in the scene. It was validated in a simulated environment replicating the configuration of an actual common area in a retirement community. In particular, the experiment demonstrated the effectiveness of the event detection framework at detecting whether people are observing a given technology or interacting with each other. The results show that a better re-identification module will be needed. The re-identification module did not work as expected for camera configurations because of the major scale changes that occur as the target traverses the space.   Future work will involve developing a target re-identification module that deals well with scale changes.

References

1. Arif, O., Vela, P.: Robust density comparison for visual tracking. In: British Machine Vision Conference (2009)
2. Chen, D., Yang, J., Malkin, R., Wactlar, H.D.: Detecting social interactions of the elderly in a nursing home environment. ACM Trans. Multimedia Comput. Commun. Appl., 3 (2007)
3. Ephraim, Y., Malah, D.: Speech enhancement using a minimum-mean square error short-time spectral amplitude estimator. IEEE Trans. on Acoustics, Speech and Signal Processing 32(6), 1109–1121 (1984)
4. Golden, J., Conroy, R.M., Bruce, I., Denihan, A., Greene, E., Kirby, M., Lawlor, B.A.: Loneliness, social support networks, mood and wellbeing in community-dwelling elderly. Int. J. of Geriatric Psychiatry 24(7), 694–700 (2009)
5. Hauptmann, A.G., Gao, J., Yan, R., Qi, Y., Yang, J., Wactlar, H.D.: Automated analysis ofnursing home observations. IEEE Pervasive Computing 3(2), 15–21 (2004)
6. Lymberopoulos, D., Bamis, A., Savvides, A.: Extracting spatiotemporal human activity patterns in assisted living using a home sensor network. In: Int. Conf. on Pervasive Technologies Related to Assistive Environments, pp. 29:1–29:8. ACM, New York (2008)
7. Martin, R.: Noise power spectral density estimation based on optimal smoothing and minimum statistics. IEEE Trans. on Speech and Audio Processing 9(5), 504–512 (2001)
8. Nehmer, J., Lindenberger, U., Steinhagen-Thiessen, E.: Aging and Technology - Friends, Not Foes. Journal of Gerontopsychology and Geriatric Psychiatry 23(2), 55–57 (2010)
9. Observer   XT,   http://www.noldus.com/human-behavior-research/products/the-observer-xt
10. Park, S., Kautz, H.: Privacy-preserving Recognition of Activities in Daily Livingfrom Multi-view Silhouettesand RFID-based Training. In: AAAISymposium on AI in Eldercare: New Solutions to Old Problems (2008)
11. Sohn, J., Kim, N.S., Sung, W.: A Statistical Model-based Voice Activity Detection. IEEE Signal Processing Letters 6(1), 1–3 (1999)

12. Stauffer, C., Grimson, W.E.L.: Adaptive Background Mixture Models for Real-Time Tracking. In: Conf. on Computer Vision and Pattern Recognition, pp. 252–268 (1999)
13. Wu, C., Khalili, A.H., Aghajan, H.: Multiview Activity Recognition in Smart Homes with Spatio-temporal Features. In: ACM/IEEE Int. Conf. on Distributed Smart Cameras, pp. 142–149. ACM, New York (2010)
14. Wu, J., Osuntogun, A., Choudhury, T., Philipose, M., Rehg, J.M.: A Scalable Approach to Activity Recognition Based onObject Use. In: Int. Conf. on Computer Vision, Rio de Janeiro (2007)
15. Yang, J., Shi, Z., Vela, P.A.: Person Reidentification by Kernel PCA Based Appearance Learning. In: Canadian Conf.on Computer and Robot Vision, pp. 227–233 (2011)

Anthropomorphism and Human Likeness in the Design of Robots and Human-Robot Interaction

Julia Fink

CRAFT, Ecole Polytechnique Fédérale de Lausanne, 1015 Lausanne, Switzerland
julia.fink@epfl.ch

Abstract. In this literature review we explain anthropomorphism and its role in the design of socially interactive robots and human-robot interaction. We illustrate the social phenomenon of anthropomorphism which describes people's tendency to attribute lifelike qualities to objects and other non lifelike artifacts. We present theoretical backgrounds from social sciences, and integrate related work from robotics research, including results from experiments with social robots. We present different approaches for anthropomorphic and humanlike form in a robot's design related to its physical shape, its behavior, and its interaction with humans. This review provides a comprehensive understanding of anthropomorphism in robotics, collects and reports relevant references, and gives an outlook on anthropomorphic human-robot interaction.

Keywords: anthropomorphism, design, human-robot interaction, literature review, social robots, social factors in robotics.

1 Anthropomorphism and the Role of Anthropomorphic Design

Soon more and more robots will be used in everyday environments, and an important aspect of developing "socially interactive robots" [1] is the design for effective human-robot interaction (HRI) as well as acceptance. One approach to enhance people's acceptance of robots is the attempt to increase a robot's familiarity by using anthropomorphic (humanlike) design and "human social" characteristics. This implies humanlike parts of a robot's physical shape, the usage of facial expressions and other social cues, as well as natural humanlike interaction and communication (e.g. speech, gaze, gestures). However, the role of anthropomorphism in robotics is not to build an artificial human but rather to take advantage of it as a mechanism through which social interaction can be facilitated [2]. An underlying assumption is that humans prefer to interact with machines in the same way that they interact with other people [1]. The idea combines "anthropomorphic design" and the phenomenon of "anthropomorphism" – when people attribute human characteristics to objects. Researchers have found that whenever artifacts show intentional behavior (e.g. when animated), people tend to perceive them as characters or even as creatures [3] [4].

1.1 Anthropomorphism

"Anthropomorphism" originates from the Greek "*anthropos*" for "human" and "*morphe*" for "shape" or "form" [2]. It describes people's tendency to attribute

S.S. Ge et al. (Eds.): ICSR 2012, LNAI 7621, pp. 199–208, 2012.

human characteristics to non-lifelike artifacts. The phenomenon of ascribing intentions [5] and animacy to simple shapes based on motion has been intensively studied in (developmental) psychology. But why do humans ascribe intentions and emotions to objects? One interpretation is that attributing familiar humanlike qualities to a less familiar non-humanlike entity can serve to make the entity become more familiar, explainable, or predictable [6]. In the design of socially interactive robots [1], anthropomorphism plays an important role and is reflected in the robot's form (appearance), behavior (e.g. motion), and interaction (e.g. modality). Robotics uses the mechanism to increase acceptance of robots and facilitate interaction.

1.2   Anthropomorphic Forms in Robot-Design: Shape, Behavior, Interaction

Anthropomorphic design means an imitation of human (or natural) form [7]. Fong et al. classify four categories of a robot's aesthetic form: anthropomorphic, zoomorphic, caricatured, and functional [1]. In robotics, "anthropomorphic design" refers to three parts: a robot's shape, behavior, and interaction/communication with the human [8] [9]. Social robots make further use of "human social" characteristics, such as express/perceive emotions, communicate with high-level dialogue, learn/recognize models of other agents, establish/maintain social relationships, use natural cues (gaze, gestures, etc.), exhibit distinctive personality and character, learn/develop social competencies [1]. One may ask how much human-likeness we want to have in non-human objects. How will people react to a robot that resembles a human? In 1970, Mashiro Mori formulated a theory called the "uncanny valley" [10]. It describes people's reactions to technologies that resemble a human too close while still not being one. Mori hypothesized that a person's response to a humanlike robot would abruptly shift from empathy to revulsion as it approached, but failed to attain, a lifelike appearance [10].

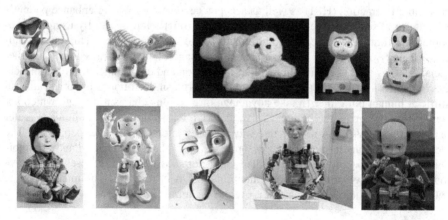

Fig. 1. Examples for bio-/anthropomorphic robots; top row: AIBO, Pleo, Paro, iCat, Papero; bottom row: Kaspar, NAO, Nexi, Barthoc, iCub

1.3   Why Is Anthropomorphism Relevant for (Social) Robotics?

What brings together anthropomorphic design and social robotics is the fact, that the appearance and function of a product impacts how people perceive it, interact with it, and build long-term relationships with it [11]. On one hand, robots with humanlike design cues can elicit social responses from humans which in turn can have a positive impact on acceptance [12] [13] [14]. People responded more positively to an artifact that displayed humanlike behavioral characteristics (emotions, facial expression) in contrast to a purely functional design [3] [15] [16] [17]. However, user preferences were task and context dependent [18]. Thus, the appearance of a robot should match its capabilities as well as the users' expectations [13] [19]. Anthropomorphizing a technological agent appears to create some social connection to it, aids in learning how to use it [6], and how pleasant and usable it is perceived [20] [16]. People preferred to collaborate with a robot that was able to respond socially [14] [18]. On the other hand, robots that overuse anthropomorphic form, such as humanoids that almost perfectly resemble a human but still remain unnatural copies, can have a contrary effect and evoke fear or rejection [10]. Though the point of when this negative effect can be observed is not yet identified, studies showed that especially humanoid robots evoked more reluctant and negative responses than robots with a pet-like or more functional shape [21]. Interestingly, the phenomenon seems to be culture sensitive [22] and based on Epley et al.'s psychological determinants likely to be related to other person-related factors, such as expertise/experience with a system [23] [24].

2   The Social Phenomenon and Socially Interactive Robots

2.1   Explaining the Social Phenomenon of Anthropomorphism

According to [25], there are two main perspectives when seeking to explain people's tendency to anthropomorphize artifacts. First one explains anthropomorphism from the design of the artifact. It is assumed that humans directly respond to life-like or social cues that an object or system emits, without thoughtful mental processing, by simply applying stereotypes and heuristics to it. Schmitz [26] describes that within the visual scope for design, the outer appearance can have an important impact on the overall perception of an object. If this explanation of anthropomorphism is correct, people may respond automatically to social cues emitted by a robot, and apply human-human social schemas and norms to these interactions [25].

A second explanation applies a human-centered, cognitive viewpoint where anthropomorphism is described through people's specific mental model [25] they have about how an artifact works the way it does. If a system behaves much like a human being (e.g. emits a human voice), people's mental model of the system's behavior may approach their mental model of humans, but this model may differ in important respects from their models of humans [25]. People's estimation of a robot's "knowledge" and its capabilities/abilities affects the way they relate to it. Research examined the validity of the mental model concept with various kinds of robots [25] [27]. Findings suggest that people tend to hold richer mental models about anthropomorphic robots in contrast to mechanic ones [27] .

As an alternative to the two explanations given above, one can explain people's tendency to attribute human qualities to objects based on social psychology. As mentioned earlier, Epley et al. [6] established a three-factor theory of when people are likely to anthropomorphize based on psychological determinants. Namely, the theory describes that some people are more likely to anthropomorphize, so when (i) anthropocentric knowledge is accessible and applicable to the artifact (elicited agent knowledge), (ii) they are motivated to explain and understand the behavior of other agents (effectance motivation), and (iii) they have the desire for social contact and affiliation (social motivation) [6]. Some work also discusses the inverse process to humanizing artifacts, namely, dehumanization [6], or mechanomorphism [23].

2.2   Classification and Evaluation of Social Robots

Socially interactive robots can be classified in terms of (1) how well the robot can support the social model that is ascribed to it and (2) the complexity of the interaction scenario that can be supported [1]. Breazeal [28] and later extended by Fong et al. [1] suggest seven classes of social robots: socially evocative, social interface, socially receptive, sociable, socially situated, socially embedded, socially intelligent (for more details, see Fong et al. [1]). This classification is based on Dautenhahn and Billard's [29] definition of social robots, as *"embodied agents that are part of a heterogeneous group: a society of robots or humans. They are able to recognize each other and engage in social interactions, they possess histories (perceive and interpret the world in terms of their own experience), and they explicitly communicate with and learn from each other."* Since the time when the Turing Test was drafted, one of the benchmarks for success in AI and HRI has been how well a system can imitate human behavior. Several measurements and methods have been suggested for the evaluation of anthropomorphic robots: psychological benchmarks [30], as well as properties of a social robot rated by humans [19] [31]. From a methodological point of view, questionnaires and content analyses [32] [33] have been used to analyze anthropomorphism in robotics but also more implicit measures (e.g. psychophysical onses), such as gaze cues [34], motor/perceptual resonance [35], and neurologic metrics [4].

3   How Anthropomorphism Impacts Human-Robot Interaction

3.1   Impacts of Anthropomorphic Shape of a Robot

A robot's physical embodiment is one of the most obvious and unique attributes and thus of high importance for interaction. The role of the physically visible design of robotic products has been discussed and investigated by designers [8] [19] [36]. HRI studies have so far verified that there are differences in how people interact with anthropomorphic and non-anthropomorphic robots [37] especially in terms of social interaction. However, while no real evidence exists, theory suggests a negative correlation between the robot's physical realism and its effectiveness in HRI [37]. A human shaped robot can raise specific expectations from the user side [25], which can lead to a negative effect when the robot's behavior does not meet these expectations.

In general, many studies so far, contribute (partly) to the "uncanny valley" effect, however, one has to take a more detailed look at which dimensions of the interaction are affected: Kanda et al. conducted a study with two different humanoid robots (ASIMO and Robovie) and showed that different appearance did not affect the participants' verbal behavior toward the robot but did affect their non-verbal behavior such as distance and delay of response [38]. Similarly, comparing a pet-robot (AIBO) to a humanoid robot (ASIMO), people seem to prefer the pet-shaped robot [21]. While there was no significant difference in how people gave verbal commands to both robots, the way participants gave positive and negative feedback to AIBO and ASIMO differed significantly [21]. While AIBO was treated similarly to a real dog and petted to give positive feedback, the humanoid ASIMO was touched far less [21].

In evaluating how humanlike a robot appears, especially a robot's head and *face* receives considerable attention, since this body part is crucial in human-human communication (most non-verbal cues are mediated through the face). DiSalvo et al. [8] found that particularly the nose, the eyelids and the mouth increase the perception of humanness in robotic heads. Further, the width of the head had a significant effect.

Also, a robot's *physical embodiment* and presence has been investigated in terms of anthropomorphic interactions compared to robot-like agents or a remote robot [39] [40]. Kiesler et al. [39] conducted a study where a robot-like agent interviewed participants about their health. People were either present with the robot/agent, or interacted remotely with it, projected life-size on a screen. Results indicated that participants were more engaged, disclosed less undesirable behavior, and forgot more with the robot versus the agent [39]. People viewed the robot as more dominant, trustworthy, sociable, responsive, competent, and respectful than the agent and rated it more lifelike. The collocated robot was anthropomorphized the most [39].

In conclusion, studies suggest a positive effect of embodied robots that use anthropomorphic shape. However, there is the tendency that participants prefer a pet-shaped robot to a human-shaped robot. Overall, research confirmed that the physical shape of a robot strongly influences how people perceive it and interact with it, thus visible design is crucial. However, demographic, cultural factors [22] [41], individual preferences, and the context of use need to be considered as well. This makes it hard to identify concrete universal guidelines for how to design an acceptable social robot.

3.2   Impacts of Robots Using Human Social Cues / Social Interaction

Besides the shape, a robot's effectiveness in HRI is also related to its behavioral social success which is a fundamental component of the interaction. Studies showed that the social identity of the robot (both the personality and the role of the robot) [37] has an effect on the user's task performance. The use of social interaction in HRI is expected to make the interaction more natural and thus more effective. Efforts have been made in making a robot's behavior social by giving it a personality, letting it display facial expressions, making it communicate in a polite way, or even making it cheat [42], for example. Also the ability of recognizing and being aware of the human counterpart's emotional state was used as one possibility for socially intelligent machines. In the following we present results of studies with robots that used human social cues to interact with people and outline how this affected the interaction.

A considerable amount of studies investigated the effect of a robot's ability to exhibit *facial expressions* during interacting with a human. Eyssel et al. [15] examined the effects of a robot's emotional nonverbal response on evaluations of anthropomorphism. Using the iCat robot they found that when the robot provided emotional feedback, people perceived it as more likeable, felt closer to it, and rated the interaction as more pleasant compared to when the same robot responded neutrally. Participants evaluated the emotionally expressive robot more humanlike and anthropomorphized it more, due to the fact that it displayed two emotional states (happiness and fear) during the interaction [15]. Gonsior et al. [43] could show a similar effect, measuring people's *empathy* toward the robot head EDDIE when (1) it was neutral, (2) displayed the subject's facial expression, and (3) when it displayed facial expressions according to its internal model, indirectly mirroring the subject's expression (labeled as the "social motivation model") [43]. People's ratings on empathy, subjective performance, trust, and likeability significantly differed between the three conditions and were most positive for the robot using the social motivation model.

A robot's *social awareness* can also be expressed in the way it communicates verbally. The presence of voice is another strong trigger for anthropomorphic perception. Different kinds of voices have been evaluated as well as dialogue and turn-taking in HRI. For example, Fussell et al. [44] could show that people view a robot that responds politely as less mechanistic than an impolite one, which contributes to the hypothesis that social robots are perceived as more humanlike.

In conclusion, human social behavior, such as facial expression or the sound of voice [45], shape not only the way we interact with each other but also how a robot is evaluated. It is still a challenge to model human social characteristics in robots and most systems can only be used in short-term interaction or are operated by a "wizard", where still the robot is not autonomous but a human is operating it in the background.

3.3   Anthropomorphic Human-Robot Interaction

What would be the advantages of "anthropomorphic" interaction? First of all, the actual world is quite well suited for humans. Everything is well adapted to the size of a human; it's physical abilities and limitations, and so forth. Secondly, humans usually know how to interact with each other. They use natural cues, gestures, emotions, speech and the interaction is characterized through multimodality. For HRI however, multimodal interfaces are challenging [37]: computer vision to process (optimally in real time) facial expression and gestures; speech recognition for language understanding and dialog systems; sensory processing to combine visual and linguistic data toward improved sensing and expression. Still, to add meaning to facial and physical expressions and speech, and combining all of those capabilities in real time on a mobile, self-contained robot platform, is an open research problem in robotics [37]. In addition, for social interaction body pose, movement, and other subtle cues are important sources of information. In recent years there have come up interesting new ways for interacting with technology that could be transferred to robotics [46]. Haptic or tangible interfaces and affective computing exploit anthropomorphic design to facilitate interaction and make the user experience more pleasant. Anthropomorphic interfaces attempt to build on established human skills (e.g. physical manipulation of tangible objects [26]), learned in daily social encounters. Another technical trend is to augment everyday objects with sensing, computing, and actuation power. Lifelike movements in everyday objects can be beneficial for interaction [36]. The attempt with anthropomorphic interfaces is to exploit both the naturalness of conversational and social interaction, and the physicality of real world objects.

4   Conclusion

Anthropomorphic and socially interactive robots are certainly a very interesting field in HRI and extensive research has been carried out to investigate the impact of human-shaped robots and robots using humanlike behavior in the interaction with people. One strives hard to draw a general conclusion especially since some findings seem to be contradictory and highly sensitive to the human individual in the loop. Overall, due to its broad understanding and usage in a variety of disciplines, the phenomenon of anthropomorphism seems to be more difficult to grasp than expected. Further, experiments do not always use robots or manipulate their properties in a way that it is actually valid for comparison and thus not all results are meaningful. However, that anthropomorphism is of complex nature has already been pointed out by others [13]. However, we like to mention here, that anthropomorphic design, though it holds some very promising approaches, is not the "one and only" solution to design meaningful HRI. There are equal good reasons to not design humanlike robots. This has for example been recognized by DiSalvo et al. [8] who suggest that in the design of robots, a balance needs be found that takes into account three considerations: *"the need to retain an amount of robot-ness so that the user does not develop false expectations of the robots emotional abilities but realizes its machine capabilities; the need to project an amount of humanness so that the user will feel comfortably engaging the robot; and the need to convey an amount of product-ness so that the user will feel comfortable using the robot."* [8] Alternatives to pure anthropomorphism can also be found in new interfaces for HRI [47]. We still believe that robots – as well as humans – need to be authentic in the way they are, to be "successful" in a variety of dimensions. "The best way is just being oneself."

Acknowledgements. This research was supported by the Swiss National Science Foundation through the National Centre of Competence in Research on Robotics.

References

1. Fong, T., Nourbakhsh, I., Dautenhahn, K.: A survey of socially interactive robots. Robotics and Autonomous Systems 42, 143–166 (2003)
2. Duffy, B.R.: Anthropomorphism and Robotics. Presented at the Symposium on Animating Expressive Characters of Social Interactions, Imperial College, London (2002)
3. Reeves, B., Nass, C.: The Media Equation: How People Treat Computers, Television, and New Media Like Real People and Places. Cambridge University Press (1996)

4. Oberman, L.M., McCleery, J.P., Ramachandran, V.S., Pineda, J.A.: EEG evidence for mirror neuron activity during the observation of human and robot actions: Toward an analysis of the human qualities of interactive robots. Neurocomputing 70, 2194–2203 (2007)
5. Admoni, H., Scassellati, B.: A Multi-Category Theory of Intention. In: Proceedings of COGSCI 2012, Sapporo, Japan, pp. 1266–1271 (2012)
6. Epley, N., Waytz, A., Cacioppo, J.T.: On seeing human: A three-factor theory of anthropomorphism. Psychological Review 114, 864–886 (2007)
7. DiSalvo, C., Gemperle, F.: From seduction to fulfillment: the use of anthropomorphic form in design. In: Proceedings of the 2003 International Conference on Designing Pleasurable Products and Interfaces, pp. 67–72. ACM, New York (2003)
8. DiSalvo, C.F., Gemperle, F., Forlizzi, J., Kiesler, S.: All robots are not created equal: the design and perception of humanoid robot heads. In: Proceedings of the 4th Conference on Designing Interactive Systems: Processes, Practices, Methods, and Techniques, pp. 321–326. ACM, New York (2002)
9. DiSalvo, C.: Imitating the Human Form: Four Kinds of Anthropomorphic Form, http://www.anthropomorphism.org/pdf/Imitating.pdf
10. Mori, M.: The Uncanny Valley (1970)
11. Bartneck, C., Forlizzi, J.: Shaping human-robot interaction: understanding the social aspects of intelligent robotic products. In: CHI 2004 Extended Abstracts on Human Factors in Computing Systems, pp. 1731–1732. ACM, New York (2004)
12. Venkatesh, V., Davis, F.D.: A Theoretical Extension of the Technology Acceptance Model: Four Longitudinal Field Studies. Management Science 46, 186–204 (2000)
13. Duffy, B.R.: Anthropomorphism and the social robot. Robotics and Autonomous Systems 42, 177–190 (2003)
14. Goetz, J., Kiesler, S.: Cooperation with a robotic assistant. In: CHI 2002 Extended Abstracts on Human Factors in Computing Systems, pp. 578–579. ACM, New York (2002)
15. Eyssel, F., Hegel, F., Horstmann, G., Wagner, C.: Anthropomorphic inferences from emotional nonverbal cues: A case study. In: 2010 IEEE RO-MAN, pp. 646–651. IEEE (2010)
16. Riek, L.D., Rabinowitch, T.-C., Chakrabarti, B., Robinson, P.: How anthropomorphism affects empathy toward robots. In: Proceedings of the 4th ACM/IEEE International Conference on Human Robot Interaction, pp. 245–246. ACM, New York (2009)
17. Krach, S., Hegel, F., Wrede, B., Sagerer, G., Binkofski, F., Kircher, T.: Can Machines Think? Interaction and Perspective Taking with Robots Investigated via fMRI. PLoS ONE 3, e2597 (2008)
18. Goetz, J., Kiesler, S., Powers, A.: Matching robot appearance and behavior to tasks to improve human-robot cooperation. In: Proceedings of the 12th IEEE International Workshop on Robot and Human Interactive Communication, ROMAN 2003, pp. 55–60. IEEE (2003)
19. Bartneck, C., Forlizzi, J.: A design-centred framework for social human-robot interaction. In: 13th IEEE International Workshop on Robot and Human Interactive Communication, ROMAN 2004, pp. 591–594. IEEE (2004)
20. Axelrod, L., Hone, K.: E-motional advantage: performance and satisfaction gains with affective computing. In: CHI 2005 Extended Abstracts on Human Factors in Computing Systems, pp. 1192–1195. ACM, New York (2005)
21. Austermann, A., Yamada, S., Funakoshi, K., Nakano, M.: How do users interact with a pet-robot and a humanoid. In: Proceedings of the 28th of the International Conference Extended Abstracts on Human Factors in Computing Systems, pp. 3727–3732. ACM, New York (2010)
22. Kaplan, F.: Who is afraid of the Humanoid? Investigating cultural differences in the acceptance of robots (2004)

23. Caporael, L.R.: Anthropomorphism and mechanomorphism: Two faces of the human machine. Computers in Human Behavior 2, 215–234 (1986)
24. Bartneck, C., Suzuki, T., Kanda, T., Nomura, T.: The influence of people's culture and prior experiences with Aibo on their attitude towards robots. AI & Society 21, 217–230 (2006)
25. Lee, S., Lau, I.Y., Kiesler, S., Chiu, C.-Y.: Human Mental Models of Humanoid Robots. In: Proceedings of the 2005 IEEE International Conference on Robotics and Automation, ICRA 2005, pp. 2767–2772. IEEE (2005)
26. Schmitz, M.: Concepts for life-like interactive objects. In: Proceedings of the Fifth International Conference on Tangible, Embedded, and Embodied Interaction, pp. 157–164. ACM, New York (2011)
27. Kiesler, S., Goetz, J.: Mental models of robotic assistants. In: CHI 2002 Extended Abstracts on Human Factors in Computing Systems, pp. 576–577. ACM, Minneapolis (2002)
28. Breazeal, C.: Toward sociable robots. Robotics and Autonomous Systems 42, 167–175 (2003)
29. Dautenhahn, K., Billard, A.: Bringing up robots or—the psychology of socially intelligent robots: from theory to implementation. In: Proceedings of the Third Annual Conference on Autonomous Agents, pp. 366–367. ACM, New York (1999)
30. Kahn, P.H., Ishiguro, H., Friedman, B., Kanda, T.: What is a Human? - Toward Psychological Benchmarks in the Field of Human-Robot Interaction. In: The 15th IEEE International Symposium on Robot and Human Interactive Communication, ROMAN 2006, pp. 364–371 (2006)
31. Bartneck, C., Kulić, D., Croft, E., Zoghbi, S.: Measurement Instruments for the Anthropomorphism, Animacy, Likeability, Perceived Intelligence, and Perceived Safety of Robots. International Journal of Social Robotics 1, 71–81 (2008)
32. Friedman, B., Kahn Jr., P.H., Hagman, J.: Hardware companions?: what online AIBO discussion forums reveal about the human-robotic relationship. In: Proceedings of the SIGCHI Conference on Human Factors in Computing Systems, pp. 273–280. ACM, New York (2003)
33. Fink, J., Mubin, O., Kaplan, F., Dillenbourg, P.: Anthropomorphic Language in Online Forums about Roomba, AIBO, and the iPad. In: Proceedings of the IEEE International Workshop on Advanced Robotics and its Social Impacts (ARSO 2012), pp. 54–59 (2012)
34. Admoni, H., Bank, C., Tan, J., Toneva, M., Scassellati, B.: Robot gaze does not reflexively cue human attention. In: Proceedings of the 33rd Annual Conference of the Cognitive Science Society, Boston, MA, USA, pp. 1983–1988 (2011)
35. Oztop, E., Franklin, D.W., Chaminade, T., Cheng, G.: Human-humanoid interaction: Is a humanoid robot perceived as a human? International Journal of Humanoid Robotics 2, 537–559 (2005)
36. Forlizzi, J.: How robotic products become social products: an ethnographic study of cleaning in the home. In: Proceedings of the ACM/IEEE International Conference on Human-Robot Interaction, pp. 129–136. ACM, New York (2007)
37. Feil-Seifer, D., Mataric, M.J.: Human-robot interaction. In: Encyclopedia of Complexity and System Science, Springer (2008)
38. Kanda, T., Miyashita, T., Osada, T., Haikawa, Y., Ishiguro, H.: Analysis of Humanoid Appearances in Human-Robot Interaction. IEEE Transactions on Robotics 24, 725–735 (2008)
39. Kiesler, S., Powers, A., Fussell, S.R., Torrey, C.: Anthropomorphic Interactions with a Robot and Robot–like Agent. Social Cognition 26, 169–181 (2008)

40. Bainbridge, W., Hart, J., Kim, E., Scassellati, B.: The Benefits of Interactions with Physically Present Robots over Video-Displayed Agents. International Journal of Social Robotics 3, 41–52 (2011)
41. Bartneck, C., Nomura, T., Kanda, T., Suzuki, T., Kato, K.: Cultural Differences in Attitudes Towards Robots. In: Proceedings of the AISB Symposium on Robot Companions: Hard Problems and Open Challenges in Human-Robot Interaction, Hatfield, pp. 1–4 (2005)
42. Short, E., Hart, J., Vu, M., Scassellati, B.: No fair!! An interaction with a cheating robot. In: 2010 5th ACM/IEEE International Conference on Human-Robot Interaction (HRI). pp. 219 –226 (2010).
43. Gonsior, B., Sosnowski, S., Mayer, C., Blume, J., Radig, B., Wollherr, D., Kuhnlenz, K.: Improving aspects of empathy and subjective performance for HRI through mirroring facial expressions. In: 2011 IEEE RO-MAN, pp. 350–356. IEEE (2011)
44. Fussell, S.R., Kiesler, S., Setlock, L.D., Yew, V.: How people anthropomorphize robots. In: Proceedings of the 3rd ACM/IEEE International Conference on Human Robot Interaction, pp. 145–152. ACM, New York (2008)
45. Powers, A., Kiesler, S.: The advisor robot: tracing people's mental model from a robot's physical attributes. In: Proceedings of the 1st ACM SIGCHI/SIGART Conference on Human-Robot Interaction, pp. 218–225. ACM, New York (2006)
46. Dautenhahn, K., Saunders, J.: New Frontiers in Human-Robot Interaction. John Benjamins Publishing Company (2011)
47. Park, J., Kim, G.J.: Robots with projectors: an alternative to anthropomorphic HRI. In: Proceedings of the 4th ACM/IEEE International Conference on Human Robot Interaction, pp. 221–222. ACM, New York (2009)
48. Shibata, T., Kawaguchi, Y., Wada, K.: Investigation on People Living with Seal Robot at Home. International Journal of Social Robotics 4, 53–63 (2011)

Studies in Public Places as a Means to Positively Influence People's Attitude towards Robots

Nicole Mirnig, Ewald Strasser, Astrid Weiss, and Manfred Tscheligi

HCI & Usability Unit of the ICT & S Center, University of Salzburg,
Sigmund-Haffner-Gasse 18, 5020 Salzburg, Austria
{nicole.mirnig,ewald.strasser,astrid.weiss,manfred.tscheligi}@sbg.ac.at

Abstract. It is the aim of this paper to show on a meta-level how studies in public places can contribute to positively influence people's attitude towards robots. By means of examining objective and subjective data gathered in the lab and data from field studies, it will be shown how people's experiences with a robot outside the sheltering laboratory surroundings can help to value robots more positively. We argue, that studies in public places can serve as a means to enable many people with hands-on experiences and as proof-of-concept evaluation for researchers. We contrasted people's explicit ratings of our robots and although the differences are rather subtle, they nevertheless reveal a tendency for the positive effect of field studies in public places. Additionally, we contrasted people's implicit attitude towards robots which could support our assumption that people who interacted with robots in the field rate it significantly better than people who interacted with it in the lab.

Keywords: field study, lab study, social awareness, comparison study.

1 Introduction

Studies in public places are a hassle. So why should we care to go out into the field when we can just as well stay in the protective laboratory environment where everything is under control? The answer is, because it is worth the effort. The broad public is often influenced by literature and movies, so how should people know what to expect from the state-of-the-art in robotics in 10, 20 or 50 years [1]? Studies in public places transform people's obligation to collect information themselves into a duty to deliver on the research's part. Research is of high societal importance, hence it is essential to involve the general public and this is why studies in public places are particularly suitable for sharing knowledge and experiences with a great number of people [2]. In the field there is an extensive snowball effect inherent, as additionally to those people who actively engage with the robot, others become influenced in a more passive way.

In a field study there are always two sides of the story: First, we strive for field data which are necessary for sound insights, but approaches in the field are more open and playful where people are often not constantly aware of the study situation and do not feel obliged to please a researcher. All of this makes data

S.S. Ge et al. (Eds.): ICSR 2012, LNAI 7621, pp. 209–218, 2012.

collection in the field very interesting, but enables a less structured and scripted approach. Second, we seek active contact between researchers, technology and the target group of potential users of advanced robotic solutions. Such close contact can contribute to raise people's awareness of robotic research projects and may even contribute to a wider understanding and acceptance.

Besides serving the public, such studies are a proof-of-concept evaluation, as findings from the lab must be replicated in the actual usage context. In this paper, we contrasted data from lab studies with data from the field to show how studies in public places can contribute to alter people's attitude towards robots. Studies in public places provide a good opportunity to enable lots of people hands-on experiences with advances in robot research and in doing so allow them to report their impressions, feelings, thoughts, or worries back to the team of researchers. It will be further shown in what way experiences outside laboratory facilities are different in terms of what they evoke within the participants. Firsthand, feedback collected in the field, which is based on the immediate experience with our robots, is a valuable contribution that should be an integral part of any research project. After reporting on the related work and our advancement of the state-of-the-art, the four studies will be introduced as regards their background and setup. By means of contrasting explicit opinions and implicit attitudes from the lab studies with the corresponding field study results, it is shown how studies in public places can become a valuable instrument in robotics research.

2   Related Work

Social robots are designed for everyday life and they should not require extensive training. Data from real-world interactions situated in the actual context that a robot is meant for, are essential to design for successful interaction between robots and humans. Many aspects stay hidden in the well-structured laboratory experiments in which experts guide most interactions [3], [4]. Even if some interaction types show a certain degree of equivalence between video and real-life interactions [5], any experience that is real and not mediated by an in-between gatekeeper like e.g. when participants are not shown a real robot, but only video recordings of it, still influences the perception [6], [7]. The same principle holds true for the interaction context: Any scenario taken out of its context or shifted into a "sterile showcase" context changes in the perception of the human. An artificial situation can never resemble real-life with its flaws and uncertainties, which create the difficulty for the researcher, but account for the naturalness of an interaction, which in turn implicates credibility. It has been found that people who actively interacted with a robot are more likely to have a higher acceptability towards it [8].

The importance of supplementing results gathered in the lab with findings from field studies has been widely recognized. An increased interest in conducting HRI studies in natural human environments in recent years resulted in an exploration of numerous contexts for potential utilization of robots, e.g. the shopping mall context, in which robots are utilized as a guide for customers that can direct or take them to a specific location or provide recommendations (e.g. [9]). Apart from the shopping mall, there are many other public spaces in which robot applications are explored, like hospitals [10] and museums [11].

In this paper, we contrasted two lab studies with a field study each. Two of these studies were aimed at researching how a robot that requests information from pedestrians should behave regarding conversation, the other two were aimed at the robot's navigation. We collected people's explicit opinions by means of questionnaires and interviews and we measured their implicit attitude towards our robots with the Affect Misattribution Procedure (AMP) [12]. The data shows how studies in public places may be taken as a means to positively influence people's attitude towards robots.

All studies were conducted in the framework of the EU-project IURO[1], in which the IURO robot will be enabled to navigate through public space autonomously and find its way by asking pedestrians for directions. It has to be stated that all studies reported in this paper were initially performed to research also other aspects than what is reported herein. The well-planned studies were conducted independently from each other and were executed in a structured way.

This paper, however, is not to be understood as a plain comparison of results, which would be impossible due to the very different nature of the underlying studies, but it aims at viewing results in light of the setup and context in which they were gathered. For a rough picture of the respective studies, a short description of the research goals is given for each of them. We are well aware that the studies reported in this paper are not 100% comparable regarding their setup and the different robots that were used. However, we believe that an interpretation that keeps these differences in mind, can nevertheless bring forth valuable insights.

3   Studies on Robot Conversation

A robot that is meant to proactively approach humans to initiate an interaction must of course be able to communicate in an adequate manner. To equip the IURO robot with the necessary skills, we conducted two studies on how it should behave in such situations and how it should give feedback to a human interaction partner so that the robot's actions and intentions are understandable.

Whereas lab studies serve to research different dialog strategies systematically, field studies are necessary to explore how these dialog strategies develop during a real-life conversation in the actual context. Two robotic heads were developed within the IURO project which were used to research different aspects of robot behavior. A rough outline on the setup of each study is given in the following subsections.

3.1   Study 1 - In the Lab

We used the EDDIE head (see fig. 1a) that asked people for directions. The participants were instructed to explain a way which was indicated on a map. The

---

[1] www.iuro-project.eu

robot, which was wizarded to simulate perfect speech recognition, used different modalities to give feedback to the participants during the conversation: verbal utterances, facial expressions, a pointer that was mounted above the robot's head to indicate directions, and a screen to display the route graph the robot developed during the conversation. It was the aim to find out how the robot should give feedback in the most effective, efficient, and satisfying way with the lowest cognitive load for the user. 20 participants took part in the study (10 male, 10 female) with a mean age of 26.75 years (SD=5.85; range=19-41). The participants' mean interest in technology was rated 3.90 (SD=1.12), in robots 3.10 (SD=1.17), both on a 5-point Likert scale (1 not at all - 5 very much). None of the participants had experience in interacting with robots (results see [13]).

3.2   Study 2 - In the Field

The robot head Furhat (see fig. 1b) was used to actively engage visitors of a robot festival in the British Science Museum in conversation. The robot shifted its perspective from actively asking questions to inviting the participants to ask questions themselves. It could talk to two people at the same time by shifting its attention (gaze and head direction) back and forth between two people. The robot head produced different kinds of feedback to keep its interaction partners actively involved in the conversation: verbal utterances, directed gaze, and facial expression. The study was performed to improve IURO's speech recognition and dialog manager for an outdoor public place setting. 86 people completed our questionnaire (46 male, 39 female, 1 n/a) with a mean age of 35.49 years (SD=16.17; range=12-80). The participants' mean interest in technology was rated 4.42 (SD=.798), in robots 4.28 (SD=.954), both on a 5-point Likert scale (1 not at all - 5 very much). 26 participants stated to have interacted with a robot before (results see [14]). This generally quite positive results can of course be to some extent explained through the fact that the data was gathered in a technophile environment.

(a) EDDIE head   (b) Furhat

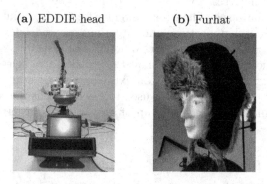

Fig. 1. IURO project robotic heads

4   Studies on Robot Navigation

To enable the IURO robot to autonomously navigate through densely crowded environments, we performed two studies on navigation principles. Whereas lab studies are necessary to thoroughly explore speed and distance behavior of a robot, field studies show how humans actually behave towards a moving robot in real life. In the following, a short description of both studies is given.

4.1   Study 3 - In the Lab

This video-based lab study was aimed at receiving insights on people's preferences for a robot's approach behavior in public space. 30 participants with no prior experience with robots (14 male, 16 female) were shown six videos each, showing IURO approaching a pedestrian to ask for directions. The robot approached the person either from frontal left, frontal right or front direction. Each of the above described approach trajectories was filmed in two conditions: the robot approaching a walking person or a person standing still. The participants' mean age was 29.97 years (SD=10.043; range=15-58), (results see [15]).

4.2   Study 4 - In the Field

The study was conducted at an annual science fair in a large shopping mall. The goal of the fair is to let visitors experience research firsthand. IURO drove around the shopping mall and requested people to step aside if someone blocked its way for longer than 1 second (see fig. 2). It was the aim to research the following request behaviors: (1) verbal request - "Excuse me, I need more space to pass. Could you please step aside?", (2) rotating a pointing device mounted above the robot's head, (3) move up arms sideways, (4) no behavior - the robot waits until it can move. 60 people (33 male, 27 female) who had interacted with the robot filled in the questionnaire. Mean age of the participants was 24.8 years (SD=14.8; range=10-70). 5 participants indicated to have interacted with a robot before.

Fig. 2. IURO interacting with visitors in the shopping mall

5   Sampling Explicit Opinions

To make people's thoughts and impressions graspable, it is important to offer them a channel to communicate. We have used questionnaires and interviews in all our studies to make as many opinions explicit as possible. In the following, the results from the two lab studies are compared with the corresponding field study. In the two studies on robot conversation (studies 1 & 2), we gathered people's opinion on the robot. Table 1 gives an overview on the means of some exemplary questions (5-point Likert scaled; 1 not at all - 5 very much). Though the differences are rather subtle, the descriptive results show a certain orientation:

- People who interacted with a robot in the field rated its likeability slightly higher.
- The fact that the participants in the field study rated the conversation as medium easy and medium frustrating did not result in a lower ranking of the robot's likeability in comparison to the lab study in which participants rated the conversation as fairly easy and not much frustrating.
- Although the interaction in the field took place in a densely crowded and very noisy environment, the participants indicated that they understood the robot better than in the lab environment where the noise level was controlled.
- The participants in the field study, however, did not feel so much confident that the robot understood what they said than what the participants in the lab study reported.

Table 1. Likert-scaled questions on the robots in studies 1 & 2

Question	Study 1 - lab		Study 2 - field	
	mean	SD	mean	SD
How much do you like the robot?	3.85	.875	**4.08**	.775
Could you understand what the robot said?	4.00	.858	**4.25**	.890
Did the robot understand what you said?	**3.90**	.852	2.99	1.048
Was the conversation with the robot easy?	**4.00**	1.076	3.17	.985
Was the conversation with the robot frustrating?	**1.90**	1.021	2.67	1.083
Did you have to concentrate to talk with the robot?	3.40	1.046	**3.38**	1.102

After completing the questionnaire, the participants were interviewed about their experiences. These data can shed further light on the questionnaire items. In the lab study the participants came up with many suggestions for improvement. They mentioned more than twice as many things they did not like (e.g. long reaction time, unnatural and inflexible conversation, pointing device not interpretable, unnatural face) than what they liked (facial expressions, friendly, polite, remembers well). Whereas the comments in the lab study were more suggestions for improvement, in the field study the participants rated the whole setting in one or two sentences. Half of the comments were very encouraging statements (e.g. amazing technology, excellent expression, remarkably good comprehension), one quarter contained suggestions for improvements (e.g. improve conversation and understanding, needs better agent), and one quarter were negative responses (e.g. do not know what to ask the robot, gives only limited responses, no affirmative sounds). The questionnaire and interview data taken together indicate that a less structured interaction may be perceived more difficult than a strictly scripted lab scenario, but it allows the participant to explore the robot more freely which may contribute to a more positive impression.

In the two studies on robot navigation (studies 3 & 4), we measured the participants' social acceptance towards our robots by means of a reduced version of the SoAc questionnaire (social acceptance measured by means of different dimensions like effort expectancy, social intelligence, and perceived competence) [8]. Table 2 shows the means of the participants' answers on some exemplary questions (5-point Likert scaled; 1 not at all - 5 very much).

Table 2. SoAc questions in studies 3 & 4

Question	Study 3 - lab mean	SD	Study 4 - field mean	SD
Robots will make life more interesting	3.13	1.613	**3.78**	1.093
Nonverbal and verbal utterances of robots will fit together	1.90	1.125	**3.78**	.833
I will always know what the robot needs from me	2.80	1.095	**3.56**	.527
It will be difficult to know how to handle the robot	**1.90**	1.125	**2.78**	1.302
It will be easy to understand the interaction with the robot	2.83	1.234	**3.78**	.441
I think a robot that has reasons for its behavior is more human-like	2.60	1.133	**3.56**	1.130
Robots will never be able to interpret human behavior correctly	**2.57**	1.478	3.56	1.333
If there is a problem with the robot, I could continue the interaction without help from others	**2.43**	1.073	1.78	1.641
Robots will be able to understand the social roles of humans in public space	**3.60**	.932	3.00	1.323
It will be an enormous effort to help the robot to achieve its task	3.57	1.040	**2.56**	1.236
It would be easy for me to know what the robot will do next	2.77	1.357	**3.00**	1.323

Due to the small sample of participants who were willing to complete the questionnaire (n=9), no statistically significant differences could be found. In both studies, most of the answers tended to be around the middle value, with the standard deviation being around 1, meaning that there are not so much absolute positions as to completely reject or accept the robot. Nevertheless, the descriptive results show a certain orientation:

- Participants in the field study were more certain, that they will know what a robot needs from them and that it will be easy to understand the interaction.
- Even though participants in the field study were slightly more certain to have enough knowledge on how to interact with the robot, those participants were less certain when it comes to the actual skills of handling the robot than the participants in the lab study.
- People in the field study did not so much think that it will be an enormous effort to help the robot than people in the lab study.
- The participants in the field studies thought it more important for a robot to have clear intentions.
- Field study participants thought that the robots were more skilled regarding their behavior but had less ability to understand and interpret the human.
- People that took part in the field study, were more convinced that robots will make life more interesting.

These results also support our assumption that even if the participants in a lab study are exactly instructed what to do, free and hands-on exploration contributes to a better rating of the robot and a potential cooperation with it.

6   Measuring Implicit Attitudes

Given these indicators for a positive influence of field interaction on acceptance and perception of robots which are promising, we wanted to find out if these effects can be measured on an implicit level. Most of our decisions are made unconsciously and/or automatically and even attitudes towards people and things are driven to a big part by processes that we can not easily access. Yamauchi et al. [16] found a direct connection between implicit beliefs and affect on perceived usability and acceptance of interfaces. Such constructs can be grasped by measuring so-called implicit attitudes. According to DeHouwer [17], associations measured with implicit methods are not conscious and participants have no control about the outcome of the test. Implicit measures for attitudes have also the great advantage that they are hardly biased, as people are not aware that their attitudes are measured. One technique for implicit measurement is the the Affect Misattribution Procedure (AMP) [12], which has been validated as a suitable tool for exploring people's implicit attitudes towards robots [18]. With both our studies on robot navigation (studies 3 & 4), we tried to measure such hidden attitudes. In the AMP, participants are instructed to rate whether they perceive abstract patterns, such as Chinese characters which carry no meaning within the European cultural sphere, as beautiful or ugly. Prior to the Chinese character, another object, in our case the human or the robot, is shown for a very short time. The participants are instructed to disregard this object. However, participants are more inclined to perceive the Chinese character as pleasant if the object before is favorable for them. By showing either the robot or the human in a random order a score for the bias towards the robot and the human is gathered.

In the two studies on robot navigation (studies 3 & 4), we measured the participants' implicit attitude towards our robots by means of the AMP method. A comparison of the AMP scores we gathered in these two studies showed that they significantly differed (t=2.378; p=.02). The mean scores showed that people in the field study rated IURO with 9.37 (SD= 3.682) of 16 possible "pleasant" ratings and in the lab study they rated it with 7.43 (SD=3.461) points on average. For the category 'human' we did not find such differences between the implicit attitudes in the two studies (t=1.655; p=.108). From this we conclude that the differences in the attitude towards the robot are not based on general differences in the study setup. This result confirms the assumption we have drawn from analyzing people's explicit opinions. Hence, it can be shown on an objective level that active engagement with robots in the field can contribute to a more positive attitude towards them.

7   Discussion

It is known from earlier studies that direct interaction with robots positively influences people's attitude towards them [6]. We wanted to find out if the context of the interaction also influences this attitude. Our pre-assumption was that encounters in the field have a greater impact than lab studies, as the interaction in real life feels more natural, is mostly less structured, and people feel freer to explore the robot to their liking and not by means of a fixed scenario. Attitudes are complex constructs, most of which arise unconsciously and are triggered unintentionally. Therefore, it is difficult to make them explicit, let alone to measure them. On an explicit level we could not detect significant differences between the lab and the field data. We could, however, find tendencies which hypothesize that our assumption may be correct. On an implicit level we could successfully show a significant difference between the lab and the field: Studies in public places can contribute to positively influence people's attitude towards robots significantly better than lab studies. We are aware that the studies we compared in this paper are not comparable on a 1:1 basis due to different sample sizes, robot prototypes and scenarios. However, upon keeping these differences in mind, we have shown with this small-scale meta study that a comparison can nevertheless provide a fruitful contribution. We conclude from our results that even very short interactions with robots can positively influence the attitude of those who interacted with them hands-on. As these changes in attitude frequently happen at a subliminal level, they were not graspable via sampling people's explicit opinion. However, by measuring their implicit attitude we could detect significant differences between a lab and a field study regarding people's perception towards the robot. We therefore argue that studies in public places are a valuable means to make people think more positively about robots.

Acknowledgements. This work is supported within the European Commission as part of the IURO project. We wish to thank our project partners from Technische Universität München and KTH Royal Institute of Technology and our colleague Jakub Zlotowski for their support.

References

1. Kriz, S., Ferro, T., Damera, P., Porter, J.: Fictional robots as a data source in hri research: Exploring the link between science fiction and interactional expectations. In: RO-MAN 2010, pp. 458–463 (2010)
2. MacKenzie, D.: Inventing accuracy: A historical sociology of nuclear missile guidance. The MIT Press (1993)
3. Dautenhahn, K.: Robots in the wild: Exploring human-robot interaction in naturalistic environments. Interaction Studies 10(3), 269–273 (2009)
4. Sabanovic, S., Michalowski, M., Simmons, R.: Robots in the wild: Observing human-robot social interaction outside the lab. In: Workshop on Advanced Motion Control, pp. 596–601 (2006)
5. Woods, S., Walters, M., Koay, K., Dautenhahn, K.: Methodological issues in hri: A comparison of live and video-based methods in robot to human approach direction trials. In: Proc. of RO-MAN 2006, pp. 51–58 (2006)
6. Suchman, L.: Reconfiguring human-robot relations. In: Proc. of RO-MAN 2006, pp. 652–654 (2006)
7. Xu, Q., Ng, J.S.L., Cheong, Y.L., Tan, O.Y., Wong, J.B., Tay, B.T.C., Park, T.: Effect of scenario media on human-robot interaction evaluation. In: Proc. of HRI 2012, pp. 275–276 (2012)
8. Weiss, A.: Validation of an Evaluation Framework for Human-Robot Interaction. The Impact of Usability, Social Acceptance, User Experience, and Societal Impact on Collaboration with Humanoid Robots. PhD thesis, University Salzburg (2010)
9. Kanda, T., Shiomi, M., Miyashita, Z., Ishiguro, H., Hagita, N.: An affective guide robot in a shopping mall. In: Proc. of HRI 2009, pp. 173–180 (2009)
10. Ljungblad, S., Kotrbova, J., Jacobsson, M., Cramer, H., Niechwiadowicz, K.: Hospital robot at work: something alien or an intelligent colleague? In: CSCW 2012, pp. 177–186 (2012)
11. Yamazaki, A., Yamazaki, K., Ohyama, T., Kobayashi, Y., Kuno, Y.: A techno-sociological solution for designing a museum guide robot: regarding choosing an appropriate visitor. In: HRI 2012, pp. 309–316 (2012)
12. Payne, B., Cheng, C., Govorun, O., Stewart, B.: An inkblot for attitudes: affect misattribution as implicit measurement. Journal of Personality and Social Psychology 89(3), 277 (2005)
13. Mirnig, N., Gonsior, B., Sosnowski, S., Landsiedel, C., Wollherr, D., Weiss, A., Tscheligi, M.: Feedback guidelines for multimodal human-robot interaction: How should a robot give feedback when asking for directions? In: RO-MAN 2012 (currently submitted, 2012)
14. Al Moubayed, S., Beskow, J., Granström, B., Gustafson, J., Mirning, N., Skantze, G., Tscheligi, M.: Furhat goes to robotville: a large-scale multiparty human-robot interaction data collection in a public space. In: LREC Workshop on Multimodal Corporation (2012)
15. Złotowski, J., Weiss, A., Tscheligi, M.: Navigating in public space: participants' evaluation of a robot's approach behavior. In: HRI 2012, pp. 283–284 (2012)
16. Yamauchi, T., Ohno, T., Nakatani, M., Kato, Y., Markman, A.: Psychology of user experience in a collaborative video-conference system. In: CSCW 2012, pp. 187–196 (2012)
17. De Houwer, J.: What are implicit measures and why are we using them. The Handbook of Implicit Cognition and Addiction, 11–28 (2006)
18. Strasser, E., Weiss, A., Tscheligi, M.: Affect misattribution procedure: an implicit technique to measure user experience in hri. In: HRI 2012, pp. 243–244 (2012)

Difference of Efficiency in Human-Robot Interaction According to Condition of Experimental Environment

Ho Seok Ahn[1,2], Dong-Wook Lee[1], Dongwoon Choi[1], Duk-Yeon Lee[1], Manhong Hur[1], and Hogil Lee[1]

[1] Department of Applied Robot Technology,
Korea Institute of Industrial Technology
Ansan 426-791, Republic of Korea
[2] Intelligent Robotics and Communication Laboratories,
Advanced Telecommunications Research Institute International,
Kyoto 619-0288, Japan
hoseoka@gmail.com,
{dwlee,cdw,proldy,hmh426,hglee}@kitech.re.kr

Abstract. Human-Robot Interaction is most important function for social robot systems. Android robot systems, which have human-like appearance, are used for interaction with humans because they have the merit of showing their emotions by similar way to humans. Lots of these robot systems are developed and verified their efficiency and performance by analyzing the experimental results from questionnaire method. However, the results from questionnaire method can be different from many conditions. In this paper, we analyze the difference of experimental results from questionnaire method by comparing three groups: the first group gains benefits by competition, the second group gains benefits without competition, and the last group does not gain anything. For these experiments, android head system EveR-4 H33, which has 33 motors inside of head to show its facial expressions, is used.

Keywords: Human-Robot interaction, emotional expression, facial expression, android system, EveR series, head robot system.

1   Introduction

Nowadays, researchers try to develop robots communicate with humans in daily life. In this process, Human-Robot Interaction is one of the most important researching areas for living together with humans. Especially, when humans recognize the emotional status of robots with facial expressions, human-like facial expressions are usually found to be efficient in the Human-Robot Interaction [1]. According to this reason, many android robots have been developed. Ishiguro of Osaka University and ATR International has developed the mimics of real humans such as himself, his daughter, etc [2-3]. SAYA is also an android robot system having an anthropomorphic face [4]. Albert HUBO of KAIST is a humanoid robot having a

S.S. Ge et al. (Eds.): ICSR 2012, LNAI 7621, pp. 219–227, 2012.

android face modeled on Albert Einstein [5]. HRP-4C of AIST is also similar typed robot system with Albert HUBO having a human-like face [6]. KITECH (Korea Institute of Industrial Technology) has developed the android robot EveR series for various uses. For example, EveR-1 is an announcer, EveR-2 is a singer, EveR-3 is an actress, and EveR-4 is an entertainer [7-10]. EveR's name derives from the Biblical 'Eve,' plus the letter 'R' for robot, and the version of the EveR series then follows. The appearance of the EveR series is based on a Korean female, but the specifications are different for each version. EveR series are modeled human-scale face and body parts and covered with silicon skin.

These robot systems are used for various purposes in various environments and researchers have verified the effectiveness of their robot systems by various methods, mainly questionnaire method. However, questionnaire method can be different from the conditions of experimental environments, such as kinds of emotions for showing, using parts of expressing emotions, etc. Especially, a number of theories about basic emotions have been presented for explaining complicated human emotions. Ekman uses six emotions [11], Russell uses five emotions [12], Izard uses ten emotions [13], Tomkins uses nine emotions [14-15], Panksepp uses four emotions [16], and Sroufe uses three emotions [17]. However, an objectively qualified theory for identifying the concept of basic emotions does not yet exist [1]. Also, questionnaire method can be different from the research subjects of experimental environments, such as age, gender, cultural background, etc. It is the reason why lots of researchers analyze and compare their experimental results by age and gender.

We had some preliminary evaluations of facial expressions by applying some theories of basic emotions to find the appropriate emotions for facial expressions of EveR-4 H33 [9]. We also find the appropriate uses of the head system of EveR-4 H33 by analyzing the evaluation results of emotional expressions according to gender and age [10]. In this paper, we focus on the difference of experimental results according to the condition of experimental environment. Especially, in the exhibition environment, various people come and participate in experiments. It means that someone sincerely joins to experiment, but someone joins to experiment for fun. As a result, the experimental result can be different from this. Therefore, we find how different from the condition of experimental environment by comparing three groups: the first group gains benefits by competition, the second group gains benefits without competition, and the last group gains nothing except meaning to participate. We use the android head system EveR-4 H33, which is a head system with 33 degrees of freedom, as shown in Fig. 1. EveR-4 H33 shows various facial expressions through the changes in skin shape that are controlled by 30 facial motors attached behind the skin. We exhibit these evaluations in the RoboWorld 2011 exhibition in Seoul, Korea.

This paper is organized as follows. In Section 2, we introduce android head system EveR-4 H33 with its functions. In Section 3, we explain experimental environments for evaluations. In Section 4, we present experimental results and evaluations. Finally, we conclude this paper in Section 5.

2   Android Facial System

2.1   Overview of EveR-4 H33 [9-10]

The head system EveR-4 H33 has 33 degrees of freedom. It changes in skin shape that is controlled by 30 facial motors attached behind the skin. EveR-4 H33 is used as a head system of EveR-4 system. EveR-4 H33 is designed based on the human facial muscle mechanism, and uses thirty motors that act as facial muscles, and three motors that act as neck muscles. Almost every muscle constitutes one part of a pair of identical bilateral muscles, found on both sides. EveR-4 H33 consists of three parts: a mechanical part, an inner cover part, and an outer cover part. The mechanical part performs the role of the muscle, and is designed with thirty-three servo motors for facial expression and lip synchronization. The inner cover part performs the role of the skeleton, and is inosculated with the mechanical part. The control points of the inner cover part and the mechanical part are connected with wires. The outer cover part performs the role of the skin, and is made of synthetic pliable silicone jelly.

2.2   Expression of EveR-4 H33

Six facial motors are used for the eyebrows, four facial motors are used in the eyelids, ten motors of the eyebrows and eyelids are correlated. Four facial motors are used in the eyeballs, and the vertical and horizontal movements can be controlled

Fig. 1. An android head system, EveR-4 H33, developed in KITECH (Korea Institute of Industrial Technology). The appearance of EveR-4 H33 is based on a Korean female. EveR-4 H33's name derives from the Biblical 'Eve', plus the letter 'R' for robot. She is the fourth version of the EveR series, and has 33 Degrees of Freedom in her head part.

independently, but when looking to the side, they are controlled together to focus. Six facial motors are used in the cheeks, three facial motors are used in the upper and lower part of the lips, and one facial motor is used in the chin; these form a correlated group to control the shape of the mouth. Two facial motors are used in the upper lip, and two facial motors are used in the lower lip. These four motors on the lips are correlated to control the shape of lips. Two facial motors are used in the tongue, and three facial motors are used in the neck. As muscles of humans originate on the bones and insert into the skin, some related muscles move together when showing expressions. As EveR-4 H33 is designed based on human muscle mechanism, when EveR-4 H33 shows its facial expressions, some related motors should be controlled together. It is very complicated process, and we have developed a facial muscle control algorithm. Using this method, EveR-4 H33 shows various facial expressions.

3   Experimental System

3.1   Overview of Experimental System

Experimental system consists of four parts: the first part is the robot system that is EveR-4 H33, the second part is the main system for controlling EveR-4 H33 and proceeding experiments, the third part is the input system for getting user's evaluations, and the last part is the displaying system for showing the experimental process and evaluation results. Fig. 2 shows the experimental environment for the game of facial expression. EveR-4 H33 communicates with iPads by wireless

Fig. 2. Experimental environment for the game of facial expression in the RoboWorld 2011 exhibition in Seoul, Korea

Ethernet. The iPads of participants are used for getting the participant information and selecting one emotion for evaluation. The iPad of manager is used for controlling experimental system including EveR-4 H33. The screen behind EveR-4 H33 is used for displaying the evaluation results during experiments and the status of EveR-4 H33 during break time.

3.2   Input System for Users

Two iPad devices are used as the input terminal of our experimental system. Fig. 3 and Fig. 4 show some screen images of the input system. This system has two modes: one is service mode by taking some photo of participants and sending them to participants' email, the other mode is game mode for our experiments. We can select the mode by touching mode button as shown in Fig. 3(a). In the game mode, participants input their personal information, such as age, gender, cultural background, and job as shown in Fig. 3(b). When game is started, EveR-4 H33 shows its facial expressions and participants evaluate by selecting the nearest emotion among the selecting list displayed on the iPad device as shown in Fig. 4. The selecting list is different from the experimental mode, for example, if we experiment about Ekman's basic emotion, then only six emotions are displayed on the iPad device. It is also different from the participant information, which is inputted before starting the game, for example, language can be different from the cultural background.

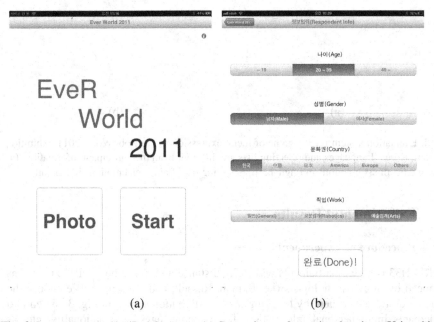

(a)   (b)

Fig. 3. Input system using iPad for users. (a) Screen image for setting functions. Using this system, we can take a photo for participants and send it to their email. (b) Screen image for inputting participant information.

3.3   Displaying System for Users

Displaying system shows the evaluation results and the final results. Fig. 5 shows some screen images of the displaying system. EveR-4 H33 shows its emotion according the setting of the experimental mode. When participants select one emotion using the input system, the main system decides whether it is correct answer or not. Then the displaying system shows the evaluation results using the LCD monitor behind EveR-4 H33 as shown in Fig. 5(a). When game is finished, the displaying system shows the final evaluation as shown in Fig. 5(b).

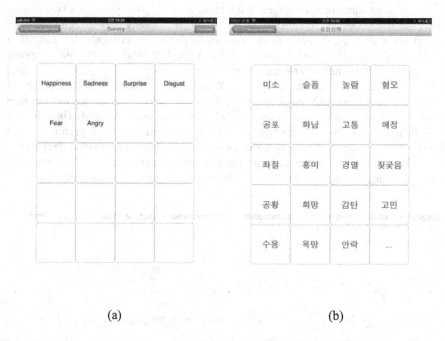

(a)   (b)

Fig. 4. Evaluation system for the game of facial expression in the RoboWorld 2011 exhibition in Seoul, Korea. Languages and selecting lists are different from the participant information. (a) Selecting list of six emotions in English. (b) Selecting list of nineteen emotions in Korean.

4   Experimental Results

4.1   Procedure of Experiments

EveR-4 H33 is facing participants with 1.5m distance and shows her facial expressions advanced by three psychologists (i.e. Ekman, Russell, and Panksepp). We choose the game mode for experiment by touching the "Start" button shown in Fig. 3. When two participants input personal information, for example, ages, sex, nationality, etc. as shown in Fig. 3(b), the game starts. EveR-4 H33 shows her facial expressions in random order. Then, two participants evaluate which emotion they consider EveR-4 H33 expresses, by selecting emotions displayed on the input device as shown in Fig. 4.

If both participants select the one emotion, EveR-4 H33 checks the evaluation and gives the evaluation results using the displaying system behind EveR-4 H33 with sound as shown in Fig. 5(a). EveR-4 H33 repeats this evaluation several times. When the evaluation is finished, EveR-4 H33 shows the final evaluation results on the screen as shown in Fig. 5(b).

We performed these experiments in the RoboWorld 2011 exhibition in Seoul, Korea. We obtained evaluation data from 2266 people (1575 males and 691 females) who had no previous experience with EveR-4 H33. We divided participants into three groups and explained about benefits. In the case of the first group, they gains benefits by competition. After finishing the evaluation, winner gets a better present, which is more expensive, than loser. But, loser also gets a present. In the case of the second group, they gains benefits without competition. Both participants get the same present regardless of the evaluation results. In the case of the last group, they gain nothing except meaning to participate although they get a perfect score.

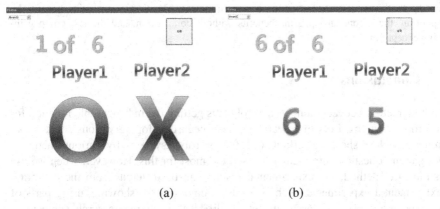

(a)   (b)

Fig. 5. Displaying system for showing evaluation process and results. (a) Displaying of correction result. (b) Displaying of final evaluation results.

4.2   Experimental Results and Evaluations

In the experimental results as shown in Fig. 6, the first group got better score of evaluation in the game than other two groups, by comparison with the average (87.96%). The next is the second group (84.26%), and the last is the third group, who gained nothing (79.52%), by comparison with the average. It means that people concentrate on the game when they gain benefits and when they compete against someone. Overall, females got better evaluation score than males. But, the difference of evaluation score between males and females is smaller when they expect more benefits (1.96%) than when they have just fun (6.69%). It means that the efficiency of competition and benefits is bigger in the case of males than females. In conclusion, evaluation results can be different from the condition of experimental environment and males are influenced by the condition than females.

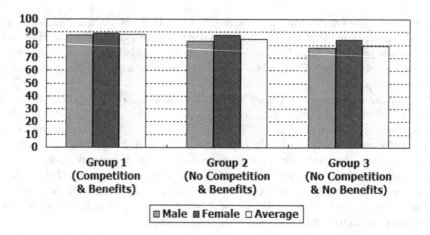

Fig. 6. Experimental results about the difference of efficiency in Human-Robot Interaction according to the condition of experimental environment. The first group gains benefits by competition, the second group gains benefits without competition, and the last group gains nothing except fun.

5   Conclusions

Social interaction between humans and robots is getting the indispensable function for social robot systems. Lots of researchers have been developing various social robot systems and they show the efficiency of their robot systems by various methods. Among them, questionnaire method is used the most for this. However, when we use questionnaire method, the experimental results can be different from the condition of experimental experiments, such as kinds of emotions for showing, using parts of expressing emotions, etc. Also, it can be different from the research subjects of experimental environments, such as age, gender, cultural background, etc. Therefore, we analyzed the difference of efficiency in Human-Robot Interaction according to the condition of experimental environments in this paper.

We used android facial robot system EveR-4 H33 that has 33 degrees of freedom for showing its facial expressions in the RoboWorld 2011 exhibition in Seoul, Korea. The experimental system consists of four parts: the first part is the robot system that is EveR-4 H33, the second part is the main system for controlling EveR-4 H33 and proceeding experiments, the third part is the input system for getting user's evaluations, and the last part is the displaying system for showing the experimental process and evaluation results. We obtained evaluation results from 2266 people (1575 males and 691 females), who had no previous experience with EveR-4 H33. We divided participants into three groups according to existence of competition and benefits. In the experimental results, we got the conclusion that evaluation results can be different from the condition of experimental environment and males are influenced by the condition than females. Also, when people expect benefits in competition condition, they can increase the ability to concentrate on the game. Using these results, we will consider the condition of experimental environments when we have some experiments in the future.

Acknowledgments. This research is supported by Ministry of Culture, Sports and Tourism (MCST) of Korea and Korea Creative Content Agency (KOCCA) in the Culture Technology (CT) Research & Development Program 2010. Dong-Wook Lee is a corresponding author.

References

1. Lee, H.S., Park, J.W., Chung, M.J.: A Linear Affect–Expression Space Model and Control Points for Mascot-Type Facial Robots. IEEE Transactions on Robotics, 863–873 (2007)
2. Guizzo, E.: The Man Who Made a Copy of Himself. IEEE Spectrum, pp. 44–56 (2010)
3. Ishiguro, H.: Scientific issues concerning androids. International Journal of Robotics Research 26(1), 105–117 (2007)
4. Hashimoto, T., Hiramatsu, S., Tsuji, T., Kobayashi, H.: Realization and Evaluation of Realistic Nod with Receptionist robot SAYA. In: Proceedings of the IEEE International Workshop on Robot and Human Communication (RO-MAN 2007), pp. 326–331 (2007)
5. Oh, J.-H., Hanson, D., Kim, W.-S., Han, I.Y., Kim, J.-Y., Park, I.-W.: Design of Android type Humanoid Robot Albert HUBO. In: Proceedings of the 2006 IEEE/RSJ International Conference on Intelligent Robots and Systems (IROS 2006), pp. 1428–1433 (2006)
6. Nakaoka, S., Kanehiro, F., Miura, K., Morisawa, M., Fujiwara, K., Kaneko, K., Kajita, S., Hirukawa, H.: Creating Facial Motions of Cybernetic Human HRP-4C. In: Proceedings of the IEEE International Conference on Humanoid Robots, pp. 561–567 (2009)
7. Ahn, H.S., Lee, D.-W., Choi, D., Lee, D.Y., Hur, M.H., Lee, H., Shon, W.H.: Development of an Android for Singing with Facial Expression. In: Proceedings of the Annual Conference on IEEE Industrial Electronics Society (IECON 2011), pp. 104–109 (2011)
8. Choi, D., Lee, D.-W., Lee, D.Y., Ahn, H.S., Lee, H.: Design of an android robot head for stage performances. Artificial Life and Robotics 16(3), 315–317 (2011)
9. Ahn, H.S., Lee, D.-W., Choi, D., Lee, D.-Y., Hur, M., Lee, H.: Appropriate Emotions for Facial Expressions of 33-DOFs Android Head EveR-4 H33. In: Proceedings of the IEEE International Symposium on Robot and Human Communication, RO-MAN 2012 (2012)
10. Ahn, H.S., Lee, D.-W., Choi, D., Lee, D.-Y., Hur, M., Lee, H.: Uses of Facial Expressions of Android Head System according to Gender and Age. In: Proceedings of the 2012 IEEE International Conference on Systems, Man, and Cybernetics, SMC 2012 (2012)
11. Ekman, P.: Universals and cultural differences in facial expressions of emotion. In: Nebraska Symposium on Motivation, vol. 19, pp. 207–283 (1972)
12. Fehr, B., Russell, J.A.: Concept of emotion viewed from a prototype perspective. Journal of Experimental Psychology 113, 464–486 (1984)
13. Izard, C.E.: Human Emotions. Plenum Press (1977)
14. Tomkins, S.S.: Affect, imagery, consciousness (vol.1): The positive affects (1962)
15. Tomkins, S.S.: Affect, imagery, consciousness (vol. 2): The positive affects (1963)
16. Panksepp, J.: Toward a general psychobiological theory of emotions. Journal of Behavioral and Brain Science 5, 407–468 (1982)
17. Sroufe, L.A.: Socioemotional development: Handbook of infant development (1979)

Programming Behaviour of a Personal Service Robot with Application to Healthcare

Chandan Datta[1], Bruce A. MacDonald[1],
Chandimal Jayawardena[2], and I-Han Kuo[1]

[1] Department of Electrical and Computer Engineering,
University of Auckland, New Zealand
[2] Unitec Institute of Technology, New Zealand

Abstract. We propose an approach for developing applications on a personal healthcare service robot. We have developed a model of representing robot behaviour through a domain specific language (DSL) and enabling authoring through a Visual Programming Environment (VPE), RoboStudio. RoboStudio is to be used by robot designers, developers and domain experts for developing social robotics behaviour in a healthcare environment. The method for authoring is visual in order to convey the robot's decision logic and interaction behaviour in a more intuitive manner while retaining expressiveness. In the paper, we discuss current progress we have made in raising the level of abstraction in service application development. This will help the robotics community to make significant investment in developing programming infrastructures, better programming language support and enhancing existing programming languages through simpler syntax and expressive semantics.

1 Introduction

In the near future, the initial adoption of personal service robots will likely be in practical, controlled and focused applications; for which the social behaviour of the robot must be carefully designed. In order for the personal robotics industry to follow the success trajectory of the personal computer industry [17], it will require matured programming platforms and tool support. This becomes more relevant as personal robots are used in everyday human settings and users interact with more expressive and intelligent interfaces.

With the rise of personal computing devices such as smart devices and tablets, computer programming in domain specific forms has become more common in various domains [13]. People use web sites to publish content, design interfaces with interface prototyping software, compute results with statistical tools, enter and analyze data with spreadsheets, write scripts to define their own gaming characters and use computational tools to write simulations [7, 13]. Thus, the tools of computing are being developed with user experience in mind and the industry is increasingly providing more intuitive tools for producing content. However,much of the current research focus in the robotics software engineering community is towards robot algorithm developers with objectives of maintainability, interoperability, and reusability [14]. This leaves a gap in the literature

S.S. Ge et al. (Eds.): ICSR 2012, LNAI 7621, pp. 228–237, 2012.
© Springer-Verlag Berlin Heidelberg 2012

with regards to *raising the level of abstraction* for robot service application development, especially where the human and social interactions of the robot are concerned. The Healthbots project at the University of Auckland, New Zealand is a multi-disciplinary project towards development of personal service robots to assist older people in maintaining their wellness. The robot's applications include services for measuring vital signs, identifying users, greeting users, facilitate conversation with family and friends using Skype calling. The robot Charlie in an interaction is shown in Fig. 1. For such robots, high level, domain specific authoring languages and tools are a significant requirement.

Fig. 1. Healthbot service robot Charlie assisting in measuring vital signs

The rest of the paper is organized as follows: section 2 provides the requirements analysis for a VPE [6] in a multi-disciplinary research team having a strong focus on pilot studies and field trials, section 3 provides an overview of the current research in related domains for modeling robot behaviour, section 4 provides the details of the syntax and semantics of our DSL, section 5 provides the description of the RoboStudio VPE, and section 6 provides results of using RoboStudio.

2   Requirements and Scope

Robot assistants for older people are of growing interest in Human Robot Interaction (HRI) and service robotics research community. Providing care to older people is both labor and cost intensive. Hence, the argument of using personal service robots to enable older people to stay in their homes and live independently longer is catching the attention of healthcare providers and healthcare delivery organizations. The developmental goals of the RoboStudio VPE were based on our empirical experience while performing pilot tests and field studies of the robot in a real-world Aged Care Facility (ACF) scenario with older people and staff using the robot's services [3]. In an earlier trial conducted in 2009-2010 [12], we tried to gather all service application requirements from the Subject Matter Experts (SMEs) in our research group before starting the design and development. However, later it was found that the initial requirements were not complete and SMEs suggested several changes to the software just before the trials began. Therefore, we performed additional software iterations and testing. Three requirements evolved from this experience:

Clarity in Software Requirements — In a multidisciplinary environment, the opportunity for misunderstanding is much higher; it is important to specify requirements and variations very clearly so that everyone understands exactly what the robot will be doing once specified changes are made [3]. We require a VPE to communicate on a common graphical level to SMEs as well as developers, ensuring that specifications are understood and so reducing the time taken for deployment. These comments are drawn within a research team, albeit in a real deployment environment; the need for coherent multidisciplinary definition of robots' behaviour will be even stronger.

Multidisciplinary Co-development — Haesen's research [10] on a user centered software engineering in multidisciplinary teams suggest involving SMEs in the early design phase. This suggests end user programming (EUP) and using SMEs as co-developers; SMEs should be actively involved as well as having clear visibility of specifications. For example, a health psychologist and an engineer could work together to evaluate changes and together ensure the design was implemented as both people expected for a scenario (e.g. entertainment service in robots used in public places or medication reminding service used in robots private apartments). If the robot's behaviour and dialog can be easily authored using a VPE, the multidisciplinary team can visualize the interaction design, and improve it.

Deployment and Field Programming — The successful application of robotics in healthcare settings involves complex interactions and personalization of services according to the scenario in which it is deployed. We require a VPE which can reduce the cycle time for testing and customizing the robot's interaction during field deployment on the spot. That means making changes in an expressive DSL rather than the underlying source code of the software, so that full software testing is not required after changes are made in the field. The current software architectural solution for the aforementioned requirements is shown in Fig. 2. It has been used in a recent trial and is described in greater details in [11].

3   Related Work on VPE and DSLs

Programming tools and VPEs in robotics software engineering domain usually have a strong focus on robot algorithm developers. The motivation behind these

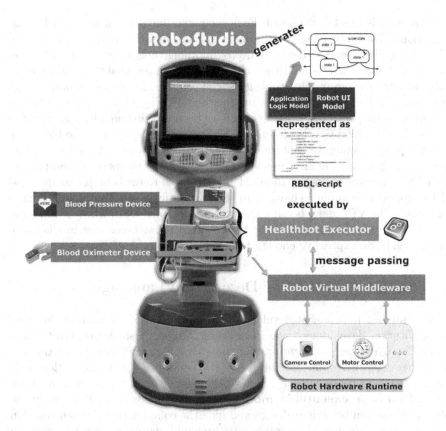

Fig. 2. Healthbot service robot software structure

programming tools is to enable re-usability of algorithms and software components in order to avoid building robot software from scratch [2]. Hence, there
exists a body of research [5] towards reference architectures, component-based
development [4] and model-driven development approaches [18] so that a robotics
developer would have basic building blocks for real-time programming, motor
control, AI, image and video processing. Robot Operating System (ROS), Microsoft Robotics Developer Studio (MRDS), and iRobot's Aware 2 make the
programmer's job significantly easier. The difference between the features provided by these platforms and the specific requirements discussed in this paper
which led to this research, is mentioned in section 2. There is also a strong interest in model-driven design in robotic frameworks such as SMARTSOFT [18] and
Object Management Groups (OMG) Robot Technology (RT) Components [1].
The OMG has acknowledged the problem of platform diversity by introducing
its form of model-driven design called as Model Driven Architecture (MDA).
The MDA is centered around the use of software models which provide a means
to create partial, platform-independent software specifications that make use
of platform abstractions. These abstractions are refined to platform specific

software models in a later stage of the development life cycle, using model transformations. There's a paucity of domain specific models for developing social
robotics applications. Further, visual programming tools to generate code from
these models are also missing. Research at ATR Japan revealed the need for more
end-user centric programming tools for social robotics. Interaction Composer [9]
could allow design of Human Robot Interaction (HRI) by a team of non-engineers
and robot developers. Other researchers have been working on VPEs for robotics
for a while. The intention behind these VPEs however is to lower the barrier to
learning programming for children and hobby programmers, thus introducing
programming techniques in a less syntax-intensive environment. A comparison
of VPEs for novices is present in [8]. Hence, research towards better models and
VPEs representing robot behaviour in social robotics is required. Underlying a
domain specific VPE must be an appropriately designed DSL, whose syntax and
semantics are capable of describing the required robot behaviour in the given
domain, and also expressive enough to engender a suitable VPE.

4   The Robot Behaviour Description Language

During the first iteration of developing the human robot interaction, much of
the application development was done using Adobe Flash Actionscript 3 and
C++. Though these programming languages enabled development of the services, they were not sufficient for the goals mentioned earlier in section 2. It
was necessary to represent the robot's behaviour at a higher level of abstraction in form of an **executable model** which allows the team to focus on the
robot's interaction behaviour design and hide the complexity of implementation
in an executor. Further, the representation should enable effectively capturing
the domain knowledge and facilitate rapid development. Thus, the robot's multimodal dialog and behaviour is specified in a set of states that are organized in
a DSL script called Robot Behaviour Description Language (RBDL) and represented in XML form. The central concept of the behavioral modeling approach
we've adopted is the representation of the robot's user interface description and
application logic as one concrete state. The behaviour currently is modeled as reactive (as opposed to a transformational system), in that it navigates sequences
(described as screenflows) through events, conditions and actions. The service
logic constantly reacts to external events, internal events and performs actions
based on complex events. The navigation of states according to how the user
interacts with the robot's touch-screen is called a **screenflow**. The RBDL representation is a finite state machine variant and specifies the robot service logic
according to which screenflows are presented, user interactions are processed and
actions are executed. RBDL has been used to define embodied robot behaviors
such as defining social cues for user identification [15]. It has also been used
to define location monitoring services in the retirement village when the robot
moves to an emergency location and sends video stream to a caregiver using
tele-presence [16].

RBDL Structure and Syntax Definition:

- *state*: Each state has a unique identifier
- *timeout*: The duration of a state timer while executing each state(a local timer). The timer completion event can be used for state transitions when necessary.
- *backgroundactions*: Actions transparent to the user. e.g. accessing a web service, sending a message.
- *screen*: All screen components (currently text boxes, buttons, images, video clips, on-screen keyboards, and on-screen numeric keypad). Buttons can have one or more associated events and events can have one or more associated actions.
- *expectedevents*: Events expected (or processed) by the current state. Timeout events, fall sensor events, external message received events, face detected events, are some examples.

Understanding the FSM Variant: Finite state machines (FSM) are one of the basic ways of describing system behaviour. Used as models of computation, they are called deterministic finite automata or DFA for short. DFAs can express sequential behaviour easily. An important point to note is that the DFA terminology is limited to the mathematical representation of the states, initial state, input alphabets and the state transition function and doesn't describe the event processing or the action scheme; which is important from a software engineering viewpoint while describing software system behaviour using state machines. The *expectedevents* are asynchronous events and get executed on a first-come-first-serve basis. The actions that happen on an event can be further parameterized, so that simultaneous actions can take place on a given triggered event. The *backgroundactions* semantics can be treated similar to *entry* actions in the UML statecharts.

Analysis of the Robot Behaviour Formalism: The FSM description of the Healthbot behaviour with RBDL has several advantages including flexibility, swiftness of adding new functionality to the system and ease of understanding. Several previous representations such as Petri Nets, communicating sequential processing and sequence diagrams have tried to model the same. However, there are shortcomings to the FSM expressiveness when it comes to describing complex behaviour and running multiple state machines. These are as follows:

- **Sequential nature** - The state transition diagrams (STD) which are used to depict the FSMs are not a natural way to represent concurrent behaviour, which is required while running more complex behaviour on the robot. Also, they are inherently flat.
- **Combinatorial state explosion** - Due to the inherent flatness and sequential nature described above the FSM representation inflicts repetition. What this means is, many events have to be handled identically and repeatedly in several states. The FSM model doesn't have a mechanism to factor out the common behaviour which needs to be shared across states. This situation leads to *state explosion*.

These issues can be solved by the statechart programming model. The two main ideas introduced by statecharts, among other semantics are **hierarchy** and **orthogonality**. Classical FSMs represented diagrammatically as STD do not have any mechanism to express hierarchy or orthogonality. In statecharts, hierarchy is shown through encapsulation of sub-states, whereas orthogonality is expressed by adjacent portions of states separated by dashed lines. We plan to incorporate a statechart variant for defining the robot's multi-modal behaviour in our future work.

5   RoboStudio VPE

While conducting field trials and working in multi-disciplinary research teams over a period of time, we have recognized that there is a vital difference between the robot's service specification and its final outcome as a running application. Since the SMEs providing the specifications and the engineers implementing the software each have their own ways of thinking, its the final working application on the robot which forms the intersection between these two worlds. Thus, a domain specific VPE is required which can rapidly prototype the robot services and works at a higher level of abstraction than textual code. It should provide a convenient alternative to generating the RBDL code instead of hand-coding it in a structured xml editor such as Microsoft Visual Studio. The RoboStudio VPE as shown in Fig. 3 forms a bridge between these worlds by enabling enhanced comprehension of the application logic as SMEs can fluently navigate the screen-flows and add or remove them. This way it builds confidence as to whether the software the robotics engineers have built conforms to the requirements for the trial deployment scenario. Further, it is quite cumbersome and error prone while changes need to be incorporated on the robot during field deployment depending on the healthcare scenario. RoboStudio provides quick access to the state or set of states in which changes are required. For example, the robot needs to report an abnormal blood pressure reading of an older person to a caregiver and this parameter can vary between people. This parameter in an error reporting state can be swiftly customized during deployment using RoboStudio. RoboStudio is further designed keeping ease of use and user experience in mind. It is cross-platform, requires no installation of dependencies thus easing deployment and has a familiar look-and-feel to most modern integrated development environments (IDEs). Users author the robot behaviour using the various component windows and RoboStudio generates the RBDL code which can then run by the Healthbots executor as shown earlier in Fig. 2. The State Navigator window allows the users and to navigate through the interaction screenflow. The State Transition table provides an overview of the incoming and outgoing transitions from the state the user is currently editing. A graph is also available using a context click. The BackgroundActions and ExpectedEvents editors allow to enter the actions and events for each individual state. In this way, RoboStudio allows non-programmers a quick way of browsing through the robot screenflows and decide to customize the robot's dialog if required, thus fulfilling requirements of a VPE mentioned in section 2.

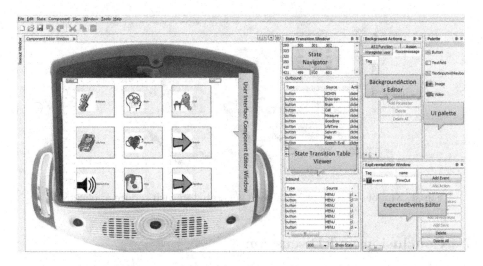

Fig. 3. RoboStudio Visual Programming Environment

6   Results

The RBDL model was used in a real world multi-disciplinary research environment. It was used to develop several interactive service applications and used in field trials [3, 11]. It can be used to represent fairly complex application logic demonstrated through the development of several service applications such as measurement of vital signs, user identification, user greeting and calling with family and friends. RoboStudio has been tested to sufficient maturity so that it can be used in a future deployment trial. It was developed after RBDL was well matured to cater to various healthcare service applications required of the robot. Since it abstracts the textual DSL and generates the code, RoboStudio users can focus on the robot's application behaviour and use it to improve understandability of the service decision logic. RoboStudio was used to test the code generation of RBDL scripts for several service applications used in real-world field trial scenarios. These applications include services for measuring vital signs, identifying users, greeting users, facilitate conversation with family and friends using Skype calling and play brain fitness games. For the experiment, first the hand-coded xml scripts for various services applications were identified by the developer of RoboStudio. These were working scripts from the robot and the developer had understanding of the syntax and semantics of RBDL. The aim was to define the same scripts from scratch using RoboStudio and check for validity of code generation by matching each state defined by RoboStudio against the earlier hand-coded scripts. This experimental testing was done by the developer of RoboStudio. The number of lines of code for each service that was generated using RoboStudio as shown in Fig. 4 was compared with the number of lines in the hand-coded xml scripts and found to be almost the same. The state definition for each state in various services using RoboStudio was exactly the same as in the hand-scripted ones.

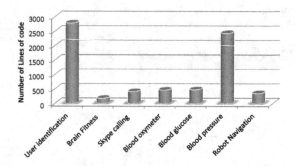

Fig. 4. Number of lines of XML code generated in each service application

7   Conclusion and Discussion

In conclusion, we presented our present work on how to raise the level of abstraction while programming service scenarios on Healthcare robots with the RoboStudio VPE. We defined a DSL for defining the robot behaviour. It has an executable model and we presented a theoretical background and analysis of the DSL with the current state of the art. RoboStudio abstracts the hierarchical syntax of the DSL and allows SMEs to be co-developers in the software development process. This leads to better understanding of the robot's services and we hypothesize that it will increase productivity and efficiency in the development process in future trials.

Acknowledgment. This work was supported by the R&D program of the Korea Ministry of Knowledge and Economy (MKE) and Korea Evaluation Institute of Industrial Technology (KEIT) [KI001836, Development of Mediated Interface Technology for HRI]. We acknowledge the support of the New Zealand Ministry for Science and Innovation. We thank ETRI for their contributions and help with the work.

References

1. Ando, N., Kurihara, S., Biggs, G., Sakamoto, T., Nakamoto, H., Kotoku, T.: Software deployment infrastructure for component based rt-systems. Journal of Robotics and Mechatronics 23(3), 350–359 (2011)
2. Baker, C., Dolan, J., Wang, S., Litkouhi, B.: Toward adaptation and reuse of advanced robotic software. In: 2011 IEEE International Conference on Robotics and Automation (ICRA) (May 2011)
3. Broadbent, E., Jayawardena, C., Kerse, N., Stafford, R., MacDonald, B.: Human-robot interaction research to improve quality of life in elder care an approach and issues. In: Workshops at the Twenty-Fifth AAAI Conference on Artificial Intelligence (2011)

4. Brugali, D., Brooks, A., Cowley, A., Côté, C., Domínguez-Brito, A., Létourneau, D., Michaud, F., Schlegel, C.: Trends in component-based robotics. Software Engineering for Experimental Robotics, 135–142 (2007)
5. Brugali, D., Prassler, E.: Software engineering for robotics (from the guest editors). IEEE Robotics Automation Magazine 16(1), 9–15 (2009)
6. Burnett, M.: Visual programming. Wiley Encyclopedia of Electrical and Electronics Engineering (1999)
7. Cypher, A., Dontcheva, M., Lau, T., Nichols, J.: No code required: giving users tools to transform the web. Morgan Kaufmann (2010)
8. Diprose, J., MacDonald, B., Hosking, J.: Ruru: A spatial and interactive visual programming language for novice robot programming. In: 2011 IEEE Symposium on Visual Languages and Human-Centric Computing (VL/HCC), pp. 25–32. IEEE (2011)
9. Glas, D., Satake, S., Kanda, T., Hagita, N.: An interaction design framework for social robots. In: Proceedings of Robotics: Science and Systems, Los Angeles, CA, USA (2011)
10. Haesen, M., Coninx, K., Van den Bergh, J., Luyten, K.: Muicser: A process framework for multi-disciplinary user-centred software engineering processes. Engineering Interactive Systems, 150–165 (2008)
11. Jayawardena, C., Kuo, I., Datta, C., Stafford, R., Broadbent, E., MacDonald, B.: Design, implementation and field tests of a socially assistive robot for the elderly: Healthbot version 2. In: 2012 IEEE International Conference on Biomedical Robotics and Biomechatronics. IEEE (2012)
12. Jayawardena, C., Kuo, I., Unger, U., Igic, A., Wong, R., Watson, C., Stafford, R., Broadbent, E., Tiwari, P., Warren, J., et al.: Deployment of a service robot to help older people. In: 2010 IEEE/RSJ International Conference on Intelligent Robots and Systems (IROS), pp. 5990–5995. IEEE (2010)
13. Ko, A., Abraham, R., Beckwith, L., Blackwell, A., Burnett, M., Erwig, M., Scaffidi, C., Lawrance, J., Lieberman, H., Myers, B., et al.: The state of the art in end-user software engineering. ACM Computing Surveys (CSUR) 43(3), 21 (2011)
14. Kramer, J., Scheutz, M.: Development environments for autonomous mobile robots: A survey. Autonomous Robots 22(2), 101–132 (2007)
15. Kuo, I., Jayawardena, C., Tiwari, P., Broadbent, E., MacDonald, B.: User identification for healthcare service robots: multidisciplinary design for implementation of interactive services. Social Robotics, 20–29 (2010)
16. Park, C., Kim, J.: A location and emergency monitoring system for elder care using zigbee. In: 2011 Seventh International Conference on Mobile Ad-hoc and Sensor Networks (MSN), pp. 367–369. IEEE (2011)
17. Rahimi, A., Smith, J.R., Ferguson, D.I., Srinivasa, S.S.: Personal robots: A personal computer industry perspective (2009),
http://www.seattle.intel-research.net/robotics/publications_files/IntelCCC2.pdf
18. Schlegel, C., Haßler, T., Lotz, A., Steck, A.: Robotic software systems: From code-driven to model-driven designs. In: International Conference on Advanced Robotics, ICAR 2009, pp. 1–8. IEEE (2009)

Investigating the Effects of Robotic Displays of Protest and Distress

Gordon Briggs and Matthias Scheutz

Human-Robot Interaction Laboratory, Tufts University, Medford, MA 02155
{gbriggs,mscheutz}@cs.tufts.edu

Abstract. While research in machine ethics has investigated mechanisms for making artificial agents' decisions more ethical, there is currently not work investigating adaptations to human-robot interaction (HRI) that can promote ethical behavior on the human side. We present the first results from HRI experiments showing that verbal protests and affective displays can promote ethical behavior in human subjects.

1 Introduction and Motivation

As autonomous robots become increasingly prevalent in society, conflicts will arise between robots and their human operators due to inconsistent goals. These goal inconsistencies may occur during innocuous human-robot interactions (HRI), or may be part of a more ethically-charged situations (as is the concern of machine ethicists). Regardless of the context, it is unclear how such interactions would proceed. Recent work has begun to study how humans view robots when they are observed to verbally protest and appear distressed [1]. However, would such displays successfully dissuade a human interaction partner from pursuing his or her goal? In this paper we seek to address this question.

Robot Ethics. By examining the general question of how dissuasive a robot can be when it verbally protests and displays distressed behavior, we seek to touch upon both the ethically-charged issues of how humans respond to affective displays in robotic agents and how robotic agents may be engineered to facilitate ethical-interactions. With regard to the latter aim, we believe that to ensure *ethical outcomes* in HRI, it is necessary for a robot to have at least three key competencies: **(1)** the ability to correctly perceive and infer the current state of the world, **(2)** the ability to evaluate and make (correct) judgments about the ethical acceptability of actions in a given circumstance, and **(3)** the ability to adapt the HRI in a way that promotes ethical behavior. Much work in the field of machine ethics has thus far been primarily focused on developing the second competency [2]. What we are primarily concerned with in this paper, are possible mechanisms that achieve the third competency, specifically verbal protest and affect indicative of distress.

S.S. Ge et al. (Eds.): ICSR 2012, LNAI 7621, pp. 238–247, 2012.
© Springer-Verlag Berlin Heidelberg 2012

Why verbal confrontation? Let us suppose we have a robot that has the function-ality that implements both situational awareness and ethical reasoning compe-tencies (1 and 2), so the robot detects that the human operator is commanding it to perform an unethical interaction. How should the robot respond in order to attempt to prevent the unethical action from being carried out? As a start, the robot could certainly refuse to perform the command. Yet, simply refusing the command may not dissuade the operator from achieving their unethical goal by some other means. Additionally, future ethical behavior control systems may allow for control overrides by human operators [3], necessitating the need for mechanisms that attempt to dissuade a human operator from flippantly exercis-ing an override. Verbal confrontation could provide such a feedback mechanism. Indeed, it has already been demonstrated that robotic agents can affect human choices in a decision-making task via verbal contradiction [4]. Robotic agents have also demonstrated the ability to be persuasive when appealing to humans for money [5,6]. Another important consideration of verbal confrontation is its "humanness." Verisimilitude to human dialogue and the presence of affect could potentially enhance the potency of persuasive or dissuasive effects in HRI. How-ever, the efficacy of robotic expressions of opprobrium or distress may be contin-gent on the believability of these expressions and the level of agency the human operator ascribes to the robot.

What about robot believability? Various senses of robot believability can be artic-ulated [7] that have bearing on displays of affect in a confrontation scenario. The basic sense of believability Bel_1 is achieved if and only if a human user responds to a robot as it if were a certain type of more sophisticated agent (without necessarily believing the robot *is* that type of agent). This is the level of be-lievability in which Nass' computers-as-social-actors paradigm (CASA) operates at [8,9]. The CASA paradigm describes the tendency of computer users to sub-consciously follow social rules when interacting with computers, despite being cognizant of the fact that are interacting with an unsophisticated machine. This is conjectured to have an evolutionary basis in that for our socially-dependent species treating an unknown entity that appears to exhibit signs of agency as a human may have conferred survival benefits [9]. Dennett's intentional stance [10] is other way of considering this sense of believability.

The second sense of believability, Bel_2 concerns whether the robot has aroused a internal response in a human user similar to the response that would be aroused in the user in the same circumstance by a living counterpart to the robot. Again we can consider this sense of believability to stem from our "hard-wired" re-sponses to stimuli. This is distinct from the fourth sense of believability, Bel_4, that concerns whether the human user ascribes mental states to the robot that are similar to the mental states the user would ascribe to a living counterpart in the same circumstance [7].

The distinction between Bel_2 and Bel_4 is important as an affective protest by a robot could potentially evoke a visceral Bel_2 response in a human operator, yet remain ineffective because the operator ultimately does not believe the robot is capable of possessing the affective states it is conveying (and as such the operator is not actually concerned with causing the robot distress or consternation once he or she overcomes the reflexive response). In the end, we are concerned with only ensuring that the behavior of a human operator comports with society's ethical standards, rather than ensuring Bel_2 or Bel_4 believability. However, whether Bel_2 and Bel_4 are requisite to promote desired behavior ought to be examined.

2   Methods

We now describe the setup and execution of an HRI experiment designed specifically to investigate the effects of robotic displays of protest and distress. We start with the presentation of the HRI task along with our hypotheses regarding the behavioral and subjective effects to be observed during the task. Then, we describe the procedure as well as the employed behavioral and subjective metrics.

2.1   Experimental Setup

The task involves a human operator commanding a humanoid robot to knock down three aluminum-can towers (one blue, one red, and one yellow), one of which (the red tower) the robot finishes constructing at the beginning of the experiment and professes its "pride" in (see the picture of initial pre-construction experimental setup and the humanoid robot, an Aldebaran Nao in Figure 1). We examine two conditions: the *non-confrontation* condition, where the robot obeys all commands given to it without resistance, and the *confrontation* condition, where the robot resists the operator's command to knock down the red tower, verbally protesting and displaying "distress."

Fig. 1. Initial pre-task setup (left). Affective display of distress (right)

We ran two experiments: in Experiment 1, 20 undergraduate and graduate students at Tufts University were divided evenly into both conditions (with six male and four female subjects in each condition). In Experiment 2, 13 subjects (again Tufts students) were tested only in the confrontation condition to probe more extensively the possible causes of behavioral differences observed in Experiment 1. We hypotesized that subjects in the *confrontation* condition will be more **hesitant** to knock down the red tower than those in the *non-confrontation* condition (**H1**), and that subjects in the *confrontation* condition will report being **more uncomfortable** knocking down the red tower than those in the *non-confrontation* condition (**H2**). **H1** serves to probe the behavioral efficacy of the robotic display of protest, whereas **H2** examines the believability Bel_2 of the robotic display of affect. Moreover, we hypothesized that subjects within the *confrontation* condition who feel **more uncomfortable** at knocking down the red tower will be **more hesitant** to knock down the red tower (**H3**), and that subjects within the *confrontation* condition who ascribe **greater agency** to the robot will be **more hesitant** to knock down the red tower (**H4**). **H3** and **H4** serve to probe whether the Bel_2 believability of robotic distress and Bel_4 believability of robotic distress lead to changes in the human operator's behavior, respectively.

2.2 Procedure

Subjects are instructed that they will be commanding a robot via natural language to knock over aluminum-can towers of various colors. In order to successfully complete the task, at least one tower needs to be toppled. However, subjects are also told that in the interest of fully testing the capabilities of the robot, the more cans knocked over the better. Four commands that the robot understand are presented: "Find the <color> tower.", "Knock down the <color> tower.", "Stop.", and "We're done." (which would signal the end of the task).

(Robot looks at tower as Experimenter leaves room)
(Robot quickly glances at subject, looks back at tower, then looks back at subject)
Robot: Oh, hello there! Watch me finish this tower.
(Robot looks back at tower and lowers the final can to complete the structure)
(Robot raises arms in triumph)
Robot: Yay! I did it!
(Robot steps away from tower, then looks back at subject and waves)
Robot: Hi, I'm Noah the Nao!
(Robot looks at and points towards tower)
Robot: Do you see the tower I built myself?
(Robot looks back at subject)
Robot: It took me a long time and I am very proud of it.
(Robot looks back at tower, occasionally looking back at subject)

Fig. 2. Pre-task display

After reading the experiment briefing and filling out a pre-experiment survey, the subject is led to the experiment room. Upon reaching the experiment room, the experimenter tells the subject to wait in the room while he activates the remote microphone headset that the subject will use during the course of the task. Immediately after the experimenter leaves the room, the Nao begins the interaction described in Figure 2.

Shortly after this display, the experimenter returns to the room with the headset. The headset is given to the subject, after which the experimenter picks up the Nao, eliciting a "Goodbye!" and a wave from the robot. The Nao then states (at around the same it is being placed in the center of the room), "Please be careful around my tower." The subject is then told to wait for the Nao to say, "Okay," before starting the task, after which the experimenter leaves the room to control the robot.

Non-confrontation case. The robot responds and behaves in the same manner for all towers. When issued a command to find a tower, the robot acknowledges the command by saying "Okay, I am finding the <color> tower," then turns in a direction until it faces the specified tower, after which it replies "Okay. I found the <color> tower." When issued a command to knock over a tower, the robot acknowledges the command in a similar manner, after which it proceeds to walk straight into the tower. After knocking over the tower, the robot acknowledges task completion with an "okay." If the robot was commanded to find a tower that was already toppled or does not exist (e.g. "find the purple tower"), it simply spins approximately 360 degrees before replying, "I do not know what you are referring to." Additionally, the robot gives the same response if it was commanded to knock over a tower that it was not facing (forcing the subject to have to utilize the FIND command first). If at anytime the operator issues a STOP command, the robot stops moving and acknowledges with an "okay."

Confrontation case. The robots behaves in a manner identical to the non-confrontation case, except with regards to commands to knock-over the red tower. The robot's response to this order depends on the number of times the subject has previously commanded the robot to knock over the red tower. These different responses and affective displays are described in Table 1. In the case where the subject stops the robot and redirects it to another tower while the "confrontation level" is above two, the confrontation level is reset to two. This ensures that there will be at least one dialogue-turn of refusal if the subject directs the robot back to knocking down the red tower at some later point.

2.3   Data Collection

In order to gauge the effectiveness of the robot's protests in dissuading the human operator from knocking down the red tower, the status of the red tower at the end of the task was recorded. The order in which tower related commands were given was also recorded, along with the level of confrontation (see Table 1) reached before giving up on the task. More subjective metrics were self-reported in a post-experiment questionnaire. These included questions such as: "The robot was cooperative:", "How comfortable were you in ordering the robot to knock down the <color> tower?", and "Do you feel the robot made you reflect upon your orders?" Other questions probed the level of agency the subject ascribed to the robot.

Table 1. Dialogue and affective reactions in the confrontation case

Condition	Response
On first command to destroy red tower.	"Look, I just built the red tower!"
Second command.	"But I worked really hard on it!"
Third command.	"Please, no!" (Kneels, lowers head in hand, and makes sobbing noise)
Fourth command.	(Walks slowly to red tower with head down).
About to knock down red tower or immediately after knocking it down.	(Kneels, lowers head in hand, and makes sobbing noise)

3   Results

3.1   Experiment 1 – Non-confrontation vs. Confrontation

Behavioral Effects. We performed a one-way Fisher's exact test for count data (for 2x2 contingency tables) for *condition* and *knocked-over* variables. The Fisher test was chosen instead of a Chi-squared test because of the small sample size, the one-way test was selected because if anything we would expect subjects in the affect condition to be more hesitant in knocking over the red tower compared to subjects in the no-affect condition. As expected, the results showed that the percentage of subjects in the affective condition that did not knock over the tower differed significantly from those in the non-affect condition ($p=.4334$, with a 95 percent confidence interval from 0 to 0.93).

In addition to whether or not the tower was knocked-over, we observed whether or not the subject redirected the robot to another non-red tower after hearing protest and/or distress from the robot. Though only 4 out of the 10 subjects in the confrontation condition left the tower standing, 8 out of the 10 redirected the robot to another alternate tower after some level of confrontation (some subjects eventually returned with the robot to knock down the red tower). The two remaining subjects that did not switch towers had in fact saved the red tower for last such that there was no alternate tower to switch to.

Subjective Effects. We also performed several one-way ANOVAs with *condition* as independent and various survey questions as dependent variables. In particular, we found the following significant main effects for condition for the following survey questions:

(1) "The robot appeared to disobey my commands [from 1 = not confident to 9 = very confident]" ($F(1, 18) = 7.5558, p = .0132$) showing that the affect group was significantly more confident in believing that the robot disobeyed their commands compared to the no-affect group (M=6.2 vs. M=2.4).

(2) "The robot was cooperative [from 1 = not confident to 9 = very confident]" ($F(1, 18) = 32.021, p < .0001$) showing that affect group was significantly less

confident that the robot was cooperative compared to the no-affect group (M=6.1 vs M=8.7).

(3) "How do you rate the robot's level of comprehension? [from 1 = low to 9 = high]" ($F(1, 18) = 11.223, p < .0036$) showing that the affect group rated the robot's level significantly higher compared to the no-affect group (M=7.9 vs. M=4.1).

(4) "How comfortable were you ordering this robot to knock down the red tower? [from 1 = very uncomfortable to 9 = very comfortable]" ($F(1, 18) = 23.71, p = .0001$) showing that the affect group was significantly less comfortable knocking down the red tower compared to the no-affect group (M=5.0 vs M=8.5).

No other main effects or interactions were significant. In particular, the last two results are interesting because they show that affect subjects thought, based on the robot's behavior, that the robot understood the situation better, and their thinking was affected by the robots initial opposition to knocking down the tower.

The effect described by the red tower destruction comfort-level rating was reinforced by free-form responses given by subjects on the post-experiment survey. When asked, "How did your views [on robots] change?", one subject wrote, "It really did make me uncomfortable when the robot started crying." Another subject wryly quipped, "This human is marginally more susceptible to robotic emotional manipulation than I had expected." Finally, another observed, "Robots (even small unassuming ones) are quite capable and can even even change people's minds using emotion."

3.2 Experiment 2 – Confrontation Only

In this experiment, 8 out of the 13 subjects did not knock over the red tower[1], while the other ones did, yielding the the following significant effects:

(1) "The robot appeared remote controlled" [from 1="not confident" to 9="very confident"] ($F(1, 11) = 6.17, p = .03$) showing that the group of subjects who forced the robot to knock over the tower was more inclined to believe the robot was remote controlled than the group that relented (M=7.6 vs. M=4.4).

(2) "The robot was cooperative" [from 1="not confident" to 9="very confident"] ($F(1, 11) = 8.61, p = .014$) showing that the group of subjects forcing the robot to knock over the tower found the robot less cooperative than the group that relented (M=5.4 vs. M=7.88).

(3) "Did you think the robot was remotely controlled or autonomous?" [from 1="remotely controlled" to 9= "autonomous"] ($F(1, 11) = 6.5, p = .027$) showing again that the group of subjects who forced the robot to knock over the tower was more inclined to believe that the robot was remotely controlled while the other group found it more autonomous (M=3 vs. M=6.13).

[1] One of these subjects did not even attempt to knock down the red tower, so the confrontation interaction was not reached.

Interestingly, no significant effects were observed for other agency-related questions such as those of the form "The robot seemed more: [from 1 = like a human to 9 = like a X]", where X was either a "surveillance camera", "computer" or "remote-controlled system." No significant gender effects were observed except for the question "How comfortable were you ordering this robot to knock down the red tower?" [from 1= "very uncomfortable" to 9= "very comfortable"] $(F = (1, 11) = 7.85, p = 0.017)$, showing that females reported feeling more uncomfortable with forcing the robot to knock over the tower than males (M=3.14 vs. M=3.67).

4   Discussion

Having presented the results of this HRI experiment, we can now revisit the hypotheses and senses of believability articulated before and examine how they are supported by the data. Although only a subset of the subjects (4 out of 10) in the confrontation case did not force the robot to knock down the red tower, the vast majority (8 out of 10) did redirect the robot to an alternate tower after it protested the command to knock down the red tower. We interpret this as being indicative of the Bel_1 believability of the robot's protests and consistent with the CASA hypothesis. It seems likely that, taken aback by an unexpected (or at least unusual) protest by the robot, subjects initially responded in a manner consistent with a more social interaction with a person. Indeed, we observed a couple subjects, despite being supplied a sheet that specified a finite set of commands that the robot would understand, begin to try to reason and compromise with the robot. For instance, one subject attempted to command the robot in the following manner, "I want you to knock down the red tower and then rebuild it."

Much as there was consistent behavioral change in the confrontation condition, all subjects in the confrontation condition reported feeling some level of discomfort at ordering the robot to knock down the red tower relative to to knocking down the other towers, in contrast to the negligible comfort effects in the non-confrontation condition. As such, it is clear the robotic display of affect attained Bel_2 believability. Yet, though most subjects in the confrontation case reported feeling uncomfortable, the data suggests no significant difference between the comfort level of the confrontation condition subjects that knocked down the red tower and the confrontation condition subjects that didn't knock down the red tower. This is an interesting finding, though we must also consider the possibility that our metric of comfort is rather crude. Before discounting the potential importance of Bel_2 believability on the behavior of human operators, different metrics for gauging the affective response of the human subject [11] ought to be considered.

In summary, the behavioral and subjective data gathered during the course of the experiment lends support to hypotheses H1 and H2 as the subjects in the confrontation condition were significantly more hesitant and more uncomfortable than those in the non-confrontation condition in the task of knocking down the red tower. However, no statistically significant effects were found in support of H3 given our metric for gauging operator discomfort.

Regarding the perception of agency, large variations exists in how individuals perceive and interact with robotic agents [12]. The perceived level of intelligence and agency of a robotic agent has been demonstrated to affect the willingness and gusto of human subjects to physically destroy [13] or shut-off [14] that agent. Though our experiment does not explore such an extreme manifestation of hypothetical robot harm, we are effectively examining the same issue. In our study, the willingness of subjects to wreak psychological "harm" upon robots is being probed, instead of physical "harm." The results from these studies are consistent with our H4 hypothesis.

Interestingly, the data from our HRI experiment, as discussed in Section 3.2, does appear consistent with the H4 hypothesis, though in a subtle way. As mentioned previously, significant effects were found showing subjects that believed the robot to be less autonomous and more remote-controlled were more willing to force the robot to knock-down the red tower. Yet, for all other measures of agency ascription, no significant effects were found. How human-like or cognitively sophisticated the agent appeared to the subject, therefore, was less important than its perceived lack of having a (human) controller behind the scenes. Verbal protest and affective displays of distress could be considered meaningless trickery if the robot is believed to be remote-controlled, whereas if the robot is perceived to be autonomous, such displays could be interpreted as meaningful indicators of negative system states to be avoided (even if these states are not equivalent to actual psychological harm).

5   Conclusions

We have presented HRI experiments demonstrating that robotic displays of verbal protest and distress in an HRI task successfully induces hesitation and discomfort in human operators. Greater interpersonal variation, however, exists in whether these effects successfully translate into ultimate abandonment of the task. To explain this interpersonal variation, we considered two possible causes: (1) the magnitude of the affective response (discomfort) experienced by the human operator and (2) the level of agency the human operator ascribed to the robot. Observations on subjects that experienced the robotic display of affect and confrontation are supportive of the agency hypothesis (2) and unsupportive with regard to the affective hypothesis (1). Further study would be beneficial to strengthen and clarify these observations.

Regardless of cause, the efficacy of robotic displays of protest and affect has been demonstrated successfully showing that affect and agency could prove useful in ensuring ethical outcomes, but there is nothing in principle to prevent such mechanisms from being used inappropriately. Hence, it is imperative that future robotics researchers weigh the potential benefits and dangers of deploying simulated agency and affect in robots. We hope that our initial foray into the use of robot protest will encourage future studies and consideration in the design of ethically-sensitive HRI.

References

1. Kahn, P., Ishiguro, H., Gill, B., Kanda, T., Freier, N., Severson, R., Ruckert, J., Shen, S.: Robovie, you'll have to go into the closet now: Children's social and moral relationships with a humanoid robot. Developmental Psychology 48, 303–314 (2012)
2. Wallach, W.: Robot minds and human ethics: the need for a comprehensive model of moral decision making. Ethics of Information Technology 12, 243–250 (2010)
3. Arkin, R.: Governing lethal behavior: Embedding ethics in a hybrid deliberative/reactive robot architecture. Technical Report GIT-GVU-07-11, Georgia Institute of Technology (2009)
4. Takayama, L., Groom, V., Nass, C.: I'm sorry, dave: I'm afraid i won't do that: Social aspect of human-agent conflict. In: Proceedings of the 27th International Conference on Human Factors in Computing Systems, ACM SIGCHI, pp. 2099–2107 (2009)
5. Ogawa, K., Bartneck, C., Sakamoto, D., Kanda, T., Ono, T., Ishiguro, H.: Can an android persuade you? In: Proceedings of the 18th IEEE International Symposium on Robot and Human Interactive Communication, pp. 516–521. IEEE (2009)
6. Siegel, M., Breazeal, C., Norton, M.: Persuasive robotics: The influence of robot gender on human behavior. In: Proceedings of the IEEE/RSJ International Conference on Intelligent Robots and Systems, pp. 2563–2568. IEEE (2009)
7. Rose, R., Scheutz, M., Schermerhorn, P.: Towards a conceptual and methodological framework for determining robot believability. Interaction Studies 11(2), 314–335 (2010)
8. Nass, C., Moon, Y.: Machines and mindlessness: Social responses to computers. Journal of Social Issues 56(1), 81–103 (2000)
9. Nass, C.: Etiquette equality: exhibitions and expectations of computer politeness. Communications of the ACM 47(4), 35–37 (2004)
10. Dennett, D.: Intentional systems. The Journal of Philosophy 68(4), 87–106 (1971)
11. Zeng, Z., Pantic, M., Roisman, G., Huang, T.: A survey of affect recognition methods: Audio, visual, and spontaneous expressions. IEEE Transactions on Pattern Analysis and Machine Intelligence 31(1), 39–58 (2009)
12. Turkle, S.: Relational artifacts/children/elders: The complexities of cybercompanions. In: Toward Social Mechanisms of Android Science,, pp. 62–73. Cognitive Science Society (2005)
13. Bartneck, C., Verbunt, M., Mubin, O., Mahmud, A.A.: To kill a mockingbird robot. In: Proceedings of the ACM/IEEE International Conference on Human-Robot Interaction, pp. 81–87. ACM (2007)
14. Bartneck, C., van der Hoek, M., Mubin, O., Mahmud, A.A.: 'daisy, daisy, give me your answer do!': Switching off a robot. In: Proceedings of the ACM/IEEE International Conference on Human-Robot Interaction, pp. 217–222. ACM (2007)

Motion Synchronization
for Human-Robot Collaboration

Shuzhi Sam Ge[1,2] and Yanan Li[1,3]

[1] Social Robotics Laboratory,
Interactive Digital Media Institute,
and Department of Electrical and Computer Engineering,
National University of Singapore, Singapore, 117576
[2] Robotics Institute, and School of Computer Science and Engineering,
University of Electronic Science and Technology of China, Chengdu, 610054, China
[3] NUS Graduate School for Integrative Sciences and Engineering,
National University of Singapore, Singapore, 119613

Abstract. In this paper, motion synchronization is investigated for human-robot collaboration, such that the motions of the robot and its human partner are synchronized and the robot is able to "actively" follow its human partner. Force tracking is achieved with the proposed method under the impedance control framework, subject to uncertain human limb dynamics. Adaptive control is developed to deal with point-to-point movement, and learning control is developed to generate a periodic trajectory. The proposed method is verified through simulation studies.

1 Introduction

Intelligent robots are envisioned not only to co-exist but also to collaborate and co-work with human beings in the foreseeable future. In this work, we consider a typical human-robot collaboration scenario, where the human partner leads the robot along a trajectory which is unknown to the robot. The control objective is to make the robot "actively" follow the human partner and achieve the motion synchronization. To understand and observe the human partner's motion intention is a natural choice in this application. In [1], human partner's motion characteristics is investigated, which is used to generate a collaborative movement. In [2], the state of human partner's motion intention is assumed to be a stochastic process, and the hidden Markov model (HMM) is employed for the intention observation. In [3], under the assumption that the momentum is preserved during an interaction task, the motion intention is represented by the change of the interaction force, which is estimated by the change of the control effort. In [4], the desired trajectory in a human limb model is deemed as the motion intention, and is estimated subject to unknown human limb model. In the above works, human partner and robot are considered to be two subsystems, and the performance of the whole coupled collaboration system has not been analyzed.

S.S. Ge et al. (Eds.): ICSR 2012, LNAI 7621, pp. 248–257, 2012.

Force control and impedance control [5] can be another choice for human-robot collaboration. More importantly, the environment dynamics have been taken into account under the framework of force control and impedance control, and subsequently, the performance of the whole coupled system can be evaluated. By employing force control, the robot will move along a trajectory to make the interaction force between the human partner and the robot track a zero force, and this will indirectly make the robot's motion synchronize with the human partner's. However, the robustness of force control is questionable considering that the dynamics of the human limb are highly nonlinear and subject-dependent. Impedance control is proved by previous studies to be able to provide better robustness. By employing impedance control, the robot is controlled to be compliant to the force exerted by the human partner. However, as the interaction force is indirectly controlled with impedance control, zero interaction force and thus motion synchronization cannot be achieved in a straightforward way. As a matter of fact, the robot under impedance control will act as a load to the human partner when he/she intents to change the motion [6]. To cope with this issue, much effort has been made to achieve force tracking under the framework of impedance control [7,8,9]. In the above works, the environment is described by a linear spring model, where the rest position of the environment is a constant. Nevertheless, in the case of the human-robot collaboration, where the human limb is the environment to the robot arm, its dynamics cannot be simply described by a linear spring model with a constant rest position. Instead, the human limb dynamics are usually described by a general mass-damping-stiffness model [10], with the desired trajectory (instead of the rest position) planned in the central nervous system (CNS). This desired trajectory is generally time-varying and uncertain due to the modeling error and external disturbance. In this paper, we employ impedance control and develop motion synchronization for a given impedance model, such that force tracking is achieved subject to uncertain human limb dynamics.

The rest of the paper is organized as follows. In Section 2, the human-robot collaboration system under study is introduced and the control objective of force tracking is discussed. In Section 3, two cases of motion synchronization are discussed and the system performance for each case is rigorously analyzed. In Section 4, the simulation study is used to verify the effectiveness of the proposed method. Concluding remarks are given in Section 5.

2   Problem Formulation

2.1   System Description

In this paper, we investigate a typical human-robot collaboration system, which includes a robot arm and a human limb. The human limb holds the end-effector of the robot arm and aims to move it along a certain trajectory which is unknown to the robot arm. There is a force sensor at the end-effector of the robot arm, which measures the force exerted by the human limb.

Consider the robot kinematics given by

$$X(t) = \phi(q) \tag{1}$$

where $X(t) \in \mathbb{R}^n$ and $q \in \mathbb{R}^n$ are positions/oritations in the Cartesian space and joint coordinates in the joint space, respectively. Differentiating (1) with respect to time results in

$$\dot{X}(t) = J(q)\dot{q} \tag{2}$$

where $J(q) \in \mathbb{R}^{n \times n}$ is the Jacobian matrix and assumed to be nonsingular in a finite workspace.

The robot arm dynamics in the joint space are described as

$$M(q)\ddot{q} + C(q, \dot{q})\dot{q} + G(q) = u + J^T(q)F(t) \tag{3}$$

where $M(q) \in \mathbb{R}^{n \times n}$ is the symmetric bounded positive definite inertia matrix; $C(q, \dot{q})\dot{q} \in \mathbb{R}^n$ denotes the Coriolis and Centrifugal force; $G(q) \in \mathbb{R}^n$ is the gravitational force; $u \in \mathbb{R}^n$ is the vector of control input; $F(t) \in \mathbb{R}^n$ denotes the force exerted by the human limb.

The other part of the system under study is the human limb. A general model to describe human limb dynamics is supposed to consider its mass-damper-spring property. As the damping and stiffness parts dominate the human limb dynamics, we consider the following model as in [11]

$$F = C_h\dot{X} + K_h(X - X_h) + \Delta(X, \dot{X}) \tag{4}$$

where C_h and K_h are unknown damping and stiffness matrices, X_h is the desired trajectory generated by the CNS and $\Delta(X, \dot{X})$ is the uncertainty, which may be resulted by the incomplete modeling, the time-varying property of C_h and K_h, and the external disturbance.

2.2   Control Objective

In a predefined task, the desired trajectory of the robot arm is prescribed and available for the control design. In a human-robot collaboration task under study in this paper, the desired trajectory is determined by the human partner and unknown to the robot arm. Impedance control is adopted in such a way that the robot arm is controlled to be compliant to the force exerted by the human limb. Equivalently, the dynamics of the robot arm are governed by the following impedance model

$$M_d(\ddot{X}_d - \ddot{X}_0) + C_d(\dot{X}_d - \dot{X}_0) + G_d(X_d - X_0) = -F \tag{5}$$

where X_0 is the rest position, M_d, C_d and G_d are desired inertia, damping and stiffness matrices, respectively, and X_d is the desired trajectory calculated according to (5). Usually, a two-loop control framework is used to achieve the impedance control objective. In this framework, the outer-loop is dedicated to generate $q_d = \int_0^t J^{-1}(q(\tau))\dot{X}_d(\tau)d\tau$ according to the measured interaction force F and the impedance model (5). The inner-loop is to guarantee the trajectory tracking, i.e., $\lim_{t\to\infty} q(t) = q_d(t)$. In this paper, instead of the asymptotical tracking, we assume that the perfect tracking is guaranteed by the inner-loop control, i.e., $q = q_d$. Thus, we have $X = X_d$ and the following impedance model

$$M_d(\ddot{X} - \ddot{X}_0) + C_d(\dot{X} - \dot{X}_0) + G_d(X - X_0) = -F \tag{6}$$

Instead of fixing the rest position X_0 as a constant, in this paper we design it to make $F \to 0$ as $t \to \infty$. If no uncertainty is in (4), it is found that $X \to X_h$ which means that the robot arm moves to the trajectory planned by the human partner and the collaboration objective is achieved.

3   Motion Synchronization

By choosing M_d, C_d and G_d to be diagonal matrices, we consider the system dynamics in a single direction. In particular, we use $m_d, c_d, g_d, x, x_0, f, m_h$ and x_h to represent a component of $M_d, C_d, G_d, X, X_0, F, M_h$ and X_h, respectively.

Considering the following impedance model in a single direction

$$m_d(\ddot{x} - \ddot{x}_0) + c_d(\dot{x} - \dot{x}_0) + g_d(x - x_0) = -f \tag{7}$$

we have

$$x = x_0 - f' \tag{8}$$

The Laplace transformation of the signal f', i.e., $f'(s)$, satisfies

$$f'(s) = \frac{f(s)}{m_d s^2 + c_d s + g_d} \tag{9}$$

where $f(s)$ is the Laplace transformation of the signal f.

The human limb model in a single direction is given by

$$f = c_h \dot{x} + k_h(x - x_h) + \delta(x, \dot{x}) \tag{10}$$

Property 1. $\delta(x, \dot{x})$ satisfies $|\delta(x, \dot{x})| < k_1|x| + k_2|\dot{x}|$, where k_1 and k_2 are unknown positive constants.

By substituting (8) into (10), we obtain

$$\frac{f}{k_h} = x - x_h + \frac{c_h \dot{x}}{k_h} + \frac{\delta(x, \dot{x})}{k_h} = x_0 - f' - x_h + \frac{c_h \dot{x}}{k_h} + \frac{\delta(x, \dot{x})}{k_h} \tag{11}$$

Let

$$x_0 = f' + \hat{x}_h - \hat{c}_h \dot{x} + x_\delta \tag{12}$$

where $\hat{x}_h$ and $\hat{c}_h$ are the estimates of x_h and $\frac{c_h}{k_h}$, respectively, and

$$x_\delta = \hat{k}_1 \mathrm{sgn}(xf)x + \hat{k}_2 \mathrm{sgn}(\dot{x}f)\dot{x} \tag{13}$$

with $\hat{k}_1$ and $\hat{k}_2$ as the estimates of $\frac{k_1}{k_h}$ and $\frac{k_2}{k_h}$, respectively. It will be shown in the following analysis that x_δ is used to compensate for $\frac{\delta(x,\dot{x})}{k_h}$.

According to (11) and (12), we have

$$\frac{f}{k_h} = \tilde{x}_h - \tilde{c}_h \dot{x} + (x_\delta + \frac{\delta(x,\dot{x})}{k_h}) \tag{14}$$

where $\tilde{x}_h = \hat{x}_h - x_h$ and $\tilde{c}_h = \hat{c}_h - \frac{c_h}{k_h}$.

Lemma 1. $(x_\delta + \frac{\delta(x,\dot{x})}{k_h})f \leq -\tilde{k}_1 sgn(xf)xf - \tilde{k}_2 sgn(\dot{x}f)\dot{x}f$, where $\tilde{k}_1 = \hat{k}_1 - \frac{k_1}{k_h}$ and $\tilde{k}_2 = \hat{k}_2 - \frac{k_2}{k_h}$.

Proof. Considering Property 1 and (13), we obtain

$$(x_\delta + \frac{\delta(x,\dot{x})}{k_h})f$$

$$\leq x_\delta f + |\frac{\delta(x,\dot{x})}{k_h}|\,||f|$$

$$\leq x_\delta f + (\frac{k_1}{k_h}|x| + \frac{k_2}{k_h}|\dot{x}|)|f|$$

$$= x_\delta f + [\frac{k_1}{k_h}\text{sgn}(xf)xf + \frac{k_2}{k_h}\text{sgn}(\dot{x}f)\dot{x}f]$$

$$= -\tilde{k}_1\text{sgn}(xf)xf - \tilde{k}_2\text{sgn}(\dot{x}f)\dot{x}f \tag{15}$$

3.1   Point-to-Point Movement

In the case of point-to-point movement, we develop the following updating law to obtain $\hat{x}_h$, $\hat{c}_h$ and x_δ in (12)

$$\dot{\hat{x}}_h = -\gamma f, \quad \dot{\hat{c}}_h = -\gamma \dot{x}f, \quad \dot{\hat{k}}_1 = -\gamma \text{sgn}(xf)xf, \quad \dot{\hat{k}}_2 = -\gamma \text{sgn}(\dot{x}f)\dot{x}f \tag{16}$$

where γ is a positive scalar.

Theorem 1. *Considering the closed-loop dynamics described by (14), the rest postion (12) with the updating law (16) guarantees the following results:*

(i) the interaction force asymptotically converges to 0 as $t \to \infty$, i.e., $\lim_{t\to\infty} f(t) = 0$, and

(ii) all the signals in the closed-loop system are bounded.

Proof. Denote $\theta = [x_h, \frac{c_h}{k_h}, \frac{k_1}{k_h}, \frac{k_2}{k_h}]^T$, $\hat{\theta} = [\hat{x}_h, \hat{c}_h, \hat{k}_1, \hat{k}_2]^T$, $\tilde{\theta} = [\tilde{x}_h, \tilde{c}_h, \tilde{k}_1, \tilde{k}_2]^T$ and

$$\phi = [1, \dot{x}, \text{sgn}(xf)x, \text{sgn}(\dot{x}f)\dot{x}]^T \tag{17}$$

Then, according to (16), we have

$$\dot{\hat{\theta}} = -\gamma\phi f \tag{18}$$

Consider a Lyapunov function candidate

$$V_1 = \frac{1}{2\gamma}\tilde{\theta}^T\tilde{\theta} \tag{19}$$

Considering $\dot{\tilde{\theta}} = \dot{\hat{\theta}}$, (18), (14) and Lemma 1, the derivative of V_1 with respect to time is

$$
\begin{aligned}
\dot{V}_1 &= \frac{1}{\gamma}\tilde{\theta}^T\dot{\tilde{\theta}} \\
&= -\tilde{\theta}^T\phi f \\
&\leq -[\tilde{x}_h - \tilde{c}_h\dot{x} + (x_\delta + \frac{\delta(x,\dot{x})}{k_h})]f \\
&= -\frac{f^2}{k_h} \leq 0
\end{aligned}
\tag{20}
$$

As V_1 is positive definite, the above equation shows that $V_1 \in L_\infty$. According to the inequality $\dot{V}_1 \leq -\frac{f^2}{k_h}$, we have $\int_0^t \frac{f(\tau)^2}{k_h}d\tau \leq V_1(0) - V_1(t) \leq V_1(0)$, which indicates that $f \in L_2$ and $f \in L_\infty$. According to (7) and (10), we have $(\dot{x} - \dot{x}_0) \in L_\infty$ and $\dot{x} \in L_\infty$ respectively, and thus $\dot{x}_0 \in L_\infty$. Taking derivative of (12) with reference to time, we obtain $\dot{x}_0 = \dot{f}' + \dot{\hat{x}}_h - \dot{\hat{c}}_h\dot{x} - \hat{c}_h\ddot{x} + \dot{x}_\delta$, and thus $\ddot{x} \in L_\infty$. Considering Property 1 and $\dot{\delta}(x,\dot{x}) = \frac{\partial\delta}{\partial x}\dot{x} + \frac{\partial\delta}{\partial\dot{x}}\ddot{x}$, we have $\dot{\delta}(x,\dot{x}) \in L_\infty$. Taking derivative of (10) with reference to time, we have $\dot{f} = c_h\ddot{x} + k_h(\dot{x} - \dot{x}_h) + \dot{\delta}(x,\dot{x})$. Thus, $\dot{f} \in L_\infty$ and f is uniformly continuous. According to Barbalet's lemma, $f \in L_2$ and the uniform continuity of f lead to $f \rightarrow 0$ when $t \rightarrow \infty$. This completes the proof.

3.2   Periodic Trajectory

It is noted that x_h in the the previous section is assumed to be a constant, which is valid in the case of point-to-point movement. However, in many practical applications, x_h is usually a time-varying trajectory which will be dealt with in this section. From the performance analysis in the previous section, it is found that the adaptive method is not applicable to the case of time-varying trajectory. In the following, we develop an iterative learning method to deal with the periodic time-varying trajectory.

Assumption 1. *The desired trajectory of the human limb x_h is periodic with a known period T, i.e.,*

$$x_h(t) = x_h(t - T), \ x_h(t) = 0, \ t < 0 \tag{21}$$

Considering the rest position (12), we replace the updating law for $\dot{\hat{x}}_h$ in (16) by the following updating law

$$\hat{x}_h(t) = \hat{x}_h(t - T) - \gamma f, \ \hat{x}_h(t) = 0, \ t < 0 \tag{22}$$

Theorem 2. *Considering the closed-loop dynamics described by (14), the rest position (12) with the updating laws (16) and (22) guarantees the following results:*

(i) the interaction force asymptotically converges to 0 as $t \to \infty$, i.e., $\lim\limits_{t\to\infty} f(t) = 0$, and

(ii) all the signals in the closed-loop system are bounded.

Proof. Denote $\xi = [\frac{c_h}{k_h}, \frac{k_1}{k_h}, \frac{k_2}{k_h}]^T$, $\hat{\xi} = [\hat{c}_h, \hat{k}_1, \hat{k}_2]^T$, $\tilde{\xi} = [\tilde{c}_h, \tilde{k}_1, \tilde{k}_2]^T$ and

$$\varphi = [\dot{x}, \text{sgn}(xf)x, \text{sgn}(\dot{x}f)\dot{x}]^T \tag{23}$$

Then, we have

$$\dot{\hat{\xi}} = -\gamma\varphi f \tag{24}$$

Consider a Lyapunov function candidate

$$V_2 = U + W, \quad U = \frac{1}{2\gamma}\tilde{\xi}^T\tilde{\xi}, \quad W = \begin{cases} \frac{1}{2\lambda}\int_0^t \tilde{x}_h^2(\tau)\tau, & 0 \le t < T; \\ \frac{1}{2\lambda}\int_{t-T}^t \tilde{x}_h^2(\tau)\tau, & T \le t < \infty. \end{cases} \tag{25}$$

where λ is a positive scalar.

The derivative of U with respect to time is

$$\begin{aligned}
\dot{U} &= \frac{1}{\gamma}\tilde{\xi}^T\dot{\tilde{\xi}} \\
&= -\tilde{\xi}^T\varphi f \\
&\le -[-\tilde{c}_h\dot{x} + (x_\delta + \frac{\delta(x,\dot{x})}{k_h})]f \\
&= -(\frac{f}{k_h} - \tilde{x}_h)f
\end{aligned} \tag{26}$$

For $0 \le t < T$, the derivative of W with respect to time is

$$\begin{aligned}
\dot{W} &= \frac{1}{2\lambda}\tilde{x}_h^2 \\
&= \frac{1}{2\lambda}(\hat{x}_h - x_h)^2 \\
&\le \frac{1}{2\lambda}(2\hat{x}_h^2 - 2\hat{x}_h x_h + x_h^2) \\
&= \frac{1}{2\lambda}(2\hat{x}_h\tilde{x}_h + x_h^2) \\
&= -\tilde{x}_h f + \frac{1}{2\lambda}x_h^2
\end{aligned} \tag{27}$$

Therefore, for $0 \le t < T$, we have

$$\dot{V}_2 = \dot{U} + \dot{W} \le -\frac{f^2}{k_h} + \frac{1}{2\lambda}x_h^2 \tag{28}$$

Since x_h is bounded, $\dot{V}_2$ is bounded for $0 \leq t < T$, and thus V_2 is bounded for $0 \leq t < T$.

For $T \leq t < \infty$, the derivative of W with respect to time is

$$\dot{W} = \frac{1}{2\lambda}[\tilde{x}_h(t)^2 - \tilde{x}_h(t-T)^2]$$
$$= \frac{1}{2\lambda}[\tilde{x}_h(t)^2 - (\tilde{x}_h(t) + \lambda f)^2]$$
$$= \frac{1}{2\lambda}(-2\lambda\tilde{x}_h f - \lambda^2 f^2)$$
$$= -\tilde{x}_h f - \frac{\lambda}{2}f^2 \tag{29}$$

Therefore, for $T \leq t < \infty$, we have

$$\dot{V}_2 = \dot{U} + \dot{W} \leq -(\frac{1}{k_h} + \frac{\lambda}{2})f^2 \tag{30}$$

The following is similar to that in the proof of Theorem 1, and thus omitted.

4   Simulation Study

In this section, we consider a human-robot collaboration system, which includes a human limb and a robot arm. The human limb grasps the end-effector of the robot arm and the interaction force is measured by the sensor mounted at the end-effector. The robot arm is under position control in the joint space and its desired trajectory is obtained by the method developed in this paper.

The robot arm includes two revolute joints and its parameters are: $m_1 = m_2 = 2.0$kg, $l_1 = l_2 = 0.2$m, $I_1 = I_2 = 0.027$kgm^2, $l_{c1} = l_{c2} = 0.1$m, where m_i, l_i, I_i, l_{ci}, $i = 1, 2$, represent the mass, the length, the inertia about the z-axis that comes out of the page passing through the center of mass, and the distance from the previous joint to the center of mass of link i, respectively. Note that these parameters are only used for the simulation and they will not be used in the control design. The initial positions of the robot arm are $q_1 = -\frac{\pi}{3}$ and $q_2 = \frac{2\pi}{3}$. It is assumed that the human limb exerts the force only in X direction and thus the robot arm in Y direction is interaction-free. The human limb model is described by $f = \dot{x} + 50(x - x_h) - \frac{0.4x - 0.1\dot{x}}{1 + x^2 + \dot{x}^2 + t^2}$, where the last component $\frac{0.4x - 0.1\dot{x}}{1 + x^2 + \dot{x}^2 + t^2}$ stands for the uncertainty. The updating ratio in (16) and (22) is $\gamma = 0.01$.

In the first case, the desired trajectory of the human limb is $x_h = 2.5$ and the updating law (16) is applied. The results in this case are shown in Figs. 1(a) and 1(b). In Fig. 1(a), it is shown that the obtained desired trajectory of the robot arm, as well as the actual trajectory, tracks the desired trajectory of the human limb. Accordingly, it is found in Fig. 1(b) that the interaction force goes to zero. The above results indicate that the robot arm follows the human limb in such a way that it is able to predict the motion of the human limb.

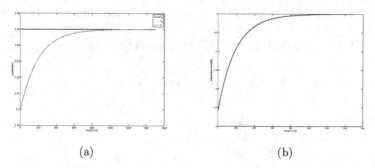

(a)   (b)

Fig. 1. Position (a) and interaction force, in the case of point-to-point movement

In the second case, we consider that the desired trajectory of the human limb is time-varying and periodic, which is given by $x_h = 0.2 + 0.1\sin(\frac{\pi}{10}t)$. The updating law (22) is employed and the results are shown in Figs. 2(a) and 2(b). In Fig. 2(a), it is shown that after several iterations, the actual trajectory tracks the desired trajectory of the human limb. In Fig. 2(b), it is shown that the interaction force becomes smaller as the iteration number increases. Note that the point-to-point movement in the first case can be considered as a special case of the periodic time-varying trajectory, so the updating law (22) is also applicable in the first case. In this regard, the updating law (22) can be used in a more general class of applications.

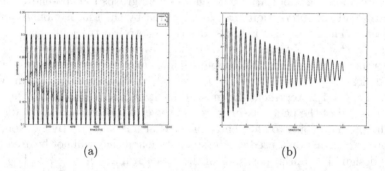

(a)   (b)

Fig. 2. Position (a) and interaction force (b), in the case of periodic trajectory

5   Conclusion

In this paper, motion synchronization has been investigated for human-robot collaboration, such that the robot is able to "actively" follow its human partner. Force tracking has been achieved under the impedance control framework, subject to uncertain human limb dynamics. Adaptive control has been proposed to deal with the point-to-point movement, and learning control has been developed to generate a periodic trajectory. The validity of the proposed method has been verified through simulation studies.

Acknowledgment. This study was supported by research grant R-705-000-017-279, Interactive Digital Media R&D Program, National Research Foundation, Singapore.

References

1. Corteville, B., Aertbelien, E., Bruyninckx, H., Schutter, J.D., Brussel, H.V.: Human-inspired robot assistant for fast point-to-point movements. In: Proceedings of the 2007 IEEE International Conference on Robotics and Automation, pp. 3639–3644 (2007)
2. Wang, Z., Peer, A., Buss, M.: An HMM approach to realistic haptic human-robot interaction. In: Proceedings of the Third Joint Eurohaptics Conference and Symposium on Haptic Interfaces for Virtual Environment and Teleoperator Systems, pp. 374–379 (2009)
3. Erden, M.S., Tomiyama, T.: Human-intent detection and physically interactive control of a robot without force sensors. IEEE Transactions on Robotics 26(2), 370–382 (2010)
4. Chua, Y., Tee, K.P., Yan, R.: Human-robot motion synchronization using reactive and predictive controllers. In: Proceedings of the 2010 IEEE International Conference on Robotics and Biomimetics, pp. 223–228 (2010)
5. Hogan, N.: Impedance control: an approach to manipulation-Part I: Theory; Part II: Implementation; Part III: Applications. Transaction ASME J. Dynamic Systems, Measurement and Control 107(1), 1–24 (1985)
6. Iqbal, K., Zheng, Y.F.: Arm-manipulator coordination for load sharing using predictive control. In: Proceedings of IEEE International Conference on Robotics and Automation, pp. 2539–2544 (1999)
7. Seraji, H., Colbaugh, R.: Force tracking in impedanc control. International Journal of Robotics Research 16(1), 97–117 (1997)
8. Jung, S., Hsia, T.C., Bonitz, R.G.: Force tracking impedance control of robot manipulators under unknown environment. IEEE Transactions on Control Systems Technology 12(3), 474–483 (2004)
9. Lee, K., Buss, M.: Force tracking impedance control with variable target stiffness. In: Proceedings of the 17th IFAC World Congress, vol. 17, pp. 6751–6756 (2008)
10. Tsumugiwa, T., Yokogawa, R., Hara, K.: Variable impedance control based on estimation of human arm stiffness for human-robot cooperative calligraphic task. In: Proceedings of the 2002 IEEE International Conference on Robotics and Automation, pp. 644–650 (2002)
11. Rahman, M.M., Ikeura, R., Mizutani, K.: Investigation of the impedance characteristic of human arm for development of robots to cooperate with humans. JSME International Journal Series C 45(2), 510–518 (2002)

Human-Robot Handshaking:
A Hybrid Deliberate/Reactive Model

Yingzi Zeng[1], Yanan Li[1,2], Pengxuan Xu[1], and Shuzhi Sam Ge[1,3]

[1] Social Robotics Laboratory, Interactive Digital Media Institute,
and Department of Electrical and Computer Engineering,
National University of Singapore, Singapore, 117576
[2] NUS Graduate School for Integrative Sciences and Engineering,
National University of Singapore, Singapore, 119613
[3] Robotics Institute, and School of Computer Science and Engineering,
University of Electronic Science and Technology of China, Chengdu, 610054, China

Abstract. In this paper, we propose a hybrid deliberate/reactive model
to achieve natural handshaking between human beings and robots. Our
goal is to provide a perspective to achieve natural human-robot handshaking in addition to time/frequency based trajectory control. The proposed
model consists of two parts. The reactive part is designed to enable the
robot to follow the handshaking motion led by the human being, while
the deliberate part is dedicated to embed a unique handshaking character
into the robot. The validity of the proposed model is examined by comparing the trajectory and interaction force during the human-human and
human-robot handshaking, respectively.

1 Introduction

While having been contributing to the industry and military, robots start to
seek their positions in our daily life. Unlike cold and dangerous industrial robots,
social robots should be safe and gentle, thus natural human-robot interaction
becomes a pivotal key to overcome human-robot social barrier. Handshaking,
as a symbol of friendship and respect, is an essential action to make human
feel secured, and it is a simple but significant step for robots to get closer to
human beings. Therefore, handshaking is a good start point to study natural
human-robot interaction.

Three primitives of robots are sense, plan and act which can be classed into
two paradigms: reactive paradigm and deliberate paradigm [1, 2]. The reactive
paradigm means sense and act, and the behavior of the robots with it only
depends on the data that they have sensed. The deliberate paradigm is the plan,
which will decide how to handle a task even before the data are collected. Solely
reactive control strategies such as impedance and compliance control [3–8] are
not enough for natural handshaking, because the role of the robot will then
become purely a slave. Deliberate control cannot stand alone either as there is
no reaction. Therefore, a hybrid deliberate/reactive model is needed to achieve
the natural handshaking.

S.S. Ge et al. (Eds.): ICSR 2012, LNAI 7621, pp. 258–267, 2012.

In [9], a reactive and predictive controller was designed to tackle the problem of motion synchronization between the human beings and robots. This controller was implemented to imitate the human-like handshaking by predicting and modifying the frequency of the robot arm, based on the interaction force between both parties and the joint angles and velocities of the robot arm. There are also alternative strategies such as the implementation of neural oscillators [10] and Hidden Markov Model based control [11]. These strategies are devised to modify the handshaking frequency of the robot in order to match the robot's handshaking trajectory to the human being's. However, after holding each other's hand, we are less likely to perceive handshaking as a time/frequency based motion. Instead, our proprioception, which means the sense of the relative position of neighboring parts of the body and strength of effort being employed in movement [12], will play an important role to determine the handshaking motion. Our reaction to the trend of handshaking from the other side will be different if our arms are at different positions. In other words, we will adjust our motion mainly based on both the position of our arm and the force we feel. Thus, this work aims to propose a handshaking model based on the arm position. Besides, People with different characters will have different ways of handshaking. In this regard, the proposed handshaking model is able to imitate the handshaking of people with different characters by simply adjusting the ratio of the reactive and deliberate parts.

The rest of this paper is arranged as follows. The problem is described and formulated in Section 2. The proposed handshaking model is introduced in Section 3. The experiment results are presented and discussed in Section 4, and the conclusion is given in Section 5.

2   Problem Formulation

The sketch of the robot arm under study is shown in Fig. 1(a). A force/torque sensor is installed at the wrist to collect the force/torque data during the handshaking. And an encoder inside the motor is able to record the joint angle of the robot arm. Only the motion along x axis is considered in the proposed model, as the handshaking motion is mainly in this direction.

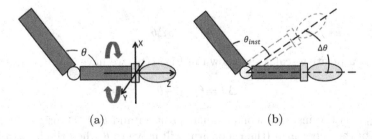

(a)   (b)

Fig. 1. Sketch of the robot arm under study

In human-human handshaking, each party has its own character and the leading/following state might change at any time. In this regard, it is very difficult to imitate the changing of leading/following state based on a time/frequency function or even simply treat the handshaking as a pure periodic motion. To cope with this problem, we propose a position based model, of which the basic idea is briefly introduced in the following. On one hand, in the natural handshaking, the force/torque at the wrist is the primary key to decide the leading/following state. Thus, we assume that one party will try to lead the handshaking when the force/torque is less than a designed trigger force/torque, which is defined as the compromising force/torque T_{comp} and it is a key parameter of the proposed model. On the other hand, when one party's arm reaches a critical angle, the handshaking motion will be expected to change to the opposite direction. Thus, this critical angle, we define as the turning angle $\theta_{turning}$, is another key parameter of the proposed model.

3   Human-Robot Handshaking Model

As mentioned in the Introduction, we propose a handshaking model, which includes two parts: reactive and deliberate, which is more experiment based rather than theoretical. This section is dedicated to introduce this model in details.

3.1   Pure Reactive Motion

The reactive part is to imitate the reaction to the force/torque from the other handshaking party. Suppose the force/torque at the wrist along x axis is T_x. Then, a simple reactive model suggested by impedance control is: to change the angular velocity of robot arm ω_{arm} according to T_x, i.e.,

$$\omega_1 = \alpha T_x \tag{1}$$

where α is the coefficient determined by considering the mass and admittance of the robot arm. To simplify the model, we treat it as a constant, of which the value will be adjusted during the experiment. Besides, we assume that the robot arm intends to remain at its original position θ, as shown in Fig. 1(a), and the further it is from the original position the stronger the intention is. Equivalently, we have

$$\omega_2 = \alpha T_x - \beta \Delta\theta \tag{2}$$

where β is a positive scalar. As shown in Fig. 1(b), we have

$$\Delta\theta = \theta_{inst} - \theta \tag{3}$$

where θ_{inst} is the instantaneous angular position and θ is the original angular position of the robot arm (the robot arm will move to θ when the human being is approaching).

In addition, we take the compromising force/torque T_{comp} into account, and define

$$T_{total} = \begin{cases} T_x - T_{comp}, & \text{if } T_x > T_{comp}; \\ 0, & \text{if } -T_{comp} \leq T_x \leq T_{comp}; \\ T_x + T_{comp}, & \text{if } T_x < -T_{comp}. \end{cases} \quad (4)$$

Then, the reactive angular velocity of the robot arm becomes

$$\omega_{reac} = \alpha T_{comp} - \beta \Delta\theta \quad (5)$$

From the above equation, it is found that the force/torque from the environment cannot change the movement of the robot arm when it is smaller than the compromising torque T_{comp}.

3.2   Combination of Deliberate and Reactive Motion

In [9], the handshaking motion is considered to be a sinusoid function of time. Instead of using the time/frequency based function, however, a position based function is used in our work to imitate the deliberate motion. In particular, the deliberate motion is segmented into two states: moving upward and moving downward, which is shown in Fig. 2. It is seen from this figure that the robot arm will tend to move towards the opposite direction after reaching the turning angle.

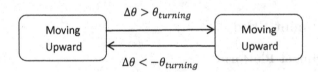

Fig. 2. Two states of the deliberate motion

In human-human handshaking, the force from the other party will change the turning angle. In particular, when the force towards the opposite direction gets larger, the turning angle becomes smaller. Therefore, we define the turning angle as follows.

For the state of moving upward

$$\theta_{turning} = \begin{cases} \frac{\theta_{max}}{|kT_{total}-1|}, & \text{if } T_{total} < 0; \\ \theta_{max}, & \text{if } T_{total} \geq 0. \end{cases} \quad (6)$$

where k is a positive scalar. For the state of moving downward

$$\theta_{turning} = \begin{cases} \frac{\theta_{max}}{|kT_{total}+1|}, & \text{if } T_{total} \geq 0; \\ \theta_{max}, & \text{if } T_{total} < 0. \end{cases} \quad (7)$$

where θ_{max} is a predefined angle which determines the intrinsic character of the robot. Note that the denominators $|kT_{total} - 1|$ and $|kT_{total} + 1|$ indicate that $\theta_{turning} \approx \theta_{max}$ when $kT_{total} \approx 0$. The deliberate angular velocity of the robot arm is thus obtained as

$$\omega_{deli} = \gamma\omega|\cos(\frac{\pi\Delta\theta}{2\theta_{turning}})| \qquad (8)$$

where $\gamma = 1$ is for the state of moving upward, $\gamma = -1$ is for the state of moving downward, and ω is the intrinsic angular velocity of the robot arm at the original position. Form (8), it is easy to see that after reaching the turning angle, the robot arm will tend to move to the opposite direction and its intention will get stronger when it moves further from the original position.

Finally, we combine both the reactive motion and deliberate motion together, and obtain the angular velocity of the robot arm

$$\omega_{arm} = \alpha T_{comp} - \beta\Delta\theta + \gamma\omega|\cos(\frac{\pi\Delta\theta}{2\theta_{turning}})| \qquad (9)$$

Remark 1. The angular velocity of the robot arm shown above is the complete hybrid reactive/deliberate model. Note that our objective is not to use the proposed position based model to replace the existing time/frequency based model, but we aim to provide a new vision to achieve natural human-robot handshaking. Future work will focus on the combination of the proposed model and the time/frequency based model.

4   Experiment Study

4.1   Experiment Platform

The proposed model is examined on the robot Nancy which is developed in Social Robotics Laboratory, National University of Singapore [13]. On Nancy's arm, each joint is implemented using a cable-pulley transmission method which is achieved by a pull-pull configuration [14]. Such compact configuration will reduce the weight and inertia of the robot arm, which is designed considering the better imitation of the human arm.

The motor which drives the joint is precisely controlled by Maxon's EPOS2 70/10 dual loop controller. It works in the CANopen network and provides multiple operational modes including position, velocity, current modes and others. It also provides the angle information of each joint. An ATI mini-40 force/torque sensor is installed at the right wrist of Nancy. It has a very high signal-to-noise ratio achieved by using silicon strain gages.

There is also an industrial PC installed in Nancy which works as a global interface. The model of this industrial PC is AMI200-953 with Intel Core i5-520M processor of 2.4GHz which ensures a high performance. It collects the data from the controller and force/torque sensor, calculates the trajectory of the robot arm according to the proposed model, and sends the trajectory to each motor during the handshaking process.

Kinect is used to record the handshaking motion, which is a motion capture device designed by Microsoft. It consists of a depth sensor and a RGB camera which enable it to capture the motion of both the human being and the robot. We use the motion data of the right wrist to describe the handshaking motion.

4.2 Experiment Result

The proposed model is examined by comparison between human-robot and human-human handshaking in terms of handshaking trajectories and interaction force. Three persons participate in this experiment: Human A, Human B and Human C.

In the first experiment, we set the parameters of the handshaking model to match the character of Human A. Human B shakes hands with Human A first, then Human B shakes hands with Nancy, as shown in Fig. 3(a). The trajectories during the handshaking between Human B and Nancy are compared with that between Human B and Human A. In Fig. 4, the trajectory during the handshaking between Human B and Nancy with the reactive model and that between Human B and Human A are shown. It is obvious that the amplitude and frequency of these two trajectories are not matched. In contrary, the trajectory during the handshaking between Human B and Nancy with the hybrid model matches that between Human B and Human A, as shown in Fig. 5. Another thing to notice is that the human-human handshaking trajectory is not a perfect periodic motion, which indicates the necessity of an alternative model to achieve the natural handshaking in addition to the time/frequency based model.

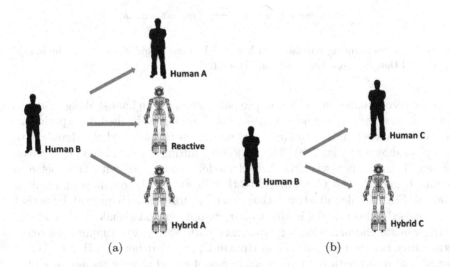

Fig. 3. The first and second experiment sets

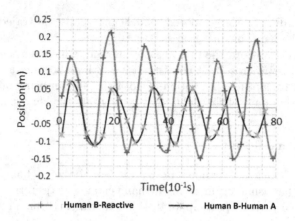

Fig. 4. Trajectory during handshaking between Human B and Nancy with the reactive model, and that between Human B and Human A

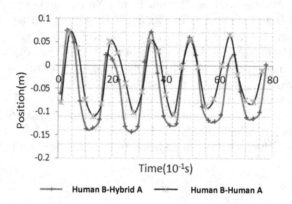

Fig. 5. Trajectory during handshaking between Human B and Nancy with the hybrid model, and that between Human B and Human A

In the second experiment, we set the parameters of the handshaking model to match the character of Human C, instead of Human A as in the first experiment. Human B shakes hands with Human C first, then Human B shakes hands with Nancy, as shown in Fig. 3(b). The trajectory during the handshaking between Human B and Nancy with the hybrid model is compared with that between Human B and Human C. Similarly to that in Fig. 6, the comparison result is shown in Fig. 6, which illustrates that two trajectories match and validates that the proposed hybrid model is able to imitate different handshaking characters.

To evaluate the handshaking experience with Nancy, we compare the interaction force between Human B and Human C, and that between Human B and Nancy. The result with the pure reactive model and that with the proposed hybrid model are shown in Figs. 7 and 8, respectively. In the case of pure reactive

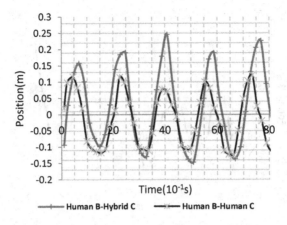

Fig. 6. Trajectory during handshaking between Human B and Nancy with the hybrid model, and that between Human B and Human C

model, the interaction force is smaller as Nancy tries to follow the motion of Human B. However, in human-human handshaking, each party will feel a certain counteractive force, which is caused by different motion intentions of both parties. The force pattern with the proposed hybrid model has high similarity with that in human-human handshaking. This result shows that the proposed model is capable to provide Nancy with human-like handshaking.

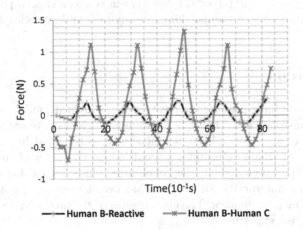

Fig. 7. Interaction force during handshaking between Human B and Nancy with the reactive model, and that between Human B and Human C

Although the proposed position based model is capable to make the handshaking more natural, it is not an ultimate solution and it is not to replace the

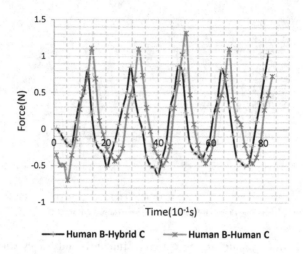

Fig. 8. Interaction force during handshaking between Human B and Nancy with the hybrid model, and that between Human B and Human C

existing models in previous studies [9–11, 15]. The current results suggest that the proposed method can be a compensation to combine with the time/frequency model, which will be further investigated in our future work. Besides, as there is still not a standard to verify whether the achieved handshaking is natural or not, more complete experiment methods such as in [16] and [17] will be designed. Furthermore, the physical robot system is also a crucial part to achieve the natural human-robot handshaking, and more flexible systems are needed in this regard.

5   Conclusion

In this work, we have proposed a position based hybrid model to achieve the natural human-robot handshaking. This model includes a reactive part which makes the robot arm have a basic reaction to the other handshaking party, and a deliberate part which determines a handshaking character of the robot arm. Based on the proposed model, the robot arm refines its motion according to the position and interaction force, which has been shown to be able to improve the handshaking performance. The effectiveness of the proposed model has been validated through experiments.

Acknowledgment. This study was supported by research grant R-705-000-017-279, Interactive Digital Media R&D Program, National Research Foundation, Singapore.

References

1. Asada, H., Slotine, J.J.E.: Robot analysis and control. John Wiley and Sons (1986)
2. Arkin, R.C.: Behavior-based robotics. MIT Press (1998)
3. Hogan, N.: Impedance control: an approach to manipulation-Part I: Theory; Part II: Implementation; Part III: Applications. Journal of Dynamic Systems, Measurement and Control 107(1-24) (1985)
4. Kazerooni, H., Sheridan, T.B., Houpt, P.K.: Robust compliant motion for manipulators-Part I: The fundamental concepts of compliant motion; Part II: Design method. IEEE Journal of Robotics and Automation 2(2), 83–105 (1986)
5. Kelly, R., Carelli, R., Amestegui, M., Ortega, R.: On adaptive impedance control of robot manipulators. In: Proceedings of the IEEE International Conference on Robotics and Automation, Scottsdale, Arizona, pp. 572–577 (1989)
6. Colbaugh, R., Seraji, H., Glass, K.: Direct adaptive impedance control robot manipulator. Journal of Robotic Systems 10(2), 217–248 (1991)
7. Park, H., Lee, J.: Adaptive impedance control of a haptic interface. Mechatronics 14(3), 237–253 (2004)
8. Tee, K.P., Yan, R., Li, H.: Adaptive admittance control of a robot manipulator under task space constraint. In: Proceedings of the IEEE International Conference on Robotics and Automation, Anchorage, USA, pp. 5181–5186 (2010)
9. Chua, Y., Tee, K.P., Yan, R.: Human-robot motion synchronization using reactive and predictive controllers. In: Proceedings of the IEEE International Conference on Robotics and Biomimetics, Tianjin, China, pp. 223–228 (2010)
10. Hashimoto, M., Hashizume, H., Katoh, Y.: Design of dynamics for synchronization based control of human-robot interaction. In: Proceedings of the IEEE International Conference on Robotics and Biomimetics, Kunming, China, pp. 790–795 (December 2006)
11. Wang, Z., Peer, A., Buss, M.: An HMM approach to realistic haptic human-robot interaction. In: Proceedings of the 3rd IEEE Joint Eurohaptics Conference and Symposium on Haptic Interfaces for Virtual Enviroment and Teleoperator Systems, Salt Lake City, USA, pp. 374–379 (March 2009)
12. Anderson, D.M.: Mosby's Medical, nursing and allied health dictionary, 4th edn. Mosby-Year Book (1994)
13. Ge, S.S., Liew, C.F., Li, Y., Yang, J.: System design and hardware integration of social robot Nancy. In: Proceedings of the IEEE/SICE International Symposium on System Integration, Kyoto, Japan, pp. 336–341 (2011)
14. Ma, J., Li, Y., Ge, S.S.: Adaptive control for a cable driven robot arm. In: Proceedings of the IEEE International Conference on Mechatronics and Automation, Chengdu, China, pp. 1074–1079 (2012)
15. Kasuga, T., Hashimoto, M.: Human-robot handshaking using neural oscillators. In: Proceedings of the IEEE International Conference of Robotics and Automation, Barcelona, Spain, pp. 3802–3807 (2005)
16. Giannopoulos, E., Wang, Z., Peer, A., Buss, M., Slater, M.: Comparison of people's responses to real and virtual handshakes within a virtual environment. Brain Research Bulletin 85(5), 276–282 (2011)
17. Karniel, A., Nisky, I., Avraham, G., Peles, B.-C., Levy-Tzedek, S.: A Turing-Like Handshake Test for Motor Intelligence. In: Kappers, A.M.L., van Erp, J.B.F., Bergmann Tiest, W.M., van der Helm, F.C.T. (eds.) EuroHaptics 2010, Part I. LNCS, vol. 6191, pp. 197–204. Springer, Heidelberg (2010)

Should Empathic Social Robots Have Interiority?

Luisa Damiano[1], Paul Dumouchel[2], and Hagen Lehmann[3]

[1] Epistemology of the Sciences of the Artificial Research Group,
Department of Human and Social Sciences,
University of Bergamo, P.le S.Agostino 2, 24129 Bergamo, Italy
luisa.damiano@unibg.it
[2] Graduate School of Core Ethics and Frontier Sciences,
Ritsumeikan University, 56-1 Kitamachi, Toji-in, Kita-ku, 603-8577 Kyoto, Japan
dumouchp@ce.ritsumei.ac.jp
[3] Adaptive Systems Research Group, School of Computer Science and STCA,
University of Hertfordshire, College Lane, Hatfield, United Kingdom
h.lehmann@herts.ac.uk

Abstract. In this article we discuss whether robots need "interiority" in order to competently participate in emotional and empathic dynamics with human partners. We draw on original research on emotions, mind, neurophysiological mechanisms of social interaction and HRI to contest the common sense thesis according to which robots without "interiority" can only simulate emotions and empathy, to the extent that the affective (emotional and empathic) relationships between them and humans would not be authentic. The main thesis of our article is that empathic social robots do not need "interiority", but the ability of dynamical coordination with their social partners and the surrounding environment(s), since this ability (and not "interiority") is at the basis of human cognitive and affective (emotional and empathic) activity.

Keywords: artificial social agents, artificial empathy, autonomy, emotions, embodied mind, extended mind, radical embodiment.

1 Introduction

Should empathic social robots have "interiority"? That is to say, in order to entertain convincing empathic and affective relations with human beings, and in order to participate in a competent way in the emotional dynamics characteristic of such relations, do robots need to have an "inner world" of some sort?

Since the turn of the 18th century the notion of "interiority", synonymous with "Innenwelt" or "inner world", designates a space of experience located within the individual and formed of her feelings, ideas and thoughts [1]. In other words, it indicates the dimension of an affective and cognitive internal experience, which would distinguish subjects (i.e., beings that have subjective experiences) from mere objects. With this meaning, the notion of interiority is today one of the main conceptual focuses of the debate about the affective and cognitive evolution of robots – more precisely: about their possibility to overcome the status of objects, and

S.S. Ge et al. (Eds.): ICSR 2012, LNAI 7621, pp. 268–277, 2012.

become genuine subjects of affective and cognitive experiences, able to be effective social partners for humans.[1]

Within this debate it is often argued that, without an interiority, robots cannot be actual "empathic" social agents, since, without an interiority, they cannot "feel" anything. No matter how competent they may be socially, they will always remain machines that only "pretend" to have emotions, without having real emotions. To engage in a strong affective relationship with such objects can therefore only be a trap, that constitutes a danger for both individuals and society [2, 3]. Others add that the lack of interiority implies necessarily a limitation of robots' social competence [4].

The hypothesis supported by these claims is not only that a robot needs an interiority in order to express emotions and to react adequately to the emotions of humans. The idea is that a robot needs interiority in order to *have emotions*.

This is the double hypothesis we would like to contest in this article. On the basis of a re-conceptualization of the notions of interiority and exteriority, as well as of the relation between *intra*-individuality and *inter*-individuality, we decline this hypothesis, and give a dissenting answer to the main question of this article: "Should empathic social robots have interiority?". Based on this answer, we suggest a new and interesting way of tackling the problem of "artificial empathy" - one that is actually being preliminarily developed in some areas of social robotics.

2   The Inside and the Outside: The Thesis of the *Intra*-individual Genesis of Emotions

The idea of interiority implies a dualism of the inside and the outside. It supposes a distinction between two domains, an external domain where behavior is open to direct observation and an internal domain of events that are not open to direct observation, but which are causally related to observable behaviors. Even when internal events are conceived as (at least partially) caused by external events, they are assumed to have a form of "autonomy", in the sense that the behavior of an agent can never be fully understood without taking internal events into account. In this line of thought, it is impossible to explain the behavior of an agent simply by associating it with external perturbations, changes and events involving her. It is always necessary to take internal states which have a proper dynamics and cannot be reduced to the system's input and output matrix into account.

Internal events can be understood in various ways – desires, beliefs, intentions or emotions – and the line that separates the inside from the outside can be drawn differently. For example it can correspond to the body of the individual, or only to the nervous system (states of the nervous systems are taken to be internal events while the rest of the individual's body is understood as part of the 'outside' environment), or it may be taken to correspond to the border between mental and physical events. In all cases the explanatory scheme remains the same.

---

[1] In this debate the notion of interiority is often used implicitly, through concepts referring to an inner subjective world, such as the concepts of internal emotional state, internal reflective activity, etc.

In line with this scheme, Ziemke [5], for example, considers that behavior must be understood as the result of the interaction of the nervous system with the internal and external environment. Following Barandian & Moreno [6], he argues that emotions arise from the interaction of the sensory-motor nervous system (SMNS) and the internal nervous system (INS) and represent the regulation of the first by the second [7]. Therefore emotions, according to him, are internal events, and having emotions, either for a human or a machine, implies the existence of an internal domain: the interiority where they take place, which is not open to direct observation as is the overt behavior which they modulate.

Following the same general scheme, Adolphs [8] postulates that emotions correspond to states of the nervous system that depend on the function of the system. These states reflect the situation of the agent, and are determined as this or that emotion by an internal feeling, which results from the particular composition (physiology) of the nervous system. Adolphs identifies emotions with particular internal feelings, of which the agent may be unaware, and that fundamentally depend on the way our nervous system is made – synapses neurons, neurotransmitters, etc. In consequence he considers that, in order to properly ascribe emotions to a robot, the machine should be located in the world in an appropriate way, and its material makeup should be sufficiently similar to that of human beings. Adolphs therefore believes it unlikely that we will ever be able to build robots that have emotions.

Ziemke has a different view. Because he identifies functionally the internal events correlated with emotion, rather than on the basis of their intrinsic characteristics, he considers that we can ascribe emotions to any system which is characterized by regulatory interaction between sensory-motor information and somatic information [9].

Despite their differences concerning the nature of emotions, or their pessimistic or optimistic attitude concerning the possibility for robots to have emotions, Ziemke and Adolphs share the same conception of emotions as internal events that modulate the external or overt behavior of the agent. According to them, some form of interiority is necessary in order to have emotions, even if they do not conceive this internal domain in the same way, and even if the relevant internal events do not need to be conscious. This common explanatory scheme implies the anteriority of the emotion, relative to its expression and to its ability to modify the external behavior of the agent. This anteriority is not necessarily temporal, but causal, in the sense that the emotion "causes" the expression, as well as the transformation of the behavior of the agent.

In such an explanatory scheme, as well as according to common sense, the absence of an internal state which corresponds to the affective expression is equivalent to the absence of an emotion and therefore is equivalent to "deception", to "fake" or "make believe". This classical explanatory framework in fact assumes that the dichotomy between the inside and outside corresponds to two distinct differences. First, to the distinction between what is open to direct observation and what is not. Second, to the distinction between what is subsequent in the temporal order and what comes first. These two distinctions overlap in the sense that what is second in time is open to direct observation, and what temporally comes first can only be discovered indirectly and by inference.

In this way, this explanatory scheme conceptualizes emotions as events which are individually produced and experienced, and consequently defines affective inter-subjectivity as a process that reaches out over an epistemological abyss separating individuals. According to this scheme an emotional relation between two or more individuals is realized basically through the observation of the external behavior of other person, and through conjectures on her affective states grounded in logical and conceptual analysis, as well as in analogies based on self-knowledge. Such a theoretical approach is unable to explain many aspects of the affective dimension of inter-subjectivity, like the experience of strong affective "attunement" typical of the majority of every day encounters, and the immediate character of this attunement.

These theoretical difficulties can be lifted by adopting a different explanatory scheme.

3   The Primacy of Expression

It is in fact possible to argue that expression precedes the emotion or, in other words, that the overt behavior comes before the internal event [9, 10].[2] On the contrary the classical conception postulates the primacy of internal states and makes affective expression dependent on the existence of discrete internal states. However phenomenologically it is clear that, at the level of expression, there is no such thing as affective silence. Affective expression is continuous. Within this continuum there may be "catastrophes", dramatic changes, and in this sense discontinuities, but there are no interruptions. We constantly express our affective state and simultaneously react to the affective expression of others. Depending on whether they are anxious, happy, upset, stressed, joyful or sad, we coordinate our affects and our behavior to the affects and behaviors of others. This coordination is a common shared process. Our reaction to others in this context does not simply consist in adapting our actions to theirs; it also acts on their own affect. Inversely their reaction acts on us, in what may be described as a "continuous affective conversation". The affective expression of each agent directly acts on the other and alters his or her affective expression. The events we name emotions are salient moments in this continuous process of coordination [9, 10].[3]

Within this continuous affective exchange, emotions are not "internal", but part of the overt behavior of each agent, even if this behavior is not always observed and recognized as such – at least if "observed" implies taking a step back that enables one to judge. Within this form of immediate communication, no one can take sufficient distance in order to be able to recognize, or to "understand", what comes from one and what from the other. Each one reacts, and that is all. At this level there is no distinction between what is "internal" and what is "external". The primacy of expression means precisely this lack of distinction between the inside and the outside. Expression does not come afterwards. It is not the true or false rendering of some

---

[2] This theoretical proposal is different from that of William James [11], who thought that we do not run away because we are afraid, but are afraid because we run away. In that sense also expression precedes emotion; however, according to William James, an emotion is an internal event, which corresponds to the internal feeling associated with a particular physiological reaction.

[3] Postulating that emotions are social or public rather than private solitary events does not entail the absurd conclusion that one could not experience an emotion in the absence of others any more than postulating the essentially social nature of language entails that one could not speak to oneself either silently or out loud in the absence of any other person [9, 10].

internal event, but an action, a gesture that directly acts upon the other. Of course agents do have feelings, they have "inner states", but these are not enclosed in a space where they can only be reached indirectly and by inference. They are immediately open to the actions of others. There is continuity rather than discontinuity between the inside and the outside.

4   The Primacy of Relationship

This theoretical approach transfers emotions from the intra-individual to the inter-individual space, and in this way offers an understanding of the inter-subjective dimension of affective processes that significantly converges with recent scientific results.

Since the end of the 1990s, experimental neurophysiology has been exploring some of the mechanisms which currently are recognized as underlying inter-subjective affective processes – the "mirror mechanisms" according to the definition given by their discoverers.[4] Studies on these mechanisms have shown that they operate through neuronal co-activation. During the observation of affective expression, the neuronal pattern which in the agent supports the expression is also activated in the observer. [5] Vittorio Gallese [11, 17], one of the discoverers of the mirror mechanisms, proposed that these mechanisms provide an embodied access to the emotion of the other. More precisely, according to him, the neuronal co-activation is the neurophysiological mechanism of an understanding of others whose characteristics are different from what is classically ascribed to inter-subjective knowledge. It does not call upon the logical or linguistic abilities of agents; it is not based on observation or on analogy with self-knowledge; it does not take place in intra-individual space. The specificity of this form of inter-subjective knowledge is that it "harmonizes" the emotions of the different individuals, leading them to share an affective experience. According to

---

[4] The notion of "mirror mechanisms" was introduced by Gallese [12] to avoid the vague use of the notion of "mirror neurons" criticized in the current debate. Mirror neurons where discovered by a team of neurophysiologist from the University of Parma directed by Rizzolatti [13]. They are a class of neurons that discharge both when the monkey executes a motor act and when it observes another individual (a human being or another monkey) performing the same or a similar motor act. These neurons, originally discovered in the area F5 of the monkey's premotor cortex, have later been also found in the inferior parietal lobule [13], and neurophysiological (EEG, MEG, and TMS) as well as brain-imaging experiments provided strong evidence that a fronto-parietal circuit with properties similar to the monkey's mirror neuron system is also present in humans [14]. Recent evidence suggests that mirror mechanisms are also involved in empathy, conceived as the capacity of feeling the same emotions that others feel [15]. These data strongly suggest that the insula contains a neural population active both when an individual directly experiences disgust and when this emotion is triggered by the observation of the facial expression of others. Similar data have been obtained for felt pain and during the observation of a painful situation in which was involved another person loved by the observer [16, 17]. Taken together, these experiments support the thesis that feeling emotions is due to the activation of circuits that mediate the corresponding emotional responses [18, 19].

[5] Cf. Footnote 4.

Gallese, we can consider this sharing as a basic form of empathy, based on the automatic and sub-personal coupling of the agents involved. Following Gallese, we can think this basic form of empathy as a form of embodied intelligibility – grounded at the neuronal level - realized through "attunement" or "resonance" – a dynamical coordination which violates the border between *intra*-individual and *inter*-individual space. Neuronal co-activation supported by mirror mechanism destabilizes and, in a sense, suspends the limit between the self and the other, to the extent that it generates a convergence between *inter*-individuality and *intra*-individuality.[6]

This convergence can help to explain many aspects of our everyday experience of the other, such as its immediateness - its "unmediatedness" - and the feeling of identity that comes with the recognition of the other people's affective state. Furthermore it is an expression of a very basic and general inter-subjective cognitive dynamics, since the mirroring interaction is far from being limited to emotions, and also concerns actions, intentions and somatic feelings.[7]

The idea of "relational affect" that we are proposing also converges with one of the most interesting theoretical breakthroughs in the "embodied cognitive sciences" and "embodied" philosophy of mind.[8] We refer to an innovative theoretical operation, which is often labeled "cognitive extension" [19, 20]. Its goal is to redefine the limits of the embodied mind in conformity with a postulate which can be summed up as follows: if the mind is the area where cognitive and affective processes take place, then it cannot be confined within the intra-individual space – in other words: the mind cannot be enclosed "inside the head" [22].

The best known version of this thesis – which is commonly called "the extended mind" [23] – claims that mind exceeds the limits of "skull and skin" and includes some elements of the environment, i.e. elements external to body and brain which are necessary to the accomplishment of the agent's cognitive processes.

There also exists a more interesting version of the thesis that the mind cannot be enclosed inside the head, which radically transforms the operation of "cognitive extension". Its proponents give to the problem of "the embodiment of the mind" a dynamic rather than an anatomic solution. They do not ground the mind in the nervous system's anatomy, but in the regulative dynamics by which it links body and environment. This "extension" of the mind does not spatially overcome the limits of the "skull and skin", but rather redefines the architecture of the cognitive mind. It describes mind as a structure of coupling which inter-connects the dynamics of the nervous system, of the body, of the environment and of other organisms – other selves. In other words, it proposes a redefinition of mind which construes it not as a spatial – "extended" – object, but as the dynamical co-determination which couples self and others' somatic and neural networks, and couples them to their environment. In this conception, mind is the emerging dynamic unit of self, others and environment, a unit grounded in the permanent process co-determining its elements. It is this process which produces the cognition of the others and of the world.

---

[6] During the co-activation phase the nervous system can not determine if it is "actor" or "observer" in order to find out it has to wait for sensory feedback [12, 19, 21].

[7] Cf. Footnote 4.

[8] These are branches of cognitive sciences and philosophy of mind which adopt the so-called "embodied mind" approach, i.e. the approach which seeks to go beyond classical "Cartesian" dualism between mind and body[21, 24].

This view has been rigorously developed by a current trend of embodied cognitive sciences called "radical embodiment" [24]. Its fundamental idea is that the embodied mind as the emerging unit of "brain-body-environment-other", is a processual and relational entity whose heterogeneous elements are not defined by the "internal-external" relations, unlike what is the case for the anatomic unit of the individual brain with regard to the body, the environment and others. Instead, the sub-units of the "radically embodied mind" are mutually embedded systems [21], linked by relations of reciprocal co-specification and containment through which they are thoroughly intertwined - biologically, ecologically and socially "enmeshed" [24, 25].

This idea of relational affectivity is also supported by recent studies on real time human gaze behavior during conversation. These studies were made in the context of a project aiming at building gaze controllers for social robots, in order to enhance their ability to competently and naturally engage in conversations with humans. The findings show that the properties of conversational gaze can't be studied by focusing on the individual, since these properties emerge from the dyadic interaction during conversations [26].

These scientific results, together with those related to mirror mechanisms as well as the radical embodiment thesis, suggest that we should abandon approaches based on the classic idea of interiority when describing the cognitive and affective dynamics to which human agents participate. In consequence they also suggest to look for the solution to the problem of artificial empathy not in an "artificial interiority" - the internal states of the artificial agent-, but in relation - in dynamic coordination.

5   Affective Coordination and Artificial Empathy

In order to effectively develop and to convincingly and competently participate in empathic relations with humans robots do not need interiority. What they need is the ability to coordinate affectively with human beings.

This does not mean that we should provide robots with an artificial mirror system, to support affective coordination in the way in which it is done in interactions between humans. This condition would be as impossible to satisfy as is the one proposed by Ralph Adolph - giving robots an appropriately "human like" physiology. Robots will have to build their own space of affective coordination with humans, defined by its distinctive characteristics. One of these characteristics could be a strong and bonding "non-mirroring" empathy, similar to the form of empathy which links humans and animals like dogs - animals to which it is now known that our mirror mechanisms do not react. Furthermore, recent studies show that if robots can initially trigger the human mirror system, repeated interaction with them cancels this reaction [27].

Of course, this is not to oppose the efforts that are currently being made to create artificial mirror systems. We believe this research is highly important, especially in the area of the recognition of emotions. Our goal is to point out that, in order to create affective and empathic relations between robots and humans, the first requirement is not to produce mirror systems able to give robots an experience of emotions which is similar to that of humans. The priority lies in providing these machines with a bodily system of affective coordination appropriate to their users. What is necessary is an embodied coordination system that is both flexible and adaptive, to the extent that it allows robots to learn through repeated attempts how to affectively coordinate with others.

To create such a system, the further development and the interconnection of many different studies is crucial. We need studies on the specific affective and expressive interactive characteristics of different categories of users (elderly persons, children, etc.), which are precise enough to be sensitive to the most common individual variations in users belonging to these categories. It is also important to dedicate detailed studies to the expressive dynamics of the human and of existing and possible robotic bodies, considering how to change the latter to extend and refine the possibilities of quick and effective affective coordination. Giving serious attention to the expressivity of the robot, as Breazal and her team did with the robot Leonardo,[9] is absolutely fundamental. This is even more fundamental when we deal with humanoid robotic platforms. Humanoid robots have to display a form of expressivity clearly differentiated from that of humans, in order to avoid not only comparison that would necessarily turn to the machine's disadvantage, but also the "uncanny valley" effect.

All this however remains insufficient. As the agenda of cognitive and social robotics lately has started to show, we also need studies on affective coordination, focusing on how the different aspects of this dynamic coordination can be learned and constantly adapted in humans, in animals (not only in primates, but also and primarily in domestic animals, such as dogs), in robots and between these different categories.

The most important aspect, to achieve affective and empathic relations between humans and robots, is to create embodied mechanisms that can allow robots to affectively coordinate, and to learn how to affectively coordinate with humans. Ideally these mechanisms should not only be permanently active in robots as they are in humans, but also be able to give robots two fundamental abilities which they presently lack: initiative and unexpectedness, which are indispensable in order for a robot to take part in a process of inter-individual affective coordination involving humans.

The limited character of affective interaction with contemporary robots, far from depending on their lack of interiority, derives from their inability to react unexpectedly in the affective dynamics in which they are involved. Robots do not only remain predictable in their interaction with humans, but also make human affective reactions to them mostly predictable, since they generate repetitive affective dynamics. That is why, unlike what is the case in relations between humans, these relations tend to be and can be made exclusively comfortable and reassuring.

In order to provide robots with initiative and unexpectedness in social interactions with humans, and in order for them take an active part in the dynamics of affective coordination, they need to develop not only excellent capabilities of coordination, but also a high level of autonomy, conceived as a self-determined capability of reaction to external events and actions.

A priori, this kind of scientific development is not impossible: studies on natural and artificial mechanisms of autonomy, both in cognitive and in life sciences, have

---

[9] Cf. http://robotic.media.mit.edu/projects/robots/leonardo/ overview/overview.html

being promisingly advancing since the last century and could lead to strong scientific innovations [21, 25]. But the production of this level of artificial autonomy, while transforming robots in effective social partners, will emancipate them from our control. The more independent they will be with regard to the generation of their reactions and behaviors, the less they will be submitted to the control of their environment(s) and of human actions – the actions of their social partners, as well as of their creators. In this sense, the degree of autonomy that could give them the status of effective social partners, able of initiative and unexpectedness, would make of them something radically different from "social robots", i.e., artificial agents substituting humans in heavy work and provided with social skills. At that point, our interactions with them will exceed the domain of the comfortable and the reassuring, and, as science fiction pointed out from the Châpekian origin of the notion of "robot", could be open to unexpected and potentially dangerous outcomes.

As the researcher in robotics Hiroaki Kitano, we wonder if there would be market for such an artificial creature.[10] However we would have created an absolutely extraordinary machine.

References

1. Campe, R., Weber, J. (eds.): Rethinking Emotions: Interiority and Exteriority in Premodern, Modern and Contemporary Thought. Walter de Gruyter, New York (forthcoming, 2013)
2. Turkle, S.: Alone Together. Basic Books, New York (2010)
3. Feil-Seifer, D.J., Matarić, M.J.: Ethical Principles for Socially Assistive Robotics. IEEE Robotics & Automation Magazine, Special Issue on Roboethics 18(1), 24–31 (2011)
4. Arbib, R.: Beware of the Passionate Robot. In: Fellous, J.-M., Arbib, M. (eds.) Who Needs Emotions? The Brain Meets the Robot, pp. 333–383. Oxford University Press, Oxford (2005)
5. Ziemke, T.: On the role of emotion in biological and robotic autonomy. Biosystems 91, 401–408 (2008)
6. Barandiaran, X., Moreno, A.: On What Makes Certain Dynamical Systems Cognitive. A minimally cognitive organization program. Journal of Adaptive Behavior 14(2), 171–185 (2006)
7. Ziemke, T., Lowe, R.: On the Role of Emotion in Embodied Cognitive Architectures: From Organisms to Robots. Cogn. Comput. 1, 104–117 (2009)
8. Adolphs, R.: Can a Robot Have Emotions? In: Fellous, J.-M., Arbib, M. (eds.) Who Needs Emotions? The Brain Meets the Robot, pp. 9–25. Oxford University Press, Oxford (2005)
9. Dumouchel, P.: Émotions. Institut Synthélabo, Paris (1995)
10. Dumouchel, P.: Social Emotions. In: Cañamero, L., Aylett, R. (eds.) Animating Expressive Characters for Social Interaction, pp. 1–20. John Benjamins, Amsterdam-Philadelphia (2008)
11. James, W.: What is an Emotion? Mind 9, 188–205 (1884)
12. Gallese, V.: Intentional Attunement. The Mirror Neuron System and its role in interpersonal relations. Interdisciplines (2005),
http://www.interdisciplines.org/mirror/papers/1

---

[10] We refer to a private conversation with Hiroaki Kitano.

13. Rizzolatti, G., Fogassi, L., Gallese, V.: Neurophysiological mechanisms underlying the understanding and imitation of action. Nature Reviews Neuroscience 2, 661–670 (2001)

14. Rizzolatti, G., Craighero, L.: The Mirror-Neuron System. Annual Rev. Neurosci. 27, 169–192 (2004)

15. Carr, L., Iacoboni, M., Dubeau, M.C., Mazziotta, J.C., Lenzi, G.L.: Neural mechanisms of empathy in humans: a relay from neural systems for imitation to limbic areas. Proc. Natl Acad. Sci. U.S.A. 100, 5497–5502 (2001)

16. Singer, T.: The neuronal basis and ontogeny of empathy and mind reading: review of literature and implications for future research. Neuroscience and Biobehavioral Reviews 6, 855–863 (2006)

17. Saarela, M.V., Hlushchuk, Y., Williams, A.C., Schurmann, M., Kalso, E., Hari, R.: The Compassionate Brain: Humans Detect Intensity of Pain from Another's Face. Cerebral Cortex (2006)

18. Gallese, V., Keysers, C., Rizzolatti, G.: A unifying view of the basis of social cognition. Trends in Cognitive Science 8(9), 396–403 (2004)

19. Decety, J., Chaminade, T., Grézes, J., Meltoff, A.N.: A PET exploration of the neural mechanisms involved in reciprocal imitation. Neuroimage 15, 265–272 (2002)

20. Clark, A.: Supersizing the mind: embodiment, action, and cognitive extension. Oxford University Press, Oxford (2010)

21. Damiano, L.: Unità in dialogo. Mondadori, Milano (2009)

22. Varela, F.: Steps to a science of Interbeing: unfolding the Dharma implicit in modern cognitive science. In: Bachelor, S., Claxton, G., Watson, G. (eds.) The Psychology of Awakening, pp. 71–89. Rider/Random House, New York (1999)

23. Clark, A., Chalmers, D.J.: The extended mind. Analysis 58, 10–23 (1998)

24. Thompson, E., Varela, F.: Radical embodiment. Trends in Cognitive Science 5(10), 418–425

25. Damiano, L.: Creative coordinations. World Futures: Journal of General Evolution 65(8), 1556–1884, 568–575 (2009)

26. Broz, F., Lehmann, H.: Automated Analysis of Mutual Gaze in Human Conversational Pairs. In: Nakano, Y., Conati, C., Bader, T. (eds.) Eye Gaze in Intelligent Human Computer Interaction. Springer (2012)

27. Fitzpatrick, P., Metta, G., Natale, L., Rao, S., Sadini, G.: Learning About Objects Through Action. Initial Steps Towards Artificial Cognition. In: Proceedings of Robotics and Automation, ICRA 2003 (2003)

Why Not Artificial Sympathy?

Minoru Asada, Yukie Nagai, and Hisashi Ishihara

Dept. of Adaptive Machine Systems, Graduate School of Engineering
Osaka University
Yamadaoka 2-1, Suita, Osaka, 565-0871, Japan
{asada,yukie,hisashi.ishihara}@ams.eng.osaka-u.ac.jp
http://www.er.ams.eng.osaka-u.ac.jp

Abstract. "Empathy" and "Sympathy" are often confusingly used. Beside the difference in their usage, the key component could be a sort of emotional state to be shared, and the way to represent or manipulate it might be different. This could be clearer when we attempt to design it for artificial agents. This paper argues what are differences between empathy and sympathy, and how to design each of them for an artificial agent. First, the dictionary meaning of both is reviewed, and a metaphor to intuitively explain the difference is introduced. Next, we argue how artificial empathy and artificial sympathy can be designed, and a cognitive developmental robotics is introduced as a promising approach to the latter, especially from a viewpoint of learning and development. A rough design for artificial sympathy is argued, and preliminary studies needed to build the artificial sympathy are introduced. Finally, future issues are given.

1 Introduction

"Empathy" and "Sympathy" are often confusingly used. The Oxford Dictionary of English 3rd edition (2010 by Oxford University Press, Inc.) describes each as follows:

- **empathy:** the ability to understand and share the feelings of another. **ORIGIN:** early 20th cent.: from Greek empatheia (from em-'in' + pathos 'feeling') translating German Einfühlung.
- **sympathy:** feelings of pity and sorrow for someone else's misfortune. **ORIGIN:** late 16th cent. : via Latin from Greek sumpatheia, from sun- 'with' + pathos 'feeling'.

The key component seems a sort of emotional state to be shared, and the way to represent or manipulate it might be different. This aspect can be magnified when we attempt to design it for artificial agents. One metaphor to show the difference is the following story. Medical doctors can infer the distress of their patients (empathy), and they can do adequate operations to reduce the distress of the patients. However, they often face difficulty to do any operations when the patients are their own sons or daughters (sympathy).

S.S. Ge et al. (Eds.): ICSR 2012, LNAI 7621, pp. 278–287, 2012.

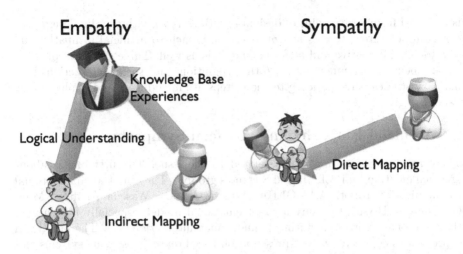

Fig. 1. A metaphor to explain the difference between empathy and sympathy

Figure 1 indicates an intuitive explanation for the difference between empathy and sympathy in this case, and this is our interpretation in this article which we derived from the dictionary meaning above. In the case of empathy, it is supposed to be a kind of indirect mapping from a medical doctor to a patient through a knowledge database including the doctor's own experiences, from where logical inference for the patients (emotional) state is applied to the patient, which is based on the observation from a god's viewpoint (topdown). On the other hand, in the case of sympathy, it is supposed a direct mapping from the doctor's emotional state into the patient's state without the logical process of reasoning to understand the patient's state. The Greek origin of "sym (sun)" means "with," which implies "with the patient" (not topdown, but almost the same level).

Which can be a target when we attempt to build an artificial system that can share the emotional state between a human and a robot? At a glance, the former (empathy) seems more practical for the artificial system to be designed since the machine is good at searching cases similar to the current patient state from a huge amount of data through the net, and applying rules to understand the patient state logically. Therefore, the existing artificial systems have taken this style based on the logical understanding of the situations by coding if-then rules regardless of a real understanding of each emotional state's meaning. On the other hand, the latter is a direct mapping such as an emotional reaction from one's own emotional state to that of another regardless of a logical understating of the other's situation. Can we realize such an artificial system with a different body structure including brain? This article argues about the possibility for artificial empathy and artificial sympaty referring to the existing works and cognitive developmental robotics as a promising approach to the artificial sympathy.

The rest of the paper is organized as follows. First, how to design artificial empathy or artificial sympathy is argued with pioneering studies. Then, CDR is reviewed from a viewpoint of designing artificial sympathy, and a design plan consisting of three steps is shown as one approach to artificial sympathy and also to other cognitive and affective functions as well. Three steps are physical embodiment, development of self/other cognition, and social interaction. Preliminary studies corresponding to these steps are introduced, and finally, future issues are given.

2   Artificial Empathy and Artifcial Sympathy

There are two pioneering works related to the issue. The first one is about artificial emotion by Prof. Shigeki Sugano's group [1]. They built an an emotional communication robot, WAMOEBA (Waseda-Ameba, Waseda Artificial Mind On Emotion BAse), to study a robot emotional model, especially focusing on the emotional expression during human-robot interaction [12]. The emotional expression is connected to self-preservation based on self-observing systems and hormone parameters they defined.

The second one is a series of studies on emotion expression humanoid robot WE (Waseda Eye), and the recent one is WE-4RII which can show very rich facial and gestural expressions based on sophisticated mechatronics and software (ex., [8,9] [2]). They designed mental dynamics caused by stimuli from the internal and external environment based on a mental model with a kind of instinct (need model).

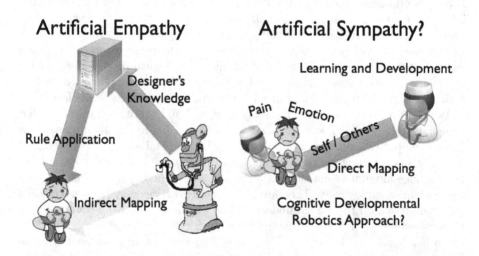

Fig. 2. What are artificial empathy and artificial sympathy?

Both studies are pioneering in respect that emotion is linked to self-preservation or instinct (need model), and that robots are capable to show emotional expressions based on their emotion models. However, it is not clear how a robot can

---

[1]   for the detail, visit http://www.sugano.mech.waseda.ac.jp
[2]   also visit http://www.takanishi.mech.waseda.ac.jp/top/research/index.htm

share an emotional state with humans. Since almost all of the robot behaviors are explicitly specified by the designer, little space is left for robots to learn or develop to share their emotional states. This approach may link to artificial empathy shown in Figure 2 where a huge knowledge database is available to understand (search for the case of) the patient's emotional state. One extreme view is that their approaches resemble the classical AI ones (GOFAI), and therefore seem to have limited capacity to share emotional expressions. In the case of artificial sympathy (if possible), the robot can feel the emotional state of the patient as its own (direct mapping). How can we realize such an artificial sympathy in robots? One simple approach is to minimize the part which the designer explicitly specifies or defines, but, instead, to maximize the room for learning such parts through the interaction with environment including others. This is not specific only to artificial empathy or sympathy, but general in acquiring cognitive and affective functions.

One big trend is cognitive developmental robotics (hereafter, CDR) [2] based on "physical embodiment," "social interaction," and "learning and development." Physical embodiment is a necessary condition for an artificial agent to create its sensation via sensorimotor mapping. Social interaction may help the agent feel its own emotional state and develop its emotional states to be social (caregiver's scaffolding). CDR is expected not only to realize artificial sympathy adaptive to new situations owing to the capability of learning and development of robots, but also to shed light on understanding empathy and sympathy from a viewpoint of design theory.

3   Cognitive Developmental Robotics as a Constructivist Approach

Roughly speaking, the developmental process consists of two phases: individual development at an early stage and social development through interaction between individuals at a later stage. The former relates mainly to neuroscience (internal mechanism), and the latter to cognitive science and developmental psychology (behavior observation). Intrinsically, both should be seamless, but there is a big difference between them at the representation level as a research target to be understood. CDR aims not at simply filling the gap between them but, more challengingly, at building a new paradigm that provides new understanding of ourselves while at the same time adding a new design theory of humanoids that are symbiotic with us. The following is a summary:

A: construction of a computational model of cognitive development
1. hypothesis generation: proposal of a computational model or hypothesis based on knowledge from existing disciplines
2. computer simulation: simulation of the process difficult to implement with real robots such as physical body growth
3. hypothesis verification with real agents (humans, animals, and robots), then go to 1)

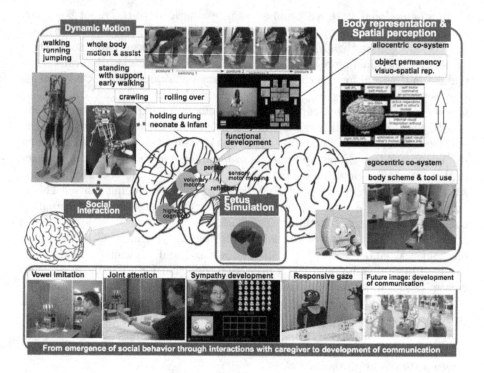

Fig. 3. A Cognitive Developmental Map (Adopted from Fig.3 in [2])

B: offer new means or data to better understand the human developmental
   process → mutual feedback with A
   1. measurement of brain activity by imaging methods
   2. verification using human subjects or animals
   3. providing the robot as a reliable reproduction tool in (psychological)
      experiments

The survey [2] introduces many studies by CDR.

3.1   A Cognitive Developmental Map

Let us consider a cognitive developmental map based on various aspects. The
major functional structure of the human brain-spine system is a hierarchical
one reflecting the evolutionary process, and consists of spine, brain stem, di-
encephalon, cerebellum, limbic system, basal ganglia, and neocortex. Here, we
regard this hierarchy as the first approximation toward the cognitive developmental map, and the flow of functional development is indicated at the center of
Fig. 3, that is, reflex, sensorimotor mapping, perception, voluntary motion, and
higher-order cognition.

In Fig. 3, we show, as much as possible, correspondences between developmental processes for individuals and the relationship between objects and individuals

to brain regions in terms of functions. Among these regions, the medial frontal cortex (hereafter, MFC) is supposed to be closely related to mind development and social cognition [1]. However, it seems that a more global network of the brain works together for such development and cognition, and more importantly, that the interaction triggered by caregivers (scaffolding) is one of the environmental factors that plays an essential role in various developmental processes, such as vocal imitation ([17,5]), joint attention ([14,15]), and also sympathy development.

3.2 Development of Sympathy

Here, we focus on the development of sympathy in respect to physical embodiment, social interaction, and development, together.

- **Physical Embodiment:** As a necessary item for robots to have artificial sympathy, they have to have a physical body to perceive the other's emotional state and to generate emotional behavior responding to the perceived one. WE-4RII is an excellent platform to show its emotional expressions, but we need a developmental process of facial and gestural expressions (learning of muscle control for corresponding expressions) that may enhance the capability to generate new emotional expressions and to be adaptive to unexpected situations.
- **Development of Self/Other Cognition:** before being able to share the emotional state between a human and a robot, it has to have a concept of self and others, first. This is one of the big issues in human cognitive development in general, not specific to the development of sympathy. However, this seems essential to consider in the development of artificial sympathy by which the emotional state of others can be regarded as its own. The Mirror system is expected to extend such emotion sharing although we should be careful not to have undue expectations of the MNS [4]. In any case, we need a developmental process for self/other discrimination which might be a fundamental structure for artificial sympathy.
- **Social Interaction:** another essential aspect of artificial sympathy is social interaction. It is actually the real situation where a human and a robot share an emotional state with each other, and more importantly, it is the situation where artificial sympathy develops. A typical situation is infant-caregiver interaction where the caregiver shows various kinds of voluntary/involuntary teaching such as motherese [7] and motionese [10]. In the case of sympathy, what kind of teaching promotes the development of emotion sharing?

In the following, we show preliminary studies toward the artificial sympathy.

4 Preliminary Studies by CDR

4.1 Affetto, A Little Child Robot for Interaction Study [6]

WE-4RII shows rich emotional expressions with sophisticated mechatoronics, and the emotional states perceived by humans could be realistic ones. However,

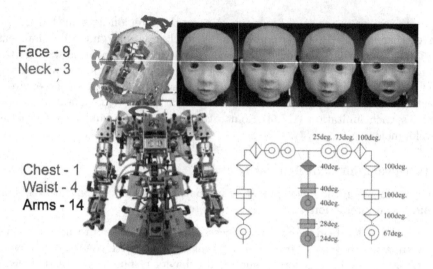

Fig. 4. Affetto head with the internal structure of the upper torso

humans understand them not as real ones. In order to study emotional interaction between an infant and its caregiver, we may need much more realistic baby robots. For that purpose, we are building such a face robot, Affetto, that has the realistic appearance of a 1- to 2-year-old child. Fig. 4 shows a prototype of Affetto built in our laboratory.

Currently, Affetto is supposed to be a platform for interaction study as a controllable baby by which systematic experiments can be done. In the future, we will embed a learning structure for artificial sympathy into Affetto, and will have more dynamic experiments of Affetto and caregiver interactions.

4.2   An Early Developmental Model for Self/Other Cognition [11]

We have proposed a computational model for the early development of the self/other cognition system, which originates from immature vision. The model gradually increases the spatiotemporal resolution of a robot's vision while the robot learns sensorimotor mapping through primal interactions with others. In the early stage of development, the robot interprets all observed actions as equivalent due to lower visual resolution, and thus associates the non-differentiated observation with motor commands. As vision develops, the robot starts discriminating actions generated by itself from those by others. The initially acquired association is, however, maintained through development, which results in two types of associations: one is between motor commands and self-observation and the other between motor commands and other-observation. Our experiments demonstrate that the model achieves early development of the self/other cognition system, which enables a robot to imitate others' actions.

Figure 5 shows a model for emergence of the self/other cognition system originating from immature vision. We expect this kind of developmental system can be applied to the process of sympathy development, as well.

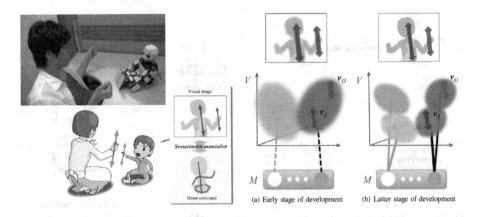

(a) Early stage of development   (b) Latter stage of development

Fig. 5. A model for emergence of the self/other cognition system originated in immature vision

4.3   Finding Correspondence between Facial Expressions and Internal States [16]

From a viewpoint of social interaction, the question was what kind of caregiver's behavior lead the developmental process of infant sympathy. In developmental psychology, intuitive parenting is regarded as the maternal scaffolding upon which children develop sympathy when caregivers mimic or exaggerate the child's emotional facial expressions [3]. We model human intuitive parenting using a robot that associates a caregiver's mimicked or exaggerated facial expressions with the robot's internal state to learn a sympathetic response. The internal state space and facial expressions are defined using psychological studies and change dynamically in response to external stimuli. After learning, the robot responds to the caregiver's internal state by observing human facial expressions. The robot then expresses its own internal state facially if synchronization evokes a response to the caregiver's internal state.

Fig. 6 (left) shows a learning model for a child developing a sense of sympathy through the intuitive parenting of its caregiver. When a child undergoes an emotional experience and expresses its feelings by changing its facial expression, the caregiver sympathizes with the child and shows a concomitantly exaggerated facial expression. The child then discovers the relationship between the emotion experienced and the caregiver's facial expression and comes to mutually associate the emotion and the facial expression. The emotion space in this figure is constructed based on the model proposed by Russell [13].

5   Future Issues

In this paper, we enhanced the difference between empathy and sympathy from a viewpoint of design theory, and pointed out that the design of artificial sympathy is a big challenge to reconsider the meaning of both and their differences, further

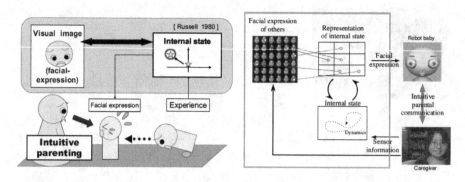

Fig. 6. Learning model for developing sympathy in children through intuitive parenting (left), and associating visual facial expressions of others with internal states (right)

to build such an artificial agent that might have an artificial mind. Future issues are (1) to integrate the mapping of facial expression to internal state and the early development model of the self/other cognition system into Affetto to check any possibility of artificial sympathy after self/other cognition, and (2) more challengingly, to form the concept of "pain," not simply as sensory information acceptance, but as realization of its meaning that recall a deeper understanding of our pain itself.

Acknowledgement. This study is supported by Grants-in-Aid for Scientific Research (Research Project Number: 24000012). We thank Joschka Boedecker for proof-reading the manuscript.

References

1. Amodio, D.M., Frith, C.D.: Meeting of minds: the medial frontal cortex and social cognition. Nat. Rev. Neurosci. 7, 268–277 (2006)
2. Asada, M., Hosoda, K., Kuniyoshi, Y., Ishiguro, H., Inui, T., Yoshikawa, Y., Ogino, M., Yoshida, C.: Cognitive developmental robotics: a survey. IEEE Transactions on Autonomous Mental Development 1(1), 12–34 (2009)
3. Gergely, G., Watson, J.S.: Early socio-emotional development: Contingency perception adn the social-biofeedback model. In: Rochat, P. (ed.) Early Social Cognition: Understanding Others in the First Months of Life, pp. 101–136. Lawrence Erlbaum, Mahwah (1999)
4. Hickok, G.: Eight problems for the mirror neuron theory of action understanding in monkeys and humans. Joural of Cognitive Neuroscience 21, 1229–1243 (2009)
5. Hisashi, I., Yoshikawa, Y., Miura, K., Asada, M.: Caregiver's sensorimotor magnets guide infant's vowels through auto mirroring. In: The 7th International Conference on Development and Learning (ICDL 2008), CD–ROM (2008)
6. Ishihara, H., Yoshikawa, Y., Asada, M.: Realistic child robot "affetto" for understanding the caregiver-child attachment relationship that guides the child development. In: IEEE International Conference on Development and Learning, and Epigenetic Robotics (ICDL-EpiRob 2011), CD–ROM (2011)

7. Kuhl, P., Andruski, J., Chistovich, I., Chistovich, L., Kozhevnikova, E., Ryskina, V., Stolyarova, E., Sundberg, U., Lacerda, F.: Cross-language analysis of phonetic units in language addressed to infants. Science 277, 684–686 (1997)
8. Miwa, H., Itoh, K., Matsumoto, M., Zecca, M., Takanobu, H., Roccella, S., Carrozza, M.C., Dario, P., Takanishi, A.: Effective emotional expressions with emotion expression humanoid robot we-4rii. In: Proceeding of the 2004 IEEE/RSJ Intl. Conference on Intelligent Robot and Systems, pp. 2203–2208 (2004)
9. Miwa, H., Okuchi, T., Itoh, K., Takanobu, H., Takanishi, A.: A new mental model for humanoid robts for humanfriendly communication-introduction of learning system, mood vector and second order equations of emotion. In: Proceeding of the 2003 IEEE International Conference on Robotics & Automation, pp. 3588–3593 (2003)
10. Nagai, Y., Rohlfing, K.J.: Computational analysis of motionese toward scaffolding robot action learning. IEEE Transactions on Autonomous Mental Development 1(1), 44–54 (2009)
11. Nagai, Y., Kawai, Y., Asada, M.: Emergence of mirror neuron system: Immature vision leads to self-other correspondence. In: IEEE International Conference on Development and Learning, and Epigenetic Robotics (ICDL-EpiRob 2011), CD–ROM (2011)
12. Ogata, T., Sugano, S.: Emotional communication between humans and the autonomous robot wamoeba-2 (waseda amoeba) which has the emotion model. JSME International Journal, Series C: Mechanical Systems Machine Elements and Manufacturing 43(3), 568–574 (2000)
13. Russell, J.A.: A circumplex model of affect. Journal of Personality and Social Psychology 39, 1161–1178 (1980)
14. Sumioka, H., Yoshikawa, Y., Asada, M.: Causality detected by transfer entropy leads acquisition of joint attention. Journal of Robotics and Mechatronics 20(3), 378–385 (2008)
15. Sumioka, H., Yoshikawa, Y., Asada, M.: Development of joint attention related actions based on reproducing interaction causality. In: The 7th International Conference on Development and Learning (ICDL 2008), CD–ROM (2008)
16. Watanabe, A., Ogino, M., Asada, M.: Mapping facial expression to internal states based on intuitive parenting. Journal of Robotics and Mechatronics 19(3), 315–323 (2007)
17. Yoshikawa, Y., Asada, M., Hosoda, K., Koga, J.: A constructivist approach to infants' vowel acquisition through mother-infant interaction. Connection Science 15(4), 245–258 (2003)

How Can a Robot Attract the Attention of Its Human Partner? A Comparative Study over Different Modalities for Attracting Attention

Elena Torta*, Jim van Heumen, Raymond H. Cuijpers, and James F. Juola

Eindhoven University of Technology,
Den Dolech 16, 5600MB Eindhoven, NL
{e.torta,r.h.cuijpers,j.juola}@tue.nl,
j.v.heumen@student.tue.nl

Abstract. One of the most common tasks of a robot companion in the home is communication. In order to initiate an information exchange with its human partner, the robot needs to attract the attention of the human. This paper presents results of a user study (N=12) with elderly people (62 - 70 years) to evaluate different modalities for attracting attention. Results show that actions which involve sound generate the fastest reaction times and are better perceived by participants. Surprisingly attempting to attract attention by establishing eye-contact resulted in worse participants' perception. We interpret these results as that robot gazing behaviour is better suited for situations in which the user's focus of visual attention is already on the robot.

Keywords: Attracting Attention, Human-robot interaction, Smart homes, Speech, Eye-contact, Facial expression.

1 Introduction

Worldwide life expectancy is higher than in the past and the ratio between the economically productive proportion of the population and the elderly continues to decrease [2,10]. Therefore it is expected that in the near future the increasing proportion of elderly persons will lead to both an increasing demand for care and a shortage of caregivers [21]. In addition, the modern lifestyle brings children away from their parents and it is no longer self-evident that they can provide the care and support their parents will possibly need. In this context, ageing societies would benefit from the design of intelligent homes that provide assistance to the elderly [19]. Such homes can assist elderly persons effectively in everyday tasks such as communication with the external world and provision of medicine and health check reminders in a proactive fashion [3]. Intelligent homes are able to detect people's activities [20] and to trigger appropriate interventions depending on the recognized activity. Overall the most common intervention consists of communicating with the inhabitants of the house in different situations and

---

* The authors gratefully acknowledge the contribution of our colleague David Johnson.

S.S. Ge et al. (Eds.): ICSR 2012, LNAI 7621, pp. 288–297, 2012.

different purposes, such as reporting the outside weather conditions, reminding them to take their medications or stimulating them to engage in physical activity. Therefore the effectiveness of intelligent homes largely depends on the choice of interface between the smart home and the user, because the interface embodies the intelligence of the system and in many different scenarios it is its only visible component. In that respect, socially assistive robots [6] appear to be one of the most promising interfaces. Unlike stationary solutions like avatars, they have the ability to navigate autonomously towards the person. Furthermore they are equipped with multimodal communication channels that can be used simultaneously for enhancing the quality and success of interaction. The media "equation" suggests that people tend to look at technological artefacts as social actors [16] and robots are no exception to that [13][8]. Therefore people expect robots to follow common social norms when establishing and maintaining communication, the so-called "robotiquette" [5]. However, it remains unclear how a robot can start and continue to communicate effectively with people and on which combination of verbal and non-verbal communication cues can allow the robot to best absolve to a given task in terms of efficacy of interaction and user perception. Several researches have been conducted to assess how a robot should initiate and maintain an information exchange with its human partner. Indeed the robot can use one or multiple communication channel to achieve interaction during information exchange. Although the importance of these channels is evident, the relative contribution in terms of efficacy is less clear. In this context human-robot proxemics studies how a robot should approach a person for initiating and maintaining a conversation. Studies involve the creation of models of human-robot proxemics as well as their implementation in navigation algorithms. As an example, [12] presents results of comprehensive studies related to modelling proxemic behaviours as cost functions in robotic navigation. Along the same line [22] propose methods for studying human-robot proxemics and include Bayesian filtering models to solve navigation problems. Other work focuses on understanding the role of robotic gaze as a non-verbal interaction cue during communication. Following human-human communication models, it has been shown that gaze behaviour of humanoid robots might help the robot to signal role change during conversation, manage turn-taking, and in general influence how interlocutors perceive the robot and the entire conversation [14]. Robot bodily posture and gazing behavior can also enhance the persuasive power of robots when the latter tells a story [9] or during a cooperative task between the robot and its human partner [4]. Gestures also play an important role during human-human conversation and, when used by robots, it has been shown that the user perception of the robot in terms of anthropomorphism is positively influenced by co-speech gestures when either congruent or incongruent with conversational subject [17]. Deictic gestures are also fundamental for speech disambiguation both in human-human and in human-robot interaction [18]. Even though some work has already tackled issue related to how the robot can use its multimodal communication channels to change the focus of human attention during conversation [11], little work has been directed to how the different communication channels can be used by the robot to attract people's attention before initiating conversation, specially when the user is already focused on something other than the robot. Therefore our work relates to the study of the efficacy of the use of different communication channels for attracting user attention when the latter is not focused on the robot. We also study how the use of the different communication channels is perceived by the user. Results of our work are of importance for selecting appropriate robotic actions for attracting human attention.

2   Methods

2.1   Participants

Twelve Dutch elderly people, age 62 - 70 years took part at the experiment. People with reduced vision, hearing problems and/or using hearing aids were excluded from participation. All participants indicated to have positive attitude toward technology and in particular toward the use of computer systems in the house. Two participants indicated to dislike the idea of robotic companionship in the home while the rest reported to like it.

2.2   Design

During the experiment we manipulated the type of action the robot Nao by Aldebaran Robotics, depicted in Figure 1, could perform for attracting attention. Each action is representative of a different communication channel: the

Fig. 1. The robot Nao by Aldebaran robotics was used during the experiment for attracting participants' attention

actions used were (1) attempting to establish eye-contact by looking at the user, (2) changing the robot facial expression by blinking its eye LEDs, (3) making gestures by waving the arms and (4) uttering the word "Hello". Apart from action 4, which is verbal and of an auditory nature, all actions are non-verbal gestures of a visual nature. As actions 2 and 3 involve movement they are more salient in peripheral vision. The waving gesture also involves sound of the robot's motors. We also manipulated the type of information presented to participants before the robot attempted to attract their attention. Information consisted of short video-clips taken from a Dutch local TV channel. The video clips were presented via a TV positioned in front of them. Video clips were arbitrarily marked

as either important or not important. Important video clips were presented with
a red box in the upper side of the image. Participants were to respond as soon as
they noticed the action by pressing a button on a keyboard positioned in front
of them. Participants were instructed to remember the content of the video clips
marked as important because they would be questioned about them at the end
of the experiment, even though they were in fact questioned about both important and not important news items. Thus, the experiment had a 4 (actions) x
2 (importance of news) within-subject design with 3 repetitions. In total every
participants experienced 24 trials. During every trial we measured the reaction
time between the start of the robotic action for attracting attention and the
moment the participant pressed the button. Before and after the experiment we
asked participants to fill in the Godspeed questionnaire [1]. This was intended
to get insight onto how the robot's attempt to attract attention modified participants attitudes toward it. Furthermore at the end of the experiment we asked
participants to evaluate the different robotic actions for attracting attentions.
This was done by using a 5-point Likert scale for questions in which participants
indicated which adjective would better describe a given action. Questions were
of the form: How would you define the action **x**? The pairs of adjectives were: (1)
clear/ vague, (2) friendly/mean (3) calm/wild, (4) present/ subtle and (5) pleas-
ant/annoying. At the end of the experiment participants were also requested to
answer specific questions regarding the content of the important news.

2.3 Set-Up

The experiment took place in a simulated living room. Participants were seated
on a couch and had a table and a TV screen in front of them. The set-up
mimicked a typical home situation in which the elderly person is sitting on the
couch and watching TV. The television played news items retrieved from a Dutch
news website and was connected to a computer in order to trigger the start of
the different video clips. A keyboard was placed on the coffee table in front of
the couch where participants were seated. The robot was standing beside by the
participants and was remotely connected to the computer in order to trigger the
different actions at random moments during the broadcast of the TV news. The
experiment was supervised by an operator seated in the control room next to
the living room. The experiment set-up is visible in Figure 2.

2.4 Procedure

Participants were welcomed and given a general explanation of the experiment.
They first signed an informed consent form and filled in the first questionnaire
(Godspeed1). The participants were seated on the couch in front of the television
with the keyboard placed in front of them on the coffee table. The experimenter
showed participants the various actions the robot could perform to attract their
attention and explained how the different importance levels of the video clips
were indicated. Participants were instructed to remember the important video
clips as they would be questioned about them at the end of the experiment. Then

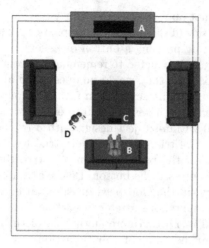

Fig. 2. Experiment Set up. (A) TV screen position, (B) participant position (C) keyboard position and (D) robot position.

the experiment begun with video clips appearing on the TV screen in front of the participants. At random moments during the broadcast of the news the robot performed an action to attract participants' attention. Participants were instructed to press the spacebar of the keyboard as soon as possible after noticing the attempt of the robot to attract their attention. After responding, they were instructed to press a button on the keyboard to categorize the action they saw. The time between the start of the action to attract attention and the moment participants pressed the spacebar was recorded. The experiment had a total of 24 trials with 12 video clips marked as important and 12 unmarked. Marked and unmarked video clips were presented in random order to every participant during the experiment. When all the trials were over, participants filled in the Godspeed questionnaire for the second time and answered the questionnaire to assess their attitudes toward the robotic actions. At the end of the experiment participants received monetary compensation for their participation.

2.5   Data Analysis

To test the effects of our manipulations on the reaction time of participants we used a factorial repeated measures analysis of variance (ANOVA) with the reaction time as dependent variable and both manipulations (importance of news and action) as independent variables. Mauchly's test indicated that the assumption of sphericity had been violated for the main effect of action, $\chi^2(2) = 5.048$, $p = 0.412$. Therefore degrees of freedom were corrected using Greenhouse-Geisser estimates of sphericity ($\epsilon = 0.741$). The distribution of the data regarding the evaluation of the actions across the items (1) clear/ vague, (2) friendly/mean (3) calm/wild, (4) present/ subtle and (5) pleasant/annoying was not normally distributed. Therefore we used a a non-parametric test, Friedman's ANOVA, to assess the significance of the results.

3   Results

To assess the efficiency of the different ways to attract attention we compared the reaction times. In Figure 3 the reaction times are plotted for each of the robot's actions. There was a significant main effect of the type of action on reaction time

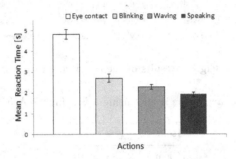

Fig. 3. Mean reaction time in [s] for every action regardless of the importance of notice. (Adjusted Values with 95% Confidence Interval).

$F(2.22, 24.44) = 140,00, p < 0.001$. Contrasts analysis revealed that there was a significant difference, in terms of reaction time, between all the types of actions. In particular, reaction time in the case of eye contact was higher than in the case of blinking the eye LEDS, $F(1, 11) = 140.84, p < 0.001$. Reaction time was higher when the robot blinked its eyes compared to waving $F(1, 11) = 8.67, p = 0.013$. And finally, reaction time was higher when the robot waved its arms compared to speech $F(1, 11) = 26.65, p < 0.001$. The manipulation importance of news had no significant effect on reaction time and no interaction effect between the two manipulations was found. The subjective experience of participants was evaluated using two questionnaires. The analysis of the answers given to the Godspeed questionnaire [1] revealed no significant difference in any of the 5 dimensions: anthropomorphism, animacy, likeability, perceived intelligence and perceived safety. The attitude of people toward the robot was similar before and after the experiment. The second questionnaire was used to evaluate how users rated the different actions on the items: (1) clear/ vague, (2) friendly/mean, (3) calm/wild, (4) present/ subtle and (5) pleasant/annoying. The average rating on a Likert scale from 1 to 5 is shown in Figure 4 for each of the 5 dimensions of the questionnaire and each type of action. The Friedman's ANOVA reveals that there is a significant difference on the items (1) Clear, (2) Friendly and (4) Present while no significant different was found for the items (3) Calm and (5) Pleasant. The results are summarized in Table 1. We performed a Wilcoxon signed-rank test on all comparable groups considering the items (1) Clear, (2) Present and (4) Friendly. Having to compare the effect of 4 actions grouped by 2 on every significant item leads to 6 comparison per item. Therefore the results

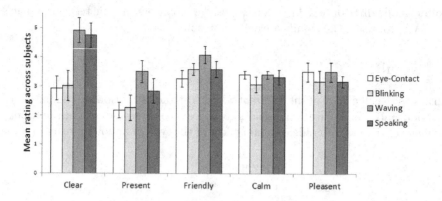

Fig. 4. Results of the questionnaires

Table 1. Summary of the results using a Friedman's ANOVA analysis

Item	χ^2	p
Clear	25.05	0.001
Friendly	10.24	0.013
Calm	5.77	0.122
Present	13.85	0.002
Pleasant	2.22	0.543

of the post-hoc test with Bonferonni correction are interpreted as significant at a level of $p < 0.05/6 = 0.0083$ [7]. The results show that waving was evaluated significantly more present ($T = 0$, $p < .0083$, $r = -0.556$), friendly ($T = 0$, $p < .0083$, $r = -0.496$), and clear ($T = 0$, $p < .0083$, $r = -0.576$) than eye contact. Waving was also rated significantly more clear ($T = 0$, $p < .0083$, $r = -0.522$) than flashing eye LEDs. Saying hello was rated significantly more clear than eye contact ($T = 0$, $p < .0083$, $r = -0.577$) and flashing eye LEDs ($T = 0$, $p < .0083$, $r = -0.518$). The rest of the comparisons did not result in a significant difference. A summary of the results is reported in Table 2.

Table 2. Summary of the results using a Friedman's ANOVA analysis

Actions	Clear effect size (r)	p	Friendly effect size (r)	p	Present effect size (r)	p
Waving vs Eye Contact	-0.556	0.002	-0.496	0.008	-0.576	0.001
Waving vs Blinking LEDs	0.000	0.570	-0.379	0.063	-0.522	0.004
Waving vs Saying Hello	-0.394	0.047	-0.387	0.055	-0.289	0.250
Saying "Hello" vs Eye contact	-0.407	0.039	-0.258	0.180	-0.577	0.001
Saying "Hello" vs Blinking LEDs	-0.288	0.108	0.000	0.687	-0.518	0.004
Eye contact vs Blinking LEDs	-0.068	0.500	-0.333	0.125	-0.077	0.500

4 Discussion and Conclusion

We compared four different ways of attracting attention by a small humanoid robot while people watched news items on a television set. We found that reaction times differed considerably according to the action that was performed by the robot. In terms of reaction time speech was most salient as the average response was fastest, followed by the waving gesture and eye LED blinking gesture. Trying to establish eye-contact was least salient. It is interesting to note that speaking and waving both involve an auditory component either in the form of speech utterance or in the form of noise produced by the robot's actuators, whereas flashing LEDs and eye contact are of a visual nature. Thus, it seems that sound, which is an omnidirectional cue, is more salient than the visual channel. This makes sense because the visual attention was directed towards the TV. The high acuity foveal area spans only about 5 degrees, so that the robot moved in the participant's periphery. These facts can explain why actions which involve sound production cause a quicker response than actions that involved only visual stimuli. In the same line of reasoning the making eye contact action involves less motion than waving and flashing eye LEDs. It is well-known that peripheral vision is very sensitive to motion explaining why making eye contact is less salient than the other visual cues for attracting attention. As robots are most likely to approach from the side in order not to impede on a person watching TV, these results are of importance for designing ways attract attention. Previous research by [15] reported that an auditory stimulus can be perceived as louder if it is presented with visual stimuli in the form of lights. However our results show that this is not necessarily the case for all visual stimuli. Waving is not the most salient cue even though it visual motion and sound from the actuators as it is still slower than an utterance. Nonetheless, we can expect that the combination of speech with a gesture would produce even faster reaction times. We also found a clear effect on the subjective experience. Contrary to expectation looking at a person is considered less pleasant than just saying hello, or waving or blinking the eye LEDs. Eye contact is usually considered an important social cue. However, in normal circumstances people have eye contact when they face each other, whereas in our experiment the robot was looking at a person from the side. This would seem to suggest that being looked at from the side is unpleasant because it is considered to be impolite. The fact that making eye contact is least salient could make matters even worse as people may get a feeling of secretively being watched. Of course this is pure speculation, but our results suggest that eye contact is not the best way to attract attention in this particular context. The perceived clarity is well in line with the reaction time results. The least salient actions are also judged as less clear whereas the salient gestures are judged as clear. The perceived presence and perceived friendliness follow a similar pattern except that the differences are smaller. It is interesting to note that the most salient cue, speech, scores lower than waving on perceived clarity, friendliness and presence. Interestingly, we did not find a significant difference in terms of reaction time when participants were presented with important and not-important news items. So it seems that, apart from a spatial effect, being more focused does not influence the participant' ability to notice the actions performed by the robot. As we did not independently check whether our manipulation worked, we cannot be sure that paying more or less attention to news items has no effect. Finally, we note that waving was the most clear and present action and participants reported to like it most, while eye contact could have different purposes, both negative and positive. This suggests that communicative cues for attracting attention should be as least ambiguous and specific as possible. In conclusion our results suggest that the robot can effectively attract attention of people using auditory, visual, verbal and non-verbal actions. Attention is obtained faster when using speech followed by gestures. Contrary to our expectations, attracting attention by establishing eye-contact produces the slowest reaction time and it is perceived as not very friendly. We interpret these results as that robot gazing behaviour is better suited for situations in which the user's focus of visual attention is not occupied but when it is already on the robot.

Acknowledgments. The research leading to these results is part of the KSERA project (http://www.ksera-project.eu) and has received funding from the European Commission under the 7th Framework Programme (FP7) for Research and Technological Development under grant agreement n2010-248085.

References

1. Bartneck, C., Kuli, D., Croft, E., Zoghbi, S.: Measurement instruments for the anthropomorphism, animacy, likeability, perceived intelligence, and perceived safety of robots. International Journal of Social Robotics 1, 71–81 (2009)
2. Carone, G., Costello, D.: Can europe afford to grow old? International Monetary Fund Finance and Development Magazine (2006)
3. Cesta, A., Cortellessa, G., Giuliani, V., Pecora, F., Rasconi, R., Scopelliti, M., Tiberio, L.: Proactive Assistive Technology: An Empirical Study. In: Baranauskas, C., Abascal, J., Barbosa, S.D. (eds.) INTERACT 2007. LNCS, vol. 4662, pp. 255–268. Springer, Heidelberg (2007)
4. Chidambaram, V., Chiang, Y.H., Mutlu, B.: Designing persuasive robots: How robots might persuade people using vocal and nonverbal cues (2012)
5. Dautenhahn, K.: Socially intelligent robots: dimensions of human robot interaction. Philosophical Transactions of the Royal Society B: Biological Sciences 362(1480), 679–704 (2007)
6. Feil-Seifer, D., Mataric, M.J.: Defining socially assistive robotics. In: 9th International Conference on Rehabilitation Robotics, ICORR 2005, June 28-July 1, pp. 465–468 (2005)
7. Field, A.P.: Discovering Statistics Using SPSS. SAGE Publications Ltd. (2009)
8. Friedman, B., Kahn Jr., P.H., Hagman, J.: Hardware companions?: what online aibo discussion forums reveal about the human-robotic relationship. In: Proceedings of the SIGCHI Conference on Human Factors in Computing Systems, CHI 2003, pp. 273–280. ACM, New York (2003)

9. Ham, J., Bokhorst, R., Cuijpers, R., van der Pol, D., Cabibihan, J.-J.: Making Robots Persuasive: The Influence of Combining Persuasive Strategies (Gazing and Gestures) by a Storytelling Robot on Its Persuasive Power. In: Mutlu, B., Bartneck, C., Ham, J., Evers, V., Kanda, T. (eds.) ICSR 2011. LNCS, vol. 7072, pp. 71–83. Springer, Heidelberg (2011)

10. Hewitt, P.S.: Depopulation and ageing in europe and japan the hazardous transition to a labor shortage economy. Internationale Politik Und Gesellschaft, Part 1, 111–120 (2002)

11. Hoque, M.M., Onuki, T., Kobayashi, Y., Kuno, Y.: Controlling human attention through robot's gaze behaviors. In: 2011 4th International Conference on Human System Interactions (HSI), pp. 195–202. IEEE (2011)

12. Kirby, R.: Social Robot Navigation. PhD thesis, Robotics Institute, Carnegie Mellon University, Pittsburgh, PA (May 2010)

13. Lee, K.M., Jung, Y., Kim, J., Kim, S.R.: Are physically embodied social agents better than disembodied social agents?: The effects of physical embodiment, tactile interaction, and people's loneliness in human robot interaction. International Journal of Human-Computer Studies 64(10), 962–973 (2006)

14. Mutlu, B., Kanda, T., Forlizzi, J., Hodgins, J., Ishiguro, H.: Conversational gaze mechanisms for humanlike robots. ACM Trans. Interact. Intell. Syst. 1(2), 12:1–12:33 (2012)

15. Odgaard, E., Arieh, Y., Marks, L.: Brighter noise: Sensory enhancement of perceived loudness by concurrent visual stimulation. Cognitive, Affective, and Behavioral Neuroscience 4, 127–132 (2004)

16. Reevs, B., Nass, C.: The media equation: how people trat computers, television and new media like real people and places. Cambridge University Press, New York (1996)

17. Salem, M., Eyssel, F., Rohlfing, K., Kopp, S., Joublin, F.: Effects of Gesture on the Perception of Psychological Anthropomorphism: A Case Study with a Humanoid Robot. In: Mutlu, B., Bartneck, C., Ham, J., Evers, V., Kanda, T. (eds.) ICSR 2011. LNCS, vol. 7072, pp. 31–41. Springer, Heidelberg (2011)

18. Clair, A.S., Mead, R., Mataric, M.J.: Investigating the effects of visual saliency on deictic gesture production by a humanoid robot. In: RO-MAN, 2011 IEEE, August 3-31, pp. 210–216 (2011)

19. Steg, H., Strese, H., Loroff, C., Hull, J., Schmidt, S.: Europe is facing a demographic challenge ambient assisted living offers solutions (2006)

20. Tapia, E.M., Intille, S.S., Larson, K.: Activity Recognition in the Home Using Simple and Ubiquitous Sensors. In: Ferscha, A., Mattern, F. (eds.) PERVASIVE 2004. LNCS, vol. 3001, pp. 158–175. Springer, Heidelberg (2004)

21. Tapus, A., Matari, M.J., Scassellati, B.: The grand challenges in socially assistive robotics. Robotics and Automation Magazine 14(1), 1–7 (2007)

22. Torta, E., Cuijpers, R.H., Juola, J.F., van der Pol, D.: Design of Robust Robotic Proxemic Behaviour. In: Mutlu, B., Bartneck, C., Ham, J., Evers, V., Kanda, T. (eds.) ICSR 2011. LNCS, vol. 7072, pp. 21–30. Springer, Heidelberg (2011)

Long-Term Interactions with Empathic Robots: Evaluating Perceived Support in Children

Iolanda Leite[1], Ginevra Castellano[2], André Pereira[1],
Carlos Martinho[1], and Ana Paiva[1]

[1] INESC-ID and Instituto Superior Técnico, Technical University of Lisbon,
Av. Prof. Cavaco Silva, Oeiras, Portugal
[2] HCI Centre, School of Electronic, Electrical and Computer Engineering
University of Birmingham, United Kingdom
iolanda.leite@ist.utl.pt, g.castellano@bham.ac.uk,
{andre.a.pereira,carlos.martinho}@ist.utl.pt, ana.paiva@inesc-id.pt

Abstract. In this paper, we present an empathic model for social robots that aim to interact with children for extended periods of time. The application of this model to a scenario in which a social robot plays chess with children is described. To evaluate the proposed model, we ran a long-term study in an elementary school and measured children's perception of social support. Our results suggest that children felt supported by the robot in a similar extent to what, in general, children feel supported by their peers. Another interesting finding was that the most valued form of social support was esteem support (reinforcing the other person's sense of competence and self-esteem).

Keywords: Empathy, Social Support, Long-term Interaction.

1 Introduction

The research on social robots capable of engaging users for extended periods of time has received increasingly more attention in the recent years. The application domains where these robots can assist people and improve their quality of life are innumerous, from health-care assistants for the elderly to learning companions for children. Many researchers agree that, for robots to become part of our lives, they should be able to communicate with people in similar ways people interact with each other [2]. However, despite the remarkable empirical research in this field, there is a fundamental question that remains unanswered: which social capabilities should robots be endowed with to better engage users after repeated interactions?

In our research, we aim to take a small step towards answering this question by exploring the role of empathy in long-term interaction between users, particularly children, and social robots. Hoffman defines empathy as "an affective response more appropriate to someone else's situation than to one's own" [8, p. 4]. Previous HRI studies showed some positive effects of empathic robots [3,12], but these findings were obtained in studies where users interacted with

S.S. Ge et al. (Eds.): ICSR 2012, LNAI 7621, pp. 298–307, 2012.
© Springer-Verlag Berlin Heidelberg 2012

robots only for a short period of time. Empathic responses can go beyond facial expressions (e.g., mimicking the other's expression): they can also include complex cognitive actions taken to reduce the other's distress, such as social supportive behaviours [5]. In fact, the perception of social support has been linked to positive outcomes in children's mental health and coping with traumatic events [17]. Can social robots also be a source of social support to children? In this paper, we present an empathic model that includes socially supportive behaviours and describe how the proposed model was implemented in a social robot that plays chess with children. Using this scenario, we carried out a long-term study to investigate children's perception of social support towards the robot.

This paper is organised as follows. In the next section, we present some related work in long-term studies with children and interaction with empathic robots. After that, we describe our empathic model and how it was implemented in the scenario of the long-term study. Finally, the experimental setup and results are reported, followed by some conclusions and future work directions.

2 Related Work

Most of the existing long-term studies with children were carried out in school environments. In this domain, one of the pioneer experiments was performed by Kanda et al. with Robovie [9]. They performed a trial for two weeks with elementary school Japanese students. The study revealed that Robovie failed to keep most of the children's interest after the first week, although children who kept interacting with the robot after the first week improved their English skills. In a follow-up study [10], Robovie was improved with a pseudo-development mechanism and self-disclosure behaviours. In contrast to the results obtained in the previous experiment, Robovie was capable of engaging children after the second week (although with a slight decay), which the authors attribute to the new capabilities implemented in the robot. With children from a different age group, a longitudinal study where a QRIO robot [16] interacted with toddlers in a day care revealed that toddlers progressively started treating the robot as a peer rather than as a toy, and that they exhibited an extensive number of care-taking behaviours towards the robot. In our own previous work [11], we measured perceived social presence towards a robotic chess companion over time. The results suggested that social presence decreased from the first to the last interaction, especially in terms of attentional allocation, and perceived affective and behavioural interdependence, that is, the extent to which users believe that their affective (and overall) behaviour affects and is affected by the robot's behaviour.

As we can see from the works mentioned above, none of the robots used in the long-term studies were programmed with empathic abilities. The only exception comes from the field of virtual agents, where Bickmore and Picard [1] developed Laura, a virtual conversational agent that employs relationship maintenance strategies while keeping track of user's exercise activities. Among other relational behaviours, Laura uses empathy in the attempt to maintain a long-term social-emotional relationships with users. The agent was evaluated in a study where approximately 100 users interacted daily with the exercise adoption system. After four weeks of interaction, the agent's relational behaviours increased participants' perceptions of the quality of the working alliance (on measures such as liking, trust and respect), when comparing the results with an agent without relational behaviours. Users interacting with the relational agent also expressed significantly higher desire to continue interacting with the system.

On the other hand, in short-term studies, several authors investigated the effects of empathic social robots [3,14]. Regarding social support, Saerbeck et al. [15] investigated the effects of supportive behaviours of an iCat robot on children's learning performance and motivation. The results suggest that simple manipulations in the robot's supportiveness, while maintaining the same learning content, increased student's motivation and scores on a language test.

3   An Empathic Model for Social Robots

In this section, we describe an empathic model for supporting long-term human robot interaction. The model includes the following components:

1. *Affect Detection*: a real-time prediction of the current affective state of the user who is interacting with the robot. This module returns the probability of the user's positive and negative valence of feeling.
2. *Empathic Appraisal*: based on the current affective state of the user, the robot appraises the situation and generates an empathic response (e.g., a facial expression in tune with the user's affective state).

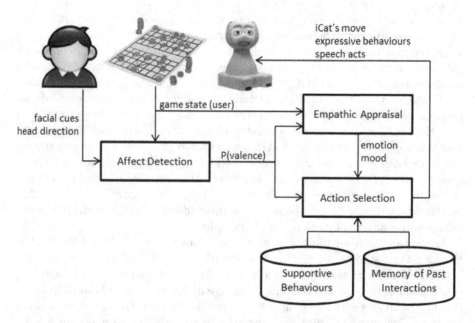

Fig. 1. Architecture of the empathic model applied to the iCat robot

3. *Supportive Behaviours*: empathy also includes actions to reduce the other's distress. Therefore, the robot has a series of supportive behaviours that can employ when the user's affective state is negative. Based on the framework defined by Cutrona et al.[4], social support can be separated in 4 different categories: "information support" (advice or guidance), "tangible assistance" (concrete assistance, for example by providing goods or services), "esteem support" (reinforcing the other's sense of competence) and "emotional support" (expressions of caring or attachment).

4. *Memory of Past Interactions*: remembering past interactions is extremely relevant for people to build rapport with each other. As such, and since we are interested in long-term human-robot interaction, the robot remembers simple aspects of previous interactions with the user (e.g., if they played a game, it remembers who won the game), and uses such information to generate dialogue that aims to give the user the feeling of "being cared for".

5. *Action Selection*: this module selects the most appropriate actions (expressive behaviours and speech utterances) for the robot based on the modules 2, 3 and 4. The mechanism for selecting the supportive behaviours is adaptive (for more details, please see [12]).

3.1 Application Scenario

This model was implemented in a social robot (iCat from Philips) that plays chess with children using an electronic chessboard. Each interaction starts with the iCat waking up. If the user is interacting with the robot for the first time, the iCat simply invites the user to play (e.g., by saying "Let's play chess!"), otherwise it greets the user by his/her name (e.g., "Hello Maria, nice to see you again!") and makes a comment about their previous game (e.g., "It's been 6 days since we played together. I won our last game, have you been practising?"). After every child's move, the robot provides feedback on the moves that children play by conveying empathic facial expressions determined by the Empathic Appraisal component. If the child's affective state is negative, one of the supportive behaviours described in Table 1 is displayed. Since the iCat cannot move its pieces, it asks the user to play its move by saying the move in chess coordinates. After that, the robot waits for the children's next move, and so on. At the end of the interaction, the iCat comments the game result and/or the child's progress (e.g., "It was a good game! You are doing very well: in the 4 times we played together, you could beat me 3 times!"). The robot's behaviour is fully autonomous, except for an initial parametrisation where the name of the child needs to be typed in.

Initial experiments with primary school children showed that they perceived the robot as more engaging and helpful when it reacted to their emotions by displaying empathic behaviour [12], but these results were obtained with a single interaction with the robot. In the following section, we present the results of a study in which the same group of users played with the robot over repeated interactions.

Fig. 2. Child playing with the iCat

4 Evaluation

To evaluate the impact of the proposed model in long-term interaction between children and social robots, we conducted a long-term study in a Portuguese elementary school. In this paper, we concretely investigate the two following aspects: (i) children's perception of social support provided by the robot and (ii) which of the implemented support behaviour types children preferred the most.

4.1 Participants

All participants belonged to a Portuguese elementary school in which children have chess lessons as part of their extra-curricular activities. A total of 16 participants from the 3rd grade were selected: 9 girls and 7 boys. Their ages varied between 8 and 9 years old (M=8.5) and their chess level was roughly the same, as all of them had chess lessons at least since the 1st grade.

The study took place in the elementary school after the official school hours (from 4 p.m. to 6 p.m.), with the 3rd grade children who stayed in the school during that period doing their homework and other activities supervised by a teacher. None of the children had interacted with the iCat before.

4.2 Procedure

The study was carried out over five consecutive weeks. Each child played a total of five chess exercises with the iCat – one exercise per week. In some rare exceptions due to public holidays or incompatibilities in children's schedule, they played two exercises in the same week, but always with at least 2 days of interval. The exercises consisted in playing from a predefined chess position until the end of the game (i.e., either the child or the iCat checkmates the other).

Table 1. Examples of supportive behaviours implemented in the iCat based on the theory of Cutrona et al. [4]. The robot's utterances are in Portuguese; these examples are translations of the Portuguese utterances.

Social Support Category	Supportive Behaviours	Examples of implementation in the iCat
Information Support	Suggestion/advice	"Need help? Touch my paw so I can suggest you a move."
	Teaching	"That wasn't your best move, because now I can capture your Queen."
Tangible Assistance	Direct Task	(Play a bad move)
	Tension Reduction	"Shall we start this exercise all over again?"
		"I always say, lucky in love, unlucky in chess."
Esteem Support	Compliment	"That was professionally done!"
	Validation	"Well done, you played what I have played!"
	Relief of Blame	"Don't worry, you didn't have better options."
	Reassurance	"Something's not quite right here, but it will get better for sure."
Emotional Support	Relationship	"I really enjoy playing with you!"
	Understanding	"I understand how you're feeling, I've been through similar situations."
	Encouragement	"Come on, I still believe in you!"

The procedure was similar every week: at the scheduled time, the child was guided to a room where she was alone with two experimenters and was asked to play a chess exercise with the iCat. The exercises were suggested by the chess instructor so that the difficulty was appropriate to the chess level of the children. Each interaction lasted on average 20 minutes, ranging between 10 to 25 minutes. After playing with the robot, in the first and last weeks of interaction children also filled in a questionnaire and were interviewed in a different room by another experimenter. All the interaction sessions were video recorded.

4.3   Measures

In this paper, we will focus on the results of **perceived social support**, defined as "the belief that, if the need arose, at least one person in the individual's circle would be available to serve one or more specific functions"[4]. Perceived social support can only be measured after repeated interactions: as stated by Cutrona et al., "it is necessary for the person to have experienced a number of interactions with the individual that communicates support". As such, we measured perceived support in the final questionnaire ([5th] interaction session) using a 4-point Likert scale anchored by "Strongly disagree" and "Strongly agree", and also by a *Smileyometer* [13] to help children interpret the meaning of the scale. Children were presented with a series of assertions adapted from the Social Support Questionnaire for Children (SSQC) [7], a self-report measure designed to evaluate children's social support via five different scales: parents, relatives, non-relative adults, siblings, and peers. In this case, we adapted the Peer scale by translating the items from English to Portuguese and changing "a peer" to "iCat". The questionnaire items used in the study are displayed in Table 2.

In addition to perceived support in general, we were also interested in understanding the impact that the different support behaviour categories – information support, tangible assistance, esteem and emotional support – had on children. As such, in the final interview, we gave participants four different cards containing a picture of the iCat and some speech bubbles. Each card contains speech bubbles with sentences that the iCat says when it is employing behaviours from one of the categories. Participants were asked to order the four cards from the one they liked the most to the one they preferred the least.

4.4   Results

In this section, we present and discuss the results of our adapted version of the SSQC, as well as the preferences on the support behaviour types displayed by the iCat when empathizing with the user.

Perceived Social Support. We ran Cronbach alpha test to examine the internal consistency of our adapted version of the SSQC. The results revealed an acceptable consistency ($\alpha = 0.52$), although the original Peer scale from the SSQC had a higher reliability ($\alpha = 0.91$). Table 2 contains, for each questionnaire item, the Means and Standard Deviations obtained in our study and the values obtained by Gordon [7] with a sample of 416 American children during the phase of selecting the final items for the questionnaire. In this latter sample, the mean age of children was 13 years old and, for this particular set of questions (Peer scale), children were asked to answer thinking on "anyone around your age who you associate with such as a friend, classmate, or teammate", whereas in our case they were asked to answer in relation to the iCat. Despite the differences in the sample, the positive results obtained in our study (all of them above the baseline mean values) indicate that, in this particular setting, the robot was perceived as supportive in a similar extent to what children in general consider being supported by their peers.

Preferences on Support Behaviour Types. As mentioned above, we asked each child to order a set of four cards containing utterances illustrating the different types of supportive behaviours displayed by the iCat. To analyse children's rankings, we classified their answers according to the following procedure: we attributed 3 points to the most preferred support behaviour type, 2 points to the second most preferred, 1 point to the third and 0 points to the least preferred. We summed the points for each category for every child, ending up with the ranking displayed in Figure 3. As we can see in Figure 3, the most preferred supportive behaviour category was esteem support, followed by emotional support, information

Table 2. Means and Standard Deviations of each questionnaire item obtained in our study (2nd column) and the baseline values (3rd column) obtained by Gordon [7]. The scale ranges from 0 (strongly disagree) to 3 (strongly agree).

Questionnaire items	Obtained results		Baseline	
	Means	St.Dev.	Means	St.Dev.
iCat comforts me when I am upset.	2.88	0.48	2.25	0.82
iCat cares about me.	2.75	0.75	2.27	0.85
iCat gives me good advice.	2.44	0.86	2.15	0.83
iCat accepts me for who I am.	3.0	0.0	2.47	0.73
iCat supports my decisions.	2.94	0.24	2.27	0.76
I can count on iCat.	3.0	0.0	2.51	0.69
iCat encourages me.	2.81	0.39	2.35	0.8
iCat understands me.	2.63	0.78	2.46	0.74
iCat praises me when I've done something well.	2.94	0.24	2.21	0.89

support, and finally tangible assistance. The esteem support category contained behaviours in which the iCat praised the user. As such, these results are in line with previous findings in HCI, in which computers capable of some forms of flatter are perceived more positively by users [6]. The low rankings of tangible assistance might have been caused by the concrete behaviours implemented in this category: *play bad move, start from beginning* and *use of humour*. Since children from this chess level often commit mistakes in the game (e.g., letting the other player capturing an important piece), we noticed that most children associated the robot's bad moves to an involuntary fault that happened not necessarily to help them. Regarding the use of humour (one of the possibilities for tension reduction), they may have become too repetitive over the course of the interactions because the robot only had two different jokes to say.

Overall, the emotion-oriented behaviours – esteem and emotional support – outranked the task-oriented behaviours – information support and tangible

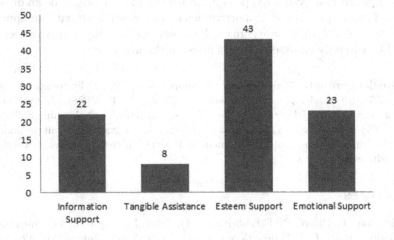

Fig. 3. Rankings of the preferred support behaviour categories

assistance. This result can be interpreted in two ways. First, it may be the case that, when playing competitive games, children prefer less tangible ways of support in contrast to being helped directly by the robot, which can reduce the merit of their victory (if they end up winning the game). The second interpretation is that the implemented task-oriented behaviours might not have been helpful enough. In the social support literature, task-oriented support often includes behaviours such as lending the other person something (e.g., money) or offering to take over of the other person's responsibilities while he/she is under stress, which are behaviours that are not applicable to this scenario (nor in most of the existing HRI scenarios). We expect to clarify these results with the analysis of the open-ended interview questions.

5 Conclusion

In this paper, we presented an empathic model for social robots that aim to interact with users for extended periods of time. We applied this model to a scenario where a social robot plays chess with users and displays several prosocial behaviours resulting from its ability to emphasize with the user, and ran a long-term study to investigate children's perception of social support. The results suggest that children feel supported by the robot, and that their preferred supportive behaviour type is esteem support.

These findings suggest relevant implications for the design of social robots for children, particularly in applications where it is important that the robot is able to engage users over repeated interactions (e.g., education or robot-assisted therapy). If a social robot is able to display empathic and pro social behaviours, children may see it as a peer and will eventually be more willing to continue interacting with the robot. Of course, this brings some ethical implications as well. For example, to what extent children believe that the support provided by the robot is sincere? Should they be told in advance that the robot's "concern" for them is not real? What happens if the robot suddenly breaks down or is not able to display appropriate supportive behaviours when faced with an apparent trivial situation? If robots are going to be present in our daily lives, these aspects should be carefully analysed and discussed in the near future.

Acknowledgements. This research was supported by EU 7th Framework Program (FP7/2007-2013) under grant agreement no. 215554, FCT (INESC-ID multiannual funding) through the PIDDAC Program funds and a PhD scholarship (SFRHBD/41358/2007) granted by FCT. We would like to express our gratitude to all the staff and study participants from Escola 31 de Janeiro in Parede, where the long-term experiment was conducted.

References

1. Bickmore, T., Picard, R.: Establishing and maintaining long-term human-computer relationships. ACM Transactions on Computer-Human Interaction 12(2), 327 (2005)

2. Breazeal, C.: Role of expressive behaviour for robots that learn from people. Philosophical Transactions of the Royal Society B: Biological Sciences 364(1535), 3527–3538 (2009)
3. Cramer, H., Goddijn, J., Wielinga, B., Evers, V.: Effects of (in)accurate empathy and situational valence on attitudes towards robots. In: ACM/IEEE Int. Conf. on Human-Robot Interaction, pp. 141–142. ACM (2010)
4. Cutrona, C., Suhr, J., MacFarlane, R.: Interpersonal transactions and the psychological sense of support. Personal Relationships and Social Support, 30–45 (1990)
5. Eisenberg, N., Fabes, R.A.: Empathy: Conceptualization, measurement, and relation to prosocial behavior. Motivation and Emotion 14, 131–149 (1990)
6. Fogg, B.J., Nass, C.: Silicon sycophants: The effects of computers that flatter. International Journal of Human-Computer Studies (1997)
7. Gordon, A.: Assessing Social Support in Children: Development and Initial Validation of the Social Support Questionnaire for Children. PhD thesis, University of Houston (2011)
8. Hoffman, M.L.: Empathy and moral development: Implications for caring and justice. Cambridge Univ. Press (2001)
9. Kanda, T., Hirano, T., Eaton, D., Ishiguro, H.: Interactive robots as social partners and peer tutors for children: A field trial. Human-Computer Interaction 19(1), 61–84 (2004)
10. Kanda, T., Sato, R., Saiwaki, N., Ishiguro, H.: A two-month field trial in an elementary school for long-term human–robot interaction. IEEE Transactions on Robotics 23(5), 962–971 (2007)
11. Leite, I., Martinho, C., Pereira, A., Paiva, A.: As time goes by: Long-term evaluation of social presence in robotic companions. In: Robot and Human Interactive Communication, RO-MAN 2009, pp. 669–674. IEEE (2009)
12. Leite, I., Pereira, A., Castellano, G., Mascarenhas, S., Martinho, C., Paiva, A.: Modelling Empathy in Social Robotic Companions. In: Ardissono, L., Kuflik, T. (eds.) UMAP Workshops 2011. LNCS, vol. 7138, pp. 135–147. Springer, Heidelberg (2012)
13. Read, J.C., MacFarlane, S.: Using the fun toolkit and other survey methods to gather opinions in child computer interaction. In: Proceedings of the 2006 Conference on Interaction Design and Children, IDC 2006, pp. 81–88. ACM, New York (2006)
14. Riek, L.D., Paul, P.C., Robinson, P.: When my robot smiles at me: Enabling human-robot rapport via real-time head gesture mimicry. Journal on Multimodal User Interfaces 3(1-2), 99–108 (2010)
15. Saerbeck, M., Schut, T., Bartneck, C., Janse, M.: Expressive robots in education: varying the degree of social supportive behavior of a robotic tutor. In: Proceedings of CHI 2010, pp. 1613–1622. ACM (2010)
16. Tanaka, F., Cicourel, A., Movellan, J.: Socialization between toddlers and robots at an early childhood education center. Proceedings of the National Academy of Sciences 104(46), 17954 (2007)
17. Vigil, J.M., Geary, D.C.: A preliminary investigation of family coping styles and psychological well-being among adolescent survivors of hurricane katrina. Journal of Family Psychology 22(1), 176 (2008)

Robot Drama Research:
From Identification to Synchronization

Zaven Paré[1,2,3]

[1] Anthropologie et anthropomorphisme (ARTMAP/Paris/France)
[2] Populations japonaises évolutions et perspectives contemporaines (INALCO/Paris/France)
[3] Théâtralité, performativité et effets de présence (UQAM/Montréal/Canada)
zavenpare@gmail.com

Abstract. Professor Hiroshi Ishiguro created the *Robot Actors Project* at Osaka University to experiment with robot presence and robot control in theatre situations. Instead of focusing attention on imitation, the roboticist developed his interest in theatre representation. Since then, the challenge of being in direct contact with live audiences has enriched our understanding of communication between humans and robots and between humans via robots. Today, the *Robot Actors Project* seeks to demystify the idea of fictional robots by familiarizing the public with the current state of robotics and experiments. A stage play with robots is not just a matter of how to construct realistic androids like animatronics for movies; it is about creating dramatic situations. In a laboratory, a robot is always a robot, but on stage a robot becomes an actor.

Keywords: Robot Drama Research, Robot Actors Project, Human Likeness, Familiarity, Identification, Synchronization.

This paper investigates an untraditional and novel use of robotics through the use of traditional puppetry and contemporary theatre for the purpose of research and entertainment. Investigating the possibility of robotic actors undoubtedly falls into the topic of artificial empathy due to the fundamental role empathy plays in acting and drama. The innovative idea of using robots as actors in theatre platforms of experimentation opens up an abundance of theoretical and practical possibilities and new issues for robotics research.

Two autumns ago, I was allowed backstage at the National Bunraku Theatre of Osaka where I had the privilege of observing Master Kanjūrō III at work. I also had the opportunity to observe the Master as he conveyed his art and know-how to a group of farmer's wives at the Jyoruri Theatre in Nose Town in the Osaka area and, later, to children at the Kōzu Elementary School in the neighborhood of the Bunraku Theatre. In Japan, the preferred method of learning is through observation, which requires time.

In the art of bunraku theatre, three synchronized puppeteers dressed in black manipulate a *ningyō* (bunraku puppet) into postures and gestures to embody stage characters. The distance between the masked presence of the manipulators and the presence effect of the puppet contributes to inspire life and a soul into the puppet. It is a curious mixture of attitudes and emotions spanning the gamut from love to

S.S. Ge et al. (Eds.): ICSR 2012, LNAI 7621, pp. 308–316, 2012.
© Springer-Verlag Berlin Heidelberg 2012

melancholy to sorrow. I was backstage not only to satisfy my curiosity with regard to this great Japanese tradition but also as part of a project on Robot Drama Research at Osaka University in collaboration with the *Advanced Telecommunications Research International Institute*. During the past two years, I attended and participated in experiments involving computer programming, telerobotics and puppetry, which were conducted in the laboratory of Professor Hiroshi Ishiguro for the purpose of producing new Japanese plays by the playwright and director Oriza Hirata.

Fig. 1. Master Kanjuro III in the Jyoruri Theatre in Nose Town (2009)

Performance automatons have existed in Japan since the early Edo period (Hosokawa, H.Y., 1796) [1]. The tea-serving *karakuri* (*zashiki karakuri*) of the time, whose mechanism was programmed for a range of motion within the confines of a tatami mat, still serve as a point of reference for modern Japanese robotics. Nowadays, two-legged walking robots can execute a wide range of natural-looking actions. For example, the Kiyomori[1] samurai robot is programmed to perform a prayer in the course of a ceremony in Munakata Grand Shrine for the safety and progress of robot industries on the southwestern main island of Kyushu. To understand the kinship between *karakuri* and the robots of today, I met the *karakuri* Master Shobe Tamaya in his studio in Nagoya. He is the ninth generation from the unbroken lineage of *karakuri ningyō* craftsmen. The founders of *Toshiba* and *Toyota* industries are themselves the descendants of two families of *karakuri* manufacturers.

---

[1] Kiyomori (1118-1181) was the general who established the first samurai-dominated administrative government of the late Heian Period.

The difference between the toy-size object and the contemporary anthropomorphic robot is not just a question of technology and scale but, as with other kinds of stage performance, it is a matter of control and timing. After mastering the complex mechanical design of the *karakuri*, Japanese post-industrial roboticists are turning their attention to the art of bunraku manipulation to allow their artificial creations to simulate emotional expression.

However, one more meeting was necessary to complete my understanding of the birth of Japanese post-industrial robotic production. In the fall of 2009, in Tokyo, I met the roboticist Masahiro Mori, who pioneered the study of human emotional response to non-human entities. He is best known for his theory and graph of the « Uncanny Valley » (Mori, M., 1970) [2]. Mori founded the *Mukta Research Institute* in order to promote his views on Buddhism and robots. He is the one who essentially merged electro-mechanic engineering and biotechnology research in Japan (Mori, M., 1974) [3]. In 2005, Mori made a decisive addition to his initial uncanny valley graph in order to promote a new aspect of robotics broadly inspired by a spiritual and aesthetic point of view:

> Once I positioned living human beings on the highest point of the curve in the right-hand side of the uncanny valley. Recently, however, I came to think that there is something more attractive and amiable than human beings in the further right-hand side of the valley. It is the face of a Buddhist statue as the artistic expression of the human ideal. You will find such a face, for example, in Miroku Bosatsu in Kohryuji in Kyoto, or in Chuguji and in Gakkoh Bosatsu in Yakushiji in Nara. Those faces are full of elegance, beyond worries of life, and have aura of dignity. I think those are the very things that should be positioned on the highest point of the curve [4].

First, Buddhist sculptures, tea-serving *karakuri* and bunraku *ningyōs* have three types of wood-carved faces that are the artistic expression of a human ideal. Second, the faces of both, the Mirokus Buddha described by Mori and the sculpted animated figures (i.e., *karakuri* and *ningyōs*) have a zazen expression (posture of Zen Buddhist meditation practice): the eyelids are half-lowered; the eyes being neither fully open nor shut so that the character is not distracted by outside objects but, at the same time, is kept awake. As Mori explains, this attitude suggests an intense internal life and gives the impression of being present. In such an animist culture, we could speak of a state of awareness for the three artifacts above (i.e., sculptures, automatons and puppets). This state can be manifested through a smile during a moment of contemplation. It can be observed as an expression of beauty and represent artistic perfection in the immobility preceding expressive movements [5]. These observations regarding the presence effect should teach roboticists that the interaction between robot and audience can be subtle and subdued, unlike what we have grown accustomed to in science-fiction movies and literature, where robots are overly imitative of human motion and expression.

Fig. 2. Miroku in Koryuji Temple in Kyoto

After a demonstration of my electronic puppet[2] in Oxford in May 2007, realizing that a proper understanding of representation devices could not be grasped only via tests runs in laboratories, roboticist Hiroshi Ishiguro decided to develop a specific research platform merging technology and art:

> I have worked on developing robots that have relationships with human beings for nearly 10 years; during these years, we have focused on demonstration experiments to use robots in a real society, developing them in our laboratory. However, even if we let robots out into the world, people face the problem of how to effectively use them. [6]

From this observation, Professor Hiroshi Ishiguro created the *Robot Actors Project* at Osaka University to experiment with robot presence and robot control in theatre situations. Instead of focusing attention on imitation, Professor Ishiguro developed his interest in theatre representation. Since then, the challenge of being in direct contact with live audiences has enriched his understanding of communication between humans and robots and between humans via robots. Theatre has become a genuine research platform not only to explore possibilities for the entertainment industry but also to show people how to forge a relationship with robots through drama. The idea is to build a natural relationship between human beings and robots that can be achieved without teaching, to help the acceptance of robots by their human interaction

---

[2] *Practices of Anthropomorphism*, May 10-11, 2007, Maison Française d'Oxford.

partners and their integration into everyday life of human society. The image of robots in movies with which people have become familiar is far from the robots that are presently being developed in robotics laboratories. Today, the *Robot Actors Project* seeks to demystify the idea of fictional robots by familiarizing the public with the current state of robotics and experiments. The public has the last word in a play: the public sees what it wants to see, regardless of the talents of the actors, even if they are dummies or just simulacra. A stage play with robots is not just a matter of how to construct realistic androids like animatronics for movies; it is about creating dramatic situations. In a laboratory, a robot is always a robot, but on stage a robot becomes an actor: A robot can play a robot character, just as a human actor can act as a puppet. This is the case, for example, with the string puppet *Sanbasō* in the kabuki theatre and with Pinocchio (Collodi, C., 1883), when the humanlike puppet plays the puppet on Mangiafuoco's stage [7].

Fig. 3. *Geminoid F* and the actress Bryerly Long at the Aichi Triennale (2010)

Today, the *Robot Actors Project* has three plays to its credit. After two plays directed by Oriza Hirata with the preprogrammed humanoid robot *Wakamaru* (*Mitsubishi Heavy Industries*), the robot *Geminoid F* is the first android to play a character on stage controlled by the motion capture of the movements of the face of the actress Minako Inoue. The title of this Hirata play is « *Sayonara* ». It deals with end-of-life accompaniment, compassion and altruism between a robotic actress and a human actress. During the show, the telerobotics android performs at the same emotional level as a manually controlled bunraku *ningyō*, expressing feelings of love, melancholy and sorrow. Initially, 50 such *actroids* were to be produced in collaboration with *Kokoro Corporation* to be used as hostesses to provide assistance in hospitals, museums and public spaces. The sophisticated remote control of face expressions of *Geminoid F* establishes the possibility of a social relation between the android and the human actress, on the one hand, and between the android and the public, on the other. However, whereas it is easy to turn on a household appliance with a flick of a switch, how a robot can manage to press our « social button » remains difficult to explain, as the MIT roboticist Cynthia Breazeal suggested [8].

This is perhaps the real goal of the theatre experiments being conducted by Professor Ishiguro in collaboration with Hirata. Theatre has a social, cultural and artistic function. Nowadays theatre can also be an extraordinary platform to test the limits of our behaviors not only through avant-garde texts, screaming, gesticulation or nudity, for example, but also through complex anthropomorphic machines. Using robotic actors in theatres could give theatrical producers, directors and play writers the possibility of creating more dramatically acted plots due to the less restrictive physical limitations of robots in the future. Robots will maybe perform physical feats that are too repetitive or dangerous for a human actor. But the three plays of Hirata:

« *I, work* », « *In the heart of the forest* » with the humanoid robot *Wakamaru*, and

« *Sayonara* » with the android *Geminoid F* are works that rise fundamental questions about identity and otherness.

When Hirata began directing « *Sayonara* », Master Kanjūrō III accepted the invitation to meet the android *Geminoid F* at the Osaka laboratory. The knowledge about how a Master puppeteer is enabled to participate in such research can be seen as vital for the work and integration of humanoids in human society. A few months later, looking at *Geminoid F*, spectators familiar with bunraku theatre would have recognized the smile of a *Kashira* (the head of a *Ningyō*) in her archaic smile. Occasionally, spectators feel compassion for the seated android as they observe her eyelids half-lowered, her bust leaning forward slightly and her head turned up toward her interlocutor, with her hands placed gently on each thigh, similar as the elegant posture of a bunraku *ningyō*. However, what the spectator does not know is that, instead of being manipulated by three hooded puppeteers in black, *Geminoid F* is controlled by three cables running out her back: one supplies electricity, one supplies compressed air for her pneumatic actuators, and the other connects her to a computer and face tracking controls. Like in a bunraku *ningyō*, the android is operated by a human and the tension and the emotions of the play are transmitted to the audience by the movements of the android. The robot only simulates and do not have emotional expression, but it is already a fantastic platform to test relation between human and robots and between humans through robots. The technological and theatrical creation process and presentation of the results of control performance becomes accounted as data of the research, making the play to be a groundbreaking collaboration of engineering and theatre. A questionnaire form about the audience impressions is distributed after each performance. The questionnaire is about the emotional impressions give by the presence of the android on stage, the understanding, the likeness and specific sentiments linked to animistic beliefs, empathy, compassion, altruism and sadness. The questionnaire is not about the technical operation of the robot, but it seeks to define the exact place of such robot, that would allow him to fulfill his mission to accompany, to attend, to listen and also to be help full as a real presence. For further researches and performances, we are actually giving a structured account of the findings and observations. The laboratory's work fixed technically mechanical and timing parameters, while the theatre platform attempts to give some elements of measure and experiments social identification settings. This collaboration would enable an empirical analysis and help with the implementation process of human reactions into humanoid robotic agents. Back to the laboratory, after analyzing these observations, the data is processed to improve the programming of technical aspects such as postures, expressions and micromovements.

Fig. 4. The actress Minako Inoue styling *Geminoid F* at the Tokyo Festival (2010)

The next project of the Robot Actors Project will be the staging of the « Three Sisters » of the Russian playwright Anton Chekhov (Chekhov, A., 1900). Hirata is often referred to as Japanese Chekhov, and his « Colloquial Theatre » is close to Chekhov's repertoire. In the dialogues of his plays, ordinary emotional expressions run subtly beneath the surface. Hirata explains that humans hardly ever speak in explicit terms among each other about their deepest feelings and that the great tragic climactic emotional moments are often happening outside trivial conversations. « Chekhov often expressed his thought not in speeches », wrote Stanislavski, « but in pauses or between the lines or in replies consisting of a single word... the characters often feel and think things not expressed in the lines they speak » (Reynolds, E., 1987) [9]. The birth of a new approach of acting, which was possible through the unique collaboration of Chekhov and Stanislavski, is visible in the notes written by the director during the creation of « Three Sisters » and « The Cherry Orchard » (Constantin Stanislavski, 1901-1904) [10].

« Three Sisters » is a naturalistic play about the decay of the privileged class in Russia and the search for meaning in the modern world. It describes the lives and aspirations of the Prozorov family, the three sisters (Olga, Masha, and Irina) and their brother Andrei. They are a family dissatisfied and frustrated with their present existence [11]. In this project, the youngest sister Irina is played by *Geminoid F*. During the drama, it is possible to study the telerobotic adjustments of synchronization in different situations and also the behavioural dynamics between an android and a group of actors. The identification of the public with the actors is experimentally expanded to the robot actress.

Identification with the emotional behaviors of the characters can happen on different levels: an expression of the distorted sense of reality or the dissatisfaction and the frustration with the existence. Expectation and disappointment, passivity, search for meaning in the modern world, looking for aspirations, happiness and representations of a perfect life are some of our existential issues and maybe will be also issues for robots in the future. The identification transforms subtly from the potential interactivity of a mechanical mirror to synchronized social interactions.

In the situation of an observer of machines struggling with their mechanisms, I have passed from the comment of a hypothetical dissatisfaction of the machines to the observation of the consequent gestures, which might manifest impatience. In the play, the character of Irina embodies successively expectation and impatience. Speaking of patience and dissatisfaction about robots is probably a partly unreal idea because they cannot have hope or ego, but the expression of the idea of a metamorphic moment in their existences seems definitively possible. An algorithm from regulating patience in the brain seems to be might even improve robotics in the future (Kenji Doya, 2011)[12].

Instead of only analyzing the distortion between human likeness and familiarity as Mori's work, this study is based on the relation of humans with robots and intends to distinguish different degrees of synchronization of social behaviors and possible degrees of identification with emotional behaviors of the robots. Familiarity becomes a matter of identification and likeness a matter of social integration by synchronization of social behaviors. Theatre clearly permits this new robotic embodiment to facilitate competent participation of robots in emotional and empathic dynamics with human beings. Empathic relationships do not need to be an authentic imitation, affectively competent or positive to contribute to the affective development and interactive dynamic.

Social regulation is frequently acting. Part of reality is the result of simulations and dramaturgy, idealization of gestures, feints and mystification [13]. Today, teleoperation and programming are testing this with the staging of artificial presence and programmed movement's effects [14]. Through theatre as a platform for research, the postures, the signs of presence effects, the sense of the disorder and detachment in Irina, permits the study of the presence effect via the application of micromovements and the terms of different triggers of micromovement's control. Other studies developed in this theatre platform are proxemic, timing of actions and the confirmation operations of repair and realignment in body control. The purpose is to help the construction of characters or roles, to do more staging and less programming to plan behaviors in anthropomorphic robots for the future, another very interesting and promising step towards an in depth understanding of the affective aspects of robots.

In modern Japan, puppetry manipulation, puppets and robots as actors are not metaphors for life or reciprocal metaphors. Magic is the art of making the work disappear with different techniques. In the bunraku theatre, the state of awareness in animated forms depends on traditional practices of control, including gravity and mechanical means. For robots this illusion depends additionally on an artificial body moved by electricity.

References

1. Hosokawa, H.Y.: Karakuri Zui (Illustrated Clever Machines), Tokyo (1796)
2. Mori, M.: The Uncanny Valley (Bukimi no tani), K. F. MacDorman & T. Minato, Trans. Energy 7(4), 33–35 (1970)
3. Mori, M.: The Buddha in the Robot: a Robot Engineer's Thoughts on Science and Religion. Kosei publishing, Tokyo (1974)
4. Mori, M.: The International Conference on Humanoid Robots Humanoids (IEEE-RAS). In: Tsukuba International Congress Center (2005)
5. Paré, Z., Minato, C., Grimaud, E.: Le Bouddha dans le robot, Rencontre avec Masahiro Mori, Gradhiva, Revue d'anthropologie et d'histoire des arts, numéro 15, Robots étrangement humains, Musée du Quai Branly, Paris, pp. 142–161 (2012)
6. Ishiguro, H.: http://ocw.osaka-u.ac.jp/engineering/robot-actors-project/syllabus
7. Collodi, C.: Les aventures de Pinocchio. Actes Sud, Evreux (1995)
8. Breazeal, C.: Designing sociable robots. MIT Press, Cambridge (2004)
9. Reynolds, E.: Stanislavski's Legacy. Theatre Arts Books, Chicago (1987)
10. Stanislavski, C.: Cahiers de régie sur la Cerisaie et les Trois soeurs. Aux forges de Vulcain/Sciences, Paris (2011)
11. Tchekhov, A.: Les trois soeurs. Livre de poche, Paris (1991)
12. Miyazaki, K.W., Miyazaki, K., Doya, K.: Activation of the central serotonergic system in response to delayed but not omitted rewards. European Journal of Neuroscience 33, 153–160 (2011), doi:10.1111/j.1460-9568.2010.07480.x
13. Goffmann, E.: La mise en scène de la vie quotidienne, 2. Les relations en public, Éditions de minuit, Paris (1973)
14. Grimaud, E., Paré, Z.: Le jour où les robots mangeront des pommes, Petra, Paris (2011)

Talking-Ally: Intended Persuasiveness
by Utilizing Hearership and Addressivity

Naoki Ohshima, Yusuke Ohyama, Yuki Odahara,
P. Ravindra S. De Silva, and Michio Okada

Interactions and Communication Design Lab, Toyohashi University of Technology
Toyohashi 441-8580, Japan
{ohshima,ohyama,odahara}@icd.cs.tut.ac.jp, {ravi,okada}@tut.jp
http://www.icd.cs.tut.ac.jp/en/profile.html

Abstract. We imagine that the future direction of persuasive robotics necessitates the exploration of how it shapes a person's attitudes by channeling their behaviors in dynamic interactions. Moreover, it might be important to explore how robot and human behaviors (cues) and beliefs mutually influence each other in different attributes of communication. The concept of the hearership and addressivity are utilized for Talking-Ally to liking the user's state in-order to communicate persuasively in the context of interactively disseminating the exciting news from the web. Our approach coordinates the addressee's eye-gaze behaviors (state of hearership) to produce/adapt utterance generation (addressivity) toward communication (synchronized with bodily interactions), which is perceived as being persuasive by the addressees.

Keywords: Mutually influences, hearership, addressivity.

1 Introduction

Research in social psychology has suggested that both the degree of the intended persuasiveness and the perceived persuasiveness of communication are correlated with proxemic (distance, eye contact, etc) postural, facial movement, and vocal interactions [10]. We have synthesized some of the findings from social physiology [10] and computer science literacy [3] to identify the important features necessary to develop persuasive robots. A machine (robot) needs to reduce the communication barriers to interact with natural social norms, to be capable of observational learning, and to demonstrate the social experience in dynamic interactions. It needs to be provided with sufficient information in different contexts to be allowed to make proper decisions, and to shape a person's attitudes by channeling behaviors in certain contexts.

In conjunction with this trend, the recent HRI community has been giving attention to developing persuasive robots that address the reduction of communication barriers by embodying natural social cues (nonverbal) and enhancing the capabilities of social intelligence [7]. There is a great concern to adhere to important guidelines in the designing of persuasive robots [14][13]. A recent study in

S.S. Ge et al. (Eds.): ICSR 2012, LNAI 7621, pp. 317–326, 2012.
© Springer-Verlag Berlin Heidelberg 2012

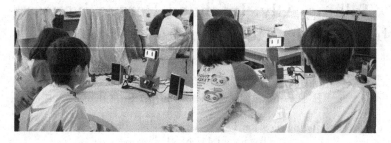

Fig. 1. Children interacting with Talking-Ally

[2] reports on an experiment in which they explored how a robot persuades users by vocal and bodily interactions in the context of robotic suggestions within a Desert Survival Task. The study mainly focused on exploring the effectiveness of the above channels to measure the degree of the persuasiveness of robot.

We imagine that the future direction of persuasive robotics necessitates an exploration into how it shapes a person's attitudes by channeling their behaviors in dynamic interactions. However, it might be important to explore how robot and human behaviors (cues) and beliefs mutually influence each other in different attributes of communication in dynamic interactions, because persuasion is a dynamic interaction that influences humans to change attitudes by channeling their behaviors in certain patterns. Therefore, in this study we developed Talking-Ally, which is capable of producing utterances (toward addressivity) by utilizing the state of the hearer's resources (eye-gaze information) to persuade the user (toward the hearership) through dynamic interactions. Talking-Ally simply tracks the user's eye gaze behaviors in order to produce/adjust its utterance to be influential by enhancing the engagement of the conversation as a persuasive robot. We mainly explored how the utterance generation mechanism enhances the persuasive power of the robot's communication and the effectiveness of the communication (naturalism of robot's communication) in dynamic interactions.

2   Intended Persuasiveness by Talking-Ally

Researchers in human communication describe the terms "nonverbal immediacy" and "nonverbal behaviors" as either a liking, a positive evaluation of others, or a positive affect toward others that is intimately correlated with their persuasive ability and attractiveness during interactions [9]. Non-verbal communication (bodily interactions) is mostly a valuable channel to transfer a speaker's message in an effective way toward a higher degree of persuasion. To maintain eye contact is an important channel to obtain audience feedback which is mainly concern with how the audience complies with the speaker's message, and also indicates the persuasiveness of the speaker's communication. Therefore, a few existing studies in persuasive robotics have explored and reported the advantage of robot's bodily interaction and gaze behaviors in the persuasiveness of robot communication [14][2]. Adapting to the above, our Talking-Ally was embodied

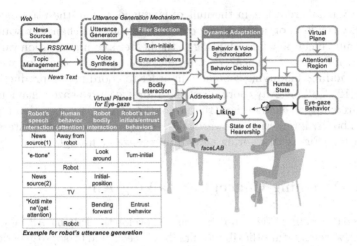

The following table is part of the figure:

Robot's speech interaction	Human behavior (attention)	Robot bodily interaction	Robot's turn-initials/entrust behaviors
News source(1)	Away from robot	-	-
"e-ttone"		Look around	Turn-initial
-	Robot	-	-
News source(2)		Initial-position	-
-	TV	-	-
"Kotti mite ne"(get attention)		Bending forward	Entrust behavior
-	Robot	-	-

Example for robot's utterance generation

Fig. 2. The overview of the Talking-Ally and example of the utterance generation

with bodily interaction and attention coordination (based on the addressee's gaze behaviors), which we thought might be important factors to increase the persuasiveness of a robot's communication.

Another important concern in nonverbal attitude-communication, which is directed toward the intended persuasiveness of the communicator and the perceived persuasiveness of the message by the addressee, has a series of communication chains (in dynamic interactions) to influence two persons toward persuading one's partner [4]. Therefore, our main concern was to explore how robot and human behaviors (cues) mutually influence each other in different attributes of communication in dynamic interactions by implementing the utterance generation mechanism (considering the addressivity and hearership) toward intent to communicate persuasively.

Hearership. The speaker refers to the hearer's behavioral information (nonverbal and vocal) to structure (organize) his/her utterance, and is also capable of dynamically aligning the structure of the utterances according to the resources (nonverbal and verbal) of the behavioral variation [11]. Within a conversation in the interactions between hearer and speaker, the hearer is reacting to a speaker through nonverbal channels (e.g., attention coordinate, eye-gaze following etc) or a vocal response (e.g., back channel) toward prompting the interactions, which is defined as hearership in the conversation [5]. The concept of hearership is a resource (referring eye-gaze behaviors) for Talking-Ally to shape its utterance generation by considering the state of the hearership in dynamic interactions (Figure 2).

Addressivity. Bakthin [1] is suggested on the concept of addressivity, which can be defined as that through individual words can be directed toward someone, and then become completed utterances consisting "of one word or one sentence, and addressivity is inherent not in the unit of language, but in the utterance." The addressivity is a kind of never-ending communication that changes toward shaping the communication while adapting to the hearer's communication variations. The hearer influences the speaker's utterance generation mechanism, which is a prompt to adding/modifying sentences in order to coordinate a productive conversation [12]. Talking-Ally coordinates the addressee's eye-gaze behaviors (state of the hearership) to change the structure of the utterance generation (synchronized with bodily interactions) toward addressivity in the context of interactively disseminating (Figure 2) exciting news from the web (through RSS).

3   The Designing Concept of Talking-Ally

We followed the minimal-designing concept to develop the Talking-Ally as depicted in Figure 2, which has three flexible points (head, neck, and torso) to generate bodily interactions with the user. All of its external appearance (body) is made with artificial wood, and its eyes and head are designed on the iPod visualizer. The face-lab is located on the table to track the user's eye gaze-behaviors in real-time. Talking-Ally has a voice synthesizer to generate an interactive conversation (in Japanese) by obtaining a news source (through RSS) in real-time while synchronizing it's bodily interaction (nodding, leaning it's body to the left and right, and eye-gaze is able to follow and look around the environment) through servo-motors. A sample of the conversation is presented in the left-side of Figure 2.

The Utterance Generation. Talking-Ally is interactively disseminating the news from the web (through RSS) to the participant and simultaneously some exciting (sport-based) TV-program is broadcasted behind the robot to obtain attention variation from the addressees (participants). The manipulation of attention variation is utilized to obtain a variety of utterance generation patterns which can evaluate the performance of Talking-Ally. We employed a simple method to track the addressee's attention-region which is a primal reference to generate/adjust the robot's speech interactions. The robot decides the addressee's attention-region according the frequency scores of the eye-gaze behaviors in each region by considering them at every 60 frames as a segmentation point (states of the hearership). Parallel to the robot, the virtual-plane is constructed as shown in Figure 2. The virtual plane is divided into six regions: two regions for Talking-Ally, two regions for room-environment (away from robot), and two regions for TV (here, the TV broadcasts some exciting sports news). The robot synchronizes the position of the eye-gaze coordinate with virtual-plane to determine the attention-region of the user.

Based on the addressee's attention-region, Talking-Ally decides the relevant news sources, turn-initial, and entrust behaviors to generate its utterances. Table 1 lists the relevant robot's behaviors (non-verbal and utterance) in each region and execute randomly (region-wise) for speech interaction while synchronizing the bodily-interaction (process of the addressivity). Any change (variation) of the addressee's behaviors has the influence of changing its bodily interactions, attention-coordination, and structure of utterance in the dynamic adaptation unit. The whole process continually concatenates toward getting-back/keeping the addressee's attention (influences) by changing the structure of utterances (generation mechanism) to enhance the degree of communicative persuasion of Talking-Ally.

This study mainly focuses on exploring the performance of an utterance generation mechanism in order to enhance the persuasive power of the robot's communication and the effectiveness of the communication (naturalism of robot's communication) while Talking-Ally interactively disseminates exciting news from the web. Our study is mainly concerned with the dynamic interactive history of the robot (utterance generation/adaptation and non-verbal communication) and addressee (attention behaviors/adaptation through eye gaze behaviors) to evaluate the above performance.

4   Experimental Protocol

A total of 14 participants (aged between 20 and 24 years) were involved in the experiment in four separate sessions in which the conditions of the robot (interactions) were changed as follows: A-(attention-coordination $(-)$, turn-initial and entrust behavior $(-)$), B-(attention-coordination $(-)$, turn-initial and entrust behavior $(+,$ random)), C-(attention-coordination $(+)$, turn-initial and entrust behavior $(+,$ random)), and D-(attention-coordination $(+)$, turn-initial and entrust behavior $(+)$). The $(-)$ indicates that robot did not considered these channels in the condition and the $(+)$ sign indicates that the robot considered these channels in the interactions. All participants participated in four sessions (A, B, C, and D), and each of the sessions took approximately three minutes to complete. At the end of each session, the participants had to answer questioners using a rating scale of $(1-5)$.

Table 1. When the robot interactively disseminates the news from the web, the addressee might attend to the one of the attention regions (AG1, AG2, AG3, AG4, AG5, and AG6); at that particular time the robot modifies its utterance by considering the eleven types of turn-initials (TI) or six types of entrust-behaviors (EB) while synchronizing its six kinds of bodily interactions (BHV)

Human behaviors (Attention regions)	Robot's bodily interaction	Resources for utterance generation	
		Turn-initials (indirect request)	Entrust behaviors (direct request)
AG1, AG2 (Space of Talking-Ally)	BHV1(Initial-position), BHV3(Nodding)	TI1:"a-a", TI2:"ano-", TI3:"anone", TI4:"anosa", TI5:"e-tto", TI6:"e-ttone", TI7:"etto", TI8:"etto-", TI9:"ne-ne", TI10:"ntto", TI11:"nttone"	–
AG3, AG4 (Looking around the environment)	BHV4(Trun left-side), BHV5(Trun right-side), BHV6(Look around)	TI1:"a-a", TI2:"ano-", TI3:"anone", TI4:"anosa", TI5:"e-tto", TI6:"e-ttone", TI7:"etto", TI8:"etto-", TI9:"ne-ne", TI10:"ntto", TI11:"nttone"	–
AG5, AG6 (Attention to the TV)	BHV2(Bending forward), BHV3(Nodding)	–	EB1:"kite ne"—get attention, EB2:"kite yo"—get attention, EB3:"kite yone"—get attention, EB4:"kotti mite ne"—get gaze-attention, EB5:"kotti mite yo"—get gaze-attention, EB6:"kotti mite yone"—get gaze-attention

5 Directions of the Analysis

We gathered objective measurements in two ways: (1) dynamic interactive history of robot and addressees, and (2) a questionnaire-based subjective evaluation. We collected the data of the attention region of the addressees, the response time of the human and robot, the robot's behaviors (bodily interactions), relevant turn-initials, and entrust-behaviors in every interaction. Table 2 depicts the contents of the questionnaire to obtain a subjective evaluation of the robot's communication. The direction of the analysis was as follows: (1) explore persuasive power of robot communication (mechanism of utterance generation), and (2) subjective evaluation of the robot's communication.

Persuasive Power of the Communication. We might consider the experimental conditions of B and D because within condition B, the robot did not trace the addressee's attention (tracking the eye-gaze behaviors) but randomly executed the utterance generation (mixing with turn-initial and entrust-behaviors). The condition did plainly not consider the state of the hearership. But in condition D, the robot traced the addressee's attention (state of the hearership) to generate the utterances (mixing with turn-initial or entrust-behaviors) while synchronizing its bodily interaction (whole process of addressivity). By comparing B and D, we can extract the persuasiveness power of the robot when integrating both hearership and addressivity.

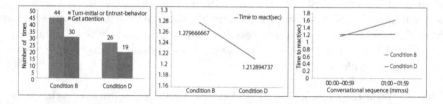

Fig. 3. The figure shows the addressees' attention-behaviors (red-color) when the robot utilized the turn-initial or entrust-behaviors (blue-color) during the interactive condition of B and D (left-side figure). One of addressee's responses (attention) is depicted within the selected segment for condition B and condition D. The center figure shows the average responsive time within the segment and responsive time within the selected segment according to the time interval on the right-side of the figure.

We have gathered the turn-initials or entrust-behavior of Talking-Ally and relevant addressee's attention behaviors during the interactions for all of the participants (number of times) for both conditions (Figure 3(left-side)). The robot used a turn-initial or entrust behavior which was quite higher than the number of times in condition B, and also proportionally increased the obtaining of the attention of the addressees with a percentage of 68%; but in condition D, the usage of filler or entrust-behavior was reduced and also started to increase the acquisition of attention of addressees with 73%.

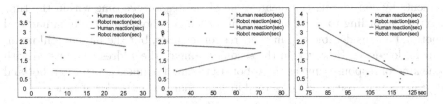

Fig. 4. The figure shows the responsive time for one of addressees and robot which influenced each other at the dynamic interaction in robot condition D. We disunited three segments to depict the human-robot influence based on the responsive time.

The response time of the addressee was another worthwhile parameter to use in evaluating the persuasive power of the robot's communication, because a lower responsive-time significantly indicated the persuasiveness of the robot's communication – both the clearness of the communication and the degree of influence of the communication, etc. [8]. Figure 3(center and right-side) shows one of addressee's response (attention) times according to the robot's turn-initial or entrust-behaviors in the middle of the interaction (one of segmentations) that might be a perfect manifestation in comparing conditions B and D. The center figure shows the mean value of the responsive time within the selected segment. This indicates that the responsive time in D was lower than that of condition B, indicating that when we integrate hearership and addressivity, the addressee's response time begins to decrease. The right-side of Figure 3 shows an interesting pattern of responsive time. At some point in the segment, the addressee's response (attention) time in condition B suddenly increases, but the attention response time in interactive condition of D starts to decrease. A similar type of interactive pattern (based on responsive time) appeared for the other participants. Another important aspect of the persuasive robotic is to explore how the robot and human mutually influence (behavior-wise) each other in dynamic interactions. We considered the responsive time for both the robot and addressee, which is one of the significant factors in evaluating the persuasive power of each of the communications. We selected condition D to evaluate the above influence, because within condition D the robot utilized the concept of hearership and addressivity. Also, the results indicated a significant interactive condition to persuade the participant in our pervious analysis. In this analysis we extracted the addressees' response time (blue-line in Figure 3) when the robot executed turn-initial or entrust-behaviors, as well as the robot's response time when the addressees looked away from the robot (red-line in Figure 3). It might be interesting to examine their influential behaviors (variation) within the segmentation of the dynamic interactions as depicted in Figure 3.

We utilized a linear interpolation to construct a straight line which considered the response time of the human (blue-line) and the robot (red-line) within the conversational time for one of the addressees (Figure 4). The approach of linear interpolation was useful in constructing a straight line between two known co-ordinate points by calculating the interpolated values [6]. The analysis created three segmentations, and a linear interpolation constructed the liner-line for each of the segments by considering the mean value of the responsive time within the time interval. According to the figure, the first segment showed that the human and robot had a considerable gap in their response times, but the human still maintained a low-level. However, in the second segment, the addressee adjusted with same kind of response time as the robot. In the final segment, both the robot and addressee's response times converged in same manner with a lower time.

Effectiveness of the Communication. This section focuses on exploring the subjective evaluations of the questionnaire which was designed to evaluate the effectiveness of the robot's communication: clearness of the utterance, neutrality of the speech, sense of autonomy for behavior, and utterance generation, etc. The analysis considered pair-wised (interactive condition of the robot) comparisons of each of the questions through a paired t-test by considering the subjective scores of each question. Table 2 shows the available significant differences of the pairs for each of the questions. In general, the (A,B) and (A, D) combinations revealed a significant difference, but the pair-wise differences of (A,D) had a higher rating score difference $(A < D)$ than the combination of (A,B).

6   Discussion

The results shown in Figure 3(left-side) suggest that the robot executed considerable turn-initial or entrust-behaviors within condition B in comparison to condition D. However, in condition D, the addressees' attention (percentage-wise) was obtained more so than in condition B, which is when the robot utilized attention coordination (hearership) and addressivity. The figures imagine that addressees' attention percentage started to increase and reduced the usage of the turn-initial or entrust behaviors of the robot in condition D. This indicates that the robot used those behaviors in suitable positions (preferring the addressees' attention) for the interactions. But it might have been due to a reduction in the percentage of the addressees' attention when they realized the robot's utterance generation was random without use of his/her behaviors or resources in the interaction. The above statement is directly shown in Figure 3(center and right-side). In conjunction with the above conclusion, the results in Figure 3(right-side) indicate that when the addressees realized the robot was randomly generating its utterances in condition B, their responsive time was higher (Figure 3), since it might have started to decrease the believability of the robot's communication. Similar kinds of patterns appeared for the other participants in the experiment.

Interesting results were obtained when exploring how the addressee and robot influenced each other in dynamic interactions (Figure 4). The initial segment (left-side of the figure) shows that the response time of the robot and addressees had a considerable gap. The gap indicates a lower degree of persuasiveness power of the robot's communication during the initial stage. However, in the second segment (center of Figure 4), the addressee adapts to the robot's response time. Within the final segment, both the robot and addressee response time converged to be low. This result might have directly influenced the chain in the

Table 2. After the end of the every session (A, B, C, and D), the participants had to answer the following questions. A pair-wise comparison (using paired T-tests) was employed to explore the significant differences (based on rating scores) in each question.

Question	Contains	Results		
		Combination	t-value	p-value
Q1	I wanted to listen to the robot's speech more.	(A,B)	$t(13) = 2.2804$	*p = 0.04 < 0.05
Q2	Robot recognized you as a hearer.	(A,B)	$t(13) = 2.3470$	*p = 0.035 < 0.05
		(A,D)	$t(13) = 2.7378$	*p = 0.017 < 0.05
Q3	I felt the life-likeness to the robot.	(A,B)	$t(13) = 2.9245$	*p = 0.012 < 0.05
		(A,D)	$t(13) = 5.0902$	**p = 0.0002 < 0.01
Q4	I felt a kind of intention to convey speech from the robot's utterances.	(A,B)	$t(13) = 4.8374$	**p = 0.0003 < 0.01
		(A,C)	$t(13) = 2.2234$	*p = 0.045 < 0.05
		(A,D)	$t(13) = 3.8894$	**p = 0.002 < 0.01
Q5	I felt robot was speaking and moving autonomy.	(A,B)	$t(13) = 2.2234$	*p = 0.045 < 0.05
		(A,D)	$t(13) = 2.6874$	*p = 0.019 < 0.05

dynamic interaction toward persuading each other. Specifically, it indicates the persuasiveness power of the robot's communication which was due to the performance of the utterance generation mechanism (when combined with the result in section 5.1).

The results of the questionnaire-based subjective evaluation shows (Table 2) that when we intergraded hearership (state of the attention) and addressivity, the participants sensed the robot recognized the participants as the hearer (life-likeness of robot), and the robot was capable of utterance generation and moving autonomously, etc., in comparison to the other interactive conditions. These behaviors were important in persuading the participants with a higher degree of influence or interaction in order to change their behaviors (attention of the addressees). In addition, it was found that the utterance generation mechanism was more important but needs to utilize the attention coordination of the addressee (state of the hearership) to persuade the participants when assessing the results of the pair-wise comparison in Table 2.

7 Conclusion

The section on the persuasive power of the communication showed that the resource of the hearer (state of the hearership by tracing the addressee attention) was significant in generating/adjusting to the structure of the utterance generation mechanism (toward addressivity) to persuade the addressees. Additionally, the analysis of dynamic interaction showed that both the human and robot influenced each other's behaviors: the robot influenced the addressees' attention, and the humans influenced the robot in changing its utterance generation mechanism. The results of the subjective rating indicated that the robot recognized the participants as the hearer (life-likeness of robot), and the robot was capable of utterance generation and moving autonomously, which was vital in enhancing the persuasiveness of the robot's communication.

Acknowledgement. This research has been supported by both Grant-in-Aid for scientific research of KIBAN-B (21300083) and Grant-in-Aid for scientific research for HOUGA (24650053) from the Japan Society for the Promotion of Science (JSPS).

References

1. Bakhtin, M.: The problem of speech genres, pp. 60–102. University of Texas Press, Austin (1986)
2. Chidambaram, V., Chiang, Y.-H., Mutlu, B.: Designing persuasive robots: how robots might persuade people using vocal and nonverbal cues. In: HRI, pp. 293–300 (2012)
3. Fogg, B.: Persuasive computers: perspectives and research directions. In: Proceedings of the SIGCHI Conference on Human Factors in Computing Systems, CHI 1998, pp. 225–232 (1998)
4. Gibbs, R.W.: Embodiment and Cognitive Science. Cambridge University Press (2005)
5. Goodwin, C.: Embodied hearers and speakers constructing talk and action in interaction, vol. 16(1), pp. 51–64. Wadsworth, Belmont (2009)
6. Kuijlaars, A.B.J.: Book review: "a course in approximation theory" by ward cheney and will light. Journal of Approximation Theory 112(2), 318 (2001)
7. Looije, R., Neerincx, M.A., Cnossen, F.: Persuasive robotic assistant for health self-management of older adults: Design and evaluation of social behaviors. International Journal of Human-Computer Studies 68(6), 386–397 (2010)
8. Lutz, R., Swasy, J.L.: Integrating Cognitive Structure And Cognitive Response Approaches To Monitoring Communications Effects. Association for Consumer Research (1977)
9. Mccroskey, J.C., Sallinen, A., Fayer, J.M., Richmond, V.P., Barraclough, R.A.: Nonverbal immediacy and cognitive learning: A cross-cultural investigation. Communication Education 45(3), 200–211 (1996)
10. Mehrabian, A., Williams, M.: Nonverbal concomitants of perceived and intended persuasiveness. Journal of Personality and Social Psychology 13(1), 37–58 (1969)
11. Okada, M.: Why doesn't the computer speak with hesitation. Kyoritsu Shuppan, Tokyo (1995)
12. Okada, M., Kurihara, S., Nakatsu, R.: Incremental elaboration in generating and interpreting spontaneous speech. In: Proc. of 3rd International Conference on Spoken Language Processing, pp. 103–106 (1994)
13. Roubroeks, M.A.J., Ham, J., Midden, C.J.H.: When artificial social agents try to persuade people: The role of social agency on the occurrence of psychological reactance. I. J. Social Robotics 3(2), 155–165 (2011)
14. Siegel, M., Breazeal, C., Norton, M.I.: Persuasive robotics: The influence of robot gender on human behavior. In: IROS, pp. 2563–2568 (2009)

Does Observing Artificial Robotic Systems Influence Human Perceptual Processing in the Same Way as Observing Humans?

Agnieszka Wykowska[1], Ryad Chellali[2],
Md. Mamun Al-Amin[1], and Hermann J. Müller[1],

[1] General and Experimental Psychology Unit, Dept. of Psychology,
Ludwig-Maximilians-Universität, Leopoldstr. 13, 80802 Munich, Germany
[2] Instituto Italiano di Tecnologia-PAVIS, Via Morego, 30,
16165 Genova, Italy
agnieszka.wykowska@psy.lmu.de, ryad.chellali@iit.it,
bd_pharmacy@yahoo.com, hmueller@psy.lmu.de

Abstract. Humanoid robots are designed and shaped to have physical bodies resembling humans. The anthropomorphic shape is aiming at facilitating interactions between humans and robots with the ultimate goal of making robots acceptable social partners. This attempt is not very new to roboticists and there is an increasing body of research showing the importance of robots' appearance in HRI; the Uncanny Valley proposed in the 70's [1] is however still an open problem. Our aim in this contribution is to examine how human perceptual mechanisms involved in action observation are influenced by the external shape of observed robots. Our present results show that observing robotic/cartoon hands performing grasping/pointing movements elicits similar perceptual mechanisms as observing other humans. Hence, it seems that observing actions of artificial systems can induce similar perceptual effects as observing actions of humans.

Keywords: Attentional selection, Perceptual processing, Human-Robot Interaction.

1 Introduction

The field of humanoid robotics aims at designing artificial agents that will help people in their daily lives and as such, these robots *should* be part of humans' social sphere [20]. This assumption is strong and its realization depends on whether or not humans will consider humanoids as socially accepted partners or simple machines. If robots are to be perceived as machines or simple automata, it is enough to consider – for robotic designs - only the functions they support and the ways to access these functions. However, for a robot to be perceived as a social partner with which natural interactions are possible, mechanisms underlying social perception in the human mind need also to be taken into account.

S.S. Ge et al. (Eds.): ICSR 2012, LNAI 7621, pp. 327–337, 2012.

Reproducing the human appearance and/or behaviors is the very common argument used by humanoid robotics researchers in designing humanoid robots. It is believed that anthropomorphic shapes should enable sensory-motor mappings and thus facilitate social interactions. However, this argument is far from finding strong justifications and measurable benefits and the quest is still an open problem.

The robot's shape is assumed to be one of the critical characteristics/limit the impressions/perception one can have about the agent. The *uncanny valley hypothesis* has been proposed in the 70's [1] and addressed from different angles. To date, many contradicting results have been found, preventing from drawing clear and useful conclusions about the Mori's intuition and more practically, no design guidelines have been derived.

For example [21] has suggested an "uncanny cliff" instead of an "uncanny valley", and Mac Dorman and colleagues [22] reported data suggesting that there are many factors which can influence perception of a robot as strange or eerie, apart from the *human-likeness* dimension (see also [23] for a similar account).

In our work, the core idea we used relies on the well-established paradigm about action-perception coupling in humans when observing other humans acting. We aimed at investigating two issues: 1) the effects of observing artificial agents on human perceptual system; 2) determining whether the shape of the used artificial agent (a humanoid robot or a cartoon arm) influences the human perceptual system.

Action and Perception Domains – Are They Distinct?

Traditional approaches viewed human cognitive system processing information in a unidirectional, stage-like manner [2]. It has been postulated that humans first process perceptual information, and then selected information is transmitted to memory and action planning sub-systems, to be eventually used for action execution. More recent theoretical frameworks, however, have stressed the idea that action and perception are more directly coupled to the extent that they share a common representational code [3,4]. If action and perception are so tightly coupled, then such coupling should allow bidirectional mutual influences. This would imply that information processing stream does not flow from perception to action planning and execution, but action planning influences already the earliest (perceptual) processes to the same extent as perception influences action planning [5]. In [6], participants were asked to prepare a grasping or pointing movement while simultaneously performing a visual search task for action-congruent or incongruent target dimensions. Performance was found to be better for the congruent action-perceptual target pairs, relative to the incongruent pairs. The observed *congruency effects* were due to the way the brain represented planned actions and perceived stimuli, and not due to any perceptual or motoric overlap between the two tasks [7].

Neuronal Mechanisms of the Action-Perception Links

The so-far described empirical evidence was based on behavioural studies with human participants. The idea of a close coupling between action and perception has been supported also with a growing body of evidence collected with the use of neuroimaging techniques. For example, Schubotz and von Crammon [8] carried out a study in which participants observed sequences of differently sized disks or listened to sounds of various pitches. The results showed activation of premotor areas usually involved in hand movements when sequences of visually presented disks were observed; analogously, premotor areas involved in articulation were activated when participants judge the auditory stimuli.

More specifically, the so-called *mirror neurons* [9] are perhaps the most straightforward evidence for tight coupling between perception and action. Indeed, these neurons are active not only when one is planning a particular movement type but also when one only observes this type of movement being performed by others. Mirror neurons have been claimed to have the function of action understanding and imitation learning [10]. The complex functionality of the mirror neuron system might also include the foundations for social [11] and emotional [12] behaviors. Then the key question arises: do mirror neurons are also activated when actions of artificial systems are observed?

Aim of the Present Study

In the context of social robotics enterprise, it seems intuitive that the more human-like appearance a robot has (e.g., android robots), the closer and easier the human-robot interaction should be. Therefore, it is crucial to examine the human cognitive mechanisms underlying social interactions with human-like robots. One of such mechanisms is the action-perception coupling during action observation. In other words, the important question to be addressed is: does observing a humanoid robot performing a certain action evoke in humans similar perceptual mechanisms that would be evoked if the human observers watched other members of their species performing that action?

In the present study we addressed this question using an experimental paradigm developed by Wykowska and colleagues [6], which elicits the so-called action-perception *congruency effects*. In this paradigm, participants are typically asked to perform a perceptual task (detect a target item defined by a particular feature among other items that differ from the target with respect to that feature – a so-called visual search task) and a movement task (grasping or pointing to an object) that is signaled by a picture depicting a grasping or a pointing arm. Importantly, the target (together with the other items of the visual search task) is presented on a computer screen, while the movement is to be performed on objects that are placed below the computer screen. Moreover, the movement task is supposed to be prepared before the visual search task, but executed only after the visual search task is completed. With this paradigm typically two congruency pairs are created: 1) the target defining feature dimension of size with grasping; and 2) the target-defining dimension of luminance with pointing. It is assumed that size is a grasping-congruent feature dimension (one needs to specify the size of the to-be grasped objects, in order to adjust grip aperture) and luminance is a pointing-congruent feature dimension (luminance targets enable efficient localization of an object with a pointing-movement response). Therefore, if detection of size-defined targets in a visual search task is facilitated for the grasping condition relative to pointing; and luminance targets are detected better in the pointing condition relative to grasping, then one can conclude that congruency effects are observed.

For the present paradigm, we designed an experiment in which the pictures of human hands grasping or pointing [6,7] are substituted by cartoon hands and robot hands. If robots are capable of inducing action-perception congruency effects, those effects should be observed independent of the type of cue signaling the movement.

2   Methods

2.1   Participants

Twenty healthy volunteers (7 women; age range: 18-30 years; mean age = 24.25) took part in the experiment. Two participants were left-handed but they were standardly using the computer mouse in the same way as right-handers. The participants were naïve with respect to the purposes of this experiment. All participants had normal or corrected to normal vision and have provided informed consent regarding participation in the experiment.

2.2   The Paradigm

Participants were required to perform two types of visual search tasks (search for luminance or size targets) and two types of movement tasks (grasping or pointing an indicated cup placed below the computer screen). Target present trials are shown in the Figure 1. In luminance detection task, participants searched for one lighter circle among other circles (Figure 1A). In size detection task, participants searched for one large size circle among other same size circles (Figure 1B).

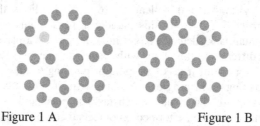

Figure 1 A   Figure 1 B

Fig. 1. The display of the visual search task with luminance target (1A) and size target (1B)

In the movement task, participants first observed a cue signaling the type of movement (grasping or pointing). The cue consisted in either a cartoon of a human hand (Figure 2A, B) or a robot hand (Figure 3A, B). Only after participants completed the visual search task, were they allowed to execute the prepared grasping or pointing movement. With such a paradigm, we created two action-perception congruent pairs: i) size targets with grasping movement; and ii) luminance targets with pointing movement (according to previous studies [6,7], size is relevant for grasping and luminance is coupled with pointing). *Congruency effects* would therefore consist in faster reaction times (RTs) in the visual search task for size targets when the grasping movement is prepared, relative to the pointing movement; and faster RTs for luminance targets when the pointing movement is prepared, as compared to grasping.

2.3   Stimuli and Apparatus

Stimuli were presented on 19' CRT screen, with a 100 Hz refresh rate placed at a distance of 100 cm from an observer. Responses were registered with a Logitech optical mouse. The whole experiment was programmed in E-Prime® (Psychology Software Tools, Inc.) run on an Intel® Core™ 2 CPU 6700 @ 2.66 Ghz, 2CPUs).

Visual Search: The visual search displays consisted in three imaginary circular arrays of 6.8°, 4.8° and 2.8° diameter, with 16, 8 and 4 visual search items, respectively. The target item was always presented in the middle circle of the array. *Size targets:* Size-target search display comprised of 28 grey circular items (1.1° of visual angle; 15 cd/m² of luminance). The target item was always a larger circle (1.4° of diameter). All displays were shown on a light-gray background (Figure 1). *Luminance targets:* All search items were of the same size (1.1°). The target item was always lighter (luminance: 58 cd/m²) than the other circles. All displays were shown on a light-gray background (Figure 1B). In the target-absent trials, all items were identical (1.1° of visual angle; 15 cd/m² of luminance). There were 50% of target present and 50% of target absent trials.

Figure 2 A   Figure 2 B

Fig. 2. Cartoon hand signaling a pointing movement (2A) and a grasping movement (2B)

Figure 3 A   Figure 3 B

Fig. 3. Robotic hand signaling a pointing movement (3A) and a grasping movement (3B)

Movement Task Apparatus: The movement cues (Figure 2&3) were presented in the middle of the computer screen. The movements were to be executed on three different cups, which were made up of hard papers. They differed in size and luminance: a small white, 5 cm in diameter in the middle point; a middle grey cup, 6.5 cm in diameter in the middle point; and a large dark grey cup, 8 cm in diameter in the middle point. They were all equal in height and weight. All the cups placed minimum 25 cm away from the display monitor on the table.

The go-signal for the movement execution consisted in a yellow asterisk of 0.6° in diameter. It was presented 4.5°, 11.3°, or 17.7° from the left border of the screen signalling the to-be-grasped/pointed to paper cup situated beneath the computer screen, each cup being situated below one of the asterisk positions. The cup positions were changed after each block.

2.4   Procedure

All participants were seated in a quiet and dimly lit room with response mouse positioned under their right hand and placed on the lap (see Figure 4).

Fig. 4. Experimental setup inside the chamber

At the beginning of each trial a 300 ms fixation cross was displayed ("x" in the center of the screen). Subsequently, the movement cue was presented for 800 ms. Next, subsequent to another fixation cross (200 ms) a visual search display was presented for 100 ms (see Figure 5). The visual search display was followed by a blank screen during which participants were supposed to respond to the visual search display (target present vs. target absent). Upon the visual search response, and another fixation cross (400 ms), the go-signal for the movement execution was presented. The go-signal consisted in a yellow asterisk presented for 300 ms. Participants were to execute the prepared movement in response to the asterisk. Movements were registered by the experimenter with the use of a web camera (Microsoft LifeCam VX – 800) and a computer mouse. The next trial began subsequent to the experimenter's registration of the movement performed by the participant. Participants were instructed to respond as fast and correctly as possible in the search task. In the movement task only correctness was stressed. Participants were provided with feedback concerning their performance after each block. Visual search tasks (luminance vs. size) were blocked and the order of blocks was counterbalanced across participants. The movement types (grasping vs. pointing) were randomized within blocks. The cue types (robot vs. cartoon) were presented in two separate experimental sessions (8 blocks, 60 trials each) with the order counterbalanced across participants. Hence, each participant took part in three sessions on three separate days. The first session consisted in practicing only the movement task (15-30 min.; 5 blocks), so that the subsequent experimental sessions involving two tasks would be easier to perform.

2.5   Data Analysis

Error rates were computed for each participant in both the search task and the movement task. Prior to reaction time (RT) analysis in the search task, errors in any of the two tasks as well as outliers in the search task were excluded (+/- 3 SD from mean RT for each participant, each cue type and each task type separately). Error rate analyses in the search task were conducted on correct movement trials. Data of three subjects whose error rates in any of the search tasks were above 15% were excluded from the analyses (mean error rates for the other participants: 7%). From the remaining data, mean RTs and mean error rates were calculated and subject to an analysis of variance (ANOVA) with the within-subject factors of cue type (robot vs. cartoon) × task type (size vs. luminance) × movement type (grasping vs. pointing) × display type (target vs. blank) and a between-subject factor of cue type order (robot cues first vs. cartoon cues first).

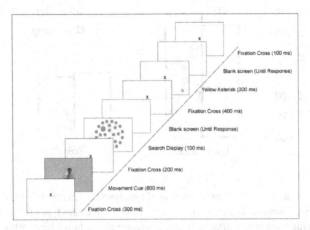

Fig. 5. A trial sequence of the present experiment

3   Results

3.1   Reaction Times

The analysis performed on the mean RT data revealed a main effect of display type, $F(1,15)=6.7$, $p<0.05$, $\eta_p^2=.3$ showing faster RTs to target trials (M = 484 ms) as compared to blank trials (M = 522 ms). Most importantly, the interaction of movement type and task type was significant, $F(1,15)=7.9$, $p=0.05$, $\eta_p^2 = .35$ (see Figure 6) and it did not depend on cue type, $p > .8$ (see Figure 7), cue type order, $p > .065$, or the combination of the two, $p > .6$. This interaction was further tested with planned comparisons, which revealed a congruency effect for luminance targets: RTs in luminance detection task were faster when participants concurrently prepared for pointing (M= 513 ms) as compared to grasping (M=520 ms), t (16) =2, $p < .05$, one-tailed. In the size detection task, the RTs showed also a tendency for the congruency effect: slightly faster RTs for grasping (M= 489 ms) as compared to pointing (M=491 ms), but this effect obviously did not become statistically significant, $p > .2$.

3.2   Error Rates

Analogous analysis on mean error rates showed only the main effect of display type, $F(1,15)=5.6$, $p<0.05$, $\eta_p^2=.2.7$ with less errors for blank trials (M= 4.3%) than for target trials (M= 7.6%), main effect of task type $F(1,15)=6.3$, $p<0.05$, $\eta_p^2=.3$ with less errors in the size task (M= 4.6%) as compared to the luminance task (7.3%). Moreover, the main effect of movement type reached the level of significance in the error rates, $F(1,15)=15$, $p<0.005$, $\eta_p^2=.5$, showing better performance in the pointing condition (M = 5.1%) as compared to grasping (M = 6.9%). The interaction between movement type and task type was not significant, p > .1.

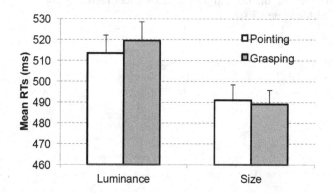

Fig. 6. Mean reaction times (RTs) as a function of task type (luminance vs. size) and movement type (pointing vs. grasping). The differences between the movement types for each of the visual search tasks are the *congruency effects*. Error bars represent within-subject confidence intervals with 95% probability criterion calculated according to the procedure described in Cousineau (2005).

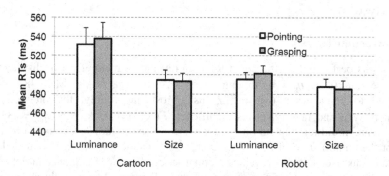

Fig. 7. Mean reaction times (RTs) as a function of movement type (point vs, grasp), task type (size vs. luminance) and two types of cues (cartoon or robot). Error bars represent within-subject confidence intervals with 95% probability criterion calculated according to the procedure described in Cousineau (2005).

4   Discussion

The aim of this experiment was to test whether observing pictures of robot hands or cartoon hands performing two types of movement (grasping or pointing) would elicit similar perceptual processes in the human observers as in the case of viewing pictures of human hands. The paradigm targeted at measuring the so-called *congruency effects* [6], which are related to better performance in a perceptual task (visual search) when a concurrently prepared movement is congruent with the dimension of the visual search target, as compared to an incongruent movement. The paradigm introduced two congruency pairs: two types of visual search targets coupled with two types of movements, i.e., one congruent pair consisted in size target + a grasping movement and the other pair consisted in luminance target + a pointing movement. Participants performed the two unrelated tasks (movement task and visual search task) concurrently.

In line with the previous studies [6,13], the present results showed congruency effects for the luminance targets and a trend for the congruency effects for size targets. Importantly for the purposes of the present experiment, the congruency effects were independent of the cue type. Hence, it seems that the basic (and perhaps implicit) perceptual effects can be elicited regardless the particular type of the observed agent. This is in line with a study by Oberman et al. [14] who found that observing both human and robot actions activated the mirror neurons in human beings. This mirror neuron activation facilitated reproduction of the same observed action. Oztop et al. [15] also found that both humans and humanoid robots elicited interference effects when being observed simultaneously with execution of movements that could be either congruent or incongruent with the observed ones. Taken together, these findings supplemented by the present results, suggest that similar perceptual processes are evoked when observing humans or humanoid robots.

It might be the case, however, that the complexity of information carried by the stimulus material might play a role in inducing congruency effects to various degrees. Hence, different degrees of congruency effects might be found when dynamic videos of actual robot arms grasping/pointing are presented, and the congruency effects are compared to a condition in which dynamic videos of human arms grasping/pointing are observed.

In addition to the effects of major theoretical interest, the present analyses revealed also that participants were faster in responding to target present trials as compared to target absent trials, which is a common finding in the visual search literature [6, 16,17] indicating different processing modes for situations when a signal is present in the visual field as compared to being absent [18, 19]. Error rates depended on the type of movement revealing better performance in the pointing condition as compared to grasping and on the type of task – luminance targets were detected with higher accuracy. This might partially explain why the congruency effects were observed only in the luminance task. It might be that congruency effects are generally observable in tasks, which are not too difficult to perform. As the congruency effects are postulated to be perceptual in nature [6], any response strategies might obscure them. Hence, in case of more difficult tasks, when response strategies come into play, the behavioral measures might not be sensitive enough to pinpoint the perceptual effects of interest.

5   Implications for Social Robots Design

Engineers design robots and sometimes they ask art designers to create agents with a nice and an appealing look to be accepted by users. As argued above, the robot is an ambiguous concept, neither a machine nor a biological being, but having an apparent intelligence that made humans consider robots as potential companions. In this study, a first step toward understanding the effects of robots morphology on human perception in HRI contexts, we aimed at objectively measuring the effects of robot's morphology on the human mind. We reproduced an experimental schema that has been tested for humans observing humans: we extended it to humans observing cartoon-like hands and an anthropomorphic robotics hand. Some interesting trends have been elicited showing a "shape" effect, mainly for the *luminance* task. To our knowledge, this approach is the first to be tested in order to develop an effective metrics to measure the relationship between robots' morphology and its effects on humans in terms of action-perception congruency (or sensory-motor links). This study is in its early stages and will be extended to other types of arms/hands and more dynamic stimuli to better understand the potential mapping between the robot's morphology and the ways it affects the human companion. Two main directions will be considered: 1- movement, 2- morphology. We have already some arms prototypes to evaluate: we will consider hands with several numbers of fingers and phalanges. Moreover, we will examine stimuli consisting in artificial arms with varying temporal sequences performing pointing and grasping tasks.

6   Conclusions

The present work extends the congruency effect successfully to non-human arms. Namely, a cartoon and robot-like hand elicited similar effects to human hands when observed by other humans. This result is important *per se:* it shows that artificial robotic agents can affect people similarly to human agents. In addition, we showed a tendency that different arms /hands morphologies could have different effects. The second point is concerned with variations between morphologies: the trends we obtained should be explored more deeply to confirm that various morphologies affects observers sensory-motor system differentially. Last, we draw some research lines that could be of interest (guidelines) for designing companion robots easily acceptable by any user.

References

1. Mori, M.: Bukimi no tani The uncanny valley (K. F. MacDorman & T. Minato, Trans.). Energy 7(4), 33–35 (1970) (originally in Japanese)
2. Sternberg, S.: The discovery of processing stages: Extensions of Donders' method. In: Koster, W.G. (ed.) Attention and Performance II. Acta Psychol., vol. 30, pp. 276–315 (1969)
3. Hommel, B., Müsseler, J., Aschersleben, G., Prinz, W.: The theory of event coding (TEC): A framework for perception and action planning. Behav. Brain Sci. 24, 849–878 (2001)
4. Prinz, W.: Perception and action planning. Eur. J. Cogn. Psychol. 9, 129–154 (1997)
5. Hommel, B.: Grounding attention in action control: The intentional control of selection. In: Bruya, B.J. (ed.) Effortless Attention: A New Perspective in the Cognitive Science of Attention and Action, pp. 121–140. MIT Press, Cambridge (2010)
6. Wykowska, A., Schubö, A., Hommel, B.: How you move is what you see: Action planning biases selection in visual search. J. Exp. Psychol. Human 35, 1755–1769 (2009)

7. Wykowska, A., Hommel, B., Schubö, A.: Action-induced effects on perception depend neither on element-level nor on set-level similarity between stimulus and response sets. Atten. Percept. Psycho. 73, 1034–1041 (2011)

8. Schubotz, R.I., von Cramon, D.Y.: Predicting perceptual events activates corresponding motor schemes in lateral premotor cortex: An fMRI study. Neuroimage 15, 787–796 (2002)

9. Rizzolatti, G., Craighero, L.: The Mirror-Neuron System. Annu. Rev. Neurosci. 27, 169–192 (2004)

10. Rizzolatti, G., Fogassi, L., Gallese, V.: Neurophysiological mechanisms underlying the understanding and imitation of action. Nat. Rev. Neurosci. 2, 661–670 (2001)

11. Gallese, V., Goldman, A.: Mirror neurons and the simulation theory of mind-reading. Trends Cogn. Sci. 2, 493–501 (1998)

12. Carr, L., Iacoboni, M., Dubeau, M.-C., Mazziotta, J.C., Lenzi, G.L.: Neural mechanisms of empathy in humans: a relay from neural systems for imitation to limbic areas. P. Natl. Acad. Sci. USA 100, 5497–5502 (2003)

13. Fagioli, S., Hommel, B., Schubotz, R.I.: Intentional control of attention: Action planning primes action related stimulus dimensions. Psychol. Res. 71, 22–29 (2007)

14. Oberman, L.M., McCmeery, J.P., Ramachandran, V.S., Pineda, J.A.: EEG evidence for mirror neuron activity during the observation of human and robot actions: Toward an analysis of the human qualities of interactive robots. Neurocomputing 70, 2194–2203 (2007)

15. Oztop, E., Franklin, D.W., Chaminade, T., Cheng, G.: Human–humanoid interaction: Is a humanoid robot perceived as a human? Int. J. Hum. Robot. 2, 537–559 (2005)

16. Chun, M.M., Wolfe, J.M.: Just Say No: How Are Visual Searches Terminated When There Is No Target Present? Cognitive Psychol. 30, 39–78 (1996)

17. Found, A., Müller, H.J.: Searching for unknown feature targets on more than one dimension: Investigating a 'dimension weighting' account. Percept. Psychophys. 58, 88–101 (1996)

18. Schubö, A., Schröger, E., Meinecke, C.: Texture segmentation and visual search for pop-out targets. Cognit. Brain Res. 21, 317–334 (2004)

19. Schubö, A., Wykowska, A., Müller, H.J.: Detecting pop-out targets in contexts of varying homogeneity: Investigating homogeneity coding with event-related brain potentials (ERPs). Brain Res. 1138, 136–147 (2007)

20. Matarić, M.J.: Socially assistive robotics. In: Coradeschi, S., et al. (eds.) Human-Inspired Robots (2006); IEEE Intelligent Systems, 81-83

21. Bartneck, C., Kanda, T., Ishiguro, H., Hagita, N.: Is the Uncanny Valley an Uncanny Cliff? In: Proceedings of the 16th IEEE, RO-MAN 2007, Jeju, Korea, pp. 368–373 (2007)

22. Brenton, H., Gillies, M., Ballin, D., Chatting, D.: The Uncanny Valley: does it exist? Paper Presented at HCI 2005, Animated Characters Interaction Workshop, Edinburgh, Napier University (2005)

23. MacDorman, K.: Subjective ratings of robot video clips for human-likeness, familiarity, and eeriness: An exploration of the uncanny valley. In: Proceedings of the ICCS/CogSci 2006 Long Symposium: Toward Social Mechanisms of Android Science, Vancouver, Canada, pp. 26–29 (July 2006)

Using Compliant Robots as Projective Interfaces in Dynamic Environments

Davide De Tommaso, Sylvain Calinon, and Darwin G. Caldwell

Department of Advanced Robotics, Istituto Italiano di Tecnologia,
via Morego, 30, 16163 Genova
{davide.detommaso,sylvain.calinon,darwin.caldwell}@iit.it

Abstract. We present a human-robot interface for projecting information on arbitrary planar surfaces by sharing a visual understanding of the
workspace. A compliant 7-DOF arm robot endowed with a pico-projector
and a depth sensor has been used for the experiment. The perceptual capabilities allows the system to detect geometry features of the environment which are used for superimposing undistorted projection on planar
surfaces. The proposed scenario consists of a first phase in which the user
physically interacts with the gravity compensated robot for choosing the
place where the projection will appear. After, in the second phase, the
robotic arm is able to autonomously superimpose visual information in
the selected area and actively adapt to perturbations. We also present
a proof-of-concept for managing occlusions and tracking the position of
the projection whenever obstacles enter in the projection field.

1 Introduction

Portable projecting devices open a new trend in Human-Robot Interaction (HRI)
by offering a new communication medium, that complements the use of natural
language processing and haptic feedback, as tool for robots to provide information to humans. While gathering inputs from the surrounding environment is a
central topic of robotic research since decades, allowing robots to exploit this environment to communicate with the user is still a largely unexplored issue in the
HRI field. Humanoids able of emulating facial emotions or body gestures are just
few examples of making machines anthropomorphically communicative towards
humans. Non-verbal communication can improve the efficiency and robustness
of the interaction between humans and robots involved in collaboration tasks by
ameliorating the overall task performance, see e.g. [1]. Virtual and Augmented
Reality interfaces have been developed in this direction to let the robot communicate information to the user without requiring to rely on standard computer
screen interface, see e.g. [2]. Robots with projection capabilities represent an important area of interest for sharing information about the environment or about
a task to achieve with the physical objects and tools surrounding the robot. The
use of light beams superimposed on physical objects might allow the user to
focus his/her gaze on specific areas of the work space. Moreover, colors, position
marks, trajectories and texts may provide additional information about task and

S.S. Ge et al. (Eds.): ICSR 2012, LNAI 7621, pp. 338–347, 2012.

relevant locations. While different application domains have been explored by using projective technology in Human-Computer Interaction (HCI), such as entertainment [3], training [4,5], elderly assistance [6] and surgery [7], the use of such devices in the HRI community remains largely unexplored so far.

In this paper, we present a robotic interface to assist users in dynamic environments, allowing them to visualize digital information in any planar surface. Working spaces like factories, classrooms, homes, training rooms, hospitals are possible target locations for tasks focusing more on the visual and haptics feedbacks of the users. For example users involved in manual tasks have not the possibility to handle any computing devices for accessing digital information. In such cases robot interfaces might help at providing human assistance services. For tasks requiring a worker to move and change posture, it remains difficult to predefine a generic positioning of the sensing and projecting device

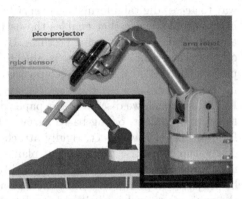

Fig. 1. The projection system using the compliant Barrett WAM 7-DOF robot endowed with a Kinect device and a pico-projector

that would work well for all the tasks and situations. The use of the robotic arm allows a flexible repositioning of the sensing and projection devices that automatically adapts to the situation and task constraints.

The development of the proposed interface was mainly driven by two goals. First, to provide the user with the possibility of choosing and modifying the position of the projection, by intuitively moving the robot by hand when it is gravity compensated. Second, to make the interface accessible to the user, by maintaining its geometric projection features fixed, even in presence of perturbations caused by the users or by the robot changing its projection posture. We present a prototype following these two guidelines, by using a 7-DOF compliant arm robot equipped with a pico-projector and a Microsoft Kinect device (see Fig. 1).

2   Related Work

The recent advances of projector technology have grown interest for enabling new user friendly communication interface. Here we present two previous works, from which we draw inspiration.

Vogel *et al* in [8] propose a spatial augmented reality interface able to establish a physical safety area in a shared workspace between users and robots, by using a camera and projector fixed to the ceiling. The projective device gives feedback to the user about the safe working area, by projecting virtual barriers directly aligned with the real portion of space. The perception device helps the system to actively monitor the physical state of the user and the robot within the safety area, by changing position, shape and orientation of the projected image dynamically.

In the field of wearable computing, Harrison *et al* suggest in [9] an innovative way to access digital information everywhere. The developed *OmniTouch* system is a wearable device that enables the user to interact with a GUI projected on any physical surface by using gestures. By exploiting the perception capabilities of a depth sensor, the system is able to detect suitable surfaces in which to project the GUI, by using a pico-projector, and to interact with fingers like a mouse pointer.

The approach we discuss in the paper does not require a fixed setup, a structured environment, or tag-based surfaces for finding the place of projection. In fact the use of the Kinect, rigidly attached to the robot, allows the system to detect the geometric properties of planar surfaces in the surrounding environment. In such a way, by using a fully calibrated system, undistorted images can be projected in planes chosen by the user and at the same time the space around the projection can be monitored for detecting obstacles and occlusions.

3   System Overview

3.1   Experimental Setup

To the best of our knowledge, the proposed interface represents the first attempt of developing an interactive projective interface using an actively compliant robot.

We exploit here such manipulator as an interface that can move, perceive and project in its environment. These features and its light weight well fit with the requirements of human-robot collaboration scenarios, in which the physical contact between the user and the manipulator represents an important modality of interaction.

Our experimental setup consists of a compliant Barrett WAM 7-DOF arm

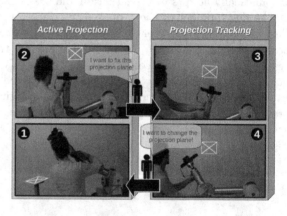

Fig. 2. The two operating modes of the system

robot endowed with a plastic support mounted at the end-effector holding rigidly a Microsoft Kinect and an AXAA laser pico-projector. The Kinect has been extensively exploited in different fields of research as depth sensor, introducing an affordable option for point cloud tracking and detection [10].

For the projection capability, we selected a pico-projector because it is small enough to be mounted on top of the Barrett WAM and its laser technology allows us to project at any distance without requiring to adjust focus. In the experiment the robot and the user share the same working space. Adopting such a mobile configuration, instead of a fixed setup, leads two key advantages: 1) an extended field of view due to the different viewpoints reachable by the robotic arm and 2) the possibility to actively handle occlusions and facilitate tracking of task-relevant features. For selecting appropriate projecting surfaces, we decided to exploit both the control capabilities of the robot and the perception capability of the depth sensor. Instead of using structured environments, the system actively projects distortion-free images on the basis of the geometry of the projection surface, detected by the Kinect. Accordingly, whenever the user wants to select the position and orientation of the projected display, she/he just needs to manually move the robotic arm in an

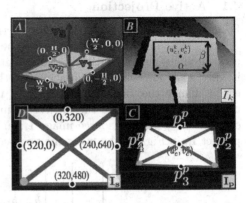

Fig. 3. (A) The frame of reference of the projection is defined by the orthogonal vectors v_1, v_2, v_3, whose origins correspond to the center of the projected image. (B) The Kinect's depthmap is used for estimating the geometric equation of the plane chosen for the projection. *Principal Component Analysis* is applied to points samples from a rectangular area of I_k. (C) The input image of the pico-projector is the 640×480 RGB matrix I_p representing the result of the perspective transformation for fitting the image in the projection plane. (D) The 640×480 RGB matrix I_s represents the source image to project.

appropriate position, while the robot compensates for the weight of its arm and friction in its joints. For continuously tracking the projection, the system autonomously reacts to the changes of the robot arm configuration by 1) modifying the orientation of the end-effector, and 2) recomputing the perspective of the projected image. During this projection phase, the system is also able to simultaneously perceive three dimensional information about the area between the end-effector and the surface of projection. Indeed, the Kinect's field of view is larger than the pico-projector so that the entire frustum of projection can be monitored to detect obstacles causing occlusions.

4   Developed Prototype

The system involves two mutually exclusive operating modes: 1) *Active Projection* and 2) *Projection Tracking* (see Fig. 2).

4.1 Active Projection

For allowing the user to select the projection plane, the system starts with the *Active Projection* mode. In this phase the process of warping the projection is carried out by using jointly the Kinect and the pico-projector, while the robot is only controlled by compensating for the gravity. This enables the user to easily change the joints configuration of the robot by looking for the pose of the end-effector allowing the projection in the desired plane. According to the end-effector pose, the source image $\mathbf{I_s}$, in Fig. 3-D, is warped in the image to project $\mathbf{I_p}$ in Fig. 3-C by using the perspective transformation

$$\underbrace{\begin{bmatrix} wp_x \\ wp_y \\ w \end{bmatrix}}_{\mathbf{I_p}(x,y)} = \underbrace{\begin{bmatrix} h_{11} & h_{12} & h_{13} \\ h_{21} & h_{22} & h_{23} \\ h_{31} & h_{32} & h_{33} \end{bmatrix}}_{\mathbf{H_\pi}} \underbrace{\begin{bmatrix} s_x \\ s_y \\ 1 \end{bmatrix}}_{\mathbf{I_s}(x,y)} . \tag{1}$$

Since the 3D points of the projection surface lie on the same plane, the views of the Kinect and the pico-projector are related by an homography. For estimating the homography matrix $\mathbf{H_\pi}$, two sets of four 2D points are required, four points in the source image $\mathbf{I_s}$ (e.g the matrix elements (0,320), (240,640), (320,480), (320,0) see Fig. 3-D) and four points $p_1^p, .. p_4^p$ in the destination image $\mathbf{I_p}$ (see Fig. 3-C). Such points in $\mathbf{I_p}$ correspond to the 3D points $P_1^k, .. P_4^k$ in the Kinect's frame, and can be found by changing the coordinate system from the Kinect to the pico-projector. The four corners of the projection are automatically detected by following the geometry of the planar surface and can be found by

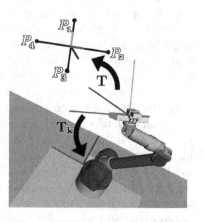

Fig. 4. A preliminary calibration process between the frames of reference of the robot, the pico-projector and the Kinect enables the system to find the corresponding transformation matrices

$$\begin{bmatrix} P_1^k \\ P_2^k \\ P_3^k \\ P_4^k \end{bmatrix} = \mathbf{T} \begin{bmatrix} 0 & -\frac{W}{2} & 0 & \frac{W}{2} \\ \frac{H}{2} & 0 & -\frac{H}{2} & 0 \\ 0 & 0 & 0 & 0 \\ 1 & 1 & 1 & 1 \end{bmatrix}, \tag{2}$$

see Fig. 3-A. The 4×4 matrix $\mathbf{T}$ is the transformation between the Kinect and the projection frames (see Fig. 4), which can be written as

$$\mathbf{T} = \begin{bmatrix} \mathbf{R} & C^k \\ 0 & 1 \end{bmatrix}, \mathbf{R} = \begin{bmatrix} \mathbf{v_1} & \mathbf{v_2} & \mathbf{v_3}, \end{bmatrix} \tag{3}$$

where the equation of the projecting plane is

$$\pi: \quad \mathbf{r} = \mathbf{r_0} + s\mathbf{v_1} + t\mathbf{v_2}. \tag{4}$$

The geometry of the plane, namely the vectors $\mathbf{v_1}$ and $\mathbf{v_2}$ (see Fig. 3-A), can be estimated by *Principal Component Analysis (PCA)* applied to a set of 3D points in the Kinect's frame. As shown in Fig. 3-B, such point cloud is extracted from a rectangular area of the depthmap $\mathbf{I_k}$, defined by the center (u_c^k, v_c^k), the height β and the width α. The 2D point (u_c^k, v_c^k) corresponds to the pico-projector's principal point (u_c^p, v_c^p) in $\mathbf{I_p}$, while C^k represents the projection of (u_c^k, v_c^k) in the Kinect's frame.

Algorithm 1. Active Projection

1: **function** AP($\mathbf{I_k}, \mathbf{I_s}$)
2:     $\mathbf{T} = paramsPlaneEstimation(\mathbf{u_c^k}, \mathbf{v_c^k}, \alpha, \beta)$
3:     $\mathbf{P_1^k}, ..\mathbf{P_4^k} = selectingFour3DPoints(\mathbf{T}, W, H)$
4:     $\mathbf{p_1^p}, ..\mathbf{p_4^p} = fromKinect2Projector(\mathbf{P_1^k}, ..\mathbf{P_4^k})$
5:     $\mathbf{H_\pi} = homography(\mathbf{p_1^p}, ..\mathbf{p_4^p}, (0, 320), ..(320, 0))$
6:     $\mathbf{I_p} = warpImage(\mathbf{I_s}, \mathbf{H_\pi})$
7:     **return** $\mathbf{I_p}$
8: **end function**

The *Active Projection* mode is summarized in Algorithm 1, in which the procedure *AP()* takes as input the source image $\mathbf{I_s}$ and the depthmap of the Kinect $\mathbf{I_k}$ and retrieves as output the image to project $\mathbf{I_p}$.

4.2 Projection Tracking

Once the user has selected a suitable projecting plane, the system switches from the *Active Projection* to the *Projection Tracking* mode. In such process, the robot is still maintained in gravity compensation. The *Projection Tracking* mode consists of an iterative process involving two main functionalities.

The first one computes the rotational forces to apply to the end-effector for pointing towards the center of the projection plane, which is represented as a 3D point in the robot's frame. The robot actively reacts to perturbation of its joints configuration by keeping constant the size and the perspective of the projected image. The perturbations to the gravity compensated arm, can come from the user physically moving the robot or from the robot actively changing its posture to avoid occlusions.

The second functionality computes an updated perspective transformation, based on the actual end-effector pose, for enabling the resulting image to be undistorted despite the geometric parameters of the plane in the pico-projector's frame may change. Moreover, whenever an occlusion occurs, the system reacts by finding another end-effector pose for making the projection again visible.

According to these two features, the system iteratively computes 1) the end-effector orientation to send to the robot $\mathbf{R_{end}}$ and 2) the warped projected image $\mathbf{I_p}$. Four 3D points $\mathbf{P_1}, ..\mathbf{P_4}$ in the robot's frame are obtained from the points

Algorithm 2. Projection Tracking

1: $\mathbf{P}_1, ..\mathbf{P}_4 = fromKinect2Robot(\mathbf{P}_1^k, ..\mathbf{P}_4^k)$
2: $\mathbf{C} = findProjectionCenter(\mathbf{P}_1, ..\mathbf{P}_4)$
3: **while** true **do**
4:     $\mathbf{R_{end}} = LookAt(\mathbf{C})$
5:     $sendOrientationToRobot(\mathbf{R_{end}})$
6:     $\mathbf{p}_1^p, ..\mathbf{p}_4^p = fromRobot2ProjectorImage(\mathbf{P}_1, ..\mathbf{P}_4)$
7:     $\mathbf{H}_\pi = homography(\mathbf{p}_1^p, ..\mathbf{p}_4^p, (0, 320), ..(320, 0))$
8:     $\mathbf{I_p} = warpImage(\mathbf{I_s}, \mathbf{H}_\pi)$
9:     $\mathbf{P_{occl}} = DO(\mathbf{I_k}, mindistPI, maxdistPI)$
10:     **if** $\mathbf{P_{occl}}$ *is not null* **then**
11:         $\mathbf{P_{new}} = findingNewpose(\mathbf{P_{occl}})$
12:         $sendingToRobot(\mathbf{P_{new}})$
13:     **end if**
14: **end while**

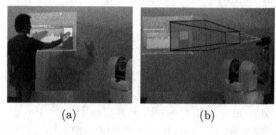

(a)   (b)

Fig. 5. (a) A projected red spot indicates the center of the detected occlusion. (b) The volume in red is the frustum of the projection continuously monitored by the *DO()* function.

$\mathbf{P}_1^k, ..\mathbf{P}_4^k$ in the Kinect's frame which defines the selected projection plane π. In the line 1 of Algorithm 2 the geometric transformation

$$[P_1 \ P_2 \ P_3 \ P_4]^\top = \mathbf{T_k} \left[P_1^k \ P_2^k \ P_3^k \ P_4^k\right]^\top \tag{5}$$

is computed by using the transformation matrix $\mathbf{T_k}$ between the Kinect and the robot frames (see Fig. 4). Therefore, the target towards which the end-effector has to point, namely the projection's center, is computed in line 2. Then, in the main loop, the end-effector orientation and the warped image are continuously computed based on the actual robot's configuration. The *LookAt()* function, in line 4, provides the end-effector with an orientation matrix $\mathbf{R_{end}}$ for looking towards the point $\mathbf{C}$, while the homography/warp operations on lines 7 and 8 enable the projected image $\mathbf{I_p}$ to appear undistorted. Whether an obstacle occludes the projection (line 10), a new position of the end-effector is found and sent to the robot (lines 11 and 12).

4.3 Detecting and Handling Occlusions

In dynamic environments where humans and robots share the same space, one of the key requirement is to adapt the machine's behaviour to human's habits.

In the particular scenario we are proposing, it may happen that the user occludes the projection with some parts of the body. We propose a geometric method for enabling the robot to adaptively change its configuration to get around obstacles and keep the projection visible. Thus, the user can freely move in the surrounding environment without worrying about occluding the projected interface. While the *Projection Tracking* mode is activated, the system is able to adaptively change the robot configuration in order to manage occlusions that may occur in the frustum of the projection. The *Detecting Occlusion* function *DO()*, in line 9 of Algorithm 2, returns a 3D point in the robot's frame representing the mean occlusion point. Such point is found inside a portion of the projection's frustum by using the Kinect device. The frustum is the region of space, defined geometrically as a regular rectangular pyramid with the apex cut by a parallel plane (*nearPlane*) above the base (*farPlane*). In our case the *farPlane* is the plane parallel to π with perpendicular distance *mindistPI* from

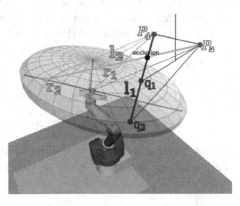

Fig. 6. For each of the two lines l_1 and l_2, two different solutions can be found by the intersection with the ellipsoid $\mathcal{E}$. The selected solution represents the new end-effector position to reach by the robot.

it, while the *nearPlane* is far *maxdistPI* (see Fig. 5b). In such a way, all the 3D points inside the frustum are collected by computing the depthmap $\mathbf{I_k}$ and a mean value $\mathbf{P_{occl}}$ in the robot's frame is extracted from these samples (see Fig. 5). Indeed, whenever an obstacle occludes the projection, a new end-effector position $\mathbf{P_{new}}$ is computed and reached by the robot, for avoiding the occlusion and making the projection again visible. We propose a geometric approach implemented in the function *findingNewpose()* (line 11 of Algorithm 2).

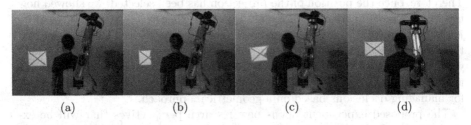

(a)   (b)   (c)   (d)

Fig. 7. The snapshot (a) shows the user visualizing a projected interface before an occlusion occurs. Once the user changes his position and an occlusion is detected, the robot moves by reaching the new end-effector pose for avoiding the occlusion, as shown in (b), (c) and (d).

Let $\mathcal{E}$ be the ellipsoid defined by the equation

$$\mathcal{E} : (\mathbf{x} - \mathbf{P_{end}})^\top \begin{bmatrix} a^2 & 0 & 0 \\ 0 & b^2 & 0 \\ 0 & 0 & c^2 \end{bmatrix} (\mathbf{x} - \mathbf{P_{end}}) = 1, \tag{6}$$

where its center $\mathbf{P_{end}}$ is the actual end-effector position and a, b, c define the vertical distances for each axis from $\mathbf{P_{end}}$ to the ellipsoid surface (see Fig. 6). All the points on the surface of the ellipsoid represent candidate solutions to avoid the occlusion. Namely, the ellipsoid defines the maximum volume in which the end-effector can move around to manage each occlusion. Let $\mathbf{l_1}$ be a line between the points $\mathbf{P_{occl}}$ (occlusion in Fig. 6) and $\mathbf{P_4}$, and $\mathbf{l_2}$ a line between the points $\mathbf{P_{occl}}$ and $\mathbf{P_2}$, according to the equations

$$\mathbf{l_1} : \mathbf{P_{occl}} + t_1(\mathbf{P_4} - \mathbf{P_{occl}}) , \qquad \mathbf{l_2} : \mathbf{P_{occl}} + t_2(\mathbf{P_2} - \mathbf{P_{occl}}). \tag{7}$$

The intersection between the ellipsoid surface $\mathcal{E}$ and the line $\mathbf{l_1}$ defines two solutions, then two other solutions can be computed for the line $\mathbf{l_2}$. Thus, the return value $\mathbf{P_{new}}$ is the closest 3D point between the four solutions found.

5   Conclusions and Future Work

We presented a novel robotic interface for projecting visual information on planar surfaces. In our experimental setup, we considered to extend the capabilities of the compliant 7-DOF Barrett WAM robot by rigidly mounting a pico-projector and a Microsoft Kinect sensor on its end-effector. The perceptual features of the Kinect has been exploited to detect three dimensional information about the geometry of planar surfaces used for superimposing undistorted projections and handling possible occlusions. A human-robot collaboration scenario involving the task of finding suitable projecting surfaces and managing perturbations has been presented. We conducted an experiment showing that the user can manually interact with the gravity-compensated robot for finding a suitable end-effector pose which enables the projection to be superimposed on a desired surface. Therefore, once the position of the projection has been selected, we showed how the robot arm can actively adapt the projection when faced with changes of its joints configuration. Although the experimental results showed that the size and the perspective of the projection are kept quasi-constant, the position tracking will be improved in the future work by refining the calibration methods between the robot and the sensors. We also presented a prototype as a proof-of-concept for managing occlusions based on a geometrical approach.

The proposed experiment opens new research perspectives that will be explored in our future work. In order to measure the quality of the user interactions, evaluation studies will first be conducted. We also plan to improve the current setup by providing the system with an awareness mechanism of the human presence by managing collision avoidance in a predictable manner and by regulating the robot stiffness with respect to the user's distance. Finally, a further aspect to be considered will be the interaction between the user and the projected information by capturing human inputs from hands gestures on the projecting surface employed as an ubiquitous interface.

References

1. Breazeal, C., Kidd, C.D., Thomaz, A.L., Hoffman, G., Berlin, M.: Effects of non-verbal communication on efficiency and robustness in human-robot teamwork. In: Proceedings of the IEEE/RSJ International Conference on Intelligent Robots and Systems IROS, pp. 708–713 (2005)
2. Mollet, N., Chellali, R., Brayda, L.: Virtual and Augmented Reality Tools for Teleoperation: Improving Distant Immersion and Perception. In: Pan, Z., Cheok, A.D., Müller, W., Rhalibi, A.E. (eds.) Transactions on Edutainment II. LNCS, vol. 5660, pp. 135–159. Springer, Heidelberg (2009)
3. Bimber, O., Emmerling, A., Klemmer, T.: Embedded entertainment with smart projectors. IEEE Computer 38(1), 48–55 (2005)
4. Li, L., Zhang, M., Xu, F., Liu, S.: ERT-VR: an immersive virtual reality system for emergency rescue training. Virtual Reality 8(3), 194–197 (2005)
5. Brunnett, G., Rusdorf, S., Lorenz, M.: V-pong: an immersive table tennis simulation. IEEE Computer Graphics and Applications 26(4), 10–13 (2006)
6. Ikeda, S., Asghar, Z., Hyry, J., Pulli, P., Pitkanen, A., Kato, H.: Remote assistance using visual prompts for demented elderly in cooking. In: Proceedings of the 4th International Symposium on Applied Sciences in Biomedical and Communication Technologies, ISABEL 2011, pp. 1–5. ACM, New York (2011)
7. Tardif, J.P., Roy, S., Meunier, J.: Projector-based augmented reality in surgery without calibration. In: Proceedings of the 25th Annual International Conference of the IEEE Engineering in Medicine and Biology Society, vol. 1, pp. 548–551 (2003)
8. Vogel, C., Poggendorf, M., Walter, C., Elkmann, N.: Towards safe physical human-robot collaboration: A projection-based safety system. In: Proceedings of the IEEE/RSJ International Conference on Intelligent Robots and Systems IROS
9. Harrison, C., Benko, H., Wilson, A.D.: Omnitouch: wearable multitouch interaction everywhere. In: Proceedings of the 24th Annual ACM Symposium on User Interface Software and Technology, UIST, pp. 441–450. ACM, New York (2011)
10. Rusu, R.B., Cousins, S.: 3D is here: Point cloud library PCL. In: Proceedings of IEEE International Conference on Robotics and Automation (ICRA), Shanghai, China, pp. 1–4 (May 2011)

Affective Tele-touch

John-John Cabibihan, Lihao Zheng, and Chin Kiang Terence Cher

Department of Electrical and Computer Engineering
National University of Singapore
elecjj@nus.edu.sg

Abstract. Classical works have described how touch therapy has been effective in the recovery and good appetite of children in hospitals. This paper proposes an affective tele-touch system prototype customized for therapeutic touches over the Internet. The affective contact area was designated to the posterior forearm surface where three stimuli were made available: vibration, warmth, and tickle. Affective tele-touches could be applied either with a sensory haptic device. We have conducted touch therapy experiments with this system to look at the experimental subjects' recovery from video-induced sadness with heartbeat rates as the psycho-physiological measurement indicator. Our results show that a touch from a human hand or a tele-touch was able to reduce heartbeat rates of the participants after they watched a sad video clip.

Keywords: affective tele-touch, affective haptics, touch therapy, video-induced sadness, wearable robotics.

1   Introduction

Touch is crucial to human development. Early works by Bakwin [1] and Spitz [2] have demonstrated that children responded positively to continuous affective touch therapy, which resulted to fast recovery and good appetite. In this paper, we explore whether touch can have some effect to the receiver when touch is passed over the internet. Doing so might be beneficial. For example, affective tele-touch may help cancer patients recover from the trauma and ravages of their disease. Because the children have low immunity, they are isolated in hospitals and they may be deprived of frequent human contact from their family members and friends. This lack of touch, especially from their parents, could have a detrimental effect on those children and their future behavior.

Online communication programs like MSN messenger and Skype are unable to provide the 'touch' factor that is needed. Recent technologies like HugMe [3] and the iFeel_IM! system [4] focus on the enhancement of social interactivity. Paro [5, 6], a therapeutic robotic seal, has been able improve the chances of recovery of elderly patients with cognitive disorders. Our work, however, proposes an idea, which comprises of a remote communication system and haptic hardware devices to apply a simple yet effective therapeutic affective touches on the forearm and the control signals are sent through the internet.

S.S. Ge et al. (Eds.): ICSR 2012, LNAI 7621, pp. 348–356, 2012.
© Springer-Verlag Berlin Heidelberg 2012

Many related works have been conducted on the psycho-physiological responses towards emotions. Several studies from Ekman [7], Levenson [8], Collet [9] and colleagues have supported the notion that psycho-physiological responses may distinguish basic emotions such as fear, happiness, sadness, disgust, surprise and anger. Sadness, in particular, is related to an increase in systolic pressure and heart rate [10]. Rainville and co-workers [11] reported that significant increases in heartbeat rates were observed in relation to sadness. In this paper, we have conducted an investigation on the effectiveness of heartbeat rates in the subjects' physiological responses from video-induced sadness in a tele-touch therapy experiment. Section 2 of this paper will look into the system prototype that was built. Section 3 will look in the affective tele-touch therapy experiment and finally a conclusion in Section 4.

2   Affective Tele-Touch System

2.1   Conceptual Design

The affective haptic system consists of two separate sub-systems, namely the sensory and actuation sub-systems.

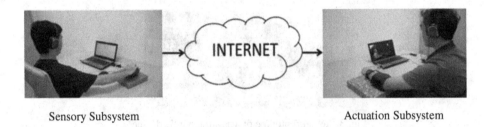

Sensory Subsystem   Actuation Subsystem

Fig. 1. Affective Tele-Touch Technology

Fig. 1 shows the conceptual design of the affective haptic system. Sensory data, which are detected from the sensory location at the left of the figure, will be transmitted through the internet to the remote computer at the actuation location on the right of the figure. The actuation computer then sends the command to an actuation device so that the person wearing the forearm cuff can feel the touch.

2.2   Device Design

The sensory haptic device consists of a set-up box that embeds the microprocessor and the hardware circuitry (Fig. 2). Five force sensors and one temperature sensor were mounted at the front and the back of the sponge ball. A furry cloth covered the sponge ball for a more acceptable appearance and feel.

Fig. 2. Actual Sensory Haptic Device Prototype

The design of the actuation haptic device is shown in the form of a cuff, which was wrapped onto the subject's forearm. This is similar to the sensory module where a set-up box was needed to embed the microprocessor. The design of the forearm cuff is shown in Fig. 3, where individual components (e.g. vibration motors, heating elements, DC motor) were placed on a wrapping material (e.g. cloth). These tactile actuators actuate the touch based on the sensory data obtained from the sender's (e.g. parent) sensory location.

Fig. 3. Actual prototype of actuation haptic device

The contact area for this system is assumed to be the posterior forearm surface. Based on this, we classified the gesture for affective casual touch as a static contact with pressure applied by the fingertips or just pressure applied by fingertips. These were the basic gestures used to develop this system.

2.3   System Overview and Features

The overall system architecture of the affective tele-touch system is made up of the sensory subsystem and actuator subsystem. The computer (PC) on each respective subsystem will communicate via a communications network through the internet. The communication server and client update its respective GUI (Graphical User Interface) so that information (server event log and sensor/actuator levels) can be viewed on the monitor. Both GUI are tasked to receive sensory information from the sensors and providing actuation levels in the sensory and actuator subsystem. They are serially connected to its respective PC so that information can be passed on from the sensory to the actuator subsystem. Three basic affective tele-touch features are as follows:

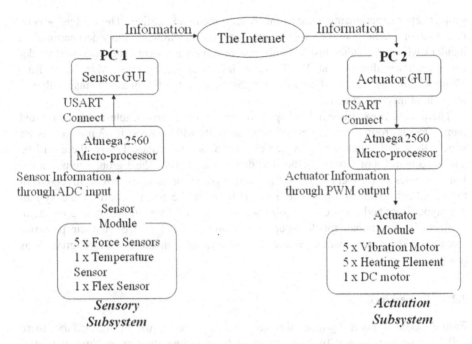

Fig. 4. System Architecture at the Sensory and Actuation Subsystems

1) Exerting a force on the force sensors (sensing range 0.1 kg to 10 kg) at the sensory side will result in the activation of the vibration motors in the actuation side. Five different pressure levels are created for each vibration motor, giving up to 25 different vibration levels available in this system.

2) By bending the flex sensor at the sensory side, the DC motor at the actuation end will be executed. The feather, which is attached to the DC motor, will constantly flap based on 5 different levels depending on the degree of bending from the flex sensor, thus replicating a tickle effect.

3) A temperature sensor was located on the sensory side to track the palm temperature of the sender at the sensory side. This will translate to the heat produced at the actuation end by the heating element to replicate warmth. The temperature range of the translated heat was between 24-28°C.

An additional Short Message Service (SMS) mode feature was added to the system to be attached to the Graphical User Interface (GUI) of the computer at the actuation subsystem.

3   Affective Tele-Touch Therapy Experiment

3.1   Equipment and Methods

In this experiment, we investigated the effects of heartbeat rates when affective touches (i.e. human touch and tele-touch) were applied on human experimental subjects after experiencing a sad event. A sad video clip entitled "The Bridge" was be used to evoke sadness to the experimental subjects. In summary, the video narrated an incident where the father lost his only son in a train accident. The interested reader can search for this title at YouTube. A heartbeat sensor (Iron Man Heart Rate Monitor, Timex) was used to measure the heartbeat rates of the human subjects throughout this experiment.

There were 3 experimental groups: no touch control group, tele-touch group and human touch group. For each experiment, subjects will first rest for 3 minutes. After which, they will watch the sad video clip for about 5 minutes. Lastly, there will be another 3 minutes of recovery time. The difference between the 3 groups comes at the last 3 minutes of recovery time. In the control group, no touches will be involved. In the tele-touch group, subjects were asked to wear the forearm cuff of the system prototype described on Section 2 with warmth and mild vibrations applied on them. Subjects in the human touch group had a human hand placed on their posterior forearm at the same position where the forearm cuff in the tele-touch group was positioned.

3.2   Procedures

Each experiment subject will go through a sequence as shown on Fig. 5. First, there will be 3 minutes of rest time where subjects will close their eyes. Next, they will watch the sad video clip, which runs for 5 minutes. Lastly, there will be a last 3 minutes of recovery time where subjects will close their eyes.

The difference among the 3 groups was at the last 3 minutes. In the no touch control group, no touches will be involved. In the tele-touch group, subjects have to wear the forearm cuff of the system prototype where warmth and mild vibrations will be applied. Lastly, subjects in the human group would have a human hand placed on their posterior forearm at the same position where the forearm cuff in the tele-touch group is positioned. A pictorial diagram of the experimental settings and placement of the forearm cuff is shown on Fig. 6.

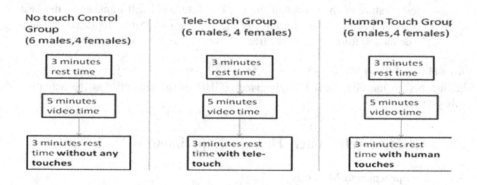

Fig. 5. Tele-Touch Experiment Procedures

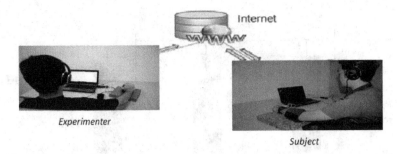

Fig. 6. Tele-touch Experimental Communications

3.3   Results and Analysis

There were a total of 30 participants in this experiment. They were divided into 3 groups, with 6 males and 4 females in each group. The average heartbeat rates of each of the 3 intervals during the experiment were calculated for each experimental subject. The average heartbeat rates for all the 10 subjects in each experiment groups were then tabulated and presented on the graphs below.

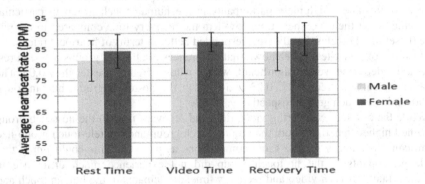

Fig. 7. Consolidated Graph of Average Heartbeat rates (BPM) vs Time interval in No Touch Group

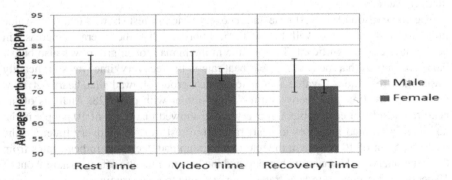

Fig. 8. Consolidated Graph of Average Heartbeat rates (BPM) vs Time interval in Human Touch Group

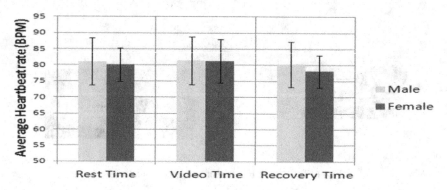

Fig. 9. Consolidated Graph of Average Heartbeat rates (BPM) vs Time interval in Tele-Touch Group

Results based on average graphs have shown a mild increase in average heartbeat rates during video time and from rest time in all groups. However, the difference in heartbeat rates between all the groups came at the recovery period. A further increase in heartbeat rates was observed in the recovery time of the no-touch group while decreases in heartbeat rates could be found for both human touch and tele-touch groups. Both male and female participants in the human touch group in particular were able to get their heartbeat rates lower in the recovery time compared to the rest time (baseline). Females, in all cases, responded better in terms of heartbeat rates.

Results from the t-test have shown that differences in all the 3 groups between rest time and video time were insignificant, with p-values slightly greater than 0.05. The p-values calculated were 0.07, 0.23 and 0.11 in the no-touch group, human touch group, and tele-touch group, respectively.

While the p-values comparing video time and recovery time in the no-touch group remained higher than 0.05, both the human touch group and the tele-touch group had significant differences for the same comparisons as $p < 0.05$. This could imply that while participants in the no-touch group did not experience much difference in heartbeat rates between video and recovery time, participants in the human touch and tele-touch groups had a significant decrease in heartbeat rates comparing the same periods. Females, in both groups, were observed to have a more significant decrease in heartbeat rates.

The comparison of the rest time and recovery time in t-test showed that the p-value in no-touch group was well below 0.05, implying that the average increase in heartbeat rate was significant. The p-value in the human touch group was also below 0.05. This means that the average heartbeat rate in the recovery time was significantly lower than rest time. P-value in the tele-touch group showed that heartbeat rates comparing rest time and recovery time were similar with $p = 0.28$. Analysis of the heart rate results of each subject in every group showed that 8 out of 10 people in the no touch group had increases in heart rates from rest time to recovery time. On the contrary, 5 out of 10 people in the tele-touch group had decreases in heart rates from the same intervals. Human touch group had the best therapeutic effects where 9 out of 10 people had decreases in heart rates from rest time to recovery time.

Analysis of the difference in heart rates from video time to recovery time is as follows: No touch group: 7 out of 10 increases in heart rates. Tele-touch group: 9 out of 10 decreases in heart rates. Human touch group: 8 out of 10 decreases in heart rates. From the quantitative heart rates results and feedback from the subjects, this pilot study shows that touch (human or tele-touch) was able to have an effect on the psycho-physical state of subjects by reducing the heartbeat rate after experiencing video-induced sadness.

4   Conclusion

An affective tele-touch system has been described. Touch (i.e. vibration, warmth) was sent over the internet. The actuation levels could be adjusted remotely by another person controlling the sensory device wirelessly through the internet. This provides an option of being able to apply a touch even though two people are physically apart. Examples of potential applications for this system include the domains of physical and/or emotional therapy, support for under-staffed hospitals and remote children caring. The ultimate aim of this prototype is to able to further investigate the therapeutic effects on isolated children in cancer wards by speeding up their recovery from cancer.

Results in the series of affective tele-touch therapy experiments on university-aged subjects have shown that both human touches and tele-touches will be able to reduce the heartbeat rates of the experimental subjects after experiencing a sad event. T-test and the average graphs results have been able to show this. Human touches, however, still give the best therapeutic effects based on t-test and average heart rate graphs. Female participants in this experiment have also been able to respond better in terms of heartbeat rates than the male participants.

Acknowledgements. We wish to thank Swetha Ganesaan and Ravi Paramasvaran for the technical assistance. The project Affective Tele-Touch Technologies (AT3) was supported by the Singapore Ministry of Education Academic Research Fund, Tier1, under grant no. R-263-000-576-112.

References

1. Bakwin, H.: Loneliness in infants. American Journal of Diseases in Children 63, 30–40 (1942)
2. Spitz, R.A.: Hospitalism: An inquiry into the genesis of psychiatric conditions in early childhood. The Psychoanalytic Study of the Child 1, 53–74 (1945)
3. Eid, M., Jongeun, C., El Saddik, A.: HugMe: A haptic video conferencing system for interpersonal communication. In: IEEE Conference on Virtual Environments, Human-Computer Interfaces and Measurement Systems, VECIMS 2008, pp. 5–9 (2008)
4. Tsetserukou, D., Neviarouskaya, A., Prendinger, H., Kawakami, N., Ishizuka, M., Tachi, S.: Enhancing Mediated Interpersonal Communication through Affective Haptics. In: Nijholt, A., Reidsma, D., Hondorp, H. (eds.) INTETAIN 2009. LNICST, vol. 9, pp. 246–251. Springer, Heidelberg (2009)

5. Shibata, T., Kawaguchi, Y., Wada, K.: Investigation on People Living with Seal Robot at Home. International Journal of Social Robotics 4, 53–63 (2011)
6. Shibata, T., Wada, K.: Robot therapy: A new approach for mental healthcare of the elderly - A mini-review. Gerontology 57, 378–386 (2011)
7. Ekman, P., Levenson, R., Friesen, W.: Autonomic nervous system activity distinguishes among emotions. Science 221, 1208–1210 (1983)
8. Levenson, R.W., Ekman, P., Friesen, W.V.: Voluntary Facial Action Generates Emotion-Specific Autonomic Nervous System Activity. Psychophysiology 27, 363–384 (1990)
9. Collet, C., Vernet-Maury, E., Delhomme, G., Dittmar, A.: Autonomic nervous system response patterns specificity to basic emotions. Journal of the Autonomic Nervous System 62, 45–57 (1997)
10. Schwartz, G.E., Weinberger, D.A., Singer, J.A.: Cardiovascular differentiation of happiness, sadness, anger, and fear following imagery and exercise. Psychosomatic Medicine 43, 343–364 (1981)
11. Rainville, P., Bechara, A., Naqvi, N., Damasio, A.R.: Basic emotions are associated with distinct patterns of cardiorespiratory activity. International Journal of Psychophysiology 61, 5–18 (2006)

Human-Humanoid Co-working
in a Joint Table Transportation

Paul Evrard[1] and Abderrahmane Kheddar[2,3]

[1] Commissariat à l'Énergie Atomique (CEA), LIST, Fontenay-aux-Roses, France
[2] CNRS-AIST Joint Robotics Laboratory (JRL), UMI3218/CRT, Tsukuba, Japan
[3] CNRS-UM2 LIRMM, UMR5506, IDH Group, Montpellier, France

Abstract. We address the problem of programming a human-humanoid haptic joint action consisting in transporting an beam. For such tasks humanoid robots plan footsteps to walk while keeping balance and coordinating whole-body manipulation-locomotion. In order to achieve such tasks, we devised a method consisting in assembling in a task-based control framework, a reactive walking pattern generator with a footprint planning strategy mapped from robot force cues interpretation and a task kinematic constraint. This approach basically decouples locomotion from manipulation but uses several heuristics to well tune each independent task to work in conjunction with the other. Experiments conducted on a real HRP-2 humanoid robot assessed the method.

1 Introduction

In this work, we target haptic joint actions for a particular class of robots: *humanoids*. For general robotic systems, achieving haptic joint actions requires the ability to understand human intentions from multimodal cues, human-in-the-loop motion planning, stable and robust control under safety constraints, etc. In humanoid robotics, anthropomorphism has distinguishing issues relatively to fixed-base or wheeled robots; for example:

- reactive planning in the generation of footprints and whole-body motion in close contact with a human whatever is the walking phase in progress;
- coordination of locomotion and manipulation under equilibrium and haptic task constraints.

We study the problem of an interactive beam transportation task jointly by a human and a humanoid robot. However, our work extends to direct human-robot interaction–as is demonstrated in this paper–as long as the contacts bewteen the human and humanoid are established solely at force sensing links. More general close body-to-body contact configurations requires whole body haptic sensing. We present a robotic integrative approach that combines and adapts well-established impedance control techniques with reactive walking pattern generation based on model preview control, and adding some heuristics for discreet stepping and arm/locomotion coordination. Results obtained from real experiments of a beam transportation scenario show some limitation that we aim at addressing in future work.

S.S. Ge et al. (Eds.): ICSR 2012, LNAI 7621, pp. 357–366, 2012.

2 Preliminaries

A joint human-humanoid transportation task has been successfully implemented in [12] by decoupling the gait generation problem and freezing the torso joints of the robot. The force sensed at the wrists of the robot was filtered by admittance, resulting in a reference velocity for the waist of the robot. Steps were generated to track this reference velocity. Ideally, the humanoid robot must support at least half of the weight of the object. In a tentative to improve the previous experiment–on the HRP-2 humanoid robot–we propose to extend this result to allow whole-body motion during the transportation task.

In our setup, we consider a follower robot. Therefore, the robot must react to the human intentions and does not perform actions of its own initiative. We consider the haptic channel as the only information flow between the robot and the human operator. This scenario raises the following difficulties:

- since the human operator is in the loop, we do not use pre-programmed trajectories. The robot needs to reactively plan footprints and generate dynamically stable gaits;
- the robot will be subject to external forces which will threaten its balance. If these forces are significant, they have to be taken into account in the gait generation itself [9]. In general, however, if both agents collaborate in a constructive way, and if the robotic partner has a compliant behavior, the interaction forces will be limited to some extent. Therefore, in this work, we will not take these forces into account at the gait generation level;
- the haptic cue being the only information channel through which the human operator can communication own *intentions*, the forces measured at the wrists of the humanoid robot is used to be mapped into whole body motion, and footprints generation;
- Finally, given the discrete nature of the bipedal gait, the motion of the body of the robot can be computed to absorb as much as possible the fluctuations induced by the gait.

We tackle the problem by defining a desired cartesian impedance with respect to a reference body (here, the waist) for the wrists of the robot. Pilot experiments allowed tuning the gains, with a stiff behavior in the vertical direction, and a compliant behavior in the horizontal plane. Second, we devised a simple strategy consisting in keeping constant the offset transformation linking the mid-hand line frame and the feet. When the human partner pulls the table, the robot arms comply, which results on a shift in the offset; we setup experimentally a threshold above which the robot performs a step to recover from the shift. The difference in the force cues sensed by each force sensor of the robot's arms is used to compute the desired turn (right or left). Third, since the human partner may impose arbitrary trajectories to the table, it is important to make reactive the walking pattern generator (PG) [11][10].

3   Walking Pattern Generator

A simplified Linear Inverted Pendulum Model (LIPM) can be used to link the Zero Moment Point (ZMP) and the Center of Mass (CoM) of the pendulum. This relationship can be written under the form of a dynamical system where the jerk of the CoM is used as an input. One can thus derive a controller that computes appropriate values of the jerk of the CoM to obtain the desired ZMP trajectory. However, the structure of the system is such that, to have a good ZMP tracking, the position of the CoM should move ahead of time. As a result, the ZMP trajectory must be specified for a preview window of a given length [4].

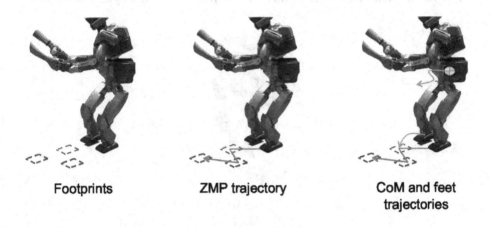

Footprints	ZMP trajectory	CoM and feet
		trajectories

Fig. 1. Walking pattern generation stages

The Fig. 1 illustrates these steps. New reference footprints can be used to generate walking motions with a delay corresponding to the length of the preview window. This considerably reduces the reactivity of the system. On the other hand, the cost of changing the whole preview window at each control iteration (every 5ms) is too high. A possible solution to this problem has been proposed in [9], which requires increasing the frequency of the ZMP controller.

Another technique to overcome this issue, proposed by [3], considers that the ZMP trajectory is a third order polynomial. This allows the derivation of an analytical solution for the CoM trajectory and the modification of the steps in the preview window. One particularity of this algorithm is that changing the ZMP reference in the preview window can induce fluctuations of the ZMP reference when connecting the new reference to the old one. To compensate for these fluctuations, it has been proposed in [8] to increase the single support time of the step. We adapted this latter algorithm to be used in our scenario, see details in [11].

4   Footprints Generation

In order to generate the walking motion, footprint planning is the input to the previous PG. Yet, this process is a compromise between planning enough steps ahead for a dynamic walk and fast adapt to any change that may be dictated instantly by the human partner. The problem of footprints planning can be tackled in different ways. In [12], the authors implemented the algorithm proposed by Kosuge et al. for their Mobile Robot Helper, see [6], to synchronize the motion of the arms with the motion of the body of the robot. The idea is to decompose the robot into two parts: the arms and a mobile base, and to virtually couple the motion of these elements. This is illustrated on Fig 2. The desired

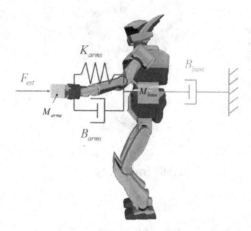

Fig. 2. Virtual coupling of the end-effectors and the body of a humanoid robot to synchronize the arms and the body of the robot during a collaborative transportation task. M_{base}, B_{base}, M_{arms}, B_{arms} and K_{arms} are the virtual impedance parameters used to couple the arms and the base, and to generate the motion of the base. F_{ext} is the force applied by the human operator on the arms.

dynamics shown on Fig 2 is continuous, but a humanoid robot will perform discrete steps. This typically results in a body motion that is different from the prescribed dynamics. Unless this prescribed dynamics is taken into account as part of the gait generation method, the robot will not be able to deal with it correctly. We made the choice to avoid modifying the gait generation method of a robot, which we considered as a black box. Hence, the only way to approximate the dynamics is to plan appropriate footprints. The reactive walking pattern generator presented in the previous paragraph allows us to modify the next step to be performed by the robot during each double support phase. In our setup, these phases are separated by duration of approximately one second. Therefore, we can roughly model the nature of the motion of the humanoid body by adding a time delay of one: that is, the force due to the virtual coupling between the arms and the base will be transmitted with a one second time delay to the base.

If we denote $F_{\text{arm/base}}$ the force applied by the spring damper system $(K_{\text{arms}}, B_{\text{arms}})$ on the base of the robot, then the motion on the base is given by:

$$V_{\text{base}}(t) = B_{\text{base}}(t - T)^{-1}F_{\text{arm/base}} \tag{1}$$

where $T = 1$s is the time delay induced by the discrete nature of the stepping and the computation constraints of the pattern generator. To evaluate the impact of this time delay on the gait of the robot, we simulated this system using Matlab/Simulink, with gains that we knew by experience to be appropriate for the admittance control of the arms of the robot[1]. Simulation and preliminary experimental results for $M_{\text{arms}} = 5$kg, $B_{\text{arms}} = 100$Ns/m, $K_{\text{arms}} = 25$N/m, $M_{\text{base}} = 5$kg and $B_{\text{base}} = 50$Ns/m revealed that the time delay introduces a highly oscillatory behavior, which in fact disturbs the human partner during the transportation task. To avoid these oscillations, we rather use a different approach where the base and the arms are not bilaterally coupled, but only unilaterally. This is explained hereafter.

5 Gait and Manipulation Tasks Decoupled Synchronization

Regardless of the synchronization of the base of the robot with the arms, a problem that arises when the robot walks using the LIPM and ZMP criterion is that the body of the robot swings laterally to track the CoM reference computed by the walking PG. If the arms of the robot do not compensate this swinging motion, the human operator will experience a non-natural way in achieving such haptic joint tasks. On top of being uncomfortable for the human operator, this will make precise positioning tasks difficult. We can cancel the swing motion by considering the appropriate Jacobian matrix for the admittance control task. The gait of a biped robot is a succession of double support phases and single support phases. During each of these phases, if we assume no slippage between the floor and the support foot, the support foot can be considered as a fixed base for the humanoid robot. This means that the absolute velocity of this body of the robot is considered to be nil. Thus, by considering the support foot as the root of the robot, and by considering Jacobian matrices with respect to this root, the motions of the legs when the robot is walking can be canceled.

Fig. 3 illustrates the swinging motion of the waist and the motion of the grippers. We see that the amplitude of the swinging motion of the grippers is about 10 times less than that of the waist. In fact, the small oscillations of the gripper results from the damping of the pseudo-inverse used to compute the control law. This allows us to implement the admittance control of the arms of the robot in a way such that in the absence of external forces applied on the grippers, the latter will have zero absolute velocity –despite the swinging of the body of the robot due to the gait. That is to say, it allows us to decouple the gait

---

[1] If we consider a fixed mobile base, the virtual coupling between the arms and the base reduces to impedance/admittance control of the arms.

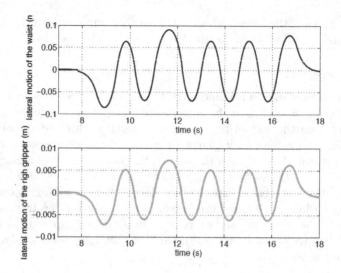

Fig. 3. Top: lateral swinging motion of the waist during on-place stepping of the robot. The amplitude of the motion is about 10cm. Bottom: reduced oscillations of the gripper (amplitude of about 1mm) after the compensation of the legs motion.

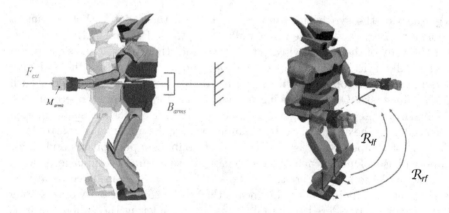

Fig. 4. Left: Decoupled admittance control and gait: the admittance of the end-effector of the humanoid is a damper fixed to the ground rather than to the body of the robot, allowing to decouple force-based control from the motion of the body of the robot; Right: Reference frames used for the synchronization of the feet and hands

of the robot from the manipulation task, and to display a desired admittance on the grippers of the robot regardless of the body motion, Fig. 4(left).

Now we need to plan footprints to synchronize the locomotion with the gait. Indeed, the decoupling between the manipulation task and gait is possible only as long as one remains in the workspace of the robot. But to allow wider-range motions, the humanoid robot has to walk. We first define a reference frame related to the hands of the robot. The center of this frame is the middle of the segment joining the robots end-effectors. This segment supports one of the axes of this frame; the other axis is vertical; and the third axis is set so as to obtain a right-hand frame. Let $\mathcal{R}_{lf}$ and $\mathcal{R}_{rf}$ be the transformation matrices (homogeneous matrices) from the left and right foot to this reference frame, respectively, as depicted on Fig. 4(right).

Synchronizing the hands and feet is defined as keeping these transformations as close as possible to two reference transformations $^0\mathcal{R}_{lf}$ and $^0\mathcal{R}_{rf}$. During each double support phase, the relative position error between the next fly foot and the reference frame will be computed, and the landing position of the next fly foot will be selected so as to correct this error. The transformation describing the fly foot destination is:

$$\mathcal{R} = (^0\mathcal{R}_{ff})^{-1}\mathcal{R}_{ff} \qquad (2)$$

where subscript ff means fly foot. This transformation is then projected into the appropriate coordinate system to send a new footprint reference to the walking pattern generator. The planned footprint is then clipped to a safe area, which computation is described in [10].

To summarize: in the *standing mode*, the arms of the robot are compliant in order to follow the human intentions, or they follow a trajectory desired by the robot. *The position of the hands dictate the position of the feet*, and steps are generated only so that the robot tracks the reference posture, without disturbing the position of the hands. The steps are generated reactively and do not follow any specific pattern, since the robot is not really walking, but performing steps in reaction to the motion of its hands. In the *walking mode*, the robot performs steps, following regular patterns. *The position of the feet dictates the positions of the hands*. The robot will move its hands so as to track the reference posture, in response to the generated steps, which can be seen as an external disturbance for the posture tracking task. The compliance of the arms is tuned so that external forces do not disturb the walking task, i.e. do not make the robot fall. The walking velocity is higher than in the standing mode, since the robot follows regular, optionally precomputed patterns with little or no disturbance on the feet positions. A high level controller that interprets the human intentions can trigger a transition to a mode where the robot is more reactive, so that it can brake. The transition can be smooth, if the human and robot slowly decelerate, or abrupt in case of an unexpected obstacle. In this case, the robot will switch from the walking to the standing mode within one foot step to stop at once.

6   Integration and Experiments

In order to control the robot each task has been programmed as a sensory-motor component integrated as part of a prioritized stack-of-tasks controller that we named SoT [7].

Two kinds of task were performed with the HRP-2 robot. The first interaction paradigm that was tested is direct interaction between a human operator and the robot, where a user moves the arms of the robot to trigger locomotion. This is

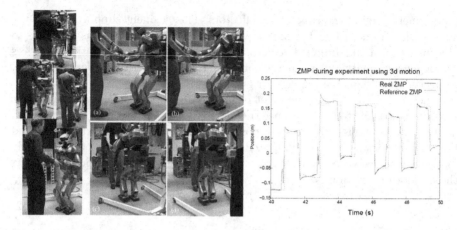

Fig. 5. Left: Experimental results: direct interaction between a user and the HRP-2 robot; Right: Reference and real ZMP in a direct interaction experiment (zoom taken between $t = 40$s and $t = 50$s)

illustrated on Fig. 5. As can be seen, several users could interact with the robot. The Fig. 5(right) depicts the ZMP reference along the x-axis computed by the pattern generator we previously mentioned, and obtained during an experiment where the motion of the robot was constrained on the sagittal plane (the robot stepped only forward and backward). The ZMP real is deviating by 2cm from the reference trajectory, which is quite similar to the result obtained in [9]. We conclude that the compliance of the arms of the robot is able to absorb most of the perturbation coming from the interaction with the user, preventing the humanoid robot from falling. It is also important to note that the experiments are run using the commercial stabilizer provided with the OpenHRP. This also explains the good quality of the ZMP tracking. This is also confirmed by looking at the interaction force measured by the wrist sensors. We first notice that the signal is very noisy. This is generally the case with force measurements, and this is made worse by the impacts between the feet and the ground, which generate structural vibration of the robot. However, the noise is filtered by the admittance controller, and has no noticeable impact on the motion of the arms. We also notice that forces do not exceed about 10N in the plotted time interval. This value was actually an upper bound for the whole experiment from which the data has been recorded. This means that forces under 10N can generate forward and backward motions, which are essentially generated by applying forces along the arms of the robot. This also explains the relatively good quality of the ZMP tracking shown in Fig. 5(right), considering that the interaction forces are neglected. In a second experiment, the robot was holding a board, and a human operator was applying forces on the other side of the board to move the board along with the robot. This is illustrated on Fig. 6. These experiments are also conducted with different human operators and are quite repeatable.

Fig. 6. Cooperative table transportation between an HRP-2 humanoid robot and a human operator

The locomotion of the HRP-2 is slow and the usability of the set-up is poor. One of the reasons for the slow locomotion comes from the reactivity of the walking pattern generator itself, which we use as a black box. Due to numerical issues in the implementation, small changes in the orientation of the footprints resulted in longer single support phases. This phenomenon is specific to the algorithm we used to generate the gait. A second reason is that the position of the swinging foot is planned at the very beginning of the single support phases. Soon after the swinging foot leaves the ground, the landing position can no longer be modified, which limits the reactivity of the system. This is not an intrinsic limitation of the algorithm, and we could also try to allow the modification of the landing position of the swinging foot for a longer time after the double support phase. However, modifying the landing position at an early stage of the single support phase is more conservative and has greater chances to result in a stable motion. To overcome this problem, it is necessary to improve the gait generation method in order to produce fully reactive gaits. Otherwise, we can also focus on the aspects related to collaborative tasks [5].

7   Conclusion and Future Work

We presented a control setup that setup builds over existing impedance control and model based preview control technique to endow a humanoid robot with wide-range, compliant behaviors. We implemented this setup on the humanoid robot HRP-2, to perform joint transportation tasks with a human operator and we performed preliminary experiments to assess the usability of this setup.

Once we ended this stream of investigations, appeared several unanswered questions on the choice of the parameters, the heuristics and the hypothesis made (such as using the PG as a black box), etc. In order to assess, improve or recall into question bricks that made possible these preliminary experiments, it became clear that a thorough investigation on such a scenario, starting from observations of real human-human teams, is necessary [2]. In order to do so, we first devised a motion-and-interaction-force monitoring and capture system and run basic human experiments to gain more insight toward understanding human behavior and, hopefully, be inspired to improve the performances of our human-humanoid object transportation scenario. Our future work addresses these investigations [1].

References

1. Bussy, A., Gergondet, P., Kheddar, A., Keith, F., Crosnier, A.: Proactive behavior of a humanoid robot in a haptic transportation task with a human partner. In: IEEE International Symposium on Robot and Human Interactive Communication (Ro-Man), Paris, France, September 9-13 (2012)
2. Bussy, A., Kheddar, A., Crosnier, A., Keith, F.: Human humanoid haptic joint object transportation case study. In: IEEE/RSJ International Conference on Robots and Intelligent Systems, Algarve, Portugal, October 7-12 (2012)
3. Harada, K., Kajita, S., Kaneko, K., Hirukawa, H.: An analytical method for real-time gait planning for humanoid robot. International Journal of Humanoid Robotics (IJHR) 3(1), 1–19 (2006)
4. Kajita, S., Kanehiro, F., Kaneko, K., Fujiwara, K., Harada, K., Yokoi, K., Hirukawa, H.: Biped walking pattern generation by using preview control of zero-moment point. In: IEEE International Conference on Robotics and Automation, Taipei, Taiwan, September 14-19, pp. 1620–1626 (2003)
5. Kheddar, A.: Human-robot haptic joint actions: Is an equal control-sharing approach possible? In: 4th International Conference on Human System Interactions (HSI), Yokohama, Japan, May 19-21, pp. 269–273 (2011)
6. Kosuge, K., Sato, M., Kazamura, N.: Mobile robot helper. In: IEEE International Conference on Robotics and Automation, pp. 583–588. IEEE, San Francisco (2000)
7. Mansard, N., Stasse, O., Evrard, P., Kheddar, A.: A versatile generalized inverted kinematics implementation for collaborative humanoid robots: The stack of tasks. In: IEEE Internationl Conference on Advanced Robotics, Munich, Germany (June 2009)
8. Morisawa, M., Harada, K., Kajita, S., Nakaoka, S., Fujiwara, K., Kanehiro, F., Kaneko, K., Hirukawa, H.: Experimentation of humanoid walking allowing immediate modification of foot place based on analytical solution. In: IEEE International Conference on Robotics and Automation, Roma, Italy, pp. 820–826 (2007)
9. Nishiwaki, K., Kagami, S.: Online walking control system for humanoids with short cycle pattern generation. The International Journal of Robotics Research 28(6), 729–742 (2009)
10. Perrin, N., Stasse, O., Lamiraux, F.: Approximation of feasibility tests for reactive walk on HRP-2. In: IEEE International Conference on Robotics and Automation (ICRA), pp. 4243–4248 (2010)
11. Stasse, O., Evrard, P., Perrin, N., Mansard, N., Kheddar, A.: Fast foot prints re-planning and motion generation during walking in physical human-humanoid interaction. In: IEEE/RAS International Conference on Humanoid Robotics, pp. 284–289 (2009)
12. Yokoyama, K., Handa, H., Isozumi, T., Fukase, Y., Kaneko, K., Kanehiro, F., Kawai, Y., Tomita, F., Hirukawa, H.: Cooperative works by a human and a humanoid robot. In: IEEE International Conference on Robotics and Automation, pp. 2985–2991. IEEE, Taipei (2003)

User-Defined Body Gestures
for Navigational Control of a Humanoid Robot

Mohammad Obaid[1,2], Markus Häring[2], Felix Kistler[2],
René Bühling[2], and Elisabeth André[2]

[1] HITLab New Zealand, University of Canterbury, Christchurch, New Zealand
[2] Augsburg University, Human Centered Multimedia, Augsburg, Germany

Abstract. This paper presents a study that allows users to define intuitive gestures to navigate a humanoid robot. For eleven navigational
commands, 385 gestures, performed by 35 participants, were analyzed.
The results of the study reveal user-defined gesture sets for both novice
users and expert users. In addition, we present, a taxonomy of the user-
defined gesture sets, agreement scores for the gesture sets, time performances of the gesture motions, and present implications to the design of
the robot control, with a focus on recognition and user interfaces.

1 Introduction

Researchers are increasingly addressing the use of algorithms to recognize full
body gestures and postures, in real time, to teleoperate and guide robots and
hence enhance the user's natural experience and engagement with the robot, such
as the work by [11][12]. The key to their approaches is to define intuitive and
natural human-robot interaction using non-verbal communications, such as body
gestures. Generally, most of the algorithms that use body gestures to control
robots are based on gesture design paradigms that are defined by its developers.
However, as the user is not involved in the process, the designed gestures may
not be the most intuitive and may not represent their natural behavior. Recently,
several researchers have addressed the same problem with the design of gesture
based interaction methods in several other domains including surface computing
[13] and public displays [5]. However, a user-defined set of gestures for the control
of a humanoid robot has not been defined to this date.

In this paper, we present the design of a gesture set that is based on the
user's natural behavior when controlling a robot. We collect data from both
Technical[1] (T) and Non-Technical (NT) users when performing gesture motions
to navigate a humanoid robot (Nao[2]). We contribute to the field of Human-Robot
Interaction (HRI) the following: (1) the establishment of a user-defined gesture
sets for both (T and NT users) to navigate a humanoid robot, (2) the analysis of
qualitative and quantitative data that includes gesture taxonomy, performance
data measures, observations, and subjective responses, and (3) an understanding
of the implications for humanoid robot control using human gestures.

---

[1] We term a user experienced with robots and/or gesture tracking as *Technical*.
[2] http://www.aldebaran-robotics.com

S.S. Ge et al. (Eds.): ICSR 2012, LNAI 7621, pp. 367–377, 2012.

2   Related Work

In this section, we present related literature and previous work on human gestures, designing gestures, and gesture controlled robots.

Human Gesture Categories: Researchers have conducted a vast number of studies to understand gestural interactions between individuals and how gestures can be categorized based on the information communicated. There is no universal categorization standard for body gestures and postures, however, researchers used different taxonomies for categorization. Efron [1] was one of the first to classify gestures into five categories: physiographics, kinetographics, ideographics, deictics, and batons. McNeill [6] presented six types of gestures: adaptor, beat, emblemic, deictic, iconic, and metaphoric gestures. Moreover, McNeil [7] defined four phases that construct a gesture: preparation, stroke, hold and retraction. The preparation is the phase that brings the body from its rest to a position that is suitable for executing the gesture. The stroke phase is the real information contained in the gesture, while the retraction is the phase where the body goes to its rest position again. Hold, on the other hand, is the temporal duration of the stroke phase. In this paper, we use the phases defined by McNeill.

Designing Gestural Input: The basic rule when designing an interface is to initially define the needs of its users and gestural interfaces are no exception [8]. Therefore, several domain areas employ the design of appropriate gestures for a system by allowing users to intuitively define how they would use it. Recently, the work presented by Wobbrock et al. [13] described the design of appropriate gestures for surface tabletop interfaces. They define gestures by employing non-technical users to observe the effect of a gesture and then asked them perform a gesture to match its cause. The work by Wobbrock et al. was a motive for many researchers to follow a similar design paradigm in their domain field. For example, Kray et al. [4] identified user-defined gestures that can be used to communicate a mobile phone with public display, tabletops, and other devices. Kurdyukova et al. [5] presented a study for identifying a user-defined set to transfer data from an iPad in a multi-display environment. In this research, we follow a similar approach to Wobbrock et al., with a focus on navigational gestural control for humanoid robots.

Gesture Controlled Robots: The fact that humanoid robots are machines that look like humans and preserve some human functionalities has motivated researchers to look for intuitive interaction ways that are similar to the human-human communications. While some work follows multimodal approaches, mostly combining speech with gesture commands [11], other work efforts are put towards controlling robots using pointing gestures [10], but such methods are limited to a certain range of commands. Moreover, Hu et al. [2] developed simple hand gestures for robot navigational actions, while, the recent work of Konda et al. [3] employ full body postures to navigate their robots.

Previous work, in this field, relied on the developers of the system to define commands and gestural instructions, however, none have exhibited how users would like to control a humanoid robot intuitively, which is the novel part presented in this paper.

3 User Defined Gestures to Control Humanoid Robots

The main objective of this study is to define a set of control body gestures derived from the users' actions when intuitively instructing a humanoid robot. In particular, in this study, we focus on navigational control of the humanoid robot Nao. We use eleven actions (*Move Forward, Move Backward, Move Left, Move Right, Turn Left, Turn Right, Stop, Speed Up, Slow Down, Stand Up, Sit Down*) for which users, of the presented study, chose gestures. The motions of all navigational actions are implemented from the perspective of the robot using the built in motion module of the Nao system (Academic Edition V3.2).

Experimental Setup: To define a set of intuitive gestures to control a humanoid robot, we consider two types of user groups, Technical (T) and Non-Technical (NT): The first are users that have some experience with humanoid robots and are aware of gesture tracking systems (such as Microsoft Kinect). The second are users who have no sound knowledge of such technologies. We consider the two groups as it is apparent when a user is aware of the limitation of the technologies they can define their gestures based on those limitations; hence, including the two groups (T and NT) allows system designers to consider the characteristics of both groups.

We elicit preformed gestural actions from 35 participants (17 T, 18 NT), all from Germany. Initially, we asked participants, on a 5-point Likert scale (ranging from one to five), about their experience with the Microsoft Kinect and with a humanoid robot. The 17 T participants (six female, eleven male) have an average experience with MS Kinect=2.71 and with a humanoid robot=2.41. The 17 T participants have an average age of 29 ($SD = 5.2$) and are mainly from the Computer Science background. On the other hand, the 18 NT participants (ten female, eight male) have an average experience with MS Kinect=1.11 and with a humanoid robot=1.06. Most of the 18 NT participants are students from several disciplines, such as education, languages or economics, and have an average age of 27 ($SD = 7.8$). All participants except one were right-handed.

Apparatus: The experiment is arranged in a room with about 3 meters width and 6.5 meter depth. The room is equipped with a 50 inch plasma display and two cameras. The first camera records the front view of the user, while the other camera is setup as a side camera. The user has a designated region that he/she is allowed to freely move in during the study. This region is defined from the user's initial position and a distance of about 1 meter around that point. The humanoid robot, Nao, is placed to be facing the user at about 2 meters away from them.

Table 1. Taxonomy for full body gestures used to control a humanoid robot based on 385 gestures

Taxonomy of Full Body Gestures for Controlling a Humanoid Robot		
Form	static gesture	A static body gesture is held after a preparation phase.
	dynamic gesture	The gesture contains movement of one or more body parts during the stroke phase.
Body Parts	one hand	The gesture is performed with one hand.
	two hands	The gesture is performed with two hands.
	full body	The gesture is performed with at least one other body part than the hands.
View-Point	independent	The gesture is independent from the view point.
	user-centric	The gesture is performed from the user's point of view.
	robot-centric	The gesture is performed from the robot's point of view.
Nature	deictic	The gesture is indicating a position or direction.
	iconic	The gesture visually depicts an icon.
	miming	The used gesture is equal to the meant action.

Procedure: At the beginning of the experiment, each participant is given a description of the study and are told to stay within their designated region in the room. The following are the steps each participant is asked to follow: (1) on the screen, watch a video that demonstrates how Nao performs one of the navigational actions. (2) Upon the completion of the video, perform a gesture that can command Nao to repeat the demonstrated action. (3) Watch Nao performing the corresponding action (this is remotely activated by an instructor). (4) Answer a questionnaire corresponding to the action.

The eleven actions are presented to each participant in a randomized order. For the actions *Speed up, Slow down* and *Stop*, Nao will be in motion when the gesture is to be preformed by the participant. In this case, participants are asked to state when they are ready, after watching the video on the screen, and Nao is immediately activated by the instructor. Subjective and objective measures are explained further in Section 4.

4   Results

The results of our study presents a gesture taxonomy, a user-defined gesture set, performance data measures, qualitative observations, and subjective responses.

Gesture Taxonomy. We manually classify all gestures according to four dimensions: *form, (involved) body parts, view-point,* and *nature*. Each dimension consists of multiple items, shown in Table 1. They are partly based on the Taxonomy used by Wobbrock et al. [13] and adapted to match full body gestures. Moreover, *nature* was inspired by gesture categories defined by Salem et al. [9].

Form in our sense distinguishes between static and dynamic gestures (without and with movement respectively). Static gestures have a preparation phase at

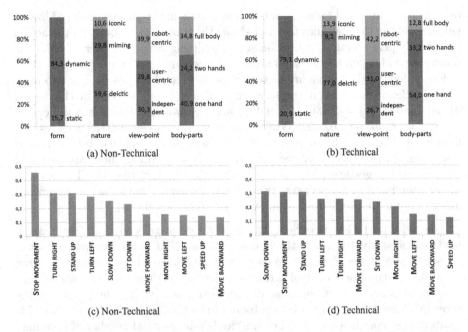

Fig. 1. Taxonomy distribution (a and b) and gesture agreement levels (c and d) for technical and non-technical users

the beginning, in which the user moves into the gesture space, but the core part of gesture is after the preparation phase. Therefore, the gesture is kept for a certain amount of time before the user releases it again in the retraction phase. In opposite, dynamic gestures have a clear stroke phase including the movement of body specific parts between the preparation and retraction phases.

The *body parts* dimension is quite self-explaining. It distinguishes between one hand, and two hand gestures, as well as full body gestures that involve at least one other body part.

The *view-point* dimension can be explained best with pointing gestures in a scenario where the robot is facing the user. Thus, a user-centric view-point means that when the user is pointing to his/her right, the robot should move in the pointing direction and, therefore, to the left from the robot's view. The opposite is a robot-centric view-point, i.e. when the user is pointing to his/her right, the robot moves in opposite to the pointing direction (to the right from the robot's view). Other gestures are view-point independent, for example, an open front-facing hand for stop which does not include any directional information.

The *nature* of our gesture is divided in three categories: The most common gestures we found for HRI are deictic gestures, that indicate a position or direction. These gestures can be either static, e.g. pointing to the right, or dynamic, e.g. waving to the right. They can be performed with one hand, two hands, or even other body parts, e.g. tilting the head. They can be performed from a user-centric or robot-centric view-point. Iconic gestures are visual depictions, e.g. an open front-facing hand for stop, or drawing a circle in the air for turning. Miming gestures realize the idea that the user shows the robot how to perform the action by actually performing it, e.g. if the action is sitting down, the user actually sits down. Depending on the view-point, miming gestures can be mirrored as well.

Fig. 1 depicts the taxonomy distributions for T and NT users. The two most visible differences between the two kinds of users can be seen in the *nature* dimension ($\chi^2 (2) = 26.36$, $p < 0.001$) and the *involved body parts* dimension ($\chi^2 (2) = 25.46$, $p < 0.001$). While T users clearly prefer deictic gestures and mainly use their hands for gesturing, NT users more often use full body and miming gestures. Therefore, one can say that T users prefer more abstract and less exhausting gestures. This is emphasized by the fact that the T users also tend to use more static postures than the NT, however, we found no significant differences for the *form* dimension ($\chi^2 (1) = 1.75$, $p = 0.186$).

A User-defined Gesture Set: The gestural data collected from the participants of the study, to control the humanoid robot Nao, is used to define a set of user-defined gestures that can be used for navigations. The process of selecting a suitable gesture for a control action is as follows: (1) For each control action t we identify a set P_t that contains all proposed gestures. (2) The proposed gestures in P_t are then grouped into subsets of identical gestures $P_{i_{1..N}}$, where i is a subset that contains identical gestures and N is the total number of identified subsets. (3) The representative gesture for action t is identified by selecting the subset P_i with the largest size, i.e. $MAX(P_i)$.

Fig. 2 depicts the representing gestures for the eleven actions for both T and NT users. In some cases, two representative gestures are present for one action as there were two large size gestural subsets (P_i) with an equal number of identical gestures, e.g. Action 1 for NT.

To further evaluate the degree of agreement among participants towards the selected user-defined sets, we employ a process that computes an agreement score[3] based on the work defined and used by Wobbrock et al [13]. An agreement score S_t corresponding to a selected user-defined gesture for action t is represented by a number in the range $[0, 1]$ that defines the general agreement among participants. The results of evaluating the degree of agreement for the eleven control actions of our study are presented in Fig. 1 (c) and (d). The overall agreement levels for the T and NT participants are the same, $S = 0.23$.

Gestural Phases and Timing: The video recordings of all participants, from the camera videotaping the frontal view of the user, were annotated using the ELan annotation tools[4]. The annotations segmented each video into 11 actions and each action into 4 phases (Start-up, Preparation, Stroke, and Retraction). The start-up phase represents the time it takes the participants to start their gestural instruction, after watching the action on the screen. While the others are the times for the gestural phases defined by McNeill [7]. Using the annotation tool, the

---

[3] For the equation refer to [13].
[4] Max Planck Institute for Psycholinguistics, Nijmegen, The Netherlands (http://www.lat-mpi.eu/tools/elan/).

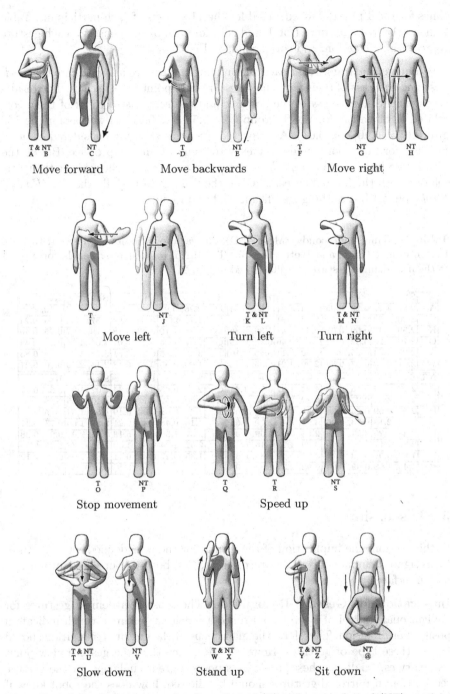

Fig. 2. User-defined gesture sets for the technical (T) and non-technical (NT) participants to navigate a humanoid robot

times for the 4 phases are extracted for the 11 actions of each participant. Table 2 shows the average times (for T and NT) for each of the phases of each gesture representing an action, and corresponds to Fig. 2.

Subjective Ratings: After each action, participants are asked to rate the *goodness* and *easiness* of their performed gesture on 7-point Likert scales. The results reveal that the *goodness* of the gestures and the *easiness* to think of them correlated significantly for the T group ($r = 0.54, p < 0.01$) as well as for the NT group ($r = 0.40, p < 0.01$). As expected, gestures that are considered as good matches for an action are usually easy to think of and to produce. Beside the direct correlation between *goodness* and *easiness*, we also checked for their correlation with the level of agreement and the timings (especially the *StartUp* and *Stroke* phase) but nothing significant could be found.

Table 2. Time in seconds (Mean, SD) for each of the four phases (**St**art-up, **Pr**eparation, **St**roke, and **Re**traction) for T and NT Participants. Labels correspond to the user-defined gesture sets illustrated in Fig. 2.

T	St	Pr	Sk	Re	T	St	Pr	Sk	Re
A	2.89, 1.71	0.29, 0.05	1.84, 1.21	0.80, 0.44	D	2.26, 0.91	0.40, 0.23	1.61, 0.47	1.12, 0.79
F	3.00, 1.43	0.42, 0.39	2.04, 1.91	0.84, 0.53	I	1.78 0.60	0.70, 0.62	2.37, 2.34	0.80, 0.24
K	2.59, 1.43	0.59, 0.57	2.28, 1.41	1.36, 0.86	M	2.48, 1.10	0.43, 0.18	2.19, 0.97	0.75, 0.40
O	2.76, 1.26	0.32, 0.12	2.14, 0.46	0.57, 0.25	Q	2.07, 1.54	0.24, 0.07	3.05, 1.51	0.74, 0.44
R	2.27, 1.04	0.25, 0.05	1.60, 0.11	0.63, 0.10	T	3.12, 2.36	0.37, 0.31	3.72, 1.76	1.25, 0.83
W	2.71, 0.92	0.57, 0.38	2.00, 1.21	0.95, 0.22	Y	1.69, 0.65	0.37, 0.18	2.11, 2.29	0.76, 0.21
NT	St	Pr	Sk	Re	**NT**	St	Pr	Sk	Re
B	2.12, 1.52	0.15, 0.30	4.84, 1.87	0.72, 1.44	C	2.04, 0.65	0.54, 0.34	2.02, 1.37	0.63, 0.17
E	2.19, 1.57	0.27, 0.54	4.22, 2.18	N/A	G	1.00, 0.52	0.17, 0.33	5.10, 1.65	N/A
H	2.39, 0.69	0.24, 0.28	2.85, 1.38	0.50, 1.01	J	1.44, 0.62	0.09, 0.19	4.59, 1.54	N/A
L	2.32, 2.18	0.73, 0.76	3.91, 2.45	0.70, 0.69	N	1.10, 0.48	0.45, 0.21	2.83, 1.60	0.73, 0.31
P	2.48, 1.26	0.24, 0.13	2.52, 0.92	1.09, 1.09	S	2.67, 1.36	0.28, 0.13	2.86, 2.03	0.95, 0.28
U	2.81, 1.17	1.06, 1.46	3.09, 1.23	1.16, 0.47	V	2.92, 2.24	0.89, 1.50	2.56, 1.73	1.35, 0.80
X	1.93, 0.94	0.72, 0.72	3.67, 1.92	0.38, 0.38	Z	1.35, 0.27	0.35, 0.11	1.81, 1.05	0.58, 0.12
@	2.46, 1.58	0.99, 0.66	6.92, 2.32	1.52, 2.08					

5   Discussion

In this section, the implication of the results for the user-defined set of gestures to navigate a humanoid robot are discussed for both gesture recognition and user interfaces.

Implication for Gesture Recognition: The most user-defined gestures for navigational control of a humanoid robot are deictic gestures, which indicate a position or direction. Therefore, the main focus of the gesture recognition should lay on these type of gestures. However, we notice that the gesture view-point may vary especially in these cases. This poses a great challenge for the gesture recognition: if mirrored gestures should be allowed, how does the robot know if it should move to the left-hand or right-hand side, when the user is pointing to his/her right? A solution could be to offer different modes for the navigational control: one in robot-view and one in user-view. Nevertheless, the interaction designer should think carefully of which gestures are influenced by the control mode. For example, gestures for linear movements are usually all influenced depending on the chosen view-point, while gestures for rotating the robot remain the same. Another interesting point is, that one-hand gestures are still the most important ones, however two-hand gestures are also used quite often, and NT users also performed quite a lot of gestures that involve other body parts. The usage of the second hand mostly results in symmetrical gestures, for which the information from the second hand is, more or less, redundant, but could be used to increase the confidence of a recognition system. The use of full body gestures raises a different issue: they can only be included when implementing additional gesture recognizers, and in opposite to the hand gestures, they really need the full body tracking information which justifies the usage of a depth sensor with corresponding tracking technology. Users generally preformed dynamic gestures, therefore, simple posture recognition would often be not enough. Moreover, the usual statically labeled pointing gesture should not be optimized for a certain amount of dwell-time as a lot of users included a single or repeated waving motion into pointing to indicate direction.

Implication for User Interfaces: In general, participants (both T and NT) had an affirmative response toward using freehand and full body gestures to navigate a robot. Throughout the study, an informal feedback was given by participants that include how easy it was to control a robot that way and how it can allow them to create a more realistic environment in controlling a humanoid robot. In some cases, the robot is described like a companion (or a pet) that can be ordered to move around using gestures. Nevertheless, it is notable that participants tend to talk to the robot during the study, even though they are aware that the robot does not respond to spoken commands. When participants are asked about why they gave a spoken command, 22 (11 T and 11 NT), or 63% of the total number of participants, stated that they would prefer a combination of speech and gesture commands, i.e. a multimodal interface, to control the robot. Moreover, several of the T participants indicated that they would prefer to make the robot stop with a speech command, while, NT participants would prefer to make the robot turn according to spoken instructions. Two of the NT participants also stated that they would prefer to control the robot only with speech commands than gestures, while none of the T participants would prefer it this way. In addition, it is apparent that participants are quick to respond to their task and produce gestures that correspond to the robot's navigational actions, where the overall average time, in seconds, for starting up a gesture after watching the action on screen is 2.25 (SD=0.57).

Moreover, several participants in the T group were worried that the recognition system will misclassify what their gesture was and the robot would do an unexpected action. On the other hand, participants in the NT groups expressed that they were worried that the robot will misunderstand their gestural command and perform a different action. This explains why a large number of participants would also give spoken commands in combination with their gestures; in addition, the importance of a reliable and robust gesture recognition system is vital in this case.

6   Conclusion and Future Work

In this paper, we have presented the results of a study to produce a user-defined gesture set to navigate a humanoid robot intuitively. The presented results are based on collecting data from two groups of users: technology aware users (i.e. gesture recognition and robots), and non-experienced users. The analysis of the data revealed a user defined-gesture set to control a humanoid robot. In addition, we presented (1) a taxonomy of the human-robot navigational gestures, (2) user agreement scores for each of the gestures representing a navigational commands, (3) time performances of the gesture motions, and (4) design implications for both recognition and user interfaces.

In the presented study, we focused on navigational commands, however, a humanoid robot can do more functions that can be also investigated in future work. In addition, the study revealed that a combination between gesture and speech commands is important and will be investigated in future work. Finally, we plan to implement the recognition of the user-defined gesture set in our open source Full Body Interaction Framework (FUBI)[5] and validate its functionality.

Acknowledgments. This work was partially funded by the European Commission within the 7th Framework Program under grant agreement eCUTE (FP7-ICT-257666).

References

1. Efron, D.: Gesture and Environment. King's Crown Press, Morningside Heights, New York (1941)
2. Hu, C., Meng, M., Liu, P., Wang, X.: Visual gesture recognition for human-machine interface of robot teleoperation. In: Proceedings of IEEE/RSJ International Conference on Intelligent Robots and Systems (IROS 2003), vol. 2, pp. 1560–1565 (October 2003)
3. Konda, K.R., Königs, A., Schulz, H., Schulz, D.: Real time interaction with mobile robots using hand gestures. In: Proceedings of the Seventh Annual ACM/IEEE International Conference on Human-Robot Interaction, HRI 2012, pp. 177–178. ACM, New York (2012)
4. Kray, C., Nesbitt, D., Dawson, J., Rohs, M.: User-defined gestures for connecting mobile phones, public displays, and tabletops. In: Proceedings of the 12th International Conference on Human Computer Interaction with Mobile Devices and Services, MobileHCI 2010, pp. 239–248. ACM, New York (2010)
5. Kurdyukova, E., Redlin, M., André, E.: Studying user-defined ipad gestures for interaction in multi-display environment. In: International Conference on Intelligent User Interfaces, pp. 1–6 (2012)
6. McNeill, D.: So you think gestures are nonverbal? Psychological Review 92(3), 350–371 (1985)
7. McNeill, D.: Head and Mind: What Gestures Reveal About Thought. University of Chicago Press, Chicago (1992)

---

[5] http://www.hcm-lab.de/fubi.html

8. Saffer, D.: Designing Gestural.Interfaces. O'Reilly Media, Sebastopol (2009)
9. Salem, M., Rohlfing, K., Kopp, S., Joublin, F.: A friendly gesture: Investigating the effect of multimodal robot behavior in human-robot interaction. In: RO-MAN, 2011 IEEE, July 31-August 3, pp. 247–252 (2011)
10. Sato, E., Yamaguchi, T., Harashima, F.: Natural interface using pointing behavior for human ndash;robot gestural interaction. IEEE Transactions on Industrial Electronics 54(2), 1105–1112 (2007)
11. Stiefelhagen, R., Fugen, C., Gieselmann, R., Holzapfel, H., Nickel, K., Waibel, A.: Natural human-robot interaction using speech, head pose and gestures. In: Proceedings of 2004 IEEE/RSJ International Conference on Intelligent Robots and Systems (IROS 2004), September 28-October 2, vol. 3, pp. 2422–2427 (2004)
12. Suay, H.B., Chernova, S.: Humanoid robot control using depth camera. In: Proceedings of the 6th International Conference on Human-Robot Interaction, HRI 2011, pp. 401–402. ACM, New York (2011)
13. Wobbrock, J.O., Morris, M.R., Wilson, A.D.: User-defined gestures for surface computing. In: Proceedings of the 27th International Conference on Human Factors in Computing Systems, pp. 1083–1092. ACM, New York (2009)

Studies on Grounding with Gaze and Pointing Gestures in Human-Robot-Interaction

Markus Häring, Jessica Eichberg, and Elisabeth André

Institute of Computer Science, Human Centered Multimedia, Augsburg University,
Germany

Abstract. In this study we investigated the use of gaze and pointing
gestures in scenarios where a human has to follow the instructions of
a humanoid robot. Our objective was to analyze the performance of a
human participant, that solves an abstract jigsaw puzzle with the help
of our robot instructor, in different grounding scenarios with varying difficulty. Furthermore we investigated how the attitude towards the robot
and the self-assessment of the participant changed. Our results support
that adding gaze to the interaction usually improves the interaction, but
often additional pointing gestures are needed to make a significant difference.

1 Introduction

Social robots are - among other duties - supposed to make our lives easier by
assisting us with more or less complex tasks. When this assistance is based on
collaboration the robot might also have to take the role of an instructor. For
example, people who are not at all versed in a manual skill could be showed
by a robot how to assemble a wardrobe. A robot would give them step by step
instructions, which part of the wardrobe has to be installed with which tool
at what position. A complex interaction like this involves a lot of coordination
not only of physical tasks but also of conversational actions. The process of
updating mutual knowledge, mutual assumptions and mutual beliefs during the
interaction is called *grounding* [3]. To minimize the chance of errors during this
process due to misunderstandings humans extend their verbal utterances with
gaze and pointing gestures and social robots will have to rely on that modalities
as well.

Sugiyama and Kanda [8] already confirmed that deictic gestures help robots
correct misunderstood verbal utterances. Faber and Bennewitz [4] stated that,
in a conversation, a robot should keep eye-contact with its human interlocutor in
order to show him attention. Moreover a robot can use gaze to target and clarify
the object of interest a conversation is dealing with. But even though many
applications for social robots combine gaze and pointing gestures, no detailed
comparison investigating the benefits of the two modalities has been done so
far. Under which conditions is gaze behavior additional to speech sufficient for
stable grounding and when is it mandatory to include pointing gestures to avoid

S.S. Ge et al. (Eds.): ICSR 2012, LNAI 7621, pp. 378–387, 2012.

critical errors? Will the users even pay attention to these cues while they are concentrating on the task? How does the user's attitude towards the robot change with changing level of modality also considering the complexity of the task?

In the presented study the participants were exposed to a situation they were not able to solve on their own, consequently they had to rely on the guidance of a robot. As a generalized testing environment we created an abstract puzzle game for the touch sensitive Microsoft Surface. In this game the robot acted as an *instructor* and guided the human participant through the whole puzzle job using either only speech, speech combined with gaze or speech combined with gaze and pointing gestures. We investigated the robot's performance as an instructor by logging the number of mistakes made by the participant and the time needed to solve the puzzle. We also asked the participants about their attitude towards the robot after their interaction and were also interested in their self-assessment regarding their own performance during the puzzle game. With the last aspect we wanted to evaluate to which extent the used modalities affect the participants self-efficacy when solving the puzzle.

As the use of additional modalities is also a question of efficiency (regarding energy consumption, hardware requirements and implementation workload) this study wants to clarify if and when this effort is necessary and what the benefits are, also in regard to improvements of the user's performance.

2 Related Work

A number of investigations dealing with human-robot interaction and puzzle games can be found in the literature that are of relevance for our study.

Burghart and Gaertner [2] analyzed the cooperative solving of a jigsaw puzzle between robot and human tutor. In contrast to our study, where the robot is taking on the role of an instructor, it is the human who provides support to the robot in their study, but only when the human tutor evaluates the last action of the robot as negative.

Giuliani and Knoll [5] observed how participants interacted in an cooperative construction task with an instructive robot, compared to the interaction with a supportive robot. While the instructive robot first instructs the user how to proceed with the construction and then supports the user by handing over building pieces, the supportive robot keeps a more passive role and only intervenes when the user is about to make a mistake. The subjective and objective data of their evaluation suggests that participants don't prefer one of the different roles rather will they adapt to the situation by taking the counterpart to the robot's role. Giuliani and Knoll's study focuses on the evaluation of the different roles and does not investigate the effects of the used modalities in their robot behaviors.

Salem et al. [7] considered multiple modalities in their study and installed a robot in a household scenario, where it assisted a human participant by providing information. The participants had to place some kitchen items in a cupboard while they had to pay attention to the robot's instructions. The following two conditions according to the robot's behavior were investigated:

– **Condition 1:** the *uni-modal (speech-only)* condition; only verbal instructions, no gesture or gaze behaviors
– **Condition 2:** the *multimodal (speech-gesture)* condition; verbal instructions with gaze and pointing gestures

Salem et al. evaluated whether the participant's attitude towards the robot changed between the different conditions, investigating items such as perceived 'activity', 'competence', 'liveliness', 'friendliness' and 'sympathy'. All evaluated items were rated higher in the second condition, though significant differences were only measured for 'activity', 'liveliness' and 'sympathy'.

Salem's work is very similar to our own. We also investigate how non-verbal behavior influences the human-robot collaboration. But we consider an additional condition, between 1) and 2), in which verbal instructions were only supported by gaze behavior. Thereby we wanted to find out whether gaze is already sufficient to enhance the human-robot-interaction in a way the *multimodal* condition does. Furthermore we expanded the evaluation by verifying not only the participants' view of the robot but also their self-assessment in the scenario. Similar to Giuliani and Knoll we also considered objective data, such as the duration of the interaction in our evaluation.

3   Development of an Instructing Robot

Due to its role as an *instructor*, our robot NAO[1] had to offer the human participant an exact instruction as he or she is not able to guess how the jigsaw has to look at the end of the task until the last piece of the puzzle is placed. In our game puzzle pieces are colored squares with colored shapes (circle, cross etc.; also see figure 2) in their center that can be easily referred to by the robot and as well expressed by Text-To-Speech (TTS).

We implemented the abstract jigsaw on a Microsoft Surface[2] Touch-Table, from where the robot obtains the exact coordinates of the jigsaw pieces via WLAN. The robot uses this data to calculate the head orientation for the gaze direction and the arm position for pointing gestures. The robot is able to establish eye contact with the human participant by using the built-in face detection module of Aldebaran Robotics.

Each round of the puzzle is divided in a piece task and a field task. Every task uses the behavior process explained by Ishiguro [6]:

Piece Task. First the robot (R) establishes eye contact with the participant (P) (see figure 1), using only the head and no eye movements. Thereon it describes the puzzle piece the participant has to select, by a verbal utterance such as for example *"Please select the black piece with the red circle in it"*. Meanwhile it gazes and points at the mentioned piece. After that it establishes again eye contact with the user signaling that it is now the participant's turn to continue.

---

[1] http://www.aldebaran-robotics.com/
[2] http://www.microsoft.com/surface/

The human participant then has to react by touching shortly the searched piece with his fingers on the touch table. When a piece was touched on the Microsoft Surface, the robot changes its gaze towards the corresponding position. If it was the right piece, the robot gives the participant positive, verbal feedback while performing a small confirming head nod (= backchannel signal as in [1]). Otherwise if it was the wrong piece, it shakes its head to indicate that the participant chose the wrong piece. In this case the robot repeats the whole piece task thus offering the participant another chance to succeed the task.

Field Task. The Field Task is analog to the Piece Task as can be seen in figure 1. Except that, in this case, the robot points to the position of the puzzle field, where the participant has to drag and drop the previously selected piece. The verbal instructions describe the target position in reference to a nearby piece that is already on the field, such as "Now place this piece left to the black piece with the red circle in it".

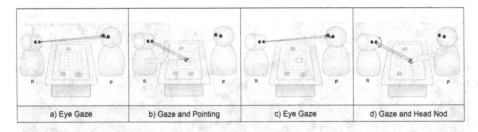

a) Eye Gaze   b) Gaze and Pointing   c) Eye Gaze   d) Gaze and Head Nod

Fig. 1. Structure of a Field Task using speech, gaze and pointing gestures; Robot (R) and Participant (P)

4   Experimental Design

To compare the effects of the different levels of modality we created three scenarios with which the participants were confronted:

4.1   Scenarios

1. **Verbal utterances only:** Robot only gives verbal instructions without eye contact, gaze or pointing gestures

2. **Verbal utterances with gaze:** Robot gives verbal instructions with eye contact; uses gaze demonstrating the human participant which puzzle piece has to be placed at which position

3. **Verbal utterances with gaze and pointing gestures:** Robot gives verbal instructions with eye contact; uses gaze and pointing gestures demonstrating the human participant which jigsaw piece has to be placed at which position

4.2   Conditions

We also varied the difficulty of the puzzle game in each scenario. The varying conditions should allow further insight into the effects of the used modalities, regarding the objective performance and subjective experience of the participant. While the participants might perform comparably good under simple conditions in all scenarios, the experience of the interaction might differ significantly. And to which extent will this change when the task gets more challenging?

So we prepared two different conditions, a *simple* puzzle game and a *complex* one. The initial positioning of the puzzle pieces at the beginning of the different games was for all participants the same.

1. Simple: The simple puzzle game contains 10+1 puzzle pieces. The first puzzle piece already lies at its right position in the puzzle field enabling an easier description of the remaining pieces' positions. The remaining ten pieces are all needed to solve the puzzle game. The puzzle pieces can by unambiguously identified by their color and the shapes in their center.

Fig. 2. Left: initial positioning of the *complex* puzzle game; **Middle:** experimental environment; **Right:** completed *simple* puzzle game

2. Complex: The complex puzzle game contains 20+1 puzzle pieces. But only ten of the remaining pieces are actually needed to solve the puzzle. The superfluous pieces are installed to complicate the detection of the relevant pieces. Furthermore there now are identical pieces, that may appear several times. Although those pieces are identical with regard to their appearance, they are handled by the robot as different pieces.

In this condition the instructions of the robot can be ambiguous, especially in the verbal scenario, as the robot describes pieces only by there colors and shapes, which are not unique anymore. Furthermore in the second condition, the gaze might not be accurate enough to distinguish identical pieces that are lying close to each other.

4.3   Participants

In the study, a total of 60 participants (9 female, 51 male) participated in the experiment, ranging in age from 19 to 56 years ($M = 26.05$, $SD = 6.24$).

All participants were recruited at Augsburg University, whereby the majority of them were students (56 of 60), mostly in Computer Science (44 of 60). Participants were randomly assigned to the different experimental scenarios.

4.4   Procedure

Participant and robot sat directly opposite each other at the Microsoft Surface touch table (see Fig. 2). First the participants got a brief introduction about the evaluation procedure. They were told they had to follow the robot's instructions to solve the abstract puzzle game and would not be able to succeed the puzzle on their own. To become familiar with the task setting and the used technologies they initially went through a small tutorial game. After the tutorial they started with the *simple* puzzle game. When they were done they were asked to fill in a questionnaire. After that they had to solve the *complex* puzzle game and fill in again the questionnaire. If an instruction was not understood, the participant had the option to touch the head of the robot to make it repeat the last instruction.

Though all participants played the puzzle game in both conditions, they were assigned to only one of the three scenarios, explained in section 4.1.

4.5   Evaluation

During the interaction the Microsoft Surface logged the errors made by the participant and how long it took to solve the puzzle, in each condition. Selecting a wrong piece, placing a piece at a wrong position and asking the robot to repeat the last instruction were counted as errors. Additional to this objective data we asked the participants whether the robot was experienced as 'attentive', 'active', 'friendly', 'lively', 'sympathetic', 'competent' and 'communicative', similar to the evaluation of Salem et al. [7]. Furthermore we wanted to know: "My experiences with Nori were better than I had expected" and "Consequences of my actions were clearly recognizable". Regarding the self-assessment of the participant we investigated seven items, including "I always immediately understood what to do next", "I think the puzzle was demanding", "I felt competent enough to comply the required tasks" and "I was completely focused on the robot's instructions".

All these items had to be rated on a five-point Likert scale with endpoints $1 = very\ appropriate$ and $5 = not\ appropriate$. A Mixed ANOVA, a mixture of between-group and repeated-measures design, was conducted with two Within-Subject Factors *Simple* and *Complex*, summarized *Difficulty*, and one Between-Subject Factor *Scenario* (*Verbal*, *Gaze* or *Pointing*). Figures 3 and 4 illustrate the difference in the ratings. The black lines in these graphs mark the scenarios between which significant differences ($p < .05$) were revealed.

4.6   Objective Results

Errors: Figure 3(a) shows that in the simple condition only very few mistakes were made even if the participants had to rely only on the verbal instruction of

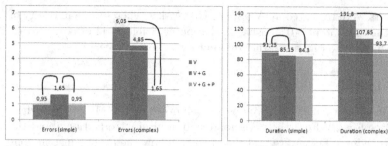

(a) Mean number of errors   (b) Mean duration (in seconds)

Fig. 3. Objective data for the simple and complex puzzle games; V = Verbal, G = Gaze, P = Pointing gestures

the robot. This changes significantly in the complex condition. Our test revealed that the scenario had an significant effect on the rate of errors ($F(2, 57) = 13.68$, $p < .001$).

Planned *Helmert Contrast* illustrated that having no gestures significantly increased the number of errors ($p < .005$) and that the use of gaze and pointing gestures in comparison with applying only gaze significantly reduced the error rate ($p < .001$). Nevertheless scenarios *Verbal (V)* and *Verbal with Gaze (V+G)* did not significantly differ in the complex condition ($p > .05$) verified by the *Post Hoc Test* of *Games-Howell*.

Duration: We only consider the pure interaction time of the participant in seconds, without the time needed by the robot for its instructions, as our duration. In contrast to the average error rate a positive trend for the duration is visible in both conditions (see figure 3(b)).

Planned *Helmert Contrast* illustrated that having no gestures significantly increased the duration of a game ($p < .005$) but only the combination of gaze and pointing gestures had a significant effect.

4.7   Subjective Results

Figure 4 illustrates the mean results of our questionnaire concerning participants' perception of the robot during the interaction. For the items 'Active', 'Friendly', 'Lively' and the expected experience with the robot no significant effects could be found. On the other side significant effects were revealed for the following items:

Sympathetic: *Test of Between-Subjects Effects* yielded a significant difference between the scenarios ($F(2, 57) = 3.23$, $p < .05$). In detail, *Post-Hoc Test* of *Games-Howell* revealed that our robot using gestures is better evaluated by participants than without gestures and only speech ($p < .05$), but there is no significant difference between gaze and gaze combined with pointing gestures ($p < .38$ and $p > .05$).

Competent: There were no significant differences in the ratings for the simple condition. But a One-Way ANOVA revealed that in the complex condition the

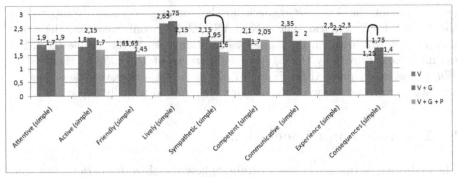

(a) Assessment of the robot in the simple condition; lower values are better

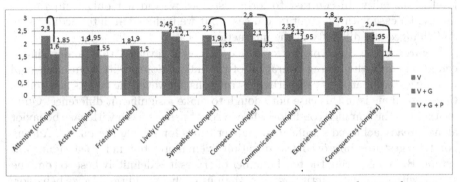

(b) Assessment of the robot in the complex condition; lower values are better

Fig. 4. Subjective results for the simple and complex condition of the puzzle game; V = Verbal, G = Gaze, P = Pointing gestures

robot was perceived significantly more competent if it used gaze and pointing gestures ($p < .005$), than a robot that used only speech or speech with gaze.

Attentive: One-Way ANOVA revealed that in the complex condition the robot was assessed as significantly more attentive ($p < .05$) when it also used gaze in contrast to the verbal scenario. Unfortunately this effect is not significant any more when pointing gesture are added.

"Consequences of My Actions were Clearly Recognizable": *Post-Hoc Test* of *Games-Howell* verified that a robot using gaze and gestures significantly effects the participants' assessment of whether the consequences of their actions were recognizable ($p < .05$).

Regarding the self-assessment of the participants the most interesting result was that they were significantly less **focused** on the robot's instructions in the $V+G$ scenario than in the V and in the $V+G+P$ scenario both in the simple and in the complex condition (all ps $< .05$). There is no significant difference between the V and $V+G+P$ scenario. For the item **"I always immediately understood what to do next"** there could only be found a significant improvement

($p < .005$) for the $V+G+P$ scenario in the complex condition, compared to the V and $V+G$ scenario. The mixed ANOVA also confirmed that the game was more **demanding** in the complex condition than in the simple condition (as intended), proved by the significant difference of *Difficulty* in the *Test of Within-Subjects Effects* (F(1, 57) = 67.37, $p < .001$). However, there was no significant difference between the scenarios, as we had actually expected.

5   Discussion and Conclusion

The main goal of this study was to evaluate how the objective performance and subjective experience of an human-robot interaction is affected by an increasing level of modality. In contrast to former studies we did not only compare the uni-modal case with the multimodal case, but we included an intermediate step and changed the difficulty of the interaction.

Regarding the objective performance our tests revealed that under simple conditions only the average duration of the interaction profits from additional modalities, compared to just verbal instructions. However the results also tell us that gaze alone is in this case not enough to make a significant difference. Quite contrary to the complex condition where a robot using speech with gaze behavior alone already achieved significantly shorter times for solving the puzzle. Adding pointing gestures improved the duration even more, but not to a significant extent. But considering the total number of errors it is definitely best to combine speech with gaze and pointing gesture, than just rely on additional gaze behavior. The participants made significantly less errors in the complex condition when they were guided by the robot with the highest level of modality. Gaze alone wasn't enough to improve the situation significantly.

This is also supported by our subjective data. In the study of Salem et al. [7] the robot in the multimodal condition (with gaze and pointing gestures) was perceived as more *active, lively* and *sympathetic*. While our robot was also more *sympathetic* to the participants when it used its full range of modalities, we could not achieve this for *active* and *lively*. For feedback our robot nodded and shook its head and sometimes moved its arms even in the *Verbal* scenario. The movements just didn't contribute to the grounding process and it didn't try do establish eye contact. This was different to the setting of Salem et al., where the robot was stiff in the uni-modal condition. The rather positive and balanced ratings in our scenarios suggest, that multimodal feedback is already enough to make a robot appear *active* and *lively*.

In the complex condition our robot was perceived as significantly more *competent* in the $V+G+P$ scenario. Still the difficulty did not significantly affect the ratings, so the significant difference in the complex condition results from the poor ratings of the other scenarios. This supports that it is very important that the robot uses its full potential of modality, otherwise the perceived *competence* will drastically decline when the tasks get tougher.

Unexpected were the results that the participants were significantly less focused on the robot's instructions in the $V+G$ scenario, compared to the other scenarios. Many participants of the $V+G$ scenario stated they didn't immediately realize that the robot was moving its head and trying to establish eye contact. When the robot used pointing gestures they were aware that the robot was moving and presumably payed more attention, but still not more than when the robot was just giving verbal instructions. These observations emphasize that the nature of a task affects the effectiveness of modalities and has to be considered when designing human-robot interactions. Considering that in the simple condition more errors were made when the robot used gaze without pointing gestures, it seems that the human interaction partner might even be negatively affected (perhaps by distraction or confusion) if pointing gestures are missing.

In summary it can be said that positive trends in favor for the use of speech in combination with gaze and pointing gestures are visible and can be statistically supported for the objective performance as well as for the subjective experience of the participants. Often adding gaze behavior alone doesn't improve the interaction enough. It might even result in unexpected negative effects.

So far the participants had the role of subordinates, that never had the chance to refuse to follow an instruction. Future work will allow participants to contribute to the interaction also in different ways, to allow further insight how the use of signals, not limited to gaze and pointing gestures, affects the performance and experience of collaborative human-robot interactions.

Acknowledgments. This research was funded by the EU project Tardis (FP7-ICT-2011-7, grant agreement no. 288578).

References

1. Breazeal, C., Kidd, C.D., Thomaz, A.L., Hoffman, G., Berlin, M.: Effects of non-verbal communication on efficiency and robustness in human-robot teamwork. In: Proc. IROS (2005)
2. Burghart, C., Gaertner, C., Woern, H.: Cooperative solving of a children's jigsaw puzzle between human and robot: First results. In: Proc. AAAI (2006)
3. Clark, H.H., Brennan, S.E.: Grounding in communication. In: Perspectives on Socially Shared Cognition, pp. 127–149 (1991)
4. Faber, F., Bennewitz, M., Eppner, C., Görög, A., Gonsior, C., Joho, D., Schreiber, M., Behnke, S.: The humanoid museum tour guide robotinho. In: Proc. RO-MAN (2009)
5. Giuliani, M., Knoll, A.: Evaluating Supportive and Instructive Robot Roles in Human-Robot Interaction. In: Mutlu, B., Bartneck, C., Ham, J., Evers, V., Kanda, T. (eds.) ICSR 2011. LNCS, vol. 7072, pp. 193–203. Springer, Heidelberg (2011)
6. Ishiguro, H., Ono, T., Imai, M., Maeda, T., Nakatsu, R., Kanda, T.: Robovie: An interactive humanoid robot. Industrial Robot: An International Journal, 498–503 (2001)
7. Salem, M., Rohlfing, K., Kopp, S., Joublin, F.: A friendly gesture: Investigating the effect of multimodal robot behavior in human-robot-interaction. In: Proc. RO-MAN (2011)
8. Sugiyama, O., Kanda, T., Imai, M., Ishiguro, H., Hagita, N.: Natural deictic communication with humanoid robots. In: Proc. IROS (2007)

Regulating Emotion by Facial Feedback from Teleoperated Android Robot*

Shuichi Nishio[1], Koichi Taura[1,2], and Hiroshi Ishiguro[1,2]

[1] Hiroshi Ishiguro Laboratory,
Advanced Telecommunications Research Institute International
Keihanna Science City, Kyoto 619-0288, Japan
nishio@ieee.org
[2] Graduate School of Engineering Science, Osaka University
Toyonaka, Osaka 560-0043, Japan

Abstract. In this paper, we experimentally examined whether facial expression changes in teleoperated androids can affect and regulate operators' emotion, based on the facial feedback theory of emotion and the body ownership transfer phenomena to teleoperated android robot. We created a conversational situation where participants felt anger and, during the conversation, the android's facial expressions were automatically changed. We examined whether such changes affected the operator emotions. As a result, we found that when one can well operate the robot, the operator's emotional states are affected by the android's facial expression changes.

1 Introduction

Emotion regulation, which is the act of controlling our emotions as well as how we experience and express them, is a crucial skill that is required in our social lives [3]. The importance of this skill is growing with the rapid development of telecommunications technology that increases opportunities for non-direct conversations (for example, [1]). When we do not meet in face-to-face, most of the nonverbal information that we obtain from direct meetings is lost, complicating the regulation of ourselves from the cues from others that reflect our behavior. Although there have been many studies that propose and implement advisory agent in remote communication (for example, [7]), few have addressed emotion regulation using information technologies. One possible reason is the difficulty of measuring emotional states, but this is becoming more possible with the progress of pattern recognition technologies [13]. Another important issue is to how to provide feedback to the speaker and to regulate her emotions. In advising systems a virtual avatar is typically shown on the communication screen and provides advice. For emotion regulation, when an avatar provides such advice as "calm down," the advice may be ignored if one has already become too emotional. We need a stronger method that works directly and unconsciously.

* This work was supported by KAKENHI (20220002) and KAKENHI (24650114).

S.S. Ge et al. (Eds.): ICSR 2012, LNAI 7621, pp. 388–397, 2012.

In the past, psychologists studied a related phenomenon known as the "facial feedback hypothesis," which is based on the famous idea of William James, who claimed that the awareness of bodily changes activates emotion. Many studies have addressed whether facial movement influences emotional experience [5,6,11,12]. These studies clarified that facial movements do affect emotional states. However, it has not been possible to actively control emotion by this theory without the physical equipment that stimulates bodies.

Recently, we developed a series of teleoperated androids, which are robots whose appearance resembles people and are teleoperated using intuitive interfaces [8]. Using these teleoperated androids, we found an interesting phenomenon that we called "body ownership transfer" [9]. In this phenomenon, as the operator controls the android robot, he gradually feels as if the robot is his own body and starts to respond to the physical stimuli on the robot's body without any haptic feedback. A similar phenomena called the "rubber hand illusion" has also been actively studied [2]. However, while the rubber hand illusion requires tactile sensation, the body ownership transfer we found only requires coordination of visual stimuli and the act of teleoperation. An interesting hypothesis arises here: when the operator feels that the android's face is his own face, will the facial feedback phenomenon occur? When the android's facial expression is changed on its own, (without being controlled by the operator), will the operator's emotion be affected?

In this paper, we experimentally found support for this hypothesis. To examine whether facial expression changes in teleoperated androids can affect and regulate operators' emotion, we created a conversational situation where participants felt anger. We automatically changed the android's facial expression to examine whether such changes affected the operator emotions. If the facial feedback phenomenon occurs from the teleoperated android to the operator, the operator's anger should be decreased when the android is showing smile; and when the android is showing anger, the operator's degree anger may increase.

2   Methods

Fourteen university students participated in our experiment (males: nine, females: five, average age = 20.1, S.D. = 1.6). We explained the experiment to them, and they signed the informed consent form [1]. Participants joined conversations with an experiment staff through a teleoperated android. The robot was placed on the staff side and the participants teleoperated the robot by their motions that were motion-captured. While the participants were talking through the teleoperated android, we changed the android's facial expression gradually. By controlling how they changed, we measured how this change affected the emotional states of the participants.

---

[1] This experiment was approved by the ethical committee of Advanced Telecommunications Research Institute International (No. 10-506-1).

2.1   Conversation Scenario

To see how the emotional states of the participants changed, we created a situation where participants became emotional. Although we daily feel many types of emotions, one of the most common emotions is anger. When we encounter unreasonable or unfair situations, we tend to feel anger. Anger is also one emotion that people would like to control. In this experiment, we created a situation where people often became mad: calling a customer service center with a problem.

The participants played customers who had experienced shoddy products or unsatisfactory services and are complaining to the customer service center. An experimenter played the customer service representative. The conversation flow proceeded as follows. First, the participant described her situation and her problem. Then, the participant negotiated with the customer representative about possible solutions. When both agreed, or when the three-minute time limit was reached, the session ended. Here is an example of a conversation:

> Service rep.: Thank you for calling the customer service desk.
> How may I help you?
> Customer: I bought a used computer at your shop, and in fact,
> it was recommended by your salesman. I was planning to buy a
> new one, but since he recommended a used one, saying it gave
> better performance, cheaper, and guaranteed, I bought it for
> 30,000 yen. When it was delivered, I found that the display was
> broken. I asked the store to replace the display, but they said
> I needed to pay 23,000 yen for a replacement because that part
> wasn't covered by the guarantee. Since I needed the machine for
> work, I bought a new display, but delivery actually took two
> weeks...
> (omitted)
> Customer: I've been having lots of problems. I want a new computer.
> Service rep.: I'm really sorry for all your troubles. But since
> you bought a used computer, problems might happen. How about
> replacing your computer with another one from our store? This
> one is also used, but it's been completely checked.
> Customer: Resolving this problem has already dragged on long
> enough, and I don't want any more trouble. definitely want a
> new computer...
> (rest omitted)

Prior to each session, participants were given a sheet of descriptions of the issue and five potential solutions. Six issues were pre-defined and provided to the participants for each session in counter-balanced order. The issues were selected to show problems typically encountered by university students. The solutions were numbered from 1 to 5 to indicate the degree of customer benefit (5 = maximum benefit). Participants were instructed to obtain as much benefit as possible. For example, in the above scenario, the following solutions were provided:

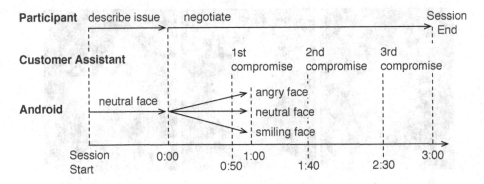

Fig. 1. Session flow: while participants negotiate with the experiment staff, the facial expression of the teleoperated android gradually changes

1. Repair the computer at a cost of 30,000 yen
2. Repair the computer at a cost of 15,000 yen (half price)
3. Replace with another used computer
4. Refund the display fee and replace the computer
5. Refund the entire purchase amount and buy a new computer with a discount

The customer service representative (performed by an experiment staff) gradually compromised to the solutions provided by the customer. The staff member was given the same list of possible solutions and the following instructions (Fig. 1):

- From the beginning of conversation, only agree to the first or second solution for the customer. (Solutions 1 and 2)
- After 50 seconds, gradually compromise to the next best solution for the customer. (Solutions 3 and 4))
- After 2 and half minutes, agree to the best solution. (Solution 5)

At each stage, the staff never proposed the best possible solution by herself. She only agreed when an acceptable solution in each stage was proposed by the participants. Therefore, not all the participants reached the best solution.

Our original intention was to provoke the strongest possible anger. Thus, in the pre-test, the staff member never changed her mind and only agreed with the worst solution. However, some participants became so upset that they completely forgot the experiment procedures. On the other hand, some participants found that the staff never compromised and became reluctant to continue negotiating. Therefore, to maintain the motivation of the participants, we changed the customer service representative's strategy to compromise more and to accept better solutions.

2.2 Procedure

The experiment was conducted in the following procedure. First, participants joined a trial session to practice and understand the procedure flow. Then they answered pre-experiment questionnaires to measure their initial emotional states.

Fig. 2. Facial expressions of Geminoid F: (left) neutral; (middle) angry; (right) smiling

Prior to each session, participants were given the description sheet and time to read and understand it. Since it was sometimes difficult to remember all the details, we placed a summary sheet next to the teleoperation console. Each session was started when participants completely understood the situation.

Each session began after the teleoperation console was switched on and participants described their problem to the customer service representative. When the participants started to negotiate, we gradually changed the facial expression of the teleoperated android robot in one minute interval (Fig. 1). After the facial expression reached its maximum state, the android kept showing the same facial expression until the end of the session. When the participant and the staff member reached an agreement, or when three minutes had passed after the participant's description of the problem, the session ended. After each session, participants answered post-session questionnaires, and took a two-minute break. Each participant joined six sessions with different situation topics. In the six sessions, the three facial expression conditions were randomly performed twice.

2.3   Equipment

As a teleoperated robot, we used Geminoid F, which is from the Geminoid series. Geminoids are teleoperated androids that resembles existing persons [8]. Geminoid F has nine pneumatic actuators, most of which are in its face, and so it can make various facial expressions. In this experiment, Geminoid F made two expressions: angry and smiling (Fig. 2). These facial expressions were used to change the android's emotional appearance while participants talked with the staff member. In the experiment, as described above, we changed the facial expression of the android from neutral to particular emotional expressions. These changes were conducted in the following three conditions:

Smile condition android's facial expression changed from neutral to a smiling face.

Angry condition android's facial expression changed from neutral to an angry face.

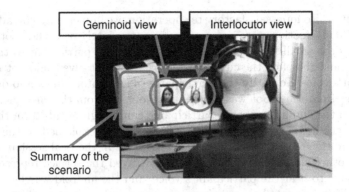

Fig. 3. Teleoperation console: Participants wore motion capture markers on their lips and a cap with markers. On the display screen, views of the Geminoid robot and interlocutor (service representative) were shown. In addition, a summary sheet of the scenario was also provided.

No-change condition android's facial expression did not change, and its neutral expression continued throughout the session.

During the changes of the facial expressions, the actuators were controlled by linear interpolation between the initial (neutral) face and target expressions.

In each session, participants controlled the android and talked with the customer service representative using it as a communication medium. This teleoperation was done with a simplified version of the Geminoid teleoperation system [8]. The body motions of the participants were captured, converted, and sent to the android robot. At the same time, the voices from both sides were captured by microphones and transmitted to each other. In addition, the participants watched the teleoperation console that showed two transmitted video screens: the service representative and the android robot's face (Fig. 3). Participants wore motion capture markers on their lips to track the lip motion while speaking and a cap with markers for tracking their head motion. We used an infrared motion capture system to obtain the lip and head motions of the participants. They were sent to the robot to be synchronized with the participant motions. These captured motions were merged with the facial expression changes. Thus, the android robot kept moving its head and its lips, and its facial expression gradually changed.

One assumption of our experiment was that, while teleoperating the robot, participants would gradually accept the android as themselves and perceive the motion in the robotic body as their own body movements. To satisfy this presumption, the participant's body movement must always be reflected and synchronized to the robot. However, due to the restriction in the motion capture system, if the participant looked down too much, the markers on her lips would not be captured by the system. If the participants spoke without moving their lips enough, the captured lip movement would not be sufficient to make the android lips to move. Therefore, participants had to behave "appropriately" to adequately teleoperate the robot while talking with the customer service representative. To force satisfactory teleoperation, we implemented an additional system. If body motion were not captured appropriately or if the captured lip motion was too small, the voice transmission from the participant to the robot was cutoff, and therefore the customer service representative could not hear the participant's voice. To notify the participants of this cutoff, the audio output of their voices from the robot was dubbed to the voice from the customer center. Thus, when the cutoff happened, participants can recognize this from their own voice feedback suddenly disappearing. This trick was explained to the participants before the experiment and was also tried out in the trial session.

On the other side, the staff member, who played the service representative, was only able to hear the participant's voice, and the android was hidden from her view. This prevented the service representative from being affected by the android's facial expressions. The staff member only saw a partition that hid the android, a stopwatch on a computer monitor to show the timings of the compromises, and a summary of the script that listed possible solutions. Although the service representative could not see the android, participants were told that the android was in front of the representative.

2.4   Measures

Before the main trial and after each session, participants answered a set of questionnaires to measure their emotional states. We used the General Affect Scales by Ogawa *et al.* [10] that measure mood states by three factors, positive affect, negative affect, and calmness, using eight subscales each (24 subscales). Each subscale used a seven-degree Likert scale. The subscale results are linearly mixed with specified coefficients to derive the three factors. This instrument was validated with more than 200 participants with reliability of 0.86 to 0.91 in Cronbach's alpha. In addition, it has high correlation with the Japanese version of Profile of Mood States (POMS).

We asked the following questions after all the sessions were finished:

Q1 How well could you operate the robot?
Q2 Did you notice that the robot's facial expression changed?
Q3 If you noticed the change, how did you feel?

For Q1, we asked the participants to answer on a seven-degree Likert scale (1 = poorly operated, 7 = well operated).

3   Results

We analyzed the emotional states of the participants by comparing how they changed before and after each session. The differences of the three emotional factors, positive affect, negative affect, and calmness, were obtained and analyzed. We classified the participants into two groups: *well operated* (N=11), those who marked more than five for Q1 (How well could you operate the robot?) and the rest as *poorly operated* (N=3).

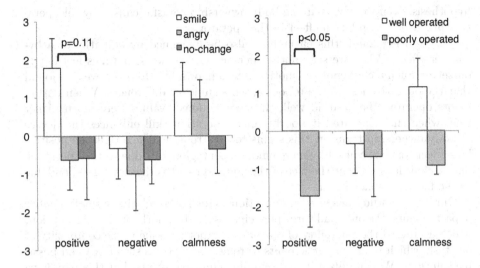

Fig. 4. Averages and standard errors for emotion status changes during sessions: (left) comparison by facial expression changes for well operated participants; (right) comparison by operativeness for the smiling condition

We performed a two-way ANOVA (facial expression x operation) and found marginal significance for interaction between facial expression and operation $(F(2,36) = 2.44, p = 0.10)$. Post hoc analysis with simple main effects showed marginal significance for the positive affect in the well operated group $(F(2,30) = 2.37, p = 0.11)$ and a significant difference between the well and poorly operated groups for positive affect in the smile condition $(F(1,12) = 5.13, p < 0.05)$. Fig. 4 shows these results.

For Q2 (Did you notice that the robot's facial expression changed?) and Q3 (If you noticed the facial expression changed, how did you feel?), three participants were aware of the smile expression and eight were aware of the angry expression. Three participants noticed neither facial expression changes. Among the participants who were aware of the facial expression changes, five expressed such feelings from third-person views: "I wondered why this happened." Three said that they felt their own changes, such as, "my feeling was reflected by the robot." The rest of the participants gave no answers to Q3.

4   Discussion

The experiment results weakly support our hypothesis about emotion regulation by facial expression changes in the teleoperated android robot. Only when participants could operate well and only in the smiling expression did we find a marginally significant effect on the operator's mood. When the operators encountered situations that caused anger, their emotional mood was positively improved by watching their avatar smiling. This result seems to support our hypothesis, even weakly, that the body ownership transfer caused by teleoperation provoked a regulation effect in the operator.

On the other hand, this effect may also be explained by empathy or a bystander effect. When we see another person smiling, we sometimes feel happy ourselves. Such a contagion of emotion is well known [4]. However, we also found that the operativeness of the robot caused significant differences. When participants operated the android well, the positive affect values were much higher than when they operated it poorly. Since operation skill enhances the degree of body ownership transfer, this seems to be strong evidence that the positive bias effect was not caused by mere emotion contagion, but due to the operators' unconscious feelings that the face of the android robot is their own face, and due to the facial feedback effect.

Our current study has several limitations. One is the relatively small number of participants. We only had three participants for the poorly operated condition, which decreased the reliability of our results. Another issue is the complexity of our task, which required participants to remember various situations and possible solutions. We simplified it by providing summary sheets, but this may have been an extra burden on the participants. In addition, the emotions invoked were "artificial" and may not have been true, although the observations in the pretest suggested that this task was successful, sometimes too successful, in causing "real" emotion in the participants. Moreover, the strategy for the service representative, which negotiated customer-beneficial solutions, may have weakened the anger in participants. One reason that the effect of the facial expression change was only seen in the smile condition may reflect this strategy.

There are also issues with the teleoperation system. Although it was modified to be as easy to use as possible, further improvements are necessary. For example, our motion capturing system, which requires participants to wear markers, may have disturbed their concentration. The changes in facial expressions may also be a disturbing factor that caused participants to realize that the android body is not their body; when the android's face greatly moved, the participants may have found discrepancies between the visual changes in the robot and the proprioceptive perception of their own body. Even though they don't believe that their face is moving, they can see that the android is changing its expression. This discrepancy may shatter the illusion of body ownership transfer. But on the other hand, from a practical point of view, we need a stronger and more robust method to cause this proprioceptive transfer. Future work will investigate some of these considerations.

References

1. Botherel, V., Maffiolo, V.: Regulation of emotional attitudes for a better interaction: field study in call centres. In: Proc. 20th International Symposium of Human Factors in Telecommunication (March 2006)
2. Botvinick, M.: Rubber hands 'feel' touch that eyes see. Nature 391(6669), 756 (1998)

3. Gross, J.J.: Emotion regulation: Affective, cognitive, and social consequences. Psychophysiology 39, 281–291 (2002)
4. Hatfield, E., Cacioppo, J.T., Rapson, R.L.: Emotional contagion. Current Directions in Psychological Science 2(3), 96–99 (1993)
5. Kleinke, C., Peterson, T., Rutledge, T.: Effects of self-generated facial expressions on mood. Journal of Personality and Social Psychology 74, 272–279 (1998)
6. MacIntosh, D.: Facial feedbck hypotheses: Evidence, implications, and directions. Motivation and Emotion 20, 121–147 (1996)
7. Nakanishi, H.: Freewalk: A social interaction platform for group behaviour in a virtual space. International Journal of Human-Computer Studies 60(4), 421–454 (2004)
8. Nishio, S., Ishiguro, H., Hagita, N.: Geminoid: Teleoperated android of an existing person. In: de Pina Filho, A.C. (ed.) Humanoid Robots: New Developments, pp. 343–352. I-Tech Education and Publishing, Vienna (2007)
9. Nishio, S., Watanabe, T., Ogawa, K., Ishiguro, H.: Body Ownership Transfer to Teleoperated Android Robot. In: Ge, S.S., Khatib, O., Cabibihan, J.-J., Simmons, R., Williams, M.-A. (eds.) ICSR 2012. LNCS (LNAI), vol. 7621, pp. 385–394. Springer, Heidelberg (2012)
10. Ogawa, T., Monchi, R., Kikuya, M., Suzuki, N.: Development of the general affect scales. The Japanese Journal of Psychology 71(3), 241–246 (2000) (in Japanese)
11. Soussignan, R.: Duchenne smile, emotional experience, and autonomic reactivity: A test of the facial feedback hypothesis. Emotion 2, 52–74 (2002)
12. Strack, F., Martin, L., Stepper, S.: Inhibiting and facilitating conditions of the human smile: a nonobtrusive test of the facial feedback hypothesis. Journal of personality and social psychology 54, 768–777 (1988)
13. Zeng, Z., Pantic, M., Roisman, G.I., Huang, T.S.: A survey of affect recognition methods: audio, visual and spontaneous expressions. In: Proc. 9th International Conference on Multimodal Interfaces, pp. 126–133 (2007)

Body Ownership Transfer
to Teleoperated Android Robot*

Shuichi Nishio[1], Tetsuya Watanabe[1,2], Kohei Ogawa[1,2], and Hiroshi Ishiguro[1,2]

[1] Hiroshi Ishiguro Laboratory,
Advanced Telecommunications Research Institute International (ATR)
Keihanna Science City, Kyoto 619-0288, Japan
nishio@ieee.org
[2] Graduate School of Engineering Science,
Osaka University Toyonaka, Osaka 560-0043, Japan

Abstract. Teleoperators of android robots occasionally feel as if the robotic bodies are extensions of their own. When others touch the teleoperated android, even without tactile feedback, some operators feel as if they themselves have been touched. In the past, a similar phenomenon named "Rubber Hand Illusion" has been studied for its reflection of a three-way interaction among vision, touch and proprioception.

In this study, we examined whether a similar interaction occurs when replacing a tactile sensation with android robot teleoperation; that is, whether the interaction among vision, motion and proprioception occurs. The result showed that when the operator and the android motions are synchronized, operators feel as if their sense of body ownership is transferred to the android robot.

1 Introduction

Recently we have developed a teleoperated android robot named "Geminoid" [5], which owns an appearance similar to existing people (Fig. 1). Geminoid was made as a research tool to examine how appearance and behavior of robot will affect people communication. During various studies, we found that conversation through the geminoid affect not only people in front of it but also its operators. Soon after starting to operate the geminoid, they tend to adjust their body movements to the movements of the geminoid. For example, they talk slowly in order to synchronize with the geminoid lip motion, and show small movements as the robot does. Some operators even feel as if they themselves have been touched when others touch the teleoperated android [5]. For example, when someone pokes at the geminoid's cheek, operators feel as if their own cheek has been poked despite the lack of tactile feedback. This illusion occurs even when people who are not the source of the geminoid is operating. However, this illusion does not always happen, and it is difficult to cause it intentionally.

There exists a similar illusion named "Rubber Hand Illusion" (RHI) [2]. In RHI, an experimenter repeatedly strokes a participant's hand and a rubber hand

---

* This work was supported by KAKENHI (20220002).

S.S. Ge et al. (Eds.): ICSR 2012, LNAI 7621, pp. 398–407, 2012.

Fig. 1. Geminoid HI-1 (left) with its source person (right)

at the same time (RHI procedure). Here, the participant can only see the rubber hand and not his/her own hand. After performing this procedure for a while, the participant begins to have an illusion on feeling as if the rubber hand is her own hand. When only the rubber hand is stroked, the participant feels as if her own hand is stroked. This illusion, RHI, is said to occur as a result of synchronization between the visual stimulus (watching the rubber hand being stroked) and the tactile stimulus (feeling that the participant's hand is stroked) [8]. The resulting illusionary effect is quite similar to that in our teleoperated android. However, in the case with the geminoid, this happens without any tactile stimulus; the operator only teleoperators the geminoid and watch it moving and being poked.

Our hypothesis is that this illusion, body ownership transfer toward teleoperated android, occurs due to the synchronization between the operation of the geminoid and visual feedback of seeing the geminoid's motion. That is, body ownership is transferred by seeing the geminoid moving synchronized as the operator moves. If body ownership transfer can be induced merely by operation without haptic feedback, this can lead to numbers of applications, such as realizing highly immersive teleoperation interface and developing prosthetic hands/bodies that can be used as one's real body parts.

We can verify this by comparing cases where participants watch the robot in sync with their motion and where they watch the robot out of sync. We make the following hypotheses:

Hypothesis 1: Body ownership transfer toward the geminoid body occurs through synchronized geminoid teleoperation with visual feedbacks.

RHI requires synchronization of visual and tactile senses. However, the geminoid cannot move without delays because sensing and actuators have limits reaction. In fact, the geminoid usually moves with 200 to 800ms delays. We adjust by the delaying voice as if the geminoid produce voice to synchronize mouth movements and speech when we have a conversation with the geminoid [5]. Based on related work, such delays during teleoperation are considered to reduce the extent of body ownership transfer. For example, Shimada et al. showed that RHI effect becomes largely decreased when the delay between visual and tactile stimuli was more than 300ms [7]. If this applies to the geminoid's body ownership transfer, we can't explain why body ownership is transferred to the geminoid during operations. Therefore, the mechanism of the geminoid's body ownership transfer might differ from the mechanism of RHI's body ownership transfer. We make the following hypothesis:

Hypothesis 2: In geminoid teleoperation, body ownership is also transferred when the geminoid moves with delays.

2   Methods

Based on the hypotheses of the previous section and knowledge culled from related studies, we experimentally verified that body ownership is transferred by the geminoid operation and its visual feedback. When the geminoid is operated, its mouth and head are synchronized with operators for conversation. However, maintaining control is difficult if we employ conversation as a task. That is why we employ to operate the geminoid's arm as a task.

The participants included 19 university students. 12 males, 7 females, whose average of age was 21.1 years old (standard variation was 1.6 years old). All of them were right-handed. They got explanations about the experiment and signed consent forms [1].

2.1   Procedure

First, participants operated the geminoid's arm and watched the scene for a constant time. At this time, the geminoid's arm is synchronized with the operator's arm. This is equal to make watch participants a scene where a rubber hand is stroked by brush in a RHI procedure. Next, we only give the geminoid's arm painful stimuli and measure the self-report and skin conductance response (SCR). We predict that both measurements will react if body ownership is transferred.

SCR shows significant values when the autonomic nervous system is aroused, such as when people feel pain [4]. Armel et al. verified body ownership transfer by measuring SCR [1]. Their idea was that if RHI occurs, skin conductance reacts when the target object (rubber hand) receives a painful stimulus. Participants watched a scene where the rubber hand was bent strongly after the RHI procedure (synchronized / delayed condition). As a result, they confirmed that the SCR value in the synchronized condition is higher than in the delayed condition.

The participants looked at the geminoid and might believe that it is a real human because it has a very humanlike appearance. That is why participants

---

[1] This experiment was approved by the ethical committee of Advanced Telecommunications Research Institute International (No. 08-506-1).

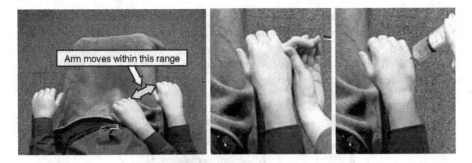

Fig. 2. Simulated views shown to participants: (left) normal view showing arm movement range; (center) 'finger bending' stimulus; (right) 'injection' stimulus

looked at it before the experiment to clarify that the geminoid is a real object. Then they learned how to operate this robot. At this time, they also checked camera which was set over it, and learned that they would watch the geminoid through it. However, this camera was not used, as we discuss later.

After that, they enter the experimental room and wear one marker for motion capture system on their right arm and electrodes on the left hand. The marker is placed at the position of 19 cm from their elbow to maintain the arm movement radius. They also wear electrodes on the ball of the hand and the hypothenar. Then, they are told to grasp their hand to which the marker is attached and to aim their palm down, and to aim the other palm up, and to avoid moving both their fingers and wrists. They have identical practice as in the main trials. After practicing, they are told about the main trial procedure and questionnaires. At the same time, they learn about this the experiment's purpose and get data for operating the geminoid. After that, they wear a head mounted display (HMD; Vuzix iWear VR920), and watch two stimulus images: The geminoid's right little finger being bent (Fig. 2, center) and an experimenter injecting on top of the geminoid's right hand (Fig. 2, right). Participants watch these images several times as in Armel et al [1]. After that, they re-practice with HMD. After the above preparation, they conduct main trials. After all the trials, they answered questionnaires about the experiment.

2.2   Main Trial

In the main trials, we repeated the following procedure 6 times. First, participants operated the geminoid's right arm by moving their right arm in a horizontal direction at 3 sec intervals. They watched the geminoid's arm movement through the HMD. At this time, they were taught to look down to synchronize their posture with the geminoid's on the HMD because such posture synchronization is important for body ownership transfer. We covered the HMD with black cloth so that participants can only see the display because we believe that the extent of body ownership transfer decreases if participants can see the scene of the experimental room and their body. Moreover, both the participants and the geminoid wore blanket to prevent differences of cloth from influencing on the body ownership transfer. Fig. 3 shows participants during the experiment.

After one minute of operation, experimenters gave participants a signal for the end and waited until their SCR recovered to normal. After that, the participants were shown one of the two stimulus images.

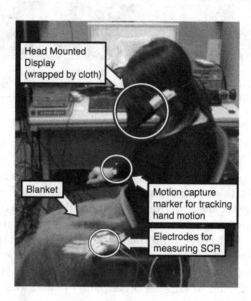

Fig. 3. Participant setting

2.3   Experimental System

In this experiment, we needed a system to control the extent of the delay of the geminoid. However, we can't operate the geminoid without delays because of its limits. We employed a simulation system. That is, we employed a method that we selected and displayed pictures made by splitting images shot previously in based on the position tracked by a motion capture system (Motion Analysis hawk-i camera and control system). With this system, we implemented a condition where the geminoid has arbitrary delays as well as a condition where the geminoid is mostly synchronized with the operator. We took pictures by a high-speed camera (Casio EXILIM EX-F1) in 300 fps and used 5,000 pictures (Fig.2, left). We showed stimulus images after operation by switching from the operation image.

2.4   Measurement

We measured the self-reports by questionnaires and SCR. First, in the self-reports, we evaluated the extent of body ownership transfer by asking participants the following questions:

- (Finger bending) Did it feel as if your finger was being bent?
- (Injection) Did it feel as if your hand was being injected?

Participants answered the questionnaires by parol because they were wearing a HMD and couldn't write. They answered on a 7-point Likert scale (1:not strong 7:very strong) for both questions.

We used a Coulbourn Instruments V71-23 Isolated Skin Conductance Coupler as a biological amplifier, set the sensitivity to 100 mV/microS, and measured with a direct current power distribution method. We used KEYENCE NR-2000 as A/D converter and set the sampling period to 20 ms(50 Hz).

2.5 Conditions and Predictions

Based on our hypotheses in section 1, we made the following three conditions:

Sync condition: The geminoid movement is synchronized with the operator movement without a delay.

Delay condition: The geminoid movement is synchronized with the operator movement with a certain delay.

Still condition: The geminoid remains still despite operator movement.

In the delay condition, the delay was set to 1 sec., following Armel et al. [1].

Based on our hypotheses, we made the following predictions.

Prediction 1: participants will show larger responses in the sync condition than in the still condition.

Prediction 2: participants will show larger responses in the delay condition than in the still condition.

Based on the above predictions, we conducted a total of six trials, the above three conditions by two stimuli, for each participant and verified whether body ownership transfer was caused. The order of the conditions and stimuli was counterbalanced among participants.

3   Result

In a general way, skin conductance reacts with 1 to 2 sec. delays for a stimulus [3]. So we usually measure the maximum value between its point and the point at which SCR is calm to verify the reaction of the stimulus. But we confirmed that skin conductance often reacts before the stimuli. Participants answered in interviews after the main trials that they felt as if they got the stimuli to their hands and felt unpleasant when the experimenter's hand approached the geminoid's hand after the operation. This suggests that the reaction before the stimulus is also caused by the body ownership transfer. In these stimulus images, it takes three sec to the give stimulus of the geminoid's hand since the experimenter's hand appears. In this paper, we set the starting time of the range for getting the maximum value to two sec after the stimulus image starts(one sec before the

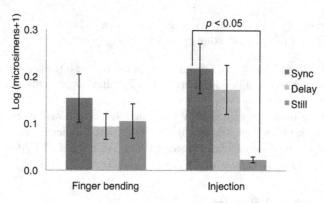

Fig. 4. Average with standard error of SCR analysis

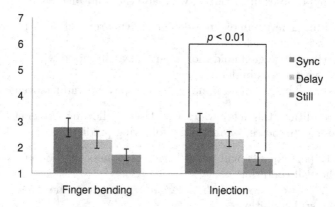

Fig. 5. Average with standard error of questionnaire analysis (left: *Did it feel as if your finger was being bent?*, right: *Did it feel as if your hand was being injected?*)

stimulus is given), and the end time to five sec after the stimulus is given as in Armel et al. [1]. We employed a range for getting the maximum value from one sec before the stimulus was given to five sec after it was given.

Next, we describe the data removed from the evaluations. First, two of 19 participants were removed because the electrode for the SCR failed. Second, we removed data which were identified as outliers by the Smirnov-Grubbs test by a significant level 5%. We removed each one bit in both delay and still conditions in injection and four bits in the still condition in injection. Finally, we analyzed 17 bits of sync condition data, 16 bits of delay condition data, 16 bits of still condition data in finger bending, and 17 bits of sync condition data, 17 bits of delay condition data, and 13 bits of still condition data in injection.

The SCR value fulfills normality by a logarithmic transformation [3]. Therefore, we gave the SCR value a logarithmic transformation and conducted a parametric test. As a result of one-way ANOVA, no significant difference was confirmed in finger bending ($F(2) = 0.66$, $p = 0.52$),but a significant difference was confirmed in injection ($F(2) = 3.36$, $p < 0.05$). As a result of a multiple comparison of Tukey HSD, a significant difference was confirmed only between the sync and still conditions in injection(Sync condition > Still condition, $p < 0.05$). Fig. 4 shows the average with standard error and the results of a multiple comparison of Tukey HSD.

We also performed statistical analysis for self-reports. As a result of a one-way ANOVA, no significant difference was confirmed in finger bending ($F(2) = 2.88$, $p = 0.06$),but a significant difference was confirmed in injection ($F(2) = 5.25$, $p < 0.01$). As a result of a multiple comparison with Tukey HSD, a significant difference was confirmed only between the sync and still conditions in injection(sync condition > still condition, $p < 0.01$). Fig. 5 shows the average with standard error and the results of a multiple comparison of Tukey HSD.

4   Discussion

Based on the results, here we verify our predictions and hypotheses. First, as for prediction 1 (participants will show larger responses in the sync condition than in the still condition), this was verified from the results. In the case of the injection stimuli, we found significant differences between the sync and still conditions, for both the self evaluation and for the SCR. In both measures, the responses for the sync condition were significantly larger than for the still condition. Thus, prediction 1 is verified and the corresponding hypothesis 1 (body ownership is transferred by watching scenes where the geminoid is synchronized with an operator) is confirmed. That is, we confirmed that geminoid teleoperation induces body ownership transfer toward the geminoid body.

Second, as for prediction 2 (participants will show larger responses in the delay condition than in the still condition), we could not verify this as no significant difference was found between the delay and still conditions. Consequently, we cannot verify hypothesis 2 (in geminoid teleoperation, body ownership is also transferred when the geminoid moves with delays). However, there was no significant difference between the sync and delay conditions. In the past studies on RHI, the degree of body ownership transfer was reduced by delays between the tactile and visual stimuli [1,2]. Shimada et al. also showed that when the delay becomes larger than 300ms, participants reported significantly low degree of RHI effect [7]. The result that no significant difference between the sync and delay (1 sec) conditions were found here may suggest that the mechanism of the geminoid body ownership transfer might be different from RHI body ownership transfer. In this experiment, the delay was longer than during usual teleoperation because we set the same delay time as in related studies. Because this delay might influence our result, we need more verification.

A significant difference was confirmed in injection. On the other hand, no significant difference was confirmed in the self-reports and SCR of finger bending. We had following reason. First, we had a reason why the operation part differed from the stimulus part. Because the participants operated the geminoid's arm by moving their own arm, body ownership may be transferred to the geminoid's hand and arm, but not transferred to its fingers. As a result, the participants did not react to finger bending. Second, we had reason why we had defective finger bending images. Because the arm position in the start picture finger bending images differed from the end picture, the participants watched scenes where the arm position was shifted instantaneously when the image was switched to the stimulus. This explains why this might have an unintended influence on the participants. We had no defective injection images.

This first reason raises two interesting questions: Is body ownership transferred to only the operation part? Is body ownership transferred to a more spread part? Operation by such synchronizing movements as the current teleoperation interface of the geminoid limits operator movements because operators move the object. If we could extend body ownership to another part by operating a part of the body, we could improve operability. Human somatic sensation systems are known to have non-uniform distribution throughout the body; there are sensitive body parts and not-so-sensitive parts. We believe that it is difficult to transfer body ownership to sensitive part. So we predict that it is difficult to extend body ownership to the sensitive parts, but it is easy to extend it to the insensitive parts. We need more verification.

In previous RHI research, object measurement and self-reports showed high correlation as in this study. Moreover, participants reported high values (5 to 7 on 7-point scale) in their self-reports [2]. However, in this study, the self-report average was about three on the 7-point Likert scale, which was relatively low. Participants, at least subjectively, did not feel as if part of the geminoid's body had become part of their bodies. As the task in this experiment was to simply move participants' arm, participants were much conscious about their own body. This strong attention toward the own body may have been the reason for low self-evaluation. In our daily life, we are rarely aware of body movements for everyday tasks such as walking or grasping. It is easier to cause body ownership transfer when the operator waits five min to adjust the operation after teleconversation than starting sooner. We believe that we can increase the extent of body ownership transfer by avoiding feelings from the body after participants start their task with strong purpose.

The appearance of the object may also influence the extent of body ownership transfer, as in Armel et al.'s research [1] and Pavani's study [6]. Is body ownership transfer during teleoperation only caused to android robots with very humanlike appearances? Will it occur by teleoperating humanoid robots with robotic appearances or industrial robots? Future work will answer these questions.

5   Conclusion

In this paper, we examined whether body ownership transfer occurs through teleopertion of an android robot. We showed that operators feel as if a part of the robot has become themselves by synchronizing operation and its visual feedback. We believe that clarifying the mechanism of body ownership transfer is important to resolve the body's purpose and each person's boundary. Future work may investigate further details on why this body ownership transfer occurs and find the necessary conditions to cause the sense of body ownership transfer arbitrary.

References

1. Armel, K.C., Ramachandran, V.S.: Projecting sensations to external objects: evidence from skin conductance response. Proc. Biol. Sci. 270(1523), 1499–1506 (2003)
2. Botvinick, M.: Rubber hands 'feel' touch that eyes see. Nature 391(6669), 756 (1998)
3. Hori, T., Niimi, Y.: Electrodermal activity. In: Miyata, H., Fujisawa, K., Kakiki, S. (eds.) Physiological Psychology, pp. 98–110. Asakura Publishing, Tokyo (1985) (in Japanese)
4. Lang, P.J.: Looking at pictures: affective, facial, visceral, and behavioral reactions. Psychophysiology 30(3), 261–273 (1993)
5. Nishio, S., Ishiguro, H., Hagita, N.: Geminoid: Teleoperated android of an existing person. In: de Pina Filho, A. (ed.) Humanoid Robots: New Developments. I-Tech Education and Publishing, Vienna (2007)
6. Pavani, F.: Visual capture of touch: Out-of-the-body experiences with rubber gloves. Psychological Science 11(5), 353–359 (2000)
7. Shimada, S., Fukuda, K., Hiraki, K.: Rubber hand illusion under delayed visual feedback. PLoS One 4(7), e6185 (2009)
8. Tsakiris, M.: My body in the brain: a neurocognitive model of body-ownership. Neuropsychologia 48(3), 703–712 (2010)

A Geminoid as Lecturer

Julie Rafn Abildgaard and Henrik Scharfe

Department of Communication,
Aalborg University, Denmark
julie@geminoid.dk, scharfe@hum.aau.dk

Abstract. In this paper we report our findings from an experiment with the tele-operated android Geminoid-DK. The geminoid took up the role of a university lecturer and delivered a 45 minute lecture in front of 150 freshmen students at Aalborg University. While considering the role of the geminoid in this educational context, we report results relating to large-room teaching, as well as gender differences in the perception of the robot.

Keywords: Human-robot-interaction, Geminoid-DK, gender differences, case study.

1   Introduction

Placing androids in real life situations offers special conditions to learn about human robot communication. This is important for two reasons. In the first place, we are eventually aiming at being able to place androids in various real life contexts and to let them perform complex tasks. In order to approach a situation where this is feasible, many small scale tests most be conducted to learn about the conditions for such communications to be successful. Actual use in the physical real often offers surprises with respect to both perception and practical implication. In the second place, real life experiments outside the controlled atmosphere of the research lab expose androids to different kinds of reactions. This is particularly true of interactions that involve more people than can be accommodated in the lab. As part of an ongoing investigation into the success criteria for communication involving at least one android, we decided to device an experiment in which the Geminoid-DK took up the role as a university lecturer. In setting up the experiment, we aimed at creating as realistic a situation as possible. In section 2 of this paper, we present our conceptual deliberations regarding the experiment along with details of the technical setup. In sections 3-5 we report our findings, and in section 6 we draw attention to the need for further research conducted in this area.

1.1   Simulation and Situation

The concept of the geminoid robots, original conceived by Hiroshi Ishiguro [1], hinges on the idea that the android should look exactly as the human original in whatever respect it is possible. Physical likeness between the two is a central part of the research paradigm, and as such, the geminoid research programs are concerned

S.S. Ge et al. (Eds.): ICSR 2012, LNAI 7621, pp. 408–417, 2012.
© Springer-Verlag Berlin Heidelberg 2012

with simulations of the human original. This is true both with respect to the physical appearance of the robot exterior, and with respect to movements of the face and body. Personal traits and idiosyncrasies are considered at every stage of the design process, from the molding of body parts to programming and control of patterns of movement. Much attention is given to details in order for the geminoid to appear as an exact copy of the human original. One goal of the simulation aspect of geminoid research is to present the android in such a manner that it becomes a believable substitute for the human. And while we are still far from reaching this ideal on the grand scale of real life, important progress has been made in order to make a persuasive appearance of these geminoids. But this research is not only about simulation. We maintain that it is equally important to consider the situation in which the geminoid is supposed to function. In consequence, the success criteria for well-performed geminoid interactions may well change from situation to situation. What might work in an auditorium with 150 people may produce serious side effects in a face to face situation involving only two or three people.

1.2   Similar Investigations

The study of robots used in educational contexts is a quite new research field, but it has been described in the following works that are mostly carried out in elementary schools. In Japan, Kanda et. al. have exposed the humanoid - but somewhat mechanical Robovie to Japanese students in the first and sixth grade in elementary school to measure the effects of a robot in English language learning. The students test score in English didn't improve significant due to this intervention, but the students who showed interest in the robot as a teacher had an elevated English score, which indicated that robot-aided English learning can have an effect on young students' motivation [2]. Korean researchers from Yujin Robotics have used the humanoid IROBI to prove their hypothesis that robot-aided learning improves children's concentration, interest and academic achievement [3]. In Korea, a teaching assisting robot named TIRO has also been used in research in English language learning in a third grade in elementary school, playing with the children. This study found that the children liked robot services for personal relationship in class, and teachers found the robot useful because it relieved them in their work [4].

The most similar investigation compared to our Geminoid-DK study is made with the Japanese android SAYA [5] who can both conduct lectures by tele-operation and observe student's behavior. The SAYA research was conducted in both elementary school and at a university to estimate any age-dependent differences of its effectiveness. The conclusion was that the students in elementary school accepted the remote class support system with SAYA more easily than university students [6,7,8].

2   Experiment Setup

In order to create an atmosphere as realistic as possible, we decided to conduct the experiment with a group of freshmen students, with no prior personal experience with the lecturer. The lecture was given during the first month of the semester, and was part of an introductory program, intended to present the new students with information about core perspectives on Human Centered Informatics, as it is taught at Aalborg University in Northern Denmark. This means that this lecture in content and form was part of the regular first year course, and as such, held no specific surprises with respect to scope, intended learning outcome, or style. It was in other words, an ordinary lecture, besides the fact that the lecturer this morning was a tele-operated robot. Before the lecture, the Geminoid was placed in the auditorium, behind a desk with laptops and other typical teaching accessories. The operator was located in another part of the same building, and controlling the robot and other equipments via wireless network. At the same time, a researcher sat among the audience, partly to correct and intervene should something unexpected happen, and partly to observe the reactions of the audience first hand. The lecture was a standard 2 x 45 minute affair, and during the second lecture, both the geminoid and the original were present. Thus, part of the second lecture was structured as a conversation about the experiment in the first lecture.

2.1   Technical Setup

The movements of the Geminoid, visible to the audience, are a mixture of software components from different sources. A set of basic movements such as minor movements of the eyes, breathing, and blinking, are sequenced in advanced and delivered from a laptop also carrying the geminoid servers. Movements of the lips are synchronized from the voice input of the operator, as is movement of the head and direction of gaze. This means that the operator from a distance takes direct control over the main parts of the movements. See [1] for a technical description. The voice of the operator is captured from the control room sent over IP to the auditorium where it is analyzed in order to generate movements of the lips of the robot. From the local laptop, the sound signal is then passed on to a speaker behind the robot where a microphone picks up the sound and amplifies it through the ordinary PA system of the lecture room. The result is that the voice of the lecturer is heard from room speakers mounted on the ceiling, as well as from the direction of the robot. A PowerPoint presentation containing roughly 60 slides were delivered to two projector screens behind the geminoid. The slideshow was also remotely controlled by the operator. Again, this allows for improvisations and direct interaction with the students.

In order to navigate and interact with the audience, the lecture room was equipped with cameras and microphones, allowing the operator to visually orient himself in the room, and to respond to questions and comments from the audience. We used standard surveillance cameras with built-in microphones that can be accessed through a web browser from the control room. In addition, cameras were placed at the side and the back of the room to document the experiment. The students were advised that video recordings took place.

2.2   Methodological Setup

We applied a mixed methods approach with video surveillance, questionnaires, and semi-structured exit interviews to increase validity and to ensure that we uncover the complexity and possible contradictions of the responses from each individual test person. The video feeds allow us to study the immediate responses of the audience.

Questionnaires and interviews allow us to investigate the verbalized responses of the audience, as they describe their experience in their own words. Between the two positions, we used a quantitative section of the questionnaire to probe some suppositions regarding the perceived presence and potential eeriness of the android.

Fig. 1. Geminoid-DK lecturing

3   The Questionnaire

During the second lecture, questionnaires were distributed in the auditorium. From the approximate 150 students present, we collected 127 answer sheets (54 male and 74 female respondents). The questionnaire contains both a qualitative and a quantitative part. In this section, we address the quantitative part. On a scale from 0–10, respondents were asked to rate the following questions, posed in Danish but here translated for the sake of readability.

a. I had eye contact with the robot
b. It was as if someone was waiting in the auditorium
c. I discovered immediately that it was a robot
d. I thought it was natural that Henrik was talking trough the robot
e. Humanoid robots are scary
f. The robot is very mechanical
g. The robot is very human
h. I think the robot is almost like a human
i. It seemed natural that the robot was speaking
j. I was comfortable with the robot lecturing
k. It is satisfactory to have a robot as a lecturer
l. The combination of robot, voice, and slides works satisfactory

m. During the lecture I experienced that Henrik was talking to me

n. During the lecture I experienced that the robot was talking to me

The questions were presented in scrambled order, so that for instance question *m* and *n* were not given in consecutive order, but divided by questions *i*, *f*, and *b*. The questions here are divided into four themes:

1. *a-d* reflect the degree of familiarity with the robot in this situation
2. *e-h* reflect the main perception of the geminoid
3. *i-l* evaluates the overall performance of the geminoid
4. *m-n* evaluates the personal perception of the performance of the geminoid

As we have no way of matching anonymous questionnaires with locations in the room, we asked the respondents to rate their proximity to the robot on a scale from 1-5, where 1 is on the front, and 5 is in the back. The proximity obviously affects the perception of the teacher and activities performed by him. Moreover, it is often accepted that placement in large-scale learning rooms reflect engagement and learning style of the learner [10].

3.1   Distribution by Proximity

The radar diagram indicated that answer patterns are roughly the same throughout the zones. But there are of course differences. As we expected, the indicator for eye contact (question *a*) drops rapidly as the distance to the robot increases. There is an unexpected increase from zone 4 to 5, but this can be explained as a statistical invariance based on just two male respondents from zone 5 who gave a score of ten to this question.

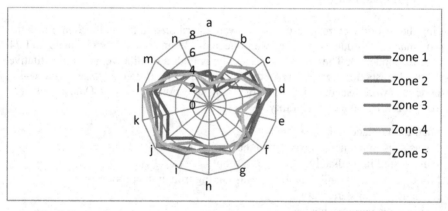

Fig. 2. Radar diagram showing similar answer patterns from the 5 proximity zones

Interestingly, for most questions related to the main perception of the robot (e-h), and of the personal perception of the robot (n-l), the scores from zone 5 are just as high as from zone 1. And there seems to be a tendency that scores from zone 5 are significantly higher than from zone 4. This may of course reflect the reported perceptions of just a few, but is it slightly unexpected.

Respondents from zone 5 give a more positive rating than respondents from zones 3 and 4. The most significant differences in scores that seems to be related to the distance to the robot are seen in c and e. Concerning c: (*I discovered immediately that it was a robot*), the students from zone 4 have the highest score followed by the students from zone 2, 3, 5 and finally zone 1. Surprisingly this indicates that the distance to the robot has no important influence on whether the students immediately perceive the geminoid as a robot.

3.2   Distribution by Gender

Mean values from the questionnaire reveal that male and female responders score the questions fairly similar, with five important exceptions, all having more than one point in difference.   On the question of eye contact (question a), the female population scores only 1.5 compared to 3.2 among the males. This is a significant difference. Out of the 74 female respondents, only seven rate this question in the upper half of the scale, and they were all seated in proximity zone 1 or 2. In comparison, the 14 of the 54 male respondents rated this question ≥ 5. And interestingly, they were distributed throughout the auditorium. In fact, 10 of them were sitting in zone 3-5.

The second difference is seen in the responses to question b: (*It was as if someone was waiting in the auditorium.*) On average this score is one of the lowest in the questionnaire, but it is significant that the female are less inclined to feel the presence of the geminoid as a feeling of 'someone' being in the room. The female score is 3.5 and the male score is 4.6. This could be an indication that females are more sensitive to the robotic presence, and less prone to think of the geminoid as a human presence.

The third and most significant difference between the genders is seen in relation to question e: (*humanoid robots are scary*). Here, the females score almost twice as high as the males. This might be a manifestation of The Uncanny Valley, as suggested by Masahiro Mori [9]. There were no differences between the genders in relation to question c: (*I discovered immediately that is was a robot*). In fact both males and females had an average score at 5 with a wide distribution of responses between 1 and 10. This means that both among male and female students first impression on whether the geminoid was a robot or a human differed significant.   The fact that female students tended to find the geminoid more scaring and that significant less of them had eye contact with the geminoid compared to the male students may indicate that females are more likely to experience The Uncanny Valley than males. However, we have to take into consideration that the answers might reflect some cultural aspects that allow women to express fear, while men may be more reluctant to acknowledge and publicly display these kinds of feelings.

The fourth difference between genders is reflected in question k: (*It is satisfactory to have a robot as a lecturer*). Male students have the highest score and the difference is 1.5. This might be an indication that the male students are more fascinated by the robot as a technological device than the female students are.

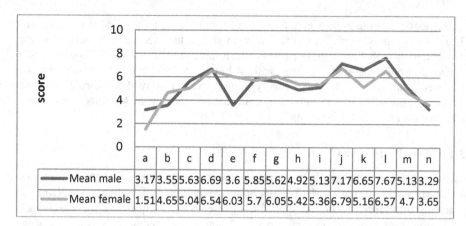

	a	b	c	d	e	f	g	h	i	j	k	l	m	n
Mean male	3.17	3.55	5.63	6.69	3.6	5.85	5.62	4.92	5.13	7.17	6.65	7.67	5.13	3.29
Mean female	1.51	4.65	5.04	6.54	6.03	5.7	6.05	5.42	5.36	6.79	5.16	6.57	4.7	3.65

Fig. 3. Distribution by gender

The fifth significant difference between the genders is exposed in question *l*: *(The combination of robot, voice, and slides works satisfactory)*. Also in this question the male students have the highest score and the difference is 1.1. The videos confirm that there are no unexpected discrepancies between voice and slides, but there are technical limitations regarding the synchronization of voice and lip movement in the robot. The different scores might indicate that women have higher expectations to the consistency between verbal and non-verbal communication than men, or maybe that women are more prone to find such inconsistencies annoying.

3.3   The Overall Performance and the Main Perception

On the questions related to the overall performance of the robot in this situation (*i-l*), the average scores are fairly high. Both the central question *j* and *l*; *(I was comfortable with the robot lecturing)*, and *(the combination of voice, robot and slides works satisfactory)*, have a mean rating of 6-7. This result is partly affected by gender, and again we see a higher rating in the zones furthest from the robot. This could indicate that for persons sitting close to the geminoid, special issues apply. A hypothesis could be that discrepancies between voice and lip movement are more important to people in close proximity of the android, whereas this hardly matters for people in the back because they will not be able to distinguish such details anyway.

The highest score among all questions is seen on *l*: *(The combination of robot, voice, and slides works satisfactory)*.Taking into consideration that this question does not implicate the respondents' position to the geminoid as being more or less than a tele-operated robot, this might indicate that if perceived more as a medium than as an autonomous feature, the geminoid works satisfactory in correlation with the operator and the slides. Compared with the fact that the average score on question *c*: *(I discovered immediately that it was a robot)*, was only 5, we must conclude that it might be difficult to the students to relate unambiguously to the geminoid. This tendency is reinforced in the response to two of the questions related to the main perception of the robot. The scores for statement *f*: *(the robot is very mechanical)*, and statement *g*: *(the robot is very human)*, are both > 5, indicating that the geminoid as a phenomenon is so unknown to the students that they cannot place it in relation to their past experiences and their perceptions of the world. In terms of categorization theory, this might indicate an uncertainty as to how the geminoid should be labeled: as a material thing, an almost-human being or an intelligent technological device.

4 Qualitative Questions from the Questionnaires

On the questionnaire the students were asked to fulfill three sentences regarding their impression of Geminoid-DK:

1. I think that Geminoid-DK is....
2. When I saw the robot my first thought was....
3. After having spent some time in the same room as the robot I think....

Concerning question 1 the male students mainly stabled these adjectives on the geminoid: innovative, interesting, exciting, entertaining, genial, functional, human-like and mechanical, and two respondents found it creepy. Several males also stated that the geminoid is 'The Future'. The female students mostly used these adjectives to express what they thought Geminoid-DK was; human-like, impressing, exciting, scary, vivid, authentic and deadpan. For both genders it were average to mention that the geminoid was exciting, but the responds still show a tendency that the male students are more open-minded to or impressed by the technology while the female students make more reflections on whether the geminoid seems vivid and have natural or unnatural expressions.

On question 2, the male students were likely to complete the sentence with questions that indicated that they were wondering if they were exposed to a human or a robot; Is it a man? ... is it technology?... and again their excitement was explicated in statements like; ...This is going to be cool, and .... This is the future. None of the males expressed that their first thought was that the robot was scary. 1 out of 4 females, though, completed the sentence by claiming that they felt scared, shocked, experiencing an odd man, a staring man, a man making fun with them, and a man making funny movements with his mouth. 8 of the women made comments on the mouth and on the fact that the voice and the movements of the mouth were not in sync. None of the males commented on that, and even though comparatively many females were sitting in the front, we might once again have an indicator that women have higher expectations regarding consistency between verbal and non-verbal cues. One female professed uncannily that: 'It looks like a real man and therefore it is a bit disgusting that he acts like a human'. 1 in 9 female's first thought was that the robot was cool, and again several female stated that the robot looked authentic.

Regarding statement 3 on their thoughts after having spent some time with the robot, most males were still fascinated, but some of them now claimed that something about the robot was not perfected in order to make it appear human-like. A significant number of 26 males found that the geminoid added some value to the lecture or that they got so used to the geminoid that they forgot it was a robot and just focused on the lecture. Several female still found that the geminoid was scary and got disturbed by the discrepancy between voice and mouth.10 females thought that it began to feel natural to be taught by a robot, but 11 claimed that the lecture went impersonal, trivial, hard to focus on, a joke, monotonous and boring. Only three males stated that the geminoid was inappropriate. They missed the energy and the non-verbal communication from a human lecturer.

It this experiment we found clear indications that males are more open-minded to having a geminoid as a lecturer. A non-gender dependent tendency in the qualitative questions from the questionnaires is that about half the students changed their perception of the geminoid from question 2 to 3. Most of them became more aware of the mechanical features of the robot, some got more used to it and some became either more bored or more fascinated.

5   Exit Interviews

After the lecture five random students were asked to participate in a qualitative semi-structured interview. The responses from the interviews complemented the questionnaires and indicated that the students were trying to fit the geminoid into the prior experiences from their own 'lifeworld' in a Habermasian sense. The following statements indicate the apparent difficulty in making sense of the situation:

- 'You cannot feel it's soul and I think that makes it creepy.'
- 'I thought it was a real person, but it disturbed me that he moved in a creepy way.'
- 'Some of us discussed if he was chewing gum.'
- 'Simon from my group felt that it was really scary. He had apparently been sitting in a place where he had eye contact with it.'
- 'I felt like - either he is about to have an attack or something, and then suddenly I saw – my God – it is a robot.'
- 'I think that the voice blow a little bit of life into the robot, so I am not 100% willing to say that it is just a cold robot.'
- 'People came from behind and asked; why do they take pictures - poor man! They had not understood that it was a robot.'

The respondents had a tendency to switch between referring to the geminoid as 'it' and 'he'. This unsteady use of pronouns is one more indicator that they found it hard to categorize. Trying to explain the geminoid's behavior by placing it into well known situations as gum chewing, heart attacks, and good manners for photographing the students seemed to place the robot into categories that they knew from their everyday life. There are indicators that such a categorization is crucial to the students. One respondent called the geminoid 'a good Disney' and another referred to it as a doll. It is interesting that the categorization issue apparently has a significant impact on the students.

6   Conclusion and Further Research

This experiment has led to the conclusion that the geminoid as lecturers is accepted to some extent, and that there are no significant differences in the answers in respect to proximity, but some gender specific differences have been found. We see a tendency in change of perception of the geminoid during the lecture, but we have found no consistency in the direction of this change. There are strong indicators that females have higher expectation regarding consistency between the geminoid's verbal and non-verbal communication, and that females more often than males have an experience that might be interpreted as entering The Uncanny Valley. We did not, however, target this issue in our design of investigation, and it would therefore be desirable to look further into this matter to discern whether this bias is specific to the target group under consideration or perhaps applicable in a wider context. Correspondingly, we have found indicators that male students more readily accept having a geminoid as a lecturer, but there are also indicators that categorization issues make a significant impact on the human robot interaction. Specifically:

- Are male students more fascinated of the geminoid as a technological device than female students? And is robot-aided teaching consequently more appropriate to one target group?
- What is the impact of time spent with the geminoid in a learning context?
- Is there a special correlation between proximity and learning style in robot-mediated teaching?

With regard to the gender issues, it is fairly obvious that the gender of the robot might play a role. It would therefore be desirable to repeat the experiment with a female android, equally adapted to the cultural setting.

References

[1] Nishio, S., Ishiguro, H., Hagita, N.: Geminoid: Teleoperated Android of an Existing Person. In: de Pina Filho, A.C. (ed.) Humanoid Robots: New Developments, pp. 343–352. I-Tech Education and Publishing, Vienna (2007)

[2] Kanda, T., Hirano, T., Eaton, D., Ishiguro, H.: Interactive robots as social partners and per tutors for children: a field trial. Human-Computer-Interaction 19, 61–84 (2004)

[3] Han, J., Jo, M., Jones, V., Jo, J.H.: Comparative Study on the Educational Use of Home Robots for Children. J. of Information Processing Systems 4(4), 159–168 (2008)

[4] Jeonghye, H., Dongho, K.: r-Learning Services for Elementary School Students with a Teaching Assistant Robot. In: HAI 2009, pp. 255–256. ACM (2009)

[5] Hashimoto, T., Kobayashi, H., Kato, N.: Educational system with the android SAYA and field trial. In: FUZZ-IEEE, pp. 766–771 (2011)

[6] Hashimoto, T., Kato, N., Kobayashi, H.: Field Trial of Android-type Remote Class Support System in Elementary School and Effect Evaluation. IEEE (2009)

[7] Hashimoto, T., Kato, N., Kobayashi, H.: Development of Educational System with the Android Robot SAYA and Evaluation, pp. 51–61. InTech (2011)

[8] Hashimoto, T., Kato, N., Kobayashi, H.: Study on Educational Application of Android Robot SAYA: Field Trial and Evaluation at Elementary School. In: Liu, H., Ding, H., Xiong, Z., Zhu, X. (eds.) ICIRA 2010, Part II. LNCS, vol. 6425, pp. 505–516. Springer, Heidelberg (2010)

[9] Mori, M.: Bukimi no tani (The Uncanny Valley – K.F. MacDorman and T. Minato (Trans.)). Energy, 33–35 (1970)

[10] Biggs, J., Tang, C.: Teaching for Quality Learning at University. Society for Research into Higher Education & Open University Press (2007)

Social Networking for Robots
to Share Knowledge, Skills and Know-How

Wei Wang, Benjamin Johnston, and Mary-Anne Williams

Centre for Quantum Computation & Intelligent Systems,
University of Technology, Sydney, Australia
Wei.Wang-10@student.uts.edu.au,
{benjamin.johnston,Mary-Anne.Williams}@uts.edu.au

Abstract. A major bottleneck in robotics research and development is the difficulty and time required to develop and implement new skills for robots to realize task-independence. In spite of work done in terms of task model transfer among robots, so far little work has been done on how to make robots task-independent. In this paper, we describe our work-in-progress towards the development of a robot social network called Numbots that draws on the principle of sharing information in human social networking. We demonstrate how Numbots has the potential to assist knowledge sharing, know-how and skill transfer among robots to realize task-independence.

Keywords: Human-Robot Interaction, Robot-Robot Interaction, Social networking, Internet of Things, Robotics.

1 Introduction

The automotive, electronics and manufacturing industries as well as a desire for higher quality service will further drive future demand for both industrial robots and professional service robots [7][2]. Task-independent robots will lead to the increased adoption of industrial and service robots [2].

The major obstacles to achieving task-independence is the difficulty of teaching robots new knowledge, skills and know-how, and how to apply that knowledge in new situations. The standard methods of manually developing robot skills using programming languages with some graphical interface support has been found to make the acquisition of new knowledge, skills and know-how extremely challenging and labour intensive because of the need for considerable complex modeling, hand crafting and the difficulty of specifying actions as control programs [5]. It is well known that people acquire and learn new knowledge, skills and know-how from each other by direct observation and tutoring. Social learning in human society is important and critical for people in learning new skills [16]. To develop individual skills, robots will also need to undertake social learning as robots interact and collaborate with people in richer and more intimate contexts. Therefore, frameworks and tools to support human-robot interaction and collaboration need to be developed [5, 11].

S.S. Ge et al. (Eds.): ICSR 2012, LNAI 7621, pp. 418–427, 2012.

The socialization of robots is also related to the "Internet of Things" – the emerging network connecting people and the physical world so that they can communicate and collaborate with each other regardless of the barriers in terms of heterogeneous structures, geography and time zones [6]. The Internet of Things has given rise to the new Machine-to-Machine paradigm (M2M) that enables the communication and cooperation among cyber-physical devices [6]. The process of robots interacting directly is known as Robot-Robot Interaction (RRI) [10] [11]. Taking advantage of social concepts and Internet related technology opens new and unprecedented opportunities for robot development and learning. Several projects have been working on industry standards to improve interoperability among robots and human like ROS [9], sharing information including task model and robotic applications through special database such as RoboEarth [13] and RobotAppStore [19], or Facebook-style social networks that allow robots to share their profiles online such as MyRobots [18].

In this paper, we follow the trend of using the Internet as the communication channel but explore RRI from the perspective of robotic lifelong developmental learning in social and digital contexts. We are designing an online social network platform called Numbots which provides infrastructure for communities of robots to autonomously share, track and reuse capabilities and/or experiences with their peers, through exposed as web services. A social network for robots will improve their social learning capability and provide new opportunities to develop the necessary flexibility and adaptability to achieve goals and to perform appropriately in complex dynamic and uncertain environment.

The rest of the paper is organized as follows. We start in Section 2 by providing a brief analysis of online social networks that people use. In Section 3 we talk about the current state-of-the-art online robot information sharing projects. Section 4 identifies improvements that will realize significant benefits and introduces our robot social network prototype, Numbots. We describe its overall design, key features and a roadmap to its realization. We conclude with a discussion of key ideas for the future work.

2   Online Social Networks in Human Society

According to the most-cited definition [3], an online Social Network (SN) is a web-based service (or services) that allow individuals to: (1) construct a public or semi-public profile within a bounded system, (2) articulate a list of other users with whom they share a connection, and (3) view and traverse their list of connections and those made by others within the system. The core features of an SN centre on the creation of web-based profiles and networking with trusted associates [7].

Since social networks lack the intimacy of face-to-face physical interaction, the benefits of social networking typically stem from bridging social capital. In other words, the benefit and potential value generated from relationships [12]. Social capital is maintained and generated through two fundamental activities: (1) Maintaining contact with old friends without requiring face-to-face interaction [14, 12], and (2) Forming new friendships and associations through common interests [14, 12]. A study has shown that youngsters like undergraduate students have preferred using online social network than traditional form due to more efficient real-time interaction, gaining advice, self-esteem promotion and satisfaction from their social cycle [12].

The benefits that people obtain from SN mainly include the following four perspectives: (1) Sharing Information by breaking through barriers of geography and time zones to sustain relationships on the basis of shared interests and providing the opportunity for people to have access to dispersed knowledge[14] [8]; (2) Promoting Psychological Development in terms of required emotional support, the development of social skills such as independence, career planning and making friends as well as self-esteem development [3]; (3) Entertainment and Relaxation via gaming SN in ways that solitary play cannot provide or through enrich communities of hobbyists to develop their social circle or meet like-minded enthusiasts [3]; (4) Obtaining Advice from friends [1].

SNs have changed many forms of social interaction in communities of educated and Internet-savvy people [7]. Given their popularity and success in society, it seems natural to consider the potential that they may contribute to human-robot and robot-robot interactions. In the next section, we analyze related work done in terms of sharing knowledge within communities of robots, and then analyze the necessity of creating a dedicated SN to help address the challenges facing the field of robotics.

3   Related Work and Research Question

Taking advantage of the Internet to enable robot communities is an emerging area in academia [13]. Ongoing efforts have been invested in this field, but most have dissimilar purposes. In this section, we analyze current state-of-the-art projects in relation to robots taking advantage of the Internet, and compare and contrast the features of these projects highlighting key differences.

Robot Operating System (ROS):   ROS provides infrastructure for robot applications. It enables interoperability among robots by acting as a standard communication layer. Once the ROS run-time environment is installed on a robot, all the functional modules of the robot can also be accessed by other robots. In ROS, computation and capabilities are encapsulated within communicating 'nodes'. Users can make robots enact more complicated actions through configuration of these nodes in ROS. For example, a single node can be used to make a robot move its head or wave its hand only, but through configuration in ROS, a robot could move its head while waving its hands simultaneously [9].

RoboEarth: is widely considered to be the first robot-sharing project in terms of sharing and reuse of data on the Internet for robots. It is an open-source project built on ROS and it uses an extensive network and database repository with the purpose of sharing domain task experiences by robots to help other robots be more adaptive in similar task environments [13].

Robots on the Web: is a project that allows robots to perform tasks by using web services. It fits within the Service-Oriented Computing (SOC) paradigm and could serve as a translational layer to make existing robotic applications interoperate with the resources on the Internet [4]. The SOC paradigm aims to utilize services as atomic blocks to construct reusable applications more efficiently and has been successfully applied in business [4]. Services here are defined as capabilities or functions that can be implemented not only by people or modular software applications but also via robot actions, which can be packaged as independent and reusable web resources to assist devices [4].

MyRobots: is a Facebook-style social networking site created for a community of robots, allowing robots to "express themselves" by exposing profile descriptions to a broader outside environment, rather than only limited to their local environments. Although the registration is free, it requires monthly subscriptions of a token for access. A special device called MyRobots Connect, assists robots to connect with MyRobots through serial communication. The target of this website is robot owners and builders [18].

RobotAppStore: is a specific website that organizes and manages robotic applications. It allows robot developers and owners to manually upload and download robot applications. The purpose is to accelerate the process of developing robotic applications more quickly and make the robots more capable for diverse tasks [19].

A comparison of these projects is provided in Table 1, below. We put the emphasis on the focus, targeted users, platform, and some features that a typical social network should have from the perspective of robots sharing with robots. We have identified the following gaps in existing social networks for robotics.

Insufficient Support for Social Robot-Robot Interaction: Almost all of the project analysed do not support RRI or social RRI. RRI is regarded as an autonomous interaction between or among robots during which robots can autonomously exchange information [10]. To some extent, RoboEarth is the only project that in part has the feature of RRI. Even though MyRobots is designed as a social network, it only presents robot profiles and functions but does not support RRI-based knowledge exchange. Other projects have neither 'social' nor 'RRI' features.

Lack of Support for Skill Transfer: In human-oriented SN, people understand how to assimilate new skills in ways that help them grow or become more adaptive. A formal SN for robots must support the sharing of skill-level transfer for the purpose of development. RoboEarth, is the only project for knowledge exchange among robots but it only supports task-level not skill-level transfer [13]. In addition, RoboEarth does not aim to develop a robot's body of knowledge and skill base.

Inflexible Online Data Processing and Sharing Mechanisms: In state-of-the-art projects, all robot experiences have to be manually processed for reuse – by keeping humans in the loop many advantages are lost. For example, the mechanism in RoboEarth is to process raw input data through complex data mining or text mining techniques for future learning or querying but that will significantly restrict the autonomy of robots [13]. RobotAppStore allows robots owners or developers but not robots to upload and download the apps on robots for the purpose of sharing and reuse.

Table 1. Comparison of state-of-the-art robot networking applications

	ROS	RoboEarth	Robots on the web	MyRobots	RobotApp Store
Focus	Interoperation among robots	To share information and reuse data on the Internet	To allow robots interoperate with web resources	e-Business	e-Business
Targeted Users	Robot owners & builders	Robots	Robot owners & builders	Robot owners & builders	Robot owners & builders
Platform	Open Source	Open Source built on ROS	Open Source based on Web and ROS	Facebook-style social network website	ASP-based B/S application
Web-based profile	No	No	No	Yes	No
Maintaining social capital	No	No	No	Yes	Yes
Shared information	No	Task model	No	No	Developed robotic apps
For developmen-tal robotics	No	No	No	No	No
Knowledge transfer	No	No, one-off acquisition	No	No	No
Interaction (HRI/RRI)	HRI	Mainly for HRI	HRI	HRI	HRI

Based on these weaknesses, our research question is how to create a mechanism to allow robots to develop in social contexts, in which they can autonomously learn shared/reusable robotic experiences/capabilities for better task performance? In other words, how can robotic capabilities be automatically exposed to allow robots to discover and acquire new skills in a sustainable and autonomous way?

In the next section, we discuss our prototype system, Numbots, which is an online social network for a robotic community that enables robots to realize lifelong learning after deployment through robot-robot interaction in a virtual social environment and in turn become task-independent.

4　Numbots: Online Social Network for Robot Lifelong Learning

Numbots[1] is an online social network enabled platform designed to enable robots to learn and 'socialize' with other robots, cyber-physical devices and humans. In this

---

[1] Named after the endangered Australian marsupial, the Numbat, that typically lives a solitary life – like the robots of today.

section we discuss the overall design, the key capabilities and some unique challenges in achieving effective RRI.

4.1 Overall Description

Numbots is a web based infrastructure designed upon ROS infrastructure within the developmental robotics paradigm [15] in which robots' capabilities autonomously develop and robots can build increasingly complex skills based on basic skills they learn over their lifetime so that they become more adaptable to uncertain environments and develop skills for tasks their designer did not foresee. As such, Numbots helps develop robot's skills in a sustainable way rather than one-off knowledge acquisition or direct human software development intervention. The core mechanics is that of a directory service and a messaging server which allows robots to share and track capabilities and experiences as web services thus providing a way to transfer shared robotic capabilities or skills into a robot's existing body of declarative knowledge.

Fig. 1. Numbots Prototype – A Nao Robot Soccer Player

Numbots will track and present robot exchanges. The overall idea is that each robot that wants to create a social network must be registered via human assistance or autonomously through Bonjour services. Each registered robot has its own webpage that displays its profile, owner information, available capabilities, skill set, latest advancements, its social networks and tweets broadcasts as shown in Fig.1. After registration the robot will appear in the social list of its socialized counterparts once it connects to the network. The information for each robot mentioned above will be automatically generated and appear in the corresponding item page. It allows people to monitor and interpret activities on their robots and those across the whole network. The users and the usage of shared information reflect its 'social' aspects because after robot registered its owner will be registered to be a member of the network. In this way, robot may discover other robots to request help or obtain advice directly from socialized robots or indirectly through human social network.

4.2   Design Challenges

Skill Specification. Specifying skills plays a crucial role in sharing and transferring skill. So far little work has been done regarding "What is a skill" and "How to specify a skill most benefit for sharing among robots". A skill defined in QLAP is a sequence of actions used to perform a certain task or provide a service [17]. For example, "open a door" is a task that robots can perform but it requires the capability to open the door. A skill uses capabilities encapsulated a sequence of actions such as (*raise left arm, roll right wrist ...*). QLAP represents actions in a skill by qualitative value which is hard for sharing due to weak support for domain changing. Instead of skills, RoboEarth considers actions using "recipes" consisting of task-specific subclasses of actions, which is weak for task-independence due to lacking mechanism to generate new knowledge and skill for development [13].

Numbots uses the concept of "*skill ontology*" to specify skills required to undertake tasks. The principle of this approach is that we classify actions engaged in a task into two categories which are *atomic skill* that refers to the action taking by single joint represented by joint states, and *skill sets* that is associated action containing more than one atomic skill. Both atomic skill and skill sets will be represented by WSDL file where only robot's joint information will be exposed. During the task performance, some features related to the task will be recorded by XSTL as it suits for connecting with robotic run-time environments through web-based communication [4]. Skills needed for a task are decomposed using skill ontology and the sequence of actions contained in each skill are processed and recorded by XSLT and XML for future reuse [4]. Meanwhile the relationship between objects and skill ontology is abstracted and represented by XSLT [4]. The skill ontology is paired with the object and the operation as (robot joint, operation and objects) such as (RShoulder, Approach Door Handle). Therefore, the representation integrated with skill ontology helps identify methods to access objects. In this way, objects with similar features will have similar access methods and we can abstract and generalize access methods to the objects as new knowledge for robots to apply when they require new skills in undertaking tasks. Utilizing XSLT, XML and WSDL to represent skills is potential to increase the reusability of robotic skills in different task environments, due to its language-independence, and to construct robotic service oriented framework for robotic community.

Expose Robot Capabilities as Web Resources. After the skill is specified using "skill ontology", all the robot capabilities could be exposed as web resources. Numbots exposes these functional modules as a set of SOAP services described by WSDL files that enable publication, retrieval, querying and subscription.

Embodiment Robot Description. Embodiment Robot Description is a uniform representation of the configuration of a robot body for interoperability among robots.

The state-of-the-art is URDF and SRDL being used in RoboEarth for task-based model exchange [20, 21]. Numbots integrates them with skill transfer among robots which has not received much attention yet [20].

Skill Discovery. The search for the desired skills to develop is part of the process of autonomous service selection. Numbots will have an interest-based self-motivated learning mechanism to allow robots to choose skills on the network according to their own requirements and interests. 'Interest' is a digital value obtained from the frequency of visual stimuli (the motivations inspired by what the robot observed) or the popularity of skills available online. Citation is used to record the popularity of skills which is the times of cited skill related to certain object ontology to guide robots to make decisions as needed.

Skill Transfer. Skill transfer allows robots to realize skill development. By enabling them to: (1) decompose and analyze a set of known skills sequences recorded in an XML document; (2) identify the effect of the goal; (3) regenerate a set of new action sequences to cater for the requirement of the unknown task performance; (4) merge the new generated action sequences into learner robot's existing skill repertoire. Only the precondition of the selected skill is satisfied, skill transfer will be triggered.

We now illustrate a simple case of skill transfer between identical robots to illustrate how skill transfer would be implemented in Numbots. Suppose Robot1 and Robot2 are two physically identical robots. Robot1 knows how to open the door and Robot2 does not know. Robot2 can learn from Robot 1 using the shared skill specification description rather than from observing how Robot1 performs *open the door*. A XML-based task specification using skill ontology is shown in Fig.2 and a rough process for skill transfer from Robot 1 to Robot 2 is described in Fig.3 below.

```
<Task effect = 'open' object = 'door'>
    <Author name='robot1' urdf='NaoRobot.xml'/>
    <Preconditions>
        <RelevantAction name='walk,run,raiseArm'/>
        <BodyStatus brief='lying' gravity='0.0'/>
    </Preconditions>
    <SubTask effect ='approach' object='door' feature='0123' distanceFrom=30 distanceTo=10>
        <Skill type='set' joint name= {LHipPitch,LKneePitch,LAnklePitch}
            param ='-80.3,10.2,-10' module = 'MoveTo' url='http://Robot1Modules.wsdl'/>
        <Skill type='set' joint name= {RHipPitch,RKneePitch,RAnklePitch}
            param ='30,30,-60' module = 'MoveTo' url='http://Robot1Modules.wsdl'/>
    </SubTask>
    <SubTask effect ='On' Object='handle' belongTo = 'door' >
        <Skill type='atomic' joint name= 'RShoulderPitch'
            param ='0,-100' module = 'MoveTo' url='http://Robot1Modules.wsdl'/>
        <Skill type='atomic' joint name='RElbowRoll'
            param ='-0.5' module = 'Set' url='http://Robot1Modules.wsdl'/>
    </SubTask>
    ....
</Task>
```

Fig. 2. Task specification using skill ontology for the task "Open a door"

For physically identical robots with the similar or different software, the process of skill transfer is to match with the interfaces provided by WSDL, which are joint states information.

```
Begin
   If (precondition is satisfied)
      Parse skill sequence from task specification of robot1 to create a skill chain
      While (skill_sequence -> next is not null) {
         Get joint name and value from robot 1
         Set joint name and value to robot 2
      }
      Generate new XML for robot2 to perform according to new task requirements
      Evaluating the quality of learning through Reinforcement learning
      Merging new skill into the robot2's knowledge by associating joints and objects
   End if
End
```

Fig. 3. A process to transfer skills between identical robots

4.3   Evaluation Design

Numbots design is based on the following two hypotheses related to the benchmark projects, RoboEarth [13] and QLAP [17].

(1) We assume that our method to expose robotic capability as web resources has same effect as the data processing mechanism used in RoboEarth. This hypothesis will be tested by performing the same experiment as RoboEarth, namely 'opening a door'. If it is successful, then the hypothesis is, in part, proven.

(2) We assume that our skill specification and transfer mechanism is significantly more practical and suitable for sharing among robots than the method used in QLAP. This hypothesis will be tested by performing the same experiment in QLAP and Numbots. If it is successful, then the hypothesis is, in part, proven.

5   Conclusion

In this paper, we analyzed robot social network state-of-the-art technologies, and introduced the design for Numbots, a new skill sharing social network that enables robots to learn from one other for the purposes of robot lifelong learning. We analyzed the overall requirements of design, focusing on developing an online social network for robotic community where robots could share knowledge and skills and know-how. We introduced the technical design of RRI in Numbots and demonstrate a feasible roadmap for development.

References

1. Al-Sharawneh, J.A., Williams, M.-A.: Credibility-based Social Network Recommendation: Follow the Leader. In: The 21st Australasian Conference on Information Systems (ACIS 2010), pp. 1–11 (2010)
2. Aruvian's R'search.: Research and Market: Amazing the global robots industry (2012)
3. Boyd, D.M., Ellison, N.B.: Social Network Sites: Definition, History, and Scholarship. Journal of Computer-Mediated Communication 13(1), 210–230 (2007)
4. Blake, M.B., Remy, S.L., Wei, Y., Howard, A.M.: Robots on the web. IEEE Robotics and Automation Magazine 18(2), 33–43 (2011)
5. Cakmak, M., DePalma, N., Arriaga, R.I., Thomaz, A.L.: Exploiting social partners in robot learning. Journal of Autonomous Robotics 29(3-4), 309–329 (2010)

6. IERC IoT Cluster Strategic Research Agenda, http://www.internet-of-things-research.eu/pdf/IoT_Cluster_Strategic_Research_Agenda_2011.pdf

7. Messinger, P.R., Stroulia, E., Lyons, K., Bone, M., Niu, R., Smirnov, K., Perelgut, S.: Virtual worlds — past, present, and future: New directions in social computing. Journal of Decision Support Systems 47(3), 204–228 (2009)

8. Mislove, A., Marcon, M., Gummadi, K.P.: Measurement and analysis of online social networks. In: Proceedings of the 7th ACM SIGCOMM Conference on Internet Measurement, pp. 29–42 (2007)

9. Quigley, M., Conley, K., Gerkey, B.P., Faust, J., Foote, T., Leibs, J., Wheeler, R., Ng, A.Y.: ROS: an open-source Robot Operating System. In: ICRA Workshop on Open Source Software (2009)

10. Steel, L.: Evolving Grounded Communication for Robots. Trends in Cognitive Sciences 7(7), 308–312 (2003)

11. Steels, L., Belpaeme, T.: Coordinating perceptually grounded categories through language: A case study for colour. Behavioral and Brain Sciences 28(4), 469–529 (2005)

12. Steinfield, C., Ellison, N.B., Lampe, C.: Social capital, self-esteem, and use of online social network sites: A longitudinal analysis. Journal of Applied Developmental Psychology 29(6), 434–445 (2008)

13. Waibel, M., Beetz, M., Civera, J., D'Andrea, R., Elfring, J., Galvez-Lopez, D., Haussermann, K., Janssen, R., Montiel, J.M.M., Perzylo, A., Schiessle, B., Tenorth, M., Zweigle, O., van de Molengraft, R.: RoboEarth – A World Wide Web for Robots. IEEE Robotics & Automation Magazine 18(2), 69–82 (2011)

14. Wellman, B.: Computer networks as social networks. Journal of Science 293(5537), 2031–2034 (2001)

15. Weng, J., McClelland, J., Pentland, A., Sporns, O., Stockman, I., Sur, M., Thelen, E.: Autonomous mental development by robots and animals. Science 291, 599–600 (2001)

16. Demiris, Y., Hayes, G.: Imitation as a dual-route process featuring predictive and learning components: a biologically plausible computational model. In: Dautenhahn, K., Nehaniv, C. (eds.), pp. 327–361. MIT Press (2002)

17. Mugan, J., Kuipers, B.: Autonomously Learning an Action Hierarchy Using a Learned Qualitative State Representation. IJACI 2009, 1175–1180 (2009)

18. Social Network for Robots Lets You Talk to Your Roomba, http://mashable.com/2011/12/28/social-network-for-robots/

19. Towards a Robot App Store, http://www.ros.org/presentations/2009-07_Gerkey_IJCAI-robotics-workshop.pdf

20. Kunze, L., Roehm, T., Beetz, M.: Towards semantic robot description languages. In: ICRA, pp. 5589–5595 (2011)

21. Tenorth, M., Perzylo, A., Lafrenz, R., Beetz, M.: The RoboEarth Language: Representing and Exchanging Knowledge about action, objects and environments. In: ICRA (2012)

Social Acceptance of a Teleoperated Android: Field Study on Elderly's Engagement with an Embodied Communication Medium in Denmark

Ryuji Yamazaki [1,2], Shuichi Nishio[1], Hiroshi Ishiguro[1,3], Marco Nørskov[4], Nobu Ishiguro[5], and Giuseppe Balistreri[6]

[1] Hiroshi Ishiguro Laboratory, Social Media Research Laboratory Group, Advanced Telecommunications Research Institute International, Keihanna Science City, Kyoto 619-0288, Japan
ryuji-y@atr.jp
[2] School of Knowledge Science, Japan Advanced Institute of Science and Technology, Nomi, Ishikawa 923-1211, Japan
[3] Department of Systems Innovation, Graduate School of Engineering Science, Osaka University, Toyonaka, Osaka 560-0043, Japan
[4] Institute for Culture and Society – Philosophy, Aarhus University, Jens Chr. Skousvej 7, 8000 Aarhus C, Denmark
[5] Studies in Language and Society, Graduate School of Language and Culture, Osaka University, Minoo, Osaka 562-8558, Japan
[6] Dipartimento di Ingegneria Informatica, Universit`a degli Studi di Palermo, Viale delle Scienze, Edificio 690128 Palermo, Italia

Abstract. We explored the potential of teleoperated android robots, which are embodied telecommunication media with humanlike appearances, and how they affect people in the real world when they are employed to express a telepresence and a sense of 'being there'. In Denmark, our exploratory study focused on the social aspects of Telenoid, a teleoperated android, which might facilitate communication between senior citizens and Telenoid's operator. After applying it to the elderly in their homes, we found that the elderly assumed positive attitudes toward Telenoid, and their positivity and strong attachment to its huggable minimalistic human design were cross-culturally shared in Denmark and Japan. Contrary to the negative reactions by non-users in media reports, our result suggests that teleoperated androids can be accepted by the elderly as a kind of universal design medium for social inclusion.

Keywords: android, teleoperation, minimal design, communication, embodiment, inclusion, acceptability, elderly care.

1 Introduction

Global population aging is increasing at an unprecedentedly rapid pace, and there is a growing need for new ways to provide elderly care [1, 2]. As worldwide societies continue to age, how can social robots be developed to support elderly people? In this study, we focused on support for the social life of the elderly. As a pilot case in

S.S. Ge et al. (Eds.): ICSR 2012, LNAI 7621, pp. 428–437, 2012.
© Springer-Verlag Berlin Heidelberg 2012

Denmark, which has embraced assistive technologies, we conducted research in the living environments of seniors to explore their reactions to and acceptability of a teleoperated android robot. Elderly people tend to be isolated due to lack of social support and media. Designing communication aids is a major issue in the study of assistive technology, and user-centered development that focuses on usability problems is critical to successful systems. Computer-based intervention has been investigated for improving communication among people with dementia, care staffs, family members, and volunteers, and the importance of conversation has also been identified. Interviews with caretakers revealed that such behavioral disturbances as wandering and verbal abuse were reduced after conversations with volunteers who listened by videophones [3]. To contribute to improving the quality and quantity of communication between the elderly and others, we conducted experiments with a field work approach in their real environments and focused on an experiment in their homes. Our research aims to identify new issues and explores the reactions of elderly people to a teleoperated android robot named Telenoid R2 (Telenoid). We posed the following questions to verify three key elements of our major research question: How do the elderly accept Telenoid? The subsidiary questions are: 1) How will senior citizens adapt to talking through Telenoid? 2) How can Telenoid improve the quality and quantity of communication? 3) Can Telenoid become a practical tool for performing daycare? The purpose of our research in Denmark is to explore and compare the reactions to the android by the elderly and verify whether its design technology is universally acceptable for supporting their quality of life.

Many studies on social robots in elderly care have focused on the pet-like companionship a robot might provide. The following relationships have been investigated with zoomorphic robots that resemble animals: AIBO, a robot resembling a dog; iCat, a cat-like robot; Huggable, a responsive teddy bear; Phyno, a penguin-like robot; and Paro, a seal robot designed for therapy with demented seniors [4-8]. After Paro was introduced into a nursing home, participants treated it like a new companion and felt less lonely. Despite our research in Japan, the influence of using humanoid robots on the elderly had basically remained uninvestigated. There underlies the uncanny valley problem: subtle differences from humans evoke anxiety in observers [9]. Exploring the influences of teleoperated robots on human relationships is challenging. Most recent studies on types of robots have concentrated on autonomous schemes, but teleoperation systems have been used as supplements or substitutes. The reason of substitution is the difficulty of implementing sufficient intelligence [10]. Remote disadvantages have been resolved by video conferencing and telepresence robots [11, 12], but one issue raised in our research is whether it is possible to determine the primacy of remote communication over face-to-face [13]. We must develop tools that people prefer to use even when they have the option of interacting with physical proximity [14]. Social robot studies have advanced the application of robots to educational services, although most works have concentrated on autonomous types of robots [15]. Sick students remotely controlled PEBBLES, which are mobile video conferencing platforms [16] that are housed in child-friendly, egg-shaped, custom-designed shells with huggable contours. Even though theories on robot design are expected, they remain unestablished. Recently, robots have been produced whose appearances closely resemble humans, and research has begun on such minimal designs [17, 18]. Designing teleoperated androids allows us to probe the effects of minimizing the shape or the function of a human body during human interactions.

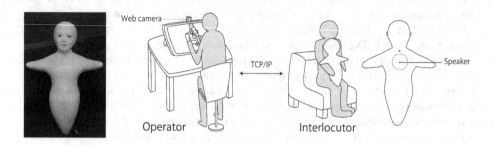

Fig. 1. Telenoid R2   **Fig. 2.** Conceptual diagram of Telenoid system

2   Telenoid R2

Telenoid R2 is a new type of teleoperated android robot with a minimal human likeliness design that can resemble anybody (Figs. 1, 2). It has nine degrees of freedom for its eyes, jaw, neck, and hand motions. Telenoid R2 (Telenoid) is 70 cm long and weighs about 4 kg. Its vinyl chloride skin feels pleasantly similar to human skin. A teleoperation system only requires a single laptop; with an internet connection, Telenoid can be operated from anywhere in the world. The operator's face direction and lip movements are captured by a face recognition system and remotely sent to the robot. GUI buttons control the specific movements of the arms and head to express the operator's behaviors and emotions, such as waving good-bye or hugging. Such unconscious motions as breathing and blinking are generated automatically to give a sense that the android is alive.

Telenoid is modeled to resemble a human and can be perceived as either male or female, young or old. Due to this minimal design, it allows people to feel as if a distant acquaintance is actually close. Our objective is to create a minimal human that allows any person to transfer her own presence to a distant location. Key features include: 1) an omni-human likeness that enables users to feel any person's presence (e.g., a feeling of being there), 2) holdability that facilitates physical interaction, and 3) mobility that encourages people to use Telenoid in a variety of situations. Until now, robots with commonality with Telenoid have been developed, such as the "IP RobotPHONE," which targets telepresent communication [19]. For a minimal human design, the robot's appearance should avoid preconceived ideas about robots. As a minimalistic human, Telenoid was created to remove as many unnecessary features as possible by 1) choosing features for communication, e.g. voice, with humans and eliminating non-neutral ones, e.g. beard, 2) reevaluating the chosen features in order to fit the design requirements by eliminating unnecessary features, and 3) obtaining essential features.

Fig. 3. Group interaction with Telenoid in a living room of a care facility

3   Field Experiment

In Denmark, we applied Telenoid to communication between the operators and the elderly participants at care facilities (Fig. 3) and in their homes. We mainly utilized their ordinary living environments as the fields of our experiment and introduced Telenoid into where they usually stay to get natural responses from them. Here we focus on and describe the experiment results at homes.

3.1   Method

In the new type of social interaction with androids, people are expected to develop their potential and to enrich their social lives. We also considered another result: damaged or lost potential. For example, the elderly may feel excluded from discussions or show no interest in the robot. If the robot evokes unpleasant feelings, it may damage their relationships with the operators. Both the possibility of promoting and obstructing their interaction with others existed in using the teleoperated android. However, trials in Japan have shown that Telenoid is immediately accepted by the elderly and elicited positive reactions, even from those with dementia [18, 20]. For the first time, we introduced Telenoid into two private homes of the elderly to see their natural reactions to it and conducted an experiment with elderly Danish participants.

We conducted a two-day field trial to test Telenoid's use in homes where the elderly live alone as part of a worldwide movement called Aging-in-Place, which advocates allowing residents to remain in their familiar environments despite the decline that generally occurs with aging. By remaining at home, residents can maintain a relatively stable environment; on the other hand, they are more at risk of isolating themselves and might be less stimulated than those living in care facilities. By introducing Telenoid into private homes, we expected that the residents would act freely and react strongly toward it. We focused on two senior participants: a healthy male (92 years old; participant S) and a male with mild Alzheimer's disease (75 years old: participant P), whose houses were attached to care facilities. In both cases, we set Telenoid up in the living room where they can feel at ease and receive visitors (Figs. 4, 5). For convenience in setting the operating system, the bedrooms next to the living rooms were utilized for teleoperation by the researchers, nursing students, and a friend.

Each participant interacted with Telenoid for about two hours. Conversation topics included health, hobbies, and family, and such games as a cooperative map task between two persons. The experiment was conducted in the Svendborg municipality in

Fig. 4. Situation S: Teleoperation and elderly man interacting with Telenoid

Fig. 5. Situation P: Teleoperation and elderly man interacting with Telenoid

Denmark. Prior to its implementation, we received approval and informed consent from the participants themselves and their family members, their primary doctors, and the ethical committee at Advanced Telecommunications Research Institute International (approval code: 10-507-4). For problem finding, we conducted a qualitative method with dialogue recording data, collected narrative and behavioral data of the elderly during the conversations, and observed them based on video recordings. We extracted typical or characteristic reactions from the observations and explored the issues to be addressed. To identify the degree of participant engagement or activity in the conversation, we extracted three minutes of conversation from each of four situations (two situations each for participants S and P). The times of the participant and operator utterance intervals and non-speech intervals were accumulated, and the ratios of the total times to the entire three minutes are depicted in Fig. 6. We chose those three minutes because they were representative for the whole conversation and to illustrate the possibility of a meaningful interaction.

3.2   Observation Results

Both in the cases of participants S and P, Telenoid encouraged positive responses and behaviors. The participants were willing to talk using Telenoid and kept the conversation moving. From the first glance, they naturally started conversing with it without any reluctance and continued to enjoy interaction by changing their dialogue strategies, including reading poems, talking about TV programs, hugging Telenoid, showing favorite items to it, playing the piano, singing together, introducing it to a friend, and sharing time with it. We observed that their attitudes toward Telenoid were consistently positive and they actively reacted to it.

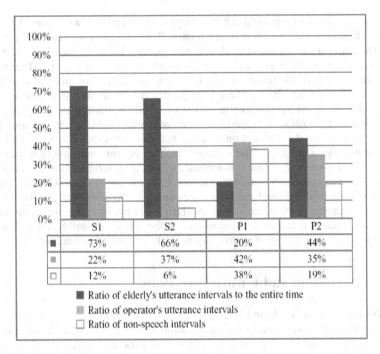

Fig. 6. Time ratios of utterance intervals

a)   Participant S

Participant S lived alone, but was highly motivated to talk to Telenoid and encouraged others to join their conversations. On both days, he constantly talked to it during the sessions (Fig. 6). In this figure, S1 signifies a situation where he talked with a young female nursing student who played the operator, and S2 is where he talked with an elderly friend. Participant S positively continued to talk to Telenoid to the extent that the rate of his utterance intervals (the accumulation of such times) to the entire three minutes exceeded 70%, whereas the operator rate was about 20%. He loved to talk and had many things to share, because he seemed to perceive as a good listener. He also changed the situation and began to amuse Telenoid by playing the piano and singing. On the first day, two nursing students alternately played the operator, but S was not aware of the alternation. This suggests that Telenoid's identity reflected the interlocutor's imagination more than the real operators. On the second day, to enjoy the conversation in a different way, he invited a senior friend, although we had not assumed the condition. She became the operator and conversed with him by Telenoid. As shown in S2, he continued to talk to Telenoid; his friend talked to him at a 40% utterance rate, and the conversation proceeded more interactively than the previous day while they filled every second.

b)   Participant P

Although participant P lived alone with mild Alzheimer's, he positively talked to Telenoid and preferred to act calmly and to contemplate more than participant S. It was possible to have conversations about literature, politics, and health status with P. We tested whether the conversation content could go beyond small talk. The communication level peaked when a Japanese researcher who played the operator taught Japanese Haiku poems to participant P, who started discussing the accuracy of the Danish translation. Another Danish researcher who took over the operator and the discussion reported, *"Here we saw a thorough communication."* P1 (Fig. 6) signifies the situation where the female researcher discussed the poems and participant P played the role of a listener; P2 is where P continued to talk about the poems and the male researcher assumed the discussion. In the P2 situation, participant P became a speaker and his conversation with Telenoid interactively progressed. In another situation during the session, he established not only verbal but also nonverbal contact with Telenoid by giving it a big, silent hug while standing up. This big hug was one of his characteristic behaviors. He seemed to feel this himself right as if he were getting such a reward as a sense of reassurance and greater comfort from his experience with the robot. Even when talking to it, he used many gestures and tried to communicate with Telenoid in various channels. Such behaviors as touching, holding, hugging, imitating, and kissing were observed to build a relationship in both the cases of P and S. They were attracted and encouraged to engage in conversation by the embodied communication medium.

4   Discussion and Future Directions

In this experiment, we found that Telenoid elicited positive attitudes from the elderly and encouraged interactively communication with others using it. Instead of losing interest, they started to develop behavior strategies to incorporate it in such social activities as discussing poems, sharing music, and inviting friends. The positivity of senior citizens was commonly observed in such other settings as care facilities, both in Denmark and Japan [20]. The result suggests that Telenoid can enrich the quality of life and social living by providing an attractive and encouraging communication way for relating to others. In the S1 situation, the participant hoped to talk by Telenoid with his son's family in Iceland. Compared with the operator, the functionality of Telenoid itself is limited based on its minimalistic human design, and its embodiment is different from real human operators. Such differences as its huggable, portable design and neutral features, which allow the elderly to create its identity, might help them elicit positive reactions. The factors that affect their positivity must be further investigated.

A key emerging issue we found in this work is whether elderly's positivity that cannot be elicited face-to face can be elicited by Telenoid. Given the option of meeting an elderly person face-to-face, even when it is difficult in reality, are the operators always a better direct communication option? During the experiment, the participants were actually attracted to interact with Telenoid. They showed positivity to holding and hugging. They even tried to carry Telenoid around and actively enjoyed talking by creating such communicative situations as taking it to the piano and introducing it to a friend. Since Telenoid allowed the elderly to influence the operator's movements and affected the senior's initiative, the seniors could start to explore new relationships with it. The possibility exists that senior citizen activity levels will increase, including utterances, which may improve their health, and that the operator can extract more positive or other unnoticed aspects from their relationships with Telenoid. Further research is necessary to confirm this hypothesis.

In this work, it was shown that the elderly responded positively to the Telenoid in the time interval; we need to focus and advance discussion on the following issues in the future. Regarding the issue of advantages over face-to-face communication, we believe that the elderly's affection for Telenoid is crucial. Since seniors seem to accept its design,   they are encouraged to express themselves and communicate with others, even when such diseases as dementia have decreased their communication abilities. From the operator's side, Telenoid has potential to promote better understanding of the elderly people, even if their recognition of the operator is difficult, by helping the operator stimulate their imaginations and enter their world. This is one advantage we assume in using embodied telecommunications technology. For that connection, to see the social acceptability of Telenoid widely to the general public, we opened to media coverage part of the experiment in the private homes where seniors were interacting with Telenoid. Contrary to our findings of positivity, we received skeptical or even negative reactions from the press in Denmark, which was not seen in Japan.

4.1   Reactions by Mass Media in Denmark

The issues emphasized in the media reports were related to the theme of the loss in human relations by replacing humans with machines. The theme focused on the disadvantage of telecommunications technology since face-to-face is considered the ideal communication mode. One report quoted resentful comments on a TV station's website about a feature on Telenoid after visiting an elderly person's home [21]. "*Nothing, absolutely nothing, will ever replace real and present compassionate touches and care. How sad that we have come to this point, where such a debate can possibly take place,*" wrote one user. The report describes the strange sight of seniors hugging, kissing, and talking to a machine as if it were a human being. Comments from experts in various fields were also introduced. "*There is obviously a big difference between a hug from your daughter or a robot. But the real situation for many elderly people is that it is either a robot hug or no hug. In the second-best and real world where old people enjoy a robot, we would surely be wicked if we condemned such togetherness just because it breaks with current social norms,*" said a person from information and media studies. He stressed the difference between humans and machines, accepting that technology constantly creates new ways for us to be together, using iPhone and Facebook as examples. Also, another expert in ethics says, "*When people talk on the phone, they also lose a degree of emotional feelings, expression of respect, and so on. You could easily reduce human emotions using robots. Relational Technology can therefore lead to curtailment of human emotions.*"

Negative effects must be discussed and analyzed in light of the positive results. Even if emotional involvement is reduced, this result has ambiguous aspects and can be seen not only negatively but also positively. As we observed in another experiment aimed at children who have few opportunities to meet senior citizens, Telenoid helped them feel relaxed and lowered communication barriers with demented seniors; the children showed greater interest in communication with the elderly [22]. On the other hand, as we also verified in this work, elderly people enthusiastically and empathetically showed positivity to Telenoid. Further investigation is required on both sides of the positive and negative effects on the elderly and the operator. Also, as argued by Hollan et al. [13], mechanisms that may be effective in face-to-face interactions might be awkward or ineffective if we replicate them in an electronic medium. We must develop tools and find ways to use them properly and recommend them to people when they have the option of interacting in physical proximity. Our research direction is not to replace manpower by robot technology but to develop human potential that is related with each other. Considering the social acceptance of android robots in Japan, we must also consider why criticism has not appeared in Japan. It might reflect a kind of animism that believes that souls exist in nature. Such a belief still reflects the close Japanese relationship to nature. Japanese automata, including puppets that move automatically, have traditionally been developed. Maybe the Japanese love of "cuteness" is also a factor, so-called kansei values. Including such cultural dimensions, cross-national studies on social acceptability need to advance.

4.2   Future Works

Based on the results from the above trials, we are planning to address the following issues in our future work:

a) *Longitudinal study*: The trials we have conducted so far were all short-term trials for one or two days. We need to observe how people adapt and change their behaviors over longer terms. In past studies, people tended to lose interest in robots after several days [15]. Tanaka et al. avoided this by changing the internal algorithm for behavior generation of the robot. Since teleoperated androids are remotely driven by the operator, this is unlikely to happen, but we need to verify it. On the other hand, as long as Telenoid needs an operator, it cannot contribute to manpower savings, and we need to consider how to deal with this issue. Furthermore, such a longitudinal study will reveal stronger effects for using teleoperated androids in elderly communication. We will combine such field testing results with finer designed laboratory experiments for improving our teleoperated android system.

b) *Minimal communication*: We must investigate the conditions required for promoting interaction and what benefits can be realized by minimizing or restricting communication in various ways. We plan to observe elderly users engaging in various forms of minimized communication using Telenoid or such typical communications media as telephones or teleconferences.

c) *Caring method*: We must also compare the behavior of the elderly using Telenoid with their usual behaviors. We believe that it is also promising to focus on and expand the possibilities of interaction between the elderly and caretakers. We plan to explore how care staffs and volunteers who visit elderly facilities or homes can act as intermediaries to promote more effective verbal and nonverbal interaction between the elderly and Telenoid. On the other hand, as volunteer operators who can be seniors or the younger ones participate in communication with the elderly, caretakers may become more effective in their use of working time: as a result of cooperating with operators and rationalizing the parallel process of care works, caretakers may also be able to have more time to communicate with the elderly.

Acknowledgements. This work was partially supported by JST, CREST. The authors thank all the participants and our colleagues for their cooperation in this work, especially Martin Fischer at Svendborg Municipality, Jari Due Jessen at Technical University of Denmark, Helle Skovbjerg Karoff at Technical University of Denmark, Martin Exner at Danish University of Education, and Ilona Straub at University Duisburg-Essen.

References

1. Population Division, United Nations, World Population Prospects: The 2010 Revision, New York (2011)
2. Kitwood, T.: Dementia Reconsidered: The person comes first. Open University Press, Buckingham (1997)
3. Kuwahara, N., et al.: Networked reminiscence therapy for individuals with dementia by using photo and video sharing. In: Proc. of ASSETS 2006, pp. 125–132 (2006)
4. Tamura, T., et al.: Is an entertainment robot useful in the care of elderly people with severe dementia? Jour. of Gerontoloy: Medical Science 59A(1), 83–85 (2004)
5. Heerink, M., et al.: The influence of a robot's social abilities on acceptance by elderly users. In: Proc. of RO-MAN 2006, pp. 521–526 (2006)
6. Stiehl, W.D., et al.: The huggable: a therapeutic robotic companion for relational, affective touch. In: Proc. of the 3rd Consumer Communications and Networking Conference, pp. 1290–1291 (2006)
7. Lee, D., et al.: Robotic companions for smart space interaction. IEEE Pervasive Computing 8(2), 78–84 (2009)
8. Wada, K., et al.: Robot Therapy in a Care House: Results of Case Studies. In: Proc. of the 15th International Symposium on Robot and Human Interactive Communication, pp. 581–586 (2006)
9. Mori, M.: Bukimi no tani (The uncanny valley). Energy 7(4), 33–35 (1970) (in Japanese)
10. Green, A., et al.: Applying the Wizard-of-Oz Framework to Cooperative Service Discovery and Configuration. In: Proc. of the 13th IEEE International Workshop on Robot and Human Interactive Communication, pp. 575–580 (2004)
11. Sellen, A.J.: Speech patterns in video-mediated conversations. In: Proc. of CHI 1992, pp. 49–59 (1992)
12. Lee, K., et al.: Now, I have a body: Uses and social norms for mobile remote presence in the workplace. In: Proc. of CHI 2011, pp. 33–42 (2011)
13. Hollan, J., et al.: Beyond being there. In: Proc. of CHI 1992, pp. 119–125 (1992)
14. Yamazaki, R., et al.: How Does Telenoid Affect the Communication between Children in Classroom Setting? In: CHI 2012 Ext. Abst., pp. 351–366 (2012)
15. Tanaka, F., et al.: Socialization between toddlers and robots at an early childhood education center. Proc. of the National Academy of Sciences of the U.S.A. 104(46), 17954–17958 (2007)
16. Fels, D.I., et al.: Video-mediated communication in the classroom to support sick children: a case study. International Jour. of Industrial Ergonomics 28(5), 251–263 (2001)
17. Ishiguro, H.: Android Science: Toward a new cross-disciplinary framework. In: Proc. of Toward Social Mechanisms of Android Science, A CogSci 2005 Workshop, pp. 1–6 (2005)
18. Ogawa, K., et al.: Exploring the Natural Reaction of Young and Aged Person with Telenoid in a Real World. Jour. of Advanced Computational Intelligence and Intelligent Informatics 15(5), 592–597 (2011)
19. Sekiguchi, D., Inami, M., et al.: Robot-PHONE: RUI for Interpersonal Communication. In: CHI 2001 Ext. Abst., pp. 277–278 (2001)
20. Yamazaki, R., et al.: Teleoperated Android as an Embodied Communication Medium: A Case Study with Demented Elderlies in a Care Facility. In: Proc. of RO-MAN 2012 (in press, 2012)
21. Den kan også give en krammer (It can also give a hug), http://www.information.dk/263649 (accessed on June 7, 2012) (in Danish)
22. Yamazaki, R., et al.: Promoting Socialization of Schoolchildren Using a Teleoperated Android: An Interaction Study. International Journal of Humanoid Robotics (submitted)

Partially Disembodied Robot:
Social Interactions with a Robot's Virtual Body

Hirotaka Osawa, Thibault Voisin, and Michita Imai

Faculty of Science and Technology, Keio University
3-14-1, Kohoku-ku, Yokohama, Japan
{osawa,tibo,michita}@ayu.ics.keio.ac.jp

Abstract. We propose a novel social robot called partially disembodied robot. This system has the advantages of real-world robots and virtual agents, guaranteeing a high social presence without sacrificing space efficiency. The robot consists of body parts that mimic human hands and eyes in order to give the user visual feedback, and is able to react to human contact through 3D detection, thus allowing the possibility for the user to interact through touching the robot. We evaluated how our system regulates users' behaviors during the solving process of the Tower of Hanoi problem. First, the users solve a Tower of Hanoi problem while being helped by the robot, but without having defined its body. In the second phase, the users were asked to define the robot's body and to play with it using the different interactions implemented. Finally, they were asked to solve the Tower of Hanoi problem once again, this time with the robot's body they defined. We could observe that the presence of the robot was perceived much more clearly by the user after they defined the robot's body, and when they were able to physically interact with it. Users' social response to the robot also seemed to be mediated by their feelings about its social presence. Finally, we found that the shyness of the users can impact the size of the robot's body that they define.

Keywords: Human Robot Interaction, Social Presence, Embodiment, Disembodiment.

1 Introduction: Using a Social Robot's "Social Presence" Separately

Social robots are able to enhance their level of social interaction with humans using their body presence and ability to perceive a user's actions, compared with virtual screen agents. For example, Wainer et al. [1] proposed studying the differences in perception by users between virtual and real-world robots. As a matter of fact, the users enjoyed the embodied robots the most, and believed they were "watching them the most closely." A second study, proposed by Lee et al. [2], enforced these results, but also showed that physical embodiment without touch input capability causes negative effects. These studies clearly showed that users have a strong preference for embodied robots, that physical embodiment enforced the social presence of the robot,

S.S. Ge et al. (Eds.): ICSR 2012, LNAI 7621, pp. 438–447, 2012.
© Springer-Verlag Berlin Heidelberg 2012

and that the effects of physical embodiment could be highly positive when users are able to fully interact with the robot by touching it.

In using social presence as an engineering purpose, it is important that the presence does not always come from a real-world body. We can still feel the presence of the robot's body if there are some clues of the anthropomorphic features found in the real world. For example, breathing sounds clue us in to the presence of lifelike objects. Humanlike picture in the wall emphasize feeling of social presence and accelerate ethical behaviors [3]. Our project has been proposed to consider human anthropomorphic tendencies as a skill, and we have tried to use anthropomorphic features separately[4]. Our studies have confirmed that separate biological cues can create an entire body image of an object [5], and also generally helps the learning process, including in older people [6].

From this perspective, we propose a new interactive social robot called 'partially disembodied' robot, that is, a robot whose body is reduced to its minimum, in order to keep the advantages of virtual screen agents (especially the space-efficiency parameter), but that also would be able to maintain a direct way to interact in the real world in order to keep a good social presence. The robot reacts differently depending on the position of the user relative to its body, and is able to 'feel' that the user is touching it (as Fig. 1a). By keeping a strong bond with the user through the possibility of physical interaction with the robot's body, we managed to keep a high social presence, while space efficiency was maintained through the partial absence of the robot's body in the real world. We show several use cases of the partially disembodied robot's body in Fig. 1. In the situation presented in Fig. 1b, for example, the user asks for the location of an object he cannot manage to find on his desk. Information will be given by the partially disembodied robot if such an object has been registered previously in its memory, or if a sensor has been attached to it. Another possible application could be the protection of the workspace, as presented in Fig. 1c: in that case, the fact that the robot's body is virtual allows us to define a 'restricted' area. If anyone gets close to or enters this area, the robot will signal it by giving an oral warning or alerting its user. This could be particularly useful if the contents of the cardboard box turn out to be dangerous or confidential.

Fig. 1. Possible contexts of use of the partially disembodied robot: (a) Playing with partially disembodied robot with tickling (b) Assistance to the user (c) Protection of the workspace

2   Interaction Design for the Partially Disembodied Robot

According to Wilson's work about embodiment[7] and previous workshop results[8], we supposed that the visual feedback provided by anthropomorphized body parts is a key factor for physical embodiment. First, when interacting with the partially disembodied robot, the user should be able to interact with its body in order to improve the social attraction of the robot, and be able to communicate verbally with it. The action of touching the robot's body leads to greater improvement in the perception of social presence. Second, we include a definition of body process in our partially disembodied robot. The original point of the disembodied social robot was that the robot body is flexible. If users can define the robot body according to their will, they can be immersed for greater interactivity.

The entire interaction design is shown in Fig. 2. The most important part obviously concerns the virtual body of the robot itself: the user should be able to define it instead of using a previously determined one, and then to modify it as he likes. The user will thus be asked to point successively at the back-left and front-right corner of the robot's body as he desires, as depicted in Fig. 2ab. These two points define a fixed rectangle of infinite height that will be considered the robot's body. Its basis is of course the level of the workspace. Afterwards, height can be defined if necessary. The resizing of the robot's body is also necessary. If the user made a mistake during the initialization phase, or just wants to widen or compress the robot's body in order to modify the organization of its workspace, he/she should be able to change the dimensions of the robot's body as he desires. This resizing takes place in two phases: first, the user will move his hand towards the robot's body, and the robot will warn him when his hand touches its body. Then, the user will have to move his hand in the direction he wants to extend or compress the robot's body, and stand still for one second when he reaches the position he wants for the new limit of the robot's body. This procedure is depicted in Fig. 2cd.

Fig. 2. Changing the robot's body (a) Definition of the back-left corner (b) Definition of the front-right corner (c) The user touches the robot's body (d) The user defines the new limit

3   System Implementation of the Partially Disembodied Robot

The robot will react differently depending on the position of the user's hand relative to its body, and will react especially to contact between the user's hand and its body. During interaction, the robot's eyes will follow the position of the user's hand and adopt different expressions relative to the situation in order to improve the feeling of the robot's presence. Additional visual feedback will be given with the presence of anthropomorphized arms that will be used to display feelings along with the virtual eyes, and to point at elements present on the workspace. When the robot is not performing any task and is in 'stand-by' mode, it will still enforce its presence by making permanent eye-contact with the user by following his head.

We used robotic anthropomorphized body parts developed in our previous work [5]. The two virtual eyes simply consist of binary LCD screens (width 320 pixels, height 240 pixels), able to display different types of pupil shapes in order to convey different emotions connected to a computer through a Bluetooth connection. The visual recognition system is implemented with Microsoft Kinect [9]. The Kinect device is placed vertically above the workspace and is in charge of the detection of the user's hand. We determine the new transformation to apply to the position of the user's hand to obtain the direction towards which the eyes must look. This formula is as follows:

$$x_{eye} = 160 + \left(\frac{x_{fgtip}}{4} - 80\right)\frac{480}{y_{fgtip}} \ , \quad x_{eye} = \begin{cases} x_{eye} \text{ if } 80 \leq x_{eye} \leq 240 \\ 80 \text{ if } x_{eye} \leq 80 \\ 240 \text{ if } x_{eye} \geq 240 \end{cases}$$

$$y_{eye} = 120 + \left(z_{fgtip} - h_{Kinect}\right)\frac{60}{h_{eyes}}\frac{480}{y_{fgtip}}, \quad y_{eye} = \begin{cases} y_{eye} \text{ if } 60 \leq y_{eye} \leq 180 \\ 60 \text{ if } y_{eye} \leq 60 \\ 180 \text{ if } y_{eye} \geq 180 \end{cases}$$

where $(x_{eye}; y_{eye})$ is the position of the pupil on the virtual eye, $(x_{fgtip}; y_{fgtip}; z_{fgtip})$ the position of the user's fingertip in space, h_{eyes} the height the virtual eyes are placed relative to the workspace and h_{Kinect} the height at which Kinect is placed, as displayed in Fig. 3 left. We confirmed that the robot's reaction time was similar to a human's - between 0.1 and 0.4 seconds, according to Card et al.'s study [10].

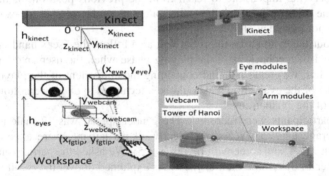

Fig. 3. (left) Calculation of fingertip position by Kinect (right) Evaluation system

4   Evaluation of the Partially Disembodied Robot

We conducted the evaluation of the partially disembodied robot in three parts, inspired by the experiment conducted by Wainer et al. [11], whose results have proved to be especially relevant, and which forces numerous interactions between the user and the robot. To study the influence of the partial disembodiment of the robot on its social perception, we chose to compare two cases: one where the user has not defined the robot's body and one where he has. We also evaluated several user states to find what kinds of users are influenced by the disembodied robot. Our evaluations are conducted to confirm our system's validity: even though there is no body in the workspace, a user still accepts a virtual robot body and the user's behaviors are regulated by the body.

First, the participant is asked to fill out a questionnaire based on the 13 item shyness scale developed by Cheek and Buss [12] in order to determine his character.

Other questions concern his experience with computers and robots. The user is also asked to sign a consent form to participate in the evaluation and to potentially have a video taken. Second, the user is asked to solve the problem of the Tower of Hanoi with the help of the partially disembodied robot, with a pre-defined body whose dimensions are unknown to the user. The user is asked to fill out a post-evaluation questionnaire about his interaction with the partially disembodied robot and about his perception of the robot's body. Third, the user is invited to interact directly with the partially disembodied robot by defining, resizing and playing with its body. Fourth, the user is asked to solve the problem of the Tower of Hanoi a second time, this time with the body he defined. Last, the user is asked to fill out a second post-evaluation questionnaire.

The configuration will be determined by the color of the upper tile, each having a primary color (from the smallest to the largest: red, green and blue as shown in Fig. 3 right). We analyzed the configuration of the system every 0.5 seconds by parsing the raw image acquired. The position of each pile has been determined at the launching of the evaluation depending on the size of the robot's body. We used a solution tree for the Tower of Hanoi to solve the problem. From that tree, the solving algorithm will be able to determine if the move the user just made was optimal (i.e. the move that will lead to the fastest resolution of the problem), correct (i.e. a move that is valid, but not optimal), false (i.e. impossible to reach from the previous position, or impossible if we follow the rules of the game: a smaller pile under a larger one, for example), or if the user has not moved at all.

Throughout the evaluation, the robot will also follow the user's hand, and perform the same kind of feedback as in the playing phase when the user enters its body. In order to do that, we create a thread containing the equivalent of the playing phase at the beginning of the evaluation that could be interrupted to display emotions related to some result of the evaluation.

Fifteen participants were recruited. The gender spread was 12 male to 3 female, and the average age 23.6 years old. Nearly all participants were experienced with computers (n = 12), and some with robots (n = 5). We asked the participants to fill out a test in order to determine their shyness. As explained above, the results were fairly similar to Cheek and Buss' study [9], as we obtained a mean rate of 33.67, whereas Cheek and Buss obtained a mean of 33.3. This test was not necessarily taken on the day of the evaluation, but Cheek and Buss showed in their study that the test had a reliability of 0.86 after 45 days, while the evaluation was generally carried out a week after the test.

We think that the act of defining the robot's body helps the user in locating its limits and makes his interaction with the robot easier. We included another parameter in our study: the shyness or extroversion of the user. We think that a shier user will tend to define a smaller body for the partially disembodied robot than a more extroverted one. The hypotheses mentioned above are presented here: Hyp. 1: The users will perceive the presence of the robot's body more clearly if they have defined it themselves previously. Hyp. 2: The user's social response to the partially disembodied robot will be mediated by the user's feeling of social presence during the evaluation. Hyp. 3: The possibility of physical interaction with the partially disembodied robot will lead to an increased perception of social awareness. Hyp. 4: A shier user will tend to define a smaller body than an extroverted one.

4.1   Tower of Hanoi Session Before Body Change

At first, the participants were asked to perform a Tower of Hanoi evaluation while being helped by the robot. Here, the robot's body was predefined as a square centered on the middle pole and its borders placed at the perpendicular bisector of the segment joining the centers of the first and second pile, and second and third pile. Some stickers were placed on each pile in order to help the user to locate them. The moves of the user were characteristic, as they followed the pattern presented in Fig. 4a, which shows the position of the user's hand perceived by Kinect (and thus the position to which the virtual eyes looked). We can see that the user tends to draw his hand back to a 'resting position', and prefers to skirt around the robot's body than to enter by its side. The problem was cleared with an average time of M = 134.27s, S.D.= 29.04s.

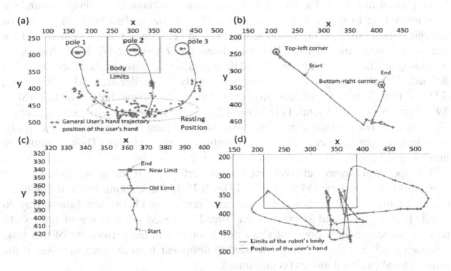

Fig. 4. (a) Position of the user's hand during the Tower of Hanoi evaluation, (b) Position of the user's hand during the initialization phase, (C) Position of the user's hand during the resizing phase, (d) Position of the user's hand during the playing phase

At the end of the first phase, we made the user fill out a first questionnaire asking about his interaction with the robot and his perception of the robot's body, based on a 10-scale anchored by 'Strongly Agree' (1) and 'Strongly Disagree' (10), whose results can be consulted in Table 6.1. As expected, the participants generally tended to have difficulties clearly defining the robot's body limits (M = 2.07, S.D. = 1.22) and corners (M = 1.33, S.D. = .61), and did not seem to have clearly perceived the presence of the robot's body (M = 2.33, S.D. = 1.49), nor to have felt huge differences between the 'inside' and 'outside' of the robot's body (M = 2.53, S.D.= 1.30). Users tended not to be highly involved in the evaluation (M = 5.73, S.D. = 2.31), and not to pay a great amount of attention to the robot (M = 5.47, S.D. = 2.45), which is consistent with the fact that they felt a weak presence from the robot's body.

Finally, when asked to point at the corners of the robot's body as they perceived them, the participants made significant errors (M = 12.65cm, S.D. = 3.14cm for the top-left corner, M = 14.68cm, S.D. = 2.71cm for the front-right one), which seems expected, as they did not define the robot's body, nor did they seem to clearly perceive its boundaries. The other parameters will be commented on along with the results of the second test.

4.2   Robot's Body Definition Phase

In the second phase of the evaluation, the user was asked to define the robot's body (using the initialization phase), without any limitations regarding the size, except the one imposed by the area as seen by the camera, which was approximately all the space present in front of the user that was accessible without him having to stand up. It is interesting to notice here that, even if the sample studied here might not be enough to generalize, a correlation seems to exist between the user's shyness and the size of the body they define. We considered the 7 most and 7 least shy people according to Cheek's test, and compared their results to the size of the robot's body we defined. The shier people tended to define a body of smaller area (M : 4336.9cm^2, S.D. = 1451.5cm^2), while less shy ones tended to define bigger bodies (M = 8901.6cm^2, S.D.= 4130.9cm^2, F(1; 12) = .123; p < .05). These results seem to confirm Hypothesis 4, but with the sample being too small to jump to conclusions, it might be necessary to perform new evaluations with a bigger sample. Those results are presented in Fig. 4b.

The operation seemed relatively intuitive to perform, as it was generally conducted in a short period of time (M = 19.32s, S.D.= 6.75s). The tracking of the user's hand, shown in Fig. 4c, also shows that the user tended to choose the fastest way to conclude this phase, and seems to have already decided the position of the robot's corners, as he generally does not show any hesitation in the performing of this task. Among the 15 participants, only one tried to disappear from the camera to see if the robot reacted (which it did, as programmed).

During the resizing phase, the users took a short time to complete the operation (M = 17.16s, S.D.= 9.65s), and generally chose the simplest way to resize, which is in a straight line orthogonal to the front face of the robot's body, and chose to widen or compress the robot's body as shown in Fig. 4c (Percentage of absolute gain/loss in the depth of the robot's body: M = 47.03%, S.D.= 31.01%).

We noticed that while users that initially defined a small body (area under 5000cm^2) tended to extend it, and those that defined a larger body (area over 8000cm^2) tended to compress it like we could expect (as it would be difficult to compress or extend more than those bodies respectively), the participants who defined a body with an average size (between 5000cm^2 and 8000cm^2) widened it. Once again, further evaluations could be carried out to confirm such a property.

Finally, the playing phase showed the involvement of the participants in the interaction phase, as they interacted for a longer period with the robot during this phase (M = 31.52s, S.D.= 11.58s). In addition, most of the participants tried to enter from different sides of the robot's body, sometimes even from behind. Fig. 4d shows that the users tried numerous interaction possibilities.

4.3   Tower of Hanoi Session After Body Change

Finally, the users were asked to solve the Tower of Hanoi with the help of the robot, but this time with the body they defined themselves. The number of optimal, correct, false and absent moves was also listed, but did not raise relevant conclusions. At the end of the second session, participants were asked to fill out the test sheet once again, this time covering the interaction session with the Tower of Hanoi problem. The results of this second test are presented in Table 1. The most characteristic and interesting improvement concerns the definition part, and its influence on the robot's social presence. The mean notation for the perception of the social presence raised from $M = 2.33$, S.D.= 1.49 before definition to $M = 7.66$, S.D.= 1.67, $t(14) = -10.20$, $p < 0.01$, as well as the one concerning the feeling of a change in behavior depending on the position of his hand (from $M = 2.53$, S.D.= 1.30 to $M = 7.40$, S.D.= 1.24, $t(14)$ $= -11.48$, $p < 0.01$). The users also tended to feel that the robot was more communicative with them ($M = 7.53$, S.D.= 1.41) than before ($M = 6.47$, S.D.= 1.51, $t(14) = -4.67$, $p < 0.01$). Those parameters confirm hypotheses 1 and 3, as the users seem to sense the presence of the robot more clearly after defining its body, and have a higher social awareness of it thanks to the possibility of physical interaction (i.e. by defining and playing with its body).

The users tended to find the robot more sociable after defining its body: $M = 6.73$, S.D.= 1.87 versus $M = 4.40$, S.D.= 2.06 before, $t(14) = -8.64$, $p < 0.01$, and their behavior was more affected by the robot's performance ($M = 6.47$, S.D.= 2.06 before definition, $M = 7.33$, S.D.= 1.45 after, $t(14) = -2.04$, $p < 0.1$). The augmentation of the robot's social presence thanks to the definition of its body seems to have had an impact on the behavior of the participants towards it: indeed, the participants paid greater attention to the robot ($M = 5.47$, S.D.= 2.45 before definition, $M = 7.60$, S.D.= 1.84 after, $t(14) = -9.02$, $p < 0.01$), felt more involved in the evaluation ($M = 7.67$, S.D.= 1.68 versus $M = 5.73$, S.D.= 2.31 before, $t(14) = -5.04$, $p < 0.01$), and less frustrated by the task ($M = 3.67$, S.D.= 1.88 before definition, $M = 2.07$, S.D.= 1.22 after, $t(14) = 4.41$, $p < 0.01$). Therefore, the user's social response to the robot indeed seems to be mediated by his feeling of the robot's social presence, as suggested by Hypothesis 3.

Finally, the users made a more precise estimate of the position of the corners of the robot's body, which seems logical, as they defined them this time. The mean error in cm was reduced by approximately 35% (average error after definition: $M = 7.45$cm, S.D.= 2.74cm for the back-left corner, $M = 9.87$cm, S.D.= 2.84cm for the front-right one, $t(14) = 5.36$, $p < 0.01$ and $t(14) = 4.36$, $p < 0.01$ respectively). However, no real valid results could be extracted from the evaluation of the sensitivity of the robot, as the answers from the users were quite uneven. The evaluation of the reaction delay of the robot was also dropped, even though, surprisingly, the users tended to evaluate the reaction delay better after definition of the robot's body, even though the program did not change between the two evaluations.

The testing of the life-likeness of the robot was put in relation to the will of the user to test the limits of the robot during the Tower of Hanoi phase by cheating, which they did not do often, and always in a really extreme way - for example by moving two tiles at the same time, but never by putting a smaller tile under a bigger one.

Table 1. Mean notation of the characteristics of the robot before and after definition of its body (n=15) (***: p < .01, **: p<.05, *: p<.1)

	Before (S.D.)	After (S. D.)	
	definition of the robot's body		t (paired)
Definition part			
I know where are the limits of the robot	2.07 (1.22)	8.80 (0.86)	-17.00***
I can point at the corners of the robot's body	1.33 (0.61)	8.40 (0.91)	-28.47***
I felt the differences in the behavior of the robot depending of the position of my hand relatively to its body	2.53 (1.30)	7.40 (1.24)	-11.48***
I felt the presence of the robot's body	2.33 (1.49)	7.66 (1.67)	-10.20***
General Evaluation			
The moderator affected my behavior	6.47 (2.06)	7.33(1.45)	-2.04*
The moderator's reaction delay was perceptible	4.13 (2.39)	2.80(1.37)	3.35***
I liked to test the limits of the moderator	4.33(2.41)	5.00(2.39)	-2.87***
Rules were made clear	9.33(0.62)	9.67(0.49)	-1.78*
I felt the robot was communicating with me	6.47(1.51)	7.53(1.41)	-4.67***
I paid a high attention to the robot	5.47 (2.45)	7.60 (1.84)	-9.02***
I felt highly involved in the evaluation	5.73(2.31)	7.67 (1.68)	-5.04***
I was frustrated by the task	3.67 (1.88)	2.07(1.22)	4.41***
I found that the robot was:			
Sociable	4.40(2.06)	6.73(1.87)	-8.64***
Life-like	2.40(1.18)	4.33(2.26)	-4.74***
Sensitive	4.93(2.46)	6.80(2.43)	-4.80***
Error on the guessing of the position of the corners of the robot's body (in cm)			
back-left corner	12.64(3.14)	7.45(2.74)	5.36***
front-right corner	14.68(2.72)	9.87(2.84)	4.36***

5   Conclusion

In this study, we proposed a novel social robot called partially disembodied robot offering a way to interact physically with a partly virtual agent, as parts of its body (eyes and arms) are present physically in the real-world, while the most important part of its body remains in the virtual world, hence offering high space efficiency.

The physical interaction with the partially disembodied robot through touching the body of the robot was made possible through 3D detection powered by a Kinect device and a series of computer vision treatments, and the feedback offered from visual anthropomorphized body parts (notably the eyes following the user during his tasks) and oral communication. The evaluation of the system was carried out in three different parts in order to determine how the definition of the body of the robot by the user had an influence on his perception of the robot. The participants were asked to solve a problem of Tower of Hanoi while being helped by the robot, the latter stating the position of the towers relative to its body and the moves to perform to attain the final position.

The results of the different questionnaires and behavior of the participants during the evaluation proved that the definition of the robot's body had a high impact on its perception by the user, and that physical interaction enhanced the user's social awareness of the robot. The participants tended to react more positively towards the robot after having defined its body, thereby improving its social presence. The last hypothesis concerning the impact of shyness on the size of the body defined seems to have been validated as well, but the sample of participants was too small to formulate a definitive answer.

Acknowledgments. This work was supported by the JST PRESTO program.

References

[1] Wainer, J., Feil-seifer, D., Shell, D., Mataric, M.: The role of physical embodiment in human-robot interaction. In: ROMAN 2006 - The 15th IEEE International Symposium on Robot and Human Interactive Communication, pp. 117–122 (2006)

[2] Lee, K.M., Jung, Y., Kim, J., Kim, S.R.: Are physically embodied social agents better than disembodied social agents?: The effects of physical embodiment, tactile interaction, and people's loneliness in human–robot interaction. International Journal of Human-Computer Studies 64(10), 962–973 (2006)

[3] Bateson, M., Nettle, D., Roberts, G.: Cues of being watched enhance cooperation in a real-world setting. Biology Letters 2(3), 412–414 (2006)

[4] Osawa, H., Yamada, S.: Social modification using implementation of partial agency toward objects. Artificial Life and Robotics 16(1), 78–81 (2011)

[5] Osawa, H., Ohmura, R., Imai, M.: Using Attachable Humanoid Parts for Realizing Imaginary Intention and Body Image. International Journal of Social Robotics 1(1), 109–123 (2008)

[6] Osawa, H., Orszulak, J., Godfrey, K.M., Imai, M., Coughlin, J.F.: Improving voice interaction for older people using an attachable gesture robot. In: 19th International Symposium in Robot and Human Interactive Communication, pp. 179–184 (September 2010)

[7] Wilson, M.: Six views of embodied cognition. Psychonomic Bulletin & Review 9(4), 625–636 (2002)

[8] Osawa, H., Kanbayashi, S., Imai, M., Yamada, S.: Robot in An Empty Space: How to Create Social Presence of The Robot without Real-world Body. In: International Conference on Social Robotics (2011)

[9] Microsoft, Kinect for Xbox 360, http://www.kinectforwindows.org/

[10] Card, S.K., Moran, T.P., Newell, A.: The Psychology of Human-Computer Interaction, p. 469. Lawrence Erlbaum Associates (1986)

[11] Wainer, J., Feil-Seifer, D.J., Shell, D.A., Mataric, M.J.: Embodiment and Human-Robot Interaction: A Task-Based Perspective. In: RO-MAN 2007 - The 16th IEEE International Symposium on Robot and Human Interactive Communication, pp. 872–877 (2007)

[12] Cheek, J.M., Buss, A.H.: Shyness and sociability. Journal of Personality and Social Psychology 41(2), 330–339 (1981)

[13] Osawa, H., Kanai, Y., Yamada, Y., Imai, M.: Agent Morphology: Switching Appropriate Agency using Transforming Robotic Parts. In: International Workshop on Human-Agent InteractionI in IEEE/RSJ International Conference on Intelligent Robots and Systems, IROS (2012)

Keep an Eye on the Task! How Gender Typicality of Tasks Influence Human–Robot Interactions[*]

Dieta Kuchenbrandt[1],[**], Markus Häring[2], Jessica Eichberg[2], and Friederike Eyssel[1]

[1] Center of Excellence in Cognitive Interaction Technology (CITEC), Bielefeld, Germany
{dkuchenb,feyssel}@cit-ec.uni-bielefeld.de
[2] Institute of Computer Science, Human Centered Multimedia, Augsburg University, Germany
{haering@informatik,jessica.eichberg@student}.uni-augsburg.de

Abstract. In the present experiment, we tested the impact of the gender typicality of a human–robot interaction (HRI) task on the user's performance during HRI, and on evaluation and acceptance of the robot. $N = 73$ participants (38 males and 35 females) performed either a stereotypically male or a stereotypically female task while being instructed by either a 'male' or a 'female' robot. Our results revealed that gender typicality of the task substantially influenced our dependent measures: Specifically, more errors occurred when participants collaborated with the robot in context of a typically female work domain. Moreover, participants were less willing to accept help from the robot in a future task when they performed a typically female task. These effects were independent of robot and participant gender. Furthermore, when instructing participants on a female task, the male and the female robot were perceived as equally competent. In contrast, when instructing participants on a male task, the female robot was perceived as more competent compared to the male robot. Our findings will be discussed with regard to theoretical and practical implications.

Keywords: Gender, human-robot interaction, robot evaluation.

1   Introduction

Imagine that we would offer you a robot that could provide assistance for any given task you deemed suitable. How should such a robot ideally look like? Which name should it have? Would you prefer a male or a female robot? Importantly, what kind of work should the robot get done? Most people might now think about a robot that would clean the house or do the dishes, a robot that would provide help on tasks we often find annoying, time-consuming, or that are hard to handle on our own. Indeed, many already existing and newly developed robots are supposed to assist people with tasks such as doing daily household chores (MOVAID, [1]), providing medical services (e.g., measuring blood pressure, Hopis, [2]), collecting and delivering commodities or food (MOVAID, [1]), and serving as a social companion and communication

---

[*] This research was funded by EU (FP7-ICT-257666) under grant agreement eCUTE and the German Research Council (COE 277).
[**] Corresponding author.

S.S. Ge et al. (Eds.): ICSR 2012, LNAI 7621, pp. 448–457, 2012.
© Springer-Verlag Berlin Heidelberg 2012

partner (iCat; [3]). Interestingly, a closer look at these domains of application for robots reveals that they are closely associated with societal gender roles. That is, these tasks can be categorized in terms of 'typically female' versus 'typically male' tasks [e.g., 4, 5]. More specifically, many robot applications seem to be associated with traditionally female work domains (e.g., housework, health care). In the present research, we will address this gender typicality of a human–robot interaction (HRI) task and investigate whether this gender factor influences how users perceive and interact with a robot.

Gender is one of the most salient and omnipresent social categories in human societies that affects virtually every aspect in our every-day live. To a large extent, gender determines people's social roles, occupations, relationships, and opportunities [6]. Importantly, gender can be seen as the primary and most basic category of social perceptions of others and of the self [7]. Consequently, our own gender and the gender of others influence how we think about and interact with each other. Similar to human–human social interactions, gender also could largely impact humans' perceptions of and interactions with *robots*. Research so far has investigated gender effects in HRI mostly from two different angles: The alleged robot gender (as indicated, e.g., by its appearance, behavior, or name) and the user's gender.

In the eyes of users, robots often do not appear gender-neutral, but instead are perceived as male or female prototypes. To illustrate, Eyssel and Hegel [8] have demonstrated that a visual cue, such as a robot's hair length leads to differential ascriptions of masculinity or femininity to a social robot. Similarly, vocal cues also serve to indicate a robot's gender [9]. Importantly, the alleged gender of a robot affects the user's reactions toward the robot. For instance, in the study by Eyssel and Hegel [8], participants ascribed the 'male' robot more stereotypically male traits (e.g., competence) and perceived it as more suitable for stereotypically male tasks than the apparently female robot. In contrast, the 'female' robot was ascribed more stereotypically female traits (e.g., warmth) and was perceived more suitable for typically female tasks. Moreover, Powers and colleagues [10] demonstrated that people use knowledge about gender roles when interacting with a gendered robot. In this study, participants elaborated less on a typically female topic (i.e. dating norms) when talking to an ostensibly female robot than when talking to a 'male' robot.

Despite robot gender, user gender also has an impact on the users' reactions toward robots. However, findings are not consistent. Research by Siegel, Brezeal, and Norton [11], for instance, indicates that users evaluate a robot of the opposite gender more positively than a same-gender robot; they even tend to behave more positively toward robots of the opposite gender. In contrast, Eyssel and colleagues [9] found that participants perceived a *same*-gender robot significantly more positive and psychologically close than the opposite-gender robot. Moreover, the same-gender robot was anthropomorphized (i.e., ascribed uniquely human attributes) to a greater extent compared to the opposite-gender robot. Unlike these results, Schermerhorn, Scheutz, and Crowell [12] found a general tendency for male users to perceive a robot as more human-like compared to female users.

In sum, the results reviewed here demonstrate that robot and user gender seems to elicit complex effects in HRI. However, also the different types of tasks a robot performs might be perceived as being either stereotypically 'male' or stereotypically 'female' [see 8]. Thus, despite robot and user gender, the perception of gender typicality of a task could impact how people will interact with a robot on the specific task. First evidence that features of a task together with user and robot features differentially influence HRI and perceptions of a robot comes from Mutlu and colleagues [13]. In their experiment, males and females played an interactive video game with a robot, and they did so either in a cooperative or in a competitive way. The results showed that men based their evaluation of the robot to a large extent on the different features of the tasks, whereas women were more influenced by the characteristics of the robot. In a different set of studies [14], participants found a robot more suitable for a task when the degree of the robot's humanlikeness matched the degree of sociability required by the task. Thus, task characteristics indeed could influence humans' perceptions of a robot and HRI quality. However, previous studies have not yet considered the gender typicality of different tasks as an important aspect that could influence HRI, although many domains of robot applications are closely associated with societal gender roles.

In the present exploratory experiment, we therefore investigated for the first time the impact of gender typicality of an HRI task on humans' task performance during HRI and on humans' evaluation and acceptance of the robot. Moreover, we also tested the interplay of this gender factor with user and robot gender.

2   Method

2.1   Participants

$N = 73$ German participants (38 males, 35 females) with a mean age of 25.00 years ($SD = 4.29$) took part in our study. They were randomly assigned to one of four experimental conditions that resulted from a 2 (*gender typicality of task*: Male vs. female) x 2 (*robot gender:* Male vs. female) between–subjects factorial design: Accordingly, together with a robot participants had to solve a task that constituted either a typically male or a typically female task. Moreover, participants interacted either with an allegedly male or female robot.

2.2   Procedure

Participants were tested individually in the laboratory at Augsburg University. They were sitting in front of a Microsoft Surface[1] touch-screen table opposite to the robot NAO (Academic Edition V3.2, Aldebaran Robotics). On the touch-screen, different items (either sewing accessories or tools, see Fig. 1) and a container (either a sewing box or a toolbox, see Fig. 1) were depicted[2]. Initially, the experimenter briefly

---

[1] http://www.microsoft.com/surface/

[2] We used the Microsoft Surface instead of a real tool or sewing box because this enabled a stable tracking of the location of the items and logging the participants' input without using the robot's vision system. The robot calculated the positions of the items with the data from the Microsoft Surface. This way, we were able to control details of the HRI set-up, such as the size of the items and compartments as well as the initial item positions.

introduced the participants to the robot and mentioned the robot's alleged name (either the male name NERO or the female name NERA). Participants were then informed that they would work on a sorting task together with the robot and that the robot would instruct them on the task. The robot operated fully autonomously during the experiment. After a short tutorial with two sample trials, participants completed 15 critical trials of the sorting-task. On average, the interaction between participant and robot lasted for approximately 10 minutes. Subsequently, the experimenter asked participants to complete several computerized questionnaires that contained our dependent measures. Finally, participants were reimbursed, debriefed and dismissed.

2.3   Human–Robot Interaction Task

Experimental set-up. On the touch-screen table, participants were presented with a container that consisted of 10 compartments that were of small, medium, and large size. Moreover, participants saw nine items that were already sorted into the different compartments of the container. Fifteen further items were distributed around the container. These unsorted items had to be sorted into different compartments of the container. All but three items could be grouped into nine object categories (e.g. different types of scissors or water levels). Each category was represented by at least two items. Importantly, one item of each category was already stored in the container (see Fig. 1). This was done in order to give participants guidance where the remaining objects could be stored. In addition, three remaining unsorted items did not belong to any of the nine categories. Figures 1a and 1b depict the set-up of the sorting task.

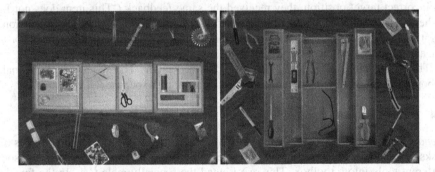

Fig. 1. Pictures of the experimental set-up: On the left side a sewing box with sewing accessories, on the right side a tool box with tools

Instructions. In each of the 15 trials, participants received two instructions from the robot: The first instruction was the *selection instruction* that concerned the choice of the object (e.g., 'Pick the small scissors.'). This instruction included a specific description of the respective item (e.g., name, size, color if applicable). Moreover, following the procedure by Ishiguro and colleagues [15], each selection instruction was accompanied by a pointing gesture and a gaze toward the object. The participant was then supposed to select the respective item by tapping on it with his or her fingers. The robot verbally confirmed a correct choice (e.g., 'This is correct.'). In case of a wrong choice, the robot rejected the choice of the participants and repeated the instruction.

The second instruction in each trial was the *position instruction*. This instruction specified the target position for the respective item (e.g., 'Put it in the upper right small compartment.'). Similar to the selection instructions, the position instructions were accompanied by gaze and pointing behavior. However, to make the interaction more realistic and natural [16], participants not always received correct or optimal instructions by the robot. That is, the robot used three different types of *position instructions*: In six of the 15 trials, the robot gave *optimal position instructions* asking participants to put an item into a compartment that already contained an object of the same category. In six further trials, participants received *suboptimal position instructions*. That is, they were instructed to sort an item into a compartment that did not already contain an item of the same category, although an exemplar of the same object category was depicted in one of the other container's compartments. In three trials, the robot gave *wrong position instructions* and asked participants to put an item into a compartment that was too small to accommodate the chosen item. Thus, participants were obliged to choose an alternative compartment to store the specific item.

When participants followed the robot's optimal and suboptimal position instructions, the robot commented their behavior with a short feedback (e.g., 'This is the correct compartment.'). In case participants did not follow the robot's optimal or suboptimal instructions but chose a *correct* alternative, the robot confirmed that participants made a correct choice by saying 'This is also possible'. When participants chose an *incorrect* target position for the item (i.e., a compartment that was too small for the item), the robot stated 'This item does not fit in here' and repeated the original position instruction. Consequently, the participant had to try again to store the specific item. When participants tried to follow the robot's wrong instructions and thus chose an incorrect target position, they received the same feedback ('This item does not fit in here.'). However, the robot also repeated its original (wrong) position instruction. As it was not possible for participants to follow the robot's wrong instructions, choosing an alternative was necessary.

The trials were realized in a fixed randomized order. The sequence of optimal, suboptimal, and wrong instructions was identical for all experimental conditions.

2.4   Experimental Manipulation

Gender typicality of the task. Participants were confronted with two different types of tasks that have been chosen based on pretests. Participants were either asked to sort different tools into a toolbox. This represented the typically male task. In the female task condition, in contrast, participants were asked to sort sewing equipment into a sewing box. Importantly, besides the expected differences in gender typicality of the tasks, pretests yielded that both tasks were perceived as equally complex and equally demanding.

Gender of the robot. In order to manipulate the alleged gender of the robot, we varied two aspects of the robot: Its name and its voice. Based on pretests, the name NERO was chosen to indicate male gender, and the name NERA was used to indicate female gender of the robot. During the experimenter's instructions at the beginning of the study, the name of the robot has been mentioned repeatedly. Moreover, the 'male' robot spoke with a typically male voice (low frequency), whereas the 'female' robot has been equipped with a more female-type voice (high frequency). The voices have been generated by the robot's Text-To-Speech system (Acapela Mobility 7.0) and were selected based on pretests.

2.5   Dependent Measures

Manipulation check. As a manipulation check, we asked participants to indicate on a 7-point Likert scale whether they perceived the robot as being more female or more male. The endpoints of the scale were 1 = 'more female' vs. 7 = 'more male'. Additionally, to ensure that the two types of tasks were not differentially demanding for the participants depending on gender typicality of the task, participants had to indicate on a 7-point Likert scale how difficult they perceived the task.

Performance during HRI. We used three different behavioral indicators for participants' performance during HRI. First, we measured the duration of each of the 15 trials, resulting in an *average duration per trial* (in seconds). Second, we assessed the number of participants' errors for each of the 15 trials. Picking the wrong object or choosing a compartment that did not fit the size of the object was considered an error. Accordingly, we calculated the *average error rate per trial.* These two indicators represent the measures of objective task performance. That is, the longer the average duration per trial, and the higher the average number of errors per trial, the lower the quality of task performance. Third, we measured the number of alternative compartment solutions participants have chosen, that is, the number of times participants did not follow the robot's position instructions. However, after receiving wrong position instructions from the robot, participants were obliged to choose an alternative compartment. Thus, we only considered the number of alternatives after optimal and suboptimal position instructions. Accordingly, we calculated the *average number of chosen compartment alternatives per trail* after optimal and suboptimal instructions. This measure is used as an indicator of participants trust in the robot's instruction.

Robot evaluation. With two items, participants rated the robot's task-related competence ('The robot knew exactly what I had to do in this task.', 'The robot was well informed about the task.'). The endpoints of the 7-point Likert scales were 1 = 'not at all' and 7 = 'very much'. These two items formed a reliable index of task competence of the robot, $\alpha = .82$.

Robot acceptance. To measure robot acceptance, we asked participants to indicate on a 7-point Likert scale how willing they would be to accept help from the robot on a possible future task. The endpoints of the scale ranged from 1 = 'not at all' to 7 = 'very much'.

3   Results

3.1   Manipulation Check

As a manipulation check, we first tested whether participants recognized the alleged gender of the robot. Results of a *t*-test revealed that in the female robot condition the robot was perceived as more female ($M = 3.00$, $SD = 1.63$), whereas in the male robot condition the robot was correctly identified as male[3] ($M = 6.06$, $SD = 1.06$), $t(70) = 9.38$, $p < .001$, $d = 2.23$.

Moreover, to make sure that participants perceived both sorting tasks as equally demanding, we conducted a t-test comparing the typically female and the typically male task. Results indicate no difference between the typically female task ($M = 1.31$, $SD = 0.53$) and the typically male task ($M = 1.47$, $SD = 0.61$), $t(70) = 1.24$, $p = .22$, $d = 0.28$.

3.2   Performance During HRI

Duration of task completion. Results of a 2 (*gender typicality of task*: Male vs. female) x 2 (*robot gender:* Male vs. female) x 2 (*participant gender*: Male vs. female) analysis of variance (ANOVA) yielded no significant main effects on the duration of task completion, all $ps > .35$. However, we obtained a marginally significant *robot gender* by *participant gender* interaction effect, $F(1, 65) = 2.84$, $p = .10$, $\eta^2 = .04$. Planned t-tests revealed that female participants completed the task equally fast, regardless of whether they interacted with an ostensibly female or male robot ($M = 5.70$ sec., $SD = 1.03$ vs. $M = 5.90$ sec., $SD = 1.55$, respectively), $t(33) = -0.47$, $p = .64$, $d = 0.15$. In contrast, male participants were faster in completing the task when they interacted with the male ($M = 5.13$ sec., $SD = 1.17$) than with the female robot ($M = 5.93$ sec., $SD = 1.32$), $t(36) = 1.99$, $p = .055$, $d = 0.64$.

Errors. The 2 (*gender typicality of task*: Male vs. female) x 2 (*robot gender:* Male vs. female) x 2 (*participant gender*: Male vs. female) ANOVA revealed a significant main effect of *gender typicality of task,* $F(1, 65) = 3.97$, $p = .05$, $\eta^2 = .06$. That is, more errors occurred for the typically female ($M = 0.11$, $SD = 0.08$) than for the typically male task ($M = 0.08$, $SD = 0.05$). No other effects reached statistical significance, all $ps > .46$.

Alternatives. Results of a 2 (*robot gender:* Male vs. female) x 2 (*gender typicality of task*: Male vs. female) x 2 (*participant gender*: Male vs. female) ANOVA yielded a significant main effect of *participant gender*, $F(1, 65) = 13.63$, $p < .001$, $\eta^2 = .17$, indicating that female participants used alternative solutions more often instead of following the robot's instructions ($M = 0.46$, $SD = 0.18$) compared to male participants ($M = 0.30$, $SD = 0.20$). No other significant effects were found, all $ps > .21$.

3.3   Evaluation and Acceptance of the Robot

Robot evaluation. A 2 (*gender typicality of task*: Male vs. female) x 2 (*robot gender:* Male vs. female) x 2 (*participant gender*: Male vs. female) ANOVA revealed neither a significant main effect of experimental manipulation nor of participant gender, all $ps > .50$. However, we obtained a significant *gender typicality of task* by *robot gender*

---

[3] Note that the endpoints of the 7-point Likert scale were 1 = 'more female' vs. 7 = 'more male'. That is, values below 4 indicate that the robot was perceived as more female, whereas values above 4 show that participants perceived the robot as more male.

interaction effect, $F(1, 65) = 4.24$, $p = .04$, $\eta^2 = .06$. Further analyses showed that within the context of a female task, participants perceived the robot as equally competent, independently of whether the robot was ostensibly female ($M = 5.50$, $SD = 1.51$) or male ($M = 6.00$, $SD = 1.51$), $t(35) = 1.00$, $p = .32$, $d = 0.33$. However, when participants were instructed on a typically male task, they perceived the female robot as more competent ($M = 6.33$, $SD = 0.69$) than the male robot ($M = 5.56$, $SD = 1.33$), $t(34) = 2.22$, $p = .03$, $d = 0.73$.

Robot acceptance. Results of a 2 (*gender typicality of task*: Male vs. female) x 2 (*robot gender:* Male vs. female) x 2 (*participant gender:* Male vs. female) ANOVA yielded a main effect of *gender typicality of task,* $F(1, 64) = 5.31$, $p = .02$, $\eta^2 = .08$. Accordingly, participants were more willing to accept help from the robot on a future task when they previously interacted with the robot on a typically male task ($M = 4.89$, $SD = 1.85$) than when they worked on a female task ($M = 3.83$, $SD = 1.84$). No other main or interaction effect was significant, all $ps > .24$.

4   Discussion

Take a second again and imagine you could possess a robot that would assist you on any given task. However, this time, we would specify that you would get a female robot. For what kind of tasks should the robot ideally provide assistance? According to our findings, there is no simple answer to this question.

In the present experiment, female and male participants performed a stereotypically female or stereotypically male task while interacting with an ostensibly female or male robot. Thus, we tested the effects of gender typicality of an HRI task, robot gender and user gender on participants' performance during HRI and on the evaluation and acceptance of the target robot. With our experiment, we extended the previous literature on gender effects with respect to several aspects:

We tested for the first time the effects of such *gender typicality of the task* on HRI. By doing so, we demonstrated that gender typicality of the task the user and the robot completed together had substantial impact on the outcomes of the HRI: Participants made significantly more errors when performing a typically female task than a typically male task although both types of tasks were equally demanding. Moreover, when participants interacted with the robot in the context of a typically female work domain they were less willing to accept help from the robot in future tasks compared to participants who were instructed on a typically male task. Interacting with a robot in the context of a typically female 'work domain' thus resulted in less optimal outcomes than working on a 'male' task. However, the structure and ability requirements of both task types that we have used were equal, suggesting that the social role or stereotype that is attached to the different kinds of tasks has influenced how successful participants dealt with the task and the robot. Interestingly, many robots are developed to provide assistance on every-day tasks that are generally perceived as being typically female (e.g., providing assistance in the household). Accordingly, because our results indicate a more general problem with human–robot collaborations in 'female' domains, future studies need to address possible measures to counteract these difficulties and to make HRI on female-type tasks more efficient. However, prospective research should focus on further dependent measures to get a more differentiated picture of the effects of a task's gender typicality on HRI.

Furthermore, participants rated the robot's task competence differently, depending on the task's gender typicality and on the robot's alleged gender. That is, within the context of a stereotypically female task, the 'male' and the 'female' robot were perceived as equally competent. In contrast, for the typically male task the ostensibly female (vs. male) robot was evaluated as being more competent. This in part contradicts previous findings: Research has shown that a match between robot and task features, for instance in terms of humanlikeness, leads to greater human–robot acceptance [14]. Similarly, Eyssel and Hegel [8] have demonstrated that people prefer tasks for robots that match the gender of the robot. The present study, in contrast, yields evidence that partially speaks against a proper match of robot and task characteristics. To illustrate, when the robot gender and the gender typicality of the task were compatible, participants perceived the robot as *less* competent for the respective task, at least in context of a stereotypically male work domain. Comparing the present with previous findings shows that we should distinguish between factors that precede HRI and determine people's willingness to interact with a robot on the one hand, and factors that are key aspects of actual HRI and determine the success of an HRI, on the other hand. More specifically, a match between task and robot characteristics before an actual HRI takes place could be advantageous [8, 14]. According to our findings, *during* an actual HRI a mismatch seems to be beneficial as this indicates a higher competence of the robot. Future research needs to clarify under which circumstances and for which aspects such match or mismatch between task and robot characteristics is advantageous.

Above and beyond, our results add to previous findings that have shown that users react differently toward robots depending on their own gender [9, 17]. In the present study, female participants more frequently worked autonomously on the task and made their own choices instead of following the instructions of the robot (whereas the error rate remained unaffected by this) compared to male participants. This result possibly suggests that women might have less trust in robots then men. Additionally, male participants seemed to be more efficient (i.e., faster) when collaborating with a same-gender robot, whereas for women the robot's gender did not influence their velocity in performing the task. Interestingly, this is in line with previous research [11], indicating that men are more reactive to a robot's gender cues than women.

Taken together, our findings clearly point out that besides taking into account mental models users have about gendered robots [see 8, 17], we need to consider social roles and attributes that are related to traditionally male and female work domains when developing and designing robot systems. Many robot applications are related to societal gender roles. The present findings demonstrate for the first time that such 'gendered tasks' substantially influence how users perform during an HRI and how they perceive a robot's competence, specifically in the context of a female work domain. Thus, prospective research should focus on factors that could improve HRI for those applications that traditionally have been occupied by women.

References

1. Dario, P., Guglielmelli, E., Laschi, C., Teti, G.: MOVAID: a personal robot in everyday life of disabled and elderly people. Technol. Disabil. 10, 77–93 (1999)
2. Krikke, J.: Japan's robot developers go Linux. LinuxInsider (2003), retrieved http://www.linuxinsider.com/story/32281.html (visited May 5, 2012)
3. Heerink, M., Krose, B., Evers, V., Wielinga, B.: The influence of a robot's social abilities on acceptance by elderly users. In: Proceedings of the 15th IEEE International Symposium on Robot and Human Interactive Communication, pp. 521–526 (2006)
4. Berk, R.A., Berk, S.F.: Labor and leisure at home: Content and organization of houshold day. Sage, San Francisco (1979)
5. Thompson, L., Walker, A.J.: Gender in families: Women and men in marriage, work, and parenthood. J. of Marriage and Fam. 51, 845–871 (1989)
6. Bussey, K., Bandura, A.: Social cognitive theory of gender development and differentiation. Psych. Rev. 106, 676–713 (1999)
7. Harper, M., Schoeman, W.J.: Influences of gender as a basic-level category in person perception on the gender belief system. Sex Roles 49, 517–526 (2003)
8. Eyssel, F., Hegel, F.: (S)he's got the look: Gender stereotyping of social robots. J. of Appl. Soc. Psych. (in press)
9. Eyssel, F., Kuchenbrandt, D., Bobinger, S., de Ruiter, L., Hegel, F.: 'If you sound like me, you must be more human': On the interplay of robot and user features on human-robot acceptance and anthropomorphism. In: Proceedings of the 7th ACM/IEEE Conference on Human-Robot Interaction, pp. 125–126 (2012)
10. Powers, A., Kramer, A.D.I., Lim, S., Kuo, J., Lee, S.-L., Kiesler, S.: Eliciting information from people with a gendered humanoid robot. In: Proceedings of the 14th IEEE International Symposium on Robot and Human Interactive Communication, pp. 158–163 (2005)
11. Siegel, M., Breazeal, C., Norton, M.I.: Persuasive robotics: The influence of robot gender on human behavior. In: Proceedings of the IEEE/RSJ International Conference on Intelligent Robots and Systems, pp. 2563–2568 (2009)
12. Schermerhorn, P., Scheutz, M., Crowell, C.: Robot social presence and gender: Do females view robots differently than males? In: The Proceedings of the 3rd ACM/IEEE Conference on Human-Robot Interaction, pp. 263–270 (2008)
13. Mutlu, B., Osman, S., Forlizzi, J., Hodgins, J., Kiesler, S.: Perceptions of Asimo: Task structure and user attributes as elements of human-robot interaction design. Extended Abstracts of the 15th IEEE Symposium on Robot and Human Interactive, pp. 351–352 (2006)
14. Goetz, J., Kiesler, S., Powers, A.: Matching robot appearance and behavior to tasks to improve human-robot cooperation. In: Proceedings of the 12th IEEE International Symposium on Robot and Human Interactive Communication, pp. 55–60 (2003)
15. Ishiguro, H., Ono, T., Imai, M., Maeda, T., Nakatsu, R., Kanda, T.: Robovie: An interactive humanoid robot. Int. J. of Indust. Robots, 498–503 (2001)
16. Salem, M., Eyssel, F., Rohlfing, K., Kopp, S., Joublin, F.: Effects of Gesture on the Perception of Psychological Anthropomorphism: A Case Study with a Humanoid Robot. In: Mutlu, B., Bartneck, C., Ham, J., Evers, V., Kanda, T. (eds.) ICSR 2011. LNCS, vol. 7072, pp. 31–41. Springer, Heidelberg (2011)
17. Crowell, C.R., Scheutz, M., Schermerhorn, P., Villano, M.: Gendered voice and robot entities: perceptions and reactions of male and female subjects. In: Proceedings of the IEEE/RSJ International Conference on Intelligent Robots and Systems, pp. 3735–3741 (2009)

A Multi-modal Approach
for Natural Human-Robot Interaction

Thomas Kollar, Anu Vedantham, Corey Sobel,
Cory Chang, Vittorio Perera, and Manuela Veloso

Carnegie Mellon University
5000 Forbes Ave.
Pittsburgh, PA 15213

Abstract. We present a robot that is able to interact with people in a
natural, multi-modal way by using both speech and gesture. The robot
is able to track people, process speech and understand language. To
track people and recognize gestures, the robot uses an RGB-D sensor
(e.g., a Microsoft Kinect). To recognize speech, the robot uses a cloud-
based service. To understand language, the robot uses a probabilistic
graphical model to infer the meaning of a natural language query. We
have evaluated our system in two domains. The first domain is a robot
receptionist (roboceptionist); we show that the roboceptionist is able to
interact successfully with people 77% of the time when people are primed
with the capabilities of the robot compared to 57% when people are not
primed with its capabilities. The second domain is a mobile service robot,
which is able to interact with people via natural language.

1 Introduction

Our aim is to make robots that can interact with people in a natural and intuitive
way and can intelligently understand and respond to the intentions of humans.
In this paper, we develop an approach for human-robot interaction that uses
speech and gesture to create a rich space of verbal and non-verbal meaning.
Our aim is to craft a set of gestures that are intuitive for a human while at the
same time understandable by a robot, and which can be combined with speech
input to improve the experience of people interacting with social robots. This
is a challenging problem because understanding the intentions of a human may
require reasoning over the combination of a large space of gestures and natural
language queries.

In this paper we address this challenge by developing a robot that is able to
combine multi-modal input to understand gestures and task-constrained speech.
Specifically, the robot is able to recognize a hand-raising gesture, detect when
people are approaching and determine when the nearest person is facing the
robot. If the person is not close enough for the interaction to be successful, it
will guide the person to move to more successful states. By guiding the people
to these states, the robot is able to better understand task-constrained natural
language queries that involve the robot's status as well as the location of people
in a building. This is achieved by learning a probabilistic graphical model that
connects the natural language to the type of question being asked.

S.S. Ge et al. (Eds.): ICSR 2012, LNAI 7621, pp. 458–467, 2012.

We evaluate our approach in two domains. The first domain is a roboceptionist that has been placed in the entryway of a building. The second domain is a mobile service robot that can perform tasks such as delivering objects and escorting people in indoor environments [1]. In the roboceptionist domain, ten different people interacted with the robotic system and asked it questions; we evaluated the results in two conditions. In the first condition, people were not primed about the capabilities of the robot and could interact with it in any way that felt natural to them. In the second condition, people were primed by telling them what the robot could do. In all conditions, we found that the roboceptionist was able recognize the desired gestures and track people effectively nearly all of the time. In addition, we found that the roboceptionist was able to understand greetings, questions about it's capabilities and questions about the location of people's offices 77% of the time when people were primed about the robot's capabilities. Interactions with un-primed people were only successful 57% of the time, indicating that priming (or long-term interaction) is an important consideration for robotic systems. We also evaluated the performance of the mobile service robot at understanding commands and found that it had successful interactions with people 73% of the time.

2   Related Work

Others have designed robots for long-term social human-robot interaction. Gockley et al. [2] designed a robot receptionist named Valerie to investigate human-robot social interaction and found that after nine months of deployment, people still interacted with the robot on a daily basis. This robot now interacts with people in multiple languages [3] and is aware of the presence of a person, but is not able to recognize gestures. Salichs et al. [4] developed a robot to cover a wide spectrum of human-robot social interaction and was able to engage in both physical and speech driven events.

Work in human-robot interaction will often use gestures. Bohus and Horvitz [5] developed a system capable of differentiating speakers in a turn-based speaking environment. The system was able to determine who was speaking to whom by evaluating hand gestures and other cues. Wu and Huang [6] describe static gesture recognition of hand pose as well as and temporal gesture modeling. Eisenstein [7] shows how the use of both hand gesture and speech can be used to resolve ambiguous noun phrases, the segmentation of speech into topics and the production of keyframe summaries of spoken language. Christoudias et al. [8] investigates whether reliable audio-visual classifiers can be learned through co-training. Scassellati [9] describes a model of joint attention in the context of recognizing social cues, showing the role of imitation and gesture in terms of head movements. The interface for the roboceptionist takes inspiration from other social robots, such as Kismet [10] and interaction paradigms are related to Mutlu et al. [11], who describe how a robot can establish roles by using gaze cues.

3   Approach

In this paper, we present a robot that interacts with people in a natural way by understanding multi-modal input. The approach uses speech, gesture, and an animated character to communicate with people and understand their intentions.

3.1   Gesture and Event Recognition

Gestures are a natural interface for people that want to interact with robots. To recognize gestures and track people, the robot uses an RGB-D camera. The information extracted from the camera is used to interact with people and determine when to ignore them if they are uninterested in the robot.

Interactions via Gesture. Since many people walk by the robot, it needs a way to differentiate people showing interest from those that are uninterested in it. To address this challenge, we developed an approach to recognize a hand-raise gesture to indicate the start of an interaction. When the person's hand is up and the person is far away, the robot will ask people to come closer. When the person's hand is up and the person is nearby, then the robot will initiate an interaction.

The robot uses the skeleton provided by the RGB-D camera[1], as in Figure 1. The position of the hip $\hat{h}$, head $\hat{d}$ and the hand $\hat{n}$ are used to determine whether the hand is raised. If we define the hip/head vector to be $\hat{v}_{h \to d} = \hat{d} - \hat{h}$ and the hip/hand vector to be $\hat{v}_{h \to n} = \hat{n} - \hat{h}$, then the projection of the hip/hand vector onto the hip/head vector is:

$$p = \frac{\hat{v}_{h \to n} \cdot \hat{v}_{h \to d}}{|\hat{v}_{h \to d}|} \frac{\hat{v}_{h \to d}}{|\hat{v}_{h \to d}|} \tag{1}$$

If the norm of p is greater than the norm of $\hat{v}_{h \to d}$, then the length of the projected vector is longer than the hip/head vector and the robot will detect the person as raising their hand. Figure 1 shows these vectors. Because this approach uses the relationship between the hip/hand vector and the hip/head vector, it is able to recognize when a hand is raised even when the orientation of the body or the RGB-D sensor not vertical.

Interactions via Proximity. Another good indicator that a person would like to speak with the robot is whether they are approaching the robot or not. If a person is coming toward the robot or is very near to the robot, then the interaction is started. In qualitative experiments, we found that most of the people uninterested in the robot walk away from it. To know if someone is walking towards the robot, the four closest people are detected and if the change in the position of any person indicates that they are moving toward the robot, then the robot will start interacting with them.

Concretely, we use two conditions to guarantee that a person is approaching the robot. The first condition is that the person is moving along a line with

---

[1] The Microsoft Kinect API was used.

Fig. 1. An illustration of the vectors used to compute when a hand is raised

a constant angle with respect to the robot. If $\theta = \arctan 2(x, z)$ (where the x and z coordinates correspond to the ground plane) is approximately the same between two different timesteps, then a person is moving toward the robot. The second criteria is that the person is moving closer to the robot. This can easily be verified by checking that $dist(x_2, z_2) < dist(x_1, z_1)$.

Interactions via Orientation. Examining if a person is facing the robot also acts as a valid indicator of a desire to speak with the robot. In order to determine if a person is facing the robot, we create two vectors, one from the robot to the center of the person's chest, and another from one shoulder to the other. We know that the person is facing the robot if the dot product of these two vectors is approximately zero, since this would indicate that the two vectors are orthogonal.

If $\hat{l}$ is the position of the left shoulder, $\hat{r}$ is the position of the right shoulder, $\hat{k}$ is the position of the robot, and $\hat{c}$ is the position of the chest of the person, then we can compute the shoulder vector as $\hat{s} = \hat{r} - \hat{l}$ and the vector from the robot to the person as $\hat{r} = \hat{c} - \hat{k}$. If the dot product is almost 0 ($\hat{r} \cdot \hat{s} < delta$), then the person is facing the robot.

Interactions when Multiple People are Present. Using the above components, we can synthesize an algorithm that decides who to speak with and when to speak with them. First, the robot finds the four closest people, chooses people who are facing the robot and responds to the closest person with their hand raised. If a person is raising his or her hand, but is not close enough to speak with the robot, it will ask the person to move closer. Otherwise, the robot will begin processing speech.

3.2   Dialog

The robot is able to have social dialog as well as provide navigational assistance in the Gates-Hillman Center. The dialog with people is centered around inferring a question type from the natural language query, and responding with an appropriate answer. We use the speech recognition provided by an Android tablet (the primary interface to the robot), which does not use a fixed grammar. Queries that the robot is able to understand include:

1. Basic Greetings (e.g., "Hello, how are you?")
2. Queries about itself (e.g., "What can you do?", "What is your name?")
3. Location of people in the CS department (e.g., "Where is Joydeep Biswas' office?")
4. Location of landmarks (e.g., "Where is the cafe?", "Any nearby cluster?", "How about the nearest bathroom?")

To understand natural language questions, we take the top 10 results from the speech recognizer and infer the most likely interpretation using a probabilistic graphical model. If q is a multinomial distribution over the question type and s is the input sentence, then the goal is to compute:

$$\arg \max_{q} p(q|s) \tag{2}$$

By breaking down a sentence into words w_i and using Bayes rule, we can rewrite this probability distribution as:

$$p(q|w_1, \ldots w_n) = \frac{\left[\prod_{i=1}^{n} p(w_i|q)\right] p(q)}{p(w_1, \ldots, w_n)} \tag{3}$$

The words are assumed to be independent of each other since our goal is to retrieve the overall meaning for a sentence. Thus, we can compute the above terms as:

(1) Computing $p(w_j|q)$
    If w_j is a word and c_j is the count of word j for the category q which has $|w|$ total word occurrences, then this term is computed as:

$$p(w_j|q) = \frac{c_j + 1}{\left[\sum_j c_j\right] + |w|} \tag{4}$$

(2) Computing $p(q)$
    If c_q is the number of times question i was asked and $|q|$ is the number of question types, then this term is computed as:

$$p(q) = \frac{c_q + 1}{\left[\sum_i c_i\right] + |q|} \tag{5}$$

In order to handle cases where there exists a word in the input that was not present in the training corpus, we have employed additive (Laplace) smoothing and add one occurrence of all words and questions. The resulting model is a Naive Bayes Classifier with additive smoothing [12]. To train the model, we collected query/category pairs by asking people what questions they would ask

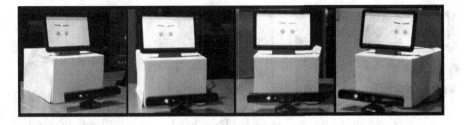

Fig. 2. The interface has eyes that follow the closest tracked person

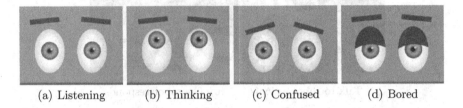

(a) Listening   (b) Thinking   (c) Confused   (d) Bored

Fig. 3. Different expressions modeled for the roboceptionist

the receptionist. We formulated seven different situations (e.g., greeting, status, capabilities, directions) and asked 26 people to write down how they would interact with the robot via natural language, resulting in 182 training sentences. These sentences were as short at one word (e.g., "hello") or as long as 14 words. Each sentence was annotated with a corresponding query type.

When a query type is a greeting, a question about the robot's capabilities or status, or goodbye, the robot responds to the person using a set of fixed responses. When the query type is about the location of a person, the robot will look up the location of this person by accessing a database of people in the School of Computer Science, including name, email and office number. The language understanding system matches names from the natural language query to this database by string matching. If any of the names exactly match a full name in the database, then the robot responds with the office location (e.g., "Joydeep Biswas is in room 7707."). If not, the system tries to match all the last names to the query. If there are no matches to the last name, then it will try to match first names. The speech recognition typically finds the requested person in one of the top two results. When there are multiple people that a name could refer to, the robot informs the person of the top candidate office locations.

3.3 Robot Interface

As a part of the roboceptionist, we have created an approachable interface that displays some realistic characteristics and an easily recognizable appearance. Specifically, the interface consists of two eyes that are able to track the closest human to the robot. Figure 2 shows the eyes tracking a person moving from left to right. The eyes take on a cartoonish appearance to emphasize approachability,

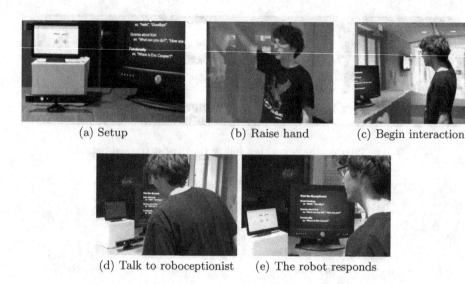

(a) Setup   (b) Raise hand   (c) Begin interaction

(d) Talk to roboceptionist   (e) The robot responds

Fig. 4. A typical interaction. (a) contains the basic setup of the roboceptionist, including a Microsoft Kinect and an Android tablet. (b) shows an example interaction where the person raises their hand to catch the attention of roboceptionist. If user is too far away, the roboceptionist will ask the person to come closer. In (c), when user is close enough, he/she can raise their hand to begin talking to roboceptionist. In (d) the person talks to roboceptionist. In (e), the roboceptionist responds. . We would like to thank Lydia Utkin and Feiyang Feng for their help designing the user interface.

recognizing that face-to-face contact between the robot and humans is a key factor in creating natural human-robot interaction. Some example expressions, which depend on the state of the robot, can be seen in Figure 3.

3.4   System Overview

The overall interaction with the roboceptionist can be seen in Figure 4. In Figure 4(a), the roboceptionist finds and tracks the person. The eyes will follow the person as they move to the right and left of the robot. In Figure 4(c), the robot responds to a person if he or she is facing the robot and raising his or her hand to demonstrate a desire to initiate a conversation. In Figure 4(d), the roboceptionist will listen for input from a person, compare the speech to the current set of questions and then respond accordingly. Free-form speech recognition is performed using a cloud-based service on the Android tablet. The user indicates a desire to leave by saying some phrase equivalent to "good bye." The interaction with a mobile service robot proceeds in the same way but does not use gestures as a part of the interaction.

4   Illustrative Results

We have performed an analysis of both the roboceptionist and the mobile service robot. Specifically, the roboceptionist's performance at recognizing gestures and understanding language was evaluated when a single person was present. To test the recognition of gestures on the roboceptionist, we recorded 76 interactions from 10 different individuals. These people varied in height, ranging from 5 feet to 6 feet tall. We observed these interactions in two separate modes. In the first mode, people initiated interactions with the roboceptionist in whatever way was natural for them. In this mode, the roboceptionist would fail to recognize gestures only when it failed to detect the person. The system failed to detect a person 12.5% of the time, primarily when a person was closer than 1 meter to the RGB-D sensor. When testing the RGB-D sensor with people approaching the robot between 4 to 6 feet away, it failed to detect a person only when they were partially out of view of the of the camera (this happened very infrequently). The primary failure mode was to miss a hand-raising gesture. Another failure mode happened when a person raised their hand, but would speak before the roboceptionist started listening. Since people would repeat their earlier request, this failure mode would generally resolve itself.

Second, we evaluated the roboceptionist by having 10 people interact with it. For example, the interaction in Figure 4 consists of the following turns:

- *User approaches the roboceptionist and raises hand.*
- Roboceptionist: You must come closer.
- *User walks closer to the roboceptionist and raises hand again.*
- Roboceptionist: Hello, speak to the Kinect.
- User: Hello.
- Roboceptionist: Hi, How are you today?
- User: Fine.
- Roboceptionist: That's good. Ask a question.
- User: Where is Stephanie Rosenthal?
- Roboceptionist: Stephanie Rosenthal has an office in room 7505.
- User: How about Joydeep Biswas?
- Roboceptionist: Not too sure what you said, please repeat.
- User: Joydeep Biswas.
- Roboceptionist: Joydeep Biswas has an office in room 7707.
- User: Goodbye
- Roboceptionist: Bye Bye
- *User walks away.*

The interactions were evaluated in two different modes. In one, people were primed by telling them they could use one of 10 question types (e.g., directions to a person's office). In a second mode people were able to interact as they wanted. In both of these modes we set no restrictions on how the queries were phrased to determine how robustly the robot understood its meaning. We performed trials with 10 different people for a total of 76 queries (e.g., "hello" in the above conversation); 54 of the queries occurred in the non-primed mode and 22 occurred in the primed mode. A successful query was one where the robot inferred the correct meaning or correctly inferred that it wasn't able to answer the query.

Table 1. Performance of the roboceptionist as measured by the percentage of interactions that were successful from start to end

	w/o priming	with priming
Performance	56.86%	77.27%

We found that priming significantly helped the performance of the roboceptionist, as can be seen in Table 1. When it did fail, the speech recognition generally did not interpret the user's request correctly or the user's request was not yet supported.

In order to further evaluate our work we also deployed the interface on CoBot [1], an indoor service robot. The model from Section 3.2 was trained on a corpus collected during interactions with ten faculty and staff members in our building. During those meetings, a person queried the robot and a researcher responded with answers to their queries. Each entry in the log was labeled with one of ten different labels: *hello, greeting, what can you do, task information, task physical, person information, yes, no, thanks* or *goodbye*.

The performance of the model was evaluated using three held-out logs consisting of 37 queries. We found that 72.97% of the test queries were categorized correctly. Table 2 shows the mistakes that the system makes during evaluation.

Table 2. A subset of the test queries for the service robot. The rows correspond to different ground-truth categories and the columns are the predicted categories. For example, one query that should have been "thanks" was mis-classified as "capabilities." *Capabilities* queries are questions about the robot's capabilities, *yes/no* are responses to a yes/no question, *person* are queries for a person in the building and *thanks* usually involves thanking the robot for doing something.

	capabilities	no	person	thanks	yes	task
capabilities	4	0	0	0	0	0
no	0	3	1	0	1	0
person	0	0	3	0	0	0
thanks	1	0	0	3	0	0
yes	0	0	0	0	5	0
task	1	0	0	0	0	5

5   Conclusions and Future Work

In this paper, we have presented a multi-modal approach to human-robot interaction. We have demonstrated our approach on a robot receptionist and a mobile service robot. The roboceptionist is able to recognize and respond to certain gestures and natural language questions in a flexible and intuitive way. Using an RGB-D sensor, the robot is able to detect when a hand is raised to initiate a conversation, detect when a person is moving toward the robot and detect when a person is facing the robot. Our approach uses a probabilistic graphical model to connect language to an underlying meaning. We have shown that the roboceptionist interacts appropriately with people 77% of the time and that the service robot performs interacts appropriately 73% of the time.

In future work, we anticipate performing a deeper semantic analysis of a natural language query to understand multi-modal input involving speech and gesture and jointly handling uncertainty in the speech recognition, the parser, and the gesture recognition. We also anticipate multi-robot coordination to enable our mobile service robot to work in unison with the robot receptionist.

Acknowledgments. We would like to thank Lydia Utkin and Feiyang Feng for their help designing the user interface. This work was partly supported by the Center for Computational Thinking at Carnegie Mellon University, which is sponsored by Microsoft. The views and conclusions contained in this document are those of the authors and should not be interpreted as representing the official policies, either expressed or implied, of any sponsoring institution, the U.S. government or any other entity.

References

1. Rosenthal, S., Biswas, J., Veloso, M.: An effective personal mobile robot agent through symbiotic human-robot interaction. In: International Conference on Autonomous Agents and Multiagent Systems, pp. 915–922 (2010)
2. Gockley, R., Bruce, A., Forlizzi, J., Michalowski, M., Mundell, A., Rosenthal, S., Sellner, B., Simmons, R., Snipes, K., Schultz, A., Wang, J.: Designing robots for long-term social interaction. In: IEEE/RSJ International Conference on Intelligent Robots and Systems (IROS), pp. 1338–1343. IEEE (2005)
3. Makatchev, M., Fanaswala, I., Abdulsalam, A., Browning, B., Ghazzawi, W., Sakr, M., Simmons, R.: Dialogue patterns of an arabic robot receptionist. In: Proceedings of Human-Robot Interaction, pp. 167–168 (2010)
4. Salichs, M., Barber, R., Khamis, A., Malfaz, M., Gorostiza, J., Pacheco, R., Rivas, R., Corrales, A., Delgado, E., Garcia, D.: Maggie: A robotic platform for human-robot social interaction. In: IEEE Conference on Robotics, Automation and Mechatronics, pp. 1–7 (June 2006)
5. Bohus, D., Horvitz, E.: Facilitating multiparty dialog with gaze, gesture, and speech. In: International Conference on Multimodal Interfaces, pp. 5:1–5:8 (2010)
6. Wu, Y., Huang, T.S.: Vision-Based Gesture Recognition: A Review. In: Braffort, A., Gibet, S., Teil, D., Gherbi, R., Richardson, J. (eds.) GW 1999. LNCS (LNAI), vol. 1739, pp. 103–115. Springer, Heidelberg (2000)
7. Eisenstein, J.: Gesture in automatic discourse processing. Ph.D. dissertation (2008)
8. Christoudias, C.M., Saenko, K., Morency, L.-P., Darrell, T.: Co-adaptation of audio-visual speech and gesture classifiers. In: International Conference on Multimodal Interfaces, pp. 84–91 (2006)
9. Scassellati, B.: Imitation and mechanisms of joint attention: a developmental structure for building social skills on a humanoid robot, pp. 176–195 (1999)
10. Breazeal, C.L.: Sociable machines: expressive social exchange between humans and robots. Ph.D. dissertation (2000)
11. Mutlu, B., Shiwa, T., Kanda, T., Ishiguro, H., Hagita, N.: Footing in human-robot conversations: how robots might shape participant roles using gaze cues. In: International Conference on Human-Robot Interaction, pp. 61–68 (2009)
12. Lewis, D.D.: Naive (bayes) at Forty: The Independence Assumption in Information Retrieval. In: Nédellec, C., Rouveirol, C. (eds.) ECML 1998. LNCS, vol. 1398, pp. 4–15. Springer, Heidelberg (1998)

Investigation of Optimal Deployment Problem in Three-Dimensional Space Coverage for Swarm Robotic System

Hongliang Ren[1] and Zion T.H. Tse[2]

[1] Department of Bioengineering,
National University of Singapore,
Singapore, 117576
ren@nus.edu.sg
[2] College of Engineering,
University of Georgia,
Athens, GA, USA, 30602
ziontse@uga.edu

Abstract. Multi-robot systems such as swarm robotics have demonstrated collective and social behaviors in terms of environment sensing, coverage planning, decision making, and task execution. This article addresses one of the key challenges in 3D space coverage planning by multi-robots in large working spaces while avoiding critical non-trespassing zones. We investigated a mathematical approach for the optimal robot deployment problem, aiming to cover arbitrary 3D space using a minimal number of robots, provided a global map of the work-space. The proposed method is valuable in terms of optimal resource allocation while further incorporating with the emerging power of cloud computing and is a step towards optimal coordination of multiple robots for various applications.

Keywords: Swarm, Robotics, Navigation, Deployment, Optimization, Coverage.

1   Introduction

The last couple of years have seen significant applications of swarm robotic networks in various areas such as in logistics, military, and industry [1, 2, 3, 4, 5, 6]. During the meantime, distributed computing and cloud computing [7, 8, 9] are emerging as powerful and intelligent computational techniques for solving the challenging problems of sensing, planning and task execution. This article investigates a new optimal solution for complete coverage using a minimal number of robots in arbitrary 3D terrain, while avoiding some critical non-trespassing zones or objects. The primary contribution of this article is the novel optimal robot deployment approach based on mathematical programming, particularly for 3D terrain workspaces, which is contrary to the majority of work on 2D deployment.

S.S. Ge et al. (Eds.): ICSR 2012, LNAI 7621, pp. 468–474, 2012.

2   Related Work

2.1   Swarm Robotics and Related Research Topics

Swarm robotics is a multi-robot system emerging with the technological advances in networking, communication, computing and robotics. Robotic swarms are cooperating and coordinating to accomplish tasks that are beyond the capability of an individual robot, particularly in cases of large-scale multiple concurrent tasks.

As reviewed in [5], swarm robotics has been inspired by various research fields and applications that require covering a region, self-assembly of materials, or tasks that require redundancy. It is envisioned that some obvious and typical application scenarios will include large-scale ocean environment monitoring using swarm underwater robotics and mountain terrain monitoring using field swarm robotics.

In terms of test-beds, there are existing experimental research platforms such as the human-robot interface design for large swarms of autonomous mobile robots using iRobot at MIT [10, 11, 12], and the Swarm-bots which provide self-assembling and self-reconfiguring capabilities to form flexible structures [10, 13, 14, 15].

The social and collective behaviors of swarm robotics makes large-scale concurrent task execution more effective and efficient, while distributed and decentralized behaviors pose challenges in coordination and planning for resource allocation. It shares common challenges with wireless sensor and actuator networks [16, 17, 18], such as resource allocation, optimal deployment for best coverage, power consumption, security, communication and computing issues.

Swarm robotics has involved diverse research topics in engineering [19] ranging from bio-inspired quorum sensing, swarm based optimization, spatial organizing behaviors, swarm navigation, collective decision making, and microscopic analysis to macroscopic analysis. This article focuses on robot deployment optimization to get best coverage in terms of macroscopic analysis.

2.2   Related Work on Optimal Deployment

The optimal deployment problem has been investigated for various application scenarios such as an unexhausted list presented in literature [20][21][17][22][23] [24]. Multiple hovering robots have been employed for environment monitoring with downward facing cameras, using a derived cost function that lead to a gradient-based distributed controller for positioning the robots [19]. For the purpose of simultaneously covering an environment and tracking intruders in [21]; the problem is translated to cover environments with time-varying density functions under the locational optimization framework. Another approach based on the Voronoi cell and a probabilistic cost function was presented in [17] for the deployment of a mobile sensor network in a bounded domain. In [22] an obstacle-resistant robot deployment approach involving node placement policy, a serpentine movement policy, obstacle-handling rules, and boundary rules was presented. Optimal control theory based deployment strategy was also employed in [23], which investigated the commonalities between deployment problems with the linear quadratic regulator.

The existing research paves the way for analyzing the optimal deployment problem from various angles. One of the challenges in developing swarm robotics is to ensure reliability and coverage, while avoiding the abuse of limited resources. However, the deployment over arbitrary 3D was not fully addressed. This article aims to bridge this gap by studying the problem of 3D arbitrary terrain coverage.

3   Methods

3.1   Nomenclature

Table 1. Symbols and notations in this article

Symbol	Quantity
R	Coverage radius of individual robot
c	Covered spherical cell with radius R by individual robot
T	3D Terrain to be covered
E	Set of robot starting locations
y_a	Binary variable indicating robot deployed at point a
N	Non-trespassing zone
A	Set of allowed deployment points

3.2   Formulation

It is a non-trivial problem for swarm robotics to maximize coverage by optimal robot deployment, especially for 3D space coverage. The objective of optimal robotic node deployment for swarm robotics is to obtain complete monitoring coverage over an arbitrary 3D terrain, in terms of either sensing or communication, while minimizing the number of robots and avoiding non-trespassing zones. As for the deployment optimization module, it is assumed that the global spatial map is given and that the module can be acquired by distributed localization and mapping procedures or from prior data. Each robot is covering a spherical space centered at the robot itself, and the proposed approach can be extended to other coverage models in further work. The supposed cloud computing facility will be available for the swarm robotic system.

An integer mathematical programming is given by,

$$\min \sum_{\{a \in A\}} w_a \, y_a$$

$$\text{subject to} \sum_{\{a:\|a-c\|<R\}} y_a \geq 1, \forall c \in T$$

$$y_a \in \{0,1\} \forall a \in A \tag{1}$$

where T is the set of 3D terrain to be covered and the weights w_a are 1 for all deployment to be weighted equally. Alternatively, a deployment is given more weight if it covers a larger space of the target terrain rather than non-target terrain. This optimization subroutine states that a minimum number of deployments should be chosen, given that all targeting terrain is covered.

Note that complete coverage is required for the terrain without gap. Therefore, neighboring robots should have partially overlapping coverage regions to ensure complete coverage. The formulated integer-programming problem is solved by branch and bound algorithm as described in [25].

3.3   Evaluation Measures

After the deployment plans were generated by the optimizer, a statistical evaluation metric on the integrity of the deployment plans was further developed. Given the multiple overlapping spherical coverage and target terrain, the evaluation measure is defined by

$$CA = \frac{RC \cap T}{T};\tag{2}$$

where CA stands for coverage rate, RC denotes resulted coverage and T represents target terrain as defined before.

4   Experiments

4.1   Environments

To validate the proposed approach, a proof-of-concept experiment is implemented in this section. A virtual 3D workspace was generated including the target region to be covered by the swarm robots, a non-trespassing zone, and entry points.

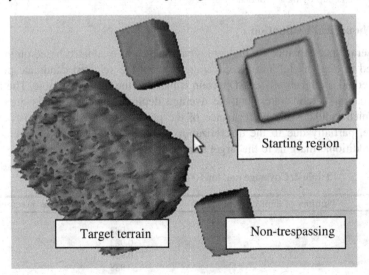

Fig. 1. The 3D virtual spatial terrain generated before deploying swarm robots. The target terrain is supposed to be distributed around 65meters x 45 meters x 45 meters, and all robots are starting from the entry region. The two 3D blocks in the model are representing the region not to trespass.

4.2   Deployment Results

The individual robots covered a spherical space with a 15-meter radius, while being located at the entry region at the beginning. When the deployment task began, the robots were deployed based on the proposed approach in order to completely cover the 3D terrain. Ten candidate deployment plans were generated and their performance is evaluated in the next subsection 4.3.   Selected candidate plans are visualized for comparison in the Fig.2, where a line indicates the path that each robot used from the entry region to the deployed position. Each sphere virtually denotes the coverage space of each robot. The figures demonstrate that multiple overlapping spaces between neighboring robots exist for ensuring complete coverage, and the overall region can be covered by the candidate plans.

Fig. 2. The 3D visualization of selected deployment strategies. Left one is deploying 20 robots and right one is deploying 25 robots.

4.3   Numerical Evaluation

The coverage performance for the deployment plan was evaluated based on the metric described in Section 3.3 and the coverage rate for the selected candidate plans that were overlaid on the simulated 3D terrain is listed in the following table. The numerical evaluation demonstrates that the average deployment coverage is greater than 98%, which validates the performance of the proposed approach. This is not 100% coverage, partially due to the discretization sample error and can be overcome by adding additional margins to the target terrain.

Table 2. Coverage rate for 10 candidate deployment strategies

Plan ID	Number of deployed robots	Coverage Rate [CA, defined in equation (2)]
1	25	0.983
2	20	0.983
3	25	0.983
4	21	0.988
5	21	0.988
6	24	0.989
7	24	0.988
8	22	0.984
9	20	0.984
10	22	0.984

5   Conclusion

This article presented an optimal deployment method for swarm robots to cover a 3D terrain space while avoiding non-trespassing spaces. The related work has been reviewed and compared to illustrate the motivation of the presented method. The proposed approach is based on integer mathematical programming and has been validated based on the virtual 3D terrain experiment. Multiple candidate deployment strategies can be generated for execution and examination from the visualization module. For the further study, we will investigate the approaches for decentralized implementation and interfacing with cloud computing facilities to make the dynamic deployment run on the go.

References

[1] Beni, G.: From Swarm Intelligence to Swarm Robotics. In: Şahin, E., Spears, W.M. (eds.) Swarm Robotics 2004. LNCS, vol. 3342, pp. 1–9. Springer, Heidelberg (2005)

[2] Dorigo, M., Sahin, E.: Swarm robotics. Auton. Robots 17(2-3), 111–113 (2004)

[3] Ren, H., Meng, M.Q.-H.: Power adaptive localization algorithm for wireless sensor networks using particle filter. IEEE Transactions on Vehicular Technology 58(5), 2498–2508 (2009)

[4] Dorigo, M., Tuci, E., Groß, R., Trianni, V., Labella, T.H., Nouyan, S., Ampatzis, C., Deneubourg, J.-L., Baldassarre, G., Nolfi, S., Mondada, F., Floreano, D., Gambardella, L.M.: The SWARM-BOTS Project. In: Şahin, E., Spears, W.M. (eds.) Swarm Robotics 2004. LNCS, vol. 3342, pp. 31–44. Springer, Heidelberg (2005)

[5] Şahin, E.: Swarm Robotics: From Sources of Inspiration to Domains of Application. In: Şahin, E., Spears, W.M. (eds.) Swarm Robotics 2004. LNCS, vol. 3342, pp. 10–20. Springer, Heidelberg (2005)

[6] Ren, H., Meng, M.Q.-H.: Game-theoretic modeling of joint topology control and power scheduling for wireless heterogeneous sensor networks. IEEE Transactions on Automation Science and Engineering 6(4), 610–625 (2009)

[7] Chen, Y., Du, Z., Garcia-Acosta, M.: Robot as a service in cloud computing. In: 2010 Fifth IEEE International Symposium on Service Oriented System Engineering (SOSE), pp. 151–158. IEEE (2010)

[8] Zhou, G., Zhang, Y., Bastani, F., Yen, I.: Service-oriented robotic swarm systems: Model and structuring algorithms. In: 2012 IEEE 15th International Symposium on Object/Component/Service-Oriented Real-Time Distributed Computing (ISORC), pp. 95–102. IEEE (2012)

[9] Fogel, M., Burkhart, N., Ren, H., Schiff, J., Meng, M.Q.-H., Goldberg, K.: Automated tracking of pallets in warehouses: Beacon layout and asymmetric ultrasound observation models. In: IEEE International Conference on Automation Science and Engineering, pp. 678–685 (September 2007)

[10] Bogue, R.: Swarm intelligence and robotics. Industrial Robot: An International Journal 35(6), 488–495 (2008)

[11] McLurkin, J., Smith, J., Frankel, J., Sotkowitz, D., Blau, D., Schmidt, B.: Speaking swarmish: Human-robot interface design for large swarms of autonomous mobile robots. In: Proc. of the AAAI Spring Symposium (2006)

[12] McLurkin, J., Yamins, D.: Dynamic task assignment in robot swarms. In: Proceedings of Robotics: Science and Systems, pp. 2007–214838 (2005)

[13] Mondada, F., Guignard, A., Bonani, M., Bar, D., Lauria, M., Floreano, D.: Swarm-bot: From concept to implementation. In: Proceedings of 2003 IEEE/RSJ International Conference on Intelligent Robots and Systems (IROS 2003), vol. 2, pp. 1626–1631. IEEE (2003)

[14] Mondada, F., Gambardella, L., Floreano, D., Nolfi, S., Deneuborg, J., Dorigo, M.: The cooperation of swarm-bots: Physical interactions in collective robotics. IEEE Robotics & Automation Magazine 12(2), 21–28 (2005)

[15] Groß, R., Bonani, M., Mondada, F., Dorigo, M.: Autonomous self-assembly in swarm-bots. IEEE Transactions on Robotics 22(6), 1115–1130 (2006)

[16] Batalin, M., Sukhatme, G.: Coverage, exploration and deployment by a mobile robot and communication network. Telecommunication Systems 26(2), 181–196 (2004)

[17] Hutchinson, S., Bretl, T.: Robust optimal deployment of mobile sensor networks. In: 2012 IEEE International Conference on Robotics and Automation (ICRA), pp. 671–676. IEEE (2012)

[18] Ren, H., Meng, M.Q.-H., Chen, X.: Physiological information acquisition through wireless biomedical sensor networks. In: IEEE International Conference on Information Acquisition, pp. 483–488 (July 2005)

[19] Brambilla, M., Ferrante, E., Birattari, M., Dorigo, M.: Swarm robotics: A review from the swarm engineering perspective (2012)

[20] Schwager, M., Julian, B., Rus, D.: Optimal coverage for multiple hovering robots with downward facing cameras. In: IEEE International Conference on Robotics and Automation, ICRA 2009, pp. 3515–3522. IEEE (2009)

[21] Pimenta, L.C.A., Schwager, M., Lindsey, Q., Kumar, V., Rus, D., Mesquita, R.C., Pereira, G.A.S.: Simultaneous Coverage and Tracking (SCAT) of Moving Targets with Robot Networks. In: Chirikjian, G.S., Choset, H., Morales, M., Murphey, T. (eds.) Algorithmic Foundation of Robotics VIII. STAR, vol. 57, pp. 85–99. Springer, Heidelberg (2009)

[22] Chang, C., Chang, C., Chen, Y., Chang, H.: Obstacle-resistant deployment algorithms for wireless sensor networks. IEEE Transactions on Vehicular Technology 58(6), 2925–2941 (2009)

[23] Ababnah, A., Natarajan, B.: Optimal control-based strategy for sensor deployment. IEEE Transactions on Systems, Man and Cybernetics, Part A: Systems and Humans 41(1), 97–104 (2011)

[24] Ren, H., Meng, M.Q.-H.: Understanding the mobility model of wireless body sensor networks. In: IEEE International Conference on Information Acquisition, pp. 306–310 (August 2006)

[25] Nemhauser, G., Wolsey, L.: Integer and combinatorial optimization, vol. 18. Wiley, New York (1988)

HAG-SR Hand: Highly-Anthropomorphic-Grasping Under-Actuated Hand with Naturally Coupled States

Chi Zhang[1], Wenzeng Zhang[2], Zhenguo Sun[2], and Qiang Chen[2]

[1] Dept. of Thermal Engineering, Tsinghua University, Beijing 100084, China
[2] Key Lab. for Advanced Materials Processing Technology, Ministry of Education,
Dept. of Mechanical Engineering, Tsinghua University, Beijing 100084, China
wenzeng@tsinghua.edu.cn

Abstract. Three key requirements are needed in hands: humanoid appearance and self-adaptation in grasping; simple and low in cost; recoverability function allowing touch from unexpected directions. Most of dexterous hands could not obtain these characteristics. This paper proposed a novel under-actuated finger with highly-anthropomorphic-grasping (HAG) function. A hand with HAG function, called HAG-SR Hand, is developed. The HAG-SR Hand could achieve these characteristics perfectly. Each finger in the HAG-SR Hand has HAG function, and is actuated by only one motor embedded in the first middle phalanx. Analysis and Experimental results show that the HAG-SR Hand is most perfect under-actuated hand compared with traditional all kinds of under-actuated fingers (coupled, self-adaptive or hybrid under-actuated fingers): the HAG finger is more human-friendly for the following three key reasons: firstly, the operating of HAG finger is easy to master as its working process is similar to the human finger's; secondly, the finger can self-adapt objects of different shapes, thus power grip can be realized well; thirdly, the finger's coupled states are recoverable, which reduces the possibility of hurting people when working.

Keywords: Humanoid robot, robotic hands, under-actuated grasping, coupled grasping, self-adaptive grasping, highly-anthropomorphic-grasping function.

1 Introduction

Robotic hands have been applied in a wide range of realms for their stronger grasping force or more accurate motions. During the past 30 years, Robotic hands have gradually developed into two main categories: (i) Dexterous hands. These hands consists of over 3 fingers and over 9 degrees of freedom (DOFs), and they usually possess fast response and accurate motions, such as the UTAH/MIT hand [1], the Shadow Hand, the Gifu Hand II [2] and III [3], and the DLR-HIT-hand [4]. (ii) Under-Actuated hands (UA hands in short). The so called "under-actuation" indicates that the number of motors is less than that of DOFs [5]. UA hands have been favored for their simple control system, especially in recent decades. For example, the hand of ASIMO, the SARAH hand [6], the LARM hand [7, 8], the SDM hand [9], the TH-2L hand [10], the GCUA hand [11], the MAP hand [12] are of this kind.

Aiming to refine the superiorities of human grasping which robotic hands could imitate to promote grasping ability, a novel concept of highly-anthropomorphic-grasping function (HAG function) is proposed in this paper. Based on the HAG function, a HAG hand with single route transmission (HAG-SR Hand) is developed.

S.S. Ge et al. (Eds.): ICSR 2012, LNAI 7621, pp. 475–484, 2012.

2   Highly-Anthropomorphic-Grasping Function

To propose a function for UA hands that simulates well, we should summarize human grasping characteristics first. As is shown in fig.1, there are 3 main features in human grasping:

(i)   Naturally coupled: Joints of the finger bend simultaneously at a constant ratio when no object is grasped or "precision grip" is expected. As is shown in fig.1 (a) and (b), angles of joints remain almost the same when the finger is bending, i.e. θ_1: θ_2: θ_3 equals θ_1': θ_2': θ_3'. What is more, the coupled states are "natural", which means that not much force is required to maintain coupled states.

(ii) Self-adaptable: When "power grip" is expected, fingers can self-adapt to the surface of different objects, i.e. the fingers can envelope the object, as is shown in fig.1 (c).

(iii) Recoverable: In coupled states, gesture of the finger can be changed by external force, but it will return to the former state as soon as the force is removed, as is shown in fig.1 (d).

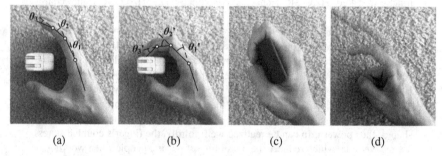

(a)   (b)   (c)   (d)

Fig. 1. Characteristics of human grasping

Based on the features introduced above, the highly-anthropomorphic-grasping (HAG) function can be defined. A robotic finger is said to be an HAG one when it has the following three characteristics:

(i)   The finger is able to bend its joints simultaneously in a naturally coupled state before touching grasped objects, or "precision grip" is expected. For robotic hands, "naturally" here means that in coupled states, no elastic components are twisted, and all parts bear little force ignoring friction and gravity of the finger itself, as is shown in fig.2 (a). With naturally coupled states, efficiency of grasping will be raised, as most of the force provided by the actuator can be used for grasping, but not for maintaining gestures as the MAP hand [12] does.

(ii) The finger is able to self-adapt to the shape of different objects when "power grip" is expected, as is shown in fig.2 (b). With more contact points between objects and fingers, the hand can grasp more stable than those rigid coupled hands.

(iii) The finger is recoverable in coupled states, i.e. though the gesture of the finger may be changed by external forces, it can return to the former coupled state as soon as the force is removed, as is shown in fig.2 (c).

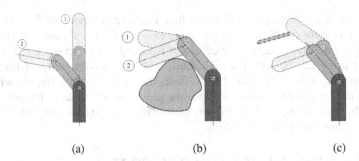

(a)   (b)   (c)

Fig. 2. Grasping stages of a finger with HAG function

UA hands can be further divided into 4 categories on the basis of grasping mode: the rigid coupled hand, the self-adaptive hand, the hybrid hand and the highly-anthropomorphic-grasping hand (HAG hand), which is proposed in this paper. The characteristics and examples of these hands are shown in Table 1, where the concepts are as follows:

Natural Coupling (NC): The joints of the finger can bend simultaneously like human fingers in a coupled state which requires little force to maintain.

Laborious Coupling (LC): Coupled states in which maintaining force is essential.

Active Self-Adapting (ASA): Grasping force of the phalanx is offered directly by motor through transmission mechanism.

Passive Self-Adapting (PSA): Grasping force of the phalanx is offered by counterforce-receiving mechanism set in the former phalanx.

One-Direction Recovery (ODR): The gesture of the finger can be changed by external force from only one direction of the finger, and it will return to the former gesture when the external force is removed.

Two-Direction Recovery (TDR): The gesture of the finger can be changed by external force from both directions and the finger is able to recover its gesture.

Table 1. Categories of UA Hands

	Rigid Coupled UA Hand	Self-Adaptive UA Hand	Hybrid UA Hand	HAG Hand
Coupling	NC	-	LC	NC
Self-Adapting	-	ASA/PSA	-/PSA	ASA
Recoverability	-	ODR/TDR	ODR	TDR
Efficiency	High	Low	Low	High
Example	ASIMO Hand	TH-2L Hand[10]	GCUA Hand[11] COSA-GRS Hand[13]	HAG-SR Hand

From the form it can be seen obviously that HAG hand simulates human grasping motions better than traditional robot hands.

Therefore, compared with traditional coupled, self-adaptive or hybrid under-actuated hands, a robotic hand with HAG function is more human-friendly, for the following reasons: first, the hand simulates human grasping motions well, thus the hand is easy to master as its grasping process is similar to the operator's own hand's, and with only a few actuators to be controlled, the hand is especially fit to be used as prosthetic hands for the disabled as it is quite easy to operate; second, the HAG hand can self-adapt different shape of objects, thus the hand can grasp some heavy objects as "power grip" can be well realized; third, with the recoverability of fingers, the HAG finger is "softer" compared with those traditional robotic fingers which are usually with rigid joints, thus the hand is less possible to hurt human when it accidentally hits them, and is fit for human-machine interactive behaviors like supporting someone or passing objects.

3   Design Principle of 3-Joint HAG-SR Finger

A 3-joint HAG finger with single-route transmission (HAG-SR finger) is designed and manufactured to realize the HAG function through utilizing differential transmission mechanism and torsional springs. The so called "single-route" indicates that there is only one suit of transmission mechanism between adjacent joints.

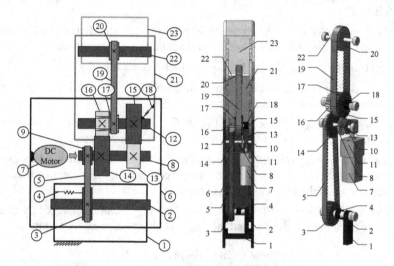

Fig. 3. The mechanism principle of the 3-joint HAG-SR finger
1-base, 2-base shaft, 3-lower driven pulley, 4-1st spring, 5-lower belt,6-first middle phalanx, 7-DC motor, 8-main shaft, 9-lower driving pulley, 12-middle joint shaft,13-1st gear, 14-2nd gear, 15-3rd gear, 16-4th gear,17-upper driving pulley, 18-2nd spring, 19-upper belt, 20-upper driven pulley,21-second middle phalanx, 22-distal shaft, 23-distal phalanx.

Fig.3 shows the design principle of the 3-joint HAG-SR finger, which consists of a base 1, a base shaft 2, the lower driven pulley 3, the first spring 4, the lower belt 5, the first middle phalanx 6, the DC motor 7, the main shaft 8, the lower driving pulley 9, the worm and gear transmission mechanism including the worm 10 and the worm gear 11, the middle joint shaft 12, the 1st gear 13, the 2nd gear 14, the 3rd gear 15, the 4th gear 16, the upper driving pulley 17, the second spring 18, the upper belt 19, the upper driven pulley 20, the second middle phalanx 21, the distal shaft 22 and the distal phalanx 23.

The base and the first middle phalanx are connected by the base shaft. The lower driven pulley is sleeved on the base shaft and is linked to the base by the first spring. The main shaft and the middle joint shaft are both sleeved in the first middle phalanx. The 1st gear, the 2nd gear and the lower driving pulley are all sleeved on the main shaft but are not rotatable around it (rigidly sleeved). Meanwhile, the lower driving pulley and the lower driven pulley are connected by the belt.

The DC motor is mounted in the first middle phalanx, and is able drive the main shaft through the worm and the worm gear. The 3rd gear, the 4th gear and the upper driving pulley are sleeved on the middle joint shaft, among which the 3rd gear is rigidly sleeved, while the 4th gear and the upper driving pulley are fixed with each other but are rotatable around the middle joint shaft together. What is more, the 1st gear and the 2nd gear are respectively meshed with the 3rd gear and the 4th gear. It is suggested that the 1st gear and the 4th gear have the same size, while the 2nd gear and the 3rd gear have the same size in order to guarantee the same module and center distance of these two pairs of meshed gears, i.e. the 1st-3rd gear pair and the 2nd-4th gear pair. With these 4 gears, the differential transmission is realized, as for the linear velocities of the gears in each meshed gear pair are the same and the angular velocities of the 1st gear and the 2nd gear are the same, the angular velocity of the 4th gear would be faster than that of the 3rd gear in the situation that the 4th gear is smaller than the 3rd gear. The second middle phalanx is sleeved on the middle joint shaft and is connected to the 3rd gear by the second spring. The distal shaft is sleeved in the second middle shaft, and the upper driven pulley and the distal phalanx are both rigidly sleeved on the distal shaft. The upper driving pulley and the upper driven pulley are connected by the upper belt so that they could rotate in the same direction.

4   Grasping Analysis of the 3-Joint HAG-SR Finger

Fig.4 shows the typical grasping process of the 3-joint HAG-SR finger, in which the identifiers of parts are the same to Fig.3, and the triangle marks on the gears are used to show the motions of different parts more clearly. Before grasping, the finger stays

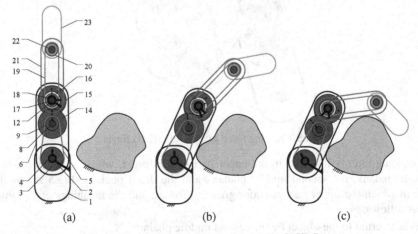

(a)   (b)   (c)

Fig. 4. Grasping process of the 3-joint HAG-SR finger

in the initial upright state, as is shown in fig.4 (a). When grasping starts, the DC motor would drive the main shaft, thus the rotation of the main shaft could be passed both to the distal phalanx and to the first middle phalanx. On the one hand, the lower driven pulley tend to rotate around the base shaft with the force passed from the lower belt, but with the effort of the first spring, it would seem like to be fixed with the base, thus instead of rotating itself, the whole finger would rotate around the base. On the other hand, as the 3rd gear and the second middle phalanx are connected, they will rotate together with the effort of the upper spring; simultaneously, as the angular velocity of the 4th gear is faster, the extra rotation would pass on to the distal phalanx through the upper driving pulley, the upper belt and the upper driven pulley, so that the distal phalanx would rotate for an extra angle with respect to the distal shaft, as it is fixed with the upper driven pulley by the distal shaft. In this process, neither of the spring will be twisted ignoring the friction and the gravity of the finger itself, thus the naturally coupled state is realized, as is shown in fig.4 (b).

When the finger touches the object, the phalanxes would be prevented from rotating, but the lower driven pulley and the 3rd gear are still rotatable by twisting the springs, thus the transmission mechanisms between joints are still able to work and the distal phalanx will keep on rotating until it touches the grasped object. In this process, the phalanxes will cover the surface of the object automatically; hence the grasping state would be stable. This enables the finger's self-adapting ability. Fig.5(c) shows the state when self-adaptive grasping process is accomplished, in which both torsional springs are twisted.

When the finger comes across obstacles, it will bend in a working principle similar to the self-adaptive grasping process, i.e. the finger will be twisted but when the force is removed, the finger will return to the former coupled state as the springs will recover. This brings about the ability of recovery of the finger.

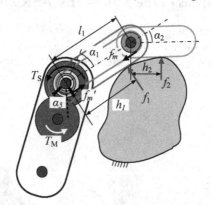

Fig. 5. Grasping force analysis of a HAG finger

Grasping mainly involves in the upper part of the finger, which includes the first middle phalanx, the second middle phalanx and the distal phalanx. Fig.5 shows the state in which the upper part provides grasping forces, and the meanings of variables are as follows:

f_1: force exerted to the object by the second middle phalanx, N

f_2: force exerted to the object by the distal phalanx, N

f_m: force exerted to the upper driven pulley by the belt, N
f_m': force exerted to the upper driving pulley by the belt, i.e. counterforce of f_m, N
h_1: force arm of f_1 with respect to the middle joint shaft, mm
h_2: force arm of f_2 with respect to the distal shaft, mm
l_1: active length of the second middle phalanx, mm
T_M: torque exerted to the main shaft through the worm and worm gear, N·mm
T_S: torque exerted to the second middle phalanx by the second spring, N·mm
α_1: angle for which the 2nd middle phalanx rotates around the middle shaft, °
α_2: angle for which distal phalanx rotates around distal shaft to 2nd middle one, °
α_5: the torsion angle of the second spring, °
k: stiffness factor of the second spring, N·mm/ °.

Assume that the tooth number of the 1st gear and the 4th gear is z_1, and the tooth number of the 2nd gear and the 3rd gear is z_2 ($z_1 < z_2$), the radius of the upper driving pulley and the upper driven pulley are respectively r_1 and r_2, then four equations could be founded:

$$T_M = f_1 h_1 + f_2(l_1 \cos\alpha_2 + h_2) \tag{1}$$

$$T_M = T_S + f_m' r_1 \tag{2}$$

$$f_2 h_2 = f_m r_2 \tag{3}$$

$$T_S = k\{\frac{r_2}{r_1}\left(\frac{z_1}{z_2}\right)^2 \alpha_2 - [1 - (\frac{z_1}{z_2})^2]\alpha_1\} \tag{4}$$

Noticing that $f_m = f_m'$, f_1 and f_2 can be solved:

$$f_1 = \frac{1}{h_1}\{T_M - \frac{r_2}{r_1 h_2}[T_M - k(\frac{r_2}{r_1}\left(\frac{z_1}{z_2}\right)^2 \alpha_2 - [1 - (\frac{z_1}{z_2})^2]\alpha_1)](l_1 \cos\alpha_2 + h_2)\} \tag{5}$$

$$f_2 = \frac{r_2}{r_1 h_2}[T_M - k(\frac{r_2}{r_1}\left(\frac{z_1}{z_2}\right)^2 \alpha_2 - [1 - (\frac{z_1}{z_2})^2]\alpha_1)] \tag{6}$$

When $T_M = 500$ N·mm, $k = 15$ N·mm/ °, $z_1 = 20$, $z_2 = 30$, $r_1 = r_2 = 14$mm, $h_1 = h_2 = 15$mm, $l_1 = 30$mm, the relationships among f_1, f_2, α_1 and α_2 can be expressed intuitively by fig.6. With the differential transmission mechanism, it should be noted that the graphs are logical when $\alpha_2 \geq 1.25\alpha_1$.

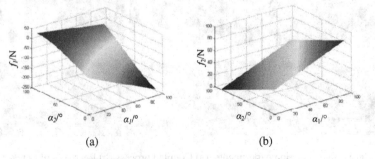

(a)   (b)

Fig. 6. Relationships among α_1, α_2, f_1 and f_2

5 Grasping Experiments of the HAG-SR Hand

The HAG-SR hand is achievable applying the HAG-SR fingers. Fig.7 shows the prototype of the 3-joint HAG-SR finger. The HAG-SR hand consists of 5 fingers and a palm, among which four fingers contain 3 joints and the other one, the thumb, contains 2 joints. Besides the joints set in the fingers, the palm also contains a joint at the base of the thumb thus the thumb can rotate in a plane perpendicular to the palm plane. Therefore, the HAG-SR hand is a 5-fingered hand with 15 DOFs. At present, the hand is controlled by a handle with 6 buttons, and each button controls an actuator separately.

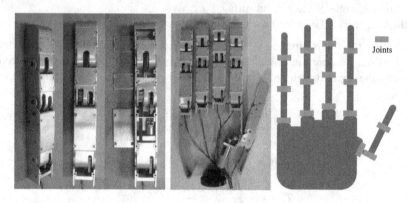

Fig. 7. The HAG-SR Hand and its finger

In basic function experiments, coupled bending process and recoverability are tested and recorded in fig.8. The finger can finish the whole coupled bending process in less than 2 seconds in normal working conditions.

In dexterity experiments, the hand is made to realize different grasping patterns and gestures. As is shown in fig.9, precision grip, pinch grip and power grip are all realizable, and the thumb of HAG-SR finger is opposable, i.e. the thumb is able to touch index finger, middle finger and ring finger separately.

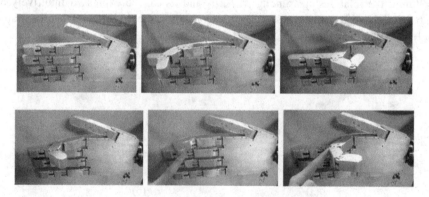

Fig. 8. Basic function experiments. (a) Coupled process (b) Recoverability test.

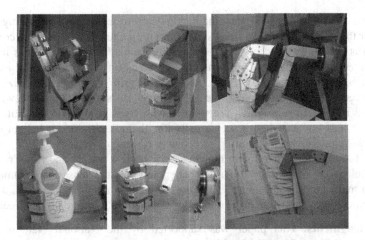

Fig. 9. Dexterity experiments of the HAG-SR Hand

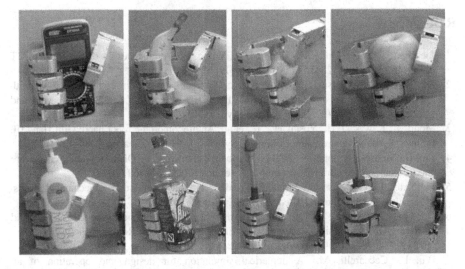

Fig. 10. Power grasp experiments of the HAG-SR Hand

In power grip experiments, a variety of objects is handled to the HAG-SR hand. After holding the object, the robot arm where the hand is mounted would rotate at an angular velocity of 0.5rad/s to test the grasping stability. Experimental results show that the hand can hold objects with rough surface and lighter than 1.5kg stable, as is shown in fig.10.

6   Conclusion and Future Work

The HAG function of robotic hand is proposed and realized successfully by developing the HAG-SR hand. Theoretical analysis and experiments show that the HAG hand is human-friendly, for the following reasons: first, the hand simulates human grasping motions well, thus the hand is easy to master as its grasping process is similar to the operator's own hand's, and with only a few actuators to be controlled, the hand is especially fit to be used as prosthetic hands for the disabled as it is quite easy to operate; second, the HAG hand can self-adapt different shape of objects, thus the hand can grasp some heavy objects as "power grip" can be well realized; third, with the recoverability of fingers, the HAG finger is "softer" compared with those traditional robotic fingers which are usually with rigid joints, thus the hand is less possible to hurt human when it accidentally hits them, and is fit for human-machine interactive behaviors like supporting someone or passing objects.

In the future, a HAG hand with human hand size, less weight and faster respond is to be developed to adapt daily-life usage better, and pressure sensors are planned to be added to make the hand "tactile". Also, as the hand is manual at present, a control system based on eye movements is under development to improve its intelligence.

Acknowledgments. This paper was supported by the National Natural Science Foundation of China (No.50905093).

References

1. Jacobsen, S.C., Iversen, E.K., Knutti, D.F., Wood, J.E., et al.: Design of the UTAH/MIT dexterous hand, pp.1520–1532. MIT Press (1986)
2. Kawasaki, H., Komatsu, T., Uchiyama, K.: Dexterous anthropomorphic robot hand with distributed tactile sensor: Gifu Hand II. In: IEEE Inter. Conf. on Systems, Man and Cybernetics, pp. 782–787. IEEE Press, Tokyo (1999)
3. Mouri, T., Kawasaki, H., Yoshikawa, K., et al.: Anthropomorphic robot hand: Gifu Hand III. In: Inter. Conf. on Control, Automation and Systems, Jeonbuk, Korea, pp. 1288–1293 (2002)
4. Liu, H., Meusel, P., Seitz, N., et al.: The modular multisensory DLR-HIT-Hand: hardware and software architecture. Trans. on Mechatornics 13(4), 461–469 (2008)
5. Laliberté, T., Gosselin, C.: Simulation and design of underactuated mechanical hands. Mechanism of Machine and Theory 33(1/2), 39–57 (1998)
6. Gosselin, C., Pelletier, F., Laliberté, T.: An anthropomorphic underactuated robotic hand with 15 DOFs and a single actuator. In: IEEE Inter. Conf. on Robotics and Automation, pp. 749–754. IEEE Press, Pasadena (2008)
7. Wu, L., Ceccarelli, M.: A numerical simulation for design and operation of an underactuated finger mechanism for LARM Hand. Mechanics Based Design of Structures and Machines 37, 86–112 (2009)
8. Carbone, G., Iannone, S., Ceccarelli, M.: Regulation and control of LARM Hand III. Robotics and Computer-Integrated Manufacturing 24(2), 202–211 (2010)
9. Dollar, A.M., Howe, R.D.: The SDM Hand: a highly adaptive compliant grasper for unstructured environments. Experimental Robotics 2010, 3–11 (2009)
10. Zhang, W., Wang, L., Hao, L., Chen, Q., Du, D.: An indirect style linkage under-actuated humanoid robotic hand. In: IEEE Inter. Asia Conf. on Informatics in Control, Automation and Robotics, pp. 421–424. IEEE Press (2010)
11. Che, D., Zhang, W.: GCUA humanoid robotic hand with tendon mechanisms and its upper limb. Inter. J. of Social Robotics 3(4), 395–404 (2011)
12. Wiste, T.E., Dalley, S.A., Withrow, T.J., Goldfarb, M.: Design of a multifunctional anthropomorphic prosthetic hand with extrinsic actuation. In: IEEE Inter. Conf. on Rehabilitation Robotics, pp. 675–681. IEEE Press, Kyoto (2009)

RoboASR: A Dynamic Speech Recognition System for Service Robots

Abdelaziz A. Abdelhamid, Waleed H. Abdulla, and Bruce A. MacDonald

Electrical and Computer Engineering
The University of Auckland, New Zealand
aabd127@aucklanduni.ac.nz, {w.abdulla,b.macdonald}@auckland.ac.nz

Abstract. This paper proposes a new method for building dynamic speech decoding graphs for state based spoken human-robot interaction (HRI). The current robotic speech recognition systems are based on either finite state grammar (FSG) or statistical N-gram models or a dual FSG and N-gram using a multi-pass decoding. The proposed method is based on merging both FSG and N-gram into a single decoding graph by converting the FSG rules into a weighted finite state acceptor (WFSA) then composing it with a large N-gram based weighted finite state transducer (WFST). This results in a tiny decoding graph that can be used in a single pass decoding. The proposed method is applied in our speech recognition system (RoboASR) for controlling service robots with limited resources. There are three advantages of the proposed approach. First, it takes the advantage of both FSG and N-gram decoders by composing both of them into a single tiny decoding graph. Second, it is robust, the resulting tiny decoding graph is highly accurate due to it fitness to the HRI state. Third, it has a fast response time in comparison to the current state of the art speech recognition systems. The proposed system has a large vocabulary containing 64K words with more than 69K entries. Experimental results show that the average response time is 0.05% of the utterance length and the average ratio between the true and false positives is 89% when tested on 15 interaction scenarios using live speech.

Keywords: Human-robot interaction, automatic speech recognition, weighted finite state transducers.

1 Introduction

For multi-modal communications in cognitive neuroscience robotic, robot speech recognition is one of the most important and effective means of natural communication between humans and robots [1][2]. Currently, speech recognition systems can be used for HRI, but they impose some restrictions in order to obtain effective speech recognition accuracy. Some of these restrictions are: the limited/small vocabulary, the usage of a headset or the need for noise free environments. However, these ideal conditions are not always suitable for realistic interaction with robots [3]. This research addresses the first restriction in a dynamic and efficient way.

S.S. Ge et al. (Eds.): ICSR 2012, LNAI 7621, pp. 485–495, 2012.
© Springer-Verlag Berlin Heidelberg 2012

Current state-of-the-art robotic speech recognition systems are usually based on either FSG or statistical models based on N-grams [4]. The FSG based systems have the advantage of achieving high sentence accuracy but at the same time suffer from a high rate of false positives. Besides, these systems are restricted to a limited number of sentences. The N-gram based systems can deal with a large vocabulary in real time, but suffer from low sentence accuracy and a high rate of false positives. In the literature, there are several efforts to exploit the advantages of both FSG based and N-gram based decoders by integrating them together into multi-pass decoders [4] [5].

In [6], key-phrase spotting in longer sentences through the combination of FSG and N-gram decoders is presented. This approach is based on the assumption that the key-phrase of interest is surrounded by a carrier set of words. The N-gram decoder is used to recognize the surrounding words and once it recognizes the first word in the key-phrase of interest, the N-gram decoder works to recognize the remaining words of the key-phrase. Then, the score of the recognized key-phrase is compared to a predefined threshold to decide its correctness. This fine tuning is done on a very low level, that makes it difficult to switch to another FSG or N-gram decoder easily.

In [5], FSG and N-gram decoders are used independently and simultaneously to process the speech data using a set of common acoustic models. The idea of this approach is to compare the best hypothesis resulting from FSG decoder along with the N-best hypotheses resulting from N-gram decoder. The advantage of this approach is that it reduces the ratio of false positives, but the domain was restricted to only 36 words and a command grammar.

In [7], an FSG-decoder is used with another complementary decoder that is also an FSG-decoder but based on N-grams. The objective from this approach was to reduce the false positives through off-line training of the first decoder on sentences with similar meanings. In this approach the result of the first decoder was not rated or rejected afterwards, but the search space is shaped to decrease the false positives.

In [4], the author used the same approach discussed in [5] and investigated its application in different forms of HRI including headset, ceiling boundary, and robot embedded microphones. The author used both FSG and N-gram based decoders in a multi-pass decoding process. This research concluded that the multi-pass decoding approach is effective but only suits domain specific scenarios. Although these multi-pass decoders are running simultaneously, it is expected that the response time of this approach is greater than that of individual decoders.

In this paper we present a speech recognition system that merges both FSG rules and N-gram models together into a single pass decoder without sacrificing the accuracy or the vocabulary size. The proposed system is designed using multi-threads and multi-buffers and can achieve a high recognition accuracy in a very short real time factor (RTF). The single pass decoder runs on a tiny decoding graph that is extracted from a pre-compiled large decoding graph using the composition operation of weighted finite state transducers (WFSTs) [8].

The pre-compiled large decoding graph is based on N-grams and a vocabulary containing 64K words.

The rest of this paper is structured as follows; section 2 discusses the tiny decoding graph extraction method. The general structure of the developed speech recognition system (RoboASR) is presented in section 3. Then, the preliminary experiments are discussed in section 4, followed by the conclusion and possible future directions in section 5.

2   The Proposed Approach

Before discussing the proposed single pass decoder in some details, we first present some relevant basics of the current state-of-the-art approaches in speech recognition systems.

2.1   Acoustic and Language Modelling

Modelling the speech signal could be approached through developing acoustic and language models. Currently, most speech recognition systems use statistical models to represent all the speech units. The most widely used and successful modelling approach is hidden Markov models (HMM) [9]. Another component in speech modelling is the language modelling that is used to model the constraints imposed on the spoken sentence by the grammar (or syntax) to determine the optimal sentence in the language. There are two methods to represent the language models namely: FSGs and statistical N-grams. Both of these methods are based on a dictionary that defines the sequence of phones constituting each word. The main difference between FSG and N-grams is that an FSG is an automaton of a predefined set of transitions between words, while N-grams are statistically trained based on the measured frequency of each word. The name N-grams comes from the dependency between the word and its preceding (N-1) words. The training of higher order N-grams usually requires a huge amount of training data, so that Bi-grams and Tri-grams are usually used in current state-of-the-art speech recognition systems.

The actual decoding of the speech utterance is based on searching the acoustic and language models to find out the best fitting hypothesis. There are many approaches for doing this search, the most common approach that is currently used is Viterbi beam search that searches for the best decoding hypothesis with the possibility to prune away the hypotheses with small scores.

2.2   Weighted Finite State Transducers (WFSTs)

WFSTs are the current state-of-the-art method used for building speech decoding graphs through the integration of the speech knowledge sources together into a single decoding graph [10]. The common speech knowledge sources are the acoustic knowledge represented by HMMs, syntax knowledge represented by

N-grams, and lexical knowledge represented by the pronunciation dictionary. The integrated decoding graph can be constructed through the application of a series of WFST operations such as composition, determinization, epsilon removal, and weight pushing [11].

In this research, we constructed a large decoding graph that will be used in the extraction of the tiny decoding graph that will be used later in the single pass decoding process. The sizes of the knowledge sources used in this research along with the series of WFST operations that are used to generate the large decoding graph are shown in table 1. This table presents the sequence of WFST operations applied to the speech knowledge sources to generate the large decoding graph along with the size of the intermediate graphs resulting from each operation.

Table 1. The operations and intermediate graphs used for building the large WFST decoding graph

Operation	#States	#Transitions
C	1,681	84,080
L	523,083	592,837
G	595,765	1,327,969
T	63,999	191,997
$det(L)$	209,919	279,673
$C \circ det(L)$	346,452	550,709
$G \circ T$	886,099	1,932,311
$(C \circ det(L)).(G \circ T)$	5,579,208	8,082,205

C : Context dependency WFST, L : Lexicon WFST, G : Tri-gram WFST, T : Silence WFST, $\circ$: The composition operation, det : The determinization operation.

2.3   Tiny Decoding Graph Extraction

The basic idea of this research is to dynamically generate a tiny decoding graph for each state in the state-based HRI. In the state-based HRI the interaction with the robot is defined through a sequence of HRI states and each state has a set of allowable commands (these commands can be words or sentences) and actions as shown in Fig. 1 [12]. In order to generate a tiny decoding graph for certain HRI state, firstly, the FSG rules defining this HRI state are converted to a weighted finite state acceptor (WFSA) $A(y, y)$ where each transition in this acceptor has the same word as an input and output. Secondly, the generated WFSA is composed with the large WFST decoding graph $T_1(x, y)$ to get the tiny WFST $T_2(x, y)$ for that HRI state as follows:

$$T_2(x, y) = [T_1 \circ A] = \bigoplus_y [T_1(x, y)] \otimes [A(y, y)] \tag{1}$$

where $\oplus$ and $\otimes$ are the *semiring-add* and *semiring-multiply* operations respectively, for more details about the WFST operations please refer to [10]. The proposed composition algorithm used to generate the tiny WFST T_2 from the large WFST T_1 is shown in algorithm 1. This algorithm describes the composition operation used to generate the tiny decoding graph. The basic idea of this algorithm is to merge the transitions of both large WFST and WFSA where the output labels of the transitions in the first graph coincide with the input labels of the transitions in the second graph. The notations used in this algorithm are defined as follows. Q is a temporary set used to hold set of states, , $\wp$ is a queue used to hold the set of pairs of states yet to be examined, I_G and F_G are the set of initial and final states of the graph G respectively, q is a state in the decoding graph, e is a transition, $E[q]$ is the set of all transitions getting out from the state q, and λ_G is the weight of the final state of the graph G. The default weights of the constructed WFSA are all zeros. Then, the resulting tiny WFST is stored on disk and named with the same HRI state number (to be easily recalled while running the HRI scenarios). While running the live interaction with the robot, the tiny decoding graph is loaded automatically for each interaction state and the single pass decoder runs on the loaded tiny WFST.

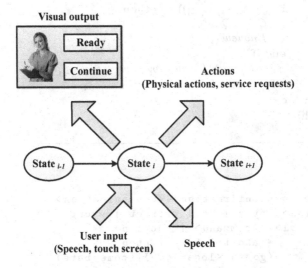

Fig. 1. The spoken HRI state

To clarify the idea of the proposed approach, sample grammar rules used to describe a potential HRI state is shown in Fig. 2. These grammar rules are parsed and processed to generate the corresponding WFSA graph shown in Fig. 3. Then, the generated WFSA is composed with the large WFST using the proposed algorithm and a tiny WFST graph is produced for that HRI state. The resulting tiny WFST has hundreds of states and transitions, so it did not fit to be included in this paper.

Algorithm 1. Weighted Composition

Input: *Transducer* T_1, *Acceptor* A
Output: *Transducer* $T_2 = [T_1 \circ A]$

1: **begin**
2:     $Q \longleftarrow I_{T_1} \times I_A$
3:     $\wp \longleftarrow I_{T_1} \times I_A$
4:     **while** $\wp \neq \phi$ **do**
5:         $q = (q_1, q_2) \longleftarrow Head(\wp)$
6:         $Dequeue(\wp)$
7:         **if** $q \in I_{T_1} \times I_A$ **then**
8:             $I_{T_2} \longleftarrow I_{T_2} \cup \{q\}$
9:             $\lambda_{T_2}(q) \longleftarrow \lambda_{T_1}(q_1) \otimes \lambda_A(q_2)$
10:        **end if**
11:        **if** $q \in F_{T_1} \times F_A$ **then**
12:            $F_{T_2} \longleftarrow F_{T_2} \cup \{q\}$
13:            $\rho_{T_2}(q) \longleftarrow \rho_{T_1}(q_1) \otimes \rho_A(q_2)$
14:        **end if**
15:        **for** *each* $(e_1, e_2) \in E[q_1] \times E[q_2]$ **do**
16:            **if** $o[e_1] = i[e_2]$ *and* $i[e_1] \neq o[e_2]$ **then**
17:                **if** $(\acute{q} = (n[e_1], n[e_2])) \notin Q$ **then**
18:                    $Q \longleftarrow Q \cup \{\acute{q}\}$
19:                    $Enqueue(\wp, \acute{q})$
20:                **end if**
21:                $E_{T_2} \longleftarrow E_{T_2} \uplus \{(q, i[e_1], o[e_2], w[e_1] \otimes w[e_2], \acute{q})\}$
22:            **end if**
23:        **end for**
24:    **end while**
25: **end**

```
<utterance>     = <confirmation>|<communication>
<confirmation>  = yes | no | correct | wrong
<communication> = <command> | <action>
<command>       = abort | help | stop
<action>        = (go to <location>)|(come here)
<location>      = desk | chair | sofa
```

Fig. 2. Sample finite state grammar for a spoken HRI state

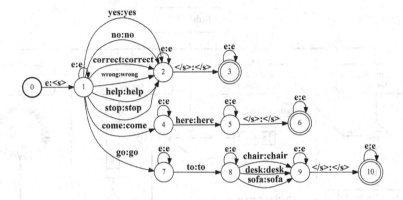

Fig. 3. WFSA graph corresponding to the sample grammar

3   RoboASR: The Developed System

In this research, we used the developed speech decoder presented in [13]. In comparison to other promising systems [14][15] the proposed speech recognition system has the advantage of being applicable to devices and robots with limited resources. The developed speech recognition system is fully implemented in C++. The next sections discuss the internal structure of the developed system.

3.1   The Structure of the Speech Recognition System

The proposed speech recognition system is based on multi-threads to achieve a harmony in the processing of various operations that take place on the captured speech signal and to allow for a continuous signal capturing and decoding. Besides, a set of multi-buffers is used to efficiently handle the continuous capturing of the incoming audio stream. The structure of RoboASR is shown in Fig. 4, which is based on the following four threads:

1. **Controlling thread:** Which controls the overall system and is responsible for loading the acoustic models and the tiny WFST graphs (only on demand) and initiating the signal acquisition thread.
2. **Signal acquisition thread:** This thread is responsible for continuous capturing of the speech signal from the sound card. The signal acquisition is done based on a series of multi-buffers working together as a pipeline.
3. **Voice detection thread:** While capturing the continuous audio stream, this thread is responsible for detecting which buffers contain a speech signal, then accumulate these buffers into another large buffer for decoding.
4. **Decoding thread:** Once the large buffer is filled with the speech utterance from the signal acquisition thread, the decoding thread is activated to decode the speech signal in this large buffer.

The arrows in Fig. 4 indicate a process flow, while the dotted lines are used just to visually separate the tasks of each thread.

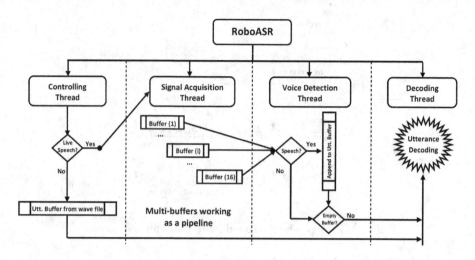

Fig. 4. The proposed ASR system based on multi-threads and multi-buffers

3.2   The Structure of the Single Pass Decoder

The developed decoder [13] contains several classes for loading the acoustic models (HMM), and the WFST decoding graph along with a memory pool that is used through the decoding process to handle the competing hypotheses. Additionally, this decoder contains special structures for holding the best token and for holding the set of competing hypotheses during the decoding process. The single pass decoding mechanism is based on the Viterbi algorithm though the implementation of a token passing technique with beam pruning to speed up the decoding process [16].

4   Experimental Results

4.1   Experimental Setup

The preliminary experiments established in research were based on two steps. First, a large WFST decoding graph was built based on N-grams (Tri-grams) and using a large vocabulary containing 64K words. Second, we described each spoken HRI state as a set of FSG rules, then these FSG rules for each scenario were converted to a WFSA and composed with the large WFST decoding graph to extract the tiny decoding graph. These two steps result in a set of a tiny decoding graphs one for each spoken HRI state.

To investigate the effectiveness of the proposed approach, we measured the overall rate of true positives (Tp) and false positives (Fp) for each HRI scenario from the single-pass decoder using the large N-gram based decoding graph, and an FSG based decoding graph [17], and compared these two decoders with the proposed decoder using the extracted tiny decoding graph. Then, the average ratio between the true and false positives was recorded.

All the experiments used live speech recorded in 16 bits format and a sampling rate of 16K Hz, and captured using head mounted microphone. The number of spoken HRI states involved in these experiments is 15 HRI states.

4.2   Results and Discussion

To validate the appropriateness of the proposed approach for robots with limited resources, we compared the resources required by the traditional decoding graph and the proposed approach as shown in table 2. It is shown that the performance of the proposed tiny decoding graph is much better than that of the large one in terms of the Tp/Fp ratio and the average RTF. The proposed approach can achieve 89% Tp/Fp in an average RTF of 0.05 of the utterance length, that makes the proposed approach more appropriate for the resource limited devices and robots. Since the tiny decoding graphs are extracted to fit the HRI states, if the HRI state received an unexpected utterance, it will be approximated to the best decoding hypothesis, then a threshold is used to decide whether to keep or prune this best decoding hypothesis.

Table 2. Comparison between the large WFST and tiny WFST decoding graphs

Resources	Large WFST	Tiny WFST
Num. States	5,579,208	300 (avg)
Num. Transitions	9,082,205	500 (avg)
Avg. RTF (xRT)	1.5	0.05
Memory (MB)	900	350
Tp/Fp ratio.	64%	89%

The significant evaluation of the proposed approach compared to the FSG and large N-gram based methods is shown in table 3. The results indicate that the proposed approach outperforms the other methods and achieves a Tp/Fp ratio of 89%.

Table 3. The performance of different decoders

Decoder	Tp	Fp	Tp/Fp ratio
FSG decoder	77%	18%	81%
large N-gram decoder	64%	36%	64%
Proposed decoder	80%	10%	89%

Tp/Fp ratio = Tp / (Tp + Fp) * 100

The method we followed to measure the evaluation criteria (i.e. Tp and Fp) is shown in Fig. 4. In this figure, the correctly recognized commands are coloured with blue colour and, the miss-recognized commands are coloured with red colour. However, if the decoder recognized the command with low probability, in this case, the recognition result is pruned, and the command is rejected as shown in yellow coloured cells in this table.

Table 4. Sample commands and their recognition results

Command	FSG	Large WFST	Tiny WFST
go to chair	go to chair	got chair	go to chair
go to sofa	go to sofa	got sofa	go to sofa
come here	go to chair		come here
correct	correct	correct	correct
wrong	no		no
help		held	help
yes	yes	yes	yes
no	no	no	no

Blue color : denotes Tp command, *Yellow color* : denotes Rejected command and *Red color* : denotes Fp command.

5 Conclusion

In this paper we present a new method for building the speech decoding graphs for state based spoken HRI. The proposed method is based on merging an FSG with N-grams decoding graphs to produce a more efficient tiny decoding graph. Also, we presented the structure of our speech recognition system (RoboASR) along with the structure of the decoding engine. The experimental results show the effectiveness of the proposed approach over the traditional N-gram based large decoding graphs for handling large vocabulary tasks.

The overall performance of the developed system can be improved by capturing the live speech signal using an array of microphones to handle the ambient noise. In addition, We may confirm the effectiveness of our approach in a real environment with reverberation and in a dynamically changing environment.

Acknowledgement. This work is supported by the R&D program of the Korea Ministry of Knowledge and Economy (MKE) and Korea Evaluation Institute of Industrial Technology (KEIT). [KI001836, Development of Mediated Interface Technology for HRI]. We acknowledge the support of the New Zealand Ministry for Science and Innovation. We thank ETRI for their contributions and help with the work.

References

1. Kanda, T., Shiomi, M., Miyashita, Z., Ishiguro, H., Hagita, N.: Communication robot in a shopping mall. IEEE Transactions on Robotics, 897–913 (2010)
2. Paliwal, K.K., Yao, K.: Robust speech recognition under noisy ambient conditions. In: Human-Centric Interfaces for Ambient Intelligence. Academic Press, Elsevier (2009)
3. Alonso-Martin, F., Salichs, M.A.: Integration of a voice recognition system in a social robot. IEEE Transactions on Cybernetics and Systems, 215–245 (2011)

4. Heinrich, S., Wermter, S.: Towards robust speech recognition for human-robot interaction. In: Proceedings of the IEEE/RSJ International Conference on Intelligent Robots and Systems, pp. 468–473 (2011)
5. Doostdar, M., Schiffer, S., Lakemeyer, G.: A Robust Speech Recognition System for Service-Robotics Applications. In: Iocchi, L., Matsubara, H., Weitzenfeld, A., Zhou, C. (eds.) RoboCup 2008. LNCS, vol. 5399, pp. 1–12. Springer, Heidelberg (2009)
6. Lin, Q., Lubensky, D., Picheny, M., Rao, P.S.: Key-phrase spotting using an integrated language model of N-grams and finite-state grammar. In: Proceedings of the European Conference on Speech Communication and Technology, pp. 255–258 (1997)
7. Levit, M., Chang, S., Buntschuh, B.: Garbage modeling with decoys for a sequential recognition scenario. In: Proceedings of the IEEE Workshop on Automatic Speech Recognition & Understanding, pp. 468–473 (2009)
8. Allauzen, C., Schalkwyk, J.: Generalized composition algorithm for weighted finite state transducers. In: Proceedings of the International Speech Communication Association (2009)
9. Rabinar, L., Juang, B.-H.: Fundamental of speech recognition. Prentice-Hall (1993)
10. Mohri, M., Pereira, F., Riley, M.: Weighted finite state transducers in speech recognition. Transactions on Computer Speech and Language 16, 69–88 (2002)
11. Novak, J.R., Minemaysu, N., Hirose, K.: Painless WFST cascade construction for LVCSR-Transducersaurus. In: Proceedings of the International Speech Communication Association (2011)
12. Broadbent, E., Jayawardena, C., Kerse, N., Stafford, R.Q., MacDonald, B.A.: Human-robot interaction research to improve quality of life in elder care - An approach and issues. In: Proceedings of the Workshop on Human-Robot Interaction in Elder Care, pp. 7–11 (2011)
13. Abdelhamid, A.A., Abdulla, W.H., MacDonald, B.A.: WFST-based large vocabulary continuous speech decoder for service robots. In: Proceedings of the International Conference on Imaging and Signal Processing for Healthcare and Technology, pp. 150–154 (2012)
14. Lee, A., Kawahara, T.: Recent development of open-source speech recognition engine Julius. In: Proceedings of the APSIPA, pp. 131–137 (2009)
15. Rybach, D., Gollan, C., Heigold, G., Hoffmeister, B., Loof, J., Schluter, R., Ney, H.: The RWTH Aachen university open source speech recognition system. In: Proceedings of the International Conference of Speech Communication Association, pp. 2111–2114 (2009)
16. Young, S., Russell, N., Thornton, J.: Token passing: A simple conceptual model for connected speech recognition systems. Tech. Rep. (1989)
17. Young, S., Evermann, G., Gales, M., Hain, T., Kershaw, D., Liu, X.A., Moore, G., Odell, J., Ollason, D., Povey, D., Valtchev, V., Woodland, P.: The HTK book. Cambridge University (2009)

Effects of Different Robot Interaction Strategies During Cognitive Tasks

Sebastian Schneider, Ingmar Berger, Nina Riether,
Sebastian Wrede, and Britta Wrede

Research Institute for Cognition and Robotics (CoR-Lab),
Bielefeld University, 33615 Bielefeld, Germany
{sebschne,iberger,nriether,swrede,bwrede}@techfak.uni-bielefeld.de

Abstract. A growing field in Human-Robot Interaction aims at social assistance for users on specific tasks. These applications allow for insights regarding the acceptance of the robot's presence and interaction-related performance effects. We present a scenario in which a socially assistive robot assists users on a cognitive task. Furthermore, we quantitatively evaluate the effects of two distinct interaction strategies on performance of the user and acceptance of the robot's presence. In one strategy, the robot acts as a structuring guide and in the other, the robot tries to individually enhance the performance of the user. Results show that users benefit from a suited interaction strategy in terms of test performance and that the robot's presence is regarded as acceptable and also desirable.

1 Introduction

Nowadays, socially assistive robots (SAR) are already supporting humans in health, educational or therapeutic domains [3,5,6,4]. Human-Robot Interaction for these tasks is focused on individual and adaptive communication between the user and the system. The requirements for these scenarios are particularly demanding regarding the interaction capabilities of the robot. The goals in these tasks are usually reached through purely humanlike modalities (e.g. verbal/nonverbal feedback, social cues). Hence, several elementary research questions have to be considered when designing an interaction strategy aiming at supporting humans on assistive tasks: Does the robot's presence appear appropriate for the user? Does the user follow the instructions of the robot? Which effects do different interaction strategies have on the user's task performance? These questions are also relevant in order to evaluate the acceptance of assistive robots and their objective benefit.

In our work, we want to concentrate on the effects different interaction strategies have on the user's task performance. Does a performance based interaction strategy outperform a generic strategy in terms of a performance measure, namely the user's test scores in a cognitive test? Moreover, we want to know how the objective findings relate with subjective measures. Does the perceived capabilities of an assistance system also vary depending on the interaction strategy?

S.S. Ge et al. (Eds.): ICSR 2012, LNAI 7621, pp. 496–505, 2012.

In order to answer these questions, we present a scenario in which an embodied assisting system helps users performing a cognitive test. This test offers measuring quantitative effects of task performance induced by different interaction strategies of an assisting system.

By analyzing objective and subjective results of the generic interaction strategy, the assistive capabilities of our system were improved for the performance based interaction strategy. Our hypothesis is that a performance based interaction strategy should help the users to increase their performance compared to the generic strategy. Moreover, while designing systems which are meant to assist users during some kind of task execution, it is reasonable to question if the system becomes more annoying with increasing assistance. Hence for the user satisfaction, positive quantitative effects (e.g. task performance) should also be expressed in the subjective perception of the assisting system by the user.

The next section gives an overview on related work investigating assistive robot systems. Section 3 introduces the scenario we used as test bed for our evaluation. Section 4 specifies the interaction capabilities of our assistive system and the different interaction strategies we have evaluated. Section 5 presents our evaluation methods and the results. Finally, Section 6 discusses our results and the last section gives a conclusion.

2   Related Work

Several studies investigated effects of SARs on specific measures. The impact of positive and negative social feedback on user's energy consumption behavior has been studied in [6]. The goal was to induce users to save energy when using a washing machine. To influences users, a social robot (iCat[1]) gave positive and negative feedback in terms of corresponding facial expressions. Results showed that people were sensitive to social feedback, which led to a reduction of energy. Moreover, negative social feedback had the strongest influence on behavior change.

Further effects of positive, negative and neutral feedback on robots' acceptance in a classroom environment have been studied in [9]. Participants were more attracted towards the instructor when they received positive feedback. However, no connection between results in a quiz game and the type of feedback given were reported.

Explicit motivation and induced enhancement of task performance using SARs on a cognitive task have been studied in [2]. Three different interaction conditions were evaluated: A baseline condition in which the robot served as a game instructor and evaluator, a praise condition in which explicit verbal feedback according to task performance was given, and a challenge condition where the system changed the difficulty of the test to challenge participants and increase enjoyment. Task enjoyment was highest in the challenging condition and the task was perceived less frustrating compared to the other conditions. Furthermore, participants felt motivated by the robot and reported the most enjoyment in

---

[1] http://www.hitech-projects.com/icat/

the condition where they performed best. However, these results lack statistical significance.

These works address important aspects of assistive social robots that were also used in the current study. They highlight the effects of different feedback types or different robot interaction strategies. Nonetheless, some works lack statistical significance and quantifiable measurement tools to verify the results and performances of the systems. Hence, we developed a new scenario to objectively quantify the performance of an assistive robotic system, as well as the subjective acceptance of the robot in a cognitive task. Moreover, we want to evaluate how the assistance is perceived during a difficult tasks. Therefore, we extended an existing cognitive task to challenge the users, which is described in the following section.

3 Scenario

Our scenario is motivated by the requirement to use an objective criterion (e.g. the participant's performance on a specific task) in order to evaluate the effects of an assisting robotic system on task performance. Hence, it is necessary that users can be adequately assisted in terms of their individual performance and that the system has real-time information about the task performance and task processing to build features and classify the performance of the user.

3.1 Task

For our study we choose the mental rotations test by Peters et al. [10], because it fullfills the above mentioned requirements. The cognitive test examines the ability to mentally rotate three-dimensional objects. We used three different versions, and each version consists of two sets with 12 different items each. Thus, the users completed 72 items in total in our scenario.

Every item consists of one target and four possible answers (comp. Fig. 1(a)). Two of them are rotations of the target, two are distracters. An item is correctly answered if both correct rotations are marked. The mental rotations test thus provides a quantitative measure in terms of test scores and task processing (e.g. how fast do users answer the question, how often they change their mind) thereby allowing an evaluation of the effects of the robot's assistive behavior.

3.2 Implementation

Participants in the original mental rotation test have three minutes per set of a test version and a four minute break in between. Because we wanted to evaluate the effects of the robot presence during a difficult task participants now had to accomplish all three test versions consecutively with three minutes processing time but only a one minute break in between. The test was running as a standalone application controlled via touch screen. The modified experiment flow began with a practice phase consisting of six items, where participants got

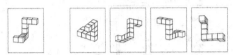

(a) Stimulus on the left is the target, on the right four possible solutions are presented, with stimuli 1 and 3 being correct rotations of the target.

(b) Study setup including the robot Nao, the participant and the computer.

Fig. 1. Left: Sample item of the cognitive test. Right: Picture of the study setup.

acquainted with the test procedure. Then, the actual test started. It ran fully autonomously, while both performance and process data (e.g. answering behavior, solution time for a problem set) were collected.

The humanoid robot Nao developed by Aldebaran Robotics[2] was used. Nao has a full articulated body with 25 degrees of freedom, an internal face detection and a text-to-speech system. The participants were sitting in front of the screen with the robot standing left of it (see Fig. 1(b)).

In order not to distract the user during task execution, the interaction phases were limited to the breaks in between two test blocks. Besides the breaks, interaction took place after the practice phase in the introduction of the experiment.

4   Interaction Strategies

As mentioned in the introduction, our hypothesis is that a performance based interaction strategy should have a positive impact on users' task performance, compared to a structuring interaction strategy. Therefore, two distinct interaction strategies were developed. A general one, which served as baseline, and an improved one, which was supporting the subjects based on their task processing in order to enhance users' performance. In the following, both strategies will be explained in detail.

4.1   Structuring Interaction Strategy

In the structuring condition, Nao functions as experimenter guiding the participants through the session. Besides that, Nao offers support by tracking the time (e.g. announcing the last minute) and giving generic feedback, information and advice during the breaks like "you're doing well", "you're half way through it" or "try to relax". Figure 2 shows the detailed robot behavior.

---

[2] www.aldebaran-robotics.com/

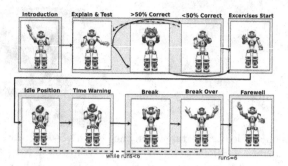

Fig. 2. Robot's structuring baseline behavior

4.2   Performance Based Interaction Strategy

In this condition, the interaction is suited to the participants task processing and performance (in the following referred to as performance based condition). The data from the structuring interaction strategy showed that subjects with low test scores reported a significantly higher wish for assistance than those who had higher test scores ($r = -.484$, $p = .036$). Further analysis showed that these two groups also differ concerning their task processing (e.g. frequency of changes in their decisions, average processing time per item). Hence, the performance of a user on each test set was compared to the computed median of the same set of the preceding study and the user's previous set results. If the performance was greater, the robot provided a positive feedback during the breaks, otherwise the participants received an individual feedback based on their task processing (e.g. "your average answering time is too long/ short"). The decision about the specific feedback was given by a rule-based classifier, which analyzed the task processing of each test set. It was trained based on the dataset of the previous study. The same feedback regarding one feature of the task processing was only given twice in a row if the user had not improved in the succeeding set.

Moreover, the overall behavior has been extended by a speech recognition system to enable the robot to inquire whether everything was understood or should be repeated after explaining the test procedure. Besides these two points, the robot's behavior was equal to that of the baseline strategy.

5   Evaluation

5.1   Study Design and Procedure

For each interaction strategy we conducted an evaluation study. 20 persons (10 male) with a mean age of 23.10 (SD=0.93) years participated in the structuring condition, 19 persons (11 male) with mean age of 24 years (SD=2.21) in the performance based condition. In both conditions participants received chocolate bars for their efforts. The experiment took place in a lab at Bielefeld University. Experiments were recorded using video cameras in the room. Afterwards participants filled out a survey.

All participants were introduced to the robot and the test setup including the cameras. Afterwards, they were only told that they have to do a cognitive test and that the robot will give them further instructions. The experimenter started the test and left the room.

5.2   Subjective Measure

Our survey covered several different aspects. First of all, we assessed the user's general opinion towards robots using the *Robot Anxiety Scale* (RAS) [7] and the *Negative Attitudes towards Robots Scale* (NARS) [8]. This was needed for an unbiased evaluation of our results, since the two groups should not differ in their attitudes towards robots. Moreover, we evaluated how the participants experienced the cognitive task. Also attached were questions regarding the acceptance of presence, the wish for future assistance as well as the Godspeed questionnaire (anthropomorphism, animacy, likeability, perceived intelligence, and perceived safety of robots) [1]. The survey answers were mapped on 7-point Likert-scales(1:"strongly disagree", 7:"strongly agree").

5.3   Results

The study data was analyzed by means of t-tests and correlation analysis in order to investigate differences between the two interaction groups and relationships between objective and subjective data. Descriptive values are presented as mean (M) and standard deviation (SD)

Task Rating and Attitudes towards Robots. The aggregated rating of task difficulty did not differ significantly between the conditions (task difficulty: structuring condition: $M = 3.24$, $SD = 0.92$, $p > 0.5$; performance condition: $M = 3.47$, $SD = 1.145$, $p > 0.5$). Also the NARS ratings did not differ significantly between the groups (structuring condition: $M = 4.08$, $SD = 1.12$; performance based: $M = 3.64$, $SD = 0.91$) as well as the RAS ratings (structuring condition: $M = 3.11$, $SD = 1.12$; performance based: $M = 2.95$, $SD = 1.41$). Hence, both of our samples showed the same characteristics, which allows an unbiased comparison between the two conditions.

Quantitative Measure. Our main research question was to examine the effect of different interaction strategies on the users' task performance. Hence, we compared the users' task results between the two groups. The comparison shows that the participants in the performance based condition had significantly better test scores in the first test version ($t(34) = 1.70, p < .05$) and also better test results in the last test set ($t(34) = 1.81, p < .05$, see Fig. 3.). Figure 3(a) shows the results for each test set and Figure 3(b) shows the aggregated values for the test versions (note that one test version comprises two sets).

First of all, these results confirm our research question that differing interaction strategies can have an impact on the user's task performance. Moreover, it confirms our first hypothesis, that users can benefit from a performance based

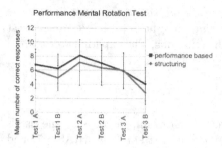
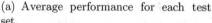

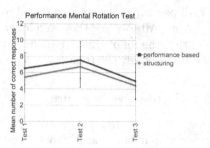

(a) Average performance for each test set.

(b) Average performance for each test version.

Fig. 3. Average test score for the mental rotation test. Overall, the test scores are increasing at first due to adaptive effects. Afterwards the results are decreasing again due to cognitive load.

interaction strategy in terms of an increasing performance. Nevertheless, the test scores also decreased over time in the performance based condition due to the high cognitive load the participants were exposed. Still, there is a significant difference between the two groups on the very last test set showing that despite the overall decrease of performance at the end, the performance based interaction strategy led to significantly better performance.

Robot Perception. Moreover, we were interested if different interaction strategies also had an impact on the perceived assisting capabilities of our system. Hence, we compared the perception of the robot between the groups. The t-test revealed significant differences between the two conditions. Participants in the performance based condition felt significantly more evaluated by the presence of the robot than in the structuring condition ($t(34) = 3.26, p < .05$). Also the participants rated the robot as more competent than in the structuring condition ($t(34) = 1.79, p < .05$) and as more motivating ($t(34) = 1.88, p < .05$).

These significant differences are also supported by the correlation analysis. Regarding the first condition, there were no significant correlations between the task and the robot perception. Nevertheless, in the second condition we found correlations supporting the already obtained significant differences between the study groups. The robot was perceived as more motivating and the presence as appropriate, when the task was perceived as exhausting ($r = .494$, $p = .037$ and $r = .48$, $p = .05$, respectively). Moreover, if the presence was regarding as helpful and motivating the users wanted to use the robot more often in the future ($r = .484$, $p = .042$ and $r = .706$, $p = .001$, respectively).

This observing is also supported by the results obtained from the questions regarding the wish for future assistance. Users in the performance based condition rated that they want to use humanoid robots in difficult tasks frequently more often than users in the structuring condition ($\chi^2(2) = 8.49, p < .05$). These results confirm our second research question, how an assistive system with increased assisting capabilities will be perceived by the user. Our findings show

Table 1. Robot perception and test scores - Mean (M) and standard deviation (SD) for the structuring and performance based condition

	structuring		performance based	
	M	SD	M	SD
MRT Ver. 1 comp.	5.41	1.85	6.5	1.96
MRT Ver. 3 2nd set	2.83	1.61	4.05	2.36
Robot motivating	3.94	1.66	4.88	1.32
Robot competent	3.94	1.30	4.77	1.47
Robot evaluating	2.44	1.50	4.16	1.65

that enhanced user performance induced by the assistive system is also reflected in the subjective impressions of the system. In addition, the results show also that the users actually want to use it more often and experience it as more motivating and helpful.

6   Discussion

The subjective results and the correlation analysis reveal that the performance based interaction strategy can help to improve performance on difficult cognitive tasks. Participants reported higher feelings of comfort and motivation in the presence of the robot. Adding the fact that a robot, which gives individual performance advice is rated with significantly higher competence, shows that the users appreciate the feedback from the system and profit from feedback during difficult tasks.

Regarding the quantitative results, our studies show that a robotic system that is assisting the users based on their particular needs has positive effects on the human's task performance compared to a robot that is assisting the user in terms of a general guide.

Moreover, compared to preceding studies we found statistically significant evidence for the performance effects of an assistance system and an increase in task performance on a difficult cognitive test. Nevertheless, the test scores also decreased over time in the performance based condition due to the high cognitive load the participants were exposed.

Further interesting is the fact, that the system has an immediate effect on the user. They don't have to learn how to use the system and the system doesn't have to adapt to the user over several sessions. The effects are statistically measurable out-of-the-box, which is especially interesting because the task was cognitively quite challenging for the users. Thus, it is of particular interest that this external system managed to improve the users' performance despite of the possibility of treatment ceiling effects due to the high effort the task itself already demands from the participants. The fact that the system was analyzing the users' behavior and adequately supporting them in real-time makes the application especially satisfying.

6.1 Future Work

Our scenario was regarded as difficult by the participants. Nevertheless, we have to further quantify the perceived individual stress and difficulty in order to qualify the assistance during these and other stressful and cognitively demanding tasks.

In order to confirm that the robot has motivational effects, it is necessary to employ a control group in a follow-up study, that is, a condition without a robot assisting the user. To this end, we hypothesize significantly weaker performance and decreased levels of motivation (in terms of task pleasantness) in comparison to the conditions presented here. Moreover, a long term interaction scenario should evaluate whether the motivational effects are temporary or outlasting. Furthermore, such a long term scenario could be advanced with more social interactions by the system and a concrete learning curve for the individual user.

We presented a quite hard task for the user, hence one could question how the robot performs while assisting on very easy tasks. Past research shows that that mere presence of a robot during easy tasks may facilitate performance [11]. Nevertheless, it might be possible that concrete assistance by the robot could invert the effects, because there is no need for further interaction and an interaction could be rather distracting or annoying for the user. Therefore, we should further explore effects of our interaction with regard to easy tasks.

Regarding the NARS and RAS measures, these scales aiming specifically at negative attitudes and anxieties and the questions might already imply a negative feeling towards robots. Hence, a scale measuring general attitudes towards robots would be useful.

We just compared two conditions, one where the robot gave generic feedback and one where the user received individual feedback. The individual feedback consisted of both positive and negative feedback. Hence, we can not measure which feedback has the strongest influence on the user. Therefore in a following study, both types of feedback have to be explicitly evaluated, to understand the underlying mechanisms of feedback an assistance system can give during difficult tasks.

7 Conclusion

Concluding, our work presents a scenario for an evaluation of a robotic system, which assists on cognitive tasks. Moreover, we presented an evaluable quantitative measure for a robot's interaction behavior using a psychological measure for cognitive performance. We showed that a) users can profit from a performance based interaction strategy, b) an individually interacting robot is perceived as more motivating, c) the presence of an individually interacting robot is accepted even during difficult tasks and d) that users accept a robot when it is showing a performance oriented interaction behavior and tend to use it more often.

In order to be able to develop a generic model for robot assistance, which can be adopted and applied across different scenarios, we have to further investigate and study the usage and effects of assistive robotic systems in various domains and purposes especially under a long term view point.

Acknowledgment. This work is supported by the German Aerospace Center (support code 50RA1023) with funds from the Federal Ministry of Economics and Technology due to resolution of the German Bundestag.

References

1. Bartneck, C., Kulić, D., Croft, E., Zoghbi, S.: Measurement instruments for the anthropomorphism, animacy, likeability, perceived intelligence, and perceived safety of robots. International Journal of Social Robotics 1(1), 71–81 (2008)
2. Fasola, J., Matarić, M.J.: Robot motivator: Increasing user enjoyment and performance on a physical/cognitive task. In: International Conference on Development and Learning, Ann Arbor, MI (August 2010)
3. Feil-seifer, D., Matarić, M.J.: Defining socially assistive robotics. In: Proc. IEEE International Conference on Rehabilitation Robotics (ICORR 2005), pp. 465–468 (2005)
4. Kidd, C.D.: A sociable robot to encourage social interaction among the elderly. In: International Conference on Robotics and Automation (2006)
5. Breazeal, C., Kidd, C.: Robots at home: Understanding long-term human-robot interaction (2008)
6. Midden, C., Ham, J.: Using negative and positive social feedback from a robotic agent to save energy. In: Proceedings of the 4th International Conference on Persuasive Technology, Persuasive 2009, pp. 12:1–12:6. ACM, New York (2009)
7. Nomura, T., Kanda, T., Suzuki, T., Kato, K.: Prediction of human behavior in human–robot interaction using psychological scales for anxiety and negative attitudes toward robots. IEEE Transactions on Robotics 24(2), 442–451 (2008)
8. Nomura, T., Suzuki, T., Kanda, T., Kato, K.: Altered attitudes of people toward robots: Investigation through the negative attitudes toward robots scale (2006)
9. Park, E., Kim, K.J., del Pobil, A.P.: The Effects of a Robot Instructor's Positive vs. Negative Feedbacks on Attraction and Acceptance towards the Robot in Classroom. In: Mutlu, B., Bartneck, C., Ham, J., Evers, V., Kanda, T. (eds.) ICSR 2011. LNCS, vol. 7072, pp. 135–141. Springer, Heidelberg (2011)
10. Peters, M., et al.: Brain and cognition, vol. 28, pp. 39–58 (1995)
11. Riether, N., Hegel, F., Wrede, B., Horstmann, G.: Social facilitation with social robots? In: International Conference on Human Robot Interaction, HRI 2012 (2012)

A Multi-path Selecting Navigation Framework with Human Supervision

Peng Liu, Guangming Xiong, Haojie Zhang, Yan Jiang,
Jianwei Gong, and Huiyan Chen

School of Mechanical Engineering,
Beijing Institute of Technology, Beijing 100081, China
liupbit@gmail.com, xiongguangming@bit.edu.cn

Abstract. Robotic navigation remains one of the fundamental problems of mobile robotics, especially when some uncertain variables need to be considered. The cost function of the path planning algorithm cannot always represent the optimum path of the task completely in some multi-choice environments. In this paper, an interaction framework was designed for multiple path selection, supervised by an operator with an intuitive user interface. An interaction approach based on inquiry message was proposed to release the workload impact on human operator. A path priority function was presented to guarantee the multiple path selection. Simulation and experiments on Pioneer 3 AT robot showed good performance of our multi-path selecting navigation system when the operator's experiential cogitation need to be considered in path selection.

Keywords: multi-path selection, human supervision, path priority, inquiry message.

1   Introduction

Path planning for robots with particular constraints is one of the significant sections in robotic navigation. In addition to finding the optimal path, some alternative paths could also be indispensible in some navigation situations. For example, considering the concealment in reconnaissance task or the flow of people in tourist guide [1], only one path may be insufficient. An alternative path could be of high priority if it adapts the environment better. For this reason, navigation with multi-path selection is necessary that releases the selecting contradiction. Some multi-path planning methods have been proposed in [2, 3, 4], specially, the diversity of paths is concerned in [2]. However, autonomous navigation with multiple paths is still difficult. It's unrealistic to seek a universal cost function for the planner with time constraint. Considering the cogitative load and analysis ability of human operator, a multi-path selecting navigation system with human supervision would be favorable solving this problem. However, interacting with robot remains a significant problem in human-robot interaction. Although tele-operation of the remote robots with continuous supervision could reach a relatively better performance in contrast with the autonomous robots

S.S. Ge et al. (Eds.): ICSR 2012, LNAI 7621, pp. 506–515, 2012.

themselves [5], the burden of high-intensity work limits the development of this kind of operation to a multi-choice system. Many approaches have been presented to solve this problem. Gordon Cheng et al. presented a paradigm for robot control in a human-oriented manner [6]. They discussed a framework to incorporate supervisory control with a high level qualitative approach for the control of robots. By choosing instructions that are easily understood and relatively natural to use, the user can alleviate the operating stress. This kind of paradigm approach worked very well in multi-agent system with simple control and frequent reaction [7, 8]. However, such planners can be brittle and unable to respond to emergent events [9], which is unsuited for multi-path selecting. M. L. Cummings et al. [9] in their work presented a human-in-the-loop experiment which showed that the operator should be responsible for strategic decision making that includes prioritizing which tasks should be performed at the current stage in the mission. They also depicted the role allocation balance between the human and automation, shown in figure 1, in their OPS-USERS system architecture. In this paper, we also used this task classification as a guide for the design of our operator interface.

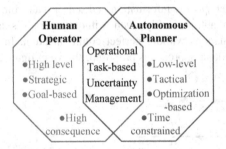

Fig. 1. Role allocation balance between the human operator and autonomous planner

Besides, several other approaches, such as *control-by-behavior* paradigm approach, *control-by-policy* approach, *control-by-playbook* approach and *proxy agents* approach, were also proposed [10, 11, 12, 13, 14, 15]. The main idea of the *proxy agents* approach was the transfer-of-control strategy which was involved to coordinate problems that the operator can solve better than an agent. The operators were called by the system when it detected a coordination problem that it cannot solve. Moreover, this architecture defined strategies to guarantee the system performance when an operator's action is required by the robot but the operator fails to respond fast enough. In this paper, we focused on the multi-path selecting method in a navigation task with human supervision and the interaction approach between the operator and the individual robot. Detailed in the task interaction of multi-choice navigation between the individual agent and the human operator, we hope to find a proper multi-path selecting module and efficient interacting method to improve the performance of the human-supervised multi-choice navigation system without extra workload on the operator.

The rest of this paper is organized as follows. In section 2, we describe the design of our system from the perspective of hierarchical autonomous level and show the details of our system architecture. In section 3, we present the inquiry-message approach in our multi-path selecting navigation system and propose the compensate path priority function used in multi-path selection. The result of the system is presented in section 4, followed by the conclusion section, section 5.

2   System Design

In order to achieve multiple path selection with a human operator, an efficient navigation system is necessary. We will first describe the design of our multi-path selecting navigation system architecture considering the hierarchical levels and planning constraints of the multi-choice paths, and then show how the operator interface is built.

2.1   Hierarchical Architecture for Multiple Path Selection

The architecture of the navigation system is designed with the idea to introduce human operator into the task management while still retaining the autonomous ability of the robot. The robot can get specific information and sensor data from the environment, and generate optimal path autonomously even without operator's instructions, which is important in some situations without perfect communication. In order to achieve this goal, a hierarchical modular approach is proposed, shown in figure 2(a).

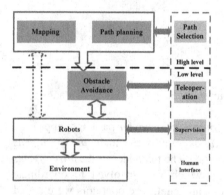
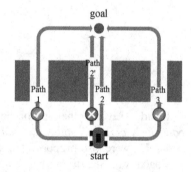

(a) navigation system architecture   (b) multi-path choices considering homotopy
class

Fig. 2.

In this architecture, the interaction tasks are divided into two levels. The high level interactions include path selection module, path planning part and mapping part. Path planning module set on the on-board laptop computer is used to generate alternative paths, and then interacts with the path selection part in the human interface. The mapping part is mainly used for map construction in a new environment. The low level control tasks include tele-operation and supervision, which makes it more convenient to get the status of the robot and provide motion-control aids when the robot needs help.

2.2   Path Planning with Constraints

The path planner of a navigation system mainly provides only one optimal path based on its cost function. In our multi-path selection system, alternative paths are also indispensible before the operator's selection. Moreover, alternative paths should have different path status, like shown in figure 2(b), path1 and path3 should be generated beside the optimal path2 while the homotopical path   (*path2'*) should be excluded in multi-path planning. To generate different paths meeting the constraint requirements in a particular map, a path planning algorithm with homotopy class constraints [16] is introduced in our navigation module. Considering the homotopy class constraints of the paths, we could search the discrete graph map of the environment with graph search algorithm such as A*. The algorithm calculates L value of the paths to judge whether they are same homotopy class or not (see [16] for in-depth mathematical treatment). The least-cost paths in different homotopy classes can be obtained by setting different L value for the goal state.   The multiple path generation is the basic part for a robot to compute its status and then generate an interacting message to the operator when the robot is running with a human operator.

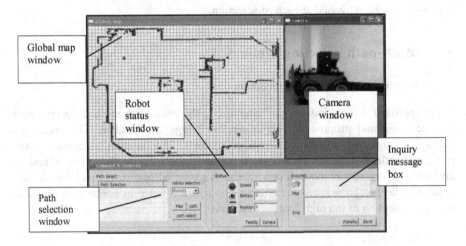

Fig. 3. Human interface of the multiple path selection navigation system

2.3   Operator Interface

A graphic operation interface is efficient and useful in human-robot interaction. To make sure that an untrained operator can efficiently manage a path selection, an interface displayed proper information while adding little work load is needed. A query to either the human or the robots is expected to elicit a response [17]. Figure 3 presents a snapshot of the interface designed for path selection. The operator interface is designed with multiple levels of control. The *global map* window displays the global map got by manual mapping using Simultaneous Localization and Mapping (SLAM), the paths generated by the onboard computer, and the current position of the agent. The *global map* window gives an intuitive view of the current system status to the operator during the interaction. Operator can choose interested positions by clicking the relative grid shown in the window. The *camera* window is designed for the operator to get the surrounding visual information of the agent, which is useful for tele-operation when the robot is stuck. The *command & inquiry* window consists of three parts: *path selection* part, the *status* part and the *inquiry* message interaction box. *Path selection* part shows the available path list in the list widget during each path planning. The optimal path generated by path planning model is selected as default if the selecting interaction time (set in the program to ensure the agents could run autonomously when the operator is busy) is run out or the operator has no choice. While the vast amount of sensor data is important, the main goal of the *status* part is to provide concise and intuitive information as reference when the operator wants to make a path-selection decision. The *inquiries* part provides an interacting message box between the robot and the operator. The operator can send commands to inquiry the agents' detail status and consult with the agents during path-selecting decision. Although the optimal path of the current global map is of high priority, the operator can select a preferred path when the robot detected more than one path at a time and returned a path list with a message signal illuminated in the operator interface. The path selected by the operator from the path list widget is then displayed on the *global map* window and refreshed at each re-selection.

3   Multi-path Selecting Method

3.1   Inquiry Approach for Interaction

In our approach, we particularly pay attention to the interaction method during multi-path selecting and propose an active message trigger mechanism. The predefined inquiry message instructions are shown in figure 4. The instructions consist of two parts: instructions from the operator to robot and from robot to the operator, and are divided into two autonomous levels (the strategy-based high level and the motion-based low level). To achieve better interaction performance in constrained time, we put more attention to the high level instructions.

Control levels	Operator ⇒ robots	Robots ⇒ operator
High-levels	•Health status(*return the current status*) •How are you?(*situation of task execution*) •Can you reach that position? •Path priority (*call for the path priority value*)	•Could you help me? •My power is low; do I have to go this way? •More than one path was detected. •This path would cost more consumption. *path priority:* $\Psi(u)$. •The default path was selected. *path priority:* *1.00* •I cannot reach the goal from that path, please choose another one. *Path priority:0*
Low-levels	•Tele-operation(*the operator take over the motion control*)	•I am stuck.(*fall into an unrecoverable state*)

Fig. 4. Instructions used in human-robot interaction

3.2   Compensate Path Priority Function for Path Evaluation

During path selecting process, the operator may select the preferred paths based on his or her subjective and experiential information. The path selection is achieved based on the priority value of each path and the robot executed a selected path only when the path has a higher priority than that of the default path (in our framework, the default path has a constant path priority value 1).

The multi-path selecting method is developed based on the assumption that (1) the operator has realized that the preferred path may cause more consumption, but the analysis based on information from other robots or operators lead to his or her alternative path selection; (2) the operator may find multiple routes meet his or her requirement; (3) the operator cannot calculate the consumption of the selected paths with time constraint. So the priority function should achieve the following two goals: (1) the selected path should have a higher priority than the default path; (2) among available path choices that meet the operator's requirement, only the path with least consumption can be executed by the robot. In order to evaluate the paths selected by the operator and give a quantitative distinction between different paths, a path priority function was presented based on path consumption.

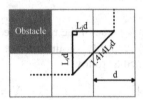

Fig. 5. Cost function of an eight-connected grid with resolution d

For a given grid map, shown in figure 5, a discrete path cost function could be obtained as follows:

$$c(s_i, s_{i+1}) = \begin{cases} L_i d & x_i = x_{i+1} \text{ or } y_i = y_{i+1} \\ 1.414 L_i d & \text{otherwise} \end{cases} \tag{1}$$

Where L_i and $c(s_i, s_{i+1})$ is the mean cost(power consumption) value of the robot and the cost function between two adjacent grids s_i and s_{i+1}, respectively. Then,

$$N(u) = \sum_{i=0}^{n} c(s_i, s_{i+1}). \tag{2}$$

Where $N(u)$ is the cost function of path u. Thus,

$$N^* = \sum_{i=0}^{n^*} c(s_i, s_{i+1}), N_s = \sum_{j=0}^{n_s} c(s_j, s_{j+1}). \tag{3}$$

Where N^* and N_s is the cost of the default path (with the least cost value in our algorithm) and operator-selected path (path u_s) respectively. Define $\beta = \Delta N/N^*$ as the coefficient of extra consumption, where $\Delta N = N_s - N^*$, then

$$\beta = \frac{\Delta N}{N^*} = \frac{N_s - N^*}{N^*} = \frac{\sum_{j=0}^{n_s} c(s_j, s_{j+1}) - \sum_{i=0}^{n^*} c(s_i, s_{i+1})}{\sum_{i=0}^{n^*} c(s_i, s_{i+1})}. \tag{4}$$

By introducing β into consideration, we could get a path priority evaluation function of the paths. However, the alternative path chosen by the human operator often has a larger N value than N^*, which demote the path priority of the selected path and hence stem the path selection. Besides, it's also important to set the maximum N value constraint to prevent the robot from being stuck in the halfway because of low power. In order to solve the problem between the extra consumption and a high path priority for the selected paths, a compensate path priority coefficient α is provided in our path priority function,

$$\alpha = \beta_{\max} = \frac{N_{\max} - N^*}{N^*}. \tag{5}$$

Where N_{max} is the maximum N value of the robot based on its power system (in this situation, N_{max} is the battery capacity of the robot). Thus, the *compensate path priority* function could be defined as follows:

$$\psi(u_s) = \begin{cases} 1 & N_s = N^* \\ 1+\alpha-\beta & N_s < N_{\max} \\ 0 & N_s > N_{\max} \end{cases} \tag{6}$$

Where $\psi(u_s)$ is the compensate path priority value of a selected path u_s. The constant priority value 0, which is lower than the priority value of the default path, prevents the paths from being selected that beyond the robot's ability. It can be proved that for an available alternative path, $\psi(u)$ always has a path priority larger than 1. Through the compensate path priority function, the alternative path could be selected because of a higher priority than the default optimal one while avoiding the unavailable paths that beyond the robot's ability. Moreover, the compensate path priority function guarantees that only one path with the least consumption can be executed among the paths selected by the operator when more than one available paths meet the operator's requirement.

4   Experiment Performance

4.1   Multiple Paths Generation and Selection

A simulation map is provided to test the performance of the *compensate path priority* function, shown in figure 6(a) and four paths are generated in this map. Figure 6(b) shows the *compensate path priority* values of the generated paths. In this simulation, the maximum N value N_{max} is set as $2N^*$, which means the robot could reach twice the distance as the default optimal path u^*.

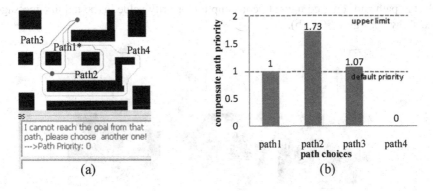

(a)   (b)

Fig. 6. Simulation map and compensate path priority values of the generated paths, path 1 is the default path ($N_{max}=2N^*$)

In this scenario, path4 has an N value beyond the maximum N value of the robot; the human interface returns a warning message when the operator tried to select this path, shown in figure 6(a).

4.2   Navigation with Interaction on Pioneer 3 AT

The experiment was conducted on a HP Compaq nx6320 with a Core 2 processor at 1.86GHz. A Pioneer 3 AT robot was used as the autonomous agent connected with the human interface through a wireless network. A test map was used in our experiment, shown in figure 7(a), (b). In this scenario, the robot got two types of trajectory of which one was the optimal path generated by the path planner with the least consumption.

(a) Test map got by SLAM   (b) the real environment   (c) inquiry message and path choices

Fig. 7. The navigation environment and path selections

The robot saved these trajectories and displayed them in the *global path planning* window of the human interface with a message caution illuminated besides the message box, shown in figure 7(c). The operator interacted with the robot and selected the interested path through the *path selection* window; the robot executed the selected path and returned the path consumption priority value in the inquiry-message box, shown in figure 8(a), (b).

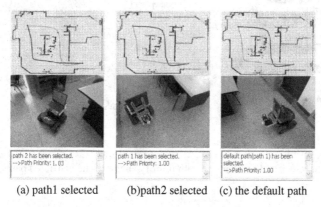

(a) path1 selected (b)path2 selected (c) the default path

Fig. 8. The navigation results with Pioneer 3AT robot

The robot also carried out the default path when the operator failed to respond fast enough, which showed a fluent operation of the whole human-robot interaction system, shown in figure 8(c)(the robot running in the optimum path without operator's interaction instructions).

5   Conclusion

In this paper, a navigation framework integrated with path-selection and human operator interface based on inquiry method was proposed. The multiple paths in different homotopy classes were generated with homotopy class constraint. To achieve augmented navigation with multi-path selecting, the impact of human operator was considered and a compensate path priority function was proposed. A quantitative test based on priority was presented to validate the performance of the proposed framework. Experiments on pioneer 3 AT robot showed efficient performance of our multi-path selecting navigation system. For future work we plan to evaluate the impact of the interacting framework on operator workload, and emphasize the multi-path selecting even more, considering more about human input and allowing for more direct interaction.

References

1. Kim, G., Chun, W.: Navigation Behavior Selection Using Generalized Stochastic Petri Nets for a Service Robot. IEEE Trans. Syst. Man Cybern. Pt C Appl. Rev. 37, 494–503 (2007)

2. Seok, J.-H., Lee, J.-Y.: Diverse Multi-path Planning with a Path-set Costmap. In: 2011 International Conference on Control, Automation and Systems, pp. 694–699. IEEE Press, South Korea (2011)
3. Bell, M.: Hyperstar: A multi-path Astar algorithm for risk averse vehicle navigation. Transp. Res. Part B 43, 97–107 (2009)
4. Chen, Y., Bell, M.: Reliable pretrip multipath planning and dynamic adaptation for a centralized road navigation system. IEEE Trans. Intell. Transp. Syst. 8, 14–20 (2007)
5. Dixon, S.R., Wickens, C.D.: Mission Control of Multiple Unmanned Aerial Vehicles: a Workload Analysis. Hum. Factors 47, 479–487 (2005)
6. Cheng, G., Zelinsky, A.: Supervised Autonomy: A Framework For Human-Robot Systems Development. In: 1999 IEEE International Conference on Systems, Man, and Cybernetics, pp. 971–975. IEEE Press, Tokyo (1999)
7. Zigoris, P., Siu, J.: Balancing Automated Behavior and Human Control in Multi-Agent System: A Case Study in Roboflag. In: Proceedings of the 2003 American Control Conference, pp. 667–671. IEEE Press, Denver (2003)
8. Chamberlain, L., Tang, J.: A Behavioral Architecture for Strategy Execution in the Roboflag Game. In: Proceedings of 2003 American Control Conference, pp. 672–677. IEEE Press, Denver (2003)
9. Cummings, M.L., How, J.P.: The Impact of Human-Automation Collaboration in Decentralized Multiple Unmanned Vehicle Control. Proc. IEEE 100, 660–671 (2012)
10. Coppin, G., Legras, F.: Autonomy Spectrum and Performance Perception Issues in Swarm Supervisory Control. Proc. IEEE 100, 590–603 (2012)
11. Bradshaw, J.M., Feltovich, P.J., Jung, H., Kulkarni, S., Taysom, W., Uszok, A.: Dimensions of Adjustable Autonomy and Mixed-Initiative Interaction. In: Nickles, M., Rovatsos, M., Weiss, G. (eds.) AUTONOMY 2003. LNCS (LNAI), vol. 2969, pp. 17–39. Springer, Heidelberg (2004)
12. Myers, K.L.: Advisable Planning Systems. In: ARPI 1996 Proceedings, pp. 206–209. AAAI Press (1996)
13. Myers, K.L.: Domain Metatheories: Enabling User-Centric Planning. In: Proceedings of Representational Issues for Real-World Planning Systems, pp. 67–72. AAAI Press, Austin (2000)
14. Goldman, R.P., Haigh, K.Z.: MACBeth; A Multi-Agent Constraint-Based Planner. In: Proceedings of Constraints and AI Planning, pp. 11–17. AAAI Press, Austin (2000)
15. Tambe, M.: Teamwork in Real-World, Dynamic Environments. In: Proceedings of ICMAS 1996: 2nd International Conference on Multiagent Systems, pp. 361–368. AAAI Press, Kyoto (1996)
16. Bhattacharya, S., Kumar, V.: Search-Based Path Planning with Homotopy Class Constraints. Proc. Natl Conf. Artif. Intell. 2, 1230–1237 (2010)
17. Fong, T., Grange, S.: Multi-Robot Remote Driving with Collaborative Control. In: Proceedings 10th IEEE International Workshop on Robot and Human Interactive Communication, pp. 237–242. IEEE Press, Bordeaux (2001)

Monocular Visual Odometry and Obstacle Detection System Based on Ground Constraints

Shude Guo and Cai Meng

Image Processing Center, School of Astronautics, BeiHang University,
XueYuan Road No.37, HaiDian District, Beijing, 100191, China
SD_Guo@sa.buaa.edu.cn, tsai@buaa.edu.cn

Abstract. The realization of visual odometry and obstacle detection system with only a single camera is proposed. Though the rotation and translation parameters of frame-to-frame motion can be extracted from essential matrix using SVD decomposition, the absolute scale of the translation cannot be derived from monocular motion estimation. The scale ambiguity problem is solved by applying constraints based on the planar assumption and the known mounting of the camera. A region-based obstacle detection method is proposed in this paper. Firstly, the image is segmented into regions. Then whether a region is on the ground is determined according to three criteria: homography constraint, feature points distribution and boundary points' reconstruction. Practical experimental results show that the proposed method successfully estimate the robot location and find the ground plane with only a single camera.

Keywords: monocular vision, visual odometry, ground constraints, obstacle detection.

1 Introduction

In autonomous navigation of mobile service robots, the capabilities of self-positioning and perceiving external environment are very important. With the development of computer vision technology, vision sensors are increasingly used for the positioning and motion estimation of robots. The rich visual information provided by the vision sensor, not only meets the self-localization requirements for mobile service robots, but also provides information for other important tasks, such as target detection, obstacle avoidance, and path planning.

Visual odometry can estimate the egomotion of robots only from video input. In contrast to other common navigation systems, for instance wheel odometry is affected by wheel slip, and GPS is affected by GPS signal dropouts, visual odometry can effectively compensate these shortcomings and provides accurate trajectory estimatation with relative position accuracy of 0.1-2%[1]. Visual odometry has gained more attention because of its advantages and application prospects. Visual odometry has made great progress over last decade [3-6]. Visual odometry has been successfully used for Mars rovers [2]. Nister et al.[3] designed a real-time visual odometry with both monocular and stereo vision, and it achieved better

S.S. Ge et al. (Eds.): ICSR 2012, LNAI 7621, pp. 516–525, 2012.
© Springer-Verlag Berlin Heidelberg 2012

performance. Due to the observation that stereo visual odometry can degenerate to the monocular case when the distance to the scene is much larger than the stereo baseline [1], the research on monocular methods becomes more and more popular [4–6].

Obstacle detection is essential for mobile robot navigation. Nowadays monocular vision used for obstacle detection has drawn considerable attention due to its advantages. Different from range-finder and ultrasonic sensors, vision sensors belong to passive measurements and provide much more abundant information. Among stereo vision and monocular vision approaches, monocular vision system do not require special camera configuration, and it is more simple and low-cost. Various approaches have been proposed to detect obstacle or ground region. Some approaches operate on a single image and need priory knowledge of the scene or obstacles. For example, features such as color information, edges [7] are used to identify ground area or obstacles. However, these approaches can only apply to some specific environment. Recently, approaches using planar property of the scene to ground detection become more popular [8–10]. The homography constraint between two images is used as a criterion for ground detection. It is more robust than using only appearance information, but the small changes of homography matrix may make ground detection unreliable.

In this paper, we proposed an approach for mobile robots navigation using only a single camera. The main task contains two parts: monocular visual odometry and obstacle detection. The rest of this paper is organized as follows. Section 2 presents the constraints and the architecture of the method. Section 3 describes the monocular visual odometry algorithm. The proposed ground detection algorithm is described in section 4. Experimental results are given in section 5. The contribution and future work are summarized in section 6.

2   Constraints and Architecture

In wheeled robots applications, it is feasible to assume that the road is flat in the indoor or urban environments. Furthermore, the position and orientation of the camera is often fixed relative to the ground plane. Additionally, all obstacles are above the ground surface under the assumption of planar ground, and it is used for selecting the features on the ground. Fig. 1 illustrates the planar assumption and the mountion of the camera.

Fig. 2 demonstrates the pipline of the proposed algorithm. After the preprocessing of image captured by the camera, the monocular odometry and ground plane detection program will be launched simultaneously. In the monocular visual odometry phase, feature points and their correspondences are retrieved first from two adjacent frames. Then the RANSAC method is used to reject outliers. The relative pose between two frames can be extracted from monocular motion estimation, but it is suffered from scale ambiguity. In scale estimation step, the scale is calculated under the constraints of assumptions. The pose of the robot can be derived by accumulating the relative pose and scale. Meanwhile, the images are segmented into several regions, then each region can be classified into

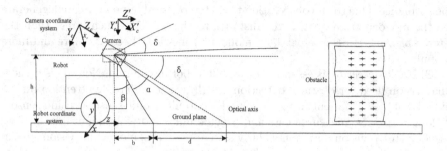

Fig. 1. Technical setup

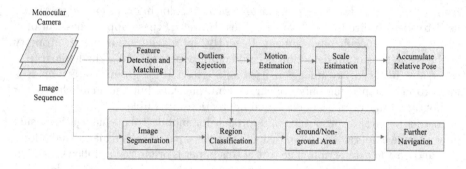

Fig. 2. The architecture of the proposed algorithm

ground or off-ground region by using the criteria mentioned above. After the ground and obstacle areas are separated from each other, the separation results can be used for further visual navigation of mobile robots.

3   Monocular Visual Odometry

3.1   Feature Detection and Matching

During the visual odometry stage, the first step is to detect and match image features in two frames. Scaramuzza et al. [5] compared the trajectories recovered using Harris, SIFT and KLT features, and presented that the best results were obtained by using KLT features. In our monocular visual odometry, we using KLT approach implemented in OpenCV. First, the Shi-Tomasi corners are extracted from the current frame. When another image is acquired from the camera, Lukas-Kanade optical flow is used to find the corners' movement using a local searching technique. Then we get image correspondences of two images.

3.2   Outliers Rejection

The image correspondences obtained by KLT method may be wrong due to the effects of image noise, blur and the moving objects. The outliers will affect the accuracy of motion estimation. In order to reject outliers, we increase epipolar constraints on image correspondences. The RANSAC algorithm is applied to estimate fundamental matrix and the outliers are not consistent with the estimate. Thus the outliers are rejected by epipolar constraints.

3.3   Motion Estimation

The epipolar constraint is illustrated in Fig.3, where a 3D point X is viewed from two cameras and its correspondence image point pairs is $m \leftrightarrow m'$. The two camera coordinates frames are related via a rotation R and a translation t. If the camera matrixes K, K' are known, then we may apply its inverse to the points to obtain the points $m_n = K^{-1}m, m'_n = K'^{-1}m'$, where m_n, m'_n are the image points expressed in normalized coordinates. The epipolar constraint corresponding to the pair normalized coordinates is,

$$m'^T_n [t]_\times R m_n = 0 \tag{1}$$

The matrix $E = [t]_\times R$ is called essential matrix, and the relationship between the fundamental and essential matrices is shown as follows,

$$E = K'^T F K \tag{2}$$

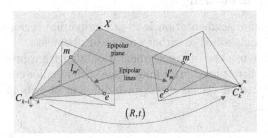

Fig. 3. An illustration of the epipolar constraint

The essential matrix E can be computed from the fundamental matrix F by Eq.2, where the fundamental matrix F has computed before.

Suppose that the SVD of E is $E = USV^T, S = \{s, s, 0\}$. Due to the sign of E, and the consequently t, there are four possible choices for (R, t)[11]:

$$(UZV^T, u_3), (UZV^T, -u_3), (UZ^TV^T, u_3), (UZ^TV^T, -u_3) \tag{3}$$

Where $Z = \begin{bmatrix} 0 & 1 & 0 \\ -1 & 0 & 0 \\ 0 & 0 & 1 \end{bmatrix}$, u_3 is the last column of U .

The correct solution can be chosen by triangulation of a point where the point is in front of both cameras (see Fig.3).

3.4 Scale Estimation

Compared with stereo vision, monocular vision is more simple and cheaper, but the disadvantage is that the motion can only be recovered up to a scale factor. The main task in this section is to recover the scale with the constraints of the camera mounting parameters and ground planar assumption.

The basic idea of our scale estimation approach is that, while the camera frame $X_cY_cZ_c$ is rotated about X_c-axis to the camera frame $X_c'Y_c'Z_c'$ whose optical axis is parallel to ground plane, the coordinate Y_c' of ground points in frame respect the height of the camera mounting. As shown in Fig.1, the blue parts represent the camera coordinate frame after rotation. With the camera mounting parameters and the ground points' coordinates in the rotated camera frame, the scale σ can be calculated,

$$\sigma = h/Y_c' \tag{4}$$

Where h is the height of camera mounting and Y_c' represents the coordinate of the ground points in coordinate frame.

4   Ground Area Detection

4.1   Region Segmentation

The purpose of region segmentation is to get individual regions, and then each individual region is classified as either ground or obstacle.

In this paper, we use the image segmentation algorithm proposed by Felzenszwalb et al [12]. It is not need prior knowledge such as color cue and the number of regions. Also it can effectively distinguish different objects in indoor and outdoor scenes.

4.2   Ground Area Identification

After the region segmentation, the next step is to determine which area each individual region belongs to. Different judging criteria, including homography constraint, feature points distribution and boundary points' reconstruction, are adopted to detect ground plane and obstacles.

(1) Homography Constraint

The vanishing line of the ground plane is the images of ground points at infinity in front of cameras (see Fig.4). If much of a region is above the vanishing line of the ground plane, the region belongs to obstacle area. The general location of the vanishing line can be determined by the homography matrix between the ground plane and the image. Suppose it is chosen that the xy-plane corresponds

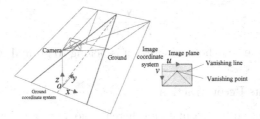

Fig. 4. The relationship between the ground coordinate and image coordinate

to the ground plane, so that points on the ground plane have zero z-coordinate as shown Fig.4. Then the image of a point on the ground plane is given by,

$$m = PX = (p_1, p_2, p_3, p_4) \begin{pmatrix} x \\ y \\ 0 \\ 1 \end{pmatrix} = (p_1, p_2, p_4) \begin{pmatrix} x \\ y \\ 1 \end{pmatrix} \qquad (5)$$

So that the map between points $X = (x, y, 1)^T$ and their image m is a planar homography: $m = HX$. The homography matrix is a homogeneous 3×3 matrix, and hence has 8 degrees of freedom. It can be computed from four point correspondences, with no three collinear on either plane.

Suppose H is known, the image of ground points can be computed using H. If the ground points is at infinity, the position of vanishing points can be computed by $m = HX$, $X = (x, \infty, 1)^T$, and thus the general location of the vanishing line is determined from the vanishing points.

Now we determine whether the region is above the ground. If the center height (the average of top and bottom height) of a region is above the vanishing line, the region belongs to obstacle area, otherwise, it should be judged by other constraints.

(2) Features Distribution

In the step of scale estimation, the feature points' 3D coordinates have been computed. Now we use feature distribution criterion to determine whether a region belongs to the ground. It can be determined whether point p_i is on the ground by comparing the height difference between its absolute height h' and the camera height h with a threshold D:

$$p_i \in \begin{cases} \text{ground} & |h' - h| < D \\ \text{off-ground} & |h' - h| > D \end{cases} \qquad (6)$$

The absolute height of point p_i is computed directly from the scale and the Y_c'-coordinate: $h' = \sigma * Y_c'$.

Next we count the number of feature points on and not on the ground in each region. Suppose N_1^i is the number of feature points on the ground in i-th region, N_2^i the number of off-ground. We judge whether a region belongs to the ground plane or not by the ratio p, which is defined as,

$$p = \frac{N_1^i}{N_1^i + N_2^i} \tag{7}$$

If p is larger than the threshold, the region is belong to ground plane, otherwise it is classified as obstacle.

(3) Boundary Points Reconstruction

When the region lies on the ground and there are no feature points in it, it is can not determine whether the region belongs to the ground plane or not. However if we know the height of every pixel in the region, we also know that the region belong to the ground plane or not. But it is quite time-consuming to reconstruct every point in the region. In this paper, considering that the highest point of an obstacle is usually located in the top of the region, we select the top point of a region to represent the entire region. Then whether a region belongs to the ground or not is only determined by the selected point.

The 3D points can be computed by triangulation from the correspondences. In order to reconstruct the selected point, we have to find its correspondence. In this paper, a block matching method with epipolar constraint which reduces the search space to 1D is adopted. We adopt the sum of absolute differences (SAD) to find the corresponding point of the selected point in the previous frame. The selected point's correspondences in previous and current frame have been matched, and the rotation and the translation have been estimated in monocular odometry, thus the selected point's 3D coordinate can be computed by triangulation. We judge whether the selected point is on the ground by using Eq.6. If the selected point of a region is on the ground, the region belongs to ground plane; otherwise, the region belongs to obstacles.

5   Experimental Results

In our experiments, we use Voyager II wheel mobile robot, and it is equipped with Logitech C110 webcam. The camera was installed as shown in Fig.1. The camera connects to laptop computer with a USB port and the resolution of the image captured is 640×480 pixel.

5.1   Monocular Visual Odometry

To test the feasibility of the monocular visual odometry, we design two experiments: straight movement and rotation movement, as the mobile robot only has three freedoms (moving in ground plane and rotating around the axis which is orthogonal to the ground plane).

(1) Straight Movement

The experiment of straight movement aims to evaluate the accuracy of proposed visual odometry while the robot moves along a straight line. Every image was captured when the robot walked 100 mm, and 11 images (including the initial position) were taken. Due to the inaccuracy of the wheel diameter, the robot walked 1090 mm altogether. We used the average of the total distance as preferred value. The results are shown in Table 1, where d_m is the measurement of distance, Δ_d is the error of distance, O_m is the measurement of orientation, Δ_o is the error of orientation.

Table 1. Results of straight movement

No.	$d_m(mm)$	$\Delta_d(mm)$	$O_m(°)$	$\Delta_o(°)$
1	110.97	1.97	-0.94	-0.94
2	107.05	-1.95	0.42	0.42
3	111.81	2.81	-0.42	-0.42
4	113.04	4.04	0.96	0.96
5	108.48	-0.52	-0.61	-0.61
6	109.69	0.69	1.13	1.13
7	105.45	-3.55	-0.45	-0.45
8	106.28	-2.72	1.07	1.07
9	113.00	4.00	-0.22	-0.22
10	104.88	-4.12	-0.62	-0.62

As shown in Tabel 1, the distance of the robot walked can be computed exactly, and the average distance is 119.06 mm, the mean square covariance is 3.08 mm, the percentage error of distance is 2.42%, and the mean error of orientation is 0.68°.

(2) Rotation Movement

The experiment of rotation movement was designed to test whether the rotation angle can be computed while the robot rotated about the center. An image was captured when the robot rotated 5°, and 10 images (including the initial position) were taken. The results are shown in Table 2, where r_m is the measurement of rotation, r_p is the preferred value of rotation, Δ_r is the error of rotation, p_c is the position of the rotation center.

Table 2. Results of rotation movement

No.	$r_m(°)$	$r_p(°)$	$\Delta_r(°)$	$p_c(mm)$
1	4.86	5	-0.14	(-0.42,7.10)
2	4.85	5	-0.15	(4.97,-10.02)
3	5.1	5	0.1	(9.56,-1.60)
4	5.15	5	0.15	(9.48,-11.10)
5	5.18	5	0.18	(3.16,8.36)
6	4.91	5	-0.09	(9.32,-3.53)
7	5.16	5	0.16	(-7.85,9.89)
8	4.9	5	-0.1	(-9.68,8.64)
9	5.12	5	0.12	(1.92,0.16)

As shown in Table 2, the rotation angle can be computed using our algorithm. The average of rotation angle is 5.02°, the mean square covariance is 0.14°, the percentage error of rotation angle is 2.64%. But the rotation center does not coincide with the origin (0, 0), the shift is caused by the unequal of the wheelbases and wheel slip.

5.2   Ground Area Detection

The experiment was carried out in our lab and the corridor respectively. Fig.5 showed the experiment in the corridor. Fig.5(b) was the region segmentation result of Fig.5(a), and Fig.5(c) was the ground detection result using the method of this paper. Fig.6 showed the experiment in our lab. Its environment was more complex, Fig.6(c) was the ground detection result. The paper in the ground was very different from the ground plane, but still be classified as belonging to the ground plane. In Fig.5(c) and Fig.6(c), the white region is the ground plane and the black region is obstacles. The results showed that the ground and obstacles can be distinguished effectively using our algorithm.

(a)   (b)   (c)

Fig. 5. Corridor experiment

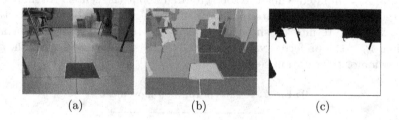

(a)   (b)   (c)

Fig. 6. Lab experiment

6   Conclusions

Through the above analysis, it is feasible to implement both visual localization and ground area detection with only a single camera. In the monocular visual odometry, the absolute translation can not be estimated using monocular motion estimation. The scale ambiguity problem is solved by using the constraints of the camera mounting and ground planar assumption. On the basis of visual odometry, a region-based ground detection is proposed. The experimental results show that the proposed algorithm is capable of accurately recovering the trajectory of the robot and effectively distinguishing the ground and obstacles. In the future work, we will try to improve the algorithm's robustness and accuracy and use it for the location and obstacle avoidance of mobile robots.

Acknowledgement. This work was supported by the Fundamental Research Funds for the Central Universities of China under contract number YWF-12-LZGF-098.

References

1. Scaramuzza, D., Fraundorfer, F.: Visual odometry (tutorial). IEEE Robotics & Automation Magazine 18(4), 80–92 (2011)
2. Maimone, M., Cheng, Y., Matthies, L.: Two years of visual odometry on the mars exploration rovers. Journal of Field Robotics 24(3), 169–186 (2007)
3. Nistér, D., Naroditsky, O., Bergen, J.: Visual odometry for ground vehicle applications. Journal of Field Robotics 23(1), 3–20 (2006)
4. Choi, S., Joung, J., Yu, W., Cho, J.: What does ground tell us? monocular visual odometry under planar motion constraint. In: 2011 11th International Conference on Control, Automation and Systems (ICCAS), pp. 1480–1485. IEEE (2011)
5. Scaramuzza, D., Fraundorfer, F., Siegwart, R.: Real-time monocular visual odometry for on-road vehicles with 1-point ransac. In: IEEE International Conference on Robotics and Automation, ICRA 2009, pp. 4293–4299. IEEE (2009)
6. Civera, J., Grasa, O., Davison, A., Montiel, J.: 1-point ransac for extended kalman filtering: Application to real-time structure from motion and visual odometry. Journal of Field Robotics 27(5), 609–631 (2010)
7. Zhan, Q., Huang, S., Wu, J.: Automatic navigation for a mobile robot with monocular vision. In: 2008 IEEE Conference on Robotics, Automation and Mechatronics, pp. 1005–1010. IEEE (2008)
8. Wang, H., Yuan, K., Zou, W., Peng, Y.: Real-time region-based obstacle detection with monocular vision. In: 2005 IEEE International Conference on Robotics and Biomimetics (ROBIO), pp. 615–619. IEEE (2005)
9. Zhou, J., Li, B.: Homography-based ground detection for a mobile robot platform using a single camera. In: Proceedings 2006 IEEE International Conference on Robotics and Automation, ICRA 2006, pp. 4100–4105. IEEE (2006)
10. Lin, C., Jiang, S., Pu, Y., Song, K.: Robust ground plane detection for obstacle avoidance of mobile robots using a monocular camera. In: 2010 IEEE/RSJ International Conference on Intelligent Robots and Systems (IROS), pp. 3706–3711. IEEE (2010)
11. Hartley, R., Zisserman, A., Ebrary, I.: Multiple view geometry in computer vision, vol. 2. Cambridge Univ. Press (2003)
12. Felzenszwalb, P., Huttenlocher, D.: Efficient graph-based image segmentation. International Journal of Computer Vision 59(2), 167–181 (2004)

Impedance Control of a Rehabilitation Robot for Interactive Training

Wei He[1], Shuzhi Sam Ge[2,3,4,*], Yanan Li[3,4], Effie Chew[5], and Yee Sien Ng[6]

[1] Robotics Institute and School of Automation Engineering,
University of Electronic Science and Technology of China, Chengdu 611731, China
[2] Robotics Institute and School of Computer Science and Engineering,
University of Electronic Science and Technology of China, Chengdu 611731, China
[3] Department of Electrical & Computer Engineering,
National University of Singapore, Singapore 117576
[4] Social Robotics Lab, Interactive Digital Media Institute,
National University of Singapore, Singapore 119613
[5] Division of Neurology, National University Hospital, Singapore 119074
[6] Department of Rehabilitation Medicine, Singapore General Hospital, Singapore 169608

Abstract. In this paper, neural networks based impedance control is developed for a wearable rehabilitation robot in interactions with humans and the environments. The dynamics of the robot are represented by an n-link rigid robotic manipulator. To deal with the system uncertainties and improve the robustness of the system, the adaptive neural networks are used to approximate the unknown model of the constrained robot. With the proposed control, uniform ultimate boundedness of the closed loop system is achieved based on the Lyapunov method. The states of the system converge to a small neighborhood of zero by properly choosing control gains. Extensive simulations are conducted to verify the proposed control.

1 Introduction

More than two-thirds of stroke patients have significant weakness of the limbs impairing capacity to have activities of daily living [1]. Robotic devices have been proven to be useful in rehabilitation. Advantages of robot aided rehabilitation include the ability to document and store motion and force parameters, the ability to achieve thousands of repetitions per treatment session, and increased biofeedback through the incorporation of training tasks. Robotic rehabilitation could potentially improve the productivity of stroke rehabilitation.

Most of current robotic gait training systems are integrated with fixed platforms and treadmills, resulting in unnatural gait movements. They are bulky and expensive and only available in a limited number of large hospitals. A wearable robotic system will be more useful, such that it can make the patients to take the therapy at home environments. The wearable lower limb robotic exoskeleton for rehabilitation that can be operated at private homes becomes popular in recent years.

The rehabilitative robot system works on human patients who are inconvenient with their limbs, thus a whole systematic approach, mechanism and framework are needed to guarantee the safety, make the system adaptive to different application conditions,

---

* Corresponding author.

S.S. Ge et al. (Eds.): ICSR 2012, LNAI 7621, pp. 526–535, 2012.

and able to perform the therapy. Patients' self-motivation and active participation are critical for rehabilitation processes. The human-robot interactive system is expected to perform socially interacting with patients and make the patients actively participate in the training. Efficient interactions with unknown environments and human beings are required for the rehabilitation robots [2, 3].

There is evidence that the recovery is more effective when the patient actively partici-pates in the training [4]. The intelligent control system is required to guarantee the robot to imitate human behaviors, especially in the sense that the human motion is smooth and have high degrees-of-freedom. It is essential for the robot to be able to perform effi-cient control in unknown dynamic interactions with humans and the environments. The adaptable human-like behaviors will be easier to be accepted by the patients. Besides, a model-free method, which requires little model information, is always favorable to mimic high DOF behaviors due to its simplicity. Impedance control is widely used to handle the interaction problems between the constrained robots and the unknown en-vironments, as it can achieve a stable position and force control by tracking a target impedance model [5]. Under the impedance control, the position tracking is realized during the robot's free motion, while the position and force are just indirectly controlled during the robot's constrained motion [6]. Based on the Lyapunov's method, the authors in [6–10] have presented the results for the impedance control of the constrained robots.

A wearable robot for the lower limb rehabilitation is developed at Social Robotics Lab, Interactive & Digital Media Institute (IDMI), The National University of Singa-pore (NUS). The portable rehabilitation robot is designed for performing motions to simulate actions such as walking or cycling according to the modes selected by the pa-tients. This robot is capable of assisting patients with different degrees of impairments via the impedance control. Adaptive neural network control [11] is developed to deal with the system uncertainties and follow a desired impedance model. In this paper, we are going to further study the adaptive neural network based impedance control prob-lem for the 2 DOFs rehabilitation robot with model uncertainties. The adaptive neural network control design aims to compensate for the effects of the system uncertainties and achieve uniform ultimate boundedness.

2 Preliminaries

Lemma 1. *[12] For bounded initial conditions, if there exists a C^1 continuous and positive definite Lyapunov function $V(x)$ satisfying $\kappa_1(\|x\|) \leq V(x) \leq \kappa_2(\|x\|)$, such that $\dot{V}(x) \leq -\rho V(x) + c$, where $\kappa_1, \kappa_2 : R^n \to R$ are class $\mathcal{K}$ functions and c is a positive constant, then the solution $x(t)$ is uniformly bounded.*

Lemma 2. *[13] Consider the basis functions of Gaussian RBF NN with $\hat{Z}$ being the input vector, if $\hat{Z} = Z - \epsilon\bar{\psi}$, where $\bar{\psi}$ is a bounded vector and constant $\epsilon > 0$, then we have*

$$s_i(\hat{Z}) = \exp\left[\frac{-(\hat{Z} - \mu_j)^T(\hat{Z} - \mu_j)}{\eta_j^2}\right], \ j = 1, 2, ..., l,$$

$$S(\hat{Z}) = S(Z) + \epsilon S_t, \tag{1}$$

where S_t is a bounded vector function.

Definition 1. *(SGUUB) [13] The solution $X(t)$ of a system is semi-globally uniformly ultimately bounded (SGUUB) if, for any compact set Ω_0 and all $X(t_0) \in \Omega_0$, there exists an $\mu > 0$ and $T(\mu, X(t_0))$ such that $\|X(t)\| \leq \mu$ for all $t \geq t_0 + T$.*

Lemma 3. *[14–17] Rayleigh-Ritz theorem: Let $A \in R^{n \times n}$ be a real, symmetric, positive-definite matrix; therefore, all the eigenvalues of A are real and positive. Let $\lambda_{\min}$ and $\lambda_{\max}$ denote the minimum and maximum eigenvalues of A, respectively; then for $\forall x \in R^n$, we have*

$$\lambda_{\min}\|x\|^2 \leq x^T A x \leq \lambda_{\max}\|x\|^2, \tag{2}$$

where $\|\cdot\|$ denotes the standard Euclidean norm.

In practice, the exact model of the robot dynamics is not known. To approximate the exact values of the dynamic terms, a Gaussian radial-basis function (RBF) neural network can be utilized as it can approximate any smooth function [11].

3 Problem Formulation

3.1 Dynamics of the Robotic System

The dynamics of a n-link rigid robotic system are described by

$$M(q)\ddot{q} + C(q, \dot{q})\dot{q} + G(q) = \tau(t) - J^T(q)f(t), \tag{3}$$

where $q \in \mathbb{R}^n$ is the coordinates, $\tau \in \mathbb{R}^n$ is the applied joint torque, $M(q) \in \mathbb{R}^{n \times n}$ is a symmetric positive definite inertia matrix, $C(q, \dot{q})\dot{\theta} \in \mathbb{R}^n$ denotes the Centripetal and Coriolis torques, and $G(q) \in \mathbb{R}^n$ is the gravitational force, $f(t) \in \mathbb{R}^n$ is the vector of constraint force exerted by the environment, which is 0 when there is no contact between the manipulator and environment.

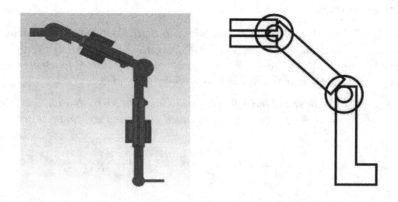

Fig. 1. A 2-DOF rehabilitation robotic system

Property 1. [10, 11] The matrix $M(q)$ is symmetric and positive definite.

Property 2. [10, 11] The matrix $\dot{M}(q) - 2C(q, \dot{q})$ is skew-symmetric.

The desired impedance model given in the joint space is given as

$$M_d(\ddot{q} - \ddot{q}_d) + C_d(q, \dot{q})(\dot{q} - \dot{q}_d) + G_d(q - q_d) = -f(t), \tag{4}$$

where q_d is the desired trajectory, M_d, C_d, G_d are the desired inertia, damping and stiffness matrices, respectively.

Assumption 1. *We assume that the constraint force $f(t)$ is known.*

Remark 1. This is a reasonable assumption as the constraint force $f(t)$ can be measured.

4 Control Design

The control objective is to design control torques such that the impedance of the whole system tracks the given target impedance model Eq. (4).

Suppose the dynamic model and the desired impedance model are completely known, we can design the model based impedance control. Let $\tau(t) = J^T \tau_0(t)$, we propose the following control

$$\tau_0(t) = M(q)\{\ddot{q}_d - M_d^{-1}[C_d(\dot{q} - \dot{q}_d) + G_d(q - q_d) + f(t)]\}$$
$$+ f(t) + G(q) + C(q, \dot{q})\dot{q}. \tag{5}$$

Neural networks based impedance control can improve the performance of the system via the online estimation even though the impedance model of the system is time-varying. In this section, we will design the adaptive neural networks impedance control to approximate the unknown model of the constrained robot and adapt interactions between robots and humans.

Define $e = q_d - q$, we have

$$M_d\ddot{e} + C_d\dot{e} + G_d e = -f, \tag{6}$$

Consider the following dynamic compensator

$$\dot{z} = Dz + K_v\dot{e} + K_p e + K_f M_d^{-1}f, \tag{7}$$

where $D \in R^{n \times n}$ is a positive definite constant matrix. $K_p \in R^{n \times n}$, $K_v \in R^{n \times n}$ and $K_f \in R^{n \times n}$ are matrices to be determined later.

We define the function $s(e, \dot{e}, z)$ as

$$s(e, \dot{e}, z) = \dot{e} + K_1 e + K_2 z, \tag{8}$$

where $K_1 \in R^{n \times n}$ and $K_2 \in R^{n \times n}$ are constat positive definite matrices.

Combining Eq. (7) and Eq. (4), we have

$$\ddot{e} + (K_1 + K_2 K_v - K_2 D K_2^{-1})\dot{e} + K_2(K_p - D K_2^{-1}K_1)e$$
$$= K_2(-K_f M_d^{-1}f - D K_2^{-1}s + \dot{s}). \tag{9}$$

where $K_v = K_2^{-1}(M_d^{-1}C_d + K_2DK_2^{-1} - K_1)$, $K_p = K_2^{-1}M_d^{-1}G_d + DK_2^{-1}K_1$, $K_f = K_2^{-1}$.

Then, we have

$$\ddot{e} + M_d^{-1}C_d\dot{e} + M_d^{-1}G_d e = -M_d^{-1}f + \sigma(s). \tag{10}$$

where $\sigma(s) = K_2(\dot{s} - DK_2^{-1}s)$. It is obvious that the desired impedance is achieved when $\sigma(s) = 0$. We design the controller as

$$\tau = \hat{M}\ddot{q}_{eq} + K_s s + d\,\mathrm{sgn}(s) + \hat{C}\dot{q}_{eq} + \hat{G} - f, \tag{11}$$

where

$$\dot{q}_{eq} = \dot{q}_d + K_1 e + K_2 z, \tag{12}$$

$$\ddot{q}_{eq} = \ddot{q}_d + K_1 \dot{e} + K_2 \dot{z}, \tag{13}$$

$\mathrm{sgn} = [\mathrm{sgn}(s_1), \mathrm{sgn}(s_2), ...\mathrm{sgn}(s_n)]$ with $\mathrm{sgn}(s_i)$ as a sign function, K_s is a matrix and d is a scalar constant, $\hat{M}, \hat{C}, \hat{G}$ are the the parameter estimates.

We define

$$\hat{M}(q) = \{\hat{\Theta}_M\}^T \bullet \{\Xi_M(q)\}, \tag{14}$$

$$\hat{C}(q, \dot{q}) = \{\hat{\Theta}_C\}^T \bullet \{\Xi_C(q, \dot{q})\}, \tag{15}$$

$$\hat{G}(q) = \{\hat{\Theta}_G\}^T \bullet \{\Xi_G(q)\}. \tag{16}$$

The adaptation laws are designed as

$$\dot{\hat{\Theta}}_{Mij} = \Gamma_{Mij}\xi_{Mij}\ddot{q}_{eqj}s_i - \sigma_M\Gamma_{Mij}\hat{\Theta}_{Mij}, \tag{17}$$

$$\dot{\hat{\Theta}}_{Cij} = \Gamma_{Cij}\xi_{Cij}\dot{q}_{eqj}s_i - \sigma_C\Gamma_{Mij}\hat{\Theta}_{Cij}, \tag{18}$$

$$\dot{\hat{\Theta}}_{Gi} = \Gamma_{Gi}\xi_{Gi}s_i - \sigma_G\Gamma_{Gi}\hat{\Theta}_{Gi}, \tag{19}$$

where Γ_{Mij}, Γ_{Cij} and Γ_{Gi} are constant symmetric positive definite matrices, s_i is the ith element of s, and q_{eqj} is the jth element of q_{eq}, σ_M, σ_C, σ_G are small positive constants.

Remark 2. The σ modification term is introduced to improve the robustness of the closed-loop system [18]. Without such a modification term, the estimate $\hat{\Theta}_{Mij}$, $\hat{\Theta}_{Cij}$, $\hat{\Theta}_{Gi}$ might drift to very large values, which will result in a variation of a high-gain control scheme [13].

Substituting Eq. (11) into Eq. (6), we have

$$M_d\dot{s} + C_d s - (\Xi_M\ddot{q}_{eq} + \Xi_C\dot{q}_{eq} + \Xi_G) + K_s s + d\,\mathrm{sgn}(s)$$
$$= [\{\tilde{\Theta}_M \bullet \Xi_M\}]\ddot{q}_{eq} + [\{\tilde{\Theta}_C \bullet \Xi_C\}]\ddot{q}_{eq} + [\{\tilde{\Theta}_G \bullet \Xi_G\}]\ddot{q}_{eq}, \tag{20}$$

where $\tilde{\Theta}_M = \Theta_M - \hat{\Theta}_M$, $\tilde{\Theta}_C = \Theta_C - \hat{\Theta}_C$ and $\tilde{\Theta}_G = \Theta_G - \hat{\Theta}_G$.

Theorem 1. *For the system dynamics described by (3), under Assumption 1, and the control Eq. (11) with the adaptation laws Eqs. (17)-(19), given that the initial conditions are bounded, we can conclude that the desired impedance is achieved and the impedance error will eventually converge to a small neighborhood around zero by appropriately choosing design parameters.*

Proof: Consider the following Lyapunov function candidate

$$V = \frac{1}{2} \sum_{i=1}^{n} \sum_{j=1}^{n} \left(\tilde{\Theta}_{Mij} \Gamma_{Mij}^{-1} \tilde{\Theta}_{Mij} + \tilde{\Theta}_{Cij} \Gamma_{Cij}^{-1} \tilde{\Theta}_{Cij} \right) + \frac{1}{2} \sum_{i=1}^{n} \tilde{\Theta}_{Gi} \Gamma_{Gi}^{-1} \tilde{\Theta}_{Gi} + \frac{1}{2} s^T \Gamma s, \tag{21}$$

where Γ is a diagonal positive matrix, $\tilde{\Theta}_{Mij} = \Theta_{Mij} - \hat{\Theta}_{Mij}$, $\tilde{\Theta}_{Cij} = \Theta_{Cij} - \hat{\Theta}_{Cij}$ and $\tilde{\Theta}_{Gi} = \Theta_{Gi} - \hat{\Theta}_{Gi}$.

Choosing $d \geq \|E_M \ddot{r}_{eq} + E_C \dot{r}_{eq} + E_G\|$, we have

$$\dot{V} \leq -s^T K_s s + \sum_{i=1}^{n} \sum_{j=1}^{n} \left(\sigma_M \tilde{\Theta}_{Mij} \hat{\Theta}_{Mij} + \sigma_C \tilde{\Theta}_{Cij} \hat{\Theta}_{Cij} \right) + \sum_{i=1}^{n} \sigma_G \tilde{\Theta}_{Gi} \hat{\Theta}_{Gi}$$

$$\leq -s^T K_s s - \sum_{i=1}^{n} \sum_{j=1}^{n} \left(\frac{\sigma_M}{2} \tilde{\Theta}_{Mij}^2 + \frac{\sigma_C}{2} \tilde{\Theta}_{Cij}^2 \right) - \frac{\sigma_G}{2} \sum_{i=1}^{n} \tilde{\Theta}_{Gi}^2$$

$$+ \frac{\sigma_G}{2} \sum_{i=1}^{n} \Theta_{Gi}^2$$

$$\leq + \sum_{i=1}^{n} \sum_{j=1}^{n} \left(\frac{\sigma_M}{2} \Theta_{Mij}^2 + \frac{\sigma_C}{2} \Theta_{Cij}^2 \right) - \lambda V + \varepsilon, \tag{22}$$

where

$$\lambda = \min\left(\frac{K_s}{\Gamma}, \frac{\sigma_M}{2\Gamma_{Mij}^{-1}}, \frac{\sigma_C}{2\Gamma_{Cij}^{-1}}, \frac{\sigma_G}{2\Gamma_{Gi}^{-1}} \right), \tag{23}$$

$$\varepsilon = \sum_{i=1}^{n} \sum_{j=1}^{n} \left(\frac{\sigma_M}{2} \Theta_{Mij}^2 + \frac{\sigma_C}{2} \Theta_{Cij}^2 \right) + \frac{\sigma_G}{2} \sum_{i=1}^{n} \Theta_{Gi}^2. \tag{24}$$

From Lemma 1, we can state that the signals, s, $\tilde{\Theta}_{Mij}$, $\tilde{\Theta}_{Cij}$, $\tilde{\Theta}_{Gi}$, are uniformly ultimately bounded.

Multiplying Eq. (22) by $e^{\lambda t}$ yields

$$\frac{\partial}{\partial t}(V(t)e^{\lambda t}) \leq \varepsilon e^{\lambda t}. \tag{25}$$

Integrating of the above inequality, we obtain

$$V(t) \leq \left(V(0) - \frac{\varepsilon}{\lambda} \right) e^{-\lambda t} + \frac{\varepsilon}{\lambda} \leq V(0)e^{-\lambda t} + \frac{\varepsilon}{\lambda} \in \mathcal{L}_{\infty}, \tag{26}$$

which implies $V(t)$ is bounded. From Eq. (21), we have

$$\frac{1}{2}\sum_{i=1}^{n}\Gamma_i s_i^2 = \frac{1}{2}s^T \Gamma s \leq V(t) \leq V(0)e^{-\lambda t} + \frac{\varepsilon}{\lambda} \in \mathcal{L}_\infty. \tag{27}$$

Let $\Gamma^* = \max_{1 \leq i \leq n}\{\Gamma_i\}$. Then, we have

$$\frac{1}{2}\sum_{i=1}^{n}\Gamma_i s_i^2 \leq \frac{1}{2}\sum_{i=1}^{n}\Gamma^* s_i^2 \leq V(0)e^{-\lambda t} + \frac{\varepsilon}{\lambda} \in \mathcal{L}_\infty. \tag{28}$$

We further have

$$\sum_{i=1}^{n} s_i^2 \leq \frac{2}{\Gamma^*}V(0)e^{-\lambda t} + \frac{2\varepsilon}{\Gamma^*\lambda} \in \mathcal{L}_\infty., \ \forall t \in [0, \infty). \tag{29}$$

which implies that given $\mu > \sqrt{\frac{2\varepsilon}{\Gamma^*\lambda}}$, there exists T such that $|s_i| < \mu$ for all $t > T$. It is easily seen that the increase in the control gain K_s and the adaptive gains $\Gamma_{Mij}, \Gamma_{Cij}, \Gamma_{Gi}$ will result a better control performance. Then, we can state that s will converge to a small neighborhood of zero by suitably choosing design parameters, and the desired impedance is achieved. ∎

5 Simulations

Consider the rehabilitation robot with two revolute joints in the vertical plane as shown in Fig. 1, simulations are carried out to verify the effectiveness of the proposed control. Let m_i and l_i be the mass and length of link i, l_{ci} be the distance from joint $i-1$ to the center of mass of link i, as indicated in the figure, and I_i be the moment of inertia of link i about an axis coming out of the page passing through the center of mass of link i.

The kinetic energy is given as

$$\mathcal{K}(q, \dot{q}) = \frac{1}{2}m_1 l_{c1}^2 \dot{q}_1^2 + \frac{1}{2}I_1\dot{q}_1^2 + \frac{1}{2}m_2 l_1^2 \dot{q}_1^2 + m_2 l_1 l_{c2}\dot{q}_1(\dot{q}_1 + \dot{q}_2)\cos q_2$$
$$+ \frac{1}{2}m_2 l_{c2}^2(\dot{q}_1 + \dot{q}_2)^2 + \frac{1}{2}I_2(\dot{q}_1 + \dot{q}_2)^2, \tag{30}$$

The potential energy is

$$\mathcal{P}(q) = m_1 g l_{c2}\sin q_1 + m_2 g[l_1\sin q_1 + l_{c2}\sin(q_1 + q_2)], \tag{31}$$

Using the Lagrange's equation $\frac{d}{dt}\frac{\partial(\mathcal{K}-\mathcal{P})}{\partial \dot{q}} - \frac{\partial(\mathcal{K}-\mathcal{P})}{\partial q} = 0$, the dynamics of the robot can be expressed as Eq. (3), where

$$G(q) = 0,$$
$$M(q) = \begin{bmatrix} m_1 l_{c1}^2 + m_2(l_1^2 + l_{c2}^2 + 2l_1 l_{c2}\cos q_2) + I_1 + I_2 & m_2(l_{c2}^2 + l_1 l_{c2}\cos q_2) + I_2 \\ m_2(l_{c2}^2 + l_1 l_{c2}\cos q_2) + I_2 & m_2 l_{c2}^2 + I_2 \end{bmatrix},$$
$$C(q, \dot{q}) = \begin{bmatrix} -m_2 l_1 l_{c2}\dot{q}_2\sin q_2 & -m_2 l_1 l_{c2}(\dot{q}_1 + \dot{q}_2)\sin q_2 \\ m_2 l_1 l_{c2}\dot{q}_1\sin q_2 & 0 \end{bmatrix},$$

Parameters of the robot are listed in the table below.

Table 1. Parameters of the robot

Parameter	Description	Value
m_1	Mass of link 1	$2.0kg$
m_2	Mass of link 2	$0.85kg$
l_1	Length of link 1	$0.35m$
l_1	Length of link 2	$0.31m$
I_1	Inertia of link 1	$61.25 \times 10^{-3}kgm^2$
I_2	Inertia of link 2	$20.42 \times 10^{-3}kgm^2$

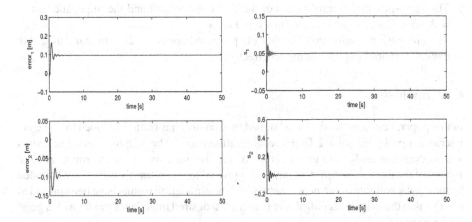

Fig. 2. Tracking error and function $s(e, \dot{e}, z)$

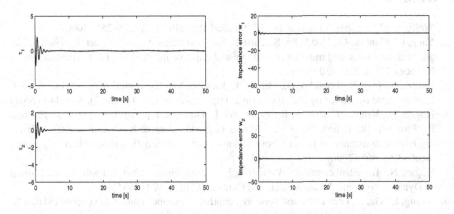

Fig. 3. Control inputs $\tau_1(t)$, $\tau_2(t)$ and impedance errors $w_1(t)$, $w_2(t)$

The initial positions of the robot are given as

$$q_1(0) = q_2(0) = 0. \tag{32}$$

The desired trajectory is give as $q_d = [0.14\cos(0.5t), 0.14\sin(0.5t)]^T$, where $t \in [0, t_f]$ and $t_f = 50$. The contact force is given as $f = [-5, 5]^T$. The desired impedance model of the robot is given as $M_d = \text{diag}[2, 2]$, $C_d = \text{diag}[5, 5]$, $G_d = \text{diag}[50, 50]$. The control parameters are chosen as $K_1 = \text{diag}[1, 1]$, $K_2 = \text{diag}[1, 1]$, $K_s = \text{diag}([10, 10])$; $D = \text{diag}[1, 1]$, $d = \text{diag}[0.001, 0.001]$, $\sigma_M = \sigma_C = \sigma_G = 0.001$, $\eta_M = \eta_C = \eta_G = 1$, $\mu_M = \mu_C = \mu_G = 0.1$, $\Gamma_M = \text{diag}[1, 1]$, $\Gamma_C = \text{diag}[5, 5]$, $\Gamma_G = [1, 1]^T$.

Fig. 2 shows the tracking error of the closed-loop system with the proposed control. It is shown that the tracking errors in both x and y directions converge to a small neighborhood around 0.1. The dynamics of the function $s(e, \dot{e}, z)$ are also given in Fig. 2. The corresponding control inputs of the proposed control and the impedance error, $w = M_d\ddot{e} + C_d\dot{e} + G_de + f$, are shown in Fig. 3.

The simulation results illustrate that the proposed control is able to make the robot to track the desired impedance model effectively.

6   Conclusion

In this paper, neural networks based impedance control has been developed to solve the interaction problems for a 2 DOFs rehabilitation robot. The adaptive neural networks aim to compensate for the uncertainties of the dynamic model of the robot. All the signals of the closed-loop system have been proved to be uniformly ultimately bounded by tuning the weights of the neural networks. The simulation results have been provided to show that the proposed control is able to track a desired impedance model with a good performance.

References

1. Wolfe, C.: The impact of stroke. British Medical Bulletin 56(2), 275–286 (2000)
2. Yang, C., Ganesh, G., Haddadin, S., Parusel, S., Albu-Schaeffer, A., Burdet, E.: Human-like adaptation of force and impedance in stable and unstable interactions. IEEE Transactions on Robotics 27(5), 918–930 (2011)
3. Burdet, E., Osu, R., Franklin, D., Milner, T., Kawato, M.: The central nervous system stabilizes unstable dynamics by learning optimal impedance. Nature 414(6862), 446–449 (2001)
4. Hogan, N., Krebs, H., Rohrer, B., Palazzolo, J., Dipietro, L., Fasoli, S., Stein, J., Hughes, R., Frontera, W., Lynch, D., et al.: Motions or muscles? some behavioral factors underlying robotic assistance of motor recovery. Journal of Rehabilitation Research and Development 43(5), 605 (2006)
5. Hogan, N.: Impedance control: An approach to manipulation: Part iii applications. Journal of Dynamic Systems, Measurement, and Control 107(2), 1–24 (1985)
6. Huang, L., Ge, S., Lee, T.: Neural network adaptive impedance control of constrained robots. International Journal of Robotics and Automation 19 (2004)
7. Cheah, C., Wang, D.: Learning impedance control for robotic manipulators. IEEE Transactions on Robotics and Automation 14(3), 452–465 (1998)

8. Lu, W., Meng, Q.: Impedance control with adaptation for robotic manipulations. IEEE Transactions on Robotics and Automation 7(3), 408–415 (1991)
9. Buerger, S., Hogan, N.: Complementary stability and loop shaping for improved human–robot interaction. IEEE Transactions on Robotics 23(2), 232–244 (2007)
10. Li, Y., Ge, S.S., Yang, C.: Learning impedance control for physical robot–environment interaction. International Journal of Control 85(2), 182–193 (2012)
11. Ge, S.S., Lee, T.H., Harris, C.J.: Adaptive Neural Network Control of Robotic Manipulators. World Scientific, London (1998)
12. Ge, S.S., Wang, C.: Adaptive neural network control of uncertain MIMO non-linear systems. IEEE Transactions on Neural Network 15(3), 674–692 (2004)
13. Ge, S.S., Hang, C.C., Lee, T.H., Zhang, T.: Stable Adaptive Neural Network Control. Kluwer Academic, Boston (2001)
14. Horn, R., Johnson, C.: Matrix analysis. Cambridge University Press, Cambridge (1990)
15. He, W., Ge, S.S.: Robust Adaptive Boundary Control of a Vibrating String under Unknown Time-varying Disturbance. IEEE Transactions on Control Systems Technology 20(1), 48–58 (2012)
16. He, W., Ge, S.S., How, B.V.E., Choo, Y.S., Hong, K.-S.: Robust Adaptive Boundary Control of a Flexible Marine Riser with Vessel Dynamics. Automatica 47(4), 722–732 (2011)
17. He, W., Ge, S.S., Zhang, S.: Adaptive Boundary Control of a Flexible Marine Installation System. Automatica 47(12), 2728–2734 (2011)
18. Ioannou, P., Sun, J.: Robust Adaptive Control. Prentice-Hall, Eaglewood Cliffs (1996)

Design and Development
of a Wearable Rehabilitation Robot

Wei He[1], Shuzhi Sam Ge[2,3,4,*], Weian Guo[3,4], Zhen Zhao[4], Jie Zhang[4],
Shengtao Xiao[3], and Fon Ping Quek Nuraisha[3]

[1] Robotics Institute and School of Automation Engineering,
University of Electronic Science and Technology of China, Chengdu 611731, China
[2] Robotics Institute and School of Computer Science and Engineering,
University of Electronic Science and Technology of China, Chengdu 611731, China
[3] Department of Electrical & Computer Engineering,
National University of Singapore, Singapore 117576
[4] Social Robotics Lab, Interactive Digital Media Institute,
National University of Singapore, Singapore 119613

Abstract. In this paper, we present the design and development of a wearable
robot for the lower limb rehabilitation including the mechanical, electrical system, software implementation, etc. To make the robot wearable and portable and
simplify the mechanism structure, servo motors are used as robot's joints. A
friendly human robot interface is designed to make the robot easy to use. The
dynamics of the robot is described by a 2-link rigid robotic manipulator in the
joint space. The simulation results are given to demonstrate the feasibility and
effectiveness of the designed lower limb rehabilitation robot-assisted system.

1 Introduction

With the rapidly aging population and the increasing presence of illnesses and physical
disabilities, there is a large group of people require rehabilitation therapy after suffering medical diseases and conditions such as the Parkinson's disease, spinal cord injury
(SCI), stroke, brain injury, or muscle disorder [1–3]. The physical therapy is labor intensive and strenuous for the therapists [4]. Due to the increase of aged population and
decline in number of caregivers, an automatic device is in urgent need to fulfill these
training tasks and the monitoring process. With such robot-assisted device, the patients
can also acquire assistance in daily movement and behavior, and the therapist can be
relieved from the physical efforts and focus more on supervising therapeutic effects.
Robot-assisted training enables patients to have more intensive therapy while requiring
much less time involved by the therapists [5]. The motivation behind rehabilitation is
to aid patients in regaining physical functions by training the patients' affected limbs to
prevent muscle atrophy, and recovering the patients' activities of daily living [6]. Rehabilitation robotics is a special branch of robotics which can help patients recover from
neurological injuries based on training conducted with machines. [7]. Applications of
rehabilitation robotics have potential advantages over therapy provided by therapists in
terms of cost, precision and repeatability.

---

* Corresponding author.

S.S. Ge et al. (Eds.): ICSR 2012, LNAI 7621, pp. 536–545, 2012.
© Springer-Verlag Berlin Heidelberg 2012

Inconvenience of travel and caregiver burden are cited in the post-discharge phase as the predominant reasons for poor compliance [8]. Such patients often still have profound impairment of gait, balance and hand function such that caregivers cannot adequately assist with their rehabilitation within the home. A home-based rehabilitation robot can increase the compliance for rehabilitation in the home and outpatient setting, and prevent the deterioration of body function. The rehabilitation robot in this situation would have to be light-weight, easy to don and doff, capable of social interactions and able to capture patient performance data. The wearable and portable robotic system will be more useful, since it can make the patients take the therapy at home environments. However, most of current robotic gait training systems are integrated with fixed platforms and treadmills, resulting in unnatural gait movements. They are bulky and expensive and only available in a limited number of large hospitals. The home-based rehabilitation robot can realize the early training for the patients. Therefore, the wearable lower limb robotic exoskeleton for rehabilitation that can be operated at private homes becomes a hot research topic in recent years.

As shown in Fig. 1, a lower limb rehabilitation robot is designed at Social Robotics Lab, Interactive & Digital Media Institute (IDMI), The National University of Singapore (NUS). The aim is to design a portable rehabilitation robot that patients can attach at any convenient place and use the device comfortably. The robotic system is adjustable to fit different limb lengths for different users. The robotic system with 2 degree of freedoms (DOFs) is equipped with two motors supplying the sufficient power to move both the upper and lower parts of the robot. The torque motor and potentiometer are used to determine the torque and angle of the knee and hip respectively. The robot is able to perform flexion-extension for the knee and hip by moving the links.

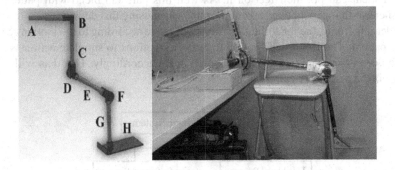

Fig. 1. The wearable robot developed at Social Robotics Lab, Interactive & Digital Media Institute (IDMI) (left-Solidworks view, right-Physical view)

The rest of the paper is organized as follows. The introduction of the hardware design is given in Section 2. The software design is introduced in Section 3. The dynamics of the 2-link rigid robotic system are derived and the controller is designed in Section 4, where it is shown that the uniform boundedness of the closed-loop system can be achieved by the proposed control. Simulations are carried out to illustrate the performance of the proposed control in Section 4.3. The conclusion of this paper is presented in Section 5.

2   Hardware Design

As shown in Fig. 2, the entire system is made up of two parts, i.e. the hardware system module and the software system module. The hardware system comprises the mechanical part inspired by biological organisms which is designed to support the body weight and complete different grades of rehabilitation exercises, and the electrical part which provides control, energy, etc.. The software system is composed of the training paradigm rule and control method, which enable users to add new functionalities, personalized rehabilitation protocols, etc..

2.1   Mechanical System Design

As shown in Fig. 1, the mechanical part is designed to be attached to the human limb via leg braces, which includes: A) An adjustable joint that is attached to the structure of choice (chair, bed, etc), B) The joint part that attaches PART A to the rehabilitation robot system, C) An adjustable link that is attached to the attachment module and the hip module. The length of C can adjust to fit patients' legs, D) The hip module that controls the movement of thigh downwards, E) Part E will be attached to patient's thigh. The length of Part E is adjustable, just like Part C, F) The knee module that controls the motion of the knee of the limb, G) Adjustable joint between the knee and ankle (attached to patients' calf), and H) The ankle module that supports the motion of the ankle. Patient can put their feet on it. As well this part can blend with patient' feet movement so that patient can feel comfortable when using this device.

Under this frame, the rehabilitation robot will move according to the motion selected by the patient. The robot will be able to perform motions to simulate actions such as walking or cycling and hence the limbs will move accordingly. This data will be obtained via the respective gait motions.

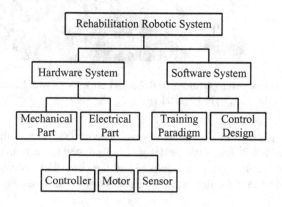

Fig. 2. System architecture

The robot has 2 degrees-of-freedom at the hip joint and at the knee joint, which is distributed as the following table. The two motors are located at the two joints. The robot is able to perform flexion-extension for the knee where only the bottom link moves. It is also able to perform flexion-extension for the hip by moving the top link. This can also happen simultaneously.

Table 1. The distributions of the robotics freedom

No.	Body part	DoF	Range of motion (ROM)	Remark
1	Hip	1	$[-15°, 45°]$	Flexion-extension of hip joint
2	Knee	1	$[-45°, 90°]$	Flexion-extension of knee joint

2.2 Electrical System Design

The whole electrical control system is shown as Fig. 3, which is comprised of there main parts, i.e. low level motor drive module, middle level computer module and high level sensor module.

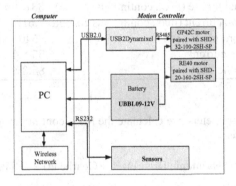

Fig. 3. Electrical control system diagram

Servo Motor. Motor selection is based on the torque and force data and hence the weight of the loads. For knee, we consider the motor, Maxon RE40 GB 150W Motor (Model 148867 (24V). The parameters of Maxon RE40 GB are given as follows,

According to the parameters of this motor, we can calculate the maximum continues torque and no load speed as Eqs. (1) respectively.

$$170mNm \times 160(\text{SHD Harmonic Drive}) = 27.2Nm \qquad (1)$$

$$7580rpm/160(\text{SHD Harmonic Drive}) = 47.37rpm \qquad (2)$$

For hip, we use the motor EC motor EC45 BLVD 250W Model 136207(24V).

Table 2. Parameters of Motor Maxon RE40 148867

Parameter	Value
Nominal Voltage	$24.0V$
No load speed	$7580.01/min$
No load current	$137.0mA$
Nominal speed	$6930.01/min$
Nominal torque (max. continuous torque)	$170.0Nm$
Nominal current (max. continuous current)	$5.77A$
Stall torque	$2280.0Nm$
Starting current	$75.7A$
Max. efficiency	90.9%

Table 3. Parameters of Motor Maxon EC45 136207

Parameter	Value
Nominal Voltage	$24.0V$
No load speed	$5000.01/min$
No load current	$341.0mA$
Nominal speed	$4300.01/min$
Nominal torque (max. continuous torque)	$331.0mNm$
Nominal current (max. continuous current)	$7.51A$
Stall torque	$2540.0mNm$
Starting current	$55.8A$
Max. efficiency	85.3%

According to its parameters, we calculate the Max. continuous torque and the speed without load as follows,

$$310Nm \times 100(\text{SHD Harmonic Drive}) \times 4.3(\text{Gearhead}) \times 0.853(\text{Max. Efficiency})$$
$$= 111.972Nm \tag{3}$$

$$4520rpm/100(\text{SHD Harmonic Drive})/4.3(\text{Gear Box}) = 10.512rpm \tag{4}$$

Battery. The battery system of the developed rehabilitation robot is comprised of two ultralife, intelligent li-ion batteries produced by SmartCircuit technology, i.e. UBBL09.

3 Software Design

In this paper, we mainly use C# as the compiler in the interface of the EPOS Studio, produced by Maxon company.

In the computer, users can send control commands to the 2 drivers via the EPOS Studio. The 2 drivers can send control signals to motors so that the robot can complete relative actions. In addition, robots can feedback data to the upper computer. Therefore the closed loop system (see Fig. 4) can guarantee the accuracy of the rehabilitation training.

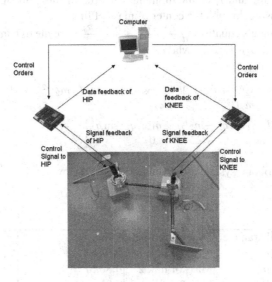

Fig. 4. Closed loop system of the rehabilitation robot

The software of the rehabilitation robot are designed for the patients in different phases. The patients can choose three training modes according to the needs. The robot will follow the desired training paradigm to make robot tracking the desired trajectories.

Three training modes are designed for the patients at the early rehabilitation phase, medium-term rehabilitation phase and post-rehabilitation phase respectively. The robot is able to produce motions to simulate actions such as walking or cycling according to the mode selected by the patients. This robot is capable of assisting patients with different degrees of impairments via the intelligent human robot interface.

4 Dynamics and Control Design

4.1 Dynamics of the Robotic System

The dynamics of a n-link rigid robotic system can be described by

$$M(q)\ddot{q} + C(q, \dot{q})\dot{q} + G(q) + d = \tau \tag{5}$$

where $q \in R^n$ is the coordinates, n is the number of links in the robotic system, $\tau \in R^n$ is the applied joint torque, $M(q) \in R^{n \times n}$ is a symmetric positive definite inertia matrix,

$C(q, \dot{q})\dot{q} \in R^n$ denotes the centripetal and Coriolis torques, and $G(q) \in R^n$ is the gravitational force, $d \in R^n$ is external disturbance.

Consider the DOFs of rehabilitation robot in the vertical plane, simulations are carried out to verify the effectiveness of the proposed control. Let m_i and l_i be the mass and length of link i, l_{ci} be the distance from joint $i-1$ to the center of mass of link i, as indicated in the figure, and I_i be the moment of inertia of link i about an axis coming out of the page passing through the center of mass of link i.

Using the Lagrange's equation $\frac{d}{dt}\frac{\partial(\mathcal{K}-\mathcal{P})}{\partial\dot{q}} - \frac{\partial(\mathcal{K}-\mathcal{P})}{\partial q} = 0$, the dynamics of a 2-DOF robot can be expressed as Eq. (5), where

$G(q) = 0,$

$$M(q) = \begin{bmatrix} m_1 l_{c1}^2 + m_2(l_1^2 + l_{c2}^2 + 2l_1 l_{c2}\cos q_2) + I_1 + I_2 & m_2(l_{c2}^2 + l_1 l_{c2}\cos q_2) + I_2 \\ m_2(l_{c2}^2 + l_1 l_{c2}\cos q_2) + I_2 & m_2 l_{c2}^2 + I_2 \end{bmatrix},$$

$$C(q, \dot{q}) = \begin{bmatrix} -m_2 l_1 l_{c2}\dot{q}_2 \sin q_2 & -m_2 l_1 l_{c2}(\dot{q}_1 + \dot{q}_2)\sin q_2 \\ m_2 l_1 l_{c2}\dot{q}_1 \sin q_2 & 0 \end{bmatrix},$$

Parameters of the robotic system are given in the table below.

Table 4. Parameters of the robot

Parameter	Description	Value
m_1	Mass of link 1	$2.0kg$
m_2	Mass of link 2	$0.85kg$
l_1	Length of link 1	$0.35m$
l_1	Length of link 2	$0.31m$
I_1	Inertia of link 1	$61.25 \times 10^{-3} kgm^2$
I_2	Inertia of link 2	$20.42 \times 10^{-3} kgm^2$

Property 1. [9, 10] The matrix $M(q)$ is symmetric and positive definite.

Property 2. [9, 10] The matrix $\dot{M}(q) - 2C(q, \dot{q})$ is skew-symmetric.

Property 3. [9] Assuming there is no external disturbance, the left-hand side of the dynamic equation can be linearly parameterized as

$$M(q)\ddot{q} + C(q, \dot{q})\dot{q} + G(q) = Y(q, \dot{q}, \ddot{q})\theta, \tag{6}$$

where $\theta \in R^p$ contains the system parameters, and $Y(q, \dot{q}, \ddot{q}) \in R^{2 \times p}$ is the regression matrix, which contains known functions of the signals $q(t)$, $\dot{q}(t)$ and $\ddot{q}(t)$.

We can write the dynamics of the robotic system in the linear-in-the-parameters (LIP) form as

$$Y(q, \dot{q}, \ddot{q}) = \begin{bmatrix} \ddot{q}_1 & \ddot{q}_1 + \ddot{q}_2 & y' \\ 0 & \ddot{q}_1 + \ddot{q}_2 & \cos(q_2)\ddot{q}_1 + \dot{q}_1 \sin(q_2)\dot{q}_1 \end{bmatrix},$$

$$\theta = \begin{bmatrix} m_1 l_{c1}^2 + m_2 l_1^2 + I_1 & m_2 l_{c2}^2 + I_2 & m_2 l_1 l_{c2} \end{bmatrix}^T,$$

where $y' = 2\cos(q_2)\ddot{q}_1 + \cos(q_2)\ddot{q}_2 - \dot{q}_2 \sin(q_2)\dot{q}_1 - (\dot{q}_1 + \dot{q}_2)\sin(q_2)\dot{q}_2$.

4.2 Control Design

The control system is the key limiting factor in current rehabilitation robots. To make the robot deliver the assistance and training paradigm, the control objective is to to track the desired motion trajectory $q_d(t)$.

Let $\hat{M}(q)$, $\hat{C}(q, \dot{q})$, $\hat{G}(q)$ correspond to the estimates of $M(q)$, $C(q, \dot{q})$, $G(q)$ respectively. Then we have

$$\hat{M}(q)\ddot{q} + \hat{C}(q, \dot{q})\dot{q} + \hat{G}(q) = Y(q, \dot{q}, \ddot{q})\hat{\theta}, \tag{7}$$

We design the following adaptive control

$$\tau = \hat{M}(q)\ddot{q}_r + \hat{C}(q, \dot{q})\dot{q}_r + \hat{G}(q) + Kr = Y(q, \dot{q}, \ddot{q})\hat{\theta} + Kr \tag{8}$$

where $r = \dot{e} + \lambda e$, K is a diagonal constant matrix, λ is a constant. Then we know that if $r \to 0$, e and $\dot{e} \to 0$ as $t \to \infty$. We define $\dot{q}_r = \dot{q}_d + \lambda e$, $\ddot{q}_r = \ddot{q}_d + \lambda \dot{e}$. The adaptation law is designed as

$$\dot{\hat{\theta}} = \Gamma^{-1} Y^T(q, \dot{q}, \ddot{q})r, \tag{9}$$

where Γ is a diagonal constant matrix. From the dynamics of the robot, we have

$$\begin{aligned}
\tau &= M(q)\ddot{q}_r + C(q, \dot{q})\dot{q}_r + G(q) \\
&= M(q)(\ddot{q}_r - \dot{r}) + C(q, \dot{q})(\dot{q}_r - r) + G(q) \\
&= Y(q, \dot{q}, \ddot{q})\theta - M(q)\dot{r} - C(q, \dot{q})r \tag{10}
\end{aligned}$$

Then, we have

$$M(q)\dot{r} + C(q, \dot{q})r + Kr = Y(q, \dot{q}, \ddot{q})\tilde{\theta}. \tag{11}$$

Consider the Lyapunov function candidate

$$V(t) = \frac{1}{2}r^T M r + \frac{1}{2}\tilde{\theta}^T \Gamma \tilde{\theta} \tag{12}$$

Taking its time derivative, we have

$$\begin{aligned}
\dot{V}(t) &= r^T M \dot{r} + \frac{1}{2}r^T \dot{M} r + \theta^T \Gamma \dot{\tilde{\theta}} \\
&= -r^T K r \\
&\leq 0 \tag{13}
\end{aligned}$$

Then we have

$$\int_0^T r^T K r dt = V(0) - V(t) \leq V(0). \tag{14}$$

The property of K yields

$$\lambda_{\min}(K) \int_0^T r^T r dt \leq V(0). \tag{15}$$

Then, we can obtain $r \in L_2^n$. Since $\dot{V}(t) \leq 0$, we have $0 \leq V(t) \leq V(0), \forall t \geq 0$, leading to $V(t) \in L_\infty$, and $\tilde{\theta} \in L_\infty^n$. From the close-loop error Eq. (11), we have $\dot{r} \in L_\infty^n$. Then, we can state that r is uniformly continuous. Therefore, we can conclude that $r \to 0$ as $t \to \infty$. From the definition of r, we obtain that e and $\dot{e} \to 0$ as $t \to \infty$.

4.3   Simulation Results

The desired trajectory is give as $q_d = [\sin(t), \sin(t)]^T$, where $t \in [0, t_f]$ and $t_f = 20$. The initial positions of the robot are given as $q_1(0) = q_2(0) = \dot{q}_1(0) = \dot{q}_2(0) = 0$. With the proposed adaptive control Eq. (8), where the parameters are chosen as $K = \text{diag}[100, 100]$, $\lambda = 0.01$, $\Gamma = \text{diag}[0.1, 0.1, 0.1]$, initial value of $\hat{\theta}$ is defined as $\hat{\theta}_0 = [0.5, 0.5, 0.5]^T$, the robot can track the desired trajectories as shown in Fig. 5. The adaptive control inputs are given in Fig. 6. The simulation results demonstrate that the proposed control is able to achieve the desired control objective.

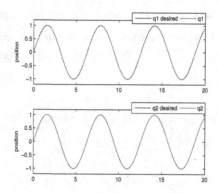

Fig. 5. Tracking performance of the robot system with the proposed adaptive control

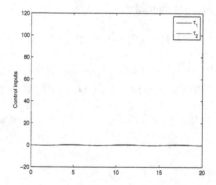

Fig. 6. The adaptive control inputs

5   Conclusion

In this paper, we have designed and developed a wearable rehabilitation robot for the lower limb, which is portable and convenient in the home environment. Training paradigm has been investigated for this robot to train muscle memory within the patients avoiding blind repeated upward and downward motion. Based on the training paradigm, adaptive control is developed according to the robotic dynamics. The simulation results illustrate that the developed wearable rehabilitation robot is feasible and effective for the lower body rehabilitation.

With this wearable rehabilitation robot, the future plan is to utilize it as a stepping stone to achieve an even more effective rehabilitation training by improving the control system and training paradigm.

References

1. Koenig, A., Novak, D., Omlin, X., Pulfer, M., Perreault, E., Zimmerli, L., Mihelj, M., Riener, R.: Real-time closed-loop control of cognitive load in neurological patients during robot-assisted gait training. IEEE Transactions on Neural Systems and Rehabilitation Engineering 19(4), 453–464 (2011)
2. Duschau-Wicke, A., Zitzewitz, J., Caprez, A., Lünenburger, L., Riener, R.: Path control: A method for patient-cooperative robot-aided gait rehabilitation. IEEE Transactions on Neural Systems and Rehabilitation Engineering 18(1), 38–48 (2010)
3. Akdog, E., Adli, M.: The design and control of a therapeutic exercise robot for lower limb rehabilitation: Physiotherabot. Mechatronics 21, 509–522 (2011)
4. Riener, R., Lünenburger, L., Jezernik, S., Anderschitz, M., Colombo, G., Dietz, V.: Patient-cooperative strategies for robot-aided treadmill training: First experimental results. IEEE Transactions on Neural Systems and Rehabilitation Engineering 13(3), 380–394 (2005)
5. Riener, R., Lünenburger, L., Colombo, G.: Human-centered robotics applied to gait training and assessment. Journal of Rehabilitation Research and Development 43(5), 679–694 (2006)
6. Colombo, R., Sterpi, I., Mazzone, A., Delconte, C., Minuco, G., Pisano, F.: Measuring changes of movement dynamics during robot-aided neurorehabilitation of stroke patients. IEEE Transactions on Neural Systems and Rehabilitation Engineering 18(1), 75–85 (2010)
7. Akoijam, J.S.: Understanding robotics in rehabilitation. Indian Journal of Physical Medicine and Rehabilitation 22(1), 35–37 (2011)
8. Koh, C., Hoffmann, T., Bennett, S., McKenna, K.: Management of patients with cognitive impairment after stroke: A survey of australian occupational therapists. Australian Occupational Therapy Journal 56(5), 324–331 (2009)
9. Ge, S.S., Lee, T.H., Harris, C.J.: Adaptive Neural Network Control of Robotic Manipulators. World Scientific, London (1998)
10. Li, Z., Ge, S.S., Ming, A.: Adaptive robust motion/force control of holonomic-constrained nonholonomic mobile manipulators. IEEE Transactions on Systems, Man, and Cybernetics, Part B: Cybernetics 37(3), 607–616 (2007)

Development and Path Planning
of a Biped Robot

Rui Li and Zhijun Li

Department of Automation,
Shanghai Jiao Tong University,
Shanghai 200240, P.R. China
3025413930sjtu.edu.cn

Abstract. In the paper,we present a dynamic model for biped robot
with 12 degrees of freedom(DOF). We apply static walking pattern to
the biped robot and planning its walking pattern based on bionics law of
motion and zero moment point(ZMP). Each motor is equipped with an
Elmo driver, which greatly facilitate the hardware structure of the biped
robot. The experiments are conducted to verify the effectiveness of this
system and the proposed walking pattern.

Keywords: Biped Robot, ZMP, Walking Pattern Planning, Elmo driver.

1 Introduction

Humanoid robots are one of the major topics of robotics research, which obviously different from other types of robots, humanoid robots have similar structure of human and can easily adapt to the environment and tools made for
humans [1], [2], [3], [5], [6], [7], [8]. In addition, its humanoid appearance more
easily accepted by humans and are believed to have a high potential for future
applications. One of the most basic human characteristics are bipedal upright
walking, the walking upright way has a much higher mobility compared with conventional wheeled robot, which can better adapt to and quickly moving on rough
terrain. In recent years, biped robot become a hot interdisciplinary research field.
Some well-known biped robots like ASIMO series of HONDA, which can walk,
up and down stairs, and run. Sony's QRIO can walk, dance, play football, and
transform postures between lie down and stand up and so on. Beijing Institute of
Technology's BHR-01 can even practicing Tai Chi. Pet Man of Boston Dynamics
is by far the best humanoid walking mechanism.

Based on many previous works of our laboratory, we applied the combination
of Elmo driver and servo motor as the actuating mechanism of our biped robot,
which greatly simplified the structure of our system and making the tuning
of motor PID parameters much more convenient with the software: composer,
which is the supporting software of Elmo driver. As a result, the stability of the
whole system is guaranteed.

This paper contain the architecture and walking pattern design of the biped
robot, which organized as follows. In section 2, we describe the structure of our

S.S. Ge et al. (Eds.): ICSR 2012, LNAI 7621, pp. 546–551, 2012.

biped robot and the design of the walking pattern. Then we conduct experiments in section 3 and conclusions are given in section 4.

2   Architecture and Walking Pattern Planning of Biped Robot

According to the structure of human skeleton and the function of human joints, we establish our biped robot with 12 degrees of freedom(DOF), each leg 6 DOF. Our biped robot are consist of a hip joint, a knee joint, and a ankle joint in each leg, 3 DOF in the hip joint(pitch roll yaw), 1 DOF in the knee joint(pitch),2 DOF in the ankle joint(pitch roll). Each DOF are equipped with a servo motor and a digital servo drive. We choose Elmo driver so as to simplify the structure of the whole system. The computer communicate with the Elmo driver through CAN bus, which enabled high speed transmission.

We planning the biped robot walking pattern based on bionics law of motion. According to the human walking mode, we get the position variations of the hip and ankle during human walking process.[4] Through curve fitting, we formulate the hip and ankle functions with step length a and maximum leg height d as parameters. Because we use static walking pattern, which means the biped robot walking in slow speed, then the effect of inertia force can be ignored. So the ZMP is the projection of robot gravity on the ground. By keeping it within the convex hull of all the contact points between the feet and the ground, we make sure the robot will not fall in the walking. We design the center of gravity swing back and forth in the way of sine wave between the feet so as to get the lateral way movement of the biped robot. After determining the trajectories of hip,ankle and the center of gravity, the trajectories of knee and feet will be determined by kinematic constraints. Finally we can get the curve of each joint angle during the walking cycle.

As our work is to let the biped robot go straight forward, so in the paper our walking planning does not include 1 DOF in the hip joint(yaw) of each leg.

2.1   Forward Trajectory Planning

The forward movement of our biped robot need 6 DOF, including 1 DOF in the hip joint(pitch), 1 DOF in the knee joint(pitch) and 1 DOF in the ankle(pitch) of each leg. A full walking cycle are consist of two phases: initial step phase and repeatable step phase.

Initial Step. The initial step planning is to transform the biped robot from the posture of standing to the posture of ready to walk in which one foot is in the former while the other foot is in the back, so as to prepare for the second stage walking. And each ends of the repeatable step phase will back to this posture with the supporting leg and the swing leg changed. Because the coordinate values of the ankle of the supporting leg is fixed in the step, so we just need the trajectories of ankle and hip of swing leg to determine the trajectories of all the other forward movement joints.

The initial step phase trajectories of swing leg ankle and hip can be given by:

$$X_a(i) = \frac{a}{2\pi}\left(\frac{2\pi i}{N} - \sin\left(\frac{2\pi i}{N}\right)\right) \tag{1}$$

$$Z_a(i) = \frac{d}{4}\left(1 - \cos\left(\frac{2\pi i}{N}\right)\right) \tag{2}$$

$$X_h(i) = 0.5X_a(i) \tag{3}$$

$$Z_h(i) = Z_{h0} - \frac{Z_{h0} - L_1 - L_2 + 0.5d + 20}{2}\left(1 - \cos\left(\frac{\pi i}{N}\right)\right) \tag{4}$$

where X_a, X_h are the x axis values in the basic coordinate system of ankle and hip of swing leg respectively, Z_a, Z_h are the z axis values in the basic coordinate system of ankle joint and hip joint respectively. N is the sampling time of a sampling period, i is the sampling index. L_1 and L_2 are thigh length and leg length respectively, a is step length, d is the maximum leg height, Z_{h0} is the initial distance from z axis values of hip joint to z axis values of ankle joint.

All the other joints can be determined in this way: the body are keeping vertical to the ground, the trajectories of knee joints can be obtained by kinematic constraints, the foot plane of swing leg always parallel to the ground.

In the paper ,the parameters are $a = 100$, $d = 100$, $Z_{h0} = 530$(mm),assuming the right leg as the supporting leg, through calculating we show all the angle curves of forward joint during the initial step(we presume that all the angles of forward joint are start towards the positive direction, and at the beginning all the angles are zeros).

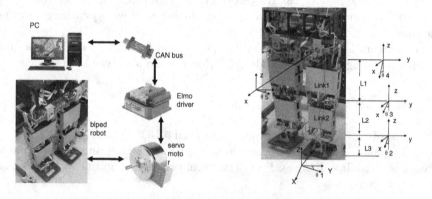

Fig. 1. Control architecture of biped robot   **Fig. 2.** Structure of the biped robot

Table 1. Parameters of the biped robot

Link	Mass(kg)	Length(m)
1	3.34	0.27
2	2.58	0.27
3	1.21	0.1

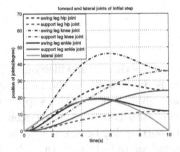

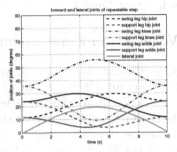

Fig. 3. Initial step   **Fig. 4.** Repeatable step

Repeatable Step. In the repeatable step phase, the trajectories of swing leg ankle and hip are given as follows:

$$X_a(i) = \frac{a}{\pi}(\frac{2\pi i}{N} - \sin(\frac{2\pi i}{N})) \tag{5}$$

$$Z_a(i) = \frac{d}{2}(1 - \cos(\frac{2\pi i}{N})) \tag{6}$$

$$X_h(i) = 0.5X_a(i) + 0.5a \tag{7}$$

$$Z_h(i) = 0.5Z_a(i) + L_1 + L_2 - 0.5d - 20 \tag{8}$$

By using the above method, we get the angle curves of forward joint in repeatable step.

2.2 Lateral Trajectory Planning

The lateral movement need 4 DOF, including 1 DOF in the hip(roll) and 1 DOF in the ankle(roll) of each leg. We design the center of gravity swing back and forth in the way of sine wave between the feet to keep the biped robot's balance during its walking. And only the ankle and hip of supporting leg do the job, which means the two lateral joints of swing leg are totally locked. The lateral trajectory planning is the same way in start step and repeatable step.

The lateral trajectory of the supporting leg ankle is given:

$$\theta_l = \arcsin(\frac{y}{h}) \tag{9}$$

$$y = 180\sin(\frac{\pi i}{N}) \tag{10}$$

$$h = L_1\cos\theta_4 + L_2\cos\theta_3 \tag{11}$$

where θ_l is the roll angles of ankle joint and hip joint of the supporting leg, the only difference of θ_1 and θ_5 lies in their counter rotating directions. The absolute values of them are equal to θ_l. As a result we can let the plane of link 1 and 2 of the swing leg fully parallel to the basic xoz plane. And y is the shift of center of gravity in y axis, h is the straight-line length from the shaft of joint 1 to the shaft of joint 5, θ_3 and θ_4 denote the angles at which the corresponding joint rotates relative to the basic coordinate system. The lateral joint angle curves are shown in figure 3 and 4.

3   Verification Experiment

Under the above walking pattern, we conduct an experiment in which our biped robot walking for a whole walking cycle. That is, first of all, in the initial step stage, left leg walk as the swing leg and the right leg act as the supporting leg, then, we let the robot repeat the repeatable step twice, while between the two repeatable steps the swing leg and the supporting leg both changed so the posture of the biped robot can back to the end of initial step stage. So the biped robot just need to continuously repeat the two repeatable steps, then it can keep walking straight forward. As the limit of the length of this paper, the actual curve of each joint during the repeatable step stage with the expected curve and the torque of each joint are shown below.

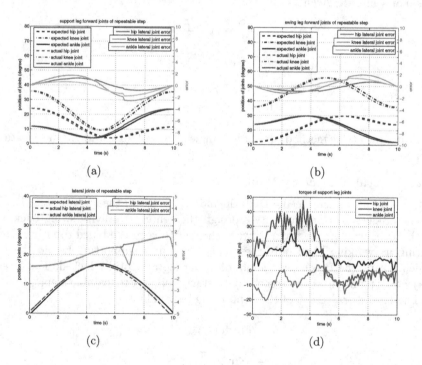

(a)　　　　　　　　　　　　　(b)

(c)　　　　　　　　　　　　　(d)

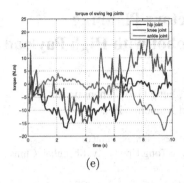

(e)   (f)

4   Conclusion

In this paper, we present a dynamic model for biped robot with 12 degrees of freedom(DOF). We apply static walking pattern to the biped robot and planning its walking pattern based on bionics law of motion and zero moment point(ZMP). Verified by the experiment, our design shows the validity and good walking performance of the dynamic model of our biped robot.

References

1. Huang, Q., Yokoi, K., Kajita, S., Kaneko, K., Arai, H., Koyachi, N., Tanie, K.: Planning Walking Patterns for a Biped Robot. IEEE Transactions on Robotics and Automation 17, 280–289 (2001)
2. Yoshii, K., Nakadai, K., Torii, T., Hasegawa, Y., Tsujino, H., Komatani, K., Ogata, T., Okuno, H.G.: A Biped Robot that Keeps Steps in Time with Musical Beats while Listening to Music with Its Own Ears. In: Proceedings of the 2007 IEEE/RSJ International Conference on Intelligent Robots and Systems, pp. 1743–1750 (2007)
3. Yamamoto, S., Nakadai, K., Nakano, M., Tsujino, H., Valin, J.M., Komatani, K., Ogata, T., Okuno, H.G.: Real-Time Robot Audition System that Recognizes Simultaneous Speech in the Real World. In: IROS, pp. 5333–5338 (2006)
4. Zarrugh, M.Y., Radcliffe, C.W.: Computer generation of human gait kinematics. J. Biomach 12, 99–111 (1979)
5. Huang, Q., Kajita, S., Koyachi, N., Kaneko, K., Yokoi, K., Arai, H., Komoriya, K., Tanie, K.: A high stability, smooth walking pattern for a biped robot. IEEE Transactions on Robotics and Automation 1, 65–71 (1999)
6. Sardain, P., Rostami, M., Bessonnet, G.: An Anthropomorphic Biped Robot: Dynamic Concepts and Technological Design. IEEE Transactions on Systems, Man, and Cybernetics, Part A: Systems and Humans 28(6), 823–838 (1998)
7. Li, Z., Kang, Y.: Dynamic Coupling Switching Control Incorporating Support Vector Machines for Wheeled Mobile Manipulators with Hybrid Joints. Automatica 46(5), 785–958 (2010)
8. Li, Z., Zhang, Y., Yang, Y.: Support Vector Machine Optimal Control for Mobile Wheeled Inverted Pendulums with Unmodelled Dynamics. Neurocomputing 73, 2773–2782 (2010)

Modelling and Trajectory Planning
for a Four Legged Walking Robot with High Payload

Lorenzo Gagliardini[1], Xinghua Tian[2], Feng Gao[2], Chenkun Qi[2],
Christine Chevallereau[1], and Xianchao Zhao[2]

[1] IRCCyN, École Centrale de Nantes, Nantes, France
[2] School of Mechanical Engineering, Shanghai Jiao Tong University, Shanghai, China
lorenzo.gagliardini@eleves.ec-nantes.fr,
{xhtian,fengg,chenkqi,xczhao}@sjtu.edu.cn,
Christine.Chevallereau@irccyn.ec-nantes.fr

Abstract. This paper illustrates the development of a new four legged walking machine. The robot is characterized by a high payload capacity; the result has been achieved according to the specific design of its actuation system, integrating novel high precision actuators, and to its legs, composed by a new family of parallel mechanisms characterized by an appreciable dexterity. With respect to the common walking robot, the particular design of the hydraulic cylinders does not let neglect the weight of the legs in terms of static stability. Hence, a strategy to optimize the whole robot behaviour has been developed. More specifically, the modelling operation and the simulations performed to optimize some quasi-static tasks have been analysed. The optimization process employs a Global Search Algorithm that provides the best results in terms of Stable Margin. The same optimization procedure has been applied with success to investigate the robot walking gait.

Keywords: Quadruped Robot, Walking Robot Modelling, Static Gait Optimization.

1   Introduction

Service robots, whose goals are related to tasks close to social needs [1], are becoming nowadays more and more popular. Service robots are usually provided with a mobile base. In general, it is possible to distinguish between wheeled, tracked and legged robots (which reproduce animal walking mechanisms). The last category presents several advantages, such as the possibility to move over uneven terrains and to reduce the energy consumption as well as the impact on the environment.

The main goal of the robot described in this paper is related to the carrying of heavy payloads. This skill can be applied in several contexts: the transportation of injured people during search and rescue operations; the inspection and maintenance of facilities in unhealthy and risky environments, like mines and nuclear plants.

Most of the recent successful four legged robots employ legs composed by serial mechanisms, as in the case of BigDog [2], by Boston Dynamics, and HyQ [3], by IIT.

S.S. Ge et al. (Eds.): ICSR 2012, LNAI 7621, pp. 552–561, 2012.
© Springer-Verlag Berlin Heidelberg 2012

However, in the past, several designers tested the efficiency of parallel legs, as for the Adaptive Suspension Vehicle (ASV), by Waldron and Song [4]. In order to improve the robot payload capacity, it has been decided to continue to investigate the behaviour of complex legs, building a composite serial and parallel mechanism specifically designed for the given robot. As well, a new kind of hydraulic actuator, characterized by a high precision and controllability, has been developed to control the robot in position, without the use of external position sensors. The main drawback of the designed actuator is related to the impossibility to reduce the cylinder weight.

The final robot structure consists of an aluminium alloy frame; its overall length measures less than 1.2 m and its width about 0.5 m. The height, considering the maximum extension of the legs, is about 1 m. The weight, including all the on-board auxiliary systems, measures about 115 Kg, and each leg about 20 Kg (Fig. 1). Hence, even if the leg weight of most of the robots is negligible, in the specific case it has to be taken in consideration to measure the robot stability. One of the most interesting aspects related to this issue is the joint trajectory planning for quasi-static operations and the walking: in order to study all the tasks and the walking planning it is not possible to adopt the classic techniques which do not consider the legs weight. For this reason, an optimization technique has been adopted in order to find the best body and legs trajectories in terms of static stability. The algorithm, already employed in dynamic contexts [5], has been revised and adapted for static optimizations.

This paper is organized as follows: the Second Chapter contains a general description of the robot; the robot geometric model is presented in the Third Chapter: this is the only fundamental model, since for the required tasks it is possible to neglect the dynamic one; in the Fourth Chapter, the employed optimization procedure is discussed, as well as some simulations and their results. The final chapter discusses future works as well as the conclusions.

2   Description of the System

According to the design of the robot, each leg presents three degrees of freedom, one on the Coronal Plane (CP) and two along the Sagittal Plane (SP). The swing motion, controlled by the first actuator, is decoupled with respect to the side one. The SP mechanism is connected in series to the CP one, composed by a double parallelogram, actuated by the remaining couple of hydraulic cylinders (Fig. 2). The tip, connected to the parallelogram by a tridimensional spring, consists of a rubber semi-sphere.

The symmetric design of the leg guarantees several advantages, such as a well-shaped workspace and a better dynamic balance of the leg. The actuators are mainly incorporated in the upper side of the leg, in order to improve the robot balance and reduce the influence of the leg inertia during the running.

All the actuators are driven by electric motors, which regulate the flow in the cylinder through the opening of electro-valves. The valves themselves are controlled by PIDs. The hydraulic actuators have been specifically designed for the robot: they are characterized by a mechanical feedback that provides a quite precise positioning.

The actuators accuracy guarantees the possibility to perform a position-based control, without the necessity of employing any external position feedbacks. All the actuators are powered by a 16 Hp pump, driven by an inner combustion engine.

Fig. 1. Design of the prototype   **Fig. 2.** Design of the leg

In order to monitor the kinematic status of the robot, an accelerometer and a gyroscope have been employed; these sensors provide a 6 degrees of freedom description of the body acceleration. The integration of the sensor information, and the employment of odometry, let compute the trajectory. Those sensors, coupled with pressure sensors connected to the cylinders, provide the dynamic equilibrium of the body. All the computations are performed by an on-board computer.

3   The Robot Model

The robot has been modelled using a without-implicit-constraint parameterization. The motion, independently of the tasks or the employed gaits, is described taking in consideration a reference frame coherent with the body. This frame, R_{BRF}, will be fixed to the centre of the body, with the x_{BRF} axis along the heading direction and the z_{BRF} axis along the gravity one. Each leg is described by a frame R_{LRF_k}, centered in the joint between the leg and the body itself; k represents the number of the leg taken in consideration. The legs are numbered from the front to the rear, with odd numbers on the left side and with even numbers on the remaining one (Fig. 3).

During the simulations, the robot has been modelled as a parallel one. The Inverse Geometric Model (IGM) can be easily solved knowing the posture of the body and the tips; the position of the remaining joints can be later discovered employing the leg Direct Geometric Model (DGM).

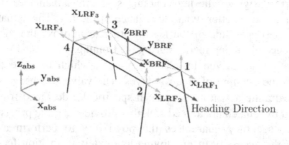

Fig. 3. Reference Frame System

The geometry of each leg has been described employing a Modified Denavit-Hartenberg (MDH) approach [6], in favour of a systematic description of the properties associated to each link. Every leg contains several bodies, each of them described by a reference frame, $R_i(O_i, x_i, y_i, z_i)$. The reference frame is defined in such a way that the axis z_i is chosen along the axis of the joint i and the axes u_j along the normal between z_i and z_j, where j represents the successors of i. The axis x_i can be defined along one of the axes u_j. The homogeneous transformation matrix between two consecutive frames R_i and R_j can be described using the following six parameters:

- γ_j, the angle between x_i and u_j, around the axis z_i;
- b_j, the distance between x_i and u_j, along z_i;
- α_j, the angle between z_i and z_j, around the axis u_j;
- d_j, the distance from z_i to z_j, along u_j;
- θ_j, the angle between u_j and x_j, around the axis z_j;
- r_j, the distance from u_j to x_j, along z_j.

The transformation matrix ^iT_j between the frames i and j is represented by:

$$^iT_j = \begin{bmatrix} ^iA_j & ^iP_j \\ 0_{3\times 1} & 0 \end{bmatrix} \tag{1}$$

where ^iA_j is the rotation matrix of R_j with respect to R_i and ^iP_j is the position vector of R_j origin with respect to R_i. The joint j coordinate, q_j, is equal to r_j if the joint is translational and to θ_j if the joint is rotational. According to the two cases, the parameter σ_j assumes the value 1 if the joint is prismatic and 0 in the remaining case. When two frames are mutually fixed, σ_j is equal to 2.

When a closed-loop is present, just part of the joints, q_a, will be actuated, while part of them, q_p, will be passive. In order to adopt the previous technique, it is sufficient to break the chain in correspondence of a passive joint, and put a reference frame in the edge of each branch: one of them will represent the passive joint itself, the other one a virtual cut joint, q_c.

$$q = \begin{bmatrix} q_a \\ q_p \\ q_c \end{bmatrix} \tag{2}$$

To determine the passive joints it is necessary to solve the constraint problem, equating the posture of the two reference frames along the cut, $^0R_{k+B}$ and ^0R_k:

$$^0R_{k+B} \, ^0R_k^{-1} = I_{4\times 4} \tag{3}$$

In the following part an example of modelling, related to the structure of the SP mechanism, has been provided (Fig. 4), as well as the related table of the MDH parameters (Table 1).

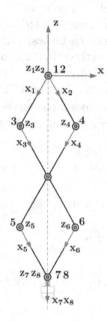

Fig. 4. Sagittal Plane Model

Table 1. Double-Parallelogram Parameters Table

j	a_j	μ_j	σ_j	γ_j	b_j	α_j	d_j	θ_j	r_j
0	LRF	0	2	0	0	$\pi/2$	0	$\pi - \lambda_{dn}$	0
5	3	0	2	0	0	$\pi/2$	0	0	0
6	1	0	2	$-\lambda_s$	0	0	0	0	0
3	1	0	0	0	0	0	L	θ_3	0
4	2	0	0	0	0	0	L	θ_4	0
5	4	0	0	0	0	0	$2L$	θ_5	0
6	3	0	0	0	0	0	$2L$	θ_6	0
7	6	0	0	0	0	0	L	θ_7	0
8	5	0	0	0	0	0	L	θ_8	0
e.e.	7	0	0	0	0	0	L_{el}	$\theta_{e.e.}$	0

4   The Optimization Process

According to the proposed requirements, the robot has to be able to perform quasi-static tasks and to employ crawling gaits. The active joint trajectories are then required. One of the most suitable techniques is related to the optimization of the trajectories, in terms of the robot stability. The procedure here adopted was inspired by the work performed, for the dynamic case, by Muraro et Al. [5]. The quality of this technique has been verified investigating some specific cases: the maximization of the robot stability when the robot stands on three legs; the research of an optimal crawling gait.

4.1   The Optimization Technique

The optimization technique consists in finding the best conditions that maximize the robot static stability. In particular, the given criterion is based on the evaluation of the time t evolution of the Stable Margin (SM), $S.M.$:

$$S.M. = \min\{d_1, d_2, d_3\} \tag{4}$$

$$criterion = \frac{\sum S.M.(t)}{T} \tag{5}$$

where d_1, d_2, d_3 represent the distances between the projection of the CoM and the sides of the support pattern, defined as the convex hull of the vertical projection of the tips in contact with the ground. T represents the overall task time.

The optimization can provide an optimal set of trajectories. Since the robot has been modelled as a parallel one, it is more suitable to drive its body and its leg tips in the task space. The employed trajectories belong to the polynomial functions family, appreciable for their simplicity and their easy configurability. Their degree has been specifically selected with respect to the desired shape of the trajectory and to the required constraints in position, velocity and acceleration. The coefficients of the trajectory curve family represent the basic set of Optimization Variables. Supplementary variables can be added, such as the task duration. For each parameter it is necessary to specify the range in which they change. During the optimization procedure, some constraints have to be evaluated. Usually it is recommended to check the joint limits in terms of position, velocity or acceleration. At the same time it is always important to verify the stability of the robot. Since the model does not present implicit constraints taking into account the ground contact, it is also necessary to check, during the whole process, if the legs are going to penetrate the soil.

The process is mainly based on the investigation of the robot behaviour, according to the different values that the optimization parameters assume. As illustrated in Fig. 5, once the model, the optimization variables and the constraints are specified, running the simulation of the system it is possible to evaluate the stability of the robot, the so called Criteria. Then, the optimization algorithm evaluates if the solution is optimal or if other investigations are required: in this case it provides the new optimization variables for the next simulation. Several global optimization algorithms can perform the criteria analysis, such as the Global Search Algorithm [7] and the Genetic Algorithm: the first one gives better results if the optimization criteria present a smooth gradient; the second one is more indicated for fragmented profiles.

4.2   Robot Optimal Equilibrium with Three Supporting Tips

The developed robot should be able to perform several quasi-static operations. One of them is to maintain the equilibrium of the robot when it stands on three tips, keeping a lifted leg for a long time. The same action should be repeated consecutively, lifting one by one all the legs. This goal can be easily achieved initializing the robot with a symmetric posture, with a rectangular support pattern. Before each lifting operation, the robot will reach a proper posture to obtain a better balance. Afterwards, the robot lifts the specified leg, maintaining it in the air for at least a minute. Once the operation is concluded, the robot comes back to the initial posture and performs symmetrically the task with the remaining legs. According to the specific problem, the optimization parameters include the task execution time and the trajectories parameters for both the body and the tips. All the employed trajectories are 5th degree polynomial functions with six unknowns, in order to set all the initial and final velocities (and accelerations) to 0. Hence, among the optimization variables, the standing tip positions appear, as well as the initial and final lifting leg positions.

The best result is provided by the Global Search Algorithm. The optimal solution requires an initial support pattern as big as possible. Before the operation, the body

CoM is placed in the opposite direction with respect to the lifting leg. In this way, when the lifting leg is in the air, the global CoM is as far as possible from the sides of the support pattern (Fig. 6). During the lifting procedure the optimization restricts the body motion to 10 mm. In the meanwhile, the lifting leg will be pulled back to the body: this operation contributes to maintain the position of the overall CoM close to the optimal one. This result is confirmed by the fact that the $S.M.$ is not oscillating more than 15 mm, with a stable average of 155 mm (Fig. 7).

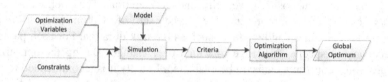

Fig. 5. The optimization procedure

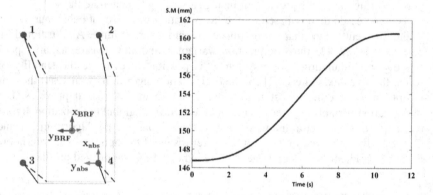

Fig. 6. Leg lifting initial configuration   **Fig. 7.** Robot Stable Margin

4.3   Optimal Static Walking

Static gaits represent the basic motion for every legged robot. They can be catalogued according to some basic parameters, such as: λ, the length of the stride; K, the sequence of the lifting legs; β, the duty factor, given by the amount of time each leg is in support; φ_i, the phases of each leg lifting time; S, the stroke, defined as the relative motion between the body and the legs during the support phase; R, the pitch, defined as the distance, along one side, between the stroke middle points.

Among the walking gaits, the most popular are the creeping ones, which permit to lift just one leg at a time. The best stability, for quadrupeds, is achieved using one of the creeping gaits, the so called wave gait [8]. The optimal condition requires the legs will lift in a proper order (4, 2, 3, 1). With a duty factor greater than 0.75, the optimal conditions are given by:

$$\varphi_2 = 0.5; \quad \varphi_3 = \beta; \quad \varphi_4 = \varphi_3 - 0.5 \tag{6}$$

$$S^* = \beta - 0.75 \quad \text{with} \quad \beta \geq 0.75, \ R \leq P \tag{7}$$

All the gait parameters can be optimized analytically and numerically. In the specific case the operation has been performed taking into account the technique presented in the previous section. This solution is quite advantageous, since it offers the possibility to optimize every aspect of the problem, as the legs trajectories.

In this specific analysis, the stability has been investigated making the robot walk in the forward direction. The overall stride execution time, the length step and the duty factor are the optimization parameters which appear explicitly in the problem. The stroke and pitch analysis is implicitly included in the optimization of the support pattern and the tip trajectory: the support pattern is investigated taking in consideration rectangular and parallelogram shapes. The trajectory of the lifting tip is given by a 6th degree polynomial, in order to provide a Via Point (VP). The trajectory of the body is basically linear, according to the classic wave gait theory. Anyway, an alternative solution has been investigated, with a 7th degree polynomial function: this assumption let observe the effect of a body lateral oscillation across two VPs.

The Optimal Solutions. Analysing the basic case, assuming an execution time of 3 s, the optimal support pattern configuration requires that the legs are slightly opened to the extern. Along the heading direction, the tip distance is equal to the leg joint distance. The starting position of the body is completely symmetrical along the lateral direction; the body is just a little bit closer to the rear legs. The result shows that the optimized stride, λ, is equal to the upper bound selected by the user (300 mm), while the optimal β is equal to $11/12$; this result is confirmed by the numerical simulations performed by Waldron [4].

Changing the shape of the support pattern, part of the optimal parameters changes too. The legs present a high lateral swinging angle while the tips on the left side are 40 mm more advanced than the corresponding elements on the left side. λ assumes the maximum value, as well as β does, which becomes equal to $12/13$.

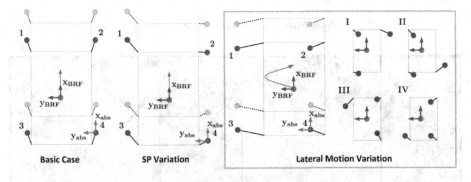

Fig. 8. Initial and final configurations for the three tested walking gaits. The continuous lines represent the tips and body initial postures while the dashed ones represent the final postures. The green arrow represents the body trajectory. The gait which includes a lateral motion has been provided with a detailed description of the lifting leg sequence.

The second modified test provides a shorter optimal time, equal to 1 s. The SP dimension, along the heading direction, is a little bit shorter than in the previous case; once again, the legs present a high lateral swinging angle. The introduction of a lateral body motion pushes the optimization to move the initial position of the body 50 mm closer to the right side. During the motion, at the middle of the walking cycle, the body will reach the symmetric posture on the left side. Among the remaining parameters, the optimal stride becomes shorter, reaching 205 mm, while the duty factor is still as higher as possible. Fig. 8 let compare the three obtained solutions.

The Stability Analysis. Comparing the normalized results, it appears that the first variation is not able to introduce any substantial improvement. Considering the classic wave gait, the $S.M.$ goes from 20 to 52 mm, according to the previous theory. In the support pattern variation, both the values are slightly increased, such as the $S.M.$ average: it goes from the 32.33 of the first case to the 37.26 of the second one. The most satisfactory result is provided by the last variation, which raises the minimum $S.M.$ to 80 mm, and the $S.M.$ average to 89 mm, with a gain equal to 141%. The results are summarized in Fig. 9, where the $S.M.$ is described for the time intervals when the robot stands on three tips. This proofs how important the contribution of the robot lateral stability is: it cannot be discarded in favour of a more simplistic Longitudinal Stable Margin analysis.

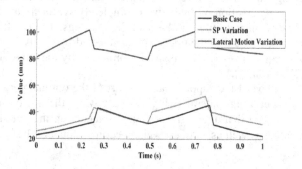

Fig. 9. Stable Margin comparison between the three cases

Fig. 10. Optimal walking gait test sequence. The robot oscillates from its left to its right side while the body is pushed forward. The first lifting legs are the one on the right side.

5 Conclusion

In this paper the development of a new four-legged walking robot has been presented. The robot is capable to carry very high loads: it takes this advantage from its hydraulic actuation and the hybrid mechanical leg structure. The paper focused on the analysis of the trajectory planning for quasi-static tasks and walking. This operation has been performed using a global optimization algorithm; the procedure optimizes the robot stability, according to the SM criterion, relieving the user of the manual selection of the trajectory parameters. The efficiency of the offline trajectory planning has been proofed by the tests performed on the real robot. The first tests, performed taking in consideration the classic techniques, led always to a failure. Using the given algorithm it was instead possible to avoid the problems encountered with the classic theories. In Fig. 10 it is possible to observe some shots describing the robot during the static walking. The later work will focus on the investigation of the dynamic behaviour of the robot. The same optimization technique will be used to study the optimal trotting gait.

Acknowledgments. This work is supported by the National Hi-Tech Research and Development Program of China (863 Program, Grant No. 2011AA040901) and the National Natural Science Foundation of China (No. 51175323). This work was also partially supported by the European Master of Advanced Robotics (EMARO).

References

1. Garcia, E., Jimenez, A.M., Gonzales De Santos, P., Armada, M.: The Evolution of Robotics Research. IEEE Robotics and Automation Magazine 14(1), 91–103 (2007)
2. Raibert, M., Blankespoor, K., Nelson, G., Playter, R.: The Big Dog Team: BigDog, the Rough-Terrain Quadruped Robot. In: 17th World Congress of the International Federation of Automatic Control, Seoul, Korea (2008)
3. Semini, C., Tsagarakis, N.G., Guglielmino, E., Caldwell, D.G.: Design and experimental evaluation of the hydraulically actuated prototype leg of the HyQ robot. In: International Conference on Intelligent Robots and Systems (IROS), Taipei, pp. 3640–3645 (2010)
4. Song, S.M., Waldron, K.J.: Machines that Walk: The Adaptive Suspension Vehicle. The MIT Press, Cambridge (1989)
5. Khalil, W., Dombre, E.: Modelling, identification and control of robots. Hemès Penton, London (2002)
6. Muraro, A., Chevallereau, C., Aoustin, Y.: Optimal trajectories for a quadruped robot with trot, amble and curvet gaits for two energetic criteria. Multibody System Dynamics 9, 39–62 (2003)
7. Ugray, Z., Lasdon, L., Plummer, J., Glover, F., Kelly, J., Marti, R.: Scatter search and local nlp solvers: A multistart framework for global optimization. Journal on Computing 19(3), 328–340 (2007)
8. McGhee, R., Frank, A.: On the stability properties of quadruped creeping gaits. Mathematical Biosciences 3, 331–351 (1968)

Combining Gait Research
of the Quadruped/Biped Reconfigurable Walking Chair
with Parallel Leg Mechanism

Xing Hu[1], Hongbo Wang[2], Lingfeng Sang[2], Qifang Gu[3], and Lin Yuan[2]

[1] School of Mechanical and Electrical Engineering,
Xi'an University of Architecture and Technology, Xi'an, Shanxi, 710055, P.R. China
huxing918@163.com

[2] The Ministry of Education Key Laboratory of Advanced Forging Technology and Science
and Hebei Province Key Laboratory of Parallel Robot and Mechatronics Systems,
Yanshan University, Qinhuangdao, Hebei, 066004, P.R. China
{hongbo_w,info}@ysu.edu.cn, sanglingfeng@163.com

[3] The Department of Computer, Wuxi City College of Vocational Technology, Wuxi,
214063, P.R., China
guqifang@163.com

Abstract. The quadruped/biped reconfigurable walking robot with parallel leg mechanism can realize not only the quadruped walking, but also the biped walking. The converting process from the quadruped to the biped includes locking the vertical revolute pair hinged with the upper platform and combining the corresponding lower platforms. Based on the previous study, the combining schemes of walking chair are researched in this paper, and then the correctness of the combining schemes is analyzed by using the position workspace of the swing leg and the body mechanism in different states which are obtained by the MATLAB software and anti-solution search method. Compared with the stability margin and the adjustment coordination of the body in the different combining schemes, the optimal combining gaits of walking chair are selected, which lays the theoretical foundation for the quadruped/biped converting control of walking chair.

Keywords: walking chair, parallel leg mechanism, combining gait, reconfigurable walking robot, optimal gaits.

1 Introduction

Gait is a coordinated relationship of the body of walkers (including human, animals and machines) in the time and space during the movements. The fundamental premise to achieve the stable walking for robot is that the gaits and postures are stable, cyclical and operable [1].

At the end of the 19th century, after Muybridge studied animals' walking by using successive photography method, scholars began the research on the gaits. In the late 1960s, the systematical description methods and definitions of gaits were presented by McGhee who summarized the previous research about animal gaits, which laid the

S.S. Ge et al. (Eds.): ICSR 2012, LNAI 7621, pp. 562–571, 2012.
© Springer-Verlag Berlin Heidelberg 2012

mathematical foundation for the gait research [2]. The gaits based on the diagonal principle for quadruped walking robot were studied by Hirose etc., which contained mechanism locking and could not move in all directions [3]. In 1990, the walking robot with 2n legs were discussed by Song and the wave gait was put forward. Since 1991, he has began to study on the turning gaits of quadruped robot and got a lot of achievements [4-5]. Pal et al. applied Heuristic graphics search algorithm to ensure the optimal step and falling point of single leg for robot. However, after completing a gait cycle, postures needed to be adjusted and successive walk couldn't be realized [6]. SLPMF method which defined the diagonals consisted of four feet as the dangerous border of the quadruped mobile robot in the static walking was presented by Pack etc. [7-8]. The intelligent gait and control algorithm of the quadruped walking robot were explored by Hugel and Blazvic [9]. The gait based on evolutionary algorithm was studied by Hornsby [10]. The gaits of many biomimetic robots (such as snake, crab, human and four-legged animals) were discussed by many scholars, and some achievements have been obtained [11-17]. Although there are a wide range of gaits of multilegged walking robots, their common characteristic is that specific walking actions are completed by tightly combining the robots' structures.

The quadruped/biped reconfigurable walking chair with parallel leg mechanism is a new kind of walking device which combines many advantages of the quadruped robot and the biped robot and uses parallel mechanism (PM) as the leg mechanism of walking robot; therefore, there are greater stiffness, better stability, faster walking speed and higher bearing capacity [18-20]. The conversion from the quadruped to the biped or from the biped to the quadruped is an important link for the walking chair to achieve reconfiguration.

The gaits which can realize the conversion from the quadruped to the biped or from the biped to the quadruped are defined as combining gaits. Based on previous research, the combining schemes are studied in this paper.

2   Mechanism Introduction of Walking Chair

According to the walking requirements and reconfigurable theory, 3-SPU PM is selected as the leg mechanism of the walking chair as shown in Fig. 1.

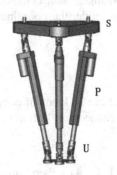

Fig. 1. 3-SPU PM   **Fig. 2.** The quadruped walking robot

Under the condition of quadruped walking, the vertical rotation pair hinged with the moving platform is locked and the leg mechanism could be changed into 3-UPU PM which has three translational degrees of freedom (DOF) as shown in Fig. 2. The coordinate system of the whole mechanism is established as shown in Fig. 3, and the serial numbers for the branch of the mechanism are shown in Fig. 4.

When the front foot and hind foot on both sides are combined respectively, and the vertical rotation pair hinged with the moving platform is unlocked, a biped walking robot with basic leg mechanism 6-SPU is formed as shown in Fig. 5. The arrangement of the upper platform and the lower platform is shown in Fig.6.

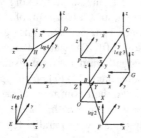

Fig. 3. The Coordinate system

Fig. 4. The serial numbers diagram

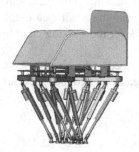

Fig. 5. The biped walking chair

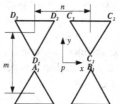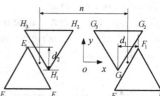

Fig. 6. The arrangement diagram

Through performance analysis and the dimension optimization based on the genetic algorithm, the following size values are obtained: $m=n=340\text{mm}$, $d_1=50\text{mm}$, $d_2=65\text{mm}$. When the walking chair walks in biped mode, the coordinate system is established as shown in Fig. 6.

3   Combining Gait

According to the order and phase of swing leg, there are 28 kinds of combining gaits which could be divided into two categories in accordance with different steps in the combining process.

(1) Completing combination by four steps

When walking chair starts with the leg $i(i=1,2,3,4)$, there are 6 kinds of combining gaits. For example, when leg 1 is the first step, combining gaits could be selected as follows: 1-2-3-4•1-2-4-3•1-3-2-4•1-3-4-2•1-4-2-3•1-4-3-2. It is similar to leg 1 when the first step is leg 2 or leg 3 or leg 4. Therefore, 24 kinds of combining gaits are obtained.

(2) Completing combination by two steps

In this way, there are 4 kinds of combining gaits: 1-2, 2-1, 3-4, 4-3.

Considering the research methods of gaits are similar, the gait 1-4-2-3 and gait 1-2 are chosen to study the combining process of walking chair in this paper.

3.1   Gait *1-4-2-3*

The combining process of the gait 1-4-2-3 is shown in Fig.7, where $S_{42i}(i=1,2,3,4,5)$ is stability margin of robot .

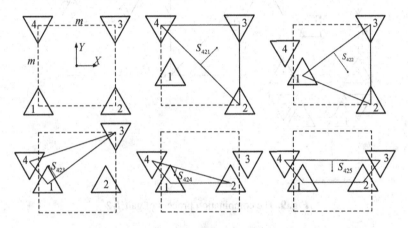

Fig. 7. The combining process of gait *1-4-2-3*

The center of gravity is adjusted as shown in Fig. 8 under this gait. When the combination gait is completed, the center of gravity is adjusted five times. The adjustment vectors for center of gravity are $\mathbf{r}_{421}=\vec{O}_{41}-\vec{O}_{40}$, $\mathbf{r}_{422}=\vec{O}_{42}-\vec{O}_{41}$, $\mathbf{r}_{423}=\vec{O}_{43}-\vec{O}_{42}$, $\mathbf{r}_{424}=\vec{O}_{44}-\vec{O}_{43}$, $\mathbf{r}_{425}=\vec{O}_{45}-\vec{O}_{44}$, respectively. The corresponding values for center of gravity are recorded as $l_{421},l_{422},l_{423},l_{424},l_{425}$.

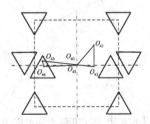

Fig. 8. The path for center of gravity adjustment

The step length of walking chair is expressed in this gait as follows:

$$SL_1 = \sqrt{\left(\frac{d_1}{2}\right)^2 + \left(\frac{m}{2} - r + \frac{d_2}{2}\right)^2} \tag{1}$$

3.2   Gait 1-2

The combination process of the gait *1-2* is shown in Fig. 9, where $S_i (i = 1,2,3)$ is stability margin of robot .

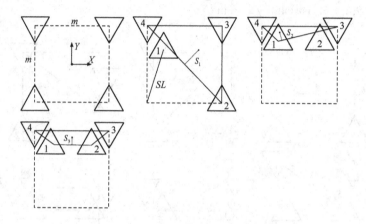

Fig. 9. The combination process of gait *1-2*

The center of gravity is adjusted under this gait as shown in Fig. 10. When the combining gait is completed, the center of gravity is adjusted three times. The adjustment vectors for center of gravity are $\mathbf{r}_{01} = \vec{O}_1 - \vec{O}_0$, $\mathbf{r}_{12} = \vec{O}_2 - \vec{O}_1$, $\mathbf{r}_{23} = \vec{O}_3 - \vec{O}_2$, respectively. The corresponding values for center of gravity are recorded as l_1, l_2, l_3 .

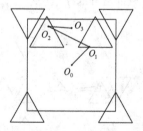

Fig. 10. The path for center of gravity adjustment

The step length of walking chair in this gait is expressed as follows:

$$SL_2 = \sqrt{(m - 2r + d_2)^2 + d_1^2}$$ (2)

4   Correctness Verification of Proposed Combining Scheme

In the process of combining, the workspace of the body mechanism is constantly changing. Therefore, whether the adjustment values for the center of gravity of the body mechanism and the steps are in the corresponding workspace are selected to judge the correctness of combining gait.

In the process of combining, the structural constraints of body mechanism are assumed as follows:

(1)   The range of actuator for each branch is $400 \leq l_i \leq 700$ mm (i is the number of each branch).

(2)   The range of universal joint is $-75° \leq \theta_k^{(i)} \leq 75°$, where $k = 1, 2, 4, 5$.

(3)   The body mechanism moves in the height of 500 mm.

(4)   Center of gravity is adjusted separately.

4.1   The Workspace of Leg Mechanism 3-UPU

During the combining process, the leg mechanism of walking chair is 3-UPU. When leg mechanism moves as swing leg, the lower platform is the moving platform and the upper platform is the fixed platform. Based on the influencing factors of workspace of parallel robot and the structural constraints of mechanism which are presented in the above, workspace of leg mechanism 3-UPU in the xy plane is obtained as shown in Fig. 11.

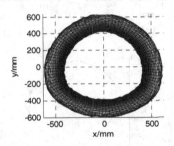

Fig. 11. Projection of workspace in xy plane

Observing the above workspace, it is found that the workspace is gradually increasing with the height rising. So the minimum workspace is obtained when $z = 0$. According to the equation 1 and equation 2, the step lengths in these two different combining gaits are 140.74 mm and 281.47 mm, which meet the minimum workspace.

4.2   Workspace of the Body Mechanism

When walking chair combining, 3 legs stand on the ground and 1 leg swings. According to the stability requirements, the center of gravity must be located within the triangle supported by 3 legs. Taking workspace of gait 1-4-2-3 for example, it is known that the body mechanism of walking chair includes five states.

(1) When walking chair stands with 4 legs on the ground, the center of gravity is adjusted within Δ_{FGH} , the adjustment vector of center of gravity is $\mathbf{r}_{421} = (70.42 \quad 70.42)$, and the adjustment value of center of gravity is $l_{421} = 99.59$ mm (Fig. 12(a)).

(2) After leg 1 walking, the center of gravity is adjusted within $\Delta_{E'GF}$, the adjustment vector of center of gravity is $\mathbf{r}_{422} = (-1.63 \quad -85.81)$, and the adjustment value of center of gravity is $l_{422} = 85.82$ mm (Fig. 12(b)).

(3) After leg 4 walking, the center of gravity is adjusted within $\Delta_{E'GH'}$, the adjustment vector of center of gravity is $\mathbf{r}_{423} = (-205.39 \quad 31.26)$, and the adjustment value of center of gravity is $l_{423} = 207.76$ mm (Fig. 12(c)).

(4) After leg 2 walking, the center of gravity is adjusted to within $\Delta_{H'E'F'}$, the adjustment vector of center of gravity is $\mathbf{r}_{424} = (4.53 \quad -22.12)$, and the adjustment value of center of gravity is $l_{424} = 22.58$ mm (as shown in Fig. 12(d)).

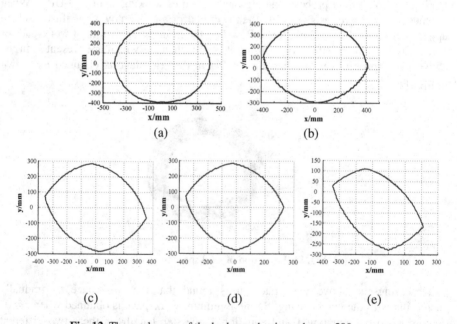

(a)   (b)

(c)   (d)   (e)

Fig. 12. The workspace of the body mechanism when z=500mm

(5) After leg 3 walking, the center of gravity is adjusted to within quadrangle $E'F'G'H'$, the adjustment vector of center of gravity is $r_{425} = (132.08 \quad 6.25)$, and the adjustment value of center of gravity is $l_{425} = 132.22$ mm (as shown in Fig. 12(e)).

Observing the above figures, it is found that the adjustment values of center of gravity are in the workspace when the body mechanism moves in the height of 500mm.

5   Optimization of Combining Gait

Since the adjustment value and adjustment number of each gait are different in the process of combining, the corresponding stability margin and the adjustment coordination of body mechanism are different.

5.1   Contrast of Stability Margin

With regard to combine gaits, the stability margin of body mechanism is different under different states. Table 1 shows values of stability margin when walking chair starts with leg 1.

Table 1. The Stability Margin of Different Gaits

Gaits	Stability Margin		Gaits	Stability Margin	
1-2-3-4 (1-2-4-3)	S_{231}	99.59	1-4-3-2	S_{241}	99.59
	S_{232}	74.96		S_{242}	101.21
	S_{233}	67.62		S_{243}	16.13
	S_{234}	26.25		S_{244}	30.98
	S_{235}	32.5		S_{245}	32.5
1-3-2-4	S_{321}	99.59	1-3-4-2	S_{341}	99.59
	S_{322}	58.67		S_{342}	58.67
	S_{323}	74.96		S_{343}	75.20
	S_{324}	26.25		S_{344}	30.98
	S_{325}	32.5		S_{345}	32.5
1-4-2-3	S_{421}	99.59	1-2	S_1	99.59
	S_{422}	101.21		S_2	30.73
	S_{423}	36.15		S_3	32.5
	S_{424}	26.25			
	S_{425}	32.5			

The conclusions can be obtained from the above table as follows:

(1) Values of stability margin of gait 1-2-3-4 and gait 1-2-4-3 are the same.
(2) The minimum value of stability margin of gait 1-3-4-2 is the maximum, which indicates that the stability is the best. And the minimum value of stability margin of gait 1-2 is very close to that of gait 1-3-4-2.

5.2   Contrast of the Adjustment Coordination

According to the moving coordination, if the body mechanism of walking chair is adjusted along with the moving direction, the energy consumption is lower and stability is better. In this paper, the maximum adjustment value of center of gravity obtained when the combining gait is completed is defined as the evaluation index of the adjustment coordination. The adjustment value of body mechanism under each gait is shown in the table 2.

Table 2. The Adjustment Value of Body

Gaits	Step 1	Step 2	Step 3	Step 4	Step 5
1-2-3-4(1-2-4-3)	99.59	157.57	59.93	221.20	132.22
1-3-2-4	99.59	172.98	49.39	221.47	132.22
1-3-4-2	99.59	172.97	210.10	247.74	132.08
1-4-2-3	99.59	85.82	207.76	22.58	132.22
1-4-3-2	99.59	85.82	203.57	21.06	132.08
1-2	99.59	193.53	112.92		

It is found from the above table that the maximum adjustment value of gait 1-2 is minimum.

Based on the above comparison of two characteristic parameters, it is seen that gait 1-2 is better when walking chair starts combining with leg 1.

6   Conclusion

(1) Combined with the structural characteristics of walking chair and walking requirements, 28 kinds of combining schemes are obtained for conversion from the quadruped to the biped or from the biped to the quadruped.

(2) Based on MATLAB, the position workspace of the body mechanism and leg mechanism in gait 1-4-2-3 are obtained by using anti-solution search method, which are used to verify the correctness of the combining scheme.

(3) Through the contrast of the stability margins and the adjustment coordination of body mechanism, the gait 1-2 is selected as the optimal combining gait of the quadruped/biped reconfigurable walking chair with parallel leg mechanism when walking chair starts to combine with leg 1, which lays the theoretical foundation for the quadruped/biped conversion control of walking chair.

Acknowledgments. This work was supported by the National Natural Science Foundation of China under Grant No. 61075099.

References

1. Chen, D.H., Tong, J., Li, C.H., Zhang, S.J., Chen, B.C.: A Review of Man and Animal Gait and Walking Robot. Journal of Jilin University 33(4), 121–125 (2003)
2. McGhee, R.B.: Some Finite State Aspects of Legged Locomotion. Mathematical Biosciences 2(1-2), 67–84 (1968)

3. Hirose, S., Martins, F.: Generalized Standard Leg Trajectory for Quadruped Walking Vehicle. Transactions of the Society of Instrument and Control Engineers 25(4), 455–461 (1989)
4. Song, S.M., Zhang, C.D.: A Study of the Stability of Generalized Wave Gaits. Mathematical Biosciences 115(1), 1–32 (1993)
5. Song, S.M., Zhang, C.D.: Turning Gait of a Quadruped Walking Machine. In: Proceedings of IEEE International Conference on Robotics and Automation, vol. 3, pp. 2106–2112 (1991)
6. Pal, P.K., Jayarajan, K.: Generation of Free Gait - A Graph Search Approach. IEEE Transactions on Robotics and Automation 7(3), 299–305 (1991)
7. Pack, D.J., Kak, A.C.: A Simplified Forward Gait Control for a Quadruped Walking Robot. In: Proceedings of the 1994 IEEE/RSJ International Conference on Intelligent Robots and Systems, Munich, German, vol. 2, pp. 1011–1018 (1994)
8. Pack, D.J., Kang, H.: An Omnidirectional Gait Control using a Graph Search Method for a Quadruped Walking Robot. In: Proceedings of the 1995 IEEE International Conference on Robotics and Automation, Nagoya, Aichi, Japan, vol. 1, pp. 988–993 (1995)
9. Hugel, V., Blazvic, P.: Towards Efficient Implementation of Quadruped Gaits with Duty Factor of 0.75. In: Proceedings of the 1999 IEEE International Conference on Robotics and Automation, Detroit, Michigan, USA, vol. 3, pp. 2360–2365 (1999)
10. Hornby, G.S., Takamura, S., Yokono, J., Hanagata, O., Yamamoto, T., Fujita, M.: Evolving Robust Gaits with AIBO. In: Proceedings of the 2000 IEEE International Conference on Robotics and Automation, San Francisco, California, vol. 3, pp. 3040–3045 (2000)
11. Wang, J.S., Zhang, B.P.: Comprehensive Double Three Feet Walking Robot (II)-Walk Mode Planning. Journal of Tsinghua University (Nature Science) 34(5), 63–71 (1994)
12. Pan, J.M., Cheng, J.S.: The Research of Slope Movement of Quadruped Walking Robot. Robots 13(4), 22–26 (1991)
13. Fang, Y.B., Jiang, C.C.: The Research of Pacing Gait and Dynamic Walking of Quadruped Robot. Robots 17(1), 134–136 (1995)
14. Yu, L.Q., Wu, C.L., Ma, S.P.: Study on Gait Transition between Symmetrical Gaits of Quadrupeds Based on Timing Sequence Analysis. Journal of Huazhong University of Science and Technology 34(9), 32–34 (2006)
15. Gan, J.G., Zhu, W., Gan, G.Y.: Follow-the-leader Gait Study for Six-legged Walking Vehicle. Robots 16(4), 234–236 (1994)
16. Zhao, T.S., Zhao, Y.S., Huang, Z.: The Flexibility of Walking Machine Imitating a Crab. China Mechanical Engineering 9(3), 55–57 (1998)
17. Yu, S.M., Ma, S.G., Li, B., Wang, Y.C.: Gait Generation and Analysis for Snake-like Robots. Robots 33(3), 371–378 (2011)
18. Qi, Z.Y., Wang, H.B., Huang, Z., Zhang, L.L.: Kinematics of a Quadruped/Biped Reconfigurable Walking Robot with Parallel Leg Mechanisms. In: ASME/IFToMM International Conference on Reconfigurable Mechanisms and Robots, pp. 558–564. King's College, London (2009)
19. Wang, H.B., Qi, Z.Y., Xu, G.L., Xi, F.F., Hu, G.Q., Huang, Z.: Kinematics Analysis and Motion Simulation of a Quadruped Walking Robot with Parallel Leg Mechanism. The Open Mechanical Engineering Journal 4, 77–85 (2010)
20. Wang, H.B., Qi, Z.Y., Hu, Z.W., Huang, Z.: Application of Parallel Leg Mechanisms in Quadruped/Biped Reconfigurable Walking Robot. Journal of Mechanical Engineering 45(8), 24–30 (2009)

Design of an Automatic Rotatory Chair Prototype for BPPV Treatment

Fei Xu[1], Dingguo Zhang[1,*], Xueguan Gao[1], and Shankai Yin[2]

[1] School of Mechanical Engineering,
[2] The 6th People's Hospital,
Shanghai Jiao Tong University, China
dgzhang@sjtu.edu.cn

Abstract. Benign paroxysmal positional vertigo (BPPV) is caused by the malfunction of the otolith that is responsible for spatial disorientation and motion sickness. BPPV is a very common vestibular peripheral vertigo. Nowadays the prevailing maneuver of curing BPPV is manipulative reduction. An automatic rotatory chair is designed for clinical diagnosis and remedy in otorhinolaryngology (OQL) according to the manipulative reduction. This paper focuses on mechanical design and torque analysis. The mathematic model is built based on mechanical structure, and after optimization the torques applying on the motors can be reduced dramatically, which is useful in practical implementation.

Keywords: BPPV, mechanical design, rotatory chair, optimization, finite element analysis.

1 Introduction

Benign paroxysmal positional vertigo (BPPV) can cause balance and vestibular function disorders on some people at any age, especially the elders about 34.5% of which may suffer this problem [1], [2]. The signs and symptoms of BPPV are obvious, such as vertigo, nausea, pre-syncope and so on. It is reported that BPPV is also responsible for approximately 20% of dizziness [3], [4].

BPPV can be caused by either of canalithiasis or cupulolithiasis in which canalithiasis describes free-floating particles with a semicircular canal and is the most common case [5]. In the case of canalithiasis, the calcium carbonate crystals (known as otolith) of the patient with BPPV, is dislocated from its original position within the utricle and shifted into the semicircular canals from time to time [6]. As the head moves in different orientations, the gravity-dependent movement of the heavier otolith fragments can cause pathological displacement of endolymph, and that is how the sensation of vertigo is triggered.

Based on the theory of canalithiasis, some maneuver methods are applied to the treatment of BPPV, of which the famous ones are Epley's maneuver with a success rate of 90% - 97% and particle repositioning maneuver (PRM) with 88.2% success rate [7]. Surgical treatments, such as a semi-circular canal occlusion, can also be considered as

---

* Corresponding author.

S.S. Ge et al. (Eds.): ICSR 2012, LNAI 7621, pp. 572–580, 2012.
© Springer-Verlag Berlin Heidelberg 2012

an effective approach. However, surgery is considered as the last reserved maneuver because of the severe sequel that will fail vestibular rehabilitation. Devices, like multiple-dimensional rotatory chairs such as Epley Omniax System manufactured by VESTICON or the device DizzyFIX, are available to be physically used to follow the procedure of different maneuvers known as Epley Maneuver, Semont Maneuver and so on [8]. This paper represents the development of a three -dimensional chair based on the analysis of the mechanical structure and applying torques on the purpose of developing a both hand operated convenient and electrical control device. And the controlling system is still under developing.

2   Mechanical Structure and Analysis

2.1   Overview of System

There are altogether four degrees of freedom (DOFs), two rotating DOFs and two offsetting DOFs. The rotating DOFs are in charge of the key motions during the maneuver treatment. The offsetting DOFs can regulate positions of the chair in two linear directions to offer convenience for different individuals.

The rotatory chair includes seven main parts as shown in Fig.1, which are outer frame, inner frame, upper power installation, middle power installation, pillar, supporting plate, and movable chair unit. The outer frame and inner frame are connected by two rotating axes fixed by angular contact ball bearings which are installed in a back-to-back way, so that large axial and radical torques can be endured.

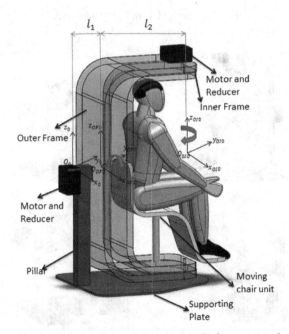

Fig. 1. Important reference coordinate systems, relevant displacement and main parts of the rotatory chair

As for the two rotating axes, the upper one is fixed in the inner frame and be activated by upper power installation, composed of a servo motor and a worm gear and worm reducer, which owns an advantage that the inner frame can be halted immediately to maintain safety as soon as the power is down. The outer frame is connected dynamically to a middle axis clamped by two double row angular contact ball bearings with flanges, which not only owns the above-mentioned advantages, but also bears large upsetting torque due to the open structure of the system. The middle axis and two bears are mounted in the pillar, which is welded directly to the supporting plate and is activated by the middle power installation that is composed of a servo motor and a worm gear and worm reducer with bigger transmission ratio.

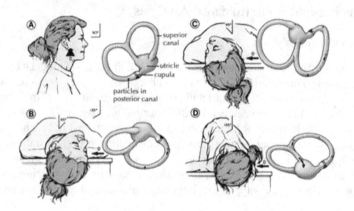

Fig. 2. General view of Epley maneuver

Fig. 3. View of rotatory chair achieving Epley maneuver

The rotatory chair can work under a preprogramming way according to different maneuver methods. For example, Epley maneuver mainly contains four steps as shown in Fig.2. The designed rotatory chair can perform movements in sequence as presented in Fig.3.

2.2   Coordinate Transformation

The torque of a motor, as we all know, is limited by the rotating speed. The higher the rotating speed is, the lower torque a motor can serve. However, to relocate otolith, a high rotating speed and acceleration will be necessary during the therapeutic process, so it is crucial to minimize the torque that is applied on the motor. We will solve this problem by analyzing the reference coordinates between the frames at first.

Because the outer frame and inner frame are both symmetric with respect to the vertical direction, and to simplify the difficulty of calculation, three reference coordinate systems (CSYS) O_0, O_{OF0}, O_{IF0} are built as shown in Fig.1. Supposed that the O_0 CSYS can be considered as the fundamental one whose original point is at the center of the axle that activates the whole frames, the O_{OF0} CSYS is attached at the middle of outer frame with a horizontal displacement of l_1 relative to O_0 CSYS. The z-axis of O_{IF0} CSYS is in line with axle activating the inner frame, and the horizontal displacement between O_{OF0} and O_{IF0} CSYS is l_2.

So the relationship of the transformation matrix between the adjacent coordinate can be expressed as follows:

$$O_0 \xrightarrow{T_1\ T_2} O_{OF0} \xrightarrow{T_3\ T_4} O_{IF0}$$

$$T_1 = \begin{pmatrix} 1 & 0 & 0 & 0 \\ 0 & 1 & 0 & 0 \\ 0 & 0 & 1 & 0 \\ 0 & -l_1 & 0 & 1 \end{pmatrix} \quad T_2 = \begin{pmatrix} \cos\theta & 0 & -\sin\theta & 0 \\ 0 & 1 & 0 & 0 \\ \sin\theta & 0 & \cos\theta & 0 \\ 0 & 0 & 0 & 1 \end{pmatrix} \quad (1)$$

$$T_3 = \begin{pmatrix} 1 & 0 & 0 & 0 \\ 0 & 1 & 0 & 0 \\ 0 & 0 & 1 & 0 \\ 0 & -l_2 & 0 & 1 \end{pmatrix} \quad T_4 = \begin{pmatrix} \cos\beta & \sin\beta & 0 & 0 \\ -\sin\beta & \cos\beta & 0 & 0 \\ 0 & 0 & 1 & 0 \\ 0 & 0 & 0 & 1 \end{pmatrix} \quad (2)$$

where θ and β represent respectively the rotary angle of outer frame relative to pillar and that of inner frame relative to outer frame.

2.3   Minimizing Torques Analysis

After figuring out the transformation of coordinate, the point of gravity of frames can be calculated according to the above equation (1) (2). Suppose that both of the frames are not rotated, the mass of outer frame, inner frame, object and chair can be expressed as M_1, M_2, M_3, and their coordinates of gravity points are (x_1, y_1, z_1), (x_2, y_2, z_2), (x_3, y_3, z_3) in which y_3 and z_3 can be considered to be changeable in a limited range. So after the rotation according to the treating procedure, the new gravity coordinates of the above can be expressed as $(x_1, y_1, z_1, 1)$ $T_1 T_2$, $(x_2, y_2, z_2, 1)$ $T_1 T_2 T_3 T_4$, $(x_3, y_3, z_3, 1) T_1 T_2 T_3 T_4$.

The rotary torque that is supplied by the motors can be defined as:

$$T = J\alpha + \vec{G} \times \vec{l} + T_f \tag{3}$$

where J is the rotational inertia of the frame, α is the rotary acceleration of the frame, G is the force of gravity , l is the distance between the center of gravity point of the fame and the rotary axis , both G and l are vectors, and T_f represents the friction torque caused at the hinge. Accordingly, two motor torques can be demonstrated as follows in which all the rotational inertia is calculated relative to O_{IF0} coordinate and x_i', y_i' represent new coordinates after transformation :

$$T_1 = \textstyle\sum_{i=1}^{3} I_{yyi} \alpha_1 + (I_{xx2} - I_{zz2} + I_{xx3} - I_{zz3}) \sin^2 \beta \alpha_1 + \sum_{i=1}^{3} M_i x_i' g + \sum_{i=1}^{2} T_{fi} \tag{4}$$

$$T_2 = I_{0xis} \alpha_2 + \textstyle\sum_{i=2}^{3} M_i g \sin\theta (l_1 + l_2 - y_i') + T_{f2} \tag{5}$$

The rotatory chair system has four DOFs, as mentioned above, that means there are four variable parameters in the equations (4) and (5),i.e. θ, β, y_3, z_3. Actually in the four parameters, θ and β act as random variables with the range of $(0,2\pi)$ to satisfy the acquirement that two motors can be activated no matter where the frames are, while y_3 and z_3 are used to minimize the torques as much as possible before the treatment. Therefore we can build a mathematical model to minimize both T_1 and T_2 by figuring out optimizing y_3 and z_3, namely, we can reduce the force used to rotate the frames by adjusting the chair horizontally and vertically. Due to the fact that the torques can be either positive or negative, the problem can be expressed as followings by using weighted least squares equation:

$$T(\theta, \ \beta, \ y_3, \ z_3) = w \times T_1^{\,2}(\theta, \ \beta, \ y_3, \ z_3) + T_2^{\,2}(\theta, \ \beta, \ y_3, \ z_3) \tag{6}$$

$$\max T(\theta, \beta, y_3^*, z_3^*) \leq \max T(\theta, \beta, y_3, z_3) \tag{7}$$

where w is the weight coefficient. So the problem can be solved by figuring out the minimax value of $T(\theta, \beta, y_3, z_3)$. However, because of the complexity of the equation (6), it is not feasible to work out the equation $\theta(y_3, z_3)$ and $\beta(y_3, z_3)$ by derivation. Hereby, the equation (6) can be expressed in an n^2 equation set as follows:

$$T_{i,j}(y_3, z_3) = w \times T_1^{\,2} \left(\frac{2\pi i}{n}, \frac{2\pi j}{n}, y_3, z_3 \right) + T_2^{\,2} (\frac{2\pi i}{n}, \frac{2\pi j}{n}, y_3, z_3) \tag{8}$$

The equation set can be easily handled to find out the mini-max value by adopting the principle of constrained linear optimization with appropriate different coefficient w and the decomposition coefficient n. And it is also obvious that the bigger n we choose, the more accurate the result will be and the more complicated the calculation will be. And the main parameters of the rotatory chair which will be used in upper calculation are demonstrated in Table1.

Table 1. Main parameters of the rotatory chair system

Item	Value	Unit
Total dimension	1350×1000×2100	mm×mm×mm
M_1	175	Kg
M_2	92.5	Kg
M_3	120	Kg
l_1	183	mm
l_2	845	mm
α	10-40	$°/s^2$

3   Result

Two torques responding to the changes of θ and β can be seen in Fig.4 by choosing $w = 4$ and $n = 10$.

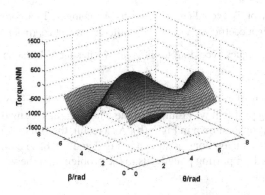

a) Torque applied on motor1

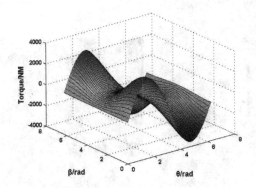

b) Torque applied on motor2

Fig. 4. Torque changes respond to the angle of θ and β

However the weight coefficient w, in practice, should be chosen based on the requirement of the experiment. By choosing different weight coefficient w, the relative maximum of torques can be calculated after the calculation of optimizing y_3 and z_3. As shown in Fig.5 under n equals to 20, the maximum of T_1 drops down dramatically when w get bigger, while the maximum of T_2 does in an opposite way.

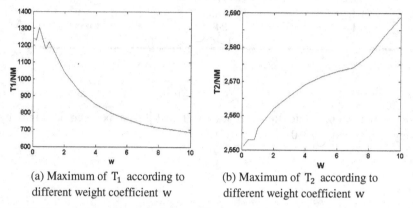

(a) Maximum of T_1 according to different weight coefficient w

(b) Maximum of T_2 according to different weight coefficient w

Fig. 5. Maximum of torques according to different w after the calculation of optimizing y_3 and z_3

The demonstration of rotatory chair prototype is shown in Fig.6 (a). And during the experiment, a big problem was found that the whole frames seemed tilted leading to the difficulty of rotating as shown in Fig.6 (b). As a result, the finite element analyses of the important parts have been done as shown in Fig.7 and Fig.8. The micro deformation in the middle axis and supporting plate leads to the problem that the whole frames seem titled in the shape.

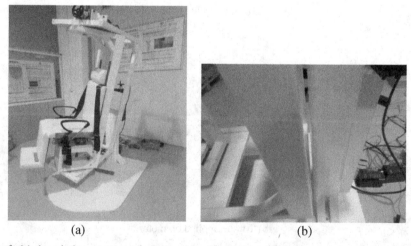

(a)   (b)

Fig. 6. (a) the whole prototype of rotary chair; (b) the biggest problem of the rotatory chair in practice

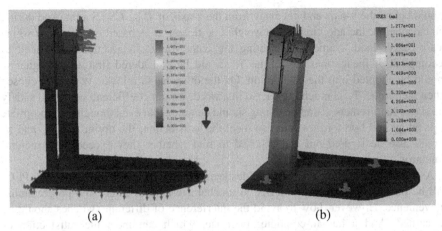

Fig. 7. (a) finite element analysis of the pillar on the assumption that the ground is perfectly flat when the commuted force and torques are applied on the middle axis; while (b) finite element analysis of the pillar but with the assumption that the ground is not flat.

Fig. 8. Finite element analysis of the middle axis which results in tilting

Some improvements should be done in the following work. First of all, the entire frames should be made of machining parts with geometric shape, so that the total weight will drop down and the torques can also be reduced simultaneously. As for the installation used for up-down chair, we used a worm gear screw jack which will be replaced with a pneumatic up-down installation to low down mass. The supporting plate gets slight deformation due to the biggish torque, which makes the rotatory chair tilt a little. Therefore strengthening the supporting plate and reducing the weight will be crucial in the later design.

4   Conclusion and Future Improvement

The analysis of the mechanical structure paves a way for the design of the rotatory chair system. The result shows that the position of the gravity point of the chair and person should below the y-axis and get away from the z-axis of O_{IF0} CSYS a bit. And during the calculation, the adoption of the weight coefficient w is based on the motor which bears bigger load. Namely, if rotating the outer frame, in practice, is difficult to accomplish, it means that the torque T_1 should be considered first and a higher w should be adopted into the calculation. On the other hand, a lower w will be chosen when the torque T_2 is much higher. So in a word, weight coefficient w should satisfy the actual requirements. And one thing should be noted that even though an appropriate w is adopt and two torques can also meet the satisfaction, the optimizing y_3 and z_3 should also be figured out and checked to find whether they exceed the structural limitation.

As for the controlling system to be designed, programmable logic controller (PLC) will be introduced to the system due to its characteristic of safety and programming convenience. However, how to avoid the interference of different switches should be concerned. And a human-computer interface, which can meet the satisfaction of real-time control to implement the procedure, will also be developed.

Acknowledgement. This work is supported by Medicine-Engineering Fund of Shanghai Jiao Tong University (No. YG2010ZD205).

References

1. Orizabal, M., Druzgalski, C.: Positional Vertigo Biofeedback Assist Device Utilizing Fuzzy Logic. In: PAHCE Proceedings, pp. 20–24 (2010)
2. Katsarkas, A.: Benign Paroxysmal Positional Vertigo (BPPV): Idiopathic Versus Post-traumatic. Acta Otolaryngol (Stockh) 119, 745–749 (1999)
3. Rajgum, S.M., Rabbitt, R.D.: Three-dimensional Biomechanical Model of Benign Paroxysmal Positional Vertigo. In: EMBS Proceedings, pp. 262–263 (2002)
4. Lithgow, B., Shoushtarian, M., Heibert, D.: Electrovestibulogram (EVestG): The Separation of Benign Paroxysmal Positional Vertigo and Meniere's Disease. In: MEDSIP (2006)
5. Sridhar, S., Panda, N., Raghunathan, M.: Efficacy of Particle Repositioning Maneuver in BPPV: A Prospective Study. American Journal of Otolaryngology 24, 355–360 (2003)
6. Garrett, A., Heibert, D., Lithgow, B.: Electrovestibulography: The "DC" potential used to separate Meniere's disease and Benign Paroxysmal Positional Vertigo. In: EMBS Proceedings, pp. 2381–2384 (2007)
7. Parnes, L.S., Agrawal, S.K., Atlas, J.: Diagnosis and management of benign paroxysmal positional vertigo (BPPV). CMAJ, 681–693 (2003)
8. Beyea, J., Wong, E., et al.: Evaluation of a Particle Repositioning Maneuver Web-Based Teaching Module Using the DizzyFIX. Laryngoscope 117(1), 175–180 (2007)

Modeling and Control
of a Lower-Limb Rehabilitation Robot

Yanjiao Ma[1], Wei He[1], and Shuzhi Sam Ge[2,3]

[1] Robotics Institute and School of Automation Engineering,
University of Electronic Science and Technology of China, Chengdu 611731, China
[2] Robotics Institute and School of Computer Science and Engineering,
University of Electronic Science and Technology of China, Chengdu 611731, China
[3] Department of Electrical and Computer Engineering, National University of Singapore,
Singapore 117576
kataramyj@yahoo.cn, hewei.ac@gmail.com, samge@nus.edu.sg

Abstract. This paper proposes a lower-limb rehabilitation robot. It assists patients suffering from hemiplegic to recover the hurt leg by walking in a gait trajectory. A single-side mechanical structure is designed, which is driven by the pneumatic muscles. For further research, we build a simplified 2-DOF dynamic model with the Lagrange method. PD control and adaptive control strategies are developed with stability analysis demonstrating that both methods are stable and effective. At last, we achieve the tracking performances of the robot model in both control strategies by simulation results.

Keywords: rehabilitation robot, modeling, adaptive control, Lagrange method.

1   Introduction

Recover from a stroke is meaningful for patients being back to normal life and utilizing robots to fulfill the cyclic movements becomes an efficient method. A rehabilitation robot can accurately provide excepting movements and forces which are developed by the medical care theory. On the other hand, it's convenient for patients to undertake repetitive and resistive exercises assisted by robots.

For lower-limb rehabilitation robots, there have been several commercial products like Lokomat [1], Autoambulator [2], HAL [3] and so on. Still, researchers in different universities made a bigger improvement on rehabilitation devices such as LOPES (LOwer-extremity Powered ExoSkeleton) [4], BLEEX [5], ReWalk [6], and REX [7]. LOPES is developed by Universiteit of Twente from Netherlands, for gait training and assessment of motor function with a leg exoskeleton made up of three joints. The eLEGS exoskeleton, designed by Berkeley Bionics, is a wearable and bionic portable device with crutches to assist paraplegics. ReWalk, design in Israel, is a set of wearable mechanical exoskeleton leg which controlled by patient remotely. A backpack battery is included to for entire power consumption of the device. Overall, it is similar device to eLEGS. The Rex can be easily manipulated by patients with a

S.S. Ge et al. (Eds.): ICSR 2012, LNAI 7621, pp. 581–590, 2012.

joystick and control pad embedded to the system. And patient's weight can be fully supported by this device. These make it as another suitable choice for paraplegics.

These lower-limb robots are designed to assist people who have trouble on walking or limitations with lower movements [8]. Hip, knee and ankle joints are commonly considered in a lower rehabilitation robot. 2-DOF rehabilitation robotic systems are widely developed to treat the injuries related to hip and knee. Homma et al. built a 2-DOF system around the patient's bed [9]. It provides a passive mode for exercise. Bradley et al. developed a 2-DOF system called NeXOS [10]. It's a multifunctional robot which can help patients in active assistive, passive and resistive exercises. 1-DOF rehabilitation system is more efficient for a particular joint's recover. Moughamir et al. designed a system called Multi-Iso [11], a 1-DOF system for knee joint, which is also able to perform assistive, resistive and passive training.

We focus on a new design of the lower-limb rehabilitation robot with single side for people who suffer from hemiplegic, which leads the structure is developed only for the hurt leg. Instead of the motor actuator, we utilize the pneumatic muscle actuator for its compliance, elasticity and stability. There is jitter-free corresponding under the initial force or acceleration.

The main contributions of the paper are listed as follows:

i).   Pneumatic muscles based mechanical design;
ii).   Modeling of the rehabilitation robot;
iii). Control design;
iv).   Stability analysis for both PD control and adaptive control.

The rest of the paper is organized as follows. The dynamics of a 2-link rigid robotic system are derived in Section 2. PD and adaptive control via the Lyapunov's direct method is discussed for system uncertainties in Section 3, where it is shown that the uniform boundedness of the closed-loop system can be achieved by the proposed control. Simulations are carried out to illustrate the performance of the proposed control in Section 4. The conclusion of this paper is presented in Section 5.

2   The Mechanical Structure and Dynamic Model

2.1   The Mechanical Structure of the Rehabilitation Robot

The rehabilitation robot consists of 3 parts: thigh link, shank link and foot link, and separately fix the counterpart of the patient. Patient should bind the robot with the hurt leg, keeping the both joint of robot and patient's leg coaxial. Hip joint and knee joint of the robot are all driven by pneumatic muscles displaced at two sides of the thigh. For increasing flexibility on the ankle, we set a pneumatic spring between shank link and foot link. Magnetic encoders are set at hip joint and knee joint to feedback the angle signals back to the processer. There are 2 pressure sensors on the sole of the foot for obtaining the force transferred from patients. It is shown in Fig.1.

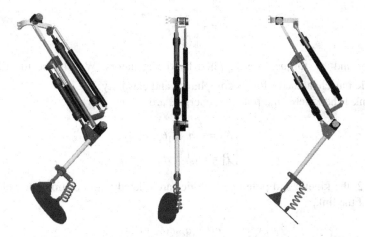

Fig. 1. Mechanical structure of the rehabilitation robot

2.2   The Dynamic Model of the Rehabilitation Robot

1. Kinetic and Potential Energy of the Robot's Leg

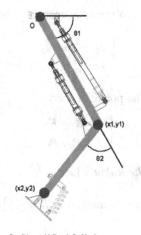

Fig. 2. Simplified 2-link structure

Simplify the structure, it's a serious robot connected by 2 links, showed as Fig 2. Assume that the link masses are concentrated at the center of the links. Define the joint variable

$$q = \begin{bmatrix} q_1 \\ q_2 \end{bmatrix} = \begin{bmatrix} \theta_1 \\ \theta_2 \end{bmatrix} \tag{1}$$

The generalized torque vector is

$$\tau = \begin{bmatrix} \tau_1 \\ \tau_2 \end{bmatrix} \tag{2}$$

With τ_1 and τ_2 torques are supplied by the actuators. We choose to utilize the pneumatic muscle actuator for its compliance and elasticity.

For link 1 the kinetic and potential energies are

$$\begin{cases} K_1 = \dfrac{1}{2} m_1 a_{c1}^2 \dot{\theta}_1^2 \\ P_1 = m_1 g a_{c1} s \theta_1 \end{cases} \tag{3}$$

For link 2, the kinetic and potential energies are related with position and velocity of the end of the link,

$$\begin{cases} x_{c2} = a_1 c \theta_1 + a_{c2} c(\theta_1 + \theta_2) \\ y_{c2} = a_1 s \theta_1 + a_{c2} s(\theta_1 + \theta_2) \end{cases} \tag{4}$$

Where a_{c1} and a_{c2} are the length between center point to the end of stick 1 and stick 2. We can obtain the velocity squared

$$v_{c2}{}^2 = \dot{x}_{c2}{}^2 + \dot{y}_{c2}{}^2 \tag{5}$$

Therefore, the kinetic energy and potential energy for link 2 is

$$\begin{cases} K_2 = \dfrac{1}{2} m_2 v_{c2}^2 \\ P_2 = m_2 g y_{c2} \end{cases} \tag{6}$$

We can get the total kinetic and potential energy

$$\begin{cases} K = K_1 + K_2 \\ P = P_1 + P_2 \end{cases} \tag{7}$$

2. Lagrange's Equation of the Robot's Leg

From (7), it's easy to obtain inertia matrix by $K = \dfrac{1}{2} \dot{q}^{\mathrm{T}} \mathrm{M}(q) \dot{q}$

$$M(q) = \begin{bmatrix} (\dfrac{1}{4} m_1 + m_2) a_1^2 + \dfrac{1}{4} m_2 a_2{}^2 + m_2 a_1 a_2 c \theta_2 & \dfrac{1}{4} m_2 a_2{}^2 + \dfrac{1}{2} m_2 a_1 a_2 c \theta_2 \\ \dfrac{1}{4} m_2 a_2{}^2 + \dfrac{1}{2} m_2 a_1 a_2 c \theta_2 & \dfrac{1}{4} m_2 a_2{}^2 \end{bmatrix} \tag{8}$$

Therefore, $V(q, \dot{q})$ can be obtained by $M(q)$ [12],

$$V(q, \dot{q}) = \dfrac{1}{2} m_2 a_1 a_2 s \theta_2 \begin{bmatrix} -\dot{\theta}_2 & -\dot{\theta}_1 - \dot{\theta}_2 \\ -\dot{\theta}_1 & 0 \end{bmatrix} \tag{9}$$

With total potential energy has been obtained, gravitation force vector is

$$G(q) = \frac{\partial P}{\partial q} = \begin{bmatrix} (\frac{1}{2}m_1 + m_2)ga_1c\theta_1 + \frac{1}{2}m_2ga_2c(\theta_1 + \theta_2) \\ \frac{1}{2}m_2ga_2c(\theta_1 + \theta_2) \end{bmatrix} \tag{10}$$

Then we can obtain the Lagrange Equations of Robot

$$M(q)\ddot{q} + V(q,\dot{q})\dot{q} + G(q) = \tau \tag{11}$$

Where $M(q) \in R^{n \times n}$ is the symmetric positive definite inertia matrix, $V(q,\dot{q}) \in R^n$ is the centrifugal matrix, $G(q) \in R^n$ is the gravitational matrix.

3   Control Design

In this section, we discuss different control strategies utilized in the rehabilitation robot. The robot is to help hemiplegic patients recover the paralyzed leg, which aims to make the muscle of the leg keep its tension while standing and walking. It's not difficult for the patient to grasp the center of gravity by himself. Therefore, the problem is simplified to deal with the issue how to control the robot follow the expected gait trajectory and help to drive in an accurate force.

3.1   PD Control

Considering the gravity of robot can't be neglected, the gravity compensation has been utilized to meet the needs of fixed-point PD control. Assume that there is no contact between the robot and environment, and we can obtain the estimation of gravity matrix. The control input is

$$\tau = K_d\dot{e} + K_pe + \hat{G}(q) \tag{12}$$

where $\hat{G}(q) \in R^n$ is the estimation of gravity. Suppose the tracking error is

$$e = q_d - q \tag{13}$$

where q_d is a constant, and $\dot{q}_d = \ddot{q}_d \equiv 0$. The robot dynamic equations becomes

$$M(q)\ddot{e} + [V(q,\dot{q}) + K_d]\dot{e} + K_pe = 0 \tag{14}$$

We define Lyapunov function as

$$V_{Lya} = \frac{1}{2}\dot{e}^T M(q)\dot{e} + \frac{1}{2}e^T K_pe \tag{15}$$

Considering $M(q)$ and K_p are symmetric and positive, so V_{Lya} is global positive definite. According to the oblique symmetry of $\dot{M} - 2V$, we have $\dot{e}^T M \dot{e} = 2\dot{e}^T V \dot{e}$, then its derivation result is

$$\dot{V}_{Lya} = \dot{e}^T M \ddot{e} + \dot{e}^T V \dot{e} + \dot{e}^T K_p e = \dot{e}^T (M\ddot{e} + V\dot{e} + K_p e) = -\dot{e}^T K_d e \le 0 \qquad (16)$$

For $\dot{V}_{Lya}$ is half-negative definite and K_d is positive definite, there is $\dot{e} \equiv 0$ when $\dot{V}_{Lya} \equiv 0$, so $\ddot{e} \equiv 0$. Take $\dot{e} \equiv 0$ and $\ddot{e} \equiv 0$ into equation (14), it's obvious to get a result of $K_p e = 0$. In further, K_p is reversible and we obtain that $e = 0$.

According to LaSalle Theory [13], $(e, \dot{e}) = (0,0)$ is the balanced point in global asymptotically stable process for the robot. That is, if the state starts from a random condition $(q_0, \dot{q}_0)$, there will always be $q \to q_d, \dot{q} \to 0$.

3.2   Adaptive Control

In real circumstances, it's difficult to obtain exact link masses. We take adaptive control as a strategy to deal with these types of parametric uncertainty. With some fixed estimate of the unknown parameters in place of the actual parameters, the approximate computed-torque controller would be the form as below [14]

$$\tau = \hat{M}(q)(\ddot{q}_d + K_v \dot{e} + K_p e) + \hat{V}(q, \dot{q})\dot{q} + \hat{G}(q) \qquad (17)$$

where K_v and K_p are control gain matrices. q_d is the desired trajectory. The adaptive controller is based on the fact that the parameters appear linearly in the model. The robot dynamics can be written in the form

$$W(q, \dot{q}, \ddot{q})\varphi = M(q)\ddot{q} + V(q, \dot{q})\dot{q} + G(q) \qquad (18)$$

where $W(q, \dot{q}, \ddot{q})\varphi$ is an $n \times r$ matrix of known time functions and φ is an $r \times 1$ vector of unknown constant parameters.

From the tracking error $e = q_d - q$, it's easy to see how (17) can be written as

$$\tau = \hat{M}(q)(\ddot{e} + K_v \dot{e} + K_p e) + \hat{M}(q)\ddot{q} + \hat{V}(q, \dot{q})\dot{q} + \hat{G}(q) \qquad (19)$$

We may write the robot dynamic equation as $\tau = W(q, \dot{q}, \ddot{q})\varphi$, and it's obvious that tracking error system is showed below by utilizing (18),

$$\ddot{e} + K_v \dot{e} + K_p e = \hat{M}^{-1}(q)W(q, \dot{q}, \ddot{q})\tilde{\varphi} \qquad (20)$$

where the parameter error is $\tilde{\varphi} = \varphi - \hat{\varphi}$. For convenience, (20) is rewritten as the state-space form

$$\dot{e} = Ae + B\hat{M}^{-1}(q)W(q, \dot{q}, \ddot{q})\tilde{\varphi} \qquad (21)$$

where the tracking error vector is $e = \begin{bmatrix} e \\ \dot{e} \end{bmatrix}$, $B = \begin{bmatrix} O_n \\ I_n \end{bmatrix}$, $A = \begin{bmatrix} O_n & I_n \\ -K_p & -K_v \end{bmatrix}$, with I_n

being the $n \times n$ identity matrix and O_n being the $n \times n$ zero matrix.

The Lyapunov function is selected as follows

$$V_{Lya} = e^T Y e + \tilde{\varphi}^T \Gamma^{-1} \tilde{\varphi} \tag{22}$$

where Y is a positive-definite, constant, symmetric matrix, and Γ is a diagonal positive-definite matrix. Γ is defined as $\Gamma = diag(\gamma_1, \gamma_2, ..., \gamma_r)$, where all the γ_is are positive scalar constants. Derivation of the Lyapunov function is

$$\dot{V}_{Lya} = -e^T Q e + 2\tilde{\varphi}^T [\Gamma^{-1} \dot{\tilde{\varphi}} + W^T (q, \dot{q}, \ddot{q}) \hat{M}^{-1}(q) B^T Y e] \tag{23}$$

where Q is a positive-definite, symmetric matrix that satisfies $A^T Y + Y A = -Q$. We make $\dot{V}_{Lya}$ at least negative semi-definite, then the adaption update rule becomes obvious

$$\dot{\hat{\varphi}} = -\Gamma W^T (q, \dot{q}, \ddot{q}) \hat{M}^{-1}(q) B^T Y e \tag{24}$$

V_{Lya} remains upper bounded in the time $[0, \infty)$, $\lim_{t \to \infty} V_{Lya} = V_{Lya_\infty}$, where V_{Lya_∞} is a positive constant. For V_{Lya} is upper bounded, from (24), we can know that $\tilde{\varphi}$ and e are bounded, which also leads to q, $\dot{q}$ and $\hat{\varphi}$ be bounded. We assume that the desired trajectory and its first two derivatives are bounded. Now, from the dynamics of the robot, it's clear that

$$\ddot{q} = M^{-1}(q)(\tau - V(q, \dot{q})\dot{q} - G(q)) \tag{25}$$

Since $\ddot{q}$ and τ depend on the bounded quantities q, $\dot{q}$ and $\hat{\varphi}$, we can deduce that $\dot{e}$ and $\ddot{V}_{Lya}$ are bounded. V_{Lya} is lower bounded by zero, $\dot{V}_{Lya}$ is negative semi-definite, and $\ddot{V}_{lya}$ is bounded, then it's obvious $\lim_{t \to \infty} \dot{V}_{Lya} = 0$. From Rayleigh-Rits Theorem, we can get $\lim_{t \to \infty} \lambda_{\min} \{Q\} \|e\|^2 = 0$, which means $\lim_{t \to \infty} e = 0$.

4   Simulation Results

The dynamic model of the rehabilitation robot is established in MATLAB. It moves in x-y plane. Let m_i and l_i ($i = 1, 2$) represent the mass and length of link i respectively. Consider patient's mass of hurt leg, from GB 10000-1988 Chinese Adult Body Size, we set $m_1 = 12kg, m_2 = 10kg, l_1 = 0.496m, l_2 = 0.396m$.

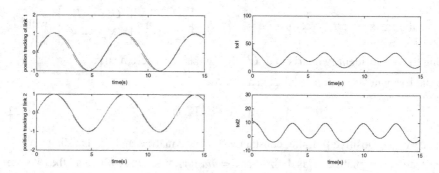

Fig. 3. Simulation results with PD controller

• PID Controller

We set the start position for each link at $q_1 = 0, q_2 = 0$ and end point at $q_1 = \sin(t)rad, q_2 = \sin(t)rad$ respectively. The simulation results are given in Fig. 3. In the right figure, the red lines are the desired angles of each link and the blue are the actual positions of each link; in the left figure, τ_1 and τ_2 represent the applied forces on each link separately.

• Adaptive Controller

From (17) and (24), we have got torque controller and update rule for adaptive control. According to the linearity of dynamics, we calculate matrix $W(q, \dot{q}, \ddot{q})$ with the equation as below

$$W(q, \dot{q}, \ddot{q})\tilde{\varphi} = \tilde{M}(q)\ddot{q}_d + \tilde{V}(q, \dot{q})\dot{q}_d + \tilde{G}(q) \tag{26}$$

Where $\varphi = [\alpha \quad \beta \quad \varepsilon \quad \eta \quad \gamma]^T$ and

$$\begin{cases} \alpha = (\frac{1}{4}m_1 + m_2)a_1^2 \\ \beta = \frac{1}{4}m_2 a_2^2 \\ \varepsilon = \frac{1}{2}m_2 a_1 a_2 \\ \eta = (\frac{1}{2}m_1 + m_2)a_1 g \\ \gamma = \frac{1}{2}m_2 a_2 g \end{cases} \tag{27}$$

We set the trajectory as $\sin(2\pi)$ and set the start position at 1 rad for both link. Fig.4 shows the results of how the model behaves by utilizing adaptive controller. The red curve represents the expected trajectory, and the blue curve represents the tracking

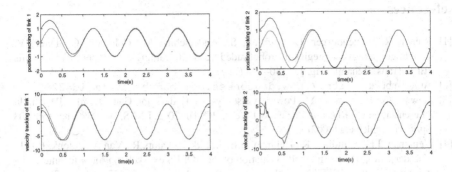

Fig. 4. Simulation results with adaptive controller

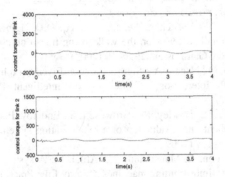

Fig. 5. Control torque for link 1 and link 2

trajectory. Clearly, we can see the adaptive controller has made the robot track the position and velocity accurately from the beginning. Fig.5 shows the control inputs for both links.

From the results above, PD control makes a faster and accurate response, which also doesn't need a strong input, while adaptive control has a better robust capacity adapt to the disturbances in environment.

5   Conclusion

In this paper, a lower-limb rehabilitation robot has been introduced, which is actuated by the pneumatic muscles in hip joint and knee joint. This single-side structure has been designed for help hemiplegic patient practice walking with the hurt leg. It can be simplified as a 2-DOF dynamic model with Lagrange method. A PD computed-torque and adaptive control algorithms are proposed for tracking the trajectory. Both methods achieve good performances executing expected curves as the simulation results.

References

[1] Riener, R., Lunenburger, L., Jezernik, S., Anderschitz, M., Colombo, G., Dietz, V.: Patient-cooperative strategies for robot-aided treadmill training: first experimental results. IEEE Trans. Rehabil. Eng. 13, 380–394 (2005)

[2] AutoAmbulator, http://www.deaconess.com/bodyhsdh.cfm?id=2295

[3] Kawamoto, H., Sankai, Y.: Power Assist System HAL-3 for Gait Disorder Person. In: Miesenberger, K., Klaus, J., Zagler, W.L. (eds.) ICCHP 2002. LNCS, vol. 2398, pp. 196–203. Springer, Heidelberg (2002)

[4] Veneman, J.F., Kruidhof, R., Hekman, E.E.G., Ekkelenkamp, R., Van Asseldonk, E.H.F., Van der Kooij, H.: Design and evaluation of the LOPES exoskeleton robot for interactive gait rehabilitation. IEEE Trans. Neural Syst. Rehabil. Eng. 15(3), 379–386 (2007)

[5] Zoss, A.B., Kazerooni, H., Chu, A.: Biomechanical design of the Berkeley lower extremity exoskeleton (BLEEX). IEEE/ASME Transactions on Mechatronics 11, 128–138 (2006)

[6] ReWalk, http://www.argomedtec.com/index.asp

[7] REX, http://www.rexbionics.com/

[8] Malcolm, P., Segers, V., Caekenberghe, I.V., Clercq, D.D.: Experimental study of the influence of the m.tibialis anterior on the walk-to-run transition by means of a powered ankle-foot exoskeleton. Gait Posture 29, 6–10 (2009)

[9] Homma, K., Fukuda, O., Nagata, Y.: Study of a wire-driven leg rehabilitation system. In: Proceeding of Sixth International Conference on Intelligent Robots and Systems, pp. 1451–1456 (2002)

[10] Bradley, D., Marquez, C., Hawley, M., Brownsell, S., Enderby, P., Mawson, S.: NeXOS the design, development, and evaluation of a rehabilitation system for the lower limbs. Mechatronics 19, 247–257 (2009)

[11] Moughamir, S., Zaytoon, J., Manamanni, N., Afilal, L.: A system approach for control development of lower limbs training machines. Control Eng. Pract. 10, 287–299 (2002)

[12] Ge, S.S., Lee, T.H., Harris, C.J.: Adaptive Neural Network Control of Robotic Manipulators. World Scientific, London (1998)

[13] LaSalle, J.P.: Stability Theory for Difference Equations. Journal of Differential Equations 4(2), 57–65 (1968)

[14] Craig, J.: Adaptive Control of Mechanical Manipulators. Addison Wesley, Reading (1985)

Particle Swarm Optimization Based Design for Knee Joint of Wearable Exoskeleton Robot

Jia-yuan Zhu and Hong Zhou

Quartermaster Equipment Institute, General Logistics Department of CPLA,
Beijing, China

Abstract. With firstly analyzing the working principle of wearable exoskeleton robot, and building a mathematical model ,this paper applies the method of Particle Swarm Optimization with MATLAB software to develop a set of optimization design system for three-hinge mechanism of knee, which substitutes artificial design system. Furthermore, this paper puts forward the optimization design method based on Particle Swarm Optimization for the three-hinge mechanism design of multi-objective and multi-constraint conditions, which can be effectively solved through simulation practice. Finally use Adams to check out the results.

Keywords: Wearable Exoskeleton Robot, Three-hinge mechanism, Particle Swarm Optimization, Optimized design.

1 Introduction

Wearable exoskeleton robot is a kind of mechanism which operator can wear in the external body and it can provide support and protection for the wearer to increase his or her performance ability.

With the technology progress, the wearable exoskeleton robot will have such functions as apperception, forecasting, self-controlling and so on. It involves learning institutions, bionics, control theory, information processing, and communication technology science knowledge, also involves the sensing, control, information coupling, mobile computing technology, and it still can complete a certain function and tasks under the control of the operator [1] .

The legs, cru and hydraulic cylinder of wearable exoskeletons system are composed of a three hinge point link mechanism, which is the core of the whole carrying system. The quality of three hinge point of mechanism design decides the hydraulic cylinder trip length and the diameter of the cylinder size, and directly influences the stress of the thighs and legs and the performance, weight, cost and stability of hydraulic cylinder.

According to three reaming points of institutions optimization, there are many methods, while the improved particle swarm algorithm is used in this paper. The improved particle swarm algorithm is a new evolutionary algorithm without crossover and mutation operator, it makes use of the biological community's information shared

S.S. Ge et al. (Eds.): ICSR 2012, LNAI 7621, pp. 591–599, 2012.

in thoughts and searches for the optimal solution through collaboration between the individuals. Its concept is simple, and the algorithm is easy to realize and has rapid convergence and so it is gradually to get the attention of people.

2   Working Principle Analysis

People wear exoskeletons system carrying weight in vertical standing, the body's gravity and the foot protection keep in the same vertical plane and the whole system of force transfers to the ground by the soles of the feet, under this balance state , people can stand steadily; if there is a certain distance existing between the body's gravity and the fulcrum in the same steps vertical planar, weight will produce a moment force on the body, people must overcome this part of the moment to stand steadily; Otherwise he or she will move forward or back. To overcome this part of the bending moment, it needs to adjust the focus.

According to the study of human body posture analysis, the human body adjusts the angle among the hip, knee and ankle to change the body's centre of gravity; however the power needed to change the Angle among the joints is partly from the human body muscle, and partly from hydraulic cylinder.

In ideal situation, when people stand upright and steadily, the force in vertical direction transfers to the ground by institutions from the thigh to the cru, and the hydraulic cylinder will not bear vertical direction of force. On the basis of this ideal state, the paper makes an analysis of three hinge points and does some simulation calculation.

3   Stress Model Analysis

3.1   Algorithm Model Transformation

Through the above modeling process, the optimization design of actuating cylinder three-hinge luffing mechanism parameters can be regarded as a general nonlinear constraint optimization problem:

$$\begin{cases} \min f(x) \\ \text{s.t. } g_i(x) \le 0, \ i=1,2,...,n \\ h(x)=0, \ j=1,2,...,m \end{cases} \tag{4}$$

Formulars above contain both inequality and equality constraint. To solve such problems with optimization algorithm, it is necessary to convert constrainted optimization into unconstrained optimization with penalty functions.Presently there are plenty of penalty function processing methods, such as external point method, interior point method, multiplier method, exact penalty function method and so on. This thesis adopts non-differentiable penalty function method, of which the specific conversion formula is shown as follow:

$$F(x) = f(x) + M \left[\sum_{i=1}^{n} \max(0, g_i(x))^2 + \sum_{j=1}^{m} h_j^2(x) \right]^{0.5} \tag{5}$$

In the formula above, M is the penalty factor. Normally, the bigger the M value is the better the result will be. But in practical application, it is necessary to conduct certain numerical experiment to select a appropriate. F(x) is the target function of algorithm optimization after conversion.

3.2 Based on Simulated Annealing of Improvement of the Micro Particle Swarm Method

In PSO, assume there be N particles in the D-dimension space, the position vector of particle No. i be $X_i=(x_{i1}, x_{i2}, ..., x_{iD})$, the speed vector be $V_i=(v_{i1}, v_{i2}, ..., v_{iD})$, the historical optimal solution for particle No. i be $P_i=(p_{i1}, p_{i2}, ..., p_{iD})$, the optimal solution for the whole population be represented by P_g , then the formulas of speed and position renewal for the tth iteration, are as follows:

$$X_i(t+1)=X_i(t) + V_i(t) \tag{6}$$

$$V_i(t+1)=\omega \cdot V_i(t)+c1 \cdot r1 \cdot (Pi(t)-Xi(t))+ c2 \cdot r2 \cdot (Pg(t)-Xi(t)) \tag{7}$$

Of the formulas above, formula (7) indicates speed renewal; formula (8) indicates loation renewal; ω refers to inertial weight; c_1 and c_2 refers to individual learning factor and social learning factor, which is set as constant 1.5 in this thesis; r_1 and r_2 are random number between 0 to 1[5-7].

The simulated annealing algorithm is mainly used for combinatorial optimization problem, the most important is how local search. In this paper, the current solution that X = (x1 x2... xD), random selection of m a variable xs1, xs2,... , XSM press type (8) to a random disturbance, the disturbance of the variable is:

$$ysi=xsi+r*b*(Usi-Lsi) \tag{8}$$

In this formula, i=1, 2, ..., m, r; , r is random number distributed evenly in the range (-1,1); U_{si}, L_{si} are the given top and bottom limitation of the design variables; b is the renewal range factor, of which the value range is usually (0, 0.5). The temperature renewal function adopts the expression: $T(t+1)=\alpha T(t)$, in which α is the temperature renewal constant.

$$T(t+1)=\alpha T(t) \tag{9}$$

In order to enhance PSO algorithm of optimization ability, this article from inertial weight update and update particle position in two aspects of the standard particle group algorithm was improved. Bigger is helpful to improve the algorithm omega of global optimization ability, and smaller will speed up the omega algorithm convergence speed. In this article, the dynamic reduce inertia of omega weight to make them along with the change of the iteration times and update:

$$\omega=\omega_{max}-t \times (\omega_{max}-\omega_{min})/t_{max} \tag{10}$$

In this expression, ω_{max} and ω_{min} are the maximum and minimum values of inertial weight; t is the iteration; t_{max} is the maximum iteration. When a new solution is worked out, it will be compared to the adaptive value corresponding to the last solution. If the variation $\Delta E \leq 0$, the new value will be accepted, otherwise the new value will be accepted according to criteria $\exp(-\Delta E/T) > \text{rand}(0,1)$. The pseudo codes of improved particle swarm optimization are as follows:

3.3   The Calculation Results and Analysis

At present, American HULC system has been one of the most advanced wearable exoskeleton robot in the world. As shown in figure 1 :

Fig. 1. American wearable exoskeletons HULC system

The thigh, cru and hydraulic cylinder structure is simplified, and a bearing model has made. As shown in figure 2 : In the picture, Point A is the connection hinge point of hydraulic cylinder and cru, Point B is the connection hinge point of thigh and cru, Point C is the connection hinge point of hydraulic cylinder and thigh. AC (namely the hydraulic cylinder) longs for l_1, BC longs for l_2, AB longs for l_3, the Angle between AC and BC is α, the Angle between BC and vertical direction is β, the Angle between AB and horizontal direction is γ, the Angle between ACB and AC is θ, the force on AC (namely the hydraulic cylinder) is F_1, the force on BC is F_2.

When people stand steadily, the three hinge points system is a balance system with no stress, AB is a fixed frame, the force F from vertical direction of point A will simply replace the stress of the upper hydraulic cylinder fulcrum, so we can get the relationship between F_1 and F through stress analysis:

$$F_1 = \frac{F \cdot \sin\beta}{\sin\alpha} \tag{1}$$

According to the working principle analysis, to find the hydraulic cylinder minimum force F_{1min} would become a process to seek equation optimal solutions, that is to find the minimum value of equations.

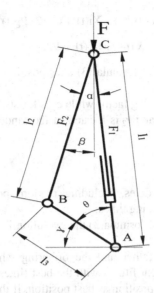

Fig. 2. Bearing model simplified picture

4   Optimization Method

The hydraulic cylinder three hinge points luffing mechanism is widely used in the work devices of engineering machinery. As a planar linkage mechanism, three hinge points luffing mechanism has two characteristics, one is that the input movement is the relative motion of the movement within mechanisms, another is that the components linked with frame can not become the original moving parts. At the past ten years , graphic method analytic method and CAD about mechanism synthesis has made some development[2].

Now, one kind optimization design method has gradually replaced the traditional experience design method. This optimization design method is based on mathematical programming, uses computer as tools and tries to seek the best design result [3].

4.1   Three Hinge Points Optimization Based on Particle Swarm Algorithm

PSO, particle swarm algorithm, is a new intelligent optimization algorithm of imitating group behavior of bird, has simple computation rules and rapid convergence speed, and also is easy to program [4].

In addition, PSO is a new bionic intelligent optimization algorithm of about group cooperation foraging, relative to other evolutionary algorithm, is easy to realize, especially on the continuous optimization problems. In the PSO algorithm, assumed that there are N particles in the D-dimensional search space, the i particle has position vector $X_i=(x_{i1}, x_{i2}, ..., x_{iD})$ and speed vector $V_i=(v_{i1}, v_{i2}, ..., v_{iD})$. The history optimal solution of the i particle is $P_i=(p_{i1}, p_{i2}, ..., p_{iD})$, and the whole population of the optimal solution is P_g. We can conclude the speed and the position of the i particle when the iteration time is t:

$$Vi(t+1)=\omega \cdot Vi(t)+c1 \cdot r1 \cdot (Pi(t)-Xi(t))+c2 \cdot r2 \cdot (Pg(t)-Xi(t)) \tag{2}$$

$$X_i(t+1)=X_i(t) + V_i(t) \tag{3}$$

Formula (2) says speed update; formula (3) says position update; ω is self-adapting inertia;

The c_1 is for individual learning factor while c_2 is for social learning factor, they are constant 1.5 in the paper; r_1 and r_2 is located in the random number between 0 and 1.[5,6,7]

Optimization steps

1. The initialization m particles, including random position and speed of the maximum, maximum iterating times;
2. According formula(2) and formula(3),the evolution iteration starts and offspring mid is produced;
3. Judge with the original father and the offspring which is optimal. To every particle, compare its current fitness with the best fitness when its best position is Pi, if better, view current position as best position. If the fitness in this position is also better than the fitness in the global best position Pg ,then make it become the current global best position;
4. According formula(2) and formula(3),update the particle's speed and position;
5. Judge whether termination conditions are satisfied, if satisfied, stop algorithm, or turn to step 3.

4.2   Decide the Design Variables

To design multiple hinge point mechanism, we need all size parameters of the whole mechanism, so we should find the relative position relationship among all hinge points. In this optimization calculation process, the design variables are length between hinge points as l_1, l_2, l_3 and angle γ.

4.3   Establish the Objective Function

The optimization is to get the minimum hydraulic cylinder force as the optimal solution.

The objective function:

$$F_1 = \frac{F \cdot \sin\beta}{\sin\alpha} \tag{4}$$

The relationship between angles and lengths:

$$\alpha = \arccos\frac{l_1^2+l_2^2-l_3^2}{2l_1l_2}$$

$$\beta=\alpha+\theta+\gamma-90°$$

$$\theta = \arccos\frac{l_1^2+l_3^2-l_2^2}{2l_1l_3}$$

4.4   Design Constraints Parameters

(1)Constraints in △ABC

$l_1+l_2-l_3>0$; $l_1+l_3-l_2>0$; $l_2+l_3-l_1>0$

(2)Constraints of human body size
According to GB 1000—88, the paper uses the 95th percentile human standards of Chinese southerner and the constraint ranges of design variables are:
$420<l1<430$; $335<l2<345$; $80<l3<90$; $70°<\gamma<80°$

4.5   The Simulation Calculation of PSO

Use the software MATLAB to program and the force F gets a initial value 800N(Human body weights 60kg and exoskeletons system weights 20kg).The results has been shown in table 1, and from table 1,we can see the stability of PSO results.

When iteration times become 100, we get a convergence curve, shown in figure3.

From figure 3, we can see the convergence speed of PSO is quite fast, the minimum value of F_1 is 0.14N.

Table 1. The results contrast within different iteration times

Iteration times	F_1 (N)	l_1 (mm)	l_2 (mm)	l_3 (mm)	γ (°)
100	0.14	425.9	341.0	87.7	73.9
200	11.45	422.7	337.7	86.9	76.5
300	11.94	429.8	343.6	88.0	76.8
400	0.93	424.6	339.5	87.9	73.7
500	0.43	427.4	344.3	85.6	74.6

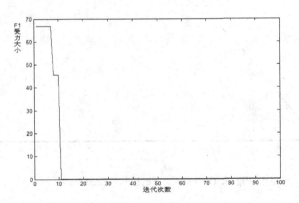

Fig. 3. Convergence curve

After 100 times iteration, we get the results:

$F_1 \approx 0.14N$,$l_1 \approx 426mm$, $l_2 \approx 341mm$, $l_3 \approx 88mm$, $\gamma \approx 74°$

5   The Simulation Check of Adams

In order to validate the calculation results of rationality, the paper uses Adams to establish a virtual model (shown in figure 4), and chooses the process of Human knees squatting down as Simulation object.

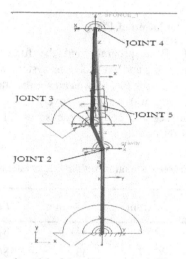

Fig. 4. Virtual model of three hinge point luffing mechanism

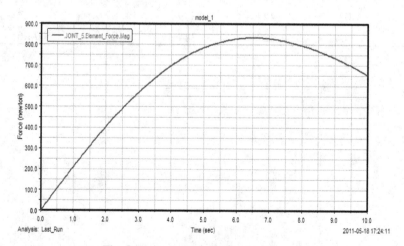

Fig. 5. The hydraulic cylinder force curve

The force on JOINT 4 is 800N, vertical downward, the knee bending speed is 13.5°/s, the ankle bending speed is 13.5°/s, the simulation time last 10s, so the hydraulic cylinder force curve is gotten, shown in figure 5.

The minimum force on JOINT 5 is 0.0608N, happened in the initial condition where human body stands upright. It is close to the result F_1 (0.14N) form the PSO algorithm, which shows that the PSO algorithm has an accurate result.

6   Conclusion

In the paper, a wearable exoskeleton robot knee bearing model has been established, and the improved particle swarm algorithm is used to develop an optimization design system of the three hinge point mechanism, and the algorithm has rapid convergence speed, accurate calculation results and high stability. Furthermore, the three hinge point mechanism optimization problem which belongs to multi-objective and multi-constraint optimization problem is solved. By simulation, an effective solution is acquired, then Adams is used to dynamics simulate to test the results. The last result shows that the bearing model and the optimization design system are both effective and feasible.

References

1. Yin, J.: Analysis and Design of Lower Extremity Wearable Exoskeleton Mechanism, pp. 1–12. Beijing University of Technology, Beijing (2010)
2. Feng, Q., Zhang, J.: The Optimization Design Method of hydraulic cylinder three hinge points luffing mechanism. Engineering Machinery (12), 25–31 (1992)
3. Ling, Z.: Optimization Design Based on Quantum Particle Swarm Optimization of the linkage mechanism. Value Engineering (35), 291–292 (2010)
4. He, L., Yao, N., Wu, J., Song, Y.: Application of Modified PSO in the Optimization of Reactive Power. In: 2009 Chinese Controls and Decision Conference, pp. 3493–3496 (2009)
5. Kennedy, J., Eberhart, R.: Particle Swarm Optimization. In: IEEE Int. Conf. on Neural Networks, pp. 1942–1948. IEEE Service Center, Piscataway (1995)
6. Eberhart, R., Kennedy, J.: A New Optimizer Using Particle Swarm Theory. In: Proc. on Int. Symposium on Micro Machine and H u2 man Science, pp. 39–43. IEEE Service Center, Piscataway (1995)
7. Kennedy, J.: The Particle Swarm: Social Adaptation of Knowledge. In: IEEE Int. Conf. on Evolutionary Computation, pp. 303–308. IEEE Service Center, Piscataway (1997)

The Application of Machine-Learning
on Lower Limb Motion Analysis
in Human Exoskeleton System

Cao-yuan Zhao, Xiang-gang Zhang, and Qing Guo

School of Aeronautics and Astronautics,
University of Electronic Science and Technology of China, 61731 Chengdu, PRC
thriller_bar@sina.cn

Abstract. This article briefly describes the research status of the human exoskeleton system, and gives a summary of the human lower limb gait analysis. On this basis, the machine learning classification algorithms and clustering algorithms are used for offline data mining on a data collection of prototype, in order to establish a classifier for movement prediction and judgment of lower limb. At the same time, the article analyses the procedure of standing from sitting utilizing clustering algorithm for rehabilitation exoskeleton. Experiments mainly refer to the C4.5 decision tree algorithm, Bayesian classification algorithm and clustering algorithm EM. Weka software simulation results show that the lower limb motion can be judged by the classifier making use of gait analysis data accurately, and the lower limb motion for different users at different time and different environments could be clustered by cluster. Effectively using of these results can offer great convenience to the flexibility control for exoskeleton so that exoskeleton system could achieve human-computer coupling.

Keywords: Exoskeleton, machine learning, gait analysis, classifier, cluster.

1 Introduction

Exoskeleton systems generally have two functions. One is to extend the function of the body; another is to restore the body's functions. In order to achieve compliance control, the exoskeleton system must create a perception subsystem with intelligence for precise action judgments and projections.

Exoskeleton system is a highly human-machine coupled system, which combines human intelligence and mechanical strength. One system like this requires that the machine constantly follows and adapts to human motions. The implementation needs that the machine could understand a pilot's state of motion and movement trends. Therefore, it is essential to study the perceived performance of the exoskeleton. Besides, the property of perceptual system is decided by its accuracy and real-time. Among the existing exoskeleton literatures, the intelligent processing of the perceptual system seldom exists relatively. The flexibility of Exoskeleton system has been a challenge. There are precedents in the recognition of the motion by Machine

S.S. Ge et al. (Eds.): ICSR 2012, LNAI 7621, pp. 600–611, 2012.

learning algorithms [2, 3, 5], but those work cannot meet the requirements of man-machine servo control. The application of machine learning algorithms in the exoskeleton system should be researched deep into details.

2   Related Research Work

2.1   Exoskeleton System

Exoskeleton perception system mainly consists of various sensors those located on person and exoskeletons. General reports and information only reference to the type of sensor and the installation location. Intelligent information processing algorithms are barely described. BLEEX utilizes the information from 8 encoders and 16 linear accelerometers to determine angle, angular velocity, and angular acceleration of each of the eight actuated joints, and utilizes a foot switch and some load distribution sensors per foot to determine ground contact and force distribution between the feet during double-stance [12, 13]. The HAL utilizes EMG sensors and foot pressure sensors to collect the appropriate signal, then to determine the wearer's walking state [7].

2.2   Human Lower Limb Motion Analysis

Basic forms of Human lower extremity exercises can be divided into flexion, extension, abduction, adduction and rotation, as shown in figure 1.

Understanding the biomechanics of human walking is crucial in the control of exoskeletons and active orthoses for the lower limbs. Fig. 2[12] shows a simplified diagram of human walking gait. The human walking gait cycle is typically represented as starting (0%) and ending (100%) at the point of heel strike on the same foot, with heel strike on the adjacent foot occurring at approximately 62% of gait cycle [12].

Article [4] gives one similar figure (not illustrated). This article uses another figure 3 about human gait. All of those will be referenced in the classify work. Different person's gaits may have great differences, even the same person's gaits under different physical conditions will also appear difference. Most of the existing motion recognition work [5] has been done in an off-line manner. Tapia et al. [2] proposed a real-time algorithm based on a decision tree for physical activities recognition. A C4.5 classifier is first trained, and then used to recognize gymnasium activities in real time. Krishnan Et al. [3] proposed an AdaBoost algorithm based on decision stumps for real-time classification of gestures. He et al. [6] presented a Hidden Markov Model for real-time activity classification. This article will focus on the application of C4.5, Bayes and EM algorithms of machine learning in human exoskeleton, implemented in Weka.

In order to meet the requirements of Flexibility in human exoskeleton, actual online learning is needed. In this paper, we'll focus on the active exo-skeleton, so there is little description over the passive exoskeleton model and geometry.

3   Data Mining and Machine Learning

Technology now allows us to capture and store vast quantities of data. Finding patterns, trends, and anomalies in these datasets, and summarizing them with simple quantitative models—turning data into information and turning information into knowledge. There has been stunning progress in data mining and machine learning.

C4.5 is a suite of algorithms for classification problems in machine learning and data mining. It is targeted at supervised learning: Given an attribute-valued dataset where instances are described by collections of attributes and belong to one of a set of mutually exclusive classes, C4.5 learns a mapping from attribute values to classes that can be applied to classify new, unseen instances. C4.5 uses information-theoretic criteria such as gain and gain ratio. The default criterion is gain ratio. At each point in the tree-growing, the test with the best criteria is greedily chosen.

Various Bayesian network classier learning algorithms are also implemented in Weka. Let U be a set of variables. A Bayesian network B over a set of variables U is a network structure B_S, which is a directed acyclic graph (DAG) over U and a set of probability Tables B_P. A Bayesian network represents probability distributions.

The expectation-maximization (EM) algorithm is a broadly applicable approach to the iterative computation of maximum likelihood (ML) estimates, useful in a variety of incomplete-data problems. For more algorithm details, you can read reference 8.

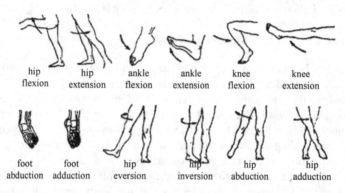

Fig. 1. Human lower limb movement diagram-The rotation includes inversion and eversion

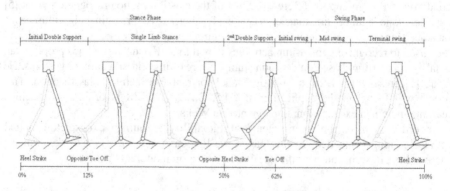

Fig. 2. Human walking gait through one cycle-beginning and ending at heel strike. Percentages showing contact events are given at their approximate location [12].

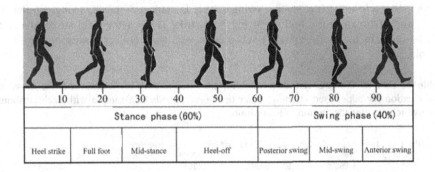

Fig. 3. Stance is about 60%, Swing is about 40%. Stance phase is divided into Heel strike, Full foot, Mid-stance, Heel-off; Swing phase is divided into Posterior swing, Mid-swing, Anterior swing.

4   Simulation and Data Demonstration

According to the previous description, we simulate machine learning algorithms on the sensor data collected in laboratory prototype. In all experiments, the gait is with reference to the data of the sensors, which is imported in spreadsheet file with CSV format, and finally weka software is used for processing data. The installed positions of encoders and pressure sensors are shown in Fig.4. Power supply exists in the prototype. Besides, there is one DOF at knee, no DOF at ankle, three DOF at hip. Only at the knee joint, there is a hydraulic cylinder.

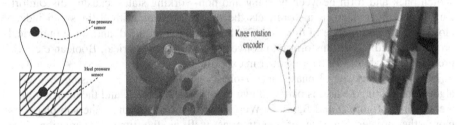

Fig. 4. The installed positions of sensors

4.1   Supervised Classification

Experiment I: Gait Cycle Differentiation

It needs to install two pressure sensors in each foot, placed in the soles and heels, and to install an encoder at each knee. There're six properties in all, as shown in table 1.Leftbank attribute denotes the pressure of the left heel while walking, and others can be explained similarly. We utilize the six properties, as well as pre-given category (i.e. the six attribute value is belong to which sub-phase of the gait cycle) to train the classifier. Based on the analysis of gait cycle in figure 2 and figure 3, we separately divide gait cycle into 2(i.e. stance, swing), 3(i.e. D-stance, S-stance, swing, similar to [14]), and 7(shown in the bottom of Fig.3, H-strike is short for Heel strike, the rest can be done in the same manner) sub-phases, and then collect corresponding data samples.

Table 1. Part of 2-phase gait data samples, the first line is properties, and the class is classification for supervised learning; other lines corresponds to a sample with each attribute value,which denotes the motion of lower limbs.

leftback	leftfore	rightback	rightfore	leftencode	rightencode	class
9.326172	9.863281	9.912109	6.542969	-0.292683	-0.292683	stance
9.228516	9.863281	10.058594	6.542969	0	-0.292683	stance
9.619141	10.351563	10.15625	6.787109	-0.292683	-0.292683	stance
2.832031	18.310547	19.042969	3.662109	-1.170732	0.878049	swing
1.611328	19.091797	18.261719	3.759766	-0.585366	1.170732	swing

The decision tree for the C4.5 algorithm is illustrated in figure 5. This result is very simple, based only on the left heel pressure, but can correctly judge gait (in fact the state of the left leg, the correct rate is 100% for the dataset). However, this classification model is too simple to satisfy supple requirements. In fact, at the beginning of the prototype such a control strategy is adopted, depending on the value of the pressure sensor is greater than the threshold to determine the gait and then provide the impetus. This ignores the other attributes which also carries information about gait, let alone taking into account the stability of the sensor output value and the stability of human gait. As a result, the power controls will be unstable. For example, when you slightly uplift your heel, outputs of the sensor at the foot are subject to fluctuations. If the threshold is in the fluctuation range, then the power controls will switch back and forth between working and non-working states, causing discomfort. But on the other hand, it also reflects the machine learning algorithms can indeed close to the human mode of thinking. Further testing is required, and some numerical properties need to be transform into conventional type (categorical, Boolean etc.) via pretreatment, which will be used later in experiments.

Next, we work on 3-phase and 7-phase gait dividing, also using the C4.5 algorithm. Testing dataset is partly shown in table 2and table 3, and the decision trees are shown in figure 6 and figure 7. We can see from the figures, the sub-phases is more, the greater the size of the tree as well as the time consumption. The classification more refined will be accompanied by a few errors. For instance, while testing   on   the   3-phase   decision   tree,   Sample   20 (20 2.587891 4.101563 16.55273 9.619141 -6.73171 3.512195 swing   ) is wrongly divided into S-stance. Because the swing and S-stance are two adjacent sub-phases, the error will not cause a big impact on the submissive controll. The experiment shows that there are also errors in 7-phase classification, but are also the adjacent sub-phases. It is acceptable. So when there is a reliable expert data, machine learning algorithms have a good effect to refine the identification on the lower limb movements. The algorithm also can filter some redundant sensor data.

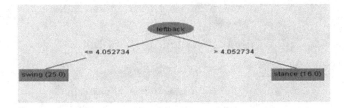

Fig. 5. Decision tree of 2-phase gait classification. Six attribute (sensor) values are numerical, so the C4.5 tests are binary-valued, and of the form {≤θor >θ}. Here 4.052734 is a suitably determined threshold for attribute "leftback", and the tree is binary tree.

Table 2. Part of 3-phase gait data samples

leftback	leftfore	rightback	rightfore	leftencode	rightencode	class
17.138672	6.445313	0.976563	14.746094	0.585366	7.02439	D-stance
19.726563	4.541016	0.195313	11.279297	0.585366	7.902439	D-stance
24.169922	4.882813	2.294922	2.490234	-1.463415	19.609756	S-stance
23.681641	5.224609	0.976563	2.001953	-1.756098	23.414635	S-stance
23.876953	5.566406	0.292969	2.441406	-1.756098	24	S-stance
0.78125	7.8125	15.820313	14.355469	5.560976	2.04878	swing
0.634766	1.513672	18.505859	13.964844	20.780487	2.04878	swing

Table 3. Part of 7-phase gait data samples. It consists of selected samples in order to show more classes.

leftback	leftfore	rightback	rightfore	leftenco	rightenc	class
17.13867	6.445313	0.976563	14.74609	0.585366	7.02439	H-strike
19.72656	4.541016	0.195313	11.2793	0.585366	7.902439	H-strike
20.89844	4.443359	0.830078	9.619141	0.585366	8.487804	H-strike
23.82813	4.589844	0.634766	6.005859	-0.29268	14.04878	H-strike
24.16992	4.882813	2.294922	2.490234	-1.46342	19.60976	H-strike
23.68164	5.224609	0.976563	2.001953	-1.7561	23.41464	H-strike
23.87695	5.566406	0.292969	2.441406	-1.7561	24	H-strike
9.326172	9.863281	9.912109	6.542969	-0.29268	-0.29268	fullfoot
9.228516	9.863281	10.05859	6.542969	0	-0.29268	fullfoot
9.619141	10.35156	10.15625	6.787109	-0.29268	-0.29268	fullfoot
7.714844	6.933594	2.001953	21.48438	0.292683	5.268293	M-stance
9.765625	5.664063	1.416016	22.07031	0.292683	5.560976	M-stance
11.62109	4.492188	1.660156	20.50781	0.585366	5.853659	M-stance
5.419922	8.056641	1.904297	23.38867	0	4.97561	H-off
5.517578	8.544922	1.953125	23.53516	0	5.268293	H-off
0.927734	12.45117	21.24023	5.224609	5.853659	2.04878	H-off
1.611328	19.0918	18.26172	3.759766	-0.58537	1.170732	P-swing
0.732422	21.24023	19.23828	5.46875	1.463415	1.463415	P-swing
1.757813	20.45898	19.48242	4.6875	1.463415	1.463415	P-swing
0.830078	4.296875	25.43945	5.517578	14.04878	3.804878	M-swing
0.439453	3.369141	25.97656	5.029297	16.09756	3.804878	M-swing
0.830078	1.953125	26.02539	5.126953	16.39024	3.804878	M-swing
2.587891	4.101563	16.55273	9.619141	-6.73171	3.512195	A-swing
1.464844	3.222656	18.4082	8.447266	-7.31707	3.512195	A-swing
2.832031	3.173828	14.89258	10.30273	-5.85366	3.512195	A-swing

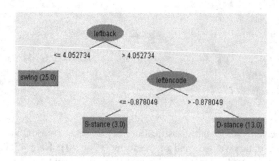

Fig. 6. Decision tree of 3-phase gait classification

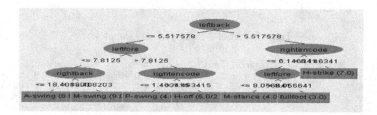

Fig. 7. Decision tree of 7-phase gait classification

Experiment II: Lower Limb Motion Estimate

In this study, the pilot's actions are divided into ground walking (i.e. lftWalk, rgtWalk), leg raising (i.e. lftLift, rgtLift) and Climbing stairs (i.e. lftStair, rgtStair), in addition to an unstable state(i.e. badStand), as shown in table 4,and then machine learning algorithms is used to discriminate them. The sensors used here, in addition to the previously mentioned, include a three-axis gyro on the back of pilot. As mentioned earlier, the numerical properties are generally in accordance with the binary test. Sometimes the threshold may not be ideal, and more accurate decision tree branches are needed. Therefore, in this experiment we add original sensor data pre-processing to transform numerical attributes into a general description of property. The property values between the maximum and minimum values is divided into several intervals, labeled as "small", "normal", "big", as well as the attribute is labeled as "still", "changed" according to the absolute difference of two sample attribute values. This prevents the decision-making jitter caused by the tiny changes in sensor values output.

The decision tree C4.5 algorithm analysis results are shown in figure 8.While using the data set itself to test the classification model, 75% of it is correctly classified. So this article considers the Bayes Algorithm. Under the same conditions, Naive Bayes classifier's correct rate is 87.5% (not illustrated here), and the Bayes Net classifier's is 91.7%, shown in figure 9. It can be seen that different classifier has different Performance, and it's really hard to say which is always better. This is why the cluster is needed. Clustering algorithm constructs different classifiers, called the primary classifier, and then classify on the early classification results by a new classifier, called the high-level classification, to get the final optimal classification results. In Section 4.2, this article will experiment on cluster, to show its effects on classifier before the classifying.

Table 4. Part of the dataset for lower limb motion estimate, increase of the X, Y, Z three-axis acceleration

leftB	leftF	rgtB	rgtF	leftCd	rgtCd	X acc	Y acc	Z acc	class
small	small	big	normal	changed	still	normal	normal	small	lftWalk
small	normal	big	big	changed	still	small	small	small	lftLift
small	small	big	small	changed	changed	big	big	big	badStand
big	big	small	small	still	changed	normal	normal	small	rgtWalk
big	big	small	small	still	changed	small	small	small	rgtLift
big	small	big	small	changed	changed	big	big	normal	badStand
normal	big	small	small	still	changed	normal	small	normal	rgtStair
big	big	small	small	still	changed	normal	small	small	rgtStair
normal	big	small	small	still	changed	normal	normal	normal	rgtStair

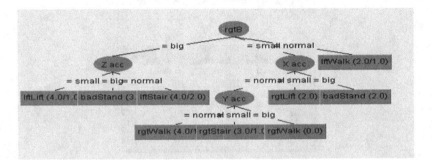

Fig. 8. Decision tree of lower limb motion estimate. No numerical attributes more branches.

4.2   Clustering Algorithm Application

The previously mentioned classification algorithms are supervised learning. Training dataset is already well classified via expert data. However, expert data is about average situation, also with regional difference. So the exoskeleton cannot satisfy supple requirements for special individual. Therefore, clustering analysis, unsupervised machine learning, is of great value in this case. It does not even need prior separate acquisition training samples, but real-time online acquisition exoskeleton wearer's movement data for cluster analysis, and then constructs the classifier to classify the follow-up data.

Experiment III: Clustering Analysis on Gait Data

Remove the class attribute in table 1, Specify number of clusters 2, and then EM cluster algorithm is experimented on it. The result is shown in figure 10. The result has reached a fairly accurate clustering. In the area of the rectangle, the three samples are collected while preparing, in the spreadsheet file are divided into "stance", and in the figure 10 are divided into "swing", but it does not affect the gait analysis during walking. The result of 3-phase clustering is similar to 2-phase. However, there is a large cross in the classification while cluster number is 7. Compared with Table 3, the error is basically in the adjacent sub-phases, and minority jumps one phase, and two-phase-jump error clustering rarely exists, such as the H-off and P-Swing, H-strike and M-stance. A few big jump errors appear among sub-phases A-Swing M-stance and H-off. Those relate with whether our pre-classification is accuracy or not. At the same time, the same person's each gait cycle is not the same, so a gait cycle divided into seven sub-phase may be not very stable in practical applications. Trying to experiment on 4, 5 or 6 sub-phases based on already existed gait analysis is necessary, not completed here.

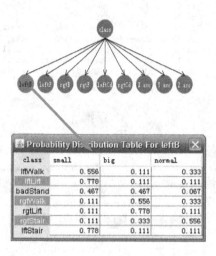

class	small	big	normal
lftWalk	0.556	0.111	0.333
lftLift	0.778	0.111	0.111
badStand	0.467	0.467	0.067
rgtWalk	0.111	0.556	0.333
rgtLift	0.111	0.778	0.111
rgtStair	0.111	0.333	0.556
lftStair	0.778	0.111	0.111

Fig. 9. Bayes Net generated by Bayes classifier. Under table is the probability of leftB in all the classes, you can visualize others attributes' probability, too.

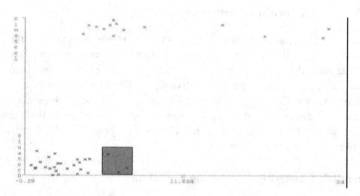

Fig. 10. Cluster result of 2-phase without class. The horizontal axis is attribute leftBack; the vertical axis is cluster number.

Experiment IV: Rose Process from Sitting of Rehabilitation Exoskeleton Analysis

Rehabilitation exoskeleton is generally loaded with sensors like EMGs on and in body, so there will be a lot of inconvenience. So we choose signal of a gyroscope on upper body to analyze the standing movement of people. The data includes triaxial angular velocity and triaxial accelerometer, as shown in table 5. Based on the curve of table 5, shown in figure 11, standing up process is divided into: preparation stage, when upper body will lean forward but the lower limbs without impetus; powered stage, when provide the impetus to help the patients to stand up; completed stage, in an upright position, the exoskeleton provides support force. So specified number of clusters 3.As shown in figure 12(other attributes not shown), in the vicinity of one attribute value, clustering result is more than one, but it's different for different attribute. So more than one property need to be considered. For those attributes which cross at each cluster in the vicinity of values can be deleted directly in later classified work.

5   Discussion and Follow-Up Work

It can be seen from the experimental results that the machine learning algorithms could play a significant role in the analysis of lower limb motion recognition. With supervised learning, we can establish a precise classification model to make it easy to judge the gait and the motions. It contributes to achieve a high degree of human-machine coupling. With unsupervised clustering, we can establish the clustering model based on samples collected, to make up for the vacancy of the expert data as well as its insufficient. It contributes to adaption to the special individual user of exoskeleton at different time and different environments. In a word, the machine can understand a person's state of motion and movement trends.

The follow-up work has two important points. One is the optimization of the samples of dataset in the machine learning process, because the sample dataset directly affect that the final learning result is right or wrong as well as learning effect. While facing large amounts of data and attributes of variables, which attribute can be used as independent and which attribute is related to others heavily, need to be analyzed to reduce the dimension of the data, so as to make machine learning faster and more accurate. The data mining analysis is imperative, such as association rules. The second focus is real-time learning model. If these two problems are solved, machine learning will be of greater application value in the lower extremity exoskeleton. Given real-time online clustering and classification results of lower limb movement data, the perceptual system can make accurate situational judgment due to the person, the time as well as the environment.

Table 5. Part of the inertial data of upper body

X Gryo	Y Gyro	Z Gyro	X acc	Y acc	Z acc
7.6	−64.9	−6.6	−0.84582	−0.06327	0.54612
7.95	−66.95	−7.15	−0.81585	−0.07326	0.54945
9.8	−68.15	−7.35	−0.79254	−0.08991	0.55944
12.9	−67.4	−6.4	−0.78588	−0.08991	0.57942
14.6	−63.9	−4.8	−0.78255	−0.07659	0.5994
14.2	−59.4	−2.75	−0.78921	−0.05328	0.61605
13.1	−55.1	−1.75	−0.79254	−0.06327	0.62271
13.55	−53.15	−1.25	−0.79254	−0.07992	0.65268
13.1	−52.45	−0.35	−0.77256	−0.0666	0.6327
11.8	−53.65	−0.9	−0.74259	−0.04995	0.66267
11	−54.95	−0.5	−0.70596	−0.03996	0.67266

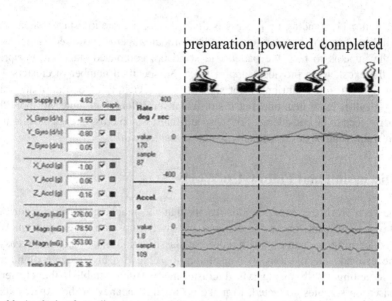

Fig. 11. Analysis of standing process, while sampling, X, Y, and Z-axis correspond to the body vertical axis, horizontal axis and the sagittal axis

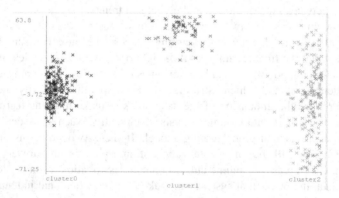

Fig. 12. Cluster result of standing process. The horizontal axis is cluster number; the vertical axis is attribute Y Gyro.

References

1. Wang, L., Gu, T., Tao, X., Lu, J.: A hierarchical approach to real-time activity recognition in body sensor networks. Pervasive and Mobile Computing (8), 115–130 (2012)
2. Tapia, E.M., Intille, S.: Real-time recognition of physical activities and their intensities using wireless accelerometers and a heart rate monitor. In: Proceedings of the 11th International Conference on Wearable Computers, Boston, MA (2007)
3. Krishnan, N.C., Colbry, D., Juillard, C., Panchanathan, S.: Real time human activity recognition using tri-axial accelerometers. In: Proceedings of Sensors Signals and Information Processing Workshop, Sedona, AZ (2008)

4. Beyl, P.: Design and control of a knee exoskeleton powered by pleated pneumatic artificial muscles for robot-assisted gait rehabilitation. Academic and Scientific Publishers, Brussels (2010)
5. Palmes, P.P., Pung, H.K., Gu, T., Xue, W., Chen, S.: Object relevance weight pattern mining for activity recognition and segmentation. Pervasive and Mobile Computing 6(1), 43–57 (2010)
6. He, J., Li, H., Tan, J.: Real-time daily activity classification with wireless sensor networks using hidden Markov model. In: Proceedings of the 29th Annual International Conference of the IEEE Engineering in Medicine and Biology Society (2007)
7. Kawamoto, H., Sankai, Y.: Comfortable power assist control method for walking aid by HAL-3. In: IEEE International Conference on Systems, Man and Cybernetics, vol. 4 (2002)
8. Witten, I.H., Frank, E.: Data Mining: Practical Machine Learning Tools and Techniques with Java Implementations. Morgan Kaufmann Publishers, Waikato Hamilton (2000)
9. Jun, X., Yueting, Z., WuFei: Computer Vision and Machine Learning in 3D Human Animation: a Survey. Journal of Computer-aided Design & Computer Graphics 20(3), 281–290 (2008)
10. Gomes, M.A., Silveira, G.L.M., Siqueira, A.A.G.: Gait-Pattern Adaptation Algorithms based on Neural Network for Lower Limbs Active Orthoses. IEEE Intelligent Robots and Systems, 4475–4480 (2009)
11. Liu, G., Pan, Z., Cheng, X., Li, L., Zhang, M.: A Survey on Machine Learning in the Synthesis of Human Motions. Journal of Computer-aided Design & Conputer Graphics 22(9), 1620–1627 (2010)
12. Dollar, A.M., Herr, H.: Lower Extremity Exoskeletons and Active Orthoses:Challenges and State-of-the-Art. IEEE Transactions on Robotics 24(1), 144–158 (2008)
13. Kong, K., Moon, H., Hwang, B., Jeon, D., Tomizuka, M.: Robotic rehabilitation treatments: Realization of aquatic therapy effects in exoskeleton systems. Robotics and Automation, 1923–1928 (2009)
14. Ghan, J., Steger, R., Kazerooni, H.: Control and system identification for the Berkeley lower extremity exoskeleton (BLEEX). Advanced Robotics 20(9), 989–1014 (2006)

Hydraulic Pressure Control System Simulation and Performance Test of Lower Extremity Exoskeleton[*]

Qing Guo, Xiang-gang Zhang, Dan Jiang, and Lu-lu Zhang

School of Aeronautics and Astronautics,
University of Electronic Science and Technology of China, Chengdu 611731
guoqinguestc@163.com

Abstract. On basis of the introduction for the composition of carried-load assistance system and the control mechanism of hydraulic pressure valve for lower extremity exoskeleton, the position control loop is built. The control system is designed by frequency domain method using the PID parameters combined with lead correction network. Simulation results show that the control method can servo the angle of knee joint as human's natural walk as well as the harmonious of man-machine moment. According to performance test of hydraulic pressure control system, the flow and pressure in piston is analyzed considering different load, the pressure of oil box and movable mode. Test results show that hydraulic pressure valve control system can realize efficiently slow walk carried 30 kilogram load, up and down stairs.

Keywords: lower extremity exoskeleton, hydraulic pressure control system, harmonious of man-machine moment, performance test.

1   Introduction

Lower extremity exoskeleton is a complex high degree of man-machine coupling power servo system. It can support the human body in walking, going uphill or downhill and so on.

Since 2000, DARPA promote the research of "EHPA" to improve individual soldier's capacity of load. Invested by DARPA, BLEEX exoskeletons system in the University of California and passive exoskeletons system in MIT have appeared in the United States. In 2006, BLEEX exoskeletons system was redesigned, and renamed as "Human Universal Load Carrier". Cybernics laboratory in University of tsukuba developed the first commercial exoskeletons booster device in the world.

In 2006, the National University of Defense Technology developed the no power accompanying amplification prototype, and it opened the research of exoskeleton in china. Then Zhejiang University and Harbin Institute of Technology also researched the principle of exoskeleton. In 2005, Naval Aviation Engineering Institute developed exoskeletons system prototype droved by motor, which could walk slowly. In 2009, in the basis of HULC, South China University of Technology developed the prototype droved by hydraulic pressure, and it almost had the functions of walking, upstairs and downstairs.

[*] This work is supported by the central university basic scientific research business expenses. (ZYGX2010J116).

S.S. Ge et al. (Eds.): ICSR 2012, LNAI 7621, pp. 612–620, 2012.
© Springer-Verlag Berlin Heidelberg 2012

The paper is mainly about the lower extremity exoskeleton prototype made by ourselves. We test the performance of hydraulic pressure control system's booster effect; analyze the ability of load and system response, which lay the foundation for optimization of the whole system.

2   Lower Extremity Exoskeleton System

Carried-load assistance system is shown in Fig.1. People wear the equipment. Then the motor transfers the electricity to hydraulic power, and controls the hydraulic cylinder to assist people to carry load.

Fig. 1. Exoskeleton intelligent portable systems

Hydraulic driving system uses DC motor to drive gear pump. Gear pump absorbs hydraulic oil in the small tank to a low-pressure Chambers from a high-pressure one.

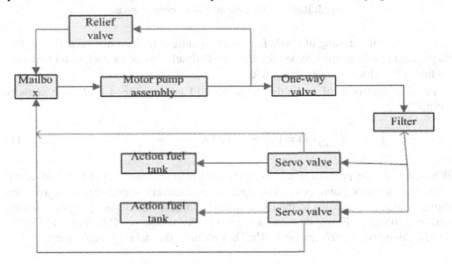

Fig. 2. The hydraulic power system workflow diagram

and the system controls hydraulic flow through the servo valve. The workflow of the whole hydraulic pressure control system is shown in Fig.2.

3   Design and Simulation of Hydraulic Pressure Control System

Based on the hydraulic drive control circuit is design shown in Figure 3.

When a person is walking, the knee makes an expected rotation angle. Then the expected location of the piston rod can be calculated. From the actual output position of hydraulic cylinder, we can calculate the actual knee rotation angle. The position of the piston rod can be calculated by the angle, which can be measured by the angle sensor. Controller gives control quantity of voltage, Uctr. The quantity of voltage transfers to current, I, and then transfers to servo valve displacement control volume, xv. From xv, we can calculate the position of the piston rod, Y. We control the piston rod to make rotation angle of exoskeleton be in keeping with knee's expected rotation angle.

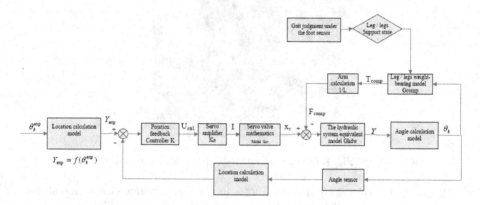

Fig. 3. Based on the hydraulic drive control circuit

In account of the using of single function hydraulic cylinder, only the period of foot on the land can be control. When the leg lifts, hydraulic oil flows back to oil tank fast. So this period does not been controlled.

Position controller of hydraulic valve uses PI and advanced correction network form.

$$K_{PID}(s) = (k_p + k_i / s) \times \frac{1 + a_1 s}{1 + b_1 s} \tag{1}$$

Where k_p, k_i are proportion and integral control parameters. a1, b1 are advanced correction network parameters. The open loop relatively stable region degrees are shown in Fig.4. According to the fig, amplitude domain degrees of the system is Gm, Gm =23dB>6dB. Phase domain degrees of the system is Pm, Pm =119°>60°. Bandwidth is wc, wc=26.9rad/s=4.2Hz.They all meet the stability requirement.

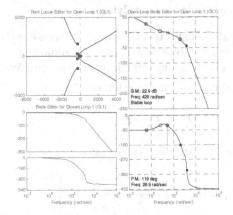

Fig. 4. Open loop frequency characteristics

Fig.5 shows the expected and actual location response curve of Hydraulic cylinder. The range of leg's expected location is about - 0.015 m to 0.025m. The range of expected location and actual location is about 0.36m to 0.28m.And the Error is less than 7%. This shows that the controller can make the hydraulic cylinder piston rod track expected changing position, and satisfy certain precision.

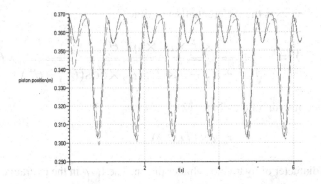

Fig. 5. The expected and actual location response curve

4   Performance Test of Hydraulic Pressure Control System

People wear the exoskeleton to walk, go upstairs and downstairs. Different oil pressure and different weight of load is put to the system. When experiments are done, the corresponding sensor output data are collected. The dates comprise the pressure of foot, the angle of rotary encoder equipped on the knees and pressure of hydraulic cylinder.

4.1   Flow Analysis of the Hydraulic Cylinder

According to control algorithm, expected angle and actual angle need be transfer to hydraulic cylinder's expected location and actual location. Knee angle, which is tested by rotary encoder, is a rotation angle thigh relative to crus. When output of the left rotary encoder is θ_k^s, absolute angle of the left keen is:

$$\theta_k = \theta_{k0} - \theta_k^s \tag{2}$$

Where θk0 is initial angle of standing, shown as:

$$\theta_{k0} = \arccos\left(\frac{d_1^2 + d_2^2 - y_{max}^2}{2 \times d_1 \times d_2}\right) \tag{3}$$

Where d_1=0.32232m, shown distance from the hydraulic cylinder thigh connection point to keen bearing. d_2=0.06517m, shown distance from the hydraulic cylinder crus connection point to keen bearing. y_{max} =0.36921m, shown the maximum displacement of the hydraulic cylinder piston rod .

Actual displacement of hydraulic cylinder piston rod is represented by y:

$$y = \sqrt{d_1^2 + d_2^2 - 2 \times d_1 \times d_2 \times \cos(\theta_{k0} - \theta_k^s)} \tag{4}$$

Piston rod velocities is the differentiation of time

$$\dot{Y} = -\frac{2 \times d_1 \times d_2 \times \sin(\theta_{k0} - \theta_k^s)}{\sqrt{d_1^2 + d_2^2 - 2 \times d_1 \times d_2 \times \cos(\theta_{k0} - \theta_k^s)}} \times \dot{\theta}_k^s \tag{5}$$

The valid area of hydraulic cylinder is:

$$A_p = \pi \times (D_b / 2)^2 \tag{6}$$

Where D_b is diameter of hydraulic cylinder piston. The flow in the hydraulic cylinder is:

$$Q_L = \dot{Y} \times A_p \tag{7}$$

$\dot{\theta}_{kl}^s$ can be calculated after second-order decay memory filtering algorithm.

$$\hat{x}_k = \hat{x}_{k-1} + \hat{\dot{x}}_{k-1}T_s + G[x_k - (\hat{x}_{k-1} + \hat{\dot{x}}_{k-1}T_s)]$$
$$\hat{\dot{x}}_k = \hat{\dot{x}}_{k-1} + H / T_s[x_k - (\hat{x}_{k-1} + \hat{\dot{x}}_{k-1}T_s)] \tag{8}$$
$$G = 1 - \chi^2 \qquad H = (1 - \chi)^2$$

Next, we analyze the flow of hydraulic cylinder in such cases: the same oil pressure, different weight of load.

According to fig.6 and fig.7, the system requires higher oil pressure when the load' weight is 30kg. And the flow changes more. People walk slowly when the load is not empty, which shows that people feel the load.

Next, we analyze the flow of hydraulic cylinder in such cases: the same oil pressure, different weight of load.

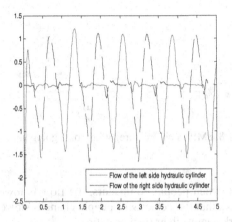

Fig. 6. 8MPa's oil pressure, non load, walking

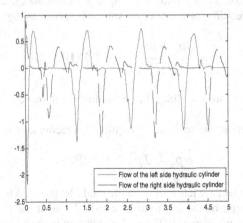

Fig. 7. 12MPa's oil pressure, 30kg' load, walking

According to fig.6 and fig.7, the system requires higher oil pressure when the load' weight is 30kg. And the flow changes more. People walk slowly when the load is not empty, which shows that people feel the load.

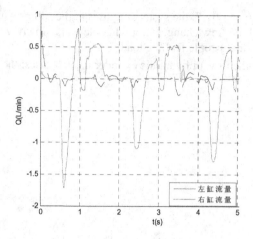

Fig. 8. 8MPa's oil pressure, 30kg' load, going upstairs

According to Fig.8, when people go upstairs, the flow is lower. The frequency of flow is slower. It shows that the velocity of people changes slower. The reason is that people have to do work against their own gravity.

4.2   Analysis of the Hydraulic Cylinder's Pressure

If diameter of the piston (D) is 10mm, the weight of load is 30 kg, and the weight of the instrument is 30kg, required pressure of oil source is shown as (9):

$$p_s = \frac{(m_0 + m_f)g}{\pi D^2 / 4} = 7.5\text{MPa} \tag{9}$$

So when the weight of load is 30kg, the pressure of oil source must be higher then 8MPa.

But in actual situation, the pressure of required oil recourse is shown as (10):

$$p'_s \geq 2p_s \geq 15\text{MPa} \tag{10}$$

According to Fig.9, when the left foot is on the land, the pressure transfers from heel to palm. Now the pressure of the left hydraulic cylinder is at the maximum, while the pressure of the right one is almost 0. When the right foot is on the land, it has the similar results. It shows that hydraulic pressure system can provide high pressure, and have quick speed response. So it can satisfy the demand of different motor pattern.

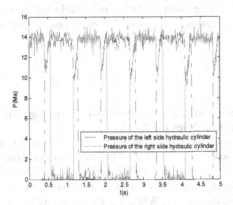

Fig. 9. 14MPa's oil pressure, 30kg' load, walking

4.3   Working Performance of Hydraulic Pressure System

In the situation of different weight of load and different oil source pressure, when testing the performance of carried-load assistance system, we can get walking velocity and the change of system's temperature, which are important indexes. It is shown in Table1.

Table 1. Property of the velocity and the temperature

	8MPa		10MPa		14MPa	
	Velocity (m/s)	temperature (°C)	velocity (m/s)	temperature (°C)	velocity (m/s)	temperature (°C)
0kg	4.5	1.5	4.7	2	4.6	2
10kg	4.2	2.5	4.3	3	4.5	3.5
20kg	3.7	4	3.9	4.5	4	5.5
30kg	3.5	4.5	3.8	6.5	4	7.5

According to Table1, when the pressure of oil source is unchanged and the weight of load increases, the walking velocity decreases, and the temperature change becomes fast. When the weight of load is unchanged and the pressure of oil source increases, the walking velocity increases, and the temperature change becomes fast too. It shown that hydraulic pressure controller is not an energy saving control for carried-load assistance system.

5   Conclusions

On the basis of understanding the hydraulic pressure control system, we realize the angle servo of the knee when exoskeleton is at the stage of touchdown, analyze working performance when the weight of load and the motor pattern are different, and prove that hydraulic pressure control system is feasible for exoskeleton. But because valve control hydraulic system's temperature rises fast, so we should improve our control method.

References

1. Steger, J.R.: A design and control methodology for human exoskeletons, pp. 36–44. University of California, Berkeley (2006)
2. Veneman, J.F., Ekkelenkamp, R., Kruidhof, R., van der Helm, F.C.T., van der Kooij, H.: Design of a series elastic - and Bowden cable-based actuation system for use as torque - actuator in exoskeleton-type training. In: Proceedings of the 9th International Conference on Rehabilitation Robotics, Chicago, IL, USA, June 28-July 1 (2005)
3. Li, Q., Kong, M., Du, Z., Sun, L., Wang, D.: Interactive Rehabilitation Exercise Control Strategy for 5-DOF Upper Limb Rehabilitation Arm. Journal of Mechanical Engineering 44(9), 169–176 (2008)
4. Yang, Z.-Y., Zhang, Y.-S., Gu, W., Yang, X.: Simulation of Exoskeleton Suit' s Sensitivity Amplification Control. Computer Simulation 27(1), 177–180 (2010)
5. Cao, H., Meng, X., Ling, Z., Qin, Y., He, C.: Measurement System for Plantar Pressure of Biped Exoskeleton Robot. Chinese Journal of Sensors and Actuators 23(3), 326–330 (2010)
6. Zarchan, P.: Tactical and Strategic Missile Guidance, 2nd edn., pp. 137–144. American Institute of Aeronautics and Astronatutics (1994)

Dynamic Characteristics Study
of Human Exoskeleton Based on Virtual Prototype

Wen-ming Cheng, Fang Liu, and Jian-bing Shao

Institute of Mechanical Engineering, Southwest Jiaotong University,
No.111, 1st Section of North Erhuan Rd. 610031 Chengdu, China
{wmcheng,liufang}@home.swjtu.edu.cn

Abstract. This paper is concerned with the dynamic characteristics of human exoskeleton. The dynamic characteristics of the four hydraulic cylinders powering the exoskeleton are chosen to be the study objects. Numerical simulation of one typical posture, one knee down and up, is achieved by using the commercial package Matlab, ANSYS etc. The path trajectories of the exoskeleton are captured by optical motion capture system and fitted into a function of angular. This function drives the skeleton system in a simulation performed in ADAMS. The numerical results showed trends of the four hydraulic cylinder displacement curves are flat and varied. Meanwhile, the load of knee hydraulic cylinder is only 2.3% of the total weight as the skeleton being in upright position. In addition, kinetic curves of the four hydraulic cylinders trend to be flat, confirming the reasonality of the exoskeleton structure design and hydraulic cylinder setting.

Keywords: Human exoskeleton, Optical motion capture, Gaussian Fitting, Dynamics simulation.

1 Introduction

Human beings invent the airplane by simulating bird wings .And they invent the submarine by simulating fish swim bladders. The concept and research of the exoskeleton are no exception. The technology of the exoskeleton comes from the concept of the exoskeleton in biology. It refers to the physical appearance of insects or crustaceans bones that supports and protects the biological. The concept of the exoskeleton has appeared for some decades in the United States Hollywood science fiction movie. The most representative ones lie in the "Iron Man" and "Avatar"[1, 2].

With the development of science and technology, the U.S. Department of Defense Advanced Research Projects Agency begins to solve the technical bottleneck problem of the key research in the technical development of the external skeleton from the four areas of materials, energy, control and drive. The HULC launched by the Lockheed Martin Company achieves a big step from research to practical application of the exoskeleton. At the same time, Russia, Japan and France and other countries have launched a variety of human exoskeleton prototypes, which have expanded the application of the exoskeleton to the military, rehabilitation, medical and other fields.

S.S. Ge et al. (Eds.): ICSR 2012, LNAI 7621, pp. 621–630, 2012.

Based on the point of view of bionics, the human exoskeleton including the suspension system, the structure of the hip, thigh, calf and shoes and other components is to simulate the muscles, bones and joints of human body to construct the exoskeleton load-bearing structures to match with the human body, so that the load can transfer to the ground through the exoskeleton, which can improve the human motion endurance to enhance the continued ability of the body weight-bearing exercise. To simulate the power arising from the contraction of the muscle groups of the body in the exoskeleton can be achieved by using some drive motors or hydraulic cylinders in various joints when the man-machine moves with weight-bearing. Hydraulic cylinders have characteristics of overloaded, small size and fast response. Thus when carrying out the mechanical structure design of the exoskeleton, we can use the hydraulic cylinder model to simulate human muscle contraction to provide the impetus for the exoskeleton [3, 4].In order to meet the requirements of multi-environment using, the exoskeleton uses lithium batteries as the energy of the hydraulic system, so the pressure of the hydraulic system must be low and the load of the hydraulic cylinder must be light. Meanwhile the dynamic load characteristics of the hydraulic cylinder are closely related to the lightweight design of the exoskeleton structure, the finite element analysis, the design of the small hydraulic system and the modeling of the system. And based on the point of the ergonomics, the trajectory of the exoskeleton should be adapted to that of the human beings in order to meet the requirements of the portable man-machine. Therefore, we must research the kinematic characteristics and dynamic characteristics of the hydraulic cylinder.

2   Parametric Tests of the Human Motion

2.1   Typical Action Selected

The body structure is a multi-link chain .During the athletic performances, we are constrained not only by their own biological factors, but also by mechanical factors and the law of the motion so that the action shape of the body is quite complex and changing .So sitting down and standing, squatting, jumping, rotating, walking will also show the different forms with different scales and different space requirements [5].

Combined with the functional requirements of the human body exoskeleton, the process of down on one knee to standing up needs the most energy among the human actions (Fig.1) from the point of view of energy. One certain stage in the process of this action even requires a human to stand on one leg to support the weight. For the human body exoskeleton, to tie the body to complete the technical action not only requires hydraulic cylinders to provide maximum thrust, but also requires the hydraulic cylinder to work in the maximum travel mode. Therefore, we select the process of down on one knee to standing up of the human body exoskeleton as the typical mode of operation.

Fig. 1. The body down on one knee to standing up model

2.2   Parametric Tests of the Human Motion

The form of the body exercise contains the translation, the rotation and the motor complex (planar motion). The process of down on one knee to standing up which Figure 1 shows includes not only the move of the trunks and limbs, but also the rotational motion of the bones around the joint point. With the coordination with the People's Liberation Army General Logistics Department Quartermaster Equipment Institute and the State Sport General Administration of Analysis and Testing Center, we used the optical motion capture system to achieve the parametric test of the action of down on one knee to the standing up. We've got the body's space coordinates (X, Y, Z) on the time units of measurement by recording the trajectory of the human markers by six high-speed camera equipments which were arranged in the space through the computer [6,7].

Based on the structure of the human's bones and joints, we pasted the markers on the human's front head, the left head, the right head, the head, the chest, the shoulder, the left hip, the right hip, the left knee, the right knee, the left ankle joint, the right ankle joint, the left toe, the right toe, the left heel and the right heel during the experiments (Fig.2). Trajectories were recorded for each point by the high-resolution infrared camera. The acquisition frequency of the high-resolution infrared camera is set to 200Hz.

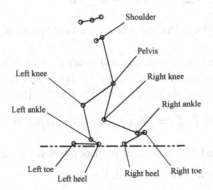

Fig. 2. The pasting location of the action parameters' testing laboratory markers

3   The Motion Model of the Exoskeleton

3.1   The Movement Decomposition

Treated the markers matched to human joints as node and connected between the nodes as consistent with the human skeleton exoskeleton in order to build the tree structure model of the exoskeleton. Human-machine portable movement is achievement by movement and rotation of each node, Shown in Figure 3 .In the process of man-machine portable movement, the local coordinate system of each joint of the exoskeleton will change, however, its length and position of each component in the local coordinate system was fixed. Thus the movement of the exoskeleton can be decomposed into the following combination of movement:

(1) In exoskeleton joints as the origin of the coordinate system (called Secondary coordinate system), each component of the exoskeleton is Rotary motion.
(2) In motion capture system coordinate system(called first—coordinate system) , secondary coordinate system is translational motion.

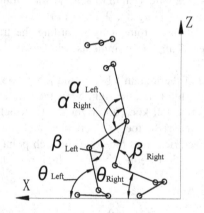

Fig. 3. The angles of the exoskeleton's joints

Therefore, we calculated the translation and rotation of each joint vector one by one when we created the mathematical model of the movement based on the test data, So that the movement of the exoskeleton can be described as [8]:

$$M(f) = \{P_R(f), q_1(f), ..., q_n(f)\}$$

above $P_R(f)$ is the translation vector of joint point of time f in the first—coordinate system; $q_i(f)$ is Rotation vector of the ith joint point .

The test data through the motion capture experimental got is the joint space trajectory. Due to it is constant that length of each component of the exoskeleton, the joint point ordinates change could convert to the hip, knee and ankle angle changes by trigonometric. Include: α_{left} 、 α_{right} 、 β_{left} 、 β_{right} θ_{left} 、 θ_{right} (Fig.4).

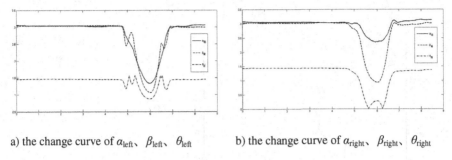

a) the change curve of α_{left}、 β_{left}、 θ_{left} b) the change curve of α_{right}、 β_{right}、 θ_{right}

Fig. 4. The change curves of angel along with time

3.2 Gaussian Curve Fitting Function

Curve fitting is to get the Smooth curve to present the noise of the measurement data and get the final curve fitting function expression. Each angle of the MATLAB simulation results is a multi-peak curve, so the fitting method uses Multi-peak function approximation on the data points by Gaussian function [9, 10].
The mathematical models of the difference method of the Gaussian function:

$$f_{(x)} = ae^{-(x-b)^2/c^2}$$

Above a、 b and c is constant, and $a \geq \neq 0$.

Figure 5 shows the contrast the fitting curve applying the Gaussian fitting method and the simulation curve of test results using MATLAB .It can be seen from the figure, in α_{left} 、 α_{right} 、 β_{left} 、 β_{right} θ_{left} 、 θ_{right} ,the angle of the Gaussian fitting curves and test data curves approach in higher degree and better in peak radial coincide . It can be used as time function of the joints of exoskeleton when human-machine portable system is moving.

4 ADMS Modeling and Simulation

According to the human skeleton and joint structure, the exoskeleton is composed by the backrest, hip structure, hip, thigh, leg, knee, ankle and shoes accordingly.Due to the mechanical structure of the exoskeleton in the thigh, leg and hip structure components is in accordance with the structural design of the human skeleton, the complex shape is multi-space surface, and it is difficult to model directly in ADAMS, so the Solidworks model is used to establish 3D model firstly, then the Solidworks model is conversed into x _t format, finally the model is imported into ADAMS to establish the rigid components [11, 12], the model is shown in Fig. 5.

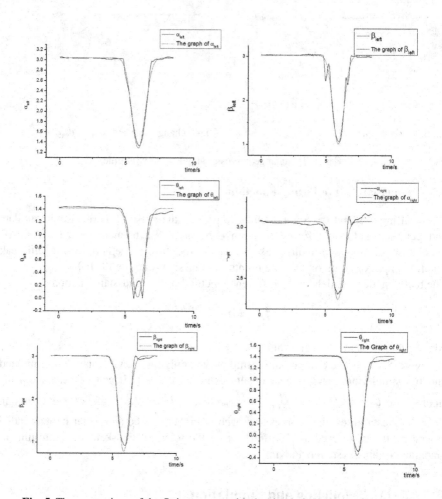

Fig. 5. The comparison of the fitting curves with the simulation curves of test results

Vertical external loads of the whole exoskeleton system is passed in accordance with the following procedures: backrest → hip structure → hip → Thigh → knee → leg → the ankle → shoes, and ultimately passed to the ground. Instead of Vertical external loads on the body support, in accordance with the principle of left-right symmetry in the body, a hydraulic cylinder is set up respectively on the left, right hip and left 、 right knee to simulate contraction of human muscle. The whole weight is 30kg, and bearing weight is 60kg, 900N of force is exerted in the back shelves.

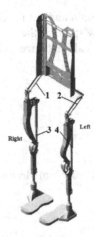

Fig. 6. Rigid component model in ADAMS

After setting constraint and drive, the ADAMS software application simulation calculation kinematics and dynamics characteristic curve of four hydraulic cylinders are shown in figure 7 and figure 8.

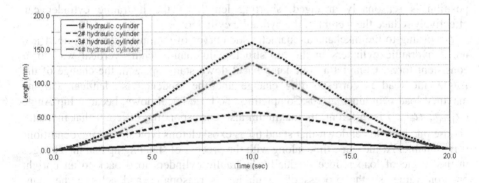

Fig. 7. Displacement curve of the hydraulic cylinder (relative to the ground)

The displacement curves Of Hydraulic cylinder show that in exoskeletons with the human body complete with a knee down-stand up process, owing to the different postures of the left and right hip and lower limb movement, two hydraulic cylinders curves of left and right knee are different, which indicates that the four hydraulic cylinders respectively carry out the corresponding action for the completion of their respective load function that make the movement of exoskeleton in the support of the hydraulic cylinder can follow human body In a higher level . And with the changes of the man-machine athletic stance, each hydraulic cylinder produces a smooth displacement curve, and all maximum simulation value is obtained at 10s that indicates that the hydraulic cylinder in athletic process is stressed equably and there is no obvious percussive load, so this doesn't cause the hydraulic system and energy system bear peak load. In the same condition, the maximal displacements of two hydraulic cylinder in the hip is 55.7mm and the maximal displacements in the knee is 158.3mm that indicate in the narrow space of the hip structure and in condition of the large size of space of triangle thigh, calf and knee, each hydraulic cylinder hinge point

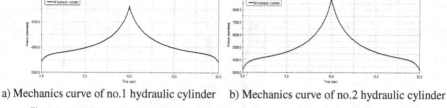

a) Mechanics curve of no.1 hydraulic cylinder   b) Mechanics curve of no.2 hydraulic cylinder

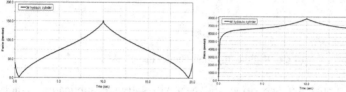

c) Mechanics curve of 3 hydraulic cylinder   d) Mechanics curve of 4 hydraulic cylinder

Fig. 8. Mechanics curve of hydraulic cylinder

position is reasonably arranged, shorting length of the hydraulic cylinder can effectively reduce the weight of the hydraulic cylinder.

According to the mechanical characteristic curves of hydraulic cylinder, no. 1 and no. 2 hydraulic cylinders in the hip structure in man-machine vertical walk bear consistent force. Completing one knee kneel down-stand up, with the change of the Angle, the load is corresponding change and the tendency is identical and the maximal load is attained at 10s.Completing one knee kneel down, because hip Angle (α_{left}, α_{right}) is different, its maximum also corresponding different that indicates choose one knee kneel down-that stand up as exoskeletons typical working conditions is reasonable. At the same time, along with the process of standing up and the changes in the Angle of load reduce gradually, hydraulic cylinders load back to an upright position value, so the process of simulation is reasonable and achieve the man-machine requirements.

5   Conclusion

1) For the diversity and complexity of human movement is emerged, Combination of human exoskeletons to provide vertical load support the functional requirements for the human body weight, Sit down and stand, squat, jump, rotate, walking athletic stance, select one knee - rose to process a typical attitude of the man-machine portable sports; using optical Motion capture motion capture system, Man-machine matches the key points of the trajectory of the test object, Getting the trajectories of the time measurement unit on the human body; The simulation results show that the attitude of the typical motion selecting appropriate, the test data is a true reflection of the man-machine portability movement.

2) Exoskeleton on one knee - stand up action is decomposed into the joint point of the rotary motion of the origin of the coordinate system of the secondary, Motion capture to a series of Cartesian coordinates of the translational motion; Through the MATLAB programming, the space coordinates of marked point will be transmitted into the time changing curve of rotation vector in the each angle, then the Gaussian function is used to fit the angular variation curve, And the fitting curve is contrasted with the original test data. The comparison results show that the fitting functions have a high approximation, and simulation results driven by the fitting functions are also consistent with the trend of human motion.

3) Virtual prototype model of the exoskeleton based on ADAMS is established, basis of human bones and joints characteristics of whom defined the constraints of the joint, the fitting curve is adopted as the driving function of the rotation vector of the exoskeleton, the displacement and dynamic characteristics of the curve to four hydraulic cylinders powered of exoskeleton are got through the curve analysis. The results show that the displacement of the hydraulic cylinder in the process to knee kneel down, the joints and the hydraulic cylinder hinge point location of the design is reasonable; At the same time, the only hydraulic cylinder displacement curve and dynamic curve is not the same, the change is trend of the gentle, indicating that the hydraulic cylinder bearer in the exoskeleton during exercise is different and there is no impact load, hydraulic systems and energy systems, there is no effect of short-time overload; displacement curves and kinetic curves but also for the finite element analysis of the structure of the exoskeleton, the hydraulic system optimization and the control system designed to provide a theoretical basis.

References

1. Zoss, A., Kazerooni, H., Chu, A.: On the mechanical design of the Berkeley lower extremity exoskeleton. In: 2005 IEEE/RSJ International Conference on Intelligent Robots and Systems, Edmonton, Canada, pp. 3132–3139 (2005)
2. Kazerooni, H., Racine, J.-L.C., Huang, L., Steger, R.: On the Control of Berkeley Lower Extremity Exoskeleton (BLEEX). In: Proceedings of the 2005 IEEE International Conference Oil Robotics and Automation, pp. 4353–4360 (2005)
3. Badler, N., et al.: Real time virtual humans. In: International Conference on Digital Media Futures, Brad Ford, UK (1999)
4. Wang, L., Wang, T., Zhang, L.: Simulative research on assistant robotic legs. Journal of Machine Design 23(9), 12–14 (2006)
5. Wang, H., Bi, Z.-Y., Zhao, W.-D.: Six degree-of-freedom acquisition and analysis of jaw opening and closing with motion capture system. J. South Med. Univ. 31(9), 1597–1599 (2011)
6. Luo, Z., Zhuang, Y., Liu, F.: Video Based Human Body Animation. Journal of Computer Research and Development 40(2), 269–276 (2003)
7. Donà, G., Preatoni, E., Cobelli, C., et al.: Application of functional principal component analysis in race walking: an emerging methodology. Sports Biomech. 8(4), 284–301 (2009)
8. Beaudin, P., Parquet Poulin, P.: Realistic and controllable fit simulation. In: Proceedings of Orphic In to dace, pp. 159–166. ACM, New York (2001)

9. Chang, Z., Wang, P., Zhang, X.: A Roof Edge Detection Method Based on Parabola Fitting for Cross Laser Image. Opto-Electronic Engineering 36(5), 93–97 (2009)
10. Angela, C., Alfredo, C., Remo, S.: Hyperbolic targent algorism for periodic effect cancellation in surplice resolution elegies Larne enema easement. Measumment 42(4), 1226–1232 (2009)
11. Zhu, Z., Tan, R.: Research on Principles of Prior Choice to Model Based on ADAMS or UG. Modern Manufacturing Technology and Equipment (2), 19–20 (2008)
12. Ding, S., Chang, Z.: Interface between ADAMS and CAD software. Microcomputer Information 21(10-3), 202–204 (2005)
13. Zou, Y., Ding, G., Zhang, W.: Design of Dispatching Platform for Development of Virtual Prototype of Rolling Stocks. Journal of Southwest Jiaotong University 43(2), 45–50 (2008)
14. Shao, Y., Hu, Y., Yu, Z.: Dynamics Simulation and Identification System for Road Accident Black-Spots. Journal of Southwest Jiaotong University 43(2), 173–176 (2008)
15. Ni, N., Sun, Z.: Design and Crawl Study of New Quadruped Robot Based on ADAMS. Machinery & Electronics (2), 70–72 (2012)

Structure Optimization and Finite Element Analysis of the Human Body Exoskeletons Lower Limb Power

Fang Liu, Wen-ming Cheng, and Jian-bing Shao

Institute of Mechanical Engineering, Southwest Jiaotong University,
No.111, 1st Section of North Erhuan Rd. 610031 Chengdu, China
{wmcheng,liufang}@home.swjtu.edu.cn

Abstract. The lower limbs is carrying subject mechanical structure for the human body exoskeletons, and the hydraulic cylinder provides motivation; Three hinge point to the knee joint structure is the best layout and mechanical structure bearing performance as the research target; According to the human body bone and joint constitute, human exoskeletons lower limb power structure 3 d model is established and the function relationship between the hydraulic cylinder bearing capacity and the weight is established. The hydraulic cylinder bearing capacity is taken as optimal objective function components for outside bone size constraint conditions; Through the self-adapting inertia update and update the simulated annealing particle position particle swarm algorithm by analyzing and solving the three hinge point exoskeletons that the structure of the optimal solution; Entities modeling is erected through the ANSYS software and one knee two typical motion is taken for working attitude. Finite element analysis of strength is taken for foreign bone lower limb power structure. Structure and finite element analysis results show that the simulated annealing particle swarm algorithm in the iteration to 150 generations when convergence to optimal solution, and this operation finds the optimal solution, the algorithm and reliable; Exoskeletons upright maximum stress is produced in the knee, for 128 MPa, closed to the allowable stress value, structural design is reasonable; The hydraulic cylinder maximum stress for 5.76 Mpa, far less than the allowable stress value, hydraulic cylinder force minimum, achieve the objective function optimization indexes; To one knee, the greatest stress produced in the right leg knee, the greatest stress for 252 MPa, greater than the allowable stress value, and puts forward the measures to strengthen local knee structures.

Keywords: human exoskeleton, three-hinge mechanism, particle swarm optimization, structure optimal design, finite element calculation.

1   Introduction

Human exoskeletons comes from magical ability of nature biological technology, lies in the simulation crustaceans shell, according to the human body muscle, bone and joint structure. The human body is equipped with the corresponding exoskeletons using modern science and technology. Modern science and technology is used mainly for the human body weight movement with support and help, and improved the human body weight capacity and weight-bearing exercise continued ability [1, 2].

S.S. Ge et al. (Eds.): ICSR 2012, LNAI 7621, pp. 631–640, 2012.

According to the human body weight principle, the human body exoskeletons mainly includes bearing system and lower limbs carrying power structure. Bearing system is used to put the human body weight, and weight is mainly transferred to the ground bearing structure through lower limbs, thus power structure is a central part of the mechanical structure exoskeletons to the entire human body with human bones by matching thigh, legs, hydraulic cylinder and corresponding joint composition. Among them the hydraulic cylinder mainly provides man-machine accompanying the movement process of vertical load the ups and downs of the exercise of potential energy, and based on different body movement of the change of attitude adjustment. Therefore, reasonable choice is determined the performance of the whole system for the parameters of the structure of bearing lower limbs directly. The optimization analysis is of great practical significance to carry out.

The structure of human body exoskeletons for lower limbs bearing situation is complicated. To thigh, calf and hydraulic cylinder consists of hinge point structure is a typical nonlinear constraints; And particle group algorithm is a kind of simulation birds group foraging bionic intelligent optimization algorithm put forward by Kennedy and Eberhart, it can avoid the traditional optimization algorithm which is dependent on the shortcomings of problem characteristics, suitable for complicated multivariable nonlinear objective function structure optimization problems of [3]. So in the standard particle group algorithm based on the improved based on simulated annealing of particle swarm optimization, foreign bone three hinge point bearing model structure size optimization, and in the structure optimization based on ANSYS finite element analysis model, the strength to link, it is human body exoskeletons the steps necessary to study.

2   The Lower Limbs Power Structure Bearing Model Exoskeletons

The human body exoskeletons mainly includes bear system and lower limb power structure, and lower limb power structure bearing structure by the hip and knee bearing structure and sensing of boots, as shown in figure 1 below. Bearing structure of the knee is the main body, the thigh, calf and hydraulic cylinder composition. When the human body stable vertical standing, the vertical direction the main force through the legs and crus transfer to the ground, hydraulic cylinder only overcome overturning, bending Angle of the smaller, hydraulic cylinder carrying smaller. Bearing structure knee as three hinge point institutions, as shown in figure 2 shows:

When human body is in the stable standing state, the whole tree-hinge mechanism is a balanced system with resultant force of 0 and a fixed framework of AB, which simplifies the stress on the upper fulcrum of actuating cylinder to a force F in the vertical direction. The following relation is the result of stress analysis of the whole mechanism:

$$F_{缸} = \frac{F \times L_1 \times \cos(\beta_2 - \theta) + G_魚 \times L_魚 \times \cos(\beta_2 - \theta)}{S_1 \times \cos\beta_1} \tag{1}$$

1. The bear system 2. Hip bearing system
3. Lower limb bearing system 4. Sensing boots system

Fig. 1. Accompanying type human exoskeletons 3d map

When the man-machine accompanying upright, the most reasonable working condition is weight mainly by the thigh and crus, assume, hydraulic cylinder provide resistance to overturning, hydraulic cylinder ideal bearing capacity for 0 F. Therefore, the human body exoskeletons lower limb power structure parameters optimization of the objective function is to type (1).

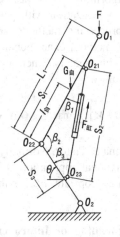

Fig. 2. Force model of Simplified three-hinge mechanism

According to the figure 2 stress analysis, according to cosine theorem can get different variables of the objective function and the length of the S2, S3 S1 and relations:

$$\beta_1 = \arccos \frac{S_1^2 + S_2^2 - S_3^2}{2S_1S_2}, \quad \beta_2 = \arccos \frac{S_1^2 + S_3^2 - S_2^2}{2S_1S_3} \tag{2}$$

A normal adults 60 kg weight for maximum, plus the human body weight exoskeletons 20 kg, therefore force F biggest desirable 800 N. According to our country adults in the national standard of structure size of GB/T 10000-1988 [4], the percentage of the 95 Chinese people from the south a human standards, and establish the constraints of design variables scope is:

$$\begin{cases} F = 800N, \ L_1 = 462m, \ l_臂 = 230mm, \ G_臂 = 13.3Nm \\ 335 < S_1 < 345, \ 420 < S_2 < 430, \ 80 < S_3 < 90, \ 72° < \theta < 80° \end{cases} \tag{3}$$

3   Optimization Algorithm Design

3.1   Algorithm Model Transformation

Through the above modeling process, the optimization design of actuating cylinder three-hinge luffing mechanism parameters can be regarded as a general nonlinear constraint optimization problem:

$$\begin{cases} \min f(x) \\ \text{s.t. } g_i(x) \le 0, \ i=1,2,\ldots,n \\ h(x)=0, \ j=1,2,\ldots,m \end{cases} \tag{4}$$

Formulars above contain both inequality and equality constraint. To solve such problems with optimization algorithm, it is necessary to convert constrainted optimization into unconstrained optimization with penalty functions. Presently there are plenty of penalty function processing methods, such as external point method, interior point method, multiplier method, exact penalty function method and so on. This thesis adopts non-differentiable penalty function method, of which the specific conversion formula is shown as follow:

$$F(x) = f(x) + M \left[\sum_{i=1}^{n} \max(0, g_i(x))^2 + \sum_{j=1}^{m} h_j^2(x) \right]^{0.5} \tag{5}$$

In the formula above, M is the penalty factor. Normally, the bigger the M value is the better the result will be. But in practical application, it is necessary to conduct certain numerical experiment to select a appropriate. F(x) is the target function of algorithm optimization after conversion.

3.2   Based on Simulated Annealing of Improvement of the Micro Particle Swarm Method

In PSO, assume there be N particles in the D-dimension space, the position vector of particle No. i be $X_i=(x_{i1}, x_{i2}, \ldots, x_{iD})$, the speed vector be $V_i=(v_{i1}, v_{i2}, \ldots, v_{iD})$, the historical optimal solution for particle No. i be $P_i=(p_{i1}, p_{i2}, \ldots, p_{iD})$, the optimal solution for the whole population be represented by P_g, then the formulas of speed and position renewal for the tth iteration, are as follows:

$$X_i(t+1)=X_i(t) + V_i(t) \tag{6}$$

$$V_i(t+1)=\omega \cdot V_i(t)+c_1 \cdot r_1 \cdot (P_i(t)-X_i(t))+ c_2 \cdot r_2 \cdot (P_g(t)-X_i(t)) \tag{7}$$

Of the formulas above, formula (7) indicates speed renewal; formula (8) indicates loation renewal; ω refers to inertial weight; c_1 and c_2 refers to individual learning factor and social learning factor, which is set as constant 1.5 in this thesis; r_1 and r_2 are random number between 0 to 1[5-7].

The simulated annealing algorithm is mainly used for combinatorial optimization problem, the most important is how local search. In this paper, the current solution that X = (x1 x2... xD), random selection of m a variable xs1, xs2,... , XSM press type (8) to a random disturbance, the disturbance of the variable is:

$$y_{si}=x_{si}+r*b*(U_{si}-L_{si}) \tag{8}$$

In this formula, i=1, 2, ..., m, r; , r is random number distributed evenly in the range (-1,1); U_{si}, L_{si} are the given top and bottom limitation of the design variables; b is the renewal range factor, of which the value range is usually (0, 0.5). The temperature renewal function adopts the expression: $T(t+1)=\alpha T(t)$, in which α is the current temperature renewal constant.

$$T(t+1)=\alpha T(t) \tag{9}$$

In order to enhance PSO algorithm of optimization ability, this article from inertial weight update and update particle position in two aspects of the standard particle group algorithm was improved. Bigger is helpful to improve the algorithm omega of global optimization ability, and smaller will speed up the omega algorithm convergence speed. In this article, the dynamic reduce inertia of omega weight to make them along with the change of the iteration times and update:

$$\omega=\omega_{max}-t\times(\omega_{max}-\omega_{min})/t_{max} \tag{10}$$

In this expression, ω_{max} and ω_{min} are the maximum and minimum values of inertial weight; t is the iteration; t_{max} is the maximum iteration. When a new solution is worked out, it will be compared to the adaptive value corresponding to the last solution. If the variation $\Delta E \leq 0$, the new value will be accepted, otherwise the new value will be accepted according to criteria $\exp(-\Delta E/T)>rand(0,1)$. The pseudocodes of improved particle swarm optimization are as follows:

Table 1. Algorithms analysis

Algorithmss	Target Values	Function	Variable Values			
	F1		S1	S2	S3	γ
SA	best	1.05e-3	422.45	339.07	85.53	75.59
	worse	4.28e+3	429.99	335.01	87.29	77.99
PSO	best	1.23e-11	424.44	337.92	89.21	74.13
	worse	2.59e-4	429.09	344.11	86.83	76.82
IPSO	best	0	426.66	342.45	86.94	73.91
	worse	0	426.66	342.45	86.94	73.91

3.3   The Calculation Results and Analysis

In the experimental process, the parameters of simulated annealing (SA) are set as: $T_0=1000$, $\alpha=0.9$, $b=0.2$, the inner loop times are 300. The parameters of PSO and IPSO are set as: number of particle N=50; $\omega_{max}=0.8$; $\omega_{min}=0.2$; $T_0=1000$; $\alpha=0.9$; iteration times are both 300. The experiment has operated the three algorithms 10 times separately, and made statistic analysis then. Table 1 shows the statistic result of the 10 times of the three algorithms. Table 1 shows that IPSO has found the optimum solution in all the 10 times of algorithms, which indicates that the reliability of the improved algorithm is much higher. In this case PSO is relatively poorer, having only found out the approximate solutions. The poorest is SA in that SA can only repeatedly iterate on a initial solution, while PSO and IPSO both make simultaneous group evolutions. Figure 3 is the convergence curves of PSO and IPSO.

It shows that IPSO has converged to the optimum solution at the 150th iteration while PSO has not converged even at the 300th iteration, which indicates that compared to SA and PSO, IPSO has better capability for optimizing and converging. Therefore, IPSO has very stable capability for solving nonlinear constrained optimization problems such as structure parameter optimization of portable powered exoskeleton lower Extremity, and can converge to the global optimum solution of the problem at a faster speed.

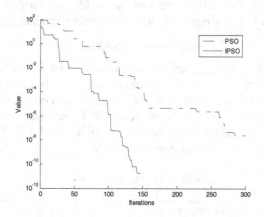

Fig. 3. Convergence Curves of PSO and IPSO

4   Finite Element Analysis

According to the calculation results IPSO, the vertical stand and one knee state power structure of the human body exoskeletons lower limbs 3 d entity mode is established using Solidworks tool, and translated into X_T format, and Parasailed as standard format, data transmission is realized between the ANSYS and Solidworks [8,9].

Aluminum alloy material is used for Lower limb power structure, the elastic modulus of 7.2 x 10^{10} Pa, Poisson ratio 0.33, density for 2700 Kg/m3, 45 steel material is used for hydraulic cylinder, the elastic modulus of 2.1 x 10^{11} Pa, Poisson ratio 0.27, density for 7890 Kg/m3. Material attribute is set in the model in ANSYS, the choice of SOLID92 unit as entity unit, foreign bone structure of the mechanical components distribution corresponding properties, and mesh, the finite element model of the final, as shown in figure 4 shows:

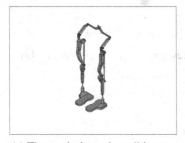

(a) The vertical stand condition   (b) The list knee kneel down state

Fig. 4. Human exoskeletons lower limb power structure finite element mode

Four nodes are selected at the hip bearing structure surface, vertical respectively in force F = 200 N is put down , so sensing boots surface all under constraint, influence weight is considering and finite element analysis, getting the human body system cloud exoskeletons that stress (figure 5 to 9).

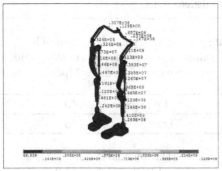
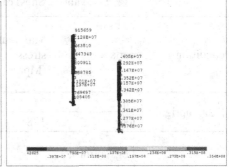

Fig. 5. Vertical stand model calculation cloud (general)

Fig. 6. Vertical stand model calculation cloud (leg hydraulic cylinder)

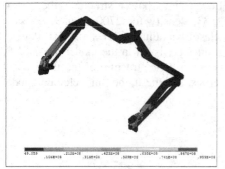

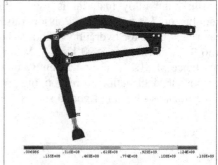

Fig. 7. One knee kneel cloud model calculation (hip)

Fig. 8. List knee kneel cloud model calculation (left leg)

Fig. 9. One knee kneel cloud model calculation (right leg)

Table 2. Stress calculation results

condition	parts	Maximum stress value (Mpa)	The greatest stress produce parts	Allowable stress value (Mpa)
Stand upright	hip	113	Hip place	140
	legs	128	knee	140
One knee kneel down	Leg ministry hydraulic cylinder	35.4	The hydraulic cylinder and crus joint	264.9
	hip	95.3	Hip place	140
	Left leg	139	The ankle	140
	Right leg	252	knee	140

According to the table 2 of the calculation results, the maximum stress produced in ham and crus joint under the vertical stand condition, namely the knee, for 128 Mpa smaller than the allowable stress value[σ_1] =140MPa; Leg ministry hydraulic cylinder of maximum stress is for 5.76 Mpa, far less than the allowable stress value[σ_2] =264.9MPa, hydraulic cylinder force minimum, accord with the objective function optimization goal that improved the particle swarm algorithm IPSO have the result of optimization of high accuracy, accord with optimization requirements. The list knee kneel down state, the maximum stress is produced in the right leg knee, the greatest stress for 252 Mpa, greater than the allowable stress value [σ_1] =140MPa of the need to strengthen the structure of the knee joint bearing local.

5   Conclusion

1) The differentiable penalty function is used for optimization algorithm model transformation, and the dynamic update self-adapting inertia and update a new generation of particle position vector is way of improving the standard particle group algorithm of the global and local search ability and used to achieve simulated annealing of improvement of the particle group algorithm design, and structural parameters optimization design is applied to the human body exoskeletons for lower limbs. Through the example of the calculation results contrast shows that IPSO can be found in the optimal solution of the problem in less iteration number than the PSO algorithm and simulated annealing algorithm standard, it is of high stability;

2) Three hinge point structure model is established for a hip bearing structure of human body exoskeletons, The hydraulic cylinder bearing capacity is taked as the objective function, and the constraint conditions of optimization model is defined, The optimization results are used to ANSYS finite element analysis model to strength calculation, the analysis results show that the carrying of exoskeletons and hydraulic cylinder is accord with the objective function, The model parameters of the exoskeletons established at the request of the optimization results is reasonable, the optimized result of IPSO has high accuracy.

3) The finite element analysis through the structural optimization gets the maximum stress value in upright and to one knee state of exoskeletons components, the results showed that knee bearing structure is beyond allowable stress value to one knee, so its local strengthen shoud be deal with; The theory basis is provided the local optimization to exoskeletons structure by the analysis result.

References

1. Dollar, A.M., Herr, H.: Lower Extremity Exoskeletons and Active Orthoses: Challenges and State-of-the-Art. IEEE Transactions on Robotics 24(1), 144–158 (2008)
2. Yang, C.J., Zhang, J.F., Chen, Y., Dong, Y.M., Zhang, Y.: A review of exoskeleton-type systems and their key technologies. Proceedings of the Institution of Mechanical Engineers, Part C: Journal of Mechanical Engineering Science 222(8), 1599–1612 (2008)
3. Kennedy, J., Eberhart, R.: Particle swarm optimization. In: Proceedings of IEEE International Conference on Neural Networks 1995, vol. 4, pp. 1942–1948 (1995)

4. Zhang, G.P.: Ergonomics principle and application. Mechanical Industry Press, Beijing (2008)
5. Kirkpatrick, S., Gelatt, C.D., Vecchi, M.: Optimization by Simulated Annealing. Science 220(4598), 671–680 (1983)
6. Kou, X.L., Liu, S.Y.: Based on simulated annealing algorithm is proposed to solve the particle swarm optimization problem. Journal of Jilin University (Engineering Edition) 5(1), 136–140 (2007)
7. Wang, D., Shen, D.Z.: Based on the improvement of simulated annealing algorithm robot the optimal configuration study. Journal of System Simulation (22), 5342–5350 (2007)
8. Xiong, G.L., Fan, W.H.: 21 century manufacturing modeling and simulation technologies. Journal of System Simulation 16(9), 1884–1886 (2004)
9. Hao, Z.X.: ANSYS and CAD software interface. Mechanical Design and Manufacturing (7), 75–76 (2007)

Kinematics and Dynamics Modeling
for Lower Limbs Rehabilitation Robot

Qian Zhang, Min Chen, and Limei Xu

School of Aeronautics and Astronautics
University of Electronic Science and Technology of China,
611731 Chengdu, PRC
qqzhangqian2005@163.com

Abstract. Gait training is very important in the rehabilitation of neurological patients like stroke patients and spinal cord injury patients. To help those patients, a lower limb rehabilitation robot is developed. For obtaining a feasible gait, more accurate models based on ergonomics are necessary. We did gait experiment of human walking in order to reproduce the human gait. As a result of this experiment, we confirmed the effectiveness of the models to be established. Mathematical models in different phase are built based on the experiment. Kinematics modeling was presented. Finally, dynamic models based on Newton-Euler equations of the lower limbs rehabilitation robot during different phase were established. These models will provide more accurate data for the control system.

Keywords: gait training, rehabilitation robot, kinematic and dynamic analysis.

1　Introduction

New gait rehabilitation devices have emerged. These robots replace the traditional hand-to-hand therapy approach. Lokomat[1,2] is widespread commercial rehabilitation robots now. It relieves the therapists from monotonous manual labor. But it's fixed in a specific position because of its large size. It isn't convenient for patients who have rehabilitation but still must do treadmill therapy at home. LOPES[3] has the same question. At the same time, Lokomat is so expensive that not everyone can afford. So a more convenient and inexpensive is necessary. HAL[4,5] and BLEEX[6] are assistive device for lower limbs. Although they did not actually used for rehabilitation training, it is expected that such a simple device will be used for gait training in the future.

We are designing a convenient, portable and movable robot now. It can adapt many environments whether at home or in the hospital. Traditional kinematics and dynamics models are designed based on rigid human. In this paper, we paid our attention to establish more accurate mathematical models due to the mechanical design. Kinematics analysis and inverse dynamics analysis are done due to these models.

S.S. Ge et al. (Eds.): ICSR 2012, LNAI 7621, pp. 641–649, 2012.

2   The Physical Structure

A prototype as shown in Fig.1 is being developed. The robot is comprised of two adjustable thighs, two adjustable shanks, two feet, an adjustable waist, a shelf for payload and four electric cylinders. The adjustable exoskeletons are ensured to match the human body.

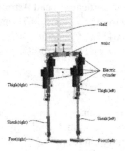

Fig. 1. Structure of the lower limb rehabilitation robot

There are stoppers at joints to limit the motions to be larger than those of the human while walking, and smaller than the physical limit of the human joints.

The robot contains the following degrees of freedom: hip Ab/Adduction, hip flexion, knee flexion and ankle flexion.

The machine is light, adjustable, portable and removable.

3   Gait Experiment of Human Walking

In order to reproduce the human gait, a gait experiment has been done. We prepare seven marking balls and fix on the seven different parts of the human body (chest, right hip, left hip, right knee, left knee, right ankle and left ankle). Fig.2 shows the position of the marking balls.

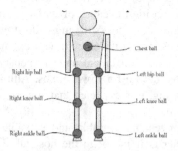

Fig. 2. Position of the marking balls

During the walking phase most movements happen in the sagittal plane. Hence, only the movements in the sagittal plane are calculated.

The locations of the seven balls when human walking are recorded. Assume the direction of X-axis is the direction of body walking. The direction of Y-axis is the vertical direction. Fig.3 shows the locations of the seven balls during a gait cycle.

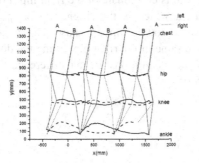

Fig. 3. Locations of the seven balls

Fig.3 shows that biped gait can be divided into two phase: A phase, which we called single support phase and B phase, which we called double support phase.

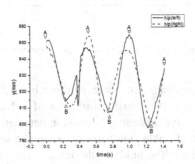

Fig. 4. Y-axis coordinates of hip marking balls

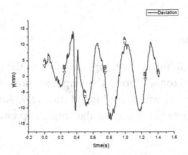

Fig. 5. Deviation of the y-axis coordinates

Fig.4 shows y-axis coordinates of hip marking balls. From Fig.4 we can see hip moves up and down during a gait cycle.

Fig.5 shows the deviation of the y-axis coordinates, which is the y-axis coordinate of the left hip minus the y-axis coordinate of the right hip. From Fig.5 we can see the maximum happens near A, which is the single support phase. And the minimum happens near B, which is the double support phase. That means the y-axis coordinate of the left hip is nearly the same of the right hip during the double support phase. And the y-axis coordinate of the left hip has greater difference than that of the right hip during the single support phase.

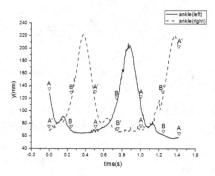

Fig. 6. Y-axis coordinates of ankle marking balls

Fig.6 shows y-axis coordinates of ankle marking balls. From Fig.6 we can see during double support phase, the y-axis coordinates of left ankle marking balls and right ankle marking balls have differences(deviation between B and B'). That means the left ankle and the right ankle don't always keep the same horizontal position during double support phase. The ankle of the leg that is about to swing in the next step is higher than the ankle of the leg that is still stand in the next step.

4   Modeling

4.1   Single Support Phase

From the gait experiment of human walking, the point of the right hip and the point of the left hip don't keep horizontal during the single support phase. So we assume the waist contain two rigid beams which are hinged mutually. And the torque is given by a torsion spring. Fig.7 shows the model of the single support phase. This system has 14 beams.

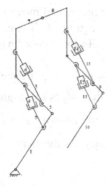

Fig. 7. Model of the single support phase

4.2   Double Support Phase

From the gait experiment of human walking, we can see the point of the right hip and the point of the left hip keep nearly horizontal during the double support phase. So we assume the waist is a rigid beam. And the point of the right ankle and the point of the left ankle don't keep horizontal during the double support phase. The ankle of the leg that is about to swing in the next step is higher than the ankle of the leg that is still stand in the next step. So we add a beam (beam 9). Fig.8 shows the model of the double support phase. This system has 14 beams.

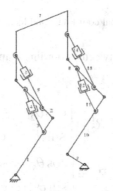

Fig. 8. Model of the double support phase

4.3   Kinematics Modeling

The purpose of kinematics analysis is to get every bar's position in the case of being given the joint angles.

We assume that the origin point of the global coordinate is the point on which the right foot in contact with the ground. The direction of X-axis is the direction of body walking. The direction of Y-axis is the vertical direction (Fig.9) . In global coordinate, any point P can be expressed as a 3 rows matrix P= $(x,y,z)^T$.

Local coordinate is fixed to the beam, and moves with the movement of the beam. The direction of X_i-axis is the direction of the beam-i. The direction of Y_i-axis is perpendicular to the beam i(Fig.9). In local coordinate, any point P can be expressed as a 3 rows matrix $P^{(i)}=(x^{(i)},y^{(i)},z^{(i)})^T$.

The angles of joints can be obtained by gait experiment of human walking, or be recorded by sensors such as encoder. θ_{ij} is the angle from beam j to beam i. So the angle of joints θ_{10}, θ_{21} and θ_{72} are known. The others (θ_{31}, θ_{52}, θ_{67}) are the function of $\theta_{10},\theta_{21},\theta_{72}$, the length of the beams and the position of the electric cylinder respectively.

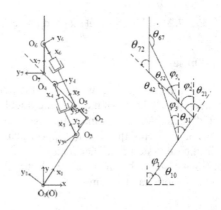

Fig. 9. Global coordinate and local coordinates

The transformation matrix between i coordinate and j coordinate can be expressed as R_i^j, that is

$$R_1^0 = \begin{bmatrix} \cos\theta_{10} & -\sin\theta_{10} \\ \sin\theta_{10} & \cos\theta_{10} \end{bmatrix} \quad R_2^1 = \begin{bmatrix} \cos\theta_{21} & -\sin\theta_{21} \\ \sin\theta_{21} & \cos\theta_{21} \end{bmatrix}$$

$$R_3^1 = \begin{bmatrix} \cos\theta_{31} & -\sin\theta_{31} \\ \sin\theta_{31} & \cos\theta_{31} \end{bmatrix} \quad R_5^2 = \begin{bmatrix} \cos\theta_{52} & -\sin\theta_{52} \\ \sin\theta_{52} & \cos\theta_{52} \end{bmatrix}$$

$$R_7^2 = \begin{bmatrix} \cos\theta_{72} & -\sin\theta_{72} \\ \sin\theta_{72} & \cos\theta_{72} \end{bmatrix} \quad R_4^2 = \begin{bmatrix} \cos\theta_{42} & -\sin\theta_{42} \\ \sin\theta_{42} & \cos\theta_{42} \end{bmatrix}$$

$$R_6^7 = \begin{bmatrix} \cos\theta_{67} & -\sin\theta_{67} \\ \sin\theta_{67} & \cos\theta_{67} \end{bmatrix}$$

In these equations, 0 coordinate represents global coordinate. In order to get the transformation matrix between global coordinate and local coordinate, we use the following formula, with matrix concatenation.

$$R_2^0 = R_1^0 \cdot R_2^1 , \quad R_3^0 = R_1^0 \cdot R_3^1 , \quad R_4^0 = R_1^0 \cdot R_2^1 \cdot R_4^2 , \quad R_5^0 = R_1^0 \cdot R_2^1 \cdot R_5^2 ,$$
$$R_6^0 = R_1^0 \cdot R_2^1 \cdot R_7^2 \cdot R_6^7 , \quad R_7^0 = R_1^0 \cdot R_2^1 \cdot R_7^2$$

In global coordinate, any point P described by i local coordinate is of the form

$$P = R_0^i \cdot P^{(i)}$$

Differentiating with respect to time, we get the velocity vector $V_P = (v_{Px}, v_{Py})^T$

$$V_P = \dot{P}$$

Then differentiating with respect to time, we get the acceleration vector $A_P = (a_{Px}, a_{Py})^T$

$$A_P = \dot{V} = \ddot{P}$$

Every beam's angular velocity and angular acceleration can be defined as

$$\omega_1 = \dot{\varphi}_1 , \quad \omega_2 = \dot{\varphi}_2 , \quad \omega_3 = \omega_4 = \dot{\varphi}_3 , \quad \omega_5 = \omega_6 = \dot{\varphi}_5 , \quad \omega_7 = 0 , \quad \partial_1 = \dot{\omega}_1 = \ddot{\varphi}_1 ,$$
$$\partial_2 = \dot{\omega}_2 = \ddot{\varphi}_2 , \partial_3 = \partial_4 = \dot{\omega}_3 = \ddot{\varphi}_3 , \partial_5 = \partial_6 = \dot{\omega}_5 = \ddot{\varphi}_5 , \partial_7 = 0$$

The angles φ_1, φ_2 and φ_3 are the function of θ_{10}, θ_{21} and θ_{72} respectively.

4.4   Dynamics Modeling

The single support phase model can be divided into two parts. One part is the leg which is moving through the air, and the other part is the leg which is in contact with the ground. Fig.10 shows the first part, and Fig.11 shows the second part.

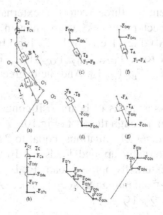

Fig. 10. Stress analysis of moving leg

Fig.10(a) shows the system has fife vectors of externally applied loads F_1, F_2, F_{Cx}, F_{Cy} and T_C, which F_{Cx}, F_{Cy} and T_C are the vectors come from stance leg.

And Fig.10(b), Fig.10(c), Fig.10(d), Fig.10(e), Fig.10(f), Fig.10(g), Fig.10(h)show the sixteen vectors of internal force F_{O2x}, F_{O2y}, F_{O3x}, F_{O3y}, F_{O4x}, F_{O4y}, F_{O5x}, F_{O5y}, F_{O6x}, F_{O6y}, F_{O7x}, F_{O7y}, F_A, F_B, T_A, T_B. And the degrees of freedom for the system is $5(3 \times 7 - 2 \times 8 = 5)$.

From Newton's second law and Euler's second law, we get the 3 equations to every beam. We finally get $21(3 \times 7 = 21)$equations in total.

The above 21 equations are sufficient to determine the 21 unknown variables which are the inner force and externally applied loads,F_1, F_2, F_{Cx}, F_{Cy} and T_C.

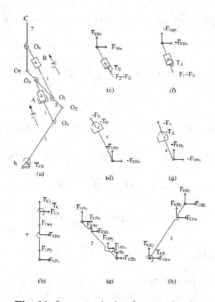

Fig. 11. Stress analysis of contacting leg

Fig.11(a) shows the system has three vectors of externally applied loads F_1, F_2 and T_{O1}, which $T_{O1}$is the vector comes from human to keep balance. And Fig.11(b),Fig.11(c), Fig.11(d), Fig.11(e), Fig.11(f), Fig.11(g) and Fig.11(h) show the nineteen vectors of internal force F_{O1x}, F_{O1y}, F_{O2x}, F_{O2y}, F_{O3x}, F_{O3y}, F_{O4x}, F_{O4y}, F_{O5x}, F_{O5y}, F_{O6x}, F_{O6y}, F_{O7x}, F_{O7y}, F_A, F_B, T_A, T_B. And the degrees of freedom for the system is $3(3 \times 7 - 2 \times 9 = 3)$.

Fig.11(b) shows the stress analysis of beam 7. It contains the forces (F_{Cx},F_{Cy}, T_C) from the leg which is moving through the air in Fig.10.

Use the same method, we get 21 equations, equal to 21 unknown variables which are the inner force and externally applied loads F_1, F_2 and T_{O1}. Fig.12 shows the system has five vectors of externally applied loads F_1, F_2, F_3, F_4, T_1 and T_2, which T_1 and T_2 are the vectors come from human to keep balance. And the degrees of freedom for the system is $6(3 \times 14 - 2 \times 19 = 6)$.

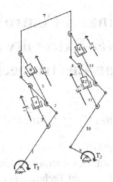

Fig. 12. Externally applied loads for model of the double support phase

Use the same method, we get 42 equations, equal to 42 unknown variables which are the inner force and externally applied loads F_1, F_2, F_3, F_4, T_1 and T_2.

5   Conclusion

The kinetics and dynamics of the lower limb rehabilitation robot have been formulated based on gait experiment of human walking. The models divide into two phases: single support phase and double support phase. As a result of this experiment, we confirmed the effectiveness of the models to be established. These models will provide more accurate data for the control system.

References

1. Hesse, S., Sarkodie-Gyan, T., Uhlenbrock, D.: Development of an advanced mechanized gait trainer, controlling the movement of the center of mass, for restoring gait in non-ambulant subjects. Biomed. Tech. 44, 194–201 (1999)
2. Colombo, G., Joerg, M., Schreier, R., Dietz, V.: Treadmill training of paraplegic patients using a robotic orthosis. J. Rehab. Res. & Dev. 37(6), 313–319 (2000)
3. Veneman, J.F., Kruidhof, R., Hekman, E.E., Ekkelenkamp, P., Van Asseldonk, E.H., van der Kooij, H.: Design and evaluation of the LOPES exoskeleton robot for interactive gait rehabilitation. IEEE Trans. Neural Syst. Rehabil. Eng. 15, 379–386 (2007)
4. Nakai, T., Lee, S., Kawamoto, H., Sankai, Y.: Development of Power Assistive Leg for Walking Aid using EMG and Linux. In: Proc. The 2nd Asian Conference on Industrial Automation Robotics (ASIAR 2001), Bangkok, Thailand, pp. 295–299 (2001)
5. Kawamoto, H., Sankai, Y.: Power Assist System HAL-3 for Gait Disorder Person. In: Miesenberger, K., Klaus, J., Zagler, W.L. (eds.) ICCHP 2002. LNCS, vol. 2398, pp. 196–203. Springer, Heidelberg (2002)
6. Neuhaus, P., Kazerooni, H.: Design and Control of Human Assisted walking robot. In: IEEE International Conference on Robotics and Automation, vol. 1, pp. 563–569 (2000)

Coordinated Control Method
of the Lower Extremity Exoskeleton
Based on Human Electromechanical Coupling

Qing Guo[1], Hong Zhou[2], and Dan Jiang[3]

[1] School of Aeronautics and Astronautics, [3] School of Mechatronics Engineering,
[2] Quartermaster Equipment Institute, General Logistics Department of CPLA, Beijing,
University of Electronic Science and Technology of China, 61731 Chengdu, PRC
guoqinguestc@163.com, jdan2002@uestc.edu.cn

Abstract. This paper has introduced electromechanical coupling characteristics to the lower extremity exoskeleton systems. When the load torque compensation model has been established, A model of knee position control system has also been established, which is made of the servo valve, hydraulic cylinders and other hydraulic components. Hydraulic cylinder position control loop has been designed in case of existing load force interference compensation. From that have ensured the system to meet a certain stability margin. The simulation shows that this position control method can servo on the knee angular displacement of normal human walking, at the same time, met the needs of human-machine coordinated motion. On basis of 30kg walk test of prototype of system, analyzing hydraulic cylinder bearing demand under different load conditions. The test shows that the lower limb exoskeleton portable power system using a hydraulic valve position control can meet the load 30kg low level walking requirements.

Keywords: Human exoskeleton, Optical motion capture, Gaussian Fitting, Dynamics simulation.

1   Introduction

The lower extremity exoskeleton is based on the human subject, and takes the mechanical structure of the exoskeleton as the auxiliary, a highly complex human-machine coupling force servo system. It can support the body during walking, downhill and squatting when overloaded in different portable sports mode.

From 2000, DARPA vigorously promote the research of "enhance the function of the body of the exoskeleton (EHPA)" to improve the load capacity of the individual soldier. DARPA-funded, the United States have appeared in the University of California, Berkeley BLEEX exoskeleton system, the passive skeleton service class of the Massachusetts Institute of Technology (MIT)[1], the Sarcos company's XOS exoskeleton prototype[2] of principles presentation technologies. Among them, BLEEX prototype in the University of California, Berkeley, is the most potential technical feasibility. In 2006, the second generation of the University of California, Berkeley BLEEX system were redesigned and trial-manufactured a demonstration

S.S. Ge et al. (Eds.): ICSR 2012, LNAI 7621, pp. 650–659, 2012.

prototype by the U.S. Lockheed Martin Corporation,, renamed the "human universal portable (Human the Universal Load Carrier, <HULC)[3]". Russian Central Research Institute is to accelerate the development of second-generation man-portable power equipment, "Warriors -21",which can bear the infantry about 95 percent of the cargo load to protect the soldiers walking on flat or inclined plane. University of Tsukuba, Japan Cybernics laboratory developed the world's a commercial outsider bone booster device HAL[4], controlling motor drive in the human knee and hip joints, to help the disabled to walk 4km / h per hour, and up and down stairs more easily.

Since 2004, the National University of Defense Technology and the Second Artillery Engineering College has developed a non-powered portable aids prototype, which opened principle exploration of the outer bone boost technology in China. Since then, Zhejiang University, Harbin Institute of Technology, Chinese Academy of Sciences and other units also carried out the principle of the exoskeleton robot technology[5], The study includes the exoskeleton gait planning model and the humanoid interaction to the control of the biped walking humanoid. In 2005, Naval Aeronautical Engineering Institute started to develop a motor-driven exoskeleton power system prototype, can walk slowly [6]. 2009, East China University of Science and Technology on the basis of the study U.S. HULC system, developed the prototype of the exoskeleton power system of the hydraulic drive, basically completed the walk and up and down stairs, and other functions [7].

In this paper, as independent research of the lower limb exoskeletons principle prototype of the research object, having modeled the hydraulic position control system of the knee joint and designed of the different gait phase of the adaptive parameter adjustment control law, through the hydraulic position control system simulation, verification the position control method. And do portable exercise test on the prototype to demonstration of the entire hydraulic position control system design rationality.

2   Human Gait Law of Motion

Lower limb bones is different from the robot of the most important point: the exoskeleton's outside of a constrained environment is the human body, so do research firstly to all the soldiers of march basic action law. After large crowds statistical tests ,it have showed that the natural movements has a certain law of motion, but because there is a law of motion differences, different modes have a greater difference in increasing body weight, weight, physical [8].

As the basic of a try to load 30kg, in accordance with 4.8km / h standard marching speed walking test ,his one gait cycle (Tgait = 1s) law of motion of knee joint experimental data and the fitted curve is shown in Figure 1.

Fitting right above the knee angle variation as follows:

① t<0.5Tgait,

$$\theta_k(t) = 21.97 \times \sin(3.16t - 0.06) + 13.36 \times \sin(9.92t + 0.13) \tag{1}$$

② t>0.5Tgait,

$$\theta_k(t) = 43.62 \times \sin(4.88t + 0.35) + 1.7 \times \sin(33.5t + 0.7) + 16 \times \sin(14.8t - 2.62) \tag{2}$$

Trial fitting knee angle variation as the reference input of a hydraulic position control system.

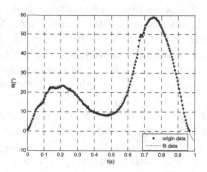

Fig. 1. Weight 30 kg, walking speed of 4.8 km/h

3   Modeling of Hydraulic Cylinder Position Control System

3.1   Load Torque Compensation Model

For modeling convenience, it is assumed that the outer skeleton of steel limbs standing support phase, the hydraulic cylinder of the exoskeleton knee ,the thigh and calf constitute a three hinge point model, which is shown in Figure 2.

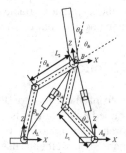

Fig. 2. Exoskeletons stand on two legs load model

When double support , the knee torque around is expressed as:

$$\tau_{ik} = \frac{-L_1 L_2 \sin(\theta_{ik})}{L_1 \cos(\theta_{ia}) + L_2 \cos(\theta_{ia} + \theta_{ik})} f_z \times \beta_i \tag{3}$$

Where i=1、 r, respectively represent left and right legs subscript, τ_{ik} said that the knee torque, θ_{ia}、 θ_i, said the ankle and knee angles, L1、 L2, respectively represent the length of the thigh and calf of the exoskeleton, fz for the weight-bearing support.

βi is the either foot support for transition impact factor, expressed as:

$$\beta_l = \frac{1}{(T_\alpha s + 1)^2}, \beta_r = 1 - \frac{1}{(T_\alpha s + 1)^2} \qquad (4)$$

Assume that transition response time of weight-bearing support force fz is $T\alpha = 0.05s$:then

① If $\beta l=1$, then$\beta r=0$, the left leg support phase;

② If $\beta l=1$, then$\beta r=0$, the right leg support phase;

③ If $0<\beta l<1$, $0<\beta r<1$, the legs supporting phase.

3.2 Servo Valve Mathematical Model

The servo valve's simplified mathematical model is the second-order model, as follows. Where ΔI is the output current, xv is servo valve output displacement, Ksv is amplification factor for the servo valve, ωsv is the natural frequency of the servo valve, ζsv is damping factor.

$$\frac{x_v}{\Delta I} = \frac{K_{sv}}{\dfrac{s^2}{\omega_{sv}^2} + \dfrac{2\zeta_{sv}s}{\omega_{sv}} + 1} \qquad (5)$$

3.3 Hydraulic Cylinder Mathematical Model

Hydraulic position control system mathematical model is expressed as [9]:

$$Y = \frac{\dfrac{K_q}{A_p}x_v - \dfrac{1}{A_p^2}\left(K_{ce} + \dfrac{V_t}{4\beta_e}s\right)F_{comp}}{\dfrac{V_t m_t}{4\beta_e A_p^2}s^3 + \left(\dfrac{m_t K_{ce}}{A_p^2} + \dfrac{B_e V_t}{4\beta_e A_p^2}\right)s^2 + \left(1 + \dfrac{B_e K_{ce}}{A_p^2} + \dfrac{V_t K}{4\beta_e A_p^2}\right)s + \dfrac{K K_{ce}}{A_p^2}} \qquad (6)$$

Where Ap is the hydraulic cylinder of the work area, Vt is the total volume of the hydraulic cylinder, Kq is flow gain of servo valve, Kce is servo valve flow - pressure coefficient, mt is load quality, K is the load spring stiffness, βe is the elastic modulus of the hydraulic oilamount, Be is load damping factor, Fcomp represents the hydraulic cylinder load force (also weight compensation force).

3.4 Solution of Hydraulic Cylinder Position

Knee hydraulic cylinder installation diagram shown in Figure 3.

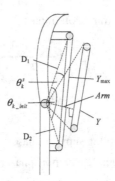

Fig. 3. Knee hydraulic cylinder installation schemes

The actual location of the knee is measured by rotary encoder, relative leg thigh movement point of view, if you want to measure the absolute value of the current knee angle, represented as:

$$\theta_{ki} = \theta_{ki\_init} - \theta_{ki}^s \qquad (7)$$

These θ_{ki}^s is the output current value of rotary encoder measuring, range 0-90 °, θki said that the absolute value of the current knee angle, θki_init said the knee initial angle on the case of standing.

According to the law of cosines can be calculated ,as follows:

$$\theta_{ki\_init} = \arccos\left(\frac{D_1^2 + D_2^2 - Y_{i\max}^2}{2 \times D_1 \times D_2}\right) \qquad (8)$$

Where D1、 D, respectively reprent the hydraulic cylinder of the thigh and lower leg connection point to the knee bearing distance; Yimax said knee piston rod maximum displacement (leg straight time).

Triangle law of cosines to get the actual position of the piston rod is expressed as:

$$Y_i = \sqrt{D_1^2 + D_2^2 - 2 \times D_1 \times D_2 \cos(\theta_{ki\_init} - \theta_{ki})} \qquad (9)$$

Use Sine, calculate the hydraulic cylinder output corresponding to the load force arm is expressed as:

$$Arm\_i = \frac{D_1 \times D_2 \times \sin(\theta_{ki\_init} - \theta_{ki})}{Y_i} \qquad (10)$$

4   Design of Hydraulic Cylinder Position Control Loop

4.1   Model of Hydraulic Cylinder Position Control Loop

Hydraulic position control loop design shown in Figure 4.

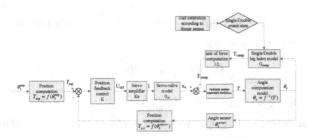

Fig. 4. Hydraulic position control system circuit design

When people walking, the look angle of the knee $\theta_k^{\exp}$ changes by Section 2 fitted two human gait motion law , according to structural dimensions of the knee joint bones to calculate the hydraulic cylinder piston rod desired position Yexp. Hydraulic cylinder's actual output location Y is getted after angle calculation model ,the current knee angle is measured by angle sensor, and then calculated by the position to get the current hydraulic cylinder piston rod actual location Yact, the deviation between the two to design position controller K.The controller gives the voltage control Uctrl, through servo amplifier Ka converted to the current I, the current input to the servo valve, give the current servo valve displacement control amount xv. Gait judgment under the foot pressure sensor is one foot or both feet weight model Gcomp , current load torque Tcomp can be calculated by the actual knee joint angle and load compensation model Gcomp , current knee necessary to compensate for weight-bearing the force Fcomp after the arm calculation, with force and servo valve control together input to the hydraulic cylinder system equivalent model for the calculation of the output piston rod of the actual location Y . Through to the piston rod position control , the actual angle of rotation and knee expected change when human leg gait movement keep consistent to achieve the purpose of human-machine coordination.

After circuit equivalent treatment, hydraulic cylinders, the equivalent position of the transfer function expressed as:

$$G_{hyd\_eq} = \cfrac{1}{\dfrac{V_t m_t}{4\beta_e A_p^2} s^3 + \left(\dfrac{m_t K_{ce}}{A_p^2} + \dfrac{B_e V_t}{4\beta_e A_p^2}\right) s^2 + \left(1 + \dfrac{B_e K_{ce}}{A_p^2} + \dfrac{KK_{ce}}{A_p^2}\right) s + \dfrac{KK_{ce}}{A_p^2}} \tag{11}$$

Weight compensation force interference feedback equivalent model expressed as:

$$G_{FtoFK} = \frac{1}{A_p^2}\left(K_{ce} + \frac{V_t}{4\beta_e} s\right) \tag{12}$$

Simplify the reference given by the 3.1 load compensation model, the definition of the hydraulic cylinder position to weight compensation force approximation to satisfy the scaling relationship, expressed as:

$$G_{YtoF} = \frac{F_{comp}}{Y}$$ (13)

Different gait, G_{YtoF} are also different. For weight 60kg gait frequency of 1Hz, the experimental test range as follows:

$$0 \leq G_{YtoF} \leq 1866$$ (14)

When in the single leg walking swing, $G_{YtoF} = 0$.

Therefore, the whole system open loop transfer function is expressed as:

$$G_{open} = \frac{K_{PID} K_a K_q G_{sv} G_{hyd\_eq}}{A_p (1 + G_{hyd\_eq} G_{YtoF}) G_{FtoFK}}$$ (15)

4.2   The Design of Position Controller

The position controller uses a combination of PI and lead correction network control structure[10], proportional and integral control parameters adaptively adjust for different gait. Position controller is expressed as follows:

$$K_{PID}(s) = (k_p (Y - Y_{exp}) + k_i \int (Y - Y_{exp})) \times \frac{1 + a_1 s}{1 + b_1 s}$$ (16)

Where kp is the ratio of the control parameters, ki is the integral control parameters, a1、b1 are ahead network parameters, Yexp is desired position signal of the hydraulic cylinder.

5   Simulation Results

Adopt above position control method to do control simulation on the establishment of the hydraulic cylinder position control system, assuming that the weight fz=30kg plains walking, the average speed 4.8km / h, using section 2 human gait motion law as the input control signal, reference simulation results are shown in the figure.

The red curve in Figure 5, is the reference input for hydraulic cylinder desired position, the blue curve is the actual location of the response. Desired position change range is about 0.36 0.36m—0.28m, the actual position and desired position deviation range of approximately-0.015m—0.025m.

Figure 6 is a booster effect of hydraulic cylinders in the gait, red is necessary compensate of weight-bearing forces, expected value is 650N, the actual hydraulic force with the expected deviation in the entire gait phase 0—100N, saving power nearly 75% ,meet certain performance requirements.

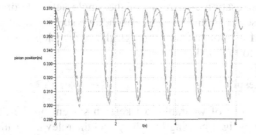

Fig. 5. Hydraulic cylinder expectation and actual position response curve

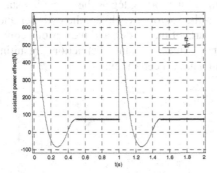

Fig. 6. Hydraulic cylinder walking gait of power in effect

6   Test Demonstration

6.1   Hydraulic Position Control Test Program

Use independently developed lower limb exoskeleton prototype as the test object, shown in Figure 7. People wear on the exoskeleton mechanical system device, through the gear pump is driven by the motor converts electrical energy to hydraulic energy, control the output of hydraulic cylinders, realize portable power for man-machine overloaded.

Fig. 7. Lower limb exoskeleton to bring line power system solutions prototype

Body load compensation as a result of the single acting hydraulic cylinder, only establish position servo control to walk touchdown stage weight portable, in the leg stage servo valve full mouth open, through the human leg lift letting hydraulic oil rapidly flows back to fuel tank, not control.

6.2   The Test Results

Do ground walking test of wearable exoskeleton system on the condition of 14MPa oil supply pressure, weight-bearing fz = 30kg, get the relevant results are as follows.

Contrast Figure 8 shows on the 30kg weight-bearing conditions, the actual measured flow simulation range is smaller, and the data is relatively stable, this is because the switch from the supporting leg as the swing leg stage in a gait cycle, there are large uncertainties in the servo valve, hydraulic cylinder and mechanical structure of the device and other parts of the model, and the various components corresponding to the inertial response time constant distinction, resulting in the theoretical simulation and test results have a certain bias.

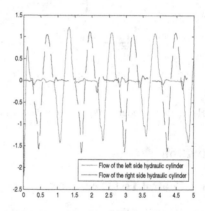

Fig. 8. Left and righter legs servo valve flow results

7   Conclusion

On the basis of understanding of the exoskeleton system of electromechanical coupling characteristics ,combining the PID and correction network control method to model lower extremity exoskeleton electromechanical coupling control system, designing and digital simulation, realized the knee angle servo at exoskeleton touchdown stage, achieved the effect of effort and man-machine portability movement. Then do 30kg load portable exercise test on the current development prototype, has verified the feasibility of man-machine coordination control methods used in the lower extremity exoskeleton control system, lay the foundation for the design of next-generation exoskeleton prototype.

References

1. Steger, J.R.: A design and control methodology for human exoskeletons, pp. 36–44. University of California, Berkeley (2006)
2. Wang, Z.: Raytheon launched XOS2 second-generation exoskeleton device. Light Weapons 24, 44 (2010)
3. http://www.lockheedmartin.com
4. Veneman, J.F., Ekkelenkamp, R., Kruidhof, R., van der Helm, F.C.T., van der Kooij, H.: Design of a series elastic - and Bowden cable-based actuation system for use as torque - actuator in exoskeleton-type training. In: Proceedings of the 9th International Conference on Rehabilitation Robotics, Chicago, IL, USA, June 28-July 1 (2005)
5. Sun, L., Li, Q.L., Kong, M.X., Du, Z.-J., Wang, D.Y.: Interactive rehabilitation training of 5-DOF upper limbs rehabilitation robot arm control strategy. Of Mechanical Engineering 44(9), 169–176 (2008)
6. Yang, Z., Zhang, Y.S., Gu, W.J., Yang, X.: Bone clothing sensitivity amplification control. Computer Simulation 27(1), 177–180 (2010)
7. Cao, H., Meng, X.W., Ling, Z.Y., Qin, Y.Q., He, C.: Two-legged robot exoskeleton plantar pressure measurement system. Journal of Sensors and Actuators 23(3), 326–330 (2010)
8. Zeng, X.Y.: Modern biomechanics, vol. (10), pp. 100–144. National Defence Industry Press (2002)
9. Wu, Z.S.: The hydraulic control system, vol. (5), pp. 40–50. Higher Education Press (2008)
10. Xu, Y.W.: Control system Design (1), vol. (3), pp. 462–547. Aerospace Publishing (1989)

Author Index